OVER PHOTO: James Randklev/FPG International

pyright © 1999 by John Wiley & Sons, Inc. All rights reserved.

part of this publication may be reproduced, stored in a retrieval system or
nsmitted in any form or by any means, electronic, mechanical, photocopying
cording, scanning or otherwise, except as permitted under Sections 107 or 108 of the
76 United States Copyright Act, without either the prior written permission of the
blisher or authorization through payment of the appropriate per-copy fee to the
pyright Clearance Center, 222 Rosewood Drive, Danvers, MA 01923, (508) 750-
0, fax (508) 750-4470. Requests to the Publisher for permission should be
dressed to the Permissions Department, John Wiley & Sons, Inc. 605 Third Avenue,
w York, NY 10158-0012, (212) 850-6008, E-mail: PERMREQ@WILEY.COM. To
der books or for customer service call 1-800-CALL-WILEY (225-5945).

brary of Congress Cataloging-in-Publication Data
oodstein, Eban S.
 Economics and the environment / Eban S. Goodstein. —2nd ed.
      p.   cm.
   Includes bibliographical references and index.
   ISBN 0-471-36439-8
   1. Economic development—Environmental aspects.   I. Title.
HD75.6.G66   1999
333.7—dc21   98-13143
                                                          CIP

inted in the United States of America

9 8 7 6 5 4 3 2

SECOND EDITION

Economics and the Environment

Eban S. Goodstein

Lewis & Clark College

WILEY

JOHN WILEY & SONS, INC.

NEW YORK • CHICHESTER • BRISBANE • TORONTO • SINGAPORE • WEINHE

By this international commerce of geese, the waste corn of Illinois is carried through the clouds to the Arctic tundras, there to combine with the waste sunlight of a nightless June to grow goslings for all the land in between. And in this annual barter of food for light, and winter warmth for summer solitude, the whole continent receives as a net profit a wild poem dropped from the murky skies upon the muds of March.

—ALDO LEOPOLD

To Anita and Marvin Goodstein, for their gifts of wisdom and strength

Contents

Preface

This book is designed to serve as a text for a one-semester course in environmental and resource economics. It is intended primarily for students who have had an introductory course in microeconomics, but it is also suitable for a course with an intermediate microeconomics prerequisite. Additionally, the text may be of interest to students taking a course in environmental studies

The book retains the three interrelated advantages of the first edition: broad content, pedagogical clarity, and timely, well-integrated examples. There are a few significant changes in the order of presentation and some major additions. Information and examples have been updated throughout. For a chapter-by-chapter analysis of what's new in this edition, please see the *Instructor's Manual*. I will hit the highlights in this preface.

In terms of content, the book provides a rigorous and comprehensive presentation of the "standard analysis," including the property-rights basis of environmental problems, efficient pollution control, benefit-estimation procedures, and incentive-based regulation. However, *Economics and the Environment* also incorporates broader topics, notably the ethical foundations of environmental economics, a safety-based approach to controlling pollution, the economic critique of growth, the potential for government failure, the promotion of "clean technology," and opportunities for sustainable development in poor countries. New in this edition is a separate chapter on ecological economics.

The second major advantage of the book is clarity. *Economics and the Environment* is centered around four cleanly focused questions:

1. How Much Pollution Is Too Much?
2. Is Government Up to the Job?
3. How Can We Do Better?
4. Can We Resolve Global Issues?

The first section of *Economics and the Environment* explicitly sets up the normative question "How much pollution is too much?" It then employs the tools of welfare economics and benefit-cost analysis to explore three possible answers.

The first is the efficient pollution level. The concept is explained, and students are introduced to the fundamentals of benefit and cost estimation. The book also features a detailed look at the use of benefit-cost analysis at the EPA. New to this edition is a discussion of the static general equilibrium efficiency impacts of pollution taxes, and the implications for a "double dividend."

The second pollution standard considered is a "safety" standard, which in fact continues to drive much environmental policy. This standard is placed solidly in the context of the economic growth debate, drawing on authors such as Hirsch, Daly, and Mishan. This second edition, in a shift from the original presentation, places the chapters on efficiency and safety back to back.

The third standard is "ecological sustainability" as proposed by the ecological economics school. This standard is contrasted in an opposing chapter with "neoclassical sustainability"—dynamic efficiency presuming automatically rising social welfare. I shied away from doing this kind of comparison in the first edition because ecological economics was really just launching itself; it has been around long enough now for me to attempt a characterization. Apologies in advance to those who feel I got it wrong!

In these two chapters on sustainability, I have developed a more thorough and well-organized presentation of basic resource economics than was available in the first edition. In particular, I have consolidated material on GDP accounting, resource rents, and Malthusian theory—previously found in part IV—into these resource-based chapters.

Finally, in this first normative section of the book, one also finds a vital discussion that is missing from other texts: the utilitarian ethical basis for the normative analysis and its relation to an "environmental ethic." Most students come into an environmental economics course thinking that saving whales is very important, without knowing exactly why. The explicit welfare-based analysis in this chapter asks students to confront the assumptions underlying their own and other's worldviews.

The text fills a second major void in the second part, "Is Government Up to the Job?" Most existing texts simply note that "government failure" is a potential problem when correcting for market externalities. In *Economics and the Environment,* the question of government's ability to regulate pollution effectively is carefully examined. The section begins with a discussion of the two primary obstacles to effective government action: imperfect information and the opportunity for political influence over government policy. It then moves on to provide a succinct review of existing legislation and accomplishments on air, water, solid and hazardous waste, toxic pollution, and, new in this edition, endangered species. Part II ends with a chapter on the often neglected subject of monitoring and enforcement.

The third section of the book, "How Can We Do Better?" tackles the (more) positive aspects of pollution regulation. Two chapters are devoted to the theory and practical application of incentive-based regulation-marketable permits and Pigouvian taxes. From here, the book examines an argument that attributes the root source of pollution to market failure in technological development, rather than in the arena of property rights. We consider the view that the market often fails to generate incentives for investment in "clean technology" as well as the feasibility of proposed solutions to this problem. In-depth discussion focuses on areas such as energy policy, pollution prevention, alternative agriculture, recycling, life-cycle analysis, and "green" consumption.

Finally, *Economics and the Environment* devotes an entire section to the resolution of global pollution and resource issues. Part IV, "Can We Resolve Global Issues?" is centered around a definition and discussion of sustainable development, as put forward by the Bruntland Commission. Topics covered include the preservation of natural capital; population and per capita consumption pressures; the relationship between poverty, sustainable development, and environmental protection in poor countries; international trade and the environment; and global pollution control agreements. Case studies here focus on our hemispheric neighbors Mexico, Costa Rica, and Brazil.

In keeping with the philosophy of incorporating examples directly in the text, *Economics and the Environment* begins with a detailed case study of a "big" issue with which many students are familiar—global warming. The text ends with a final section covering more advanced topics in environmental economics—non-convexities; regulation under uncertainty; macro level, input-output modeling of environmental impacts; and incentive-compatible regulation. The material in this last section is suitable for classes with an intermediate microeconomics prerequisite.

Economics and the Environment will appeal to three groups of instructors. The first are economists who are simply looking for a clear and concise presentation of the conventional approach to environmental and resource economics. The four-question format developed in the text provides a much simpler pedagogical handle than is available elsewhere. In addition, the book provides a wealth of examples from the current literature, as well as an explicit consideration of the government's role in environmental policy, not available in competing works. Finally, the supplemental chapters on advanced theoretical topics insure that there is enough standard material to fill out a one-semester course.

The book will clearly appeal, however, to those with an interest in expanding the scope of environmental economics. *Economics and the Environment* moves beyond the standard analysis in five important areas. It provides a rigorous normative analysis of environmental goals; an in-depth evaluation of ecological economics; serious attention to the potential for government failure in pollution control; substantial discussion of dynamic issues of path dependence and technological change; and a sophisticated presentation of sustainable development in poor countries. The book seeks to incorporate into a well-developed economic analysis ideas that have emerged in the environmental and ecological sciences over the past few decades.

Given this orientation, instructors in environmental studies courses will also find this text to be unusually user-friendly. Chapters on measuring the value of nonmarket goods, cost-benefit analysis, markets for pollution rights, incentives for investment in appropriate technology, the governmental role in pollution control, population and consumption pressures, global bargaining, and conservation in poor countries provide accessible material for environmental studies courses with a social science focus.

Ultimately, the test of any textbook comes in the classroom. *Economics and the Environment* was written with students in mind. It addresses important questions raised in their lives and introduces them to the economist's view of some solutions.

Acknowledgments

Second edition acknowledgments are fewer in number than the first-time list, but no less heartfelt. Thanks go first to Dallas Burtraw, who always keeps me up to date.

A synthetic textbook such as this one depends on the contributions of the hundreds of economists and environmental scholars working the field. Some of their names appear in the list of authors cited at the end of this book; undoubtedly many important contributors were omitted due to the scarce resource of space. At this point, I would like to acknowledge helpful discussions and exchanges with the following individuals:

Frank Ackerman	Tellus Institute
Dean Baker	Economic Policy Institute
Ralph Bradburd	Williams College
John Buell	College of the Atlantic
Margriet Caswell	U.S. Department of Agriculture
Steve Colt	University of Alaska, Anchorage
Paul Decotis	New York State Energy Office
Peter Dorman	Michigan State University
Faye Duchin	Institute for Economic Analysis
Richard England	University of New Hampshire
Peter Fox-Penner	Charles River Associates
Kittie Gillespie	Washington State Department of Ecology
David Goodman	University of California, Santa Cruz
Neva Goodwin	Tufts University
Robert Gottfried	University of the South
Ann Gramsch	U.S. Environmental Protection Agency
Douglas Greer	San José State University
Sharman Haley	Merrit College
Darwin C. Hall	California State University, Long Beach
Jonathan Harris	Tufts University
Debra Holt	Queens University
Alice Hubbard	Rocky Mountain Institute
Ann Ingerson	Sterling College
Kent Klitgaard	Wells College
Gunnar Knapp	University of Alaska, Anchorage
Michael Krasner	Queens College
Thea Lee	Economic Policy Institute
Rick Lostspeich	Indiana State University
Paul McCarthy	Ford Motor Company
Larry Mishel	Economic Policy Institute

William Moomaw	Tufts University
Frank Muller	Environmental Tax Project
Deborah Nestor	U.S. Environmental Protection Agency
Carl Pasurka, Jr.	U.S. Environmental Protection Agency
Steve Polasky	Oregon State University
Daniel Press	University of California, Santa Cruz
J. Barkley Rosser, Jr.	James Madison University
Moyara Ruehsen	Monterey Institute of International Studies
Brett Snyder	U.S. Environmental Protection Agency
Martin Spitzer	U.S. Environmental Protection Agency
Eileen Van Ravensway	Michigan State University

Debra Holt, Dallas Burtraw, Darwin C. Hall, Ann Ingerson, Kent Klitgaard, Peter Schwarz, Dennis Palmini, J. Barkley Rosser, Jr., Seid Zekavat, Matthew Forstater, Janusz Mrozek, and several anonymous reviewers provided me with excellent comments on the manuscript as it was in progress. Many of their suggestions have found their way into the final version of the book. I would also like to acknowledge the help of Rod Banister and Maureen Wilson at Prentice Hall. Finally, I would like to thank my many friends, including especially my parents and children, who helped me stay sane through the summer of 1997.

Introduction

Four Economic Questions about Global Warming

1.0 Introduction

Yesterday morning I had to deliver my older daughter, Emma, to a friend's house for a play date. Then I made a quick trip to the office to pick up some notes. After I arrived home, my wife took the car to the grocery store, then drove across town to deliver our younger daughter (Liza) to the doctor's office. When she returned, I made an afternoon trip to the landfill, then swung back over to pick up Emma. In the mid-afternoon, we all headed out to a lake north of town for a swim. We started for home when the shadows began to spread across the beach.

On this typical Saturday, we put about 90 miles on the family car; less visibly, we pumped some 80 pounds of carbon dioxide (CO_2) into the air. This was our small daily share of the more than 25 billion pounds people around the world contribute annually from the burning of carbon fuels such as coal, oil, natural gas, and wood. Carbon dioxide is a **greenhouse gas**—a compound that traps reflected heat from the earth's surface and contributes to **global warming.** Other greenhouse gases include nitrogen oxide from natural and human-made fertilizers; methane gas emitted from oil and gas production and transport, and from rice production and the digestive processes of cows and sheep; and chlorofluorocarbons (CFCs), once widely used for air-conditioning, refrigeration, and other industrial applications.[1]

As a result of industrialization and the ensuing rapid increase in greenhouse gases in our atmosphere, most scientists agree that the earth's surface temperature will rise over the next few decades. The extent of the warming is uncertain: Assuming no controls on greenhouse gas emissions, low-end estimates suggest an increase in the

---

[1]Chloroflourocarbons also deplete the earth's protective ozone shield, a separate issue from global warming discussed in more detail below.

3

earth's average surface temperature of 1.5 degrees Fahrenheit by the year 2100. Predictions at the high end are on the order of 6.5 degrees over this time period.[2] Few studies have looked beyond the "near term" of 100 years, but over the course of 250 to 300 years the outlook is obviously worse. A mid-range estimate over the long term, assuming no efforts to curtail use of fossil fuels, is a warming of 18 degrees Fahrenheit.[3]

The potential consequences of this warming range from manageable to catastrophic. The first major impact will be on **agricultural output,** a direct effect of changing temperature and rainfall patterns. Rainfall has a dominant impact on agriculture. More northerly regions may actually experience an increase in precipitation and yields, but the current grainbelts of the United States and central Europe will become drier and agricultural output in these regions will probably fall. The net global effect through the mid-century is expected to be, on balance, negative, and will be particularly harsh in many Third World countries, which lack resources for irrigation and other adaptive measures.[4]

Second, **natural ecosystems** will also suffer from climate change. The U.S. Environmental Protection Agency has estimated that by the year 2050 the southern boundary of forest ecosystems could move northward by 600 kilometers, yet forests can migrate naturally at a much lower pace. Massive disruption of ecystems and species extinction is thus a distinct possibility. Diseases might also thrive in a warmer climate.

The third concern is the possibility of a **sea-level rise** as ice caps in northern latitudes and Antarctica begin to melt. An increase in sea level of three feet—well within the realm of possibility—would flood many parts of Florida, Louisiana, Boston, and New York City, as well as much of low-lying countries like Bangladesh and the Netherlands (unless they were protected by dikes). As many as 1 billion people live in areas that might be directly impacted.[5]

Global warming is an environmental reality that presents stark choices. On the one hand, substantial, short-term reductions in the human contribution to the greenhouse effect would require substantial changes in western lifestyles. In particular, our casual reliance on fossil fuels for transportation, heat, and power would have to be dramatically scaled back. On the other hand, the consequences of inaction are potentially disastrous. By continuing to pollute the atmosphere, we may be condemning the next generation to even greater hardship.

This book focuses on the economic issues at stake in cases like global warming, where human actions substantially alter the natural environment. In the process, we will examine the following four questions.

1. How much pollution is too much? Many people are tempted to answer simply: Any amount of pollution is too much. However, a little reflection reveals that zero pollution is an unachievable and, in fact, undesirable goal. Pollution is a by-product of liv-

---

[2]IPCC (1996).

[3] Cline (1991); Hall (1997).

[4]For an optimistic assessment of the impact on U.S. agriculture, see Mendelsohn et al. (1994); for a critique, see Cline (1996); and for an overview of agricultural issues, see Hall (1997).

[5]Rosenberg et al. (1989). The most recent IPCC estimates suggest a sea-level rise of up to a meter by 2100 (but not stopping at that date!), with a best guess of 50 cm (IPCC [1996]; Watson [1996]).

ing; for example, each time you drive in a car, you emit a small amount of carbon dioxide to the air, exacerbating the greenhouse effect. The question really is "At what level are the benefits of pollution (cheap transportation in the case we started with) outweighed by its costs?"

Different people will answer this question in different ways, depending upon their value systems: "Costs" of pollution may be defined narrowly, as strictly economic, or they may be broadened to include ethical considerations, such as fairness and the protection of rights. Costs may also be very difficult to measure. Nevertheless, it is clear that a rough weighing of benefits and costs is a critical first step for deciding "how much is too much."

2. Is government up to the job? After resolving the first question, we must then rely on government to develop and implement an economic plan to control pollution. But is our government able and willing to tackle the tough job of managing the environment? The costs and mistakes associated with bureaucratic decision making, as well as the likelihood of political influence in the process, will clearly have an impact on government's ability to respond effectively to the challenge.

The first Earth Day was April 20, 1970. Also that year, the U.S. Congress passed the first major pollution control initiative, the National Environmental Policy Act, which, among other things, created the Environmental Protection Agency. Looking back over our twenty-five plus years of experience in regulating the environment, we have a record of both successes and failures to evaluate. Such an exploration can help us design policies to increase the effectiveness of the governmental response.

3. How can we do better? Suppose that as a society we decide to stabilize carbon dioxide emissions at their 1990 level in ten years. Given the limitations that government might face, identified in the answer to the second question, how can we best achieve that goal? A long list of policies might be used: regulations, taxes, permit systems, technology subsidies (or their removal), research incentives, infrastructure investment, right-to-know laws, product labeling, legal liability, fines, and jail terms. Which policies will most successfully induce firms and consumers to meet the target?

4. Can we resolve global issues? Finally, regulating pollution within a single nation is a difficult task. Yet problems such as global warming transcend national boundaries. Brazilians say that they will stop cutting down and burning their rain forests to create crop and range land as soon as we stop driving gas-guzzling cars. (Although the United States has only 5% of the world's population, we account for over 21% of the greenhouse gases.) How can this kind of international coordination be achieved? Are economic development and environmental quality necessarily in conflict? And to what extent can the explosion in population growth and per capita resource use, which ultimately drive environmental problems, be managed?

Let us return to our discussion of global warming, and see what type of answers we might develop to these four questions. Global warming is a consequence of what is known as the **greenhouse effect.** Solar energy enters the earth's biosphere in the form of visible and ultraviolet light from the sun. The first law of thermodynamics—energy can be neither created nor destroyed—requires that this energy go somewhere, and much of it is radiated back into the biosphere as infrared radiation or heat. The greenhouse gases surrounding the earth let in the visible and ultraviolet light from the sun.

Yet, like the glass surrounding a greenhouse, these gases trap the reflected infrared radiation (heat) close to the earth's surface.

Until the present time, the greenhouse effect has been primarily beneficial. Without its naturally occurring carbon dioxide shield, the average temperature on earth would be about 91 degrees Fahrenheit colder—well below the freezing point. The problem facing us today is the steady increase in human-made greenhouse gases, which began with the industrial revolution but dramatically accelerated after World War II. In less than two centuries, the concentration of greenhouse gases in the atmosphere has increased by 25%, and it is expected to double by the middle of the next century or earlier if action is not taken to reduce emissions.

Is the greenhouse effect here yet? The earth's average temperature appears to have risen a little less than 1 degree Fahrenheit over the last century, though there has been no change recorded in the United States. However, the 1980s and mid-1990s have seen several of the hottest years on record; global temperature peaked in 1995, and 1996 also made the top ten. In 1995, the Intergovernmental Panel on Climate Change (IPCC), an organization of some 2,500 scientists operating under the auspices of the United Nations, made it official—the greenhouse effect is here. According to the IPCC, "the balance of evidence suggests that there is a discernible human influence on global climate."[6]

Many obstacles stand in the way of concerted action against global warming, but perhaps the biggest is uncertainty. As previously indicated, scientists are virtually unanimous in their belief that warming will occur, but the magnitude of the warming is difficult to predict. After all, consider how often your local weather-forecaster makes a bad call on the one-day forecast; with global warming, scientists are attempting to predict the weather fifty years into the next century!

Uncertainty in predicting the degree of global warming is due primarily to the presence of **positive and negative feedback** effects. If it were only necessary to predict the impact of greenhouse gases on global temperature, the problem would be difficult enough. But changing temperatures will in turn affect many different parts of the earth and its surface, leading either to an acceleration of the warming (positive feedback) or a deceleration (negative feedback).

Two examples of the latter include the possibility that increasing cloud cover will reduce the amount of radiation entering the earth's atmosphere, or that higher rates of carbon dioxide will lead to higher rates of plant growth and thus more trapping of carbon dioxide in the air. Negative feedbacks would clearly be welcome, but unfortunately, positive feedbacks appear just as likely, if not more so, to occur. For example, higher temperatures may generate an increased rate of decay of organic material; lead to the emission of methane and CO_2 currently trapped in frozen bogs and peat fields in high latitudes; expose heat-absorbing darker earth under ice shields; or reduce the capacity of ocean organisms to fix carbon dioxide in their shells.

In the face of this uncertainty, what action should be taken to prevent or mitigate the consequences of global warming? Following the outline described above, we can begin to tackle this daunting question piece by piece.

---

[6]IPCC (1996).

1.1 How Much Pollution Is Too Much?

How much should we reduce emissions of carbon dioxide, nitrogen oxide, and methane? Weighing costs and benefits in a case like this is a tremendous task, but it is nevertheless a vital first step.

On the cost side, several recent studies have estimated the reduction in the dollar value of goods and services produced that would result if we restrained carbon dioxide emissions over the next century to their 1990 levels in the United States alone. These studies suggest costs in the range of $8 billion to $36 billion per year, in 1990 dollars. The costs would be lower initially but would rise over time as cleaner energy sources like natural gas and energy conservation opportunities are exhausted. Over the next 100 years, this adds up to a total of between $800 billion and $3.6 trillion in "lost" income.[7] (By comparison, the U.S. government currently spends about $265 billion on the military each year.)

These cost figures may be overstated because they underestimate the energy-saving potential of new technologies, particularly conservation technologies. A study by Geller et al. (1992) focused explicitly on the issue of energy efficiency—using new technologies to squeeze more energy out of available resources.[8] The study estimated that an investment of about $2.7 trillion in these new technologies from 1988 to 2030 would achieve a 50% reduction in CO_2 emissions. However, the study went on to argue that such investments would *actually save* consumers and firms $5 trillion in reduced energy bills, for a net savings of $2.3 trillion! Chapter 20 of this book looks more closely at the Geller et al. claim. For now, however, suffice it to say that achieving such dramatic results would require an effective governmental commitment to a fundamental restructuring of energy production and use in the U.S. economy.

The energy savings that are feasible via efficiency measures are a focus of intense current debate. Nevertheless, all agree that direct investment cost estimates in the trillions of dollars give a feel for the "out-of-pocket" expense involved in freezing or reducing greenhouse gas emissions.

Given these major costs, are the benefits from slowing down the warming comparable? Putting a monetary value on such benefits presents very difficult issues. Among them: How do we deal with uncertainty and the possibility of cataclysmic change? How do we value damage to future generations? Can we measure the value of intangible or "priceless" benefits such as human suffering and death averted or forests saved? How do we weigh the fact that certain countries will lose more than others in the warming process? We will explore these issues in detail later in the book. Nevertheless, in spite of these difficulties, Nordhaus (1991) has presented some initial damage estimates for the United States.[9]

Assuming that greenhouse gas levels stabilize at double pre-industrial levels, Nordhaus sees surprisingly small economic damages—ranging from $8 to $66 per ton of carbon dioxide emitted. These low estimates arise from the fact that only a small portion of U.S. economic activity is in the agricultural sector, the area most likely to

---

[7]See Nordhaus (1991) and Manne and Richels (1990, 1991).

[8]Hall (1992) and Williams (1990) take similar positions; the authors also explore the potential cost savings from new clean technology, for example, solar power. For an intermediate view, see Office of Technology Assessment (1991).

[9]Nordhaus and Yang (1996) draw similar conclusions. For a critique of Nordhaus, see Cline (1992).

be severely affected. (Indeed, elsewhere, Nordhaus, writing with Mendelson et al. [1994], finds a positive impact of global warming on U.S. agriculture!) The lower estimate includes only economic damages; the latter a rough adjustment for the value of lost species and other intangibles.

These figures do not take into account non-global warming benefits of restrained greenhouse gas emissions. Energy conservation or fuel switching will help us reduce conventional air pollutants such as sulfur dioxide, nitrogen oxide, and suspended particulates. Since transportation will also be affected, we may count as benefits reduced road congestion and traffic accidents. Finally, benefits will be reaped from improved energy security.

Economists also recognize that people are reasonably good at adapting to new environmental conditions. For example, while changing rainfall patterns will reduce harvests in some areas, improved agricultural technology may compensate for some, if not all, of that reduction. Some areas such as central Canada *may* actually experience better agricultural conditions. Dikes could be built to protect cities from sea-level rises; the EPA has estimated that such an effort in the United States would cost between $70 billion and $110 billion. Finally, mass migration from low-lying countries like Bangladesh and India could possibly be supported by the international community.

Given these benefit-cost estimates, the ability of individuals to adapt, as well as the uncertainty surrounding the ultimate greenhouse impact, and the difficulty of enforcing international agreements on the issue (discussed below), Nordhaus argues for a "go-slow" effort on restraining carbon emissions. His work suggests that a fairly modest tax on carbon-based emissions is called for. At this point, it is maintained, the benefits of major pollution reduction efforts simply do not outweigh the costs.

Nevertheless, *some significant* action is called for. In particular, Nordhaus argues for at least a reduction of around 11% in greenhouse gas emissions below their uncontrolled growth level, and a stabilization by 2050.[10] And in 1997, Nordhaus and 2,000 economists around the United States signed off on a public statement urging the U.S. government to take a more aggressive stance on reducing global warming. It read in part: "There are many potential policies to reduce green-house gas emissions for which the total benefits exceed the total costs."[11]

Note that Nordhaus and the other economists are prescribing an unstated ethical goal: Control pollution only if the measurable monetary benefits of doing so are greater than the measurable monetary costs. This is one answer to the question "How much is too much?" It is called an **efficiency standard** for pollution reduction.

Even within the efficiency framework of measurable costs and benefits, Nordhaus' somewhat timid conclusions are open to question. The Geller et al. study, for example, suggests that due to energy savings it might actually be profitable to reduce global warming. One could also argue that the lost consumption from controlling CO_2 emissions in an affluent country such as the United States really means very little over the long run. Because the happiness derived from consumption is in many ways a rel-

---

[10]See Schelling (1992) and Nordhaus (1993) for similar arguments.

[11]"Economic Scene," *New York Times,* February 13, 1997, p. C2.

ative phenomenon, a general increase in income in large measure only accelerates the "rat race," leaving few better off in absolute terms.[12]

However, there are ways of thinking about pollution standards other than through a comparison of economic costs and benefits. First there are issues of fairness: Inaction on our part today—though it may provide for somewhat higher incomes today, particularly for citizens in affluent countries—may also condemn future generations, in particular those in already poor countries, to even greater hardship. Can we justify actions today that, for example, will destroy entire island nations and their cultures?

A second answer to the question "How much is too much?" emphasizes fairness. This is called a **safety standard.** Safety requires reducing pollution to (socially defined) "safe" levels, unless the costs of doing so are prohibitive.

Finally, there is the question of fundamental uncertainty regarding our impacts on the planetary ecosystem. Nordhaus assumes an intermediate case of predictable damages, but of course, a worst-case scenario might emerge. In a related vein, can we even begin to put benefit numbers on things we know nothing about? For example, what would be the value to future generations of the unique genetic code that will be lost as species extinction accelerates? In the face of this uncertainty, a third standard emerges—**ecological sustainability.** This standard requires protecting natural ecosystems from major changes, again, unless the costs of doing so are prohibitive.

The policies flowing from the "safety" and "ecological sustainability" standards are to freeze greenhouse pollution at current levels and initiate a substantial reduction in emissions. Efficiency proponents such as Nordhaus would respond that these actions will impose excessively high costs on the current generation and, by depressing current investment in capital, research, and education, on future generations as well.

Where do we stand on global warming emission targets? At the "Earth Summit" meeting in Rio de Janeiro in 1992, attended by the leaders of more than 140 countries, the industrialized nations signed a pledge to "try" and stabilize greenhouse gas emissions at 1990 levels by the year 2000. However, in the United States, this promise is unlikely to be kept: Low energy prices and strong economic growth have boosted U.S. greenhouse gas emissions substantially.[13]

In December 1997, the major industrial countries signed an agreement in Kyoto, Japan, committing themselves to a reduction in greenhouse gas emissions averaging 5.2% below 1990 levels, with the target to be achieved between 2008 and 2012. However, the U. S. Senate threatened not to ratify the Kyoto treaty unless developing countries also made some binding commitment to future greenhouse gas reductions. By the spring of 1998, no such agreement had been reached, and President Clinton made it clear that he would not be bringing the treaty to the Senate for consideration until at least 1999.[14]

---

[12]Nordhaus' analysis also stops at the year 2050. Cline (1992), taking a 300-year framework for analysis, finds damages that are roughly twice as large as those of Nordhaus.

[13]See "How Bush Achieved Global Warming Pact with Modest Goals," *Wall Street Journal,* May 27, 1992; "Not Just Hot Air," *Time,* 141, no. 59, May 3, 1993; and Gardner (1996).

[14]"Clinton Pledges to Forge Accord in U.S. for the Battle Against Global Warming," *Wall Street Journal,* June 27, 1997, p. A2.

When the public debate over global warming reemerges in the United States (after the next hot summer?), it will be between those who maintain somewhat different **ethical** viewpoints. On one side, efficiency advocates will stress the measurable costs involved in reducing global warming and will advocate small reductions. On the other, proponents of safety and ecological sustainability will argue for major greenhouse gas cutbacks, focusing on less tangible factors that affect the quality of life of those alive both today and tomorrow.

The purpose of this book is not to sort out which answer is "correct," but rather to better understand the different positions. However, the first essential step in addressing any environmental problem is to decide, "How much pollution is too much?" Once this is resolved, it is then possible to move on to the second question.

1.2 Is Government up to the Job?

For reasons we will explore further in this book, an unfettered free-market economy will produce too much pollution by almost anyone's standards. This suggests that government needs to step in and regulate market behavior in order to protect the environment. But government itself has its own limitations. Is government up to the job?

Two obstacles stand in the way of effective government action. The first is **imperfect information.** Regulators often have a hard time obtaining accurate information about the benefits and costs of pollution reduction. Benefits such as cancers reduced, visibility improved, and ecosystems salvaged are hard to measure and even harder to quantify. Costs are also hard to gauge accurately since they depend on the details of how an industry actually operates. Under these circumstances, even well-meaning bureaucrats may have a difficult time imposing regulations that achieve cost-effective control of pollution.

The second obstacle lies in the opportunity for **political influence.** Evaluating the importance of this problem requires a theory of governmental action. Economics, like all social sciences, is not a "value-free" pursuit. This is most apparent in political economy, where scholars of different political persuasions are in the business of analyzing government activity.

Traditional **conservatives** view governmental intervention as a necessary evil and argue for as limited a governmental role as is possible in all affairs, including environmental. Conservatives argue that government legislators and regulators are self-interested individuals who desire to maximize their own well-being, rather than wholeheartedly pursue their stated public mission. Such officials, in theory, seldom act in "the public interest" but instead serve "special interests." Special interests include, for example, coalitions of particular businesses, environmental groups, women's or civil rights groups, or labor unions.

In contrast to this conservative view, **progressives** view government as capable of promoting an activist agenda to serve the general interest of the public. Like conservatives, progressives acknowledge the possibility of "government failure." Yet in contrast to the conservative position, progressives argue that the problem with government involvement in the economy is not primarily the existence of pluralistic special-interest groups, but is instead the dominance of big business and development interests in the legislative and regulatory process. For example, progressives point to fossil fuel subsidies obtained by industry as a major obstacle to the resolution of the global warming issue.

As the next section illustrates, these different perspectives on the potential for effective governmental action will determine views on the best policies for dealing with global warming.

1.3 How Can We Do Better?

As noted above, at the Rio conference, the United States committed itself to targeting 1990 greenhouse gas emission levels; in 1993 a year 2000 deadline was set. Carbon dioxide is the most important of the greenhouse gases, contributing about 60% of the total greenhouse effect. It is produced by the burning and decay of carbon-based materials: coal, oil, and plant matter. Given what we have learned above about the political economy of regulation, how do we set about controlling CO_2 emissions?

Government could take many possible actions to control carbon dioxide emissions. In a rough way, we can divide such measures into three categories. First is so-called **command-and-control regulation,** the current, dominant approach to environmental protection. Under command and control, government would regulate CO_2 emissions by mandating the adoption of *particular types of CO_2 abatement technology* on, for example, coal-burning power plants. Other types of technology would be required for automobiles, still others for natural gas plants.

As we shall see, command-and-control regulation has been widely criticized as centralized and inflexible and, thus, much more costly than necessary. Many economists have advocated a switch to **incentive-based regulation.** Incentive-based approaches set emission targets and leave it up to industry to figure out the best way to comply. Incentive-based regulation gets its name from the fact that firms are provided with incentives to reduce emissions: A tax on pollution is one example.

Finally, government can intervene more directly to encourage the development and diffusion of new **clean technology.** For example, government can force firms to meet energy-efficient design standards such as building codes. Or government could promote clean technological change through its investment activities—for example, by favoring rail transport infrastructure over autos or providing research and development funding for clean fuels. Which of these is the best method?

Of all the pollution control methods available, by and large economists of all stripes do agree that pollution taxes (and their kin, marketable permit systems introduced below) can be a good policy.[15] To deal with CO_2 emissions, for example, a tax based on the carbon content of fuels (a carbon tax) is one of the most effective policies we could impose. Under this kind of scheme, non-CO_2 fuels would be promoted over carbon-based fuels in the marketplace, and cleaner CO_2 fuels like natural gas would be promoted over dirtier ones such as coal.

Nordhaus, based on his efficiency perspective, argues that while meeting the Rio target is a good idea, we don't need to do much more than that. Nevertheless, his analysis suggests that the United States impose a modest carbon tax of approximately

---

[15]As we will discuss in chapters 16 and 17, the appeal of incentive-based approaches depends on the adequacy of monitoring and enforcement. For a comprehensive discussion of carbon taxes, see Poterba (1991).

$8 per ton of emissions. Such a tax would first generate some reduction in CO_2 emissions as firms switched to existing technologies employing relatively cheaper fuel sources. Second, it would provide companies with the financial incentive to develop carbon-free technologies. The benefits of such a gradual approach would be to avoid serious disruption of economic affairs in countries like the United States, prevent an overcommitment of resources to global warming given the current uncertainty, and obviate the need for obtaining a complicated and difficult-to-enforce international agreement. The Rio targets could be exceeded at a later date if evidence for substantial warming becomes more compelling.

In contrast to Nordhaus, other economists have argued for an ecological sustainability standard: Given the irreversibility of global warming, aggressive action is warranted sooner rather than later.[16] Holders of this viewpoint press for a tax with substantial teeth. Estimates of around $100 per ton of greenhouse gas emissions seem to be consistent with the 1990 level target and may even achieve some rollback. Such a tax would generate substantial revenues and could be made politically palatable were the funds rebated back to the public in the form of income tax cuts.

Such tax cuts should be targeted disproportionately to poorer citizens to reduce the impact of higher prices for necessities—gasoline, heat, and electricity. Table 1.1 provides some estimates for price increases from a British study of a $96 per ton tax. Prices for these necessities rise substantially under such a scenario. A more recent study for the United States finds that a $100 per ton tax would raise gasoline prices an estimated $.26 per gallon and electricity prices by $.02 per kWh.[17]

In addition to the market-based approach represented by carbon taxes, progressive economists would argue for policies to promote energy efficiency and for a reorientation of government investment priorities. The Geller et al. study, for example, recommends that fuel, lighting, and power efficiency standards be strengthened or introduced. The authors also envision major government efforts to revamp our transportation infrastructure, including promotion of high-speed railways as a substitute for short plane flights, zoning laws to encourage denser residential patterns, greater investment in mass transit, and taxes to discourage auto transport.

Finally, governmental-funded research and development into new energy technologies, in particular those that utilize renewable, non-carbon-based sources, such as

TABLE 1.1 Carbon Taxes and Fuel Price Increases ($96 per ton Carbon Tax)		
	Coal	*Oil*	*Natural Gas*
Expected Price Increase	87%	96%	49%

Source: Some data taken from a study by Symons et al. (1990) as cited in David Pearce, "The Role of Carbon Taxes in Adjusting to Global Warming," *The Economic Journal,* 101, no. 407 (1991), 946.

[16]See Pearce (1991) for example.
[17]"White House Predicts Lower Costs for Controlling Emissions," *New York Times,* July 16, 1997, p. A10.

energy efficiency, solar, wind, and hydrothermal power, might be promoted. High carbon taxes combined with substantial government-sponsored research and development into clean energy technologies and an aggressive approach to promoting efficient energy use is the "progressive" position on global warming.

Conservative economists would be suspicious of government regulations mandating energy efficiency or government-funded research and development (R&D) of the alternative technologies recommended by the progressive program. The question they would ask about such an agenda would be: Can the government do a better job developing appropriate technologies than the market already does? First, conservatives would charge that the R&D pool is likely to become just another government pork barrel. Second, even granting efficient operation, some would maintain that government bureaucrats would have a hard time "picking winners"; that is, determining which potential technologies are feasible, cost-effective, and environmentally benign. As a result, conservatives prefer a "wait and see" position, with taxes imposed only as a last resort.

On the global warming issue, Nordhaus falls between the extreme conservative and progressive positions, in that he does advocate a minimal carbon tax and the devotion of some governmental resources to R&D in energy technologies. Yet he offers a typically conservative caution against more aggressive efforts to slow global warming: "Don't forget that humans have the capacity to inflict great damage on themselves through ill-designed economic and regulatory schemes, as the Communist experiment clearly shows."[18]

Progressive economists would respond that the "Communist experiment" has little relevance for policy makers in a modern capitalist country. Existing government decisions such as energy tax breaks for fossil fuels, highway construction funds, and other subsidies for auto transport, tax and zoning policies that encourage suburbanization, and high levels of poorly targeted R&D funding already constitute a defacto "plan" with major negative environmental and economic effects. The choice, therefore, is not between free markets and central planning, but rather between myopic and farsighted government policy. Quoting from the Geller et al. study: "The policies here do not call for a return to price controls and crash programs to promote specific fuels. But they recognize the market biases and barriers that currently favor energy production over energy efficiency. . . ."

Progressives maintain that on energy policy, our market system (which is *already* affected by substantial government involvement) has failed miserably to deliver appropriate technology. Because private investors do not take into account the tremendous costs to society of carbon-based fuels, incentives do not exist to develop appropriate technologies. In addition, a network of vested interests, inappropriate government subsidies already in existence, and substantial economies of scale all justify government involvement. Due to the massive nature of the market failure, the argument is that picking winners would not be hard: among the obvious candidates—energy efficiency technologies, photovoltaic solar cells, and wind power to name a few.

How can we do better? Most economists would argue that a greater reliance on incentive-based approaches like pollution taxes makes sense. Economists who hold a progressive viewpoint argue that, in addition, government should take a more active hand in promoting the development and diffusion of clean technology.

---

[18]Nordhaus (1990: 45).

1.4 Can We Resolve Global Issues?

Whether the U.S. government relies primarily on traditional regulatory mechanisms to achieve the Rio targets or also employs more incentive-based regulations and direct investment tools, our efforts will be in vain if other nations do not also comply with the treaty. Global warming requires a global solution. Many economists are pessimistic about the prospects for enforceable global agreements that substantially reduce carbon dioxide emissions in the near future.

CO_2 reduction is what is known as a **public good,** a good that is consumed in common. This means, for example, that if the United States cuts back CO_2 emissions 20%, the whole world benefits. Thus, each country would prefer to see the other cut back and then "free ride" on its action. With every country being in this position, there is great incentive for signatories to a treaty to cheat on any agreement. One reason that nations are reluctant to commit to substantial carbon dioxide reductions is the fear that other countries will not go along, and thus their sacrifice will be meaningless in the long run.

However, economists are eager to be proven wrong. An ongoing experiment may shed some light on the potential for the success of the Rio agreement. In 1987 most countries of the world signed on to the Montreal Protocol, an agreement to drastically reduce the production of one of the greenhouse gases, CFCs, by 1996. In 1992 the treaty was strengthened and now calls for a complete ban. (The impetus to the agreement was actually *not* global warming, but rather destruction of the ozone layer—the primary problem with CFCs.) We will examine the success of the protocol and other international agreements in chapter 23, where we also return for a final discussion of global warming. However, much hinges on whether poor countries such as India and China can be induced to adopt the more expensive CFC substitutes that have been developed to provide such basic goods as refrigeration.

This issue highlights another obstacle facing the Rio global warming treaty: the economic needs of Third World countries. Poor countries currently contribute about 30% of the world's CO_2 emissions. But high rates of population growth, increasing energy use per capita, and accelerated deforestation are expected to increase their contribution to 50% by the year 2025. Some would argue that it is both unrealistic and unfair to expect these countries to sacrifice economic growth by reducing CO_2 emissions in exchange for uncertain environmental gains.

Yet economic growth in many poor countries has its own environmental costs and may prove **unsustainable.** The economic growth process is often rooted in exploitative colonial relationships that have encouraged the establishment of lopsided, resource-dependent economies. In the modern context, debt has replaced colonial status as the mechanism by which wealth flows from the poor to the rich. Deforestation, overgrazing, and massive pollution from mineral and oil development persist, reinforced by a network of government policies favoring local elite and multinational corporate interests, all occurring in an environment where common property resources are available for exploitation. When economic growth fails to compensate for natural resources depleted in the process, the economic development process is unsustainable: That is, growth today comes at the expense of future generations. (For a more careful definition of sustainable development, see chapter 21.)

It is clear that the economic needs of the world's poor nations must be placed at the forefront of an effort to reduce global warming. In this fashion, global agreements to control pollution are most likely to succeed. But it is also true that Third World countries have more to lose from global warming because they have fewer resources to finance adaptive measures, from resettlement to irrigation to dike building. It is possible that a combination of energy efficiency and conversion to renewable energy sources (biomass and solar) can substantially slow the rate of growth of CO_2 emissions while at the same time promoting sustainable development, which in turn will lower population growth rates. A commitment to the development and transfer of this kind of technology by wealthy nations would have to be part of a successful treaty to reduce greenhouse gas emissions.

Along these lines, an incentive-based pollution control approach pioneered by economists has been suggested for resolving equity issues between the First and Third worlds: a **marketable permit system.**[19] Such a system would work in the following way. First, a global treaty would determine a worldwide greenhouse gas emission target and then assign each country a quota, based on its total population. Thus, each person in the world would initially be permitted to make an equal contribution to global warming. But because the average Indian, for example, uses only 4% as much energy as the average American, Third World countries would have an excess supply of permits, while we in the First World would have an excess demand.

Because the permits are marketable, we would buy some from the poorer countries of the world to maintain our energy-intensive lifestyles. The funds generated could then be used to support the kind of investments in poor countries in non-carbon fuels that they will require to develop. Moreover, because we would now be paying directly for our global warming, we would have the incentive both to conserve energy and to seek out new technologies.

The advantages of the marketable permit system in this case are threefold. First, it may allay some of the equity concerns of Third World countries, encouraging them to reduce their CO_2 emissions. Second, as we shall see, economists argue that marketable permit systems provide highly efficient ways of allocating a scarce resource—such as the ability to pollute. Finally, the price of the permits encourages private parties to seek out less expensive ways of doing business.

However, a tradeable permits treaty such as this would clearly be costly to the First World. As always, the essence of the economic debate is: Do the benefits of action outweigh these costs? At this point, on the issue of substantially reducing the emission of carbon dioxide to slow global warming, the case is not closed. Some economists say reduce a little. Others say reduce a lot. This book challenges you to make up your own mind.

1.5 Summary

This chapter has provided an introduction to the scientific issues surrounding the buildup of greenhouse gases in our atmosphere and the resultant possibility of global warming. But global warming is only one of the myriad environmental challenges posed by human activity. From the siting of landfills at the local level, to regulations

---

[19]For a more extended discussion, see chapters 16, 17, and 23 and Oates and Portney (1991).

on chemical emissions from manufacturing plants that are issued by national governments, to international agreements designed to preserve species diversity, the need for a public informed of the underlying scientific issues is great.

Environmental economists must also rely on scientific assessments of the dangers posed by environmental degradation to ourselves and our descendants. However, this book is *not* focused on specific environmental concerns arising from our economic activity. Instead, the point is to *illustrate the framework* that economists use for approaching pollution problems. For any such concern, from landfill siting, to chemical regulation, to loss of species diversity, three general questions must be answered:

1. How much pollution is too much?
2. Is government up to the job?
3. How can we do better?

When, as is increasingly common, the issue is an international one, a fourth question must also be addressed:

4. Can we resolve global issues?

To this point, I have both outlined the questions raised and provided a sketch of the answers that arise when one grapples with the economics of environmental protection. As indicated, there is often lively debate among economists regarding the right answers. But what we do agree on is the centrality of these four questions. The rest of the book moves on to explain and explore a number of possible solutions. It is my hope that the reader will come away better equipped to address the local, national, and global environmental problems that we and our children will have to overcome in the twenty-first century.

APPLICATION 1.0

Benefits of Urban Air Pollution?

Sulfur dioxide (SO_2) is a common urban air pollutant created by the combustion of fossil fuels, and is responsible for both acid rain and respiratory problems in humans. One of the ironic conclusions to emerge from the study of global warming is that sulfur dioxide actually cools the earth by blocking sunlight. (This effect was evident globally in the early 1990s when Mount Penetubo erupted in the Philippines, producing a great amount of SO_2, which lead to a couple of cooler than usual years.) This so-called "aerosol" effect led scientists to downgrade their predictions for global warming by a few degrees Fahrenheit between 1990 and 1995.

As a final twist to the story, these sulfur aerosols are fairly short-lived, as compared to the carbon dioxide emissions that cause global warming. So the SO_2 produced from burning fossil fuels is masking an underlying buildup of greenhouse gases. Put another way, as long as we continue to burn coal, which emits both SO_2 and CO_2, then the sulfur dioxide aerosols will partially offset the warming. A few years after we stop burning the coal, however, a much more serious greenhouse problem will emerge.

Question: Suppose you were in charge of evaluating a proposed tightening of the SO_2 emission regulations. In a benefit-cost analysis of reducing sulfur dioxide emissions, would you count as a benefit their cooling impact? Why or why not?

APPLICATION 1.1

Reading Economists on Global Warming

A study by Shah and Larson (1992) of carbon taxes designed to reduce the emission of greenhouse gases makes some interesting points. Here you are asked to identify the "answers" they provide to three of the four economic questions posed in this chapter.

1. Shah and Larson state: "A [national] carbon tax . . . offers significant benefits in terms of local pollutant reductions in addition to CO_2 reductions. The cost benefit analyses presented in this paper for selected countries suggest that countries with low or non-existent energy taxes can receive substantial net gains from a carbon tax on local environmental considerations alone. . . ."

What is meant by "local" pollutants? Do Shah and Larson think that carbon dioxide pollution levels are "too high" for the countries they are studying? If so, which of the three pollution standards are they using?

2. I noted in the text above that by raising the price of necessities, carbon taxes can have a large, unfair impact on poor people. Shah and Larson, however, argue that such an effect is not likely if national carbon taxes are substituted for income taxes, due in part to widespread evasion of income taxes.

The authors are clearly touching here on the question, "Is government up to the job?" What is their proposal for making government work better?

3. Shah and Larson state: "Total world energy subsidies in 1990 are estimated to be in excess of $139 billion. . . . An elimination of these subsidies would translate into a 17% reduction in carbon emissions in subsidizing countries. To achieve an equivalent reduction in tons of emissions in OECD [some of the rich] countries, a carbon tax of $50 would have to be imposed." Such a tax would cost rich countries $10.4 billion. Instead of imposing such a tax, it might be cheaper for rich countries to pay up to that amount to eliminate subsidies.

Here Shah and Larson don't really address the first two questions: How much pollution is too much? or Is government up to the job? Instead, they offer a possible way of "doing better." What is it?

Key Ideas in Each Section

1.0 Global warming, arising from the accumulation of **greenhouse gases** and the resulting **greenhouse effect,** poses a potentially severe threat to human welfare and natural ecosystems. Changing rainfall patterns that accompany warming may lead to reductions in **agricultural output,** particularly in poor countries, and major changes in **natural ecosystems,** including accelerated species extinction and higher rates of disease, are likely to occur. **Sea level** might also rise. Although scientists largely agree that *global warming is already a reality,* the magnitude of the warming will ultimately depend on **positive and negative feedback** effects. Economists need to answer **four questions** to address a problem like global warming.

1.1 The first question is "**How much pollution is too much?**" Answering this question requires at least a rough weighing of costs and benefits; an **efficiency standard** relies solely on benefit-cost analysis; **safety** and **ecological sustainability standards** argue for reducing pollution to much lower levels. This is fundamentally an **ethical debate** over the proper way to weigh both costs and benefits. Initial attempts to define an efficient level of global warming have also provoked a technical debate centered on to what extent and how fast we can adopt energy efficiency and other cleaner energy technologies.

1.2 Government action is necessary to reduce pollution in a market economy, but "**Is government up to the job?**" Two basic obstacles to effective government action are **imperfect information** and the **opportunity for political influence. Conservatives** view environmental regulation as a necessary evil best kept at the absolute minimum, believing that government action primarily serves special interests. By contrast, **progressives** see no way around an activist government role in environmental protection. From the progressive point of view, government failure results primarily from the influence of big business and development interests.

1.3 Command-and-control regulation is the dominant approach to pollution control today. In response to the question "**How can we do better?**" many economists have advocated adoption of **incentive-based** regulatory approaches, such as pollution taxes. Another option is the direct promotion of **clean technology** through actions such as R&D funding, infrastructure investment, zoning laws, and efficiency standards. Conservatives dispute the ability of government to achieve environmental goals by promoting clean technology.

1.4 Resolving global issues often requires international agreement. Such agreements, in turn, face two major obstacles. The first of these is the **public good** nature of environmental agreements. Once an agreement is signed, the incentives to free ride are great. Second, poor countries often cannot afford to invest in environmental protection. At the same time, they cannot afford not to; economic growth may lead to **unsustainable development.** In practice, this means funds to resolve global pollution problems must come from rich countries. A **marketable permit system** for controlling global CO_2 emissions (1) provides a way to fund poor country efforts and (2) provides rich countries with the right incentives to seek out less polluting technology.

References

Cline, William R. (1996). "The Impact of Global Warming on Agriculture: Comment." *The American Economic Review,* 86, no. 5, 1309–1311.

Cline, William R. (1992). *The Economics of Global Warming.* Washington, DC: Institute for International Economics.

Cline, William R. (1991). "Scientific Basis for the Greenhouse Effect." *The Economic Journal,* 101, no. 407, 904–919.

Firor, John (1990). *The Changing Atmosphere.* New Haven, CT: Yale University Press.

Gardner, David (1996). "Opening Remarks." *Climate Change Analysis Workshop, Post-Conference Proceedings.* Washington, DC: US EPA.

Geller, Howard, Daniel Lashoff, Alden Meyer and Mary Beth Zimmerman (eds.) (1992). *America's Energy Choices: Investing in a Strong Economy and a Clean Environment.* Cambridge, MA: Union of Concerned Scientists.

Hall, Darwin C. (1997). "Impacts of Global Warming on Agriculture." Paper delivered at the Western Economic Association Meetings, July.

Hall, Darwin C. (1992). "Social Cost of CO_2 Abatement from Energy Efficiency and Solar Power in the United States." *Environmental and Resource Economics,* vol. 2, 491–512.

IPCC (1996). *Climate Change 1995: The Science of Climate Change.* Oxford: Cambridge University Press.

Manne, A. S. and R. G. Richels (1991). "Global CO_2 Emission Reductions—the Impacts of Rising Energy Costs." *The Energy Journal,* 12, no. 1, 87–108.

Manne, A. S. and R. G. Richels (1990). "CO_2 Emission Limits: An Economic Cost Analysis for the USA." *The Energy Journal,* 11, no. 2, 51–74.

Mendelson, R., W. Nordhaus and D. Shaw (1994). "The Impacts of Global Warming on Agriculture: A Ricardian Analysis." *The American Economic Review,* 84, no. 4, 753–771.

Nordhaus, William D. (1993). "Optimal Greenhouse Gas Reductions and Tax Policy in the DICE Model." *American Economic Review,* 83, no. 2, 313–317.

Nordhaus, William D. (1991). "To Slow or Not to Slow: The Economics of the Greenhouse Effect." *The Economic Journal,* 101, no. 407, 920–937.

Nordhaus, William D. (1990). "A Perspective on Benefits and Costs." *The EPA Journal,* March–April, 44–45.

Nordhaus, William D. and Zili Yang (1996). "A Regional Dynamic General-Equilibrium Model of Alternative Climate-Change Strategies." *American Economic Review,* 86, no. 4, 741–765.

Oates, Wallace E. and Paul R. Portney (1991). "Policies for the Regulation of Global Carbon Emissions." *Discussion Paper CRM 91-02.* Washington, DC: Resources for the Future.

Office of Technology Assessment (1991). *Changing by Degrees: Steps to Reduce Greenhouse Gases.* Washington, DC: US GPO.

Pearce, David (1991). "The Role of Carbon Taxes in Adjusting to Global Warming." *The Economic Journal,* 101, no. 407, 938–948.

Poterba, James M. (1991). "Designing a Carbon Tax." In *Economic Policy Responses to Global Warming,* eds. R. Dornsbusch and James M. Poterba. Cambridge, MA: MIT Press.

Rosenberg, Norman J., Pierre Crosson, William E. Easterling III, Kenneth Frederick and Roger Sedjo (1989). "Policy Options for Adaption to Climate Change." *Discussion Paper ENR 89-05.* Washington, DC: Resources for the Future.

Schelling, Thomas C. (1992). "Some Economics of Global Warming." *American Economic Review,* 82, no. 1, 1–14.

Shah, Anwar and Bjorn Larson (1992). "Global Warming, Carbon Taxes and Developing Countries." Paper presented at the American Economic Association Meetings, January. The paper was abridged from Shah and Larson (1991), "Carbon Taxes, the Greenhouse Effect and Developing Countries." *WDR Working Paper 6.* Washington, DC: World Bank.

Watson, Robert T. (1996). "Balancing Risks and Uncertainties: Impacts of Climate Change." *Climate Change Analysis Workshop, Post-Conference Proceedings.* Washington, DC: US EPA.

Williams. R. H. (1990). "Low Cost Strategies for Coping with CO_2 Emission Limits." *The Energy Journal,* 11, no. 4, 35–60.

PART

I

HOW MUCH POLLUTION IS TOO MUCH?

The first step in protecting the environment is setting a goal: how clean do we want it to be? There is no "right" answer to this question, but whatever answer we choose, implicitly or explicitly, the costs of clean-up will get weighed against the benefits. Here we explore three different clean-up targets, each comparing costs and benefits in different ways: efficiency, safety, and sustainability. The focus is on both ethical and practical issues. We begin with a discussion of the utilitarian ethical framework that economists use, and then explore two fundamental reasons why unregulated markets tend to produce too much pollution from *any* perspective. We look carefully at the techniques economists have developed to measure the benefits of environmental protection as well as it costs, the strengths and limitations of benefit-cost analysis, and the broader relationship between growth in material consumption and growth in well-being. How much is too much? This part of the book provides the tools to help you make up your mind.

Ethics and Economics

2.0 Introduction

After reading the brief introduction to global warming, you are now more informed about the issue than 95% of the U.S. population. Suppose there were a presidential election tomorrow, and candidate A was supporting an efficiency standard. Based on the current benefit-cost analyses of reducing greenhouse gas emissions, he was advocating only a minimal carbon tax. Candidate B, by contrast, believed in an ecological sustainability standard and was pushing a much higher tax, combined with aggressive government action to promote clean technology. If you were a single-issue voter, for whom would you vote? Why?

If you voted "A," you might have done so out of a concern for "economic growth" or "jobs." You might even have reasoned that the economic slowdown brought on by increased regulation would actually penalize future generations more than the warming by reducing investment in education, capital, and new technology. If, on the other hand, you voted "B," perhaps you did so because you thought it was unfair to punish our descendants for our wasteful consumption habits and that endowing them with an unpolluted environment was more important than providing them with a new, improved form of breakfast cereal. You might also have thought that we had a moral duty to preserve the species of the earth themselves. Finally, you might have reasoned that new jobs would be created in the process of controlling carbon emissions.

The question "How much pollution is too much?" is what economists call a **normative** issue—it focuses our attention on what should be, rather than what is. Some are tempted to dismiss normative or ethical questions saying "it's just a matter of opinion." But, in fact, in our society opinion matters. The underlying ethical viewpoints held by lawmakers, regulatory and industry officials, and voters fundamentally influence the making of pollution policy. Like most countries, the United States already has a system of laws and regulatory agencies responsible for controlling the amount of pollutants emitted from factories, offices, farms, cars, and in the case of cigarettes, even people's lungs. Are the current laws too strict (as many in industry maintain) or do they need tightening up (as environmentalists argue)? Examining the ethical foundations of our own opinions will help us evaluate what is the "right" amount of pollution that these laws ought to permit. Without a well-reasoned answer to this question, sensible environmental regulation becomes impossible.

In the first part of this book we will examine three different pollution standards: an **efficiency standard,** which carefully weighs benefits and costs; a **safety standard** emphasizing human health; and an **ecological sustainability standard,** which argues for the preservation of current ecosystems. Along the way we will explore the complex issues involved in measuring the costs and benefits of cleaning up our environment. Wrestling with this material probably will not change where you stand on the "growth versus environment" debate, but it should help you clarify why you think the way you do. This in turn will make you a more effective advocate of your position. And convincing others that your opinion is "better"—either more logical or more consistent with widely held social norms—is the basis for taking action to make our world a better place.

2.1 Utility and Utilitarianism

Economic analysts are concerned with *human* welfare or well-being. From the economic perspective, the environment should be protected for the material benefit of humanity and not for strictly moral or ethical reasons. To an economist, saving the blue whale from extinction is valuable only insofar as doing so yields happiness (or prevents tragedy) for present or future generations of people. The existence of the whale independent of people is of no importance. This human-centered (or anthropocentric) moral foundation underlying economic analysis, which has as its goal human happiness or utility, is known as **utilitarianism.**

There are, of course, different perspectives. One such view is known as an **environmental ethic.** It can be put rather simply: *Independent of the utility of doing so,* people have a moral responsibility to treat the earth with respect. From the Native Americans, to Henry David Thoreau and John Muir, to Earth First! activism, this is an old and familiar idea in American culture. (Of course, a celebration of the unbridled exploitation of nature has also played a dominant role in American intellectual history.)[1] Aldo Leopold, considered by many to be the most influential environmental thinker of this century, stated it this way: "We abuse land because we regard it as a commodity belonging to us. When we see land as a community to which we belong, we may begin to use it with love and respect."[2]

As this quote suggests, many environmentalists are hostile to utilitarian arguments for protecting the environment. Indeed, an economic perspective on nature is often viewed as the primary problem, rather than part of the solution. The philosopher Mark Sagoff (1995: 618) puts it this way:

> . . . the destruction of biodiversity is the crime for which future generations are the least likely to forgive us. The crime would be as great or even greater if a computer could design or store all the genetic data we might ever use or need from the destroyed species. The reasons to protect nature are moral, religious and cultural far more often than they are economic.

The focus on anthropocentric, utilitarian arguments in this book is not meant to discount the importance of other ethical views. Indeed, over the long run, nonu-

---

[1]See Nash (1989).
[2]Leopold (1966).

tilitarian moral considerations will largely determine the condition of the planet that we pass on to our children and theirs. But economic arguments invariably crop up in short-run debates over environmental protection, often playing pivotal roles.

Individual economists may in fact accept the environmental ethic as part of their personal moral code. However, in conducting their analysis, economists adopt a hands-off view toward the morality or immorality of eliminating species (or of pollution in general), because they are reluctant to impose a single set of values on the broader society. However, failing to make a judgment itself implies an ethical framework—and the moral philosophy underlying economics is utilitarianism.

Utilitarians have two hard questions to settle before they can apply their analysis to an issue like pollution. The first is, What in fact makes people happy? This is a very difficult question; the great religions of the world, for example, each offer their own spiritual answers. Economists respond at the material level, by assuming that the consumption of goods brings happiness or utility. "Goods" are defined very broadly to include any and all things that people desire. These include both **market goods** such as tomatoes, VCRs, and basketball shoes, and **nonmarket goods,** such as clean air, charitable deeds, or the view from a mountaintop. What makes something a "good" is a personal matter. Leon Walras, an economist who lived in the late 1800s, put it in this rather provocative way:

> We need not concern ourselves with the morality or immorality of any desire which a useful thing answers or serves to satisfy. From other points of view the question of whether a drug is wanted by a doctor to cure a patient, or a murderer to kill his family is a very serious matter, but from our point of view, it is totally irrelevant.[3]

One can express the positive relationship between consumption of goods and utility in a mathematical relationship known as a **utility function.** We can write a utility function for a person named Aldo on a given day as

$$\text{Utility}_{Aldo} = U_{Aldo} (\overset{+}{\text{\# of tomatoes}}, \overset{+}{\text{\# of VCRs}}, \overset{+}{\text{\# of basketball shoes}},$$

$$\overset{+}{\text{lb of clean air}}, \overset{+}{\text{\# of charitable deeds}}, \overset{+}{\text{\# of mountaintop views}} \ldots)$$

where the . . . indicates all the other items Aldo consumes over the course of the day and the "+'s" indicate that Aldo's utility rises as he consumes these "goods." Another way to present Aldo's utility function is to compress all the goods he consumes into a "consumption bundle," labeled X_A (the A is for Aldo), and write $\text{Utility}_A = U_A(X_A)$.

Now, the production of many of the market goods in his consumption bundle, X_A, also creates pollution, which Aldo doesn't like. So let us break out one element from Aldo's consumption bundle—P_A, the pollution to which Aldo is exposed. We can now write Aldo's utility function as $\text{Utility}_A = U_A(\overset{+}{X}_A, \overset{-}{P}_A)$, where the "−" above the pollution variable reminds us that Aldo's utility declines as his exposure to pollution increases.

---

[3]Walras (1874).

This utility function illustrates a key assumption underlying most economic approaches to environmental issues: A fundamental trade-off for human happiness exists between increased material consumption (economic growth) and environmental quality. Whenever P_A goes down (the environment is cleaned up), X_A goes down too (other consumption falls), and vice versa. Put another way, the opportunity cost of environmental cleanup is assumed to be slower growth in the output of market goods.

One additional assumption about this utility-consumption relationship is often made: **More is better.** That is, Aldo is always happier when given more stuff. This may seem implausible. Why should Aldo want more than one ice cream cone if he is already full? The standard reply is, give it to a friend (which would make Aldo happy), or sell it and use the money to buy something he wants.

As we shall see, the "more is better" assumption is a crucial one. On the one hand, it provides substantial power to proponents of the efficiency standard. On the other hand, proponents of a safety standard argue that it incorrectly builds in a "bias" toward economic growth—ignoring the additional pollution it creates, under the more is better assumption, growth *by definition* increases human happiness.

We will devote Chapter 11 of this book to a careful examination of this assumption. To the extent that more is *not* better, utilitarian arguments for protecting the environment at the expense of consumption growth become much stronger.

To summarize this section: In answer to the first question of what makes people happy, utilitarians argue consumption of market and nonmarket goods. The happiness trade-off between consumption and environmental quality can be conveniently expressed in the form of a utility function. A second and more controversial assumption often made is that, from the individual perspective, more of any such good always increases happiness. With this answer in hand, we can now move on to the second question facing utilitarians: how does one "add up" individual happiness into social happiness?

2.2 Social Welfare

If increases in consumption of both market and nonmarket goods make *individuals* happy, does this also mean that increases in individual consumption increase the overall welfare of a *society*? Answering this question involves incorporating issues of fairness and rights. How does one weigh a reduction in the happiness of one individual against an increase in the happiness of another? To make explicit their assumptions about fairness, economists often specify a **social welfare function,** which determines a "desirable" way of adding up individual utilities. In a society including Rachel (R), John (J), and many others ($. . .$), we can write:

$$\text{SW} = f(U_R(\overset{+}{X_R}, \overset{-}{P_R}), U_J(\overset{+}{X_J}, \overset{-}{P_J}), \ . \ . \ .)$$

where again, the "+'s" indicate that social welfare rises as each individual gets happier.

One commonly used social welfare function is just the sum of individual utilities:

$$\text{SW} = U_R(\overset{+}{X_R}, \overset{-}{P_R}) + U_J(\overset{+}{X_J}, \overset{-}{P_J}) + \ . \ . \ . \tag{1}$$

The original nineteenth-century utilitarians believed this to be the correct form, arguing that the "greatest good for the greatest number" should be the guiding principle for public policy. They thought that to implement such a policy would require measuring utility in a precise way, and they devised elaborate methods for comparing the relative happiness derived from consumption by different individuals.

Unlike classical utilitarians, modern economists do not rely on direct measurements of utility. However, to determine the "correct" level of pollution from a social welfare perspective, we do need to weigh one person's consumption against another's. One social judgment we might make is that *additions* to consumption are valued equally by individuals. This is called an assumption of **equal marginal utility of consumption,** and it allows us to weigh the welfare impact of changes in patterns of consumption directly. For example, under this assumption, if your income goes up by a dollar and mine goes down by a dollar, social welfare will remain unchanged.[4]

Given this assumption and the specification of the social welfare function in equation (1), *increases* in each person's happiness receive equal weight—social welfare goes up at the same rate when the utility of either a millionaire (John) or a street person (Rachel) rises. In fact, social welfare could potentially rise as millionaire John was made better off at street person Rachel's expense! When utility is simply added up, no allowance is made in the social welfare function for issues of fairness in the distribution of income among those alive today.

Social welfare function (1) also provides no special protection for the well-being of future generations; under the simple adding-up specification, social welfare might rise if the current generation went on a consumption binge at the expense of our descendants. This would be true, provided that the increase in consumption today more than offset the decrease in consumption tomorrow.

Finally, social welfare function (1) also assumes that pollution victims have no special rights. If, for example, Rachel lives downwind from John's steel factory and, as a result, suffers health damages of, let us say, $25 per day, this reduction in social welfare would be strictly offset by a gain in John's profits of $25. Equation (1) is thus "blind" to the distribution of the costs and benefits of economic events within the current generation, across generations, and between pollution victims and beneficiaries. All that matters for boosting social welfare is increasing net consumption of *both* market and nonmarket goods, regardless of who wins and who loses.

Equation (1) is in fact the "adding up" mechanism underlying an **efficiency standard** for pollution control. Under an efficiency standard, the idea is to maximize the **net benefits** (benefits minus costs) of economic growth, by carefully weighing the benefits (more consumption) against the costs (pollution and resource degradation). This is done without reference to who bears the costs or gains the benefits.

How can such a position be ethically defended? While pollution certainly imposes costs on certain individuals, efficiency advocates maintain that, over time, *most people*

---

[4]The assumption of equal marginal utilities of consumption within the relevant range is implicit behind the efficiency standard. See Kneese and Schulze (1985). The presentation through equation (2) follows Varian (1987). However, in the interests of clarity, I keep the "utility functions" constant across the equations and incorporate "weights" within the utility functions to illustrate changes in the underlying assumptions. One could also express the sustainability SW function as an unweighted sum subject to the constraint that the utility of the average future person is no less than that of the average current person.

will benefit if the net consumption benefits from pollution control are maximized. Put in simple terms, lower prices of consumer goods for the vast majority (including necessities like food) must be strictly balanced against protection of environmental quality and health.

The "blind" approach that efficiency supporters take toward the distribution of costs and benefits provides one extreme. By contrast, if Rachel is impoverished, we might assume that her marginal utility of income is *greater than* that of John; one dollar increases Rachel's happiness more than it increases John's. Then, in the interests of social well-being we might well want to weigh increases in Rachel's consumption more heavily than those of the affluent.[5]

In practice, the strict efficiency standard for pollution control is often modified to include "fairness weights" in the social welfare function. In particular, as we discuss further in Chapters 6 and 7, a concern for fairness to future generations is often incorporated. For example, we might wish to employ a **sustainability rule** that says social welfare does not rise if increases in consumption today come at the expense of the welfare of our children. Suppose that Rachel (now an "average" person) is not yet born, while John (also an "average" person) is alive today. Then our sustainable social welfare function would be written:

$$SW = w * \overset{+ \quad -}{U_R(X_R, P_R)} + \overset{+ \quad -}{U_J(X_J, P_J)} + \ldots \tag{2}$$

where w is a weighting number big enough to insure that increases in John's consumption do not substantially penalize Rachel. Here, and unlike in equation (1), increases in happiness for the average individual today cannot come at the expense of future generations.

Finally, bring Rachel back to the present, living downwind from John's steel factory. She is now exposed to air pollution, P_R. She consumes this pollution, but recall that it is an economic "bad," and so enters her utility function with a negative sign. Proponents of a **safety standard** will argue that in the interests of personal liberty, Rachel has a *right* to protection from unsolicited damage to her health. As a result they will weight very heavily the negative effect of pollution in her utility function:[6]

$$SW = \overset{+ \quad - \quad \quad +}{U_R(X_R, w*P_R)} + U_J(X_J) + \ldots \tag{3}$$

Now, social welfare rises substantially less with the production of steel than it does with less-polluting commodities. An extreme safety advocate, by choosing such a large value for the weighting number w, would essentially refuse to balance the benefits of the polluting steel process (cheaper steel, and all the products that steel contains) against the harmful impact of pollution.

The latter two specifications of the social welfare function—sustainability and safety—imply that a happy society is more than just the sum of its parts. Fairness cri-

---

[5]This in fact is the classical utilitarian argument for income redistribution. Rawls (1971) provides a contractual argument in favor of weighting the consumption of the least well off.

[6]Equation (3) is a crude way of representing philosopher John Rawls'(1971: 61) lexicographic preference ordering that puts personal liberty, including liberty of the person, above material consumption. Kneese and Schulze (1985) specify the libertarian position as a decision rule requiring an actual Pareto improvement from any proposed social policy.

teria based on income distribution (both within and between generations) and personal liberty must be met as well. When the more is better assumption is relaxed later in the book, we will add yet another layer of complexity: Because my happiness from consumption depends on your level of consumption in a variety of ways, happiness will depend on *relative* rather than absolute levels of material welfare. As a result, in order to correctly specify social welfare, certain "noncompetitive" consumption items such as environmental health will also be weighted in the social welfare function.

This section has illustrated three different forms for a social welfare function—efficiency, sustainability, and safety—each specifying how individual utility might be added up to equal social well-being. While these different social welfare functions may seem arbitrary, proponents of each will argue that, in fact, their vision reflects the "dominant viewpoint" in our society about the proper relationship between material consumption and social welfare.[7] Social welfare functions have the advantage of forcing advocates of utilitarian policies to precisely state and defend both their basic assumptions and the logic by which they reach their conclusions. As we proceed in this first part of the book, we shall see that the different pollution standards are defended ethically by making different assumptions about the proper form of both the utility and social welfare functions.

2.3 Summary

This chapter has provided an introductory discussion of the ethical foundations of economics. Economists maintain as a basic assumption that increases in material consumption of both market and nonmarket goods—including clean air and water—increase individual utility. Whether growth in material consumption, independent of fairness and rights, necessarily leads to an overall increase in *social* welfare depends on the form that is specified for the social welfare function. There is no "correct" social welfare function. But economists use social welfare functions to help clarify normative debates, including the one that concerns us: "How much pollution is too much?"

Three positions are often staked out in economic discussions regarding environmental protection. First, there are those who argue for a careful weighing of costs and benefits, with no attention paid to the distribution of those costs and benefits. This is an efficiency position. Second, there are safety standard supporters, who maintain that people have a right to have their health protected from environmental damage, regardless of the cost.

The third position is sustainability, which argues for protecting the welfare of future generations. While the sustainability criterion is easy to state, we will find that there is much debate about what sustainability means in practice. This is because future generations are affected by our current decisions in complex ways. For example, will our grandchildren be better off if we leave them oil in the ground, or if we exploit the oil deposits and invest the profits in developing new forms of energy? The answer to this question is not obvious.

Insofar as the debate about resources and the environment focuses on the welfare of people, it remains a utilitarian one and in the realm of economics. Again, this is not

---

[7]Arrow (1963) has analyzed the difficulties in democratically determining a social welfare function.

to downplay the importance of noneconomic ethical views about the environment. However, the economic approach asks us to think clearly about the ways in which nature serves our social needs. By examining the ethical foundations of different views about the appropriate level of pollution, we can develop a better notion of why it is that we support either a wait-and-see or an aggressive position on slowing global warming.

APPLICATION 2.0

Social Welfare and Landfill Regulation

Recently, the U.S. Environmental Protection Agency issued regulations covering the design and construction of landfills for municipal solid waste. Landfills can represent a threat to environmental health if toxic chemicals leach from the waste into surrounding ground or surface waters.

The regulations require certain design, construction and maintenance standards extending beyond the post-closure period, including, in most cases, installation of impermeable liners and covers and groundwater monitoring. The purpose of the regulations was to insure safe containment of solid waste and to prevent future generations from having to bear cleanup costs from poorly disposed waste. (For more on the landfill issue, see Chapter 10.)

Even with the new regulations, just under 10% of landfills will still pose what the EPA considers to be a "moderate" health risk for individuals who depend on contaminated groundwater: a greater than 1 in 1 million increase in the risk of contracting cancer. However, because so few people actually depend on groundwater within leaching distance of a landfill, the new regulations were predicted to reduce cancer by only two or three cases over the next 300 years. Potential benefits of the regulation not quantified by the EPA include increased ease of siting landfills, reduced damage to surface water, fairness to future generations, and an overall reduction in waste generation and related "upstream" pollution encouraged by higher disposal costs.

In aggregate, the regulations are expensive: about $5.8 billion, or around $2 billion per cancer case reduced. On a per household basis, this works out to an annual cost of $4.10 in increased garbage bills over the twenty-year life of a landfill.

1. Using the concept of social welfare represented respectively by equations (1) and (3), explain why the EPA's landfill regulation is (a) too strict and (b) not strict enough.

Key Ideas in Each Section

2.0 Normative questions ask what *should* be rather than what is. Economic analysis of normative issues proceeds by clearly stating underlying ethical assumptions.

2.1 The ethical foundation of economics is **utilitarianism,** a philosophy in which environmental cleanup is important solely for the happiness (utility) that it brings to people alive today and in the future. This philosophy is contrasted with an **environmental ethic,** which values nature for its own sake. Economists assume that consumption of both **market goods** and **nonmarket goods** makes people happy. This relationship can be expressed in a **utility function,** with pollution entering as a negative consumption element. A utility function assumes a fundamental trade-off between growth in consumption and improvements in environmental quality. Economists often make one further key assumption about the consumption-utility relationship: **More is better.**

2.2 To add up individual utility, economists use a **social welfare function.** In such a function, one might assume **equal marginal utility of consumption** so that social welfare was just the sum of individual happiness, regardless of the distribution of benefits within a generation, across generations, or between victims and polluters. This SW function underlies the **efficiency standard,** which seeks to maximize the **net benefits** from steps taken to protect the environment. Alternatively, one might want to weight the consumption of poor people more heavily than rich people, victims more heavily than polluters (**safety standard**), or adopt a **sustainability rule** insuring that consumption today does not come at the expense of future generations. No social welfare function is "correct"; their use helps clarify underlying assumptions in normative debates over the right level of pollution.

References

Arrow, Kenneth (1963). *Social Choice and Individual Values.* New York: John Wiley.

Kneese, Alan V. and William D. Schulze (1985). "Ethics and Environmental Economics." In *Handbook of Natural Resource Economics,* Vol. 1, ed. A. V. Kneese and J. L. Sweeney. New York: Elsevier.

Leopold, Aldo (1966). *A Sand County Almanac.* New York: Oxford University Press.

Nash, Roderick Frazier (1989). *The Rights of Nature.* Madison, WI: University of Wisconsin Press.

Rawls, John (1971). *A Theory of Justice.* Cambridge, MA: Harvard University Press.

Sagoff, Mark (1995). "Carrying Capacity and Ecological Economics." *Bioscience* 45, no. 9, 610–619.

Varian, H. (1987). *Intermediate Microeconomics.* New York: W. W. Norton.

Walras, Leon (1977). *Elements of Pure Economics.* Fairfield, NJ: Augustus M. Kelley.

CHAPTER 3

Pollution as an Externality

3.0 Introduction

Our first order of business is to define what exactly we mean by pollution. Consider three examples:

1. Tyler is eating in a smoky restaurant. Is he exposed to pollution?
2. Karen routinely comes in contact with low-level radioactive waste while working at a nuclear power plant. Is she exposed to pollution?
3. Marilyn is trying to get some sleep while his neighbor Tipper blares the sound system. Is he exposed to pollution?

For the purposes of this book, the correct answers are maybe, maybe, and yes. Economists define "pollution" as a **negative externality:** a human-made, unbargained for, negative element of the environment. Pollution is termed an externality because it imposes costs on people who are "external" to the transaction between the producer and consumer of the polluting product.

In the first case, what if Tyler is the one smoking? While the smoke is undeniably doing damage to Tyler's lungs, he may be aware of the damage and yet, balancing pleasure against risk, does not consider himself worse off. The second "maybe" is more difficult. Exposure to radioactive waste increases Karen's risk of cancer and is clearly a by-product of human activity. However, if she fully understands the risk to her health of performing the job, and yet shoulders it in exchange for a salary, then exposure to the waste is part of the bargain. That is, the exposure is not external to the transaction between her and her boss. Under these circumstances Karen would face a serious *occupational hazard,* which needs regulation on its own terms, but not a pollutant as we have defined it.[1] Finally, poor Marilyn is a clear-cut pollution victim. He is involuntarily being exposed to a negative by-product of Tipper's listening experience.

From an economist's point of view, market systems generate pollution because many natural inputs into the production of goods and services—such as air and water—are "underpriced." Because no one owns these resources, in the absence of gov-

---

[1]This assertion requires that Tyler and Karen *are indeed fully aware of the risks they face.*

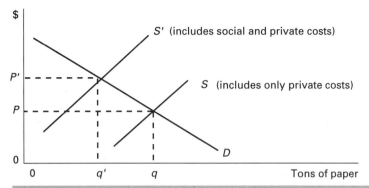

FIGURE 3.1 Social and Private Costs in the Paper Market

ernment regulation or legal protection for pollution victims, businesses will use them up freely, neglecting the external costs imposed on others. For example, suppose the Stinky Paper Co. discharges polluted water into a stream, which kills the fish that people enjoy eating downstream. If Stinky were forced to compensate the fisher people for the damages it imposed (**internalize the externality**), the firm would in effect be paying for the water it used up. Water would no longer be "underpriced." As a result, Stinky would conserve on its use of water and would seek out ways to clean up its discharge. This, in turn, would raise the production costs of the firm.

Figure 3.1 provides a simple supply-and-demand analysis of the situation and yields an immediate prediction. If all firms are forced to pay their full social costs of production, the competitive supply curve will shift up. The market price for paper will be higher, and the quantity sold will be lower. The diagram indicates a general principle: It is difficult to reduce pollution without also reducing the supply of the polluting product.

Because the river water is commonly owned and thus a "free" good, Stinky overexploits it, and the fisherfolk downstream are exposed to a negative externality of the paper production process. From an economic point of view, many pollution problems arise because environmental resources such as rivers are, by their nature, commonly owned. The rest of this chapter takes a closer look at the implications of this common ownership.

3.1 The Open Access Problem

Any economy depends on the ecological system in which it is imbedded in two fundamental ways, illustrated in Figure 3.2. First, human production and consumption processes rely on the environment as **sources** for raw materials; second, they also exploit the environment as **sinks** for waste materials. Both sources and sinks form what economists call natural capital. **Natural capital** is the input that nature provides for our production and consumption processes. Pollution is the overuse of sinks; resource degradation is the overharvesting of sources. In this sense, pollution and resource degradation are flip sides of the same process, the excessive exploitation of natural capital.

FIGURE 3.2 Natural Capital: Sources and Sinks

Many forms of natural capital, both sources and sinks, are not (and cannot) be privately owned. Because of this, pure free-market systems will generate too much pollution (or resource degradation) by any of the standards considered in this book—efficiency, safety, or sustainability. There are two related reasons for this: The first is the **open access problem,** which often arises when natural capital is commonly held. The second, addressed in the next section, is the public goods problem.

The open access problem can be stated simply: If people weigh private benefits against private (as opposed to social) costs, they will overexploit common resources when given open access. This idea was popularized in the late 1960s by Garrett Hardin, who called it "The Tragedy of the Commons." He poses the problem facing a herder whose cattle forage on common land:

> As a rational being, each herdsman seeks to maximize his gain. Explicitly or implicitly, more or less consciously, he asks: "What is the utility to *me* of adding one more animal to my herd?" This utility has two components:
>
> 1. A positive component, which is a function of the increment of one animal. Since the herdsman receives all the proceeds from the sale of the additional animal, the positive utility is nearly $+1$.
> 2. A negative component, which is a function of the additional overgrazing created by one more animal. But since the effects of overgrazing are shared by all the herdsmen, the negative utility for any particular decision-making herdsman is only a fraction of -1.
>
> Adding together the component partial utilities, the rational herdsman concludes that the only sensible course for him to pursue is to add another animal to his herd. And another, and another. . . . Therein is the tragedy. Each man is *locked in* to a system that compels him to increase his herd without limit—in a world that is limited. Ruin is the destination toward which all men rush, each pursuing his own best interest in a society that believes in the freedom of the commons.[2]

Hardin suggests a stark and inescapable connection between common ownership of resources and their ultimate exhaustion. But, in fact, grazing and fishing grounds in most traditional societies have often been commonly held and managed quite sustainably for centuries. This was achieved by informal social restraints and traditions that

---

[2]Garrett Hardin (1968), "The Tragedy of the Commons," *Science,* 168, December 13. Copyright 1969 by the AAAS. Reprinted by permission.

prevented overexploitation. However, when such restraints break down as a result of "modernization" or population pressures, the open access problem emerges, and a tragedy of the commons is likely to result.[3]

The open access problem explains not only why sources of natural capital like grazing land are degraded but also why environmental sinks like the air are polluted. For example, a factory owner might install a low-cost technology that generates substantial air pollution, in spite of the fact that he and his family live nearby and will be exposed to the toxic materials. The owner captures the full benefits of the pollution (the profit from "low-cost" production), while his family bears only a small portion of the total risk.

In combination with vastly more efficient technology, open access also explains the dramatic decline in fish catches off the New England coast over the past seven or eight years. According to the *Wall Street Journal,* "the trawler catch in New England peaked in 1983 and has since fallen sharply. Stocks of flounder and haddock are near record lows. The cod population is down. Bluefin tuna and swordfish have been depleted." But in spite of this situation, some fishers still oppose catch limits. "Straining to pay off mortgages on expensive boats, many fishermen say they don't have the luxury of *not* catching as much as they can as fast as they can."[4] Indeed, perversely, the incentive for any individual fisherperson is to employ more and more sophisticated technology to increase his or her share of a dwindling stock.

We can explore this overfishing issue further with the help of a hypothetical example. Suppose that fish cost a dollar a pound, and the marginal cost of running a vessel—including the fuel and salaries for crew and owner—is $250 per day. Then the rational response for fishing boats is to continue to fish as long as, on average, the catch exceeds 250 pounds. Suppose that the relationship between the number of vessels and the total catch in a New England bay is illustrated in Table 3.1.

TABLE 3.1	Vessels and Total Catch in a New England Bay
Number of Vessels	*Total Catch*
1	400 lb
2	800
3	1,200
4	1,600
5	1,900
6	2,100
7	2,100
8	2,000

[3]See Bromley (1991) for a full discussion.
[4]"Dead in the Water," *Wall Street Journal,* July 18, 1991.

Given this information, consider the following:

PUZZLE

Part 1.   If there were open access to the bay and seven boats were already fishing, would you fish in the bay?

Part 2.   If you ran the government fisheries board, how many boats would you allow out if you wanted to maximize total profits from the bay?

SOLUTION

Part 1.   The revenue for the eighth boat is $1 times the average catch of 250 pounds, or $250. You'd earn a day's salary and cover costs if you went out, so it is worth it.

Part 2.   Six is a common guess but it is incorrect. Six maximizes *revenue,* but profit is revenue minus cost. Table 3.2 puts together some additional information to help answer this part.

To maximize the profit from the New England bay, additional boats should be sent out up to the point where the value of the addition to the total catch just exceeds the opportunity cost of sending out the boat. The fisheries board would stop at *five boats,* since the sixth would bring in only $100 in marginal revenue, less than enough to cover its costs of $250. The final column labeled marginal profit (the *extra* profit from each additional boat) makes this clear: After five boats, losses begin to accumulate.

TABLE 3.2   Calculating the Profit-Maximizing Harvest

Number of Vessels	Total Catch	Marginal Catch	Marginal Revenue	Average Catch	Average Revenue	Marginal Profit
1	400 lb	400 lb	$400	400 lb	$400	+$150
2	800	400	400	400	400	+ 150
3	1,200	400	400	400	400	+ 150
4	1,600	400	400	400	400	+ 150
5	1,900	300	300	380	380	+ 50
6	2,100	200	200	350	350	− 50
7	2,100	0	000	300	300	− 250
8	2,000	−100	−100	250	250	− 350

Note there are two externalities here. First, after four boats, some of the catch of the new entrants is diverted from other boats. Second, after seven boats, the catch exceeds a sustained yield level, and over time the stock of fish begins to decline. When there is open access to the bay, however, individual fisherpeople don't recognize (but more importantly don't care) about these negative externalities imposed on the other boats; each bears only a small portion of the reduction in the total stock. Thus, boats continue to go out even when the total catch, and total revenue in the industry, declines. As a result of open access, in New England, a human and ecological tragedy is indeed unfolding.

Figure 3.3 below develops a graphical analysis of the open access problem. Marginal revenue first stays constant and then falls, reflecting eventual declining marginal productivity as additional boats go out. Notice the average and marginal revenue curves coincide up to four boats—but once declining marginal productivity kicks in, the marginal curve lies below the average revenue curve. (This is due to the mathematical relationship between marginal and average values: As long as the addition to revenue equals the average revenue, the average stays constant and equal to the marginal value. However, when additions to revenue fall below the average, the average is pulled down.) Finally the constant marginal cost of sending out additional boats is represented by the straight line at $250.

Again, the figure tells us that private boats will go out as long as *average* revenue covers costs, even though the total profits earned in the industry are going down. The profit-maximizing catch level occurs where *marginal* revenue just exceeds marginal costs at five boats.

The profit earned in the industry is displayed visually as the sum total of the difference between marginal revenue and marginal cost for each boat that goes out— the shaded area in the diagram.[5] The hatched area in the picture shows the *reduction in profit* for the industry as a result of overfishing. For the sixth through eighth boats,

FIGURE 3.3 The Common Property Problem

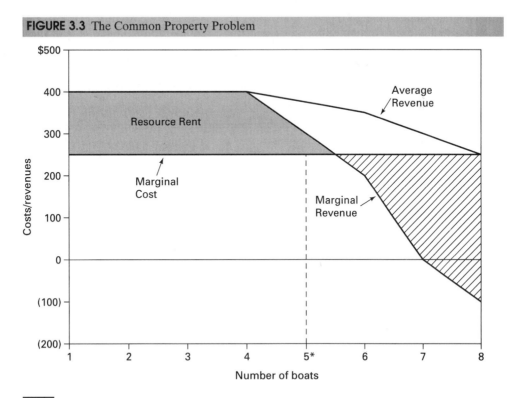

5Technically, this is not profit but producer surplus, because the example ignores fixed costs. The language is chosen for ease of exposition.

the marginal revenue is *less than* the marginal cost, leading to a drop in industry-wide profits. Clearly, the total industry-wide profit is largest at five boats.

In Chapter 2 we learned that an efficient outcome is one in which the net benefits produced by the economy are maximized. Here, the efficient number of boats is five. This is true since in this example, where the price of fish (and thus the consumer) is unaffected by the small changes in supply, net social benefits are just equal to profits.

The picture also illustrates a key feature of markets that rely on scarce natural capital either as sources or sinks. *When natural capital is used efficiently, long-run economic profits will be earned by those who retain access to the resource.* It is precisely those profits that attract entry into the market and lead to overexploitation of the source or the sink. These long-run profits, generated by restricted access to natural capital, are called **resource rents.** Comparable to rents earned by landlords at choice properties, these are rents due to ownership of (or limited access to) scarce natural resources.

In our example, open access in the fishery leads to an outcome in which profits in the industry are competed completely away. With eight boats, average revenue equals average cost, and all the boats just break even. But at the efficient level, where marginal revenue equals marginal cost, a substantial resource rent is earned. Adding up the difference between marginal revenue and marginal cost (marginal profit) for the first five boats, the resource rent turns out to be $650 per day.

In the New England case, economist Steven Edwards and biologist Steven Murawski have estimated that fishing efforts off of New England would have to be reduced by about 70% to eliminate overfishing and achieve an efficient harvest. This in turn would generate a resource rent in the industry of around $130 million.[6] The rent might go to the government in the form of fees for fishing rights or to the remaining fishermen and women in the form of profits. Edwards calculates that government revenues from a fee system would be sufficient to compensate those boats put out of business by restrictions, suggesting a politically feasible way out of this tough problem.

Fisherpeople in New England often resent governmental restrictions placed on access to fishing grounds; it is, after all, their livelihood and lifestyle at stake. However, without some kind of restraint on open access to common property resources, overuse to the point of exhaustion is the predictable consequence.

This section has illustrated three main points. First, when there is open access to common property, overexploitation will generally result since users will not take the full social cost of their action into account. Second, government-imposed restraints on access to common property like fisheries, clean air, and clean water will generate a resource rent, or long-run economic profit, for those who maintain access. Finally, this rent can sometimes be collected through taxes or fees and used to reimburse those who lose out in the process of regulating and reducing access.

3.2 The Public Goods Problem

The open access problem may explain why there is a tendency for commonly held resources such as clean air and water, or fisheries, to be overexploited. But why does the government have to decide what to do about it? Instead, why don't the victims of neg-

---

[6]Tregarten (1992).

ative externalities simply band together on their own to prevent pollution? As we noted above, this was the response to environmental degradation of common grazing and fishing grounds in traditional societies. Informal social pressure and tradition were relied on to prevent overexploitation. The modern American equivalent would be to sue an offending company or individual for damages. Indeed, a few so-called **free-market environmentalists** have advocated eliminating many environmental regulations, then relying on lawsuits by injured parties to "internalize" externalities.[7]

Such private remedies to environmental degradation run into what economists call the **public goods problem.** Public goods are goods enjoyed in common; a classic example, though a little dated, is the warning service provided by a lighthouse. Technically, economists describe public goods as "non-excludable." Once in operation, it is impossible to exclude any passing boat from utilizing the warning beacon provided by the lighthouse.[8]

The provision of public goods is a problem for the free market due to the existence of two factors: transactions costs and free riding. To illustrate, consider a good that is enjoyed in common such as, for example, the noise level after 11 o'clock at night in Marilyn's neighborhood. Now suppose that neighbor Tipper cranks her sound system. Marilyn could go to the considerable trouble of obtaining signatures from all of his neighbors, getting money from them to hire a lawyer, file a lawsuit, and possibly obtain a legal injunction requiring her to turn it down. The costs of undertaking this action are known as **transactions costs,** and they are particularly high because of the public nature of the injury.

If Marilyn does undertake the effort, he will benefit not only himself but also the entire neighborhood. Some of the neighbors might refuse to help out and instead **free ride** on Marilyn's provision of the public good. Instead, Marilyn decides it's not really worth organizing a lawsuit and tosses and turns in bed, hoping that someone else will make the effort. The result is that, although there may be considerable total demand for a quiet evening in the neighborhood, it doesn't get expressed. It is not worth it to any one individual to overcome the transactions costs and the possibility of free riding required to provide the public good of the lawsuit, though, if Marilyn did, the social benefits might far outweigh the cost.

In most towns, the response to noise pollution is a government regulation called a nuisance law. With such a regulation in place, Marilyn can just call the cops, greatly reducing the costs associated with stopping the noise. The general principle is that without government intervention, public goods—in this case, a quiet evening—will be undersupplied. This is not to say that no public goods will be supplied. Some will, but less than the amount that society collectively is willing to pay for.

To see this, consider another example: private contributions to purchase and preserve wetlands and other valuable ecosystems in the United States. The organization The Nature Conservancy currently solicits funds to do this. Suppose such an organization sends a mailing to Mr. Peabody and Mr. Massey saying it needs $50 to preserve the last 100 feet of a prime Appalachian trout stream. Now Peabody would be willing to pay $30 and Massey $40 toward the effort, for a total of $70. Thus, the monetary benefits of preservation exceed the costs by $20.

---

[7] See the introductory and concluding essays in Greve and Smith (1992).

[8] Pure public goods also have another characteristic: They are non-rival. This means that the one boat's use of the lighthouse service does not reduce the value of that service to others.

PUZZLE

Will The Nature Conservancy get enough in contributions to buy the land?

SOLUTION

Not necessarily. Peabody, figuring Massey will pay $40, may contribute only $10, while Massey, following the same logic, will contribute only $20, for a total of $30. As a result, each will try to free ride off the other's provision of the 100 feet of public good and sufficient funds will not be forthcoming.

We can approach this problem graphically, by examining the difference between the demand curve for a public good and a more conventional private good. In Figure 3.4A, let us assume that the trout stream is for sale to private individuals. Note that, for 100 feet of land, as above, Peabody would pay $30 and Massey $40, but now they do not have to share it. As you may recall from a previous course, the demand curve for a private good is the horizontal sum of the individual demand curves. At a price of $30, Peabody demands 100 feet while Massey demands 120 feet, so total demand equals 100 + 120, or 220 feet. In a market for private goods, consumers face a single price, and each individual consumes as much as she wants to buy. Thus, total demand is met.

By contrast, when goods are public, all consumers face a given public quantity and must decide how much to pay. In Figure 3.4B, the trout stream has become a public good: Massey and Peabody must share whatever is purchased. For 100 feet of land, we know their collective value is $70; following this logic we can see that their total willingness to pay (or their demand) for any given amount of preservation is the *vertical* sum of the individual demand curves.

FIGURE 3.4 Demand for Private and Public Goods

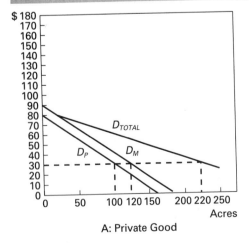

A: Private Good

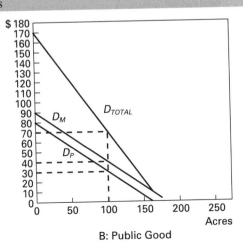

B: Public Good

The true total demand for public goods is seldom expressed in the market for two reasons. First, unlike the case for private goods, some third party must organize the collection of funds to pay for the public good or to initiate a lawsuit against a polluter. Marilyn would have to drag himself out of bed and go collect signatures on a petition from the neighbors to convince a judge to tell Tipper to shut up. More generally, there may be large costs associated with proving highly contestable environmental damages in a court of law. The need to support such efforts raises the *transactions costs*—the costs associated with making a market deal—for public goods.

Second, in the case of public goods, individuals have an incentive to *free ride* on the efforts of others. Though Massey and Peabody collectively value the land at more than its asking price, they may be unwilling to reveal their true preferences to a private agency or government collecting revenues to pay for the public good. Incentives to free ride are often dampened in small groups, where an individual can see his or her individual effort as "pivotal" to the success of the public effort, and/or a sense of group responsibility is carried by the members.[9] However, such conditions are unlikely to hold for most pollution control efforts, making free riding a serious obstacle for nongovernmental attempts to provide such goods.

To summarize this section, in contrast to private goods, public goods are consumed in common. The true demand for public goods will not be satisfied in pure market economies due to high transactions costs and free riding. Free-market environmentalists who advocate relying solely on the court system to internalize environmental externalities recognize these twin hurdles. Yet they believe these obstacles are not really that large, especially considering the costs associated with regulation. Most economists, however, argue that as a result of transaction costs and free riding, public goods such as clean air or water, rain forests, wilderness parks, and other environmental amenities, will be undersupplied in a laissez-faire market system.[10]

3.3 Summary

In this chapter we have analyzed two different aspects of communal property that contribute to the degradation of the environment. First, the open access problem explains why individuals would knowingly damage a resource upon which they depend. Second, the public goods problem explains, in part, why people cannot "buy" a clean environment, either by suing polluters or purchasing wilderness. Transactions costs are high, and there is a tendency for people to free ride on the efforts of others.

The point is that free-market forces do not provide the right incentives to insure that adequate care is taken to protect our environment. Given this, what should our response be? As we have noted, a few have argued that externalities can nevertheless be adequately internalized by means of private lawsuits. A second, more common response, which we will examine in chapters 18 through 20, has been a call for development of more environmentally benign "clean" technologies that reduce pollution

---

[9]See the review discussion in Mitchell and Carson (1989).

[10]Using the legal system to resolve externalities also involves very large administrative and transactions costs. For a general review of the economics of liability, see the symposium in the *Journal of Economic Perspectives,* 5, no. 3, Winter 1991, especially the article by Menell (1991).

problems in the first place. However, the conventional response has been government regulation of pollution, which brings us back to our principal topic: How much is too much?

Getting Government out of Pollution Control?

A recent article in the business magazine *Forbes*[11] blasted the U.S. Environmental Protection Agency for implementing ineffectual, expensive, and corrupt policies: "U.S. environmental policy is out of control, costing jobs, depressing living standards and being run by politicians, scheming business people and social extremists."

(I was actually not too surprised to find that politicians were running environmental policy, since that is, after all, part of the job they were elected to do.) Luckily, however, the article had a suggestion for eliminating our cumbersome pollution control bureaucracy:

> There is an environmental policy suited to the American Way: The development of property rights and the common law of tort. The threat of litigation will discourage pollution, with the details worked out between private parties. For example, neighbors could use "nuisance law" to sue a malodorous factory.
>
> Law students are taught in Environmental Law 101 that this approach didn't work, just as economics students are taught about "market failure"— the solution in both cases being government intervention. But modern scholarship suggests that the common law was indeed working until government intervened.

The *Forbes* article went on to cite Greve and Smith (1992) as a source of this "modern scholarship" that advocates free-market environmentalism.

1. Although the term "market failure" was not used in this chapter, we did indeed identify such a beast in the form of the public goods problem. And most economists do maintain that resolving pollution problems privately through lawsuits will result in too much pollution. Explain the two reasons why.

The Open Access Problem

Surrounding the Great Lake are four paper mills, each producing 100 tons of paper per year. The paper is sold on the national market for $2 per ton, and including all the costs of production, costs for each firm are $1 per ton. Thus each firm earns a pure economic profit of $1 per ton. These paper mills require fresh water to operate and also produce a pollutant called gunk, which the mills dump into the Great Lake.

New paper mills can also locate on the Great Lake and produce at a base cost of $1 per ton. However, for each new paper mill that arrives, the water will become more

---

[11]Peter Brimelow and Leslie Spencer, "You Can't Get There from Here," *Forbes,* July 6, 1992.

polluted with gunk, and each firm will have to install a water treatment facility to obtain freshwater. This externality associated with new plants will raise the costs of paper production at all facilities, including the new one, by $.15 per ton for each new mill.

1. Assume there is open access to the Great Lake. If paper mills will continue to locate as long as there is any economic profit to be earned, how many new mills will be built? How many mills maximize total combined profits for the paper producers? (Hint: Average revenue remains constant at $2. Create a table that compares average revenues with average and marginal costs as new firms locate around the lake.)

2. Draw a diagram of the marginal cost and marginal revenue curves with the number of mills on the horizontal axis. Assume that government regulation restricts lake access to the profit-maximizing number of firms. Show the resources rent earned by the mills that are allowed to operate.

3. Suppose that government regulation reduced the number of mills by one from the number that would have resulted given open access. Show that the increase in profits to the remaining firms (the resource rent) is sufficient to compensate the firm denied access for its lost profits.

Key Ideas in Each Section

3.0 A **negative externality** is an unbargained for, negative impact on a third party of a private transaction. **Internalizing an externality** means forcing the source of the externality to bear the external costs imposed on others.

3.1 Natural capital is the input that nature provides for our production and consumption processes. Pollution is the overuse of **sinks;** resource degradation is the overharvesting of **sources.** Negative externalities arise when there is **open access** to **common property** sources and sinks, such as air, water, or land. Traditional societies regulated access to common environmental resources using informal laws and restraints, but many of these have broken down. When access to natural capital is restricted, by either government action or private ownership, a **resource rent** is earned by those who retain access.

3.2 Is government regulation of the environment necessary to solve the open access problem? **Free-market environmentalists** believe polluters should be left unregulated and victims should sue to insure environmental quality. However, most economists argue that because a clean environment is a **public good,** the obstacles of high **transactions costs** and **free riding** mean that private negotiation in the courts would be inefficient (and also unsafe and unsustainable). Thus, government regulation is needed to internalize environmental externalities.

References

Bromley, Daniel (1991). *Environment and Economy: Property Rights and Public Policy.* Cambridge, MA: Blackwell.

Greve, Michael S. and Fred L. Smith (1992). *Environmental Politics: Public Costs, Private Rewards.* Boulder, CO: Praeger.

Hardin, Garrett (1968). "The Tragedy of the Commons." *Science,* vol. 168, December 13.

Menell, Peter S. (1991). "The Limitations of Legal Institutions for Addressing Environmental Risks." *Journal of Economic Perspectives,* 5, no. 3, 93–114.

Mitchell, Robert C. and Richard T. Carson (1989). *Using Surveys to Value Public Goods.* Washington, DC: Resources for the Future.

Tregarten, Timothy (1992). "Fishermen Find Fewer Fish." *The Margin,* vol. 7, Spring.

CHAPTER 4

The Efficiency Standard

4.0 Introduction

Some economists are fond of pointing out that achieving a goal of zero pollution not only would be prohibitively expensive but, indeed, might well be counterproductive. The view is that we should balance the costs and benefits of pollution reduction and seek, in general, to achieve an efficient amount of pollution. The idea that any level of pollution is "efficient" strikes many people as a bit odd. This chapter will thus begin by defining the efficient pollution level; next, illustrate how marginal analysis can be used, both in principle and in practice, to identify the efficient pollution level; and, finally, discuss the utilitarian ethical defense of the efficiency standard.

4.1 Efficiency Defined

To understand what is meant by an efficient level of pollution, we need to look closer at the concept of efficiency. The term "efficient" in everyday parlance means a situation in which no resources are wasted. Economists use the term in a related but more specific way. The economic definition of efficiency was introduced by the Italian economist Vilfred Pareto in 1909 and is named in his honor.

> **Pareto efficient situation:** A situation in which it is impossible to make one person better off without making anyone else worse off.

When economists say an outcome is efficient, they almost always mean "Pareto efficient." I'll drop the Pareto most of the time as well, adding the modifier only when I want to remind the reader that we are using this specific definition.

The advantage of pursuing efficiency is that, conditional on the existing distribution of income, it makes the "economic pie" as big as possible. In fact, at the efficient outcome, the **net monetary benefits** produced by the economy will be maximized. This means that the difference between all benefits that can be given a monetary value, both human-made and those generated by nature, minus all costs of production, both private and external, will be as large as possible at the efficient point.

How do we know this? By applying the definition of efficiency. If it were possible to make someone better off without making someone else worse off (meaning that we are at an *inefficient* point), we could always make the "economic pie" of net benefits bigger by moving toward efficiency.

The first point to make about efficiency is that it need not be fair. Thus, on its own, efficiency may not be much use as a guide to good social outcomes. I recall first learning about Pareto efficiency in my microeconomics class and asking the teacher if it would be possible to have an efficient slave society. The answer was yes—freeing the slaves might not be "efficient" because, in monetary terms, the masters might lose more than the slaves would gain.

Yet whenever the economic pie is enlarged, it is at least possible for everyone to get a bigger slice. Thus, any move toward efficiency can in theory be a "win-win" situation. We have already considered one such case: By restricting fishing in New England, the government could generate enough resource rent to both compensate the fisherfolks put out of business and allow the remaining boats to earn a decent living. Let us look at another such case involving the use of California's scarce water resources.

California is a semi-arid state with a vast agricultural industry and rapidly growing urban centers. Water is scarce, and an unlikely coalition of corporate farmers and environmentalists have supported moving to an open market in water rights to increase the efficiency with which existing supplies are used.[1] Farmers seek a profit from the sale of their water, while environmentalists are interested in forestalling the construction of ecologically disruptive new dams in the state.

To simplify a complex story, farmland in California comes endowed with rights to a percentage of water from a given reservoir; currently farmers use about 85% of the state's water. The price for agricultural water charged by state and federal governments is much lower than that for metropolitan use: One study put the price of the former at $10 per acre foot, while the latter was priced at $100 per acre foot. This low price for agricultural water has resulted in such clearly inefficient but profitable uses as growing irrigated hay in Death Valley. This practice is inefficient because it shrinks the size of California's economic pie. The water could be used to produce output in other sectors of the economy with a higher monetary value: other less water-intensive crops, industrial products, or perhaps even green lawns (which raise the value of homes) in metropolitan areas. A 1978 study estimated that California's gross domestic product was about $5 billion lower than it would have been had water been allocated efficiently.

We can analyze the situation by considering there to be two markets for water in California: agricultural and metropolitan, with no transfer in between. This situation is illustrated in Figure 4.1A. The state could move toward efficiency by combining the markets into one, as illustrated in Figure 4.1B, thus generating a single price of around $70.

One way to achieve this goal would be for the government bodies selling the water simply to raise the price to its market level, in this example, $70. A 1982 statewide initiative calling for a similar approach was defeated, not surprisingly, with heavy opposition from farm interests. Such an effort would clearly be efficient since the water not bought by farmers would be freed up for metropolitan use. However, it was thought to be unfair in the way it penalized farmers by changing the rules of the game in midstream.

---

[1]This analysis is drawn from Gomez-Ibanez and Kalt (1990).

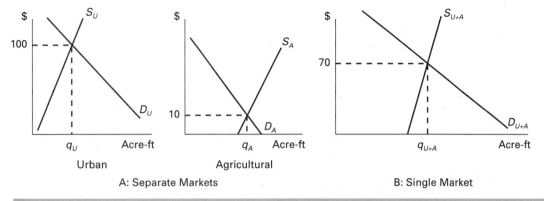

FIGURE 4.1 California Water Pricing and Efficiency

Yet, as is always the case when moving toward efficiency, a Pareto-improving alternative policy exists—one that makes everyone better off. In California, farmers could continue to purchase their old allotments at $10 but be allowed to resell them without restriction to the urban sector. In this case, the Death Valley farmer could continue to grow her hay but, by doing so, would be passing up substantial profit opportunities. By simply reselling her water she could make $90 per acre foot! Under this policy, farmers would gradually abandon inefficient farming practices and become "water tycoons." Reforms of this nature are now being sought in California.

Either policy—a single price or subsidized prices with water marketing—would put a lot of farmers out of the farming business, and the California economy would shift toward greater industrial and service-sector production. Overall, economists would predict that the monetary value of California production would rise as water flowed into higher-value uses. Thus, *both policies are efficient,* though the first one is unfair in many ways. It is worth noting that both policies would also encourage urban growth in California, itself considered a problem by many people. Are green lawns in the suburban desert really an "efficient" use of water, that is, one that makes people happier overall? We will take a close look at the complex relationship between growth and social welfare later in Chapter 11.

One reason that economists like efficient outcomes is that, as in the California case, when moving from an inefficient outcome to an efficient outcome, it is at least possible to make everyone better off without making anyone else worse off. This means that equity need not, in theory, be sacrificed when moving from a less to a more efficient outcome. More often, however, there are almost always winners and losers from any change in economic policy, even those that increase economic efficiency. The point here is that efficiency and fairness are different notions. Efficient outcomes need not be equitable (or moral or fair), though they may be. At the same time, equitable outcomes need not be efficient, though they may be.

4.2 Efficient Pollution Levels

Now you may recall that we are supposed to be discussing the right amount of pollution. How does efficiency fit in here? Let's take the simplest example of pollution one can think of, by following two workers, Brittany and Tyler, into their office in the morning.

They sit down at their desks, and Tyler pulls out a pack of smokes and proceeds to light up. Brittany hates cigarettes, but there's no rule against smoking in the office. Tyler's been smoking about five a day. Brittany is pretty desperate, so she considers a bribe. "How much would I have to pay you to smoke one less cigarette per day?" Tyler thinks it over. "One cigarette? I can put up with that for four dollars," he says. "Two per day?" she inquires. "That'll be tougher. You'd have to pay me six more dollars for that one." The third cigarette, it turns out, could be eliminated for a bribe of an additional $8.00. They keep at it, developing Table 4.1 below.

Table 4.1 reveals that, due to his addiction, Tyler is increasingly reluctant to give up each additional cigarette. Indeed, even after receiving a total of $28.00 for the first four, he would have to receive *an additional $12* to quit smoking altogether.

Brittany has her own notion of the benefits of pollution reduction in the office. Getting rid of the first cigarette is essential to making the environment tolerable: She'd be willing to pay $10 to do so. Eliminating the next cigarette would make a big improvement but is not absolutely necessary. It's worth $8. Her private benefit schedule for cigarette reduction is illustrated in Table 4.2.

The benefits of additional pollution reduction decline for Brittany as the number of cigarettes smoked falls, because the health damage and discomfort she experiences also decline. Thus, she's only willing to pay $2 to get rid of the last cigarette, perhaps because she can take her daily coffee break (choose yer poison) when Tyler chooses to light that one up.

Note here that we're focusing on reducing cigarettes (pollution) one at a time. Economists call this **marginal analysis.** The last unit of pollution reduced is called the **marginal unit;** the costs (to Tyler) of reducing that unit are called the **marginal costs,** and the benefits (to Brittany) from reducing that unit are called the **marginal benefits.** Comparison of marginal costs with marginal benefits will help us zero in on the efficient level of pollution.

To help us determine the efficient level of cigarette reduction, Figure 4.2 graphs the marginal costs and benefits of giving up cigarettes. On the horizontal axis we have the number of cigarettes reduced per day; on the vertical axis, dollars. Because marginals represent *changes* in total values as we move from one unit to the next, it is conventional to graph marginal values in between the units on the X axis. For example, the marginal cost of the fourth cigarette reduced is $10. Because this is the change in total cost as we move from 3 to 4 cigarettes reduced, you will notice that the $10 value is graphed halfway between 3 and 4.

TABLE 4.1   Marginal and Total Costs of Cleanup

Number of Cigarettes Reduced	Additional Payment Required Per Cigarette Reduced	Total Payment Required
1	$ 4.00	$ 4.00
2	$ 6.00	$10.00
3	$ 8.00	$18.00
4	$10.00	$28.00
5	$12.00	$40.00

TABLE 4.2 Marginal and Total Benefits of Cleanup

Number of Cigarettes Reduced	Additional Willingness to Pay Per Cigarette Reduced	Total Willingness to Pay
1	$10.00	$10.00
2	$ 8.00	$18.00
3	$ 6.00	$24.00
4	$ 4.00	$28.00
5	$ 2.00	$30.00

The curve labeled "marginal costs of pollution reduction" illustrates the cost to Tyler of giving up additional cigarettes. It slopes upward, reflecting the fact that the first cigarette smoked can be given up at low cost by Tyler, although he would have to be mightily bribed to give up smoking altogether. The curve labeled "marginal benefits of pollution reduction" reflects the value to Brittany of a progressively less smoky environment. It slopes downward, because the health risk and discomfort from breathing secondary smoke decreases as the number of cigarettes smoked goes down.

You can probably guess where the efficient level of pollution reduction is going to be. (*X* marks the spot.) Indeed, two cigarettes reduced is the efficient number. Why? Because *at any other level of pollution, both parties can be made better off by trading.*

FIGURE 4.2 Marginal Costs and Benefits of Cleanup

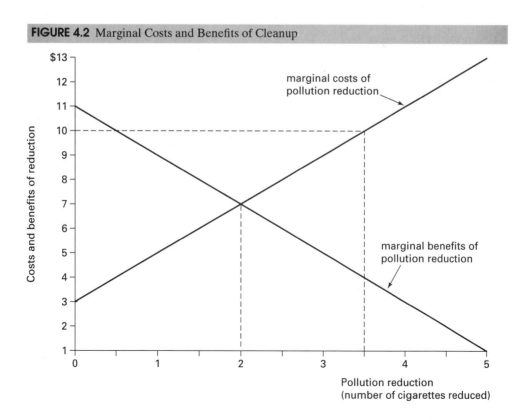

To see this, consider the following:

PUZZLE

Tyler, who loves to smoke, would puff his way through five cigarettes a day if he were in the office by himself. Tyler is a selfish individual, and he has the right to smoke as much as he wants. Would he continue smoking five cigarettes if Brittany were around?

SOLUTION

The answer is no. Tyler is willing to give up one cigarette for $4, and Brittany is willing to pay him ten dollars to do so. Thus, he can make up to six dollars in "profit" by accepting the initial bribe. Similarly, Tyler will accept six dollars for the next cigarette, and Brittany would pay up to eight dollars to get him not to smoke it. Thus, he can earn an additional profit of up to two dollars by reducing the second cigarette. Finally, Brittany would pay Tyler only six dollars to reduce the third cigarette, and that would be less than the $8 necessary to get him to give it up. Thus, Brittany will pay Tyler to eliminate two cigarettes, and *both* will be better off than if Tyler smoked all five.

Clearly Tyler would not give up the second-to-last cigarette: Brittany would have to pay Tyler ten dollars to get him to give it up, and it is worth only four dollars to her in increased comfort and safety. Only for those cigarettes where the marginal cost curve (Tyler's required compensation for reducing pollution) lies below the marginal benefit curve (Brittany's willingness to pay for pollution reduction), will Tyler be better off by striking a deal with Brittany than by smoking.

This example is worth close study (or, as I tell my students, this one will be on the test). To check to make sure you follow it, take a minute to explain to yourself why it is that, *at any level of pollution other than three cigarettes smoked (or two reduced), both parties can be made better off through a trade.* Three cigarettes smoked is the efficient level of pollution, because only at three cigarettes is it impossible to make one party better off without making the other worse off.

Here is an outcome that, while efficient, would strike many people as being unfair. Why should Brittany have to pay Tyler not to slowly poison her? This question is, as we will see, crucial in the discussion of a safety pollution standard. But efficiency defenders respond in two ways: First, they argue, whether polluters have a right to pollute or victims have a right to prevent pollution should not necessarily be settled in the victim's favor. While agreeing that fairness is an important issue, they feel ultimately that it is a matter of value judgment, thus lying outside the realm of economics.[2] But as we will see below, the efficiency standard, in fact, has its own basis in "value judgments."

---

[2]In textbook neoclassical theory, of course, equity and efficiency are the two normative criteria that should drive policy. However, in practice, some environmental economists look only at efficiency. See Bromley (1990) for a discussion.

A more consistent defense of the efficiency standard is that, since efficient outcomes maximize the monetary size of the total pie, consistently pursuing efficient outcomes will, on balance, benefit most people over time. While Brittany might lose out from this level of cigarette pollution, she will benefit from efficient regulation elsewhere. For example, she may get lower-priced strawberries if pesticide use is regulated at an efficient, as opposed to a safe, level.

In this section, we have employed marginal analysis to identify the efficient pollution level—where the marginal benefits and costs of pollution reduction are equal. At any other level of pollution, it is *possible* to make all parties better off by moving toward efficiency. This section has also illustrated that efficient outcomes need not accord with standard notions of fairness. We now move on to consider the relationship between a marginal analysis of pollution reduction and one based on total costs and benefits.

4.3 Marginals and Totals

As noted above, focusing on marginal costs and marginal benefits allowed us to isolate the efficient pollution level. This section digresses for a moment to illustrate the relationship between marginal and total cleanup costs and the marginal and total benefits of cleanup. The bottom panel of Figure 4.3 reproduces the marginal relationships in Figure 4.2 while the top panel graphs the total costs of cleanup (to Tyler) and the total benefits (to Brittany).

Both sets of curves illustrate the same information. The *total* costs of pollution reduction rise at an increasing rate, generating a curve that is bowed upward; another way of saying this is that the additional or *marginal* cost of each cigarette given up rises. Similarly, the *total* benefits of cleanup rise at a decreasing rate, producing a downward bowed curve; thus, the *marginal* benefits of pollution reduction are falling.

How can we move from one set of curves to another? The marginal cost curve represents the change in total costs. Thus, as the figure illustrates, the marginal cost of the first cigarette reduced, $4, is just the change in the total cost curve between 0 and 1 cigarette reduced. Similarly, the marginal benefit of the fifth cigarette reduced, $2, is the change in the total benefits curve between 4 and 5 cigarettes reduced. The marginal curves graph the total change in y for a 1-unit change in x. But this is just the "rise" over the "run" of the total curve. Thus, the marginal curves graph the slopes of the total curves.[3]

Moreover, the area *under* the marginal cost curve equals the total cost. For example, the marginal cost of the first cigarette reduced, $4, plus the marginal cost of the second, $6, equals the total costs of two cigarettes reduced, $10. But $4 is just the area under the marginal curve between 0 and 1, while $6 is the area under the curve between 1 and 2. We will use this relationship often in the chapters ahead.

Finally, note that *the efficient pollution level does not occur where total costs equal total benefits* (at four cigarettes reduced). At this point, since total benefits and costs are equal, the net monetary benefits to "society" are zero. Instead, the efficient level occurs where the total benefit curve lies farthest above the total cost curve. Here, the net monetary benefits to Brittany and Tyler combined are maximized. At the point

[3]For those students with a calculus background, the marginal curve graphs the derivative of the total curve.

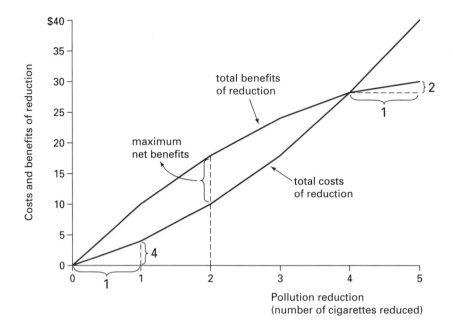

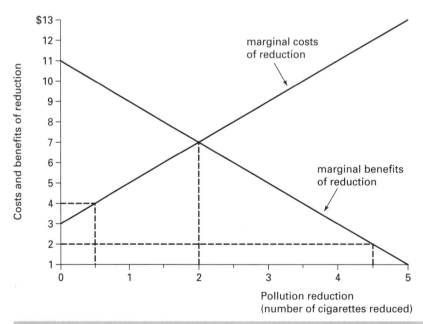

FIGURE 4.3 Marginals and Totals Compared: Costs and Benefits of Pollution Reduction

where total benefits and costs are equal, we know we have reduced pollution "too much" under an efficiency standard. At this point the *marginal* costs of reduction exceed the *marginal* benefits, given the conventional shapes of the benefit and cost curves.[4]

To summarize: The relationship between the marginal and total benefit and cost curves is a straightforward one. The marginal curves graph the change in the total curves or, equivalently, their slope. An upward slope to the marginal cost of reduction curve thus reflects total pollution costs, which rise at an increasing rate. Similarly, the downward slope to the marginal benefit of reduction curve results from an assumption that the total benefits of reducing pollution increase at a decreasing rate. Controlling pollution to a level where the total benefits of reduction equal the total costs results in too much control from an efficiency perspective.

4.4 The Coase Theorem Introduced

One interesting aspect of the efficiency perspective is that, under certain circumstances, whichever way initial rights over pollution are granted, the efficient level of pollution doesn't change! To see this, think for a minute about the case where Brittany is granted the right to ban smoking in the office. Will she do so?

Referring back to Figure 4.2, we can see that the answer is no. If Tyler were willing to give up his last cigarette for twelve dollars, he would enjoy that cigarette more than, say, $11.99 in cash. Thus, he should be *willing to pay up to that amount* to be able to smoke it! Brittany, on the other hand, is now in the position of taking bribes, and her marginal benefit curve indicates she would rather have $2 than a smoke-free environment. So the two can strike a deal on the first cigarette. Similarly, because Tyler values the second at up to ten dollars, and Brittany will sell him a "smoking right" for anything over four dollars, there is room to deal. Finally, Tyler would pay eight dollars for the third cigarette, and Brittany would accept (though she would only be making $2 in profit, it is still profit!). Notice, they would not go on to four cigarettes though, because Tyler would pay only six dollars for it, and Brittany would demand eight dollars.

We have just shown that, for a simple case of pollution reduction uncomplicated by transactions costs and free riding (discussed in the last chapter), the efficient outcome is independent of whether pollution is legal or not. If polluter and victim can bargain easily and effectively, private negotiation should arrive at the efficient outcome regardless of who has the initial right to pollute or prevent pollution. This result is known as the **Coase theorem,** after Nobel prize–winning economist Ronald Coase.

Some have interpreted the Coase theorem to imply that from an efficiency perspective it does not matter who has to pay for pollution—victims or polluters. Either way, one arrives at an efficient solution. (Of course, on fairness grounds most would argue that polluters should have to pay for damages.) However, as Coase himself recognized, the theorem holds only under highly limited circumstances.

In fact, efficiency will in general be better served under a **polluter pays principle.** This is true for two reasons. The first of these is the public good nature of pollution cleanup discussed in the last chapter. In real-world settings, a single polluter typically

---

[4]In important cases, the curves may not be shaped this way. See advanced topic chapter T1, "The Importance of Being Convex," as well as Application 4.2 at the end of this chapter.

affects a broad community. Requiring polluters to pay for the privilege of polluting is more likely to generate an efficient outcome than a policy that legalizes pollution and requires victims to pay. Having the polluter pay reduces the free riding and transactions costs associated with the latter policy.

More importantly, the assignment of liability has important long-run effects. If Brittany paid Tyler not to smoke, she would very likely soon find all the smokers in the office moving their desk close to hers! More generally, if firms are given the right to pollute (or are subsidized to reduce pollution), this lowers their costs. In the long run, this encourages entry into the market and creates more pollution.[5] For example, when taxpayers at large pay for the construction of landfills, households and firms have little long-run incentive to minimize their production of garbage. On the other hand, if landfill construction costs are financed by "pay-by-the-bag" disposal fees, waste producers have an incentive to modify their long-run waste production strategies.

As we will see later, the Coase theorem is quite useful when analyzing the initial distribution of permits in a marketable permit system. For now, though, this example illustrates clearly the claim not only that zero pollution levels are very expensive (poor Tyler suffers severe nicotine withdrawals) but also that a solution more efficient than banning exists in which all parties are made better off.

To review this section, the Coase theorem demonstrates that in the absence of transactions costs and free riding, the efficient pollution control level can be achieved through negotiation regardless of who has the legal right to pollute or prevent pollution. In the real world, however, efficiency will best be served by following a polluter pays principle. This is true both because of transactions costs and free riding, and because long-run incentives for entry into the polluting industry are reduced when the polluter pays.

4.5 Air Pollution Control in Baltimore: Calculating the Efficient Standard

To give you a feel for how the efficiency standard might be applied in practice, let us look at a study that estimated the marginal benefits and marginal costs of reducing suspended particulate emissions in Baltimore under the current type of regulation.[6] Suspended particulates are small particles of ash or soot emitted as a by-product of burning fossil fuels for power or transport. They contribute to respiratory ailments, some of which are fatal, soil clothing and buildings, and reduce visibility. Figure 4.4 graphs the estimated marginal costs and benefits of different total suspended particulate (TSP) standards.

The marginal cost curve has the same shape as that in Figure 4.2; reducing particulate emissions becomes increasingly costly. To move from a standard of 110 to 109 parts per million would cost about $3 million, while tightening the standard from 95 to 94 parts per million would cost an additional $16 million. This is because under the regulations in Baltimore, source types with relatively low costs of reduction must trim their emissions first. To meet tougher standards, facilities facing higher control costs must also reduce emissions.

[5]See Mohring and Boyd (1971).
[6]Oates, Portney, and McGartland (1989).

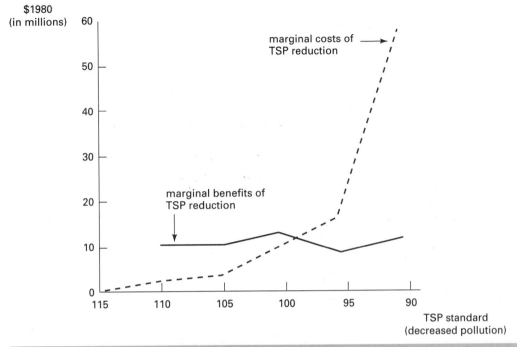

$1980
(in millions)

FIGURE 4.4 Particulate Standards in Baltimore: Identifying the Efficient Pollution Level

The marginal benefit curve is not presented in full for ease of presentation.
Source: Wallace E. Oates, Paul R. Portney, and Albert M. McGartland (1989: Figure 2), "The Net Benefits of Incentive-Based Regulation: A Case Study of Environmental Standard Setting," *American Economic Review,* December, 79, no. 5, 1233–1242. Reprinted by permission.

The marginal benefit curve, on the other hand, is relatively flat. Unlike the cigarette case, the additional benefits of reduction do not decrease as the pollution level falls. Instead, the authors of the study assume that tightening the standard from 110 to 109 parts per million yields roughly the same benefits—reduced death, sickness, and soiling, and improved visibility—as moving from a standard of 100 to 99 parts per million. They estimate these benefits to be around $10 million for each one-unit decrease in the particulate standard.

To arrive at this monetary figure for benefits, the authors value each life saved at $2 million, each lost workday at $100, and each restricted activity day at $25. Monetary benefits were also estimated for soiling and visibility. Chapter 8 discusses the means by which environmental economists attempt to estimate dollar values for these "priceless" elements of our lives. But to preview briefly, as suggested by the smoking example above, economists generally measure the benefits of pollution reduction based on society's willingness to pay for that reduction. The benefits of less smoke in the office were measured precisely by Brittany's willingness to pay for fewer cigarettes. Although this willingness-to-pay approach has problems we will explore in detail later, it captures the basic idea of trade-offs between a cleaner environment and all other goods.

The efficient standard occurs at about 98 parts per million. With a looser particulate standard, the additional benefits from reducing pollution up to 98 parts per million would be greater than the additional costs. However, moving to a standard tighter than 98 parts per million would entail additional costs exceeding the additional value of the benefits. Thus, net monetary benefits—the estimated value of clean air enjoyed by citizens of Baltimore less the cleanup costs borne by Baltimore firms (and ultimately, to some extent, Baltimore consumers)—are maximized at the efficient standard.

4.6 The Ethical Basis of the Efficiency Standard

Let us look one last time at the cigarette example and use our utility and social welfare functions to clearly focus on the ethical assumptions underlying the efficiency standard. First, there are no "equity" weightings: Tyler and Brittany's utility count equally in overall social welfare. Second, no distinction is made between the utility of pollution victims and beneficiaries—Tyler's need for cigarettes holds just as much weight as Brittany's need for clean air. Together these conditions imply that the social welfare function underlying the efficiency standard looks like this:

$$SW = U_{Tyler} (\overset{+}{\#Cigs_T}, \overset{+}{\$_T}) + U_{Brit} (\overset{-}{\#Cigs_T}, \overset{+}{\$_B})$$

Note the negative sign over Tyler's cigarette consumption in Brittany's utility function. Cigarettes are a "bad," not a "good," for her and so lower her utility. The social welfare function clearly illustrates the value judgments underlying the efficiency standard. By *not* weighting income distribution, efficiency advocates by default maintain that the *status quo* is acceptable. By treating victims and beneficiaries equally, efficiency proponents do not acknowledge a "right" to protection from harmful pollutants.

Recall that, as we have stressed, the efficiency standard does not require that losers be compensated, even though this is possible. Suppose that company policy originally banned smoking in the office, but the office manager then decreed Tyler could smoke three cigarettes a day, offering Brittany no compensation in return. *This is still an efficient outcome,* since in dollar terms, the gain to Tyler is greater than the loss to Brittany.

If overall happiness or social welfare is somehow maximized by such a policy, it must be the case that *additions to income must generate equal increases in happiness for the two people,* or in economists' terms, the two must have the same **marginal utility of income.** This in turn would imply that since the dollar gain to Tyler exceeds the dollar loss to Brittany, the happiness gain to Tyler also exceeds the happiness loss to Brittany. Thus, there is an overall gain in total happiness by a move toward efficiency, regardless of whether Brittany is compensated.[7]

For the efficiency standard to maximize social welfare, the assumption of equal marginal utilities of income must be true in general. However, this is highly unlikely: In practice, it means that a dollar to a millionaire yields equal happiness as a dollar to a street person. Thus, we must conclude that, *on its own terms,* the ethical basis of the

---

[7]This point is made in Kneese and Schulze (1985). Bromley (1990) also discusses the normative basis of the efficiency standard.

efficiency standard is a bit murky. Any individual move toward the efficiency standard will not, in general, increase social welfare.

It is worth stressing this point because many textbooks will refer to the efficient standard as "optimal" or "socially optimal." Even disregarding fairness issues (income distribution between and within generations and victims' rights), we have seen that such a claim relies on the very dubious assumption of equal marginal utilities of income.

Because a move to efficiency almost always creates losers as well as winners, such a move is not socially optimal. This does not mean that the efficiency standard is indefensible. It does, in fact, maximize the measurable *monetary* benefits to society. The best defense of the efficiency is that because of this, over time *most people* (NOT just polluters) will eventually reap net benefits from a move toward more efficient pollution standards. In concrete terms, most of us are *both* consumers of goods whose prices are raised by environmental regulation, and beneficiaries of cleaner air and water. Efficient regulation, according to its proponents, is the best way to balance these two concerns.

4.7 Summary

The efficiency approach puts the question of "How much pollution?" in a marginal cost, marginal benefit framework. In principle, we can replace "cigarettes reduced" with "pollution cleanup" in Figure 4.2, and the diagram will show us the efficient amount of nitrous oxide, sulfur dioxide, CFCs, dioxin, DDT, waste oil, particulates, heavy metals, litter, nuclear waste, or PCBs that "should" be in the environment. Of course, to make this approach operational, one needs to estimate a *dollar figure* for both the costs and benefits of reducing each unit of pollution. The benefit figure will include quantifiable savings such as those on medical care. But, as in the Baltimore case, it also must take into account less easily calculable benefits such as human lives saved and cancers avoided.

But why should any pollutant be in the environment? Society is willing to suffer pollution because it is an essential by-product of some good or service that people desire and because cleanup is not free. In Figure 4.5, the "supply curve" for pollution cleanup is just the marginal cost of reduction curve; it shows the increasing cost to society of eliminating additional units of pollution. This cost will be determined by the technology available for controlling the pollutant. The curve, for example, would shift down (toward the *x* axis) if cheaper ways of reducing pollution were discovered.

Society, on the other hand, clearly has a demand for pollution reduction. The "demand curve" for cleanup is the marginal benefits of reduction curve; it illustrates the increasing damages inflicted on people or the environment as the amount of cleanup decreases. The location of the curve depends on a variety of factors, such as the number of organisms (including people) affected, weather conditions, and defensive measures taken by those affected. In the Baltimore case, for example, the curve would shift up (away from the *x* axis) if more people moved into the city.

The efficient quantity of the pollution from the production of a desired product will occur just at the point where the additional costs of reduction are equal to the additional benefits of reduction. Any more reduction and the additional monetary costs borne by members of society exceed the additional monetary benefits; any less and there will be net social monetary benefits to be gained.

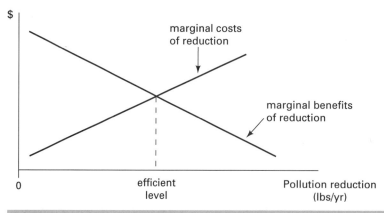

FIGURE 4.5 Marginal Costs and Benefits of Cleanup: The General Case

As our discussion of the open access and public good problems in the last chapter made clear, economists do not think that free markets generate the efficient amount of pollution. In the cigarette example, we saw that self-interested private parties, through their own negotiation, might arrive at the efficient level of pollution. But this was a rather special example, featuring perfect information about costs and damages, clearly defined property rights, zero transactions costs, and no free riding. In the real world, "markets for pollution" seldom develop naturally, and a more likely outcome in a real-world office would be an inefficient one. Until recently the open access outcome would have meant complete pollution—five cigarettes per day; more likely these days would be a safety-based regulation banning smoking completely.

This chapter has employed the notion of marginal costs and marginal benefits associated with pollution reduction to illustrate how one might identify an efficient level of pollution. The problems involved in actually measuring benefits and costs will be explored in Chapters 8, 9, and 10. We have also seen that a move to more efficient pollution control almost always generates winners and losers, and since the losers are seldom compensated, such a move cannot be considered socially optimal. The best ethical defense of efficiency is thus that, since it maximizes the size of the measurable economic pie, over time "most" people will benefit from more efficient pollution control. We now turn to a very different perspective—a safety standard.

APPLICATION 4.0

More on Efficient Smoking[8]

These smoking problems are a little silly but are good at illustrating some basic lessons about efficiency. So, this time, Groucho and Harpo work together in the same office. Groucho smokes; Harpo hates smoke. Groucho currently smokes twelve cigars per day. He faces marginal costs of reducing smoking (withdrawal pains) equal to $x, where x is the number of cigars reduced. In other words, the cost of giving up the first cigar is $1, the

---

[8]Thanks to Steve Polasky for the original version of this problem.

second, $2, and so forth. Harpo receives marginal benefits (reduced discomfort and risk of cancer) equal to $(12 − x)$ from Groucho reducing the number of cigars smoked.

It is possible to rent a Clean-Air Machine that reduces smoke in the air by 50% for $10 per day. It is also possible to relocate Groucho in a different office so Harpo would not have to breathe any smoke at all for $40 per day.

1. Draw a diagram showing the marginal costs and benefits of pollution reduction, with the number of cigars reduced on the horizontal axis. Use this diagram to determine whether machine rental or relocation is the more efficient option.

2. This problem has no transactions costs or free riding. The Coase theorem says that, in this kind of simple example, the efficient outcome should be achieved through negotiation even if Harpo has the power to banish Groucho to another office *at Groucho's expense.* Explain why.

APPLICATION 4.1

The Stray Cow Problem[9]

Rancher Roy has his ranch next to the farm of farmer Fern. Cattle tend to roam and sometimes stray onto Fern's land and damage her crops. Roy can choose the size of his herd. His revenues are $6 for each cow he raises. The schedules of his marginal cost of production (MCP) and the damage each additional cow creates (marginal cow damage or MCD) are given below.

# of Cattle	MCP	MCD
1	$3	$1
2	3	2
3	4	3
4	5	4
5	6	5
6	7	6

Farmer Fern can choose either to farm or not to farm. Her cost of production is $10, and her revenue is $12 when there are no cattle roaming loose. For each additional cow her revenue is reduced by the amount in the MCD column above.

To answer the following questions, you need to figure out four things: the profit-maximizing number of cows for Roy to own, his profits, whether or not Fern will farm, and what her profits will be. Remember that efficient outcomes maximize the net monetary benefits to both parties; in other words, total ranching plus farming profits. Finally, a diagram won't help for this problem.

1. What will be the outcome if there is no liability (Roy does not pay for any damages caused)?

2. What will be the outcome if Roy is liable for damages?
3. What is the efficient outcome (the outcome that maximizes total profits)?

---

[9]Acknowledgments are due to the unknown author of the original version of this problem, which I borrowed from a University of Michigan problem set.

4. Suppose it is possible to build a fence to enclose the ranch for a cost of $9. Is building the fence efficient?

5. Suppose the farmer can build a fence around her crops for a cost of $1. Is building this fence efficient?

APPLICATION 4.2

End-of-the-Pipe Control versus Pollution Prevention

The marginal cost of reduction curve illustrated in Figure 4.5 assumes a particular approach to reducing pollution, often called "end-of-the-pipe" control. In other words, when we draw that upward sloping MC curve, we assume that firms respond to regulation by maintaining the same basic production technology but adding on scrubbers or filters to clean up their emissions. Under these conditions, rising marginal costs of reduction are quite likely.

However, suppose that firms radically overhaul their production technology, so that they completely eliminate emissions. This is known as a "pollution prevention" strategy. An example might be a jeweler, who in the face of regulation adopts a closed loop production system. This is one in which all mineral waste products are recovered from recycled wastewater and then reused. What would the marginal cost of reduction diagram look like in this case?

1. Specifically, assume that reducing metal pollution by the first 1% required the installation of a $100,000 recycling system, but that the marginal cost of further reduction was zero. Draw the marginal cost of reduction curve.
2. Let the marginal benefit of reduction curve be equal to $(30,000 - 1/3 * x)$, where x is the percentage reduction in pollution (ranging from 0% to 100%). In this case, is installation of the recycling system efficient? What is the efficient cleanup level?

Key Ideas in Each Section

4.0 The efficiency standard argues for a careful balancing of the costs and benefits of pollution control.

4.1 Efficiency is defined as **Pareto efficient.** Pareto efficient outcomes maximize the measurable **net monetary benefits** available to a society. Thus, in any move toward efficiency, it is always *possible* for the winners to compensate the losers. However, compensation is not required for efficiency, so efficient outcomes are not necessarily fair.

4.2 Marginal analysis, which compares the **marginal costs** of pollution reduction against its **marginal benefits,** is used to pinpoint the efficient pollution level. At any point other than the efficient level, both polluter and victim can *potentially* be made better off through negotiation.

4.3 The marginal curves graph the change in the total curves. The area under the marginal cost (benefit) curve equals the total costs (benefits). At the point where total costs and benefits are equal, net benefits are zero and pollution has been "overcontrolled" from an efficiency perspective.

4.4 The **Coase theorem** states that *in the absence of transactions costs and free riding,* private negotiation will arrive at the efficient pollution level, regardless of whether victims have the right to impose a ban or polluters have the right to pollute. In the real world, however, the **polluter pays principle** will lead to a more efficient outcome, since it generally reduces transactions costs and free riding, and does not distort the incentives for entry into the market.

4.5 The case of air pollution in Baltimore illustrates how the efficiency standard might be applied in practice.

4.6 The efficiency standard weights the utility of all individuals equally: Rich and poor, current and future generations, and victims and polluters. Thus, outcomes are efficient even if the increased consumption by one group comes at the expense of another. Yet, unless an **equal marginal utility of income** is also assumed, any individual move toward efficiency does not increase social welfare. Nevertheless, efficiency can best be defended by arguing that, over time, most people will benefit in their role as consumers, if efficiency is pursued at every turn.

References

Bromley, Daniel (1990). "The Ideology of Efficiency: Searching for a Theory of Policy Analysis." *Journal of Environmental Economics and Management,* 19, no. 1, 86–107.

Coase, Ronald (1960). "The Problem of Social Cost." *Journal of Law and Economics,* vol. 3, 1–44.

Gomez-Ibanez, Jose A. and Joseph P. Kalt (1990). *Cases in Microeconomics.* Englewood Cliffs, NJ: Prentice Hall.

Kneese, Alan V. and William D. Schulze (1985). "Ethics and Environmental Economics." In *Handbook of Natural Resource Economics,* vol. 1, ed. A. V. Kneese and J. L. Sweeney, New York: Elsevier.

Mohring, Herbert and J. Hayden Boyd (1971). "Analyzing 'Externalities': 'Direct Interaction' versus 'Asset Utilization' Frameworks." *Economica,* vol. 38, 347–361.

Oates, Wallace E., Paul R. Portney and Albert M. McGartland (1989). "The Net Benefits of Incentive-Based Regulation: A Case Study of Environmental Standard Setting." *American Economic Review,* December 79, no. 5, 1233–1242.

CHAPTER 5

The Safety Standard

5.0 Introduction

In the last chapter, we explored the logic of controlling pollution at an efficient level. The efficiency approach emphasizes trade-offs—pollution control has opportunity costs that must be weighed against the benefits of environmental protection. This is not, however, the kind of language one hears in everyday discussions of pollution control. Instead, pollution is more generally equated with immoral or even criminal behavior, a practice to be stamped out at all costs. In this chapter, we will explore the pros and cons of a safety standard, which, like much popular opinion, rejects a benefit-cost approach to decisions about the "correct" amount of pollution.

The **safety standard** springs fundamentally from fairness rather than efficiency concerns. Recall that the efficiency standard makes no distinction between victims and perpetrators of pollution. Instead, efficiency weighs the dollar impact of pollution on victims' health against the dollar impact on consumers' prices and polluters' profits. Each is considered to have equal say in the matter, under the reasoning that in the long run, most people will benefit as consumers from the larger pie made possible via efficient regulation. Advocates of a safety approach, on the other hand, contend that our society has developed a widespread consensus on the following position: People have a right to protection from unsolicited, significant harm to their immediate environment. Efficiency violates this right and is thus fundamentally unfair.

There is also, curiously, an efficiency argument to be made in favor of relying on safety standards. We know that the efficiency standard requires that the costs and benefits of environmental regulation be carefully measured and weighed. However, as we shall see in Chapters 8 and 10, many important benefits of protection are often left out of benefit-cost analyses because they cannot be measured. Moreover, as will be discussed in Chapter 11, material growth in our affluent society may primarily feed conspicuous consumption, fueling a rat race that leaves no one better off. If the measured costs of protection are overstated by this rat race effect, while the benefits are understated because they cannot be quantified, then safe regulation may in reality meet a benefit-cost test. Having said this, however, safety is more often defended in terms of basic rights, rather than on efficiency grounds.

5.1 Defining the Right to Safety

There is a saying that the freedom to wave your fist ends where my nose begins. In a similar vein, many Americans believe that the freedom to pollute the environment ends where a human body begins. Preventing positive harm to its citizens is the classic liberal (in modern parlance, libertarian) justification for governmental restraint on the liberties of others. At the extreme, permitting negative externalities that cause discomfort, sickness, or death might be looked upon as the equivalent of permitting the poisoning of the population for material gain.

The safety standard can thus be defended as necessary to protect **personal liberty.**[1] Viewed in this light, we require that pollution should be reduced to levels that inflict "minimal" harm on people. What constitutes minimal harm is of course open to debate. In practice, the U.S. Environmental Protection Agency (EPA) appears to consider risks below 1 in 1 million for large populations to be acceptable, "below regulatory concern." On the other hand, the EPA and other federal agencies tend to take action against risks greater than 4 in 1,000 for small populations, and 3 in 10,000 for large populations.[2] Risks that fall in between are regulated based on an informal balancing of costs against benefits and statutory requirements. One observer characterizes this back-and-forth process as permitting "an agency to take technological and economic factors into account, on a case-by-case basis, as long as it acts in good faith to make progress toward reducing and, we hope, eventually eliminating damage to the environment and risks to human health."[3]

Based on this real-world experience, for the purposes of this book, we can define **safety** as a cancer risk level of less than 1 in 1 million; risks greater than 1 in 10,000 are **unsafe;** and risks in between are up for grabs. (For comparison, police officers bear a risk of about 1 in 10,000 of being killed by a felon on the job.)

Of course, many other health risks besides cancer are associated with pollution, such as impacts on the immune, nervous, and reproductive systems. However, the risks in these areas are much harder to quantify, and as yet there is no social consensus, as reflected in a judicial record, about exposure levels. Because noncancer health risks are not well understood, and because cancer risks can be estimated only with a substantial margin of error, the safety standard can be quite nebulous. As a result, the precise definition of safety must often be determined on a case-by-case basis through the give and take of politics. (As we will see in Chapter 10, pinning down the efficient pollution level can be quite difficult as well!)

In spite of this uncertainty, however, a safety standard in fact remains the stated goal of much environmental policy. As we explore further in Chapter 13, the basic antipollution laws covering air, water, and land pollution require cleanup to "safe" levels, period. There is no mention of a benefit-cost test in the legislation.

Ultimately, however, cost considerations *must* play a role in the political determination of safe pollution levels. Attainment of "objectively" safe standards in some areas would be prohibitively expensive. Indeed, while U.S. courts have thrown out regu-

---

[1]For a more extended discussion, see Goodstein (1994). Shrader-Frechette (1991) presents a related defense of a safety (maximin) strategy against an efficiency (expected utility) standard.
[2]Travis et al. (1987). For a good discussion of the advantages and disadvantages of legislating health-based "bright-lines," see Rosenthal et al. (1992).
[3]Sagoff (1988).

latory standards for safety legislation based solely on benefit-cost analysis, at the same time, they have allowed costs of attainment to be considered as one factor influencing the stringency of regulation. They also have interpreted safe to mean not the absence of any risk but the absence of "significant" risk. On the other hand, the courts have not allowed costs to be a factor in the determination of significant risk.

Accepting that some danger to human health is inevitable does not require abandoning the safety standard. For example, it is commonly accepted that we have a right to live free from violent behavior on the part of our neighbors. Now this right, like most others, is not enforced absolutely: We are willing to fund police departments, the court system, the construction of new jails, educational and job programs, and drug rehabilitation centers only to a certain level. Moreover, poor people receive much less protection than wealthy people do. Ultimately, the decision about how much violence to live with is a political one, influenced but not solely determined by willingness to pay.

One could characterize this approach as declaring a societal right to be the protection of all individuals from violent crime, then backing away from such a goal on a case-by-case basis in the face of rising cost. This results in a substantially different standard than would determining the police departments' homicide budget based on a benefit-cost analysis. In particular, the former will generally result in less violent crime. Returning to environmental concerns, a safety target of a maximum 1 in 1 million cancer risk may not always be economically feasible. But relaxing a safety standard that is too costly is quite different than adopting an efficiency standard.

In the real world, the safe level will certainly be influenced by the associated sacrifices in consumption. Nevertheless, safety advocates would argue that in the arena of environmental protection, costs are not and should not be a dominant factor in people's decision-making process.

Survey research seems to find widespread support for this claim. A majority of Americans consistently agree with the statement that "protecting the environment is so important that requirements and standards cannot be too high, and continuing improvements must be made regardless of the cost."[4] This is a very strong statement. Efficiency proponents suggest it represents softheaded thinking, and if the remark is taken literally, obviously it does. But, a less harsh interpretation of this survey data is that people feel that, since *current levels* of pollution significantly affect human health and well-being, within the relevant range of possibilities cleanup is justified regardless of the cost.

To illustrate, one study asked residents of a Nevada community about their willingness to accept annual tax credits of $1,000, $3,000, and $5,000 per person in exchange for the siting of a potentially dangerous hazardous waste facility nearby. Contrary to the author's expectations, increases in the rebate had no measurable impact on approval of the facility. The results were "consistent with a threshold model of choice, whereby individuals refuse to consider compensation if the perceived risk falls in the inadmissible range. For those respondents where the risk was perceived to be too high, the rebates offered were not viewed as inadequate, but as inappropriate . . . most of the Nevada sample viewed the risks as inherently noncompensable. . . ."[5]

---

[4]Blinder (1987).
[5]Kunreuther and Easterling (1990).

Behavior such as this suggests that one important benefit of environmental protection—the right not to be victimized—is unmeasurable. Casting this argument in terms of our social welfare function, in the interests of personal liberty, safety advocates put very strong weights on injuries to human health arising from pollution. To illustrate, let us return to our Chapter 4 example in which Brittany and Tyler were wrangling over smoking in the office. To a safety advocate, the social welfare function might look like this:

$$\text{SW} = U_{Tyler}(\overset{+}{\#\text{Cigs}_T}, \overset{+}{\$_T}) + U_{Brit}(\overset{-}{w * \#\text{Cigs}_T}, \overset{+}{\$_B})$$

where the weight w given to the negative impact of smoke on Brittany is a very big number, one that may well justify banning smoking altogether.[6]

Should smoking be banned in public places under a safety standard? This is a question for voters and courts to decide. One feature of the safety standard is its imprecision. No right is absolute, since rights often come in conflict with one another, and the political arena is where the issue is ultimately decided. What the safety standard maintains is that in the absence of a "compelling" argument to the contrary (which may include but is not limited to cost of attainment), damage to human health from pollution ought to be minimal. Individuals have a right to be free from the damage that secondary smoke inflicts.

5.2 The Safety Standard: Inefficient

The first objection to the safety standard is that it is, by definition, inefficient. Efficiency advocates make the following normative case against safety: Enshrining environmental health as a "right" involves committing "too many" of our overall social resources to environmental protection.

As a result of pursuing safe levels of pollution, regulators and voters have often chosen pollution control levels that may be "too high" based on a benefit-cost or efficiency standard. Consider, for example, the Clean Air Act amendments of 1990. Their first goal is to reduce acid rain, which has contributed to the sterility of lakes and death of forests in the northeastern United States. In achieving this goal, an important "side" benefit will be the reduction of sulfate- and particulate-related sickness and death; estimates of these effects are uncertain, but at the high end range to 50,000 premature deaths a year.

To accomplish this, the law imposes tighter controls on electric utility emissions of sulfur dioxide, requiring a reduction of 10 million tons per year below their 1980 level. Nitrogen oxide emissions must also be reduced by about 2 million tons per year.

To improve urban air quality and curb the emission of hazardous air pollutants (those substances that cause cancer or other illnesses), additional pollution control in urban areas and at hazardous pollutant production sites, and tighter emission standards for vehicles will be required.

While the costs and benefits of such sweeping legislation are difficult to pin down precisely, economist Paul Portney undertook this task in 1990. He estimated that by

---

[6]Kneese and Schulze (1985) formalize a libertarian social welfare function as one in which a Pareto improvement must actually take place for a policy to increase social welfare. The safety standard discussed here is not this restrictive.

the year 2005, the compliance costs will be $29 million to $36 billion per year. This works out to around $300 to $400 per household. (An additional $30 billion to $40 billion per year is already spent to comply with existing Clean Air Act regulations.) Total benefits, including intangibles such as the value of lives saved, reduced sickness, and improved visibility, Portney "speculated" will be about $14 billion per year. Thus, "If these estimates are even close to correct, Congress and the President are about to shake hands on [and have since] a landmark piece of legislation for which costs may exceed benefits by a substantial margin. Why is this so?"[7]

Portney argued that if people were better informed about the cost that they would bear as a result of the Clean Air Act, less stringent standards would have been imposed. And yet, the public debate over the Clean Air Act was clearly framed as "environment versus growth." The businesses that were most affected worked long and hard to get their message across. President Bush at one point spoke out against the measure as being too costly, though he ultimately signed on. In the midst of the debate, poll results indicated that 80% of the population felt that protecting the environment was more important than keeping prices down.[8] Thus, it seems likely that the public was aware that the environmental benefits of the act would not come without substantial sacrifice, though they may have been unaware of the exact magnitude.

The alternative explanation would be that voters tend to view environmental health as a "rights" issue. One backs away from the defense of a right only when it becomes prohibitively expensive, not on the basis of a negative net-benefit analysis.

A postcript to this particular story: As I am writing the second edition of this book (July 1997), a major study released just last week shows that the acid rain program under the 1990 Clean Air Act is in fact easy to justify on effficiency grounds. Measurable benefits (mostly from reduced death and sickness, and improved visibility) will exceed the costs under virtually any set of assumptions (Burtraw et al. [1997]). Indeed the estimated benefits for the acid rain program alone range from $23 billion to $26 billion—well above Portney's original speculation of $14 billion for the *entire* legislative package. But other components of the Clean Air Act, for example, air toxics control, probably remain inefficient.

And in other cases, pursuing safety undoubtedly generates a high degree of inefficiency. For example, consider the EPA's regulations for landfills mentioned in Application 2.0 (and discussed more fully in Chapter 10). In this case, even with the new regulations, just under 10% of landfills will still pose what the EPA considers to be a "moderate" health risk for individuals who depend on contaminated groundwater: a greater than 1 in 1 million (but less than 1 in 10,000) increase in the risk of contracting cancer. However, because so few people actually depend on groundwater within leaching distance of a landfill, the new regulations were predicted to reduce cancer by only two or three cases over the next 300 years. Potential benefits of the regulation not quantified by the EPA include increased ease of siting landfills, reduced damage to surface water, fairness to future generations, and an overall reduction in waste generation and related "upstream" pollution encouraged by higher disposal costs.

In aggregate, the regulations are expensive: about $5.8 billion, or around $2 billion per cancer case reduced. On a per household basis, this works out to an annual

---

[7]Portney (1990).

[8]"Americans Are Willing to Sacrifice to Reduce Pollution, They Say," *Wall Street Journal*, April 20, 1090.

cost of $4.10 in increased garbage bills over the twenty-year life of a landfill. An efficiency proponent would say that it is simply crazy (horribly inefficient) to spend so much money to reduce risk by so little. The $4.10 per year per household is an unjustified tax.

The landfill case illustrates a more general point; regulations that protect small groups of people from risk will almost always be inefficient, since even relatively high risks will not generate many casualties. Here is a classic situation in which efficiency and fairness (measured as equal risk protection for small and large groups) conflict.

5.3 The Safety Standard: Not Cost-Effective

The second, and perhaps most telling criticism leveled at the safety standard is its lack of **cost-effectiveness.** A cost-effective solution achieves a desired goal at the lowest possible cost. In pollution control, this goal is often defined as "lives saved per dollar spent." The cost-effectiveness criticism is not that safety is a bad goal per se, but that it gives no guidance to insure that the maximum amount of safety is indeed purchased with the available resources. If safety is the only goal of pollution control, then extreme measures may be taken to attack "minimal" risk situations.

For example, the EPA, following its mandate from the Superfund legislation, has attempted to restore to drinking level purity the groundwater at toxic spill sites. Tens of millions of dollars have been spent at a few dozen sites on such efforts, yet cleanup to this level has proven quite difficult. According to one observer, cleaning up the aquifers is "like trying to get soap out of a sponge. You can wash it out ten or twelve times but there's still some soap left." Critics have argued that rather than restoring the water to its original safe drinking quality, the goal should be simply to contain the contaminants. EPA's limited resources could then be redirected to preventing future spills. In 1990, the agency's entire groundwater protection program had an $11 million annual budget—less than the cost of many single Superfund cleanups.[9]

More generally, economist Lester Lave points out that children have about a 5 in 1 million chance of contracting lung cancer from attending a school built with asbestos materials. This is dramatically less than the threat of death from other events in their lives, and Lave suggests that if our interest is in protecting lives, we would do better spending money to reduce other risks, such as cancer from exposure to secondary cigarette smoke, auto accidents, or inadequate prenatal nutrition and care.[10]

A safety proponent might argue in response that devoting more resources to *each* of the first three problems would be a good idea, and in fact, the limits to dealing with them are not fundamentally limited resources, but rather a lack of political will. More generally, a safety advocate would respond that Lave's comparison is a false one, since funds freed up from "overcontrol" in the pollution arena are more likely to be devoted to increasing consumption of the relatively affluent than to saving children's lives. Taxpayers do put a limit on governmental resources for dealing with environmental, traffic safety, and children's welfare issues. Yet safety proponents ultimately

---

[9]"Throwing Good Money at Bad Water Yields Scant Improvement," *Wall Street Journal*, May 15, 1991.

[10]Lave (1987). Lave points also out that more people probably contract cancer from eating corn, which contains a natural carcinogen aflatoxin, than from asbestos-laden schools. To this, a safety proponent might respond that environmental protection is not about saving people from all hazards of life, but rather, in the interests of personal liberty, from hazards imposed upon them by others.

have more faith in this political allocation of funds than in an allocation based on a benefit-cost test.

However, the politically determined nature of the safety standard can also set it up to fail from a cost-effectiveness perspective. Determining "significant harm" on a case-by-case basis through a political process is a far from perfect mechanism, in which money and connections may play as large a part as the will of the electorate regarding environmental protection. For example, Crandall (1983) has argued that northeastern members of Congress advocated and helped pass strict clean air standards for new sources and in already clean areas, *not* for environmental reasons, but rather to slow down the shift of industry to the South and Southwest.

Chapter 12 of this book is devoted to a consideration of the government's role in environmental policy and will consider policies recommended to correct this kind of government failure. For now, safety proponents can respond only by saying, imperfect as the political process is, voting remains the best mechanism for people to make decisions about enforcing rights. Moreover, as we will see, the benefit-cost alternative is certainly not "value-free" and is arguably as subject to influence as the political process itself.

Ultimately, however, given the limited resources available for controlling pollution, safety alone is clearly an inadequate standard for making decisions. Requiring regulatory authorities to insure a safe environment may lead them to concentrate on eradicating some risks while ignoring others. To deal with this problem, so-called **risk-benefit** studies can be used to compare the cost-effectiveness of different regulatory options. The common measure used in this approach is lives saved per dollar spent. This kind of cost-effectiveness analysis can be a useful guide to avoid an overcommitment of resources to an intractable problem. However, adopting a cost-effective approach does not mean backing away from safety as a goal. Rather, it implies buying as much safety as possible with the dollars allocated by the political process.

To summarize the last two sections, critics charge safety standards with two kinds of "irrationality": first, inefficiency, or overcommitment of resources to environmental problems, and second, lack of cost-effectiveness in addressing these problems. Criticism (1) is fundamentally normative and thus is a subject for public debate. In this debate, benefit-cost studies can be useful in pointing out just how inefficient the pursuit of safety might be. Criticism (2), however, does not question the goal of safety. Rather it suggests that blind pursuit of safety may in fact hinder efforts to achieve the highest possible level of environmental quality.

5.4 The Safety Standard: Regressive?

The final objection to a safety standard is based on income equity. Safety standards will generally be more restrictive than efficiency standards; as a result, they result in a greater sacrifice of other goods and services. Quoting efficiency advocate Alan Blinder: "Declaring that people have a 'right' to clean air and water sounds noble and high-minded. But how many people would want to exercise that right if the cost were sacrificing a decent level of nutrition or adequate medical care or proper housing?"[11]

Blinder is worried that a fair number of people will in fact fall below a decent standard of living as a result of overregulation. While such dramatic effects are un-

---
[11]Blinder (1987: 138).

likely, given the level of hunger, poverty, and homelessness in our society, it is possible that stringent environmental standards are something poor people may simply not be able to afford. Currently, compliance with pollution regulations commits about $160 billion of U.S. gross national product (GNP). Suppose that by moving from a safety standard to an efficiency-based standard we spent $30 billion less on environmental improvement. Would the poor be better off?

The first issue is Who ultimately pays the hypothetical extra $30 billion for pollution control? It does appear that because much pollution is generated in the production of necessities—basic manufactured goods, garbage disposal, food, drinking water, electric power, and transport—the cost of environmental regulation is borne unevenly. In general, pollution control has a **regressive** impact on income distribution, meaning that the higher prices of consumer goods induced by regulation take a bigger percentage bite of the incomes of poor people than of wealthier individuals.

As one example, Walls and Hanson (1996) looked at the impact of some proposed automobile pollution taxes in California. They found that a tax on the annual emissions of each vehicle would cost poor folks (those in the bottom 20% of the income distribution) 2.35% of their annual income, while the average for all households was only 0.95% of annual income. Even if auto registration fees were lowered to compensate for the new tax, poor people would still pay substantially more when measured against annual income.

This finding of a regressive impact is fairly typical, and extends to the economy-wide impact of pollution control measures. One analyst reports that overall costs as a fraction of income ranged from 0.76 of 1% for the poorest individuals to 0.16 of 1% for the wealthiest.[12] This is in spite of the fact that wealthy individuals, through their consumption patterns, indirectly produce much more than their share of many common pollutants.[13]

On the other hand, poor and working-class people appear to benefit more from pollution control than the relatively wealthy. In the case of air pollution, for example, urban rather than suburban areas have been the primary beneficiaries of control policies. The effects are further magnified because those in the lower half of the income distribution have a harder time buying their own cleaner environment by way of air and water filters and conditioners, trips to spacious, well-maintained parks, or vacations in the country. Dramatic evidence of the exposure of low-income people comes from the autopsies of 100 youths from poor neighborhoods in Los Angeles. According to the pathologist, "Eighty percent of the youths had notable lung abnormalities . . . above and beyond what we've seen with smoking or even respiratory viruses. . . . It's much more severe, much more prevalent."[14]

Hazardous waste facilities are situated primarily in poor communities and predominantly in minority communities. Table 5.1 shows the results from a 1980s study of hazardous waste landfills in EPA's region IV, where blacks make up one fifth of the total population.

Three of the four facilities are in census areas where blacks are in the majority; in all cases the total poverty rate was at least double the state average. Over 90% of the black people in these areas were poor, compared to a 31% to 43% rural poverty rate

---

[12]Robison (1985). See also the review of earlier literature in Cropper and Oates (1992).
[13]Bingham et al. (1987).
[14]Mann (1991). See also Brajer and Hall (1992).

TABLE 5.1	Race, Poverty, and Hazardous Waste Sites, Census Data from EPA Region IV, 1980		
	Population (%)	*Poverty Population (%)*	
LANDFILL (State)	*Black*	*All Races*	*Black*
Chemical Waste Management (Alabama)	90	42	100
SCA Services (South Carolina)	38	31	100
Industrial Chemical Co. (South Carolina)	52	26	92
Warren County PCB Landfill (North Carolina)	66	32	90

Source: U.S. GAO (1983). The data are based on subdivisions of political jurisdictions used by the Census Bureau for data gathering.

for blacks in the three states. Such high poverty rates in the affected areas suggest that blacks in particular are benefiting little in economic terms from the presence of these major facilities.

This pattern of overrepresentation of minority populations in hazardous waste host communities has been borne out in studies in Atlanta and Los Angeles, where Hispanic communities are affected. Some evidence suggests the pattern holds for Native Americans as well. One of the worst PCB dumps in the country lies on the Mohawk Indian reservation along the St. Lawrence River.[15]

Although some of the correlation between waste sites and minority communities is due to higher poverty rates, race appears to be an important independent factor. In his summary of the evidence, Bullard (1991: 40) argues, "The facility siting controversy cannot be reduced solely to a class phenomenon . . . poor whites along with their more affluent counterparts have more options and leveraging mechanisms (formal and informal) at their disposal than do Blacks of equal status." More recent research confirms the independent link between race and exposure to environmental toxins.[16]

This type of inequity in siting of hazardous facilities has been dubbed **environmental racism** and has sparked a political movement among minority groups called the environmental justice movement. Indeed, some of the loudest calls for stricter enforcement of safety standards have come from poor and/or minority communities.

Because poor, working-class, and minority people, relative to their income, both pay more for and receive more from pollution control, it is difficult to evaluate its overall distributive impact. Thus, one cannot conclusively argue whether pollution control imposes net benefits or net costs on the lower half of the income distribution. Nevertheless, in important cases such as a carbon tax to slow global warming, which would dramatically raise the price of necessities, distributional issues need to be weighed carefully. Here, economists have recommended that much of the revenue raised from the tax be rebated back as income tax cuts disproportionately to those in the lower half of the income distribution.

Beyond the issue of distributional effects, efficiency critics of the safety standard point out correctly that the additional costs imposed on society—hypothetically $30 billion—are real. It is certainly possible that the money saved under an efficiency

---

[15]"Indian Tribes Contend with Some of Worst of America's Pollution," *Wall Street Journal*, November 29, 1990.

[16]Brooks and Sethi (1997) provide both supporting data and a good literature review.

JUST RELEASED
⊕ UNITED NATIONS PUBLICATIONS

Industrial Development Report 2004

Industrialization, Environment and the Millennium Development Goals in Sub-Saharan Africa

The new frontier in the fight against poverty

UNITED NATIONS INDUSTRIAL DEVELOPMENT ORGANIZATION
the industrial path out of poverty

ORDER NOW at 1-800-253-9646 or UNP.UN.ORG

PRSRT STD
US Postage
PAID
New York, NY
Permit No. 5478

JAY JOHNSON
GENERAL BUSINESS
SOUTHEASTERN LOUISIANA U
500 WESTERN AVE
HAMMOND, LA 70402-0001

UNITED NATIONS PUBLICATIONS • UNP.UN.ORG • 1-800-253-9646

Industrial Development Report 2004:
Industrialization, Environment and the Millennium
Development Goals in Sub-Saharan Africa -
The New Frontier in the Fight against Poverty

The Industrial Development Report is intended to build on development policy experience and contribute to a refinement of the international development agenda. The Report pays special attention to current needs and capabilities in the developing countries in general, and the least developed among them in particular. The 2004 edition addresses the challenges faced by Sub-Saharan African countries in furthering their efforts towards poverty reduction and reaching the Millennium Development Goals.

E.04.II.B.22 ISBN: 9211064287 2004 Pages: 240 Price: $ 50.00

Order your copy today! Mail: 2 UN Plaza, DC2-853, Dept D209, New York NY 10017
Call: 1-800-253-9646 or 212-963-8302 Fax: 212-963-3489 Internet: unp.un.org

Please send me _____ copy(ies).

Charge my: ☐ Visa ☐ Master Card ☐ American Express

Acct. No. _____ Exp. Date _____

Signature _____

Name (print) _____

Address _____

City _____ State _____ Zip _____

Country _____

Telephone _____ Fax. _____

E-mail _____

*Postage and handling: Domestic: add 5%. US$5.00 Minimum except HI, AK, PR and VI.
Orders for HI, AK, PR, VI and Overseas: US$5.00 per title in addition to US$5.00 handling charge.

standard could, as Blinder implies it will, be used to fund basic human needs. However, safety proponents might argue in response that the funds would more likely be funneled into consumption among the middle and upper classes.

The last three sections have looked at criticisms of the safety standard—inefficiency, potential for cost-ineffectiveness, and the charge of regressive distributional impacts. All have some merit. And insofar as safe regulations are regressive in their net effect, safety advocates lose the moral high ground from the claim that their approach is "fairer" than efficiency.

Yet, as we have seen, the alternative efficiency standard is open to its own criticisms. Perhaps no issue dramatizes the differences between these two standards better than the disposal of hazardous wastes.

5.5 Siting Hazardous Waste Facilities: Safety versus Efficiency

In a 1992 internal memorandum to his staff, chief economist at the World Bank, Lawrence Summers wrote: "Just between you and me, shouldn't the World Bank be encouraging more migration of the dirty industries to the [less developed countries]? . . . I think the economic logic behind dumping a load of toxic waste in the lowest-wage country is impeccable and we should face up to that." The memo, leaked to *The Economist* magazine, stirred considerable controversy. Brazil's environment minister responding to Summers' blunt analysis said, "It's perfectly logical but perfectly insane," and called for Summers' dismissal from the Bank.

Summers, in a letter to the magazine, maintained that his provocative statements were quoted out of context. "It is not my view, the World Bank's view, or that of any sane person that pollution should be encouraged anywhere, or that the dumping of untreated toxic wastes near the homes of poor people is morally or economically defensible. My memo tried to sharpen the debate on important issues by taking as narrow-minded an economic perspective as possible."[17] This "narrow-minded" view is what we have characterized as the efficiency perspective. However, we also know that the efficiency perspective—in this case, trade in waste—can be defended both morally and economically, since it provides *an opportunity* for making *all* parties better off. The morality of the trade depends upon the degree to which this promise is fulfilled.

Disposing of waste—hazardous, radioactive, or even simple nonhazardous municipal waste—has become an increasingly vexing and expensive problem. Such "locally unwanted land uses" (**LULUs**) impose negative externality costs on their immediate neighbors, ranging from the potential hazards of exposure to decreased land values, for the benefit of the broader society. This is true, even when very expensive protective measures are undertaken to reduce expected risk. For someone with a waste dump in his or her backyard, an "adequate" margin of safety means zero risk. By definition, communities do not want LULUs for neighbors, and the wealthier (and

---

[17]Summers quotes are from "Let Them Eat Pollution" and "Polluting the Poor," *The Economist,* February 8, 1992; February 15, 1992, reprinted with permission. Environment minister's quote is from *In These Times,* March 8, 1992.

better organized) the community, the higher the level of safety the community will demand.

Because the benefits to the broader society of having toxic facilities are great, one possible solution to the problem of siting is to "compensate" communities with tax revenues generated by the facility, which could pay for schools, hospitals, libraries, or sewer systems. Poorer communities of course would accept lower compensation levels; thus, to reduce disposal costs some including Summers have argued that government policy should promote this kind of "trade" in LULUs.[18] Should poor communities (or countries) be encouraged to accept dangerous facilities in exchange for dollars? The dumping controversy provides a classic example of the conflict between the efficiency and safety positions on pollution control. Both sides maintain that their policy promotes overall social welfare.

First, let us consider the logic of the efficiency position. Summers defends his trade-in-toxics stance on two counts. First, if the physical damages due to pollution rise as it increases, then pollution in cleaner parts of the world will do less physical damage than comparable discharges in dirty areas. In other words, Summers assumes the standard case of decreasing marginal benefits of cleanup. As he puts it: "I've always thought that under-populated countries in Africa are vastly under-polluted," relative to Mexico City or Los Angeles.

Summers' second point is that people "value" a clean environment less in poorer countries. In his words: "The concern over an agent that causes a one-in-a-million change in the odds of prostate cancer is obviously going to be much higher in a country where people survive to get prostate cancer than in a country where under-5 mortality is 200 per thousand." This difference in priorities shows up in the form of a much lower monetary value placed on all environmental amenities, including reduced risk of death. Thus, trading waste not only reduces the physical damage to the environment but also results in (much) lower dollar damages measured in terms of the fully informed willingness of the community to accept the waste. Firms will be able to dump their waste at a lower cost, *even including compensation costs*, thus freeing up resources to increase output and raise the gross global product.

Figure 5.1 presents a graphical analysis of Summers' position. Due to lower incomes (and lower population densities in some cases), the poor country has a marginal benefit of cleanup schedule lying below that of the rich country. In addition, because current pollution levels are relatively low in the poor country (PC_1 versus RC_1), the marginal benefits of cleanup are also low relative to the rich country. Transferring 10% of the waste from the rich country to the poor country reduces monetary damages (in the rich country) by the gray area and increases damages (in the poor country) by the hatched area. Overall, *monetary* damages from the pollution have been reduced by the trade.

Clearly there will be winners and losers in such a process. The winners include those in wealthy countries no longer exposed to the waste, those around the world

---

[18]Kunreuther and Kleindorfer (1986) recommend that communities bid against one another to elicit their willingness to accept compensation in exchange for a LULU. Under such a procedure, the site would, in general, be located in the poorest community; however, the authors envision this process as a Pareto improving mechanism. In addition, the authors are not pure efficiency advocates, since they suggest government impose standards guaranteeing that "residents in all potential sites are convinced that they are sufficiently protected against adverse environmental effects. . . ." Shrader-Frechette (1991) marshalls several arguments against toxic trade.

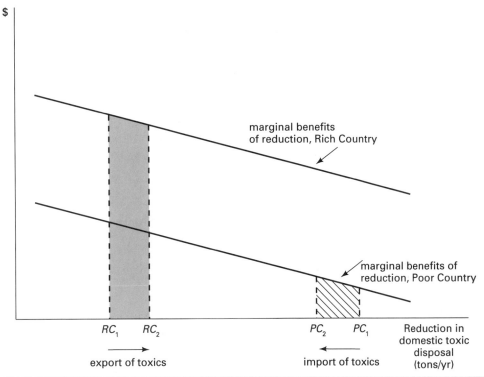

FIGURE 5.1 Efficiency and Toxic Trade

who can buy products more cheaply if output is increased, firm managers and stockholders who reap higher profits (assuming imperfect competition), and those in the poor countries who obtain relatively high wage work at the dump sites or benefit from taxes levied against the dumping firms. The losers will be those poor country individuals, alive today and as of yet unborn, who contract cancer or suffer other diseases contracted from exposure, and those who rely on natural resources that may be damaged in the transport and disposal process.

Because dumping toxics is indeed efficient, we know the total monetary gains to the winners outweigh the total monetary losses to the losers. Thus, in theory, the winners could compensate the losers, and everyone would be made "better off." A higher risk of cancer in poor countries from exposure to waste might be offset by reduced risk of death from unsafe drinking water if, for example, revenues from accepting the waste were used to build a sewage treatment facility. In practice, however, complete compensation is unlikely. Thus, as we saw in Chapter 4, toxic dumping like any efficient strategy is not "socially optimal"; it can only be defended on utilitarian grounds if, over time, the great majority of the population benefits from the action. Summers clearly believes it is in the interests of the people of poor countries themselves to accept toxic wastes.

The first response to this argument is What kind of world do we live in where poor people have to sell their health and the health of their children merely to get clean water to drink? Shouldn't there be a redistribution of wealth to prevent people from having to make this kind of Faustian bargain? But an efficiency defender might note that socialist revolution is not a current policy option. Given that rich countries or individuals are not likely to give up their wealth to the poor, who are we to deny poor people an opportunity to improve their welfare through trade, if only marginally?

A more pragmatic response to the Summers argument is that, in fact, the majority of benefits from the dumping will flow to the relatively wealthy while the poor will bear the burden of costs. The postcolonial political structure in many developing countries is far from democratic. In addition, few poor countries have the resources for effective regulation. One could easily imagine waste firms compensating a few well-placed individuals handsomely for access, while paying very low taxes and ignoring any existing regulations.

In fact, a similar process may well explain the racial disparities in toxic site locations in the United States. Firms could historically deal with a predominantly white political power structure, disregarding the needs of disenfranchised black or Hispanic majorities. A survey of black neighbors of five toxic facilities revealed substantial majorities who felt that the siting process was unfair. In four of the five communities, a clear majority disagreed with a statement that the benefits clearly outweighed the costs of the facility; the community was split evenly in the fifth case.[19]

Even if poor country (or county) governments are genuinely motivated to regulate industry at the efficient level, have the resources or expertise to do so, and spread the benefits widely, they face an additional dilemma. Stiff regulation or high taxes will increase the rate of illegal dumping; unrestricted trade in waste may thus lower the welfare of the recipient country.[20]

The basic criticism of the efficiency perspective is that the *potential* for a Pareto improvement is an insufficient condition to increase overall welfare. This is especially apparent in the case of international trade in toxics, where the benefits are likely to accrue to wealthy in both rich and poor countries, while the costs are borne by poor residents of poor countries. In fact, we expect pollution policy to *actually* increase the welfare of most of those affected by the pollution itself.

On the other hand, safety proponents face a difficult issue in the siting of LULUs. A politically acceptable definition of "safety" cannot be worked out, since a small group bears the burden of any positive risk. Nobody wants a LULU in *his* or *her* backyard.

As a result, compensation will play an increasingly important role in the siting of hazardous facilities. And firms and governments will tend to seek out poorer communities where compensation packages will be lower. Yet there are at least two preconditions for insuring that the great majority of the affected population in fact benefit from the siting. The first of these is a government capable of providing effective regulation. The second is an open political process combined with well-informed, democratic decision making in the siting process.[21]

---

[19]See the discussion in Bullard (1991: 86–95).

[20]Copeland (1991).

[21]The Environmental Impact Statement procedure described in Chapter 7 has been credited with providing a forum for such efforts in the recent siting of incineration facilities in Utah (Clough and Wann [1990]).

The siting of a LULU presents a case where the important insight of efficiency proponents—that something close to a Pareto improvement is possible—can be implemented. But to do so requires that the enforceable pollution standard be quite close to safety. It also requires an informed and politically enfranchised population.

5.6 Summary

In the last two chapters we have wound our way through a complex forest of arguments to examine two different answers to the question, How much pollution is too much? Table 5.2 provides a summary of their features.

The first standard, efficiency, relies heavily on benefit-cost estimates. In theory, it requires precise calculation of *marginal* benefits and costs, and leads to a maximization of the net monetary benefits to be gained from environmental protection. In practice, as we shall see later, benefit-cost analysts are able only to roughly balance benefits and costs. The efficiency standard requires a belief that intangible environmental benefits can be adequately measured and monetized. This in turn sanctions a "technocratic" approach to deciding how much pollution is too much.

By contrast, the safety standard ignores formal benefit-cost comparisons to pursue a health-based target defined by an explicitly political process. In theory, under a safety standard, regulators are directed to get as close to a 1 in 1 million cancer risk as they can, while also pursuing more nebulous noncancer safety goals, all conditional on the funds allocated to them by the political system. In practice, regulators often back away from safety when faced with high compliance costs.

TABLE 5.2   Comparing the Two Pollution Standards

	Efficiency	*Safety*
1. STANDARD	Marg. benefits just exceed marg. costs	Danger to marg. costs Health/environment minimized
2. RELATION TO GROWTH	Least restrictive	Most restrictive
3. LONG-RUN IMPACT ON EMPLOYMENT	Neutral	Neutral
4. ASSUMPTIONS ABOUT SOCIAL WELFARE *Pollution victim and beneficiary utility equal?	Yes	No

5. IMPLIED SOCIAL WELFARE FUNCTION:

EFFICIENCY:
$$SW = U_A \overset{+\quad -}{(X_A, P_A)} + U_R \overset{+\quad -}{(X_R, P_R)} + U_T \overset{+\quad -}{(X_T, P_T)} + \ldots$$

SAFETY:
$$SW = U_A \overset{+\qquad -}{(X_A, w*P_A)} + U_R \overset{+\qquad -}{(X_R, w*P_R)} + U_T \overset{+\qquad -}{(X_T, w*P_T)} + \ldots$$
Weights: $w > 1$

6. ADVANTAGES/DISADVANTAGES

EFFICIENCY: Maximizes measurable net monetary benefits/relies heavily on assumptions of benefit-cost analysis

SAFETY: Seems to be consistent with public opinion/often cost-ineffective and may be regressive

The social welfare function for the safety standard relies on a liberty argument, putting heavy weights on the welfare reduction from pollution. As a result, as is illustrated in Figure 5.2, a stricter pollution standard is called for than is implied by the efficiency standard. Efficiency proponents attack the "fairness" defense of safety with the charge that it is regressive—but this claim is hard to either verify or refute in general.

One new point in Table 5.2 is that the choice between the two standards does not affect the long-run employment picture. The more stringent safety standard may result in slightly more short-run structural job loss; yet it also creates more jobs in the environmental protection industry. (We will discuss this issue more fully in Chapter 9.) *The real trade-off is between increased material consumption and increased environmental quality.*

Beyond concerns of fairness, choice between the safety and the efficiency standards also depends on two related factors. First, how fully do monetary estimates capture the benefits of environmental protection? Second, what real benefits would we gain from the increased consumption that is sacrificed by tighter environmental controls? If benefit estimates leave out much that is hard to quantify, or if increased material consumption just feeds a rat race that leaves no one any happier, then safety may be "more efficient" than efficiency! We will explore these two issues later in the first part of the book.

Before that, however, the next two chapters will consider a problem we have so far left off the table: sustainability. How should we deal the interests of future generations into environmental protection measures taken today?

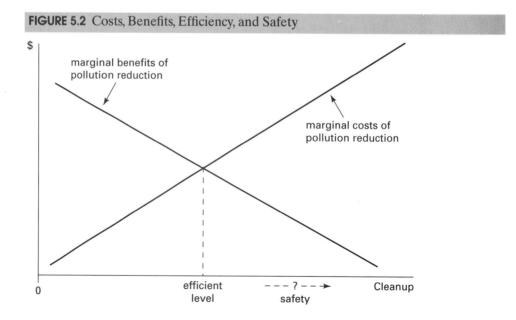

FIGURE 5.2 Costs, Benefits, Efficiency, and Safety

APPLICATION 5.0

Controlling Air Toxics

One of the Clean Air Act amendments passed by the U.S. government in 1990 was designed to control the emission of hazardous air pollutants. The EPA released a publication that year estimating that at 149 industrial facilities nationwide, cancer risks to the most exposed local residents from airborne toxics were greater than 1 in 10,000; at 45 plants risks were greater than 1 in 1000.[22]

The new air toxics law requires firms to impose control technology that, it is hoped, will reduce risks to below the 1 in 10,000 level. After the control technologies are installed, a follow-up risk analysis will be conducted to see if further control is necessary to reduce any unsafe exposure. While the legislation does not require risk reduction to the 1 in 1 million level, that remains the long-run target.[23]

1. Clearly, air toxics control is justified on safety grounds. Suppose that total benefits of the legislation just matched total costs, at $5 billion annually. Would air toxics control be justified on efficiency grounds?

2. Fortney (1990) has in fact criticized the legislation from an efficiency perspective. He puts estimated total costs at $6 billion to $10 billion per year, with total benefits at zero to $4 billion per year. The air toxics legislation attacks some fairly significant risks. How can the estimated benefits be so low (as low as zero)?

Key Ideas in Each Section

5.0 This chapter defines and then critically examines a **safety standard** for pollution control. Safety standards are defended primarily on fairness grounds. However, if unquantified benefits are large and/or the true costs of protection overstated due to rat race effects, then safe regulations may be more efficient than those passing a benefit-cost test.

5.1 Safety standards are defended on **personal liberty** grounds. A political consensus has developed that environmental cancer risks less than 1 in 1 million are considered **safe,** while risks greater than 1 in 10,000 are generally **unsafe.** There is no consensus on whether risks lying in between are safe. A precise safety standard cannot yet be defined for noncancer risks or ecosystem protection. In these areas, safe levels are determined politically on a case-by-case basis.

5.2 The first criticism of the safety standard is that it is often inefficiently strict. This is a normative criticism and is thus a proper subject for political debate.

5.3 The second criticism of the safety standard is that it fails to give sufficient guidance to insure **cost-effectiveness.** Cost-effectiveness is often measured in dollars spent per life saved. If regulators pursue safety at every turn, they may devote too many resources to eradicating small risks, while ignoring larger ones. This problem can be alleviated by using **risk-benefit analysis.** The cost-effectiveness criticism is not that too

---

[22]The report is discussed in Greider (1990).
[23]For more detail on these points, see chapter 13, and Rosenthal et al. (1992).

many resources are being devoted to environmental protection, but rather that these resources are not being wisely spent.

5.4 The final criticism of the safety standard is that it may have a **regressive** impact on income distribution. While poor people do pay a higher percentage of their income for pollution control than do rich people, poor, working class, and minority communities also benefit disproportionately. (The greater exposure borne by minorities is referred to as **environmental racism.**) Thus, the overall impact of environmental regulation on income distribution is uncertain. Moreover, it is not clear that freeing up resources from environmental control would in fact lead to increases in well-being among the poor.

5.5 The siting of a **LULU** is used to compare and contrast the efficiency and safety standards for pollution control. In such a case, efficiency is a very hard standard to implement because it ignores fairness issues. Thus, something like a safety standard is generally enforced. If a basic level of "safe" protection is afforded through effective regulation, however, Pareto improving compensation schemes can result in some movement toward efficient regulation.

References

Bingham, Taylor H., Donald W. Anderson and Phillip C. Cooley (1987). "Distribution of the Generation of Air Pollution." *Journal of Environmental Economics and Management,* vol. 14, 30–40.

Blinder, Alan (1987). *Hard Heads, Soft Hearts.* New York: Addison-Wesley.

Brajer, Victor and Jane V. Hall (1992). "Recent Evidence on the Distribution of Air Pollution Effects." *Contemporary Policy Issues,* vol. 10, 63–71.

Brooks, Nancy and Rajiv Sethi (1997). "The Distribution of Pollution: Community Characteristics and Exposure to Air Toxics." *Journal of Environmental Economics and Management,* 32, no. 2, 233–250.

Bullard, Robert D. (1991). *Dumping in Dixie: Race, Class and Environmental Quality.* Boulder, CO: Westview.

Burtraw, Dallas, Alan Krupnick, Erin Mansur, David Austin and Deirdre Farrell (1997). "The Costs And Benefits of Title IV," *RFF Working Paper.* Washington, DC: Resources for the Future.

Clough, Kerrigan and David Wann (1990). "A Burning Issue." *The Bureaucrat,* Spring, 25–29.

Copeland, Brian R. (1991). "International Trade in Waste Products in the Presence of Illegal Disposal." *Journal of Environmental Economics and Management,* vol. 20, 143–162.

Crandall, Robert W. (1983). *Controlling Industrial Pollution: The Economics and Politics of Clean Air.* Washington, DC: Brookings.

Cropper, Maureen L. and Wallace Oates (1992). "Environmental Economics: A Survey." *Journal of Economic Literature,* 30, no. 2, 675–740.

Dorfman, Robert (1965). *Measuring Benefits of Government Investments.* Washington, DC: Brookings.

Goodstein, Eban (1994). "In Defense of Health-based Standards." *Ecological Economics,* 10, no. 3, 189–195.

Greider, William (1990). *Who Will Tell the People? The Betrayal of American Democracy.* New York: Simon & Schuster.

Hamilton, J. (1995). "Testing for Environmental Racism: Prejudice, Profits, Political Power?" *Journal of Policy Analysis and Management,* vol. 14, 107–132.

Kneese, Alan V. and William D. Schulze (1985). "Ethics and Environmental Economics." In *Handbook of Natural Resource Economics,* vol. 1, eds. A. V. Kneese and J. L. Sweeney. New York: Elsevier.

Kunreuther, Howard and Douglas Easterling (1990). "Are Risk Benefit Trade-offs Possible in Siting Hazardous Facilities?" *American Economic Review,* 80, no. 2, 252–256.

Kunreuther, Howard and Paul Kleindorfer (1986). "A Sealed-Bid Auction Mechanism for Siting Noxious Facilities." *American Economic Review,* 76, no. 2, 295–299.

Lave, Lester (1987). "Health and Safety Risk Analyses: Information for Better Decisions." Science, vol. 236, 297.

Mann, Eric (1991). *LA's Lethal Air* (Labor Community Strategy Center: Los Angeles).

Norton, Bryan (1991). "Ecological Health and Sustainable Resource Management." In *Ecological Economics: The Science and Management of Sustainability,* ed. Robert Costanza. New York: Columbia University Press.

Portney, Paul (1990). "Policy Watch: Economics and the Clean Air Act." *Journal of Economic Perspectives,* 4, no. 4, 173–182.

Robison, H. David (1985). "Who Pays for Industrial Pollution Abatement?" *Review of Economics and Statistics,* 67, no. 4, 702–706.

Rosenthal, Alon, George M. Gray and John D. Graham (1992). "Legislating Acceptable Cancer Risk from Exposure to Toxic Chemicals." *Ecology Law Quarterly,* 19, no. 2, 269–362.

Sagoff, Mark (1988). *The Economy of the Earth.* Cambridge: Cambridge University Press.

Shrader-Frechette, K. S. (1991). *Risk and Rationality: Philosophical Foundations for Populist Reform.* Berkeley: University of California Press.

Travis, Curtis, S. A. Richter, E. A. Crouch, R. Wilson and E. Klema (1987). "Cancer Risk Management." *Environmental Science and Technology,* 21, no. 5, 415–420.

U.S. Government Accounting Office (1983). *Siting of Hazardous Waste Landfills and Their Correlation with Racial and Economic Status of Surrounding Communities.* Washington, DC: GAO.

Walls, Margaret and Jean Hanson (1996). "Distributional Consequences of an Environmental Tax Shift: The Case of Motor Vehicle Emission Taxes." *RFF Discussion Paper 96–11.* Washington, DC: Resources for the Future.

CHAPTER **6**

Sustainability:
A Neoclassical View

6.0 Introduction

The Iroquois Indians are said to have lived under a traditional directive to consider the impact of their decisions on the next seven generations. Due to the dramatic increase in the pace of technological change, it would be difficult for us today to even imagine with much precision the needs and wants of our descendants two hundred years hence. Yet, many decisions we make today have implications for the well-being of the seventh generation. In this chapter and the next, we will move beyond our efficiency versus safety debate over pollution control standards, and consider these long-run impacts. In the process, we will shift our focus from allowable standards for pollution to maximum targets for the exploitation of natural capital.

In fact, the two concepts are closely related. We can think of long-lived pollution as exhausting a natural resource called an **environmental sink**—the absorbative capacity of the environment. A critical feature of many of today's industrial pollutants is indeed their longevity. Each one of us carries in the fat cells of our bodies residues of the pesticide DDT even though it was banned from use in this country in the early 1970s. Chlorofluorocarbons released into the atmosphere today will continue to contribute to ozone depletion for decades. Certain types of high-level nuclear waste retain their toxicity for tens of thousands of years.

Pollutants such as these that accumulate in the environment are called **stock pollutants.** By contrast, pollutants that do their damage relatively quickly and are then either diluted to harmless levels or transformed into harmless substances are known as **flow pollutants.** Examples include acid rain, smog, and noise or heat pollution.

Stock pollutants use up the critical natural resource of environmental sinks. For example, our bodies are one sink that absorbs waste DDT to some level with minimal damage; we have already used up some, if not all, of that capacity. Stock pollutants that exhaust environmental sinks are one channel through which we of the current generation affect future generations. At the same time we also exploit scarce natural resources that are inputs into the economy—both renewable (water, wood, fish, and soil) and nonrenewable (minerals, oil, the genetic code in species). Economists refer to both these natural resource inputs and environmental waste sinks as **natural capital,** thereby stressing the notion that they are productive assets.

Most people accept that we have a responsibility to control our emission of stock pollutants and manage the planet's natural resources so as to provide future generations with a high quality of life. We can define this goal more precisely as **sustainability:** providing the typical person alive in the future with a standard of living, including both material *and* environmental welfare, at least as high as that enjoyed by the typical person today.[1] Achieving this goal may not be easy; as we have seen, material growth often comes at the expense of environmental quality and vice versa.

Discussions around sustainability have divided economists into two broad groups, which we can call **neoclassical** and **ecological.** (For purposes of argument, I'm going to draw very sharp distinctions between these two views; in reality many economists have one foot in both camps.[2]) The main bone of contention between these two groups is this: To what degree can **created capital,** or human-made capital, substitute for natural capital? In concrete terms, can we continue, for example, to replace natural topsoil with fertilizers, without substantially raising the cost of food production? Neoclassicals would say yes; ecologicals would say no.

Neoclassical economists view natural and created capital as **substitutes** in production. They are technological optimists, believing that as resources become scarce, prices will rise, and human innovation will yield high-quality substitutes, lowering prices once again. More fundamentally, neoclassicals tend to view nature as highly resilient; pressure on ecosystems will lead to steady, predictable degradation, but no surprises. This view of small (marginal) changes and smooth substitution between inputs is at the heart of the broad neoclassical tradition in economics. (If you have taken intermediate micro, let your mind drift back to a smooth, bow-shaped *isoquant*; now recall how two inputs like capital and labor could be easily substituted for each other while keeping the total output level the same!)

At the level of broad vision, neoclassicals generally believe that the global spread of market-based economies provide a powerful foundation for achieving a sustainable future. While still seeing a need for government regulations to control pollution and resource depletion, neoclassicals are generally optimistic that as markets spread, living standards around the globe will continue to rise, and population growth rates will fall, all within an acceptable range of environmental degradation. This is not to say that neoclassicals believe there are no trade-offs, only that sustainability is more or less assured in a well-functioning and properly regulated market system.

By contrast, **ecological economists** argue that natural and created capital are fundamentally **complements**—that is, they are used together in production and have low substitutability (L-shaped isoquants, for you micro fans). Technological pessimists, ecologicals believe that as the sinks and sources that make up our stock of natural capital are exhausted, human welfare will decline. Fundamentally, ecologicals view natural systems

---

[1]This definition follows Pezzey (1992), who also discusses other possible interpretations of the term.

[2]The group I call "neoclassicals" is represented by the Association of Environmental and Resource Economists (AERE) founded in 1978. AERE is housed at a think tank in Washington, DC, called Resources for the Future (RFF). RFF's home page, including access to information on AERE, is http://www.rff.org.

The "ecologicals" group is the International Society for Ecological Economics, founded in 1988; browse ISEE at http://kabir.cbl.cees.edu/isee/iseehome.html.

as rather fragile. If one component, say, of a fishery, is disturbed, the productivity of the entire ecosystem may plummet. This vision of web-like linkages between nature and the economy has led this group to refer to itself as ecological economists.

In contrast to neoclassicals, ecological economists consider the globalizing world economy to be on a fundamentally unsustainable path, and that further ecological pressure in the form of population and consumption growth is likely to lead to real disaster. While not hostile to the spread of markets or to incentive-based approaches to resolving environmental problems, ecological economists see a largely expanded role for government in aggressively protecting our dwindling stock of natural capital.

Arguments between ecological and neoclassical economists can get rather heated—ecologicals refer to the latter disparagingly as "cornucopians" (look it up) while the charge of "doomsayers" flies back. But the debate is quite useful. Neoclassical views may be more helpful in some cases, ecological views in others. The issue ultimately boils down to the degree of substitution between natural and created capital, and this differs from case to case.

This chapter and the next provide two takes on sustainability, given these very different perspectives on the role of natural capital. We will start with the more optimistic neoclassical view.

6.1 Measuring Sustainability: Net National Welfare

Economists are hands-on types, and if we can't measure something, we find it hard to talk about it. In concrete terms, how do we know if we are achieving sustainability or not? Because neoclassical economists believe in a high degree of substitutability between natural and created capital, their approach to measuring sustainability is to weigh directly the material benefits of growth against its environmental costs, both measured in dollar terms.

The most widely used measure of the health of the economy is gross domestic product, or GDP. GDP is the government's measure of the final value of all goods and services produced and consumed in the market each year; it also equals the income earned and spent by consumers.

But GDP is a bad measure of sustainability: whether the typical person is better off or not over the long run. In short, GDP has at least four well-known problems.[3]

1. *GDP fails to include the value of nonmarket production.* Housework, child care, and volunteer work are the three biggies.

2. *GDP fails to subtract the costs of growth* A true measure of welfare needs to account for the fact that rising GDP imposes costs on society. These include externalities: the direct health and productivity costs of pollution and congestion, borne by third parties. Sometimes these externality costs show up as what are called defensive expenditures—money spent to protect oneself from a deteriorating environment. Examples include increased doctor visits, water purifiers, and cell phones (to make traffic jams tolerable). Some analysts include as defensive expenditures measures to address

---

[3]For a broader and accessible critique of GDP, see Cobb et al. (1995). Clifford Cobb compiled the ISEW, discussed in section 6.6 below, for the book by his father, John Cobb, and Herman Daly. Clifford Cobb and his colleagues have updated this measure, now calling it the Genuine Progress Indicator.

crime and family breakdown, which they view as costs of economic growth.[4] When defensive expenditures boost final consumer demand, the GDP measure perversely counts them as increasing well-being!

The costs of growth also include increased spending on internalized externalities. These include the direct costs to industry and government of pollution control and cleanup (some $160 billion per year in the United States.). Here again, GDP counts on the positive side of the ledger some expenditures on pollution abatement and cleanup. Thus, after the giant oil spill in Alaska by the Exxon *Valdez,* the cleanup money spent by the company translated into a big boost to Alaskan consumer spending, and thus GDP.

3. *GDP fails to account for the depreciation of the capital used up in production.* The U.S. government actually publishes an adjusted GDP measure, called net national product (NNP), which does take into account the depreciation of physical, human-made capital. However, our main concern here is the lack of accounting for the depreciation of natural capital—both sources and sinks—used up in the production of GDP.

4. *GDP reflects the experience of the "average" rather than the "typical" person.* GDP is reported on a per capita basis, showing the *mean* (average) value for a society. But for a measure of sustainability, we are interested in the welfare of the *median* (typical) person. If the income distribution in a country is getting more equal, median welfare will rise faster than if the typical worker finds him or herself being "downsized."

Given these four problems, we need a better measure of the welfare of the typical person—let us call such a measure of sustainability **net national welfare (NNW).** Currently, there is no universally agreed-upon approach to this kind of environmental/economic accounting. However, because such a measure would be quite valuable, economists have recently been focusing a lot of attention on measuring NNW.[5]

In principle, NNW can be defined as the total annual output of both market and nonmarket goods and services minus the total externality costs associated with these products, minus the depreciation of capital, both natural and human-made, used up in production. Figure 6.1 shows the arithmetic.

The first step in calculating NNW is to augment GDP with nonmarket consumption—the value of leisure time, nonmarket work such as housecleaning and child

FIGURE 6.1 Calculating Net National Welfare

NNW = Total Output − Costs of Growth − Depreciation

= GDP + Nonmarket output
　　− Externality Costs
　　− Pollution Abatement and Cleanup Costs
　　− Depreciation of Created Capital
　　− Depreciation of Natural Capital

Note: This countrywide measure of NNW must be adjusted to reflect changes in income distribution, since sustainability requires that the *typical* person be no worse off.

_____
[4]Cobb et al. (1995).
[5]See Ahmad et al. (1989), and World Bank (1995).

care, and the value of capital services, such as owner-occupied housing. From augmented GDP, one then subtracts both market and externality costs associated with economic growth from GDP. These range from obvious pollution control expenses, to the increased congestion costs of commuting to work, to increased spending on health care due to environmental damage. Economists have developed a variety of techniques for estimating the costs of both pollution control and environmental damage. We will explore these methods in detail in Chapters 8 and 9.

As a last bit of arithmetic, one must subtract a depreciation fund—the amount of money necessary to replace the capital, both natural and created, used up in the production of GDP, and to provide for a growing population. Included in this fund would be depreciation of machines, plant, equipment and physical infrastructure, as well as much government investment in human capital, such as spending on education and health care.

The depreciation of human-made capital is relatively straightforward, but how does one value nonrenewable resources used up in production? Calculating the "right" depreciation rates for lost topsoil, species that become extinct, or exhausted petroleum reserves is difficult, controversial—and the subject of the next section.

The formula in Figure 6.1 gives a value for net national welfare on a countrywide basis. But a final adjustment for changes in income distribution is required—rather than look at the average (or per capita) NNW, we need to consider what is happening to the median individual.

Figure 6.1 gives us what we want, at least in principle—a way to measure sustainability. Our NNW figure incorporates both the (positive) material and (negative) environmental features of economic growth. Under the neoclassical assumption that reductions in environmental quality can be either remedied or substituted for by new technologies, subtracting the environmental costs of growth from the material benefits makes sense.

Recall that neoclassical economists are technological optimists. Essentially, they *assume* that NNW for the median individual has been rising over time and that we are thus, by definition, living in a sustainable economy. Is this a fair assumption? Let us defer that question until the end of the chapter and, until then, remain sustainability optimists.

Even as neoclassicals, however, we still recognize a variety of ways in which specific actions today can nevertheless lower the welfare of future generations below what it otherwise could be. Given that NNW is rising, neoclassicals argue for achieving *the maximum NNW over time*, a goal known as **dynamic efficiency.**

But maximizing NNW over time brings us back to the issue of measuring it. The next section turns to resource exploitation and its impact on the welfare of future generations. In the process, we'll tackle one of the thorny issues in sustainability accounting: measuring the depreciation of natural capital.

6.2 Natural Capital Depreciation

Any human-made capital good has a relatively fixed useful life before it wears out; a pizza delivery truck, for example, may last for five years. Each year, then, we say the truck has "depreciated" in value. Depreciation is a measure of how much of the truck is used up each year in the delivery process. How should we value the loss of natural capital—like oil, timber, or species diversity—that we use up in production?

Let's begin answering this question with a

PUZZLE

Suppose that Mr. Bill has an oil field containing 100 barrels of oil on his property. He can hire a firm from a neighboring town to pump his oil at a total economic cost of $1 per barrel, but because it is scarce, the price of oil is $2 per barrel, well above cost.[6] Scarcity of the oil means that Mr. Bill can earn a **resource rent** of $1 per barrel from its production. Resource rents develop when, due to absolute scarcity of resources, prices get bid up above the total economic cost of production (see Chapter 3). They are thus a form of economic profit.

If all the oil is produced and sold today:

1. How much will Mr. Bill's *net* income (economic profits) rise for the year?
2. If Mr. Bill spends all the income on a new 80-inch color TV (which he keeps locked up in his bedroom), how much worse off are his children?
3. If Mr. Bill's family were the sole residents of the country of Billsville, how much would Billsville GDP rise?
4. How much would Billsville NNW rise?

The big question addressed by the Billsville situation is this: To what extent does GDP overstate true NNW due to the fact that the current generation is running down the stock of natural capital? We are seeking a way to measure the wealth that we of the current generation are taking away from future generations by using up scarce natural capital.

SOLUTION

Economic profits are equal to total income ($200) minus total economic costs ($100), or $100. This is just the resource rent. If Mr. Bill blows the money on a consumption binge, his children are also worse off by the value of the resource rent (not $200, since they too would have to pay $100 to get the oil out of the ground). Thus, *none* of this increased income can be devoted to Mr. Bill's consumption and still be sustainable. He needs to invest the entire $100 of resource rent in created capital to replace his natural capital and thus insure that his children are not being made worse off by his action.[7]

Billsville GDP also rises by $100, the increase in net income. He now has the option of going on a shopping spree at the local Kmart. But, Mr. Bill *cannot* increase his consumption out of the oil profits (the resource rent) *without* penalizing his kids. Thus NNW does not rise at all! Note also that Mr. Bill is not necessarily punishing his kids by draining the oil today. If he invests the resource rent productively, his kids may well be better off than if he were to leave them the untapped field.

---

[6]Total economic costs include interest payments on borrowed capital and a "normal" profit for any equity financing. See any introductory microeconomic textbook for more on this concept.

[7]This is not strictly true if real interest rates exceed the real rate of growth of oil prices. In such a case, Bill could cream off a small portion of the profits to finance his own consumption and, utilizing the power of compound interest, not make his children any worse off.

Investing resource rents will pay off, especially if, due to technological change, oil prices may actually fall in the future. Neoclassical economists, again reflecting an underlying technological optimism, often urge early exploitation of resources for precisely this reason. Ignoring the cost of extraction, if oil prices are rising in percentage terms at less than the going rate of interest (true over the last fifty years), Bill's family will clearly be better off if he develops the field today *and* banks the rents.

The oil-rich state of Alaska has actually pursued such an approach, diverting some of its oil tax revenues into the so-called Permanent Fund. Earnings from this giant investment fund (over and above the amount reinvested to keep the fund intact) are paid out annually to all Alaskans, totaling around $900 per person per year. Alaska has also invested in a lot of created capital—roads, telecommunications, a better-educated population. The fund and the greater stock of created capital may not fully compensate future generations of Alaskans for the depletion of the resource. Nevertheless, it does suggest how the current generation can directly substitute created wealth for natural wealth, making resource depletion sustainable in economic terms.

The Mr. Bill puzzle suggests a **depreciation rule** for natural capital: *Depreciation equals the measured value of the resource rent.*[8] The resource rent, not the full market value of the resource, is what future generations are losing by our exploitation of natural capital. It is also exactly the amount that needs to be saved and invested (for example, in a permanent fund, or in education, productive infrastructure, or research and development) if resource depletion is to be sustainable.

Figure 6.2 illustrates how one might calculate the resource rent from a supply-and-demand diagram for tropical hardwoods. The long-run supply curve (as you surely recall from an introductory course) reflects the full cost of production. Area *A*, between the supply curve and the price thus shows the resource rent earned by firms in the hardwood industry.[9]

A study by Repetto (1989) sought to estimate the NNW of Indonesia by calculating resource rents from the depletion of petroleum, timber, and topsoil, and then subtracting these figures from GDP. Repetto found that while GDP increased at a rate of 7.1% from 1971 to 1984, the adjusted measure of NNW grew by around 4%. Overall, Indonesia did make genuine economic progress across the decade but considerably less than was indicated by the growth in GDP. However, Repetto also notes that at least for a few years, Indonesian development was unsustainable. Between 1979 and 1981, according to our adjustment rule, natural capital was being depleted faster than investment was creating new capital.[10]

---

[8]Solow (1992) develops this point and also provided the inspiration for the puzzle above.

[9]The area *A* is often considered to be Ricardian rent, not resource rent. However, a Ricardian rent can be thought of as a resource rent for a narrowly defined resource, for example, "low-cost timber." At any rate, all of the rent from the resource needs to be saved and invested to insure sustainability.

[10]Repetto reports that gross investment was lower than resource depletion in those years. To maintain sustainability, net investment (which includes an adjustment for the depreciation of created capital) would have to exceed the drawdown of natural capital stocks. Repetto used the value-added in these industries as a measure of the resource rent, a rather crude approximation. World Bank (1992: 35) reports on similar efforts to adjust GDP in Mexico; see also Pearce and Atkinson (1993).

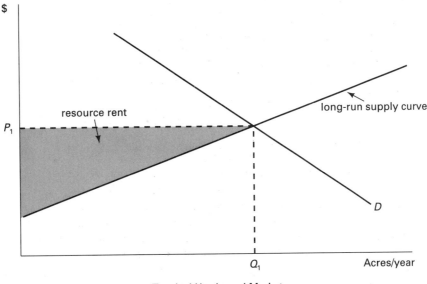

FIGURE 6.2 Measuring Resource Rent

A Problem with the Depreciation Rule Our GDP adjustment requires that we subtract the estimated value of the resource rent to account for the depreciation of natural capital. In this way we do not count as income the reduction in wealth suffered by future generations. Unfortunately, the GDP adjustment rule is not perfect. There is a basic theoretical problem with the approach: The resource rent is measured using *today's* prices. And yet, prices today may not accurately reflect the fair value that future generations are liable to place on natural capital—whether it is oil, blue whales, wilderness, or medicinal products from the rain forest.

Market systems do not completely ignore the interests of the future when scarce resources are being consumed. For example, if rain-forest logging companies expect timber prices to rise at a rapid rate due to future shortages, they will hold off exploiting their holdings in order to reap greater profits. This mechanism, known as **profit-based conservation,** is illustrated in Figure 6.3 below, using a simple supply-and-demand analysis.

The supply curves S_1 and S_2 illustrate forest depletion in the *absence* of profit-based conservation. In period 1, all timber acreage that is profitable at the equilibrium price P_1 is brought onto the market. In period 2, the forest resource has shrunk dramatically, shifting the supply curve in and driving the price up to P_2.

However, firms are likely to recognize such an effect and therefore withhold some supply in the first period. This will shift the first-period supply curve in to S_1' and increase price to P_1'. Now more supply will be available in the second period, shifting the curve out to S_2' and reducing price to P_2'. Profit-based conservation thus tempers the current rate of depletion *and* drives up the current period price to reflect the resource scarcity. Thus, resource rents do take into account, in a limited way, the interests of future generations.

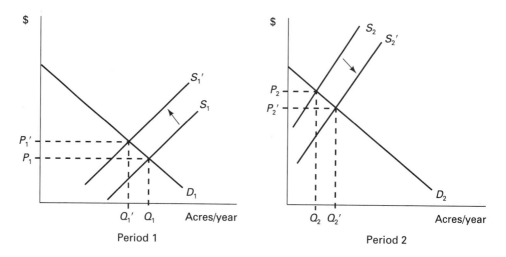

Tropical Hardwood Market

FIGURE 6.3 Profit-Based Conservation

Profit-based conservation means that resource rents today do take into account future demand. However, this does not mean that the interests of future generations are being *fairly* represented. One reason for this is that property rights in developing countries are often uncertain, leading to "use it or lose it" behavior, increasing supply, and driving down prices and resource rents. This issue is explored further in chapter 22. Uncertainty about future needs and preferences can also limit the effectiveness of profit-based conservation. A hundred years ago, it would have been virtually inconceivable to think that people would have actually wanted to have wolves and grizzly bears living close by. Thus, no private entrepreneurs contemplated establishing grizzly ranges in Montana in 1890.

However, the principal reason that today's resource rents do not capture the interests of future generations is that the wealth represented by natural resources is not equally distributed across time: We of the current generation are endowed with 100% of this wealth. This gives us **dictatorial power** over resource decisions. If we were shortsighted enough our descendants could not stop us from squandering it all today, because it is "ours" by default. Another way to say this is that, although current prices may reflect the scarcity of natural capital, the prices do not reflect a fair distribution of natural capital between those of us alive today and those who will follow.

How does dictatorial control over resource use affect prices? Since we alive today "own" all of the tropical timber, this increases our perceived wealth. Higher perceived incomes increase demand and lead to greater levels of exploitation.

Imagine instead that we "gave" the forests to future generations by setting them aside in preserves. We allow harvesting but only if we put the full value of the resource rent into a savings account on behalf of our grandchildren—similar to the Alaska Permanent Fund. This increase in cost for current harvesting would shift the supply curve back and drive up timber prices, a process illustrated in Figure 6.4. Note that (assuming inelastic demand) the *resource rent itself now rises,* from the gray area, to the gray area minus the triangle marked *x* plus the hatched area.

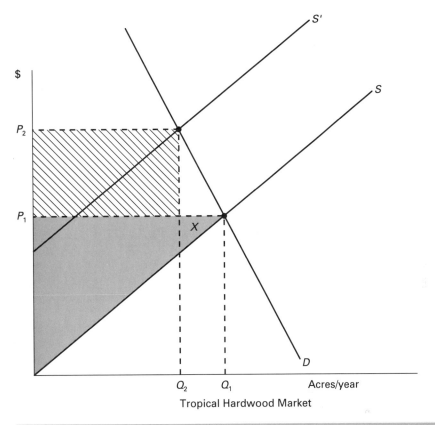

FIGURE 6.4 Dictatorial Power, Prices, and Resource Rent

This example illustrates that the "intergenerational distribution of wealth" itself affects prices, and thus resource rents. Under profit-based conservation, future generations have to indirectly buy from us the privilege of using tropical timber; if instead, we bought from them the right to use it up, the current price would be higher.[11]

In reality, profit-based conservation insures that *some* resources will be conserved to satisfy the needs of the future and, thus, that prices and resource rents today will rise. But as we will see later in this chapter, a general feature of market psychology is that people prefer current over future consumption. Combined with our dictatorial power over resources, this preference for current consumption will tend to generate unsustainably high levels of resource depletion and/or current consumption over investment. Thus, it is unlikely that today's resource rents reflect a fair accounting of the impact of resource depletion on future generations. Instead, adjusting GDP by the value of the resource rent probably reflects a *lower bound* of the true reduction in future wealth due to the drawdown in the stock of natural capital.

---

[11]Howarth and Noorgard (1990) explore this point formally in an overlapping generations, general equilibrium model. They show that all prices (and thus resource rents) are contingent on the intertemporal distribution of the stock of natural capital.

That being said, a rough approach to depreciating natural capital is to follow our depreciation rule. Let us end this section by returning to Mr. Bill's world to illustrate the two ways in which a measure of NNW that accounts for the depletion of natural capital can be useful.

1. **Indicator of progress.** If properly measured NNW rose over time, we could confidently say that the society would be better off, since increases in material welfare would not be coming at the expense of future generations. In Mr. Bill's case, draining the oil field leads to no increase in NNW, yet a $100 increase in GDP. Thus, the year the field is drained, the Bill family is not better off despite the increase in GDP.

2. **Sustainable resource use.** The difference between GDP and NNW that results from resource depletion must be "saved" in order to insure sustainability. This savings can take the form of investment in created capital (putting the money into a college fund). However, if the current generation is too consumption oriented and refuses to invest (Mr. Bill buys his TV), the savings gap would have to be made up by setting aside some natural capital for preservation, thus lowering GDP. Mr. Bill's children should cancel the development order rather than let him head off to Kmart.

More generally, suppose that GDP is $12,000 per capita, but we find that NNW is only $8000 per capita. To insure sustainability we had either (1) better be socking away $4000 per capita in savings and investment in created capital or (2) begin preserving our natural capital.

This section has addressed an important technical issue: How can we measure progress toward sustainable development? From a neoclassical perspective, properly measured NNW subtracts resource rents from GDP. In addition, we have seen that it is possible to penalize future generations by consuming, rather than investing, resource rents. This is one case where neoclassicals concede that individual resource development decisions may be unsustainable (while still assuming overall sustainability at the economy-wide level).

It is also possible to overexploit natural resources both because of the common property problem and because of our own dictatorial power over resource decisions. But why don't markets encourage investors to take a long view when it comes to protecting natural capital? We now move on to consider how the market in fact evaluates trade-offs between our needs and those of generations to come.

6.3 Future Benefits, Costs, and Discounting

In this section we will think about how to value benefits reaped by future generations that result from our actions today. Consider the following

---

PUZZLE

Would you prefer to have $100 in real purchasing power this year or next year or are you indifferent? By "real purchasing power" I mean that if you opt to take the money next year, you will be compensated for any inflation. Assume you don't "need" the money any more this year than next.

SOLUTION

This one requires a little business acumen. It's better to take the money up-front, put it in the bank, and earn interest. As a result, you will have more "real purchasing power" next year than this year. For example, suppose the interest rate on a savings account were 3%, and there was no inflation. If you banked the $100, next year you would have $103 to spend.

Now, stop to think. Where exactly did that extra $3 come from? From the bank, obviously, but where did the bank get it? The bank had loaned out your money to a businessperson (or to the government) who in turn invested it in productive real assets: machines, buildings, roads, schools. A year later, thanks to your saving effort, and other people's ingenuity and labor, the economy as a whole was capable of producing $3 more worth of stuff. At the national level, this year-to-year increase in productive capacity leads GDP to grow between 2% and 3% per year. This growth is the ultimate source of profits, interest, and wage increases.

This illustrates a crucial point: Investment is productive. As a result, at least from an individual's point of view, $100 today is worth more than $100 next year or $100 fifty years from now. From a social point of view, there is a major **opportunity cost to foregone investment.** Investment of $100 today is worth much more today than the same investment in the future.

How does this observation relate back to the environment? Let us return to a global warming example, suitably simplified. Suppose that, if unchecked, carbon dioxide emitted this year would generate global warming sufficient to raise sea levels, so in the year 2050 New Orleans would begin to flood. Let us also make the drastic simplifying assumption that this is the only damage the carbon dioxide emissions will ever do. Here are our options. First, for $15 billion spent today we could reduce our emissions enough to prevent this particular damage. Second, we could do nothing today. Then in the year 2050, for the cost of $15 billion (in today's dollar terms), a dike could be built to protect the city. Thus, our inaction would force our children to incur a $15 billion expense in fifty years (or evacuate the city). The issue on the table is this: Should we spend $15 billion this year to prevent $15 billion of damage to our descendants?

Some economists would argue no. To see why, consider the following response: We could compensate future generations for the damage we are doing to them by setting aside money today that would be available for dam construction in 2050. However, we wouldn't need to put aside $15 billion. We could put a smaller amount of money in the bank today and, by earning interest, it would grow over time to equal $15 billion. In fact, $15 billion in the year 2050 is equivalent to only $2.95 billion banked today at a 3% real (inflation-adjusted) rate of interest. Putting money aside into a bank account specifically to compensate future generations for depletion of natural capital is known as posting an **environmental bond.**

The Alaska Permanent Fund provides one example of an environmental bond. A second simple case is a bottle deposit. Currently, ten U.S. states require a refundable deposit of five to ten cents per can or bottle of soda or juice purchased. If you choose to throw your container out of the window of your car, the money is available for cleanup. (The deposit also provides an incentive for third parties to clean up the mess.)[12] On a larger scale, strip mine companies must post bonds sufficient to allow regulatory agencies to assure reclamation if the property is abandoned.[13]

The potential for posting an environmental bond offers us a rationale for spending less on prevention today than the full value of the damage we inflict on future generations. When future benefits are not weighted as heavily as current benefits, we say that the future benefits have been **discounted.** The basic rationale behind discounting is that because investment is productive, resources on hand today are more valuable than resources available at a later date.

However, because in reality bonds are seldom posted, we have not yet settled the question of how much we "should" spend today to prevent New Orleans from drowning in fifty years. Before returning to this question, however, let us look a little more closely at the mechanics of discounting.

The figure of $2.95 billion mentioned above is known as the **present discounted value** (PDV) of $15 billion paid or received in the year 2050. Formally, the PDV of $X received in T years is the amount of money one would need to invest in the present to just receive $X in T years, at a specified rate of interest, or **discount rate, *r*.**

There is a simple formula for calculating the value of a future benefit in terms of today's dollars. If the discount rate is r, then the present discounted value of $X received in T years is

$$PDV = \$X/(1 + r)^T$$

Let us consider a real-world private investment decision to see how discounting works.

6.4 An Example of Discounting: Lightbulbs

A recent technological innovation has the potential to dramatically reduce electricity use throughout the world, leading to lessened reliance on fossil and nuclear fuels and, thus, substantial improvements in environmental quality. The product is the humble lightbulb. New compact fluorescent lightbulbs can replace standard incandescent bulbs, generate a similar quality light, use somewhere between one fifth and one tenth of the electricity, and last around ten times as long. So what's the catch? The up-front investment is substantially higher. Each compact fluorescent bulb costs about $15, compared with an initial cost for a standard incandescent of around $1.

Suppose you are the physical plant manager at a new hotel with 1,000 light fixtures and have to decide whether investing in these new bulbs is a good idea. How do you proceed? The first step is to marshal the information that you have on the costs and benefits of the two options over their lifetimes. This is done in Table 6.1 below.

The numbers in Table 6.1 simplify the problem. In year 0 the investment is made: $15,000 for the compact fluorescents; $1,000 for the incandescents. The costs in subse-

---

[12]Costanza and Perrings (1990) advocate a wider use of environmental bonding.
[13]Harvey (1978).

TABLE 6.1 Cash Outlays for Investing in Lighting

	Year					
Option	*0*	*1*	*2*	*3*	*4*	*Total*
A. Compact fluorescents	$15,000	$800	$800	$800	$800	$18,200
B. Incandescents	1,000	4,800	4,800	4,800	4,800	20,200
B–A. Savings from compact fluorescents	–14,000	4,000	4,000	4,000	4,000	2,000

quent years reflect the electricity bill and are $4,000 per year higher for the incandescents. We ignore the fact that the compact fluorescents last much longer than the incandescents and assume instead that they both burn out after four years. We also assume, as we will throughout the book, zero inflation (or, alternatively, that the figures are inflation-adjusted to reflect real purchasing power). Other than that, the numbers are realistic approximations.[14] The third line represents the net outlays from investing in option A, the compact fluorescents. On the face of it, investing in the compact fluorescents appears to save $2,000 over the four years.

Unfortunately, choosing between the options is not this simple. The reason: The compact fluorescents require an extra $14,000 initial commitment. If, instead, you bought the incandescents, you could take that $14,000 (less electricity payments), put it in the bank, and earn interest on it. At a 10% interest rate, you would earn over $1,000 during the first year alone.

Things have suddenly gotten quite complex. Fortunately, there is a simple way out: Calculate the PDV of the net savings from investing in compact fluorescents. The PDV will tell you how much, in today's dollars, investment in compact fluorescents saves over the alternative option. To calculate the PDV of the investment, simply apply the formula for each year and add up the values:

$$\text{PDV} = -14{,}000/(1+r)^0 + 4{,}000/(1+r)^1 + 4{,}000/(1+r)^2 + 4{,}000/(1+r)^3 + 4{,}000/(1+r)^4$$

Table 6.2 provides the relevant calculations. How do we interpret the numbers in the table? Consider $2,732, the number in the fourth-year column and the .10 discount rate row. This is the PDV of $4,000 received in four years, if the interest rate is 10%. In other words, one would need to bank $2,732 today at a 10% interest rate to have $4,000 on hand in four years. If the interest rate were .00 (the first row), then one would have to have the full $4,000 on hand today to have $4,000 four years from now.

TABLE 6.2 PDV of Savings from Compact Fluorescents Varies with the Discount Rate

	Year					
Discount Rate	*0*	*1*	*2*	*3*	*4*	*Total*
.00	–$14,000	$4,000	$4,000	$4,000	$4,000	+$2,200
.05	–14,000	3,810	3,628	3,455	3,290	+183
.10	–14,000	3,636	3,305	3,005	2,732	–1,320

[14]The example assumes the lights are on four hours per day, and that electricity costs $.08 per kWh.

The last column of the table illustrates that if the interest rate is zero, the compact fluorescents do save $2,000. However, as the interest rate climbs to 5%, the investment looks less attractive, and at an interest rate of 10%, the compact fluorescents become the more expensive option. With this high interest rate, it is better to save the $14,000 on the initial investment and earn interest while paying out larger sums in electricity payments in later years. The main lessons to be learned here are that the higher the discount rate, (1) the less important are benefits earned down the road, and (2) the more important are initial expenses.

Private, for-profit decision makers, such as hotel managers, do not have to decide what discount rate to use when comparing future benefits with present costs. Businesses seeking to maximize profits should use the market rate of interest on investments of similar risk, that is, their opportunity cost of capital. A rate of 0%, 5%, or 10% will be determined in the financial marketplace. However, government policy makers must *choose* a discount rate for analyzing decisions about how much stock pollution to allow. What is the right discount rate for public choices, such as the level of legal carbon dioxide emissions?

6.5 Choosing the "Right" Discount Rate for Pollution Control

Let us return to our example of the New Orleans flood. Recall the essence of the case: We could spend $15 billion this year on carbon dioxide reduction to prevent $15 billion worth of damage in fifty-some years. Should we do so?[15]

We have already explored a more efficient alternative: an environmental bond. We know that if we set aside $2.95 billion this year, then at a 3% interest rate, we will have on hand the $15 billion in 2050. This option is more efficient since it leaves the current generation with an extra $12.05 billion to invest in other sectors of the economy. In the case of an environmental bond, all the externalities of the carbon dioxide pollution have been internalized, so the market rate of interest is the efficient discount rate.

In most cases, however, bonds are not posted. If future residents of New Orleans are not to be directly protected, should we then go ahead and spend the $15 billion to prevent the flooding? Not necessarily. The argument goes this way: First, *assume* that due to technological improvements net national welfare "naturally" grows at, let us say for convenience, 3% per year. For simplicity, also assume that population growth is zero so that the growth rate of NNW for the typical person is also 3%.

Now, suppose we took action costing $15 billion today to stop global warming and the flooding of New Orleans in 2050. This would divert resources—engineers, scientists, production workers, bank loans—from investment in the production of other goods and services, lowering NNW this year by, let us assume, the full $15 billion. Now if NNW is $15 billion lower this year, next year, due to the cumulative nature of the growth process, it will be $15 * 1.03 = $15.45 billion less than it would have been, *even with no additional expenditure on pollution reduction.* The following year NNW will be depressed by $15.45 * 1.03 = $15.91 billion, and so on, until in the year 2050, NNW

---

[15]Some would argue that we have a moral responsibility to prevent the sea-level rise, regardless of whether the impact on people can be eliminated by means of dike construction. There is nothing wrong with such an argument; however, it steps outside of the utilitarian framework we have established for this book.

will be $76.2 billion less than it would have been had we not made that initial investment in pollution control! Figure 6.5 illustrates the way in which "diverting" $15 billion from investment throws the economy onto a lower-growth path, impoverishing those alive in 2050 by $76.2 billion, less the $15 billion necessary to build the dike.

Under this scenario, our children's generation as a whole would actually be $61.2 billion poorer as a result of our attempts to protect them from global warming. If we had not spent the $15 billion to reduce emissions and had instead invested it in the production of goods and services, they would have enough additional resources to encircle New Orleans by a dike and still have a large sum left over. If NNW grows at 3% per year, it is **dynamically efficient** to allow the flooding, even if no bond is established.

From a benefit-cost perspective, reducing carbon dioxide emissions today would make sense only if it cost less than $2.95 billion—the PDV of $15 billion in the year 2050 at a 3% discount rate. The moral: When comparing future benefits with present costs, *dynamic efficiency requires that future benefits be discounted at the rate of growth of NNW.*[16]

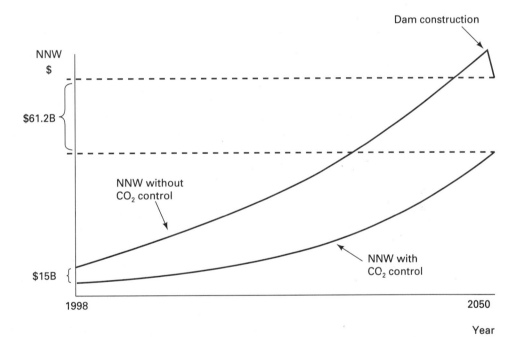

FIGURE 6.5 The Cumulative Effect of "Diverting" Resources Into Pollution Control

[16]This is the efficient discount rate that guarantees dynamic efficiency, given that sustainability as defined here is assumed. Note, this discount rate is *not* chosen on intergenerational equity grounds; sustainability is assured by the assumption of positive growth in NNW.

See Page (1977) for a similar view. Nordhaus (1991) also employs this discounting formulation, in addition to others. For an accessible presentation of discounting in the context of a growth model, see Gramlich (1982). This chapter extends the Page and Gramlich analyses to incorporate externalities. Many neoclassical authors (e.g., Nordhaus) argue for discounting at a rate equal to the growth rate of the economy *plus* the rate of time preference. But including time preference builds in an inefficient bias toward current consumption. The true opportunity cost to future generations of today's foregone investment is the rate of growth of NNW alone.

For an extended discussion of discounting, see the *Journal of Environmental Economics and Management,* special issue, 18, no. 2, March 1990.

Now, this is a very simple story that requires at least one *caveat.* Expenditures on pollution control are unlikely to be wholly "wasteful," failing to contribute to NNW whatsoever. That is, $15 billion of pollution reduction expenditure is unlikely to reduce NNW by $15 billion, even in our simplified case where the direct benefits won't be realized for fifty years. This is true for two reasons. First, if there are unemployed resources present in the economy, these can be devoted toward pollution control and, in fact, boost GDP via a multiplier. Several such opportunities will be explored in the discussion of energy policy later in the book.

Second, if technological spillovers result from investment in pollution control, these, too, will contribute to the growth of NNW. One important benefit of investing in pollution control today is that it widens the technological menu available for future generations in this vital area. By initiating the development of pollution-reducing technology early, one can substantially decrease the cost to future generations of coping with similar problems.

In spite of these criticisms, dynamic efficiency requires that future benefits be discounted at a rate close to that of the growth of NNW. In the New Orleans example, discounting future benefits in this way would mean inaction on the pollution front today. We know such inaction is efficient; that is, it maximizes the size of the economic pie for our children as a whole. Is it also a good idea?

Consider this possibility: We choose not to reduce CO_2 emissions and NNW as a result is $61.2 billion higher in 2050 than it otherwise would have been. However, due to the winds of economic fortune, most of this wealth accumulates in Kansas, and the residents there are unwilling to pay for a dike to protect New Orleans. As a result, New Orleans residents lose their beloved city and all their property and (immobile) possessions. If in turn the total damage to New Orleans is less than $15 billion, we have the now familiar case in which an outcome is efficient but in many ways unfair. Discounting at the rate of growth of NNW is efficient; as a result, it generates the *potential* for a Pareto improvement. In the case of stock pollutants, however, an environmental bond is necessary to insure that such a Pareto improvement actually occurs.

The choice of the "right" discount rate is controversial and also quite important. In the benefit-cost study of global warming discussed in the introductory chapter, its author, William Nordhaus, shows that an efficient policy response varies dramatically depending upon the choice of the discount rate. Under his "maximum damage" scenario, a discount rate of 4% implies that an efficient tax on greenhouse gases would be $2.44 per ton of carbon, leading to reductions in greenhouse gases of less than 5% from uncontrolled levels. On the other hand, a zero discount rate reflecting a "low- or no-growth economy" implies an efficient carbon tax of $65.94 per ton, which would lead to an estimated 33% reduction in greenhouse gas emissions.

6.6 Is Net National Welfare Growing?

How fast, if at all, is NNW actually growing? Knowing the answer to this question would be useful for at least two reasons. First, we just learned that this rate of growth of NNW, if positive, is the dynamically efficient discount rate when a bond is not posted. More significantly, the critical debate between neoclassical and ecological economists in large measure rides on this question—if NNW is growing, economic growth is sustainable and neoclassicals are right (at least for now). If NNW is falling, the ecological vision is more persuasive.

Unfortunately, there is no agreed-upon methodology for estimating NNW, although economists have been working hard in this area. As suggested in the earlier part of this chapter, the basic problem is that there are many judgment calls that go into the construction of such an index of NNW. This lack of consensus means that we cannot sort out in a "scientific way" whether or not our economy is sustainable in neoclassical terms; that is, whether NNW is rising or falling.

In some ways, this should be obvious. People have very differing opinions about whether the typical person is getting better off or worse off with economic growth. These differing opinions reflect an underlying complexity that makes NNW very difficult to measure.

However, the available studies do shed light onto the dynamically efficient discount rate. Moreover, some measure of "progress" is necessary; by default, many politicians and much of the general population view GDP as a measure of social welfare. Perhaps the main value in calculating NNW is to see whether growth in GDP serves as a good proxy for growth in real social welfare.

Table 6.3 summarizes the results of four major attempts to calculate NNW, using as their basis the gross national product (GNP), a measure closely related to GDP.[17]

The studies cited in Table 6.3 all make different assumptions in constructing their indices. Nordhaus and Tobin's writing in 1972 focuses more on sustainability and less on environmental damage. A decade later, Zolatas does the reverse. Both of these studies find rates of growth of NNW to be positive, but less than 1% per year.

TABLE 6.3   Estimates of Growth Rates of NNW

Source	Country	Time Period	Per Capita Annual Growth Rates NNW (%)	GNP (%)
Nordhaus and Tobin (1972)	U.S.A.	1929–1965	1.0	1.7
		1947–1965	0.4	2.2
Zolatas (1981)	U.S.A.	1947–1965	0.4	2.2
		1950–1965	0.6	2.2
		1965–1977	0.7	2.2
Daly and Cobb (1989)	U.S.A.	1950–1960	0.8	1.0
		1960–1970	2.0	2.6
		1970–1980	−0.1	2.0
		1980–1986	−1.3	1.8
Daly and Cobb (1989)	Japan	1955–1960	6.3	8.9[a]
		1960–1970	13.5	14.9

[a]NDP. This study is cited in Daly and Cobb, but was not conducted by them.

Source: This summary table is compiled from a discussion of these studies found in Herman Daly and John Cobb, *For the Common Good* (Boston: Beacon Press, 1989).

---

[17]For an update on the ISEW, see Cobb et al. (1995); an organization called Redefining Progress now publishes updates of the ISEW under a new name, the Genuine Progress Indicator (GPI). Grambsch (1992) addresses most of the conceptual problems at a more micro level in an environmental and resource accounting study of the Chesapeake Bay region.

Daly and Cobb's (1989) effort for the United States is the most ambitious and, thus, controversial: They include adjustments both for depletion of nonrenewable resources, such as petroleum, and for long-term environmental damage.[18] Daly and Cobb also use "equity weights" in constructing their index, with higher rates of income inequality leading to lower overall welfare. Daly and Cobb's results are consistent with the previous studies through 1970, but find a dramatic downturn in NNW in the 1970s and 1980s, due primarily to growing income inequality, nonrenewable resource exhaustion, and long-term environmental damage.

Not surprisingly, Nordhaus and Tobin are neoclassical economists, while Daly is one of the founders of the ecological economics school. The final measured outcomes—positive growth of NNW in the former case and negative growth in the latter—reflect underlying assumptions as much as underlying reality. Nevertheless, we can conclude two things from these studies.

First, both the Nordhaus and Tobin and Daly and Cobb studies show no clear correlation between growth in GNP and growth in NNW in the United States. For example, Nordhaus and Tobin find that the rate of growth of NNW dropped by over 50% after 1947, at the same time that the growth of GNP accelerated. From this we can conclude that the popular perception of GNP (or GDP) as a measure of economic welfare may well be misguided. However, the Japanese study suggests that very high growth rates in underdeveloped countries can lead to substantial improvements in welfare.

Second, even according to more neoclassical studies, the average historical rate of growth of NNW in the United States appears to be less than 1% over the long term. This suggests that for evaluating social decisions, a discount rate in a range from 0% to 1% is dynamically efficient. What discount rates are in fact used by the government and the private sector?

One important branch of the federal government, the Office of Management and Budget, requires a uniform 10% discount rate for most of the benefit-cost studies it reviews. Although uniformity across governmental departments is certainly desirable, a discount rate of 10% is clearly inefficient. At such a high rate, future benefits weigh in with very little force. For example, $100 received in eight years would be discounted to less than $50; the PDV of a $100 benefit received in twenty-five years falls to less than $10! Such shortsightedness cannot be justified on economic grounds. The Environmental Protection Agency typically uses a 3% discount rate.[19]

Decision makers in the private sector have even shorter time horizons. Companies often require profit rates on the order of 15% or more to initiate an investment. Private profit rates are higher than the growth of NNW for two reasons. First, they reflect only the private benefits of investment and fail to account for the external costs of growth.

Second, such high returns are required to induce people to save and invest their income, rather than consume it today. This in turn reflects what economists refer to as **positive time preference**—a widespread desire to consume today rather than save for

---

[18]However, even when they omit these adjustments, the same general pattern holds up. Although NNW growth remains positive in the 1970s, it still falls substantially, turning negative in the period 1980 to 1986 as income inequality rose.

[19]Criticisms of the OMB policy among environmental economists are widespread. See Howe (1990). For a dissenting view, based on a project selection criteria, see Quirk and Terasawa (1991).

tomorrow. The famous environmental economist A. C. Pigou called this our "faulty telescopic facility." Positive time preference leading to high market discount rates is one way in which the market penalizes investments with long-term payoffs.

It is worth noting, however, that low discount rates are not always "pro-environment." Any undertaking with high up-front costs and a long stream of future benefits will look better with a low discount rate. Huge dams may thus be favored by low discount rates, since people will enjoy the cheap electricity and recreational opportunities for decades. The point here is that using market discount rates of 5% or 10% or 15% dramatically undercount the benefits that future generations reap from current investment—whether those benefits are low-cost energy from hydro-plants or a cleaner environment.

This is a very important point. Along with open access to common property (chapter 3), high market discount rates explain how our actions today penalize the welfare of future generations. Due to high discount rates, we fail to make many long-lived investments that could benefit our descendants.

Neoclassicals assume, however, that we are still making *enough* investments to insure sustainability. They argue that, due to rapid technological progress, NNW is nevertheless still rising (though not as fast as possible). As a result, our descendants will still be better off than we are, in spite of our shortsightedness.

Ecologicals, by contrast, argue that these two fundamental economic problems—open access to common property and high market discount rates—have already led to unsustainable exploitation of natural capital. In other words, they maintain, our failure to invest in protecting natural capital has already begun to impoverish our descendants in very literal terms.

To summarize: This section has argued that, in terms of real welfare improvements for society as measured by neoclassicals, $1 "diverted" to environmental protection has an opportunity cost that grows between 0% and 1% per year. That is, investing $1 elsewhere in the economy will lead, on average, to increases in well-being of the typical person that grow in a slow but compounding fashion over time. From a neoclassical perspective, ignoring this opportunity cost in environmental decisions by government will lead to lower welfare for future generations.

While future benefits must be discounted somewhat, private decision makers use much higher discount rates than the efficient rate—the growth rate of NNW. This leads market actors to neglect investments with long-term benefits, thereby depressing future living standards below their maximum achievable levels.

6.7 Summary

Like the Iroquois Indians, we can recognize our ability to alter the welfare of our descendants dramatically, both for good and for bad. In the material sphere, we clearly have a responsibility to endow future generations with the productive capital—both natural and created—sufficient to generate a quality of life at least comparable to our own. However, the means of achieving this goal of sustainable development remain subject to intense debate.

This chapter examines the neoclassical view of sustainability. Neoclassical economists share two underlying assumptions: (1) created capital can generally substitute for natural capital in production, and (2) technological progress will uncover these substitutes as natural capital becomes scarce. These two assumptions imply that we are not "running out of resources."

When analyzing sustainability, the first task for an economist of any stripe is measurement. Neoclassicals have worked on an index of net national welfare, which includes data on economic growth and its associated environmental costs to chart the progress of "quality of life" for the typical individual. Calculating NNW requires subtracting from (adjusted) GDP both the externality costs of growth and the attendant depreciation of natural capital.

Neoclassicals do recognize that future generations can be made worse off by today's "overexploitation" of resources. More precisely, if the resource rent from an exploited resource is consumed, rather than productively invested, then the resource depletion is unsustainable. Moreover, the value of the resource rent is also our (imperfect) measure of the depreciation of natural capital that has to be subtracted from GDP to arrive at NNW. The measure is imperfect, since it is calibrated in prices that reflect the current generation's dictatorial power over resource decisions.

While neoclassicals do concede that individual resource exploitation decisions may be unsustainable, they believe generally that net national welfare rises with economic growth and that sustainability is thus assured. Implicit in this assumption is a faith that technological progress will allow us to replace the services of natural capital with those of created capital.

Under these circumstances, development decisions made with future benefits and costs discounted at the rate of growth of NNW are both dynamically efficient and sustainable. If NNW is growing, investment "diverted" to environmental protection carries with it an opportunity cost of foregone investment that also grows over time at a compound rate. This means that maximizing the overall size of the economic pie for future and current generations, *if the pie is growing,* should be done using the tools of benefit-cost analysis and discounting.

And yet, even within the neoclassical framework, discounting remains controversial. First, while discounting is efficient, it may not be fair. We saw this when our friends from Kansas, for example, failed to fund the New Orleans dike. Second, expenditures on pollution control need not "crowd out" investment in NNW, thus shifting the economy onto a lower-growth path.

Our look at discounting also revealed that, due to a positive time preference, market actors discount the future at a much higher rate than is dynamically efficient. This reduces investments in projects with long-term benefits and lowers the welfare of future generations below the maximum level that could be achieved. In spite of this, neoclassicals argue, we still currently invest enough to insure sustainability.

Finally, we have assumed in this discussion that increases in material consumption (and thus, NNW) actually increase human welfare. In other words, we have uncritically accepted the "more is better" assumption to justify some level of environmental degradation. Chapter 11 will look more closely at this issue.

Peering 200 years into the future, the neoclassical vision is fairly optimistic. Market systems, given the proper government regulation of environmental sinks and sources, will induce the technological innovation necessary to overcome any widespread shortages of natural capital. We now turn to a more challenging view of the prospects for the seventh generation.

APPLICATION 6.0

Thinking Sustainability

From an economic point of view, sustainability is about maintaining a high quality of life for future generations. To see how difficult this problem is to address, try and answer the following question: From a quality-of-life point of view, would you rather have been born in 1920, 1950, or 1980? Assume that you would have been born in the same country and region, but that you don't know your parents' income, or your gender or race ahead of time. If you prefer 1980, this may suggest we have been on a sustainable track until now. Does it also imply that we are currently on a sustainable track? If you prefer an earlier year, what unsustainable decisions did your parents' or grandparents' generations make?

APPLICATION 6.1

Dynamic Efficiency, Equity, and Sustainability

Suppose Pandora is deciding how to dispose of some hazardous waste. She can contain it safely at a cost of $175 or bury it in the local landfill. If she chooses the second option, in ten years' time the stuff will have seeped out enough to permanently ruin the vineyard of Bacchus, who lives next-door to the landfill. The vineyard has a value to him in ten years of $450 (i.e., he'd sell it then for $450). This is the only damage the hazardous waste will ever do. Assume there is no inflation.

1. What is the present value of $450 in ten years at a discount rate of 10%?
2. In the absence of regulation, Pandora is likely to bury the stuff and save $175. If the interest rate is 10%, is it *efficient* for Pandora to bury her waste in the landfill? To answer this, discuss how Bacchus could maximize his utility if he had the legal right to prevent the dumping (and was not an ardent environmentalist). What does this say about the relative size of the total net monetary benefits under the two alternatives? How do total net benefits relate to efficiency?
3. Is burying the waste equitable? Why or why not? Could the use of an environmental bond satisfy a fairness problem if it exists?
4. Is burying the waste sustainable from a neoclassical point of view? From an ecological point of view? Why or why not?

APPLICATION 6.2

Mining and Economic Development

A recent book, entitled *Mineral Wealth and Economic Development,* has focused on the "dismal" economic performance of many mineral dependent countries in the Third World. On average, they have fared very poorly: Per capita GDP has actually fallen in three quarters of the sample of fifteen countries studied, and they have accumulated some of the highest relative debt levels in the world.

This poor performance is in many ways surprising: In principle, economic rent from mineral production can be used for investment in other sectors of the economy, spurring economic growth. Tilton (1992) explains this apparent contradiction partially as a result of unproductive investment of the economic rent. "Rents lost through waste and needlessly high production costs contribute nothing to economic growth. The same holds true for rents spent on current consumption or rents captured and expatriated by foreign interests. Even those rents that are invested can retard economic growth if they are used unwisely."[20]

1. If per capita GDP had risen in these mineral-dependent countries, would they necessarily have achieved "sustainable development"? Why or why not?

2. Does the evidence presented above suggest that countries are better off not developing their mineral wealth?

Key Ideas in Each Section

6.0 We reduce the stock of natural capital available for future generations in two ways: first, the emission of **stock pollutants,** which exhaust **environmental sinks;** and second, the exploitation of natural resources. (**Flow pollutants** have no long-term impact.) Although both **neoclassical** and **ecological economists** agree on the definition of **sustainability,** they disagree on the best means of achieving it. The former believe that **created capital** can **substitute** for **natural capital** on a widespread basis; the latter believe that the two are **complements.**

6.1 Net national welfare (NNW) is the measure proposed by neoclassical economists to try and indicate whether quality of life (material *and* environmental welfare) has, in fact, been rising or falling. Measuring NNW requires correcting four major problems with GDP. If NNW is rising, then the goal of maximizing NNW over time is called **dynamic efficiency.**

6.2 This section develops a **depreciation rule** to account for the depletion of natural capital when measuring NNW: Depreciation can be approximated by the **resource rent.** Resource rents reflect the interests of future generations, *albeit* in a weak form, through **profit-based conservation.** However, the current generation's **dictatorial power** over resource use means that current resource prices are arguably still too low from a fairness point of view. Finally, a measure of NNW is important both as an **indicator of progress** and as a measure of **sustainable resource use.**

6.3 Because resources invested today are productive, there is a major **opportunity cost to foregone investment.** Therefore, future costs and benefits from today's actions must be **discounted.** For example, as illustrated by the New Orleans case, an **environmental bond** posted and invested this year will pay for much larger damages incurred in the future. The current value of benefits (costs) received (borne) at a given future date is called the **present discounted value** and can be calculated *via* a simple formula.

6.4 The use of discounting is illustrated in the light bulb example. A higher **discount rate,** in this case, the interest rate, means a lower present discounted value. High dis-

[20]Tilton also identifies two other factors: "distortions" such as wage inflation and currency appreciation induced by mineral booms; and the slow pace of mineral development arising from investor insecurity. From a sustainability perspective, however, and given the potential for waste and distortions, a slow pace of mineral development may ultimately turn out to be a plus. This will be less true if mineral prices fall in relative terms. For a strong defense of early development, see Radetzski (1992).

count rates thus mean that current costs and benefits are weighed much more heavily than those occurring in the future. Private decision makers use the market interest rate for making decisions. But when sustainability is the goal, a different, lower discount rate must be chosen.

6.5 If NNW is growing, a discount rate equal to the rate of growth of NNW is **dynamically efficient.** Dynamic efficiency means that NNW for future generations is as large as possible. However, just as for the simple efficiency concept discussed in chapter 4, dynamic efficiency need not be fair.

6.6 Several attempts to estimate NNW in the United States have found little correlation between changes in NNW and changes in the conventional progress measure, GNP. They also suggest that NNW has been growing at a rate of between 0% and 2%. One recent study by an ecological economist argues that NNW has actually been declining. Market discount rates (profit rates) are much higher than this, since they do not include the social costs of growth and do reflect a **positive time preference** on the part of consumers. Along with open access to common property, high market discount rates explain why we fail to invest at a fully efficient rate in natural capital.

References

Ahmad, Yusuf J., Salah El Serafy and Ernst Lutz (1989). *Environmental Accounting for Sustainable Development.* Washington, DC: World Bank.

Cobb, Clifford, Ted Halstead and Jonathan Rowe (1995). "If the GDP Is Up, Why Is America Down?" *The Atlantic Monthly,* October, 59–78.

Costanza, Robert and Charles Perrings (1990). "A Flexible Assurance Bonding System for Improved Environmental Management." *Ecological Economics,* vol. 2, 57–75.

Daly, Herman and John Cobb (1989). *For the Common Good.* Boston: Beacon Press.

Grambsch, Anne (ed.) (1992). *Environmental and Resource Accounting in the Chesapeake Bay Region.* Washington, DC: U.S. EPA, Economic Analysis and Research Branch.

Gramlich, Edward M. (1982). *Benefit-Cost Analysis of Government Programs.* Englewood Cliffs, NJ: Prentice-Hall.

Harvey, Michael D. (1978). "Paradise Reclaimed? Surface Mining Control and Reclamation Act of 1977." *Houston Law Review,* vol. 15, 1147–1174.

Howarth, Richard B. and Richard B. Noorgard (1990). "Intergenerational Resource Rights, Efficiency and Social Optimality." *Land Economics,* 66, no. 1, 1–11.

Howe, Charles (1990). "The Social Discount Rate." *Journal of Environmental Economics and Management,* 18, no. 2, 1–2.

Nordhaus, William D. (1991). "To Slow or Not to Slow: The Economics of the Greenhouse Effect." *The Economic Journal,* 101, no. 407, 920–937.

Page, T. (1977). *Conservation and Energy Efficiency.* Baltimore, MD: Johns Hopkins University Press.

Pearce, David and Giles D. Atkinson (1993). "Capital Theory and the Measurement of Sustainable Development: An Indicator of 'Weak' Sustainability." *Ecological Economics,* 8, no. 2, 103–108.

Pezzey, John (1992). "Sustainability: An Interdisciplinary Guide." *Environmental Values,* 1, no. 4, 321–362.

Quirk, James and Katsuaki Terasawa (1991). "Choosing a Government Discount Rate: An Alternative Approach." *Journal of Environmental Economics and Management,* 20, no. 1, 16–28.

Radetzki, Marian (1992). "Economic Development and the Timing of Mineral Exploitation." In *Mineral Wealth and Economic Development,* ed. John E. Tilton Washington, DC: Resources for the Future.

Repetto, Robert (1989). "Nature's Resources

as Productive Assets." *Challenge* 32, no. 5, 16–27.

Solow, Robert (1992). *An Almost Practical Step Toward Sustainability.* Washington, DC: Resources for the Future.

Tilton, John E. (1992). "Mineral Wealth and Economic Development: An Overview." In *Mineral Wealth and Economic Develop-ment,* ed. John E. Tilton. Washington, DC: Resources for the Future.

World Bank (1995). *Monitoring Environmental Progress: A Report on Work in Progress.* Washington, DC: World Bank.

World Bank (1992). *World Development Report 1992: Development and the Environment.* New York: Oxford University Press.

Sustainability:
An Ecological View

7.0 Introduction

Back in 1971, the well-known biologist Paul Ehrlich presented a way of thinking about environmental problems now called the **IPAT equation:**

environmental **I**mpact = **P**opulation * **A**ffluence * **T**echnology

The IPAT relation suggests that we think about three main causal factors underlying environmental problems: population growth, growth in consumption per person (affluence), and the damage per unit of consumption inflicted by the available technology. The IPAT equation also points broadly toward solutions: addressing both overpopulation and overconsumption and cleaning up dirty technologies [Ehrlich and Holdren [1971]].

To make the equation more concrete, consider the global emissions of carbon dioxide from cars in 1995:

$$\underbrace{\frac{CO_2 \text{ emissions}}{\text{per year}}}_{\mathbf{I}} = \underbrace{\{6 \text{ billion people}\}}_{\mathbf{P}} * \underbrace{\frac{\{.1 \text{ cars}\}}{\{\text{person}\}}}_{\mathbf{A}} * \underbrace{\frac{\{5.4 \text{ tons } CO_2\}}{\{\text{car per year}\}}}_{\mathbf{T}}$$

$$= 3.45 \text{ billion tons } CO_2/yr[1]$$

Now, get set for some depressing mathematics. By the year 2050, global population could easily double to 11 billion or so people. Affluence (the number of cars per person) is likely to quadruple. The IPAT equation tells us that, holding technology constant, CO_2 emissions from autos would thus rise eightfold; alternatively, to keep CO_2 emissions constant, technology would have to advance so that each auto could reduce emissions by a factor of 8.

This, in fact, is not so hard to imagine. We could, for example, develop electric cars fueled by solar power, which would omit very low levels of CO_2. But IPAT has much

---

[1] Estimates courtesy of Skip Laitner, at the American Council for an Energy Efficient Economy.

broader implications. Consider, for example, the environmental impacts of the eight-fold increase in mining, oil drilling, lumbering, and manufacturing needed to support construction of even solar vehicles for the larger and more affluent population; or consider the impacts on the natural environment if road construction expands along with auto use.

Ecological economists are technological pessimists—fundamentally they believe that rapid increases in population, and even faster increases in consumption, are putting unsustainable pressure on our natural resource base. In individual cases like solar-electric cars, created capital may substitute for natural capital. But at a general level, created and natural capital are complements in production. That is to say, eco-logicals believe that we are "running out" of the natural capital that forms the base of our economic well-being: both natural resources like freshwater and topsoil, and the environmental sinks that absorb our wastes.

What is meant by "unsustainable" pressure? First, there is the gradual reduction in human welfare as the environment is degraded, and natural resources become scarce and expensive. (This is in contrast to the neoclassical view, where the degraded environment can be either repaired or substituted for, and where technological im-provements overcome resource scarcity and rising prices.)

More radically, ecological economists view the global ecosystem in which our economy is embedded as being fragile, in the sense that accumulating stresses may lead to catastrophic changes in the system itself. For example, climate change from unchecked global warming or increased radioactive exposure from unchecked ozone depletion could radically alter the natural environment. Of course, ecosystems are subject to catastrophe all the time—for example, when lightning causes fire in a for-est. Catastrophe, when severe enough, in fact forms grist for the mill of evolution, by favoring individuals within species better adapted to new conditions. So nature itself is not threatened. "Saving the planet" is not the issue.

However, individual species (or human cultures) do not always survive environ-mental catastrophe. Ecologicals believe that our economy depends in countless, often subtle ways on the natural environment *as it exists today*. If this is true, major environ-mental changes brought on by the stress of doubling and then redoubling of popula-tion and consumption could lead to very large and sudden declines in human welfare.

The ecological economics view implies that, for the sake of future generations, governments need to engage in a much more aggressive program to rein in the twin pressures of population and consumption growth on the deteriorating stock of natural capital. In addition, although ecologicals see distinct limits to technological solutions, government needs to promote clean technology as a short-run strategy for dealing with the inexorable mathematics of IPAT. Later in this book, chapter 21 will explore solutions to the population problem; chapter 11 addresses overconsumption; and chapters 18 through 20 focus on clean technology promotion. This chapter will flesh out the ecological view and consider its implication for government resource policy.

7.1 Malthus and Ecological Economics

In 1798, the Reverend Thomas Malthus wrote a book that has given the economics profession a bad name ever since. Called *An Essay on the Principle of Population,* Malthus laid out a simple proposition with a dire and seemingly unescapable outcome. Assuming (1) that the food supply grows only *arithmetically* (increasing at a constant rate of, say, 10 million tons of grain per year), and (2) that a healthy population grows *geometrically* (doubling every thirty to fifty years), then the prospects for long-run human progress are dim. Eventually, Malthus argued, population growth would outstrip the food supply, leading to the increasing misery of the population, famine, disease, or war. This in turn would provide a "natural" check on further population growth.

This **Malthusian population trap** is illustrated in Figure 7.1. As population grows geometrically, and the food supply increases only arithmetically, available food per person declines. Eventually, some form of natural check halts or even reverses population growth. Malthus was one of the first modern economists, and this, his most famous work, led to economics being labeled "the dismal science."

Malthus's theory should sound familiar. Ecological economists in fact trace their lineage back to Malthus and are sometimes called **neomalthusians.** Malthus' theory clearly reflects technological pessimism, viewing land as an irreplaceable source of natural capital. But surely, wasn't Malthus wrong?

Certainly, his gloomy prediction has yet to come true on a global scale; population growth continues even in the face of substantial poverty worldwide. To date, we have indeed avoided a Malthusian fate because of impressive technological developments in the fields of agriculture, health care, and birth control.

These technological advances have challenged Malthus' basic assumptions. First, it need not be the case that agricultural output grows only arithmetically. From about 1950 through the 1980s, world agriculture underwent a so-called **Green Revolution.** The Green Revolution centered around new, hybrid forms of wheat, rice, and corn

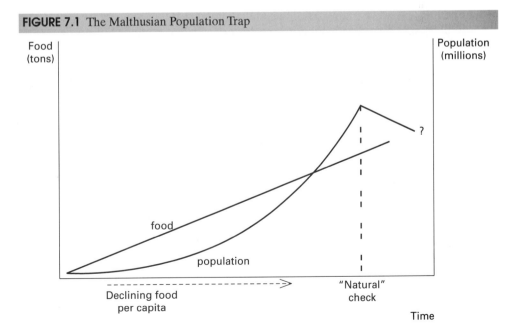

FIGURE 7.1 The Malthusian Population Trap

seeds that produced much higher yields per acre than did conventional seeds. The results were dramatic. From 1950 to 1984, world grain output increased by a factor of 2.6. Over the same period, world population roughly doubled. Thus, from 1950 to the mid-1980s, history did not validate Malthus' first assumption. Both agricultural output and population increased geometrically, with food supply actually outstripping population growth.[2]

Malthus' second assumption, that population growth grows geometrically, also does not always hold. Not including immigration, wealthy countries have very low population growth rates, often *below* zero. The availability of effective birth control, not foreseen by Malthus, has meant that families are able to control their "natural" reproductive tendencies if they so desire. As we shall see in chapter 21, as countries develop economically, most people in fact do limit their fertility.

But, in recent years classic Malthusian conditions have again begun to prevail at the global level. Between 1984 and 1995, grain output per acre improved little, and population growth began to move ahead of growth in food production. Over the period, world grain output per person fell 11%.[3]

What explains this reversal in trends? Partly, the Green Revolution has exhausted its potential. By 1985, for example, 80% of India's wheatlands had already been converted to the high-yielding seed varieties. In addition, however, some of the hidden environmental and social consequences of the Green Revolution technology have come home to roost. Growing the new Green Revolution seeds often resulted in a shift to capital-intensive, chemical-intensive, irrigation-intensive, large-scale agriculture. Brown and Young (1990) estimate that the direct environmental consequences of this shift—ranging from soil erosion, to waterlogging and salting of irrigated land, to compaction of soil from heavy equipment—have lead to annual crop losses on the order of 10 million tons per year, about half of the annual gain in production during the 1980s.

In addition, the productivity gains of the Green Revolution were not evenly shared. In many cases, the shift to large-scale agriculture displaced and impoverished small farmers, leading to greater poverty and hunger. Moreover, a substantial portion of the increased grain production went, not to feed people directly, but instead to feed cattle, pigs, and chicken. This increased meat output serviced First World markets and those of the relatively affluent urban middle class in poor countries. Finally, influenced by western consumption habits (and advertising), poor people in poor countries began to abandon traditional, balanced diets (beans and corn, lentils and rice), for processed western foods—white bread and soft drinks in particular. Thus, it is not clear that a higher percentage of the world's population was actually eating any better at the end of the Green Revolution than at its beginning.[4]

In spite of dramatic productivity gains, the Green Revolution was not able to reduce poverty and malnutrition substantially in many poor countries. Thus, as the technological revolution winds down, and its environmental and social consequences take hold, neomalthusian views are again gaining adherents. There is widespread concern that a cycle of poverty → population growth → poverty, and so on . . . will overwhelm the positive effects of economic growth on population in poor countries. And

---

[2]Brown and Young (1990).
[3]Gardner (1996).
[4]Goodman and Redclift (1991) make this case for Latin America.

unless effective population control measures are taken, global population would continue to increase well above the 10 billion level until some natural check—famine, war, or disease—emerges.

Malthus was truly the forerunner of ecological economists, because he captured both senses in which fundamental limits on natural capital lead to unsustainable development. First, there is a steady decline in available food per capita, leading to rising prices and gradual impoverishment. Second, he predicted an eventual catastrophic change in the ecosystem-economy relationship: fatally weakened immune systems in the human species; famine arising in years of bad harvest; peaceful economies suddenly giving way to economies based on theft and plunder.

Ecological economists are, however, more than reborn Malthusians. First, the sources of stress on the environment have shifted from population to both population and consumption. More significantly, ecological economists have, as we shall see in the next section, turned to ecologists for guidance in measuring sustainability. The definition of sustainability remains the same as for neoclassicals: insuring a non-declining standard of living for the typical member of a future generation. However, the means have changed. In the ecological view, because economic functions are embedded in nature, **sustainability requires handing down to future generations local and global ecosystems that largely resemble our own.**[5]

More specifically, the ecosystems we pass on must be resilient. In resilient ecosystems, external stresses do not lead to catastrophic change. **Ecosystem resilience** is in turn a function of the number and complexity of the underlying interspecies interactions. A quick example: Salmon fisheries in the Pacific Northwest have collapsed, and many are on the verge of extinction. The reasons for this are complex, but clear-cut logging has played an important role. In an old-growth forest, fallen conifers create dams, which in turn develop spawning pools; different types of hardwood trees—maple and later alder—provide food for insects upon which young salmon smolts feed. Large trees throughout the watershed protect streams from devastating debris flows during heavy rains. Slowly these trees have been removed and replaced by a much less diverse second-growth forest, destroying the resilience of the ecosystem. Now, catastrophic events like mud flows, once a part of stream rejuvenation, scour and destroy the salmon habitat.[6]

Ecological economists claim, essentially, that we are doing to ourselves what we have done to the salmon; in complex and perhaps unknowable ways, we are dismantling the delicate physical and biological structure that underlies the resilience of the ecosystems on which we depend. This in turn dramatically increases our economic vulnerability to any large-scale ecosystem shifts that we may induce. This, in a nutshell, is basic ecological economic theory. But what does it mean in practice?

---

[5]Common and Perrings (1992: 31) put it this way: "An ecological economics approach requires that resources be allocated in such a way that they do not threaten the stability either of the system as a whole or key components of the system." The authors earlier (pp. 16–17) define system stability as "Hollings-resilience": the "propensity of a system to retain its organizational structure following perturbation." Arrow et al. (1995) provide a declaration by prominent ecological economists defending ecosystem resilience as the appropriate measure of sustainability.

[6]A neoclassical economist would point out here that farmed salmon has largely replaced wild salmon in stores; in spite of the collapse of the traditional salmon ecosystems, salmon are not scarce. How would an ecological economist respond to this critique?

7.2 Measuring Sustainability

Because ecological economists do not believe that natural and created capital are substitutes, they reject the NNW approach to measuring sustainability developed in the last chapter. If environmental quality and natural resources are not, in general, capable of restoration or substitution, it does not make sense to subtract off the reductions in natural capital from the increases in created capital to arrive at a measure of welfare.[7]

Instead, ecologicals use **physical measures of ecosystem resilience and resource stocks weighed against population and consumption pressure** as their measure of sustainability. Recall that from an ecological point of view, the only way to insure that future generations are not penalized by our actions is to hand down a stock of natural capital that largely resembles our own. This means, for example, on the global warming and ozone depletion fronts, our current impacts are not sustainable. This follows since everybody agrees that, unchecked, they will lead to large-scale changes in the global environment. (Of course, neoclassicals argue that we could adapt to, and therefore do not *necessarily* need to stop, these changes.)

Ecological economists have looked to ecological studies to find other signs of "limits" to growth. For example, Vitousek et al. (1986) calculated that humans now appropriate directly or indirectly 40% of what they called the "net primary production" of organic material on land. In other words, humans are currently consuming close to half of the vegetable matter growing on earth. From the ecological point of view (no substitute for photosynthesis!): "If we take this percentage as an index of the human carrying capacity of the earth, and assume that a growing economy could come to appropriate 80% of photosynthetic production before destroying the functional integrity of the ecosphere, the earth will effectively go from half to completely full during the next . . . 35 years" (Rees and Wackernage [1994: 383]).

Let's pause for a

PUZZLE

The authors of the previous quote are applying the IPAT equation and assuming that the combined effect of increasing population and consumption will lead to a doubling of the human appropriation of biomass in thirty-five years. What are they "forgetting" and why are they "forgetting" it? Another way to phrase the question is this: How would a neoclassical economist respond to this dire prediction, and how would the ecologically-minded author reply?

SOLUTION

The neoclassical response is that the ecologicals are forgetting technology: Innovations in biotechnology and plant breeding will boost yields per acre to

---

[7]Ecological economists refer to the last chapter's neoclassical definition of sustainable resource use, in which resource rents are fully invested in created capital, as "weak" sustainability. They refer to the ecological formulation—an intact stock of natural capital—as "strong" sustainability. See Daly (1996: 79).

compensate for the growth in P (population) and A (affluence). History provides some comfort here: In spite of massive increases in food production, New England now has a much heavier forest cover today than it did in the mid-1800s. Massachusetts, Connecticut, Rhode Island, and Vermont all have close to or more than double the forested acreage found in the previous century.[8]

The ecological comeback is that history provides little guide for assessing the impact of geometric economic growth. While technology may have been able to accommodate the last 100 years of increase on an initially "empty" planet to 6 billion people and their consumption needs, we are now facing a 35-year doubling of combined population-consumption impacts on an already crowded planet. Yes, technology will improve, but ecologists argue that available land poses a fundamental, relatively short-term constraint. Therefore, "forgetting" technology is justified. We will return to this core area of disagreement again at the end of the chapter.

One last example of an ecological accounting of sustainability relates to freshwater use. Postel et al. (1996) find that humans now use about 54% of the surface water runoff that is geographically accessible. They do consider one technology option, calculating that new dam construction could increase accessible runoff by 10% over the next thirty years, but note that population is expected to increase by 45% over the same period. Of course, other technological possibilities exist, chief among them increases in the efficiency of water use. However, ecological economists would argue that freshwater prices are likely to increase substantially over the next few decades and that adequate substitutes are unlikely to be forthcoming.

More fundamentally, however, ecologicals following the IPAT logic would have us consider the broader ecological impacts of significant increases in the demand for water. Dam construction in remote areas, for example, often has high ecological externality costs. Water conflicts throughout the world are already driving many freshwater creatures to the brink of extinction and beyond, destroying industries and livelihoods in the process. Some have argued that water wars between nations are not far behind (Postel [1996]). Beyond the "simple" question of access to cheap water, ecological economists believe that resource scarcity will lead us to fundamentally damage many of the ecosystems on which our economic and cultural lives depend.

In this section, we have seen that ecological economists rely on physical measures of either resource stocks or the absorption capacity of environmental sinks, to judge whether or not our use of natural capital is sustainable. If natural resources have no good substitutes on the horizon, and demand is a large portion of current supply (water or primary vegetation, ecologicals argue) then our use is unsustainable. If the absorptive capacity of environmental sinks is exceeded, leading to long-term alterations in the environment from stock pollutants (ozone-depleting CFCs, carbon dioxide), then our use of those sinks is unsustainable.

Since ecologicals reject the notion that, in general, created capital can substitute for natural capital, they reject as well the neoclassical idea that protecting natural capital

---

[8]Sedjo (1991).

carries with it a large opportunity cost in terms of foregone investment. If future generations need to be handed down local and global ecosystems very much like our own for their economy to function at a reasonable level, then the best thing we can do for them is to "protect natural capital." But if ecological economists argue that much of our current activity is unsustainable, how do we know in any particular case? And more importantly, if we are supposed to protect natural capital, which pieces do we protect first?

7.3 The Daly Rule

The underlying question from the ecological perspective is this: To what extent, if any, can we afford to further run down the existing stock of natural capital? The concept of "sustainability" was originally used in the context of a specific resource. For example, a "sustained yield" of timber can be generated when the harvest rate does not exceed the rate of growth of new forest. One of the founders of ecological economics, Herman Daly, has raised this idea to the economy-wide level, by proposing the following:

> **DALY RULE**[9]
> Never reduce the stock of natural capital below a level that generates a sustained yield unless good substitutes are currently available for the services generated.

The first thing to note about the Daly Rule that it is like a commandment—it says, "Thou shalt protect natural capital without good substitutes," *regardless of the cost* of do so. In other words, under the presumption that future generations will benefit from preserving resources, the Daly Rule requires that the current generation make potentially large sacrifices on their behalf. While this is fine in theory, in practice the rule must be modified. At some point, the costs of preserving natural capital might simply become so high that political support for the Daly Rule would disappear.

Given this caveat, we first need to address what we mean by the "yield" of a resource. The important aspect of natural capital from our utilitarian perspective is not the capital itself: that is, the oil, the old-growth forest, or the clean air. Rather the important feature is the flow of services from that capital: inexpensive transportation, biodiversity resources and wilderness experiences, environmental health.

To determine the availability of substitutes requires focusing on two factors: **uniqueness** and **uncertainty combined with irreversibility.** First of all, do the services provided by the natural capital in question currently *have* substitutes? Each day, for example, over a hundred species of plants or animals are destroyed as a consequence of tropical deforestation. The primary use value from this natural capital is its medicinal and genetic properties; currently, an average of one in four pharmacy purchases contains rain-forest-derived compounds. Suppose that, of the millions of species alive in the forest, one and only one contains a chemical compound effective in curing many types of cancer. In that case, clearly that species and the rain forest that harbors it are unique natural capital.

---

[9]Daly (1996: 81–82) puts it this way for renewables: "Keeping the annual offtake equal to the annual growth increment (sustainable yield) is equivalent to maintenance investment," and then adds, "The general rule would be to deplete non-renewables at a rate equal to the development of renewable substitutes." The way I reformulate it, the rule applies to both renewables and nonrenewables.

A question closely related to uniqueness is the *technological potential* for substitution. Each species, for example, represents a unique DNA blueprint that has evolved over millions of years. While we may be able to imagine substitutes for rain-forest products generated by advanced technology, are such options feasible within the relevant time frame? In cases of unique natural capital—where good substitutes do not now, or will not soon, exist for the services flowing from the natural capital being destroyed—then according to the Daly Rule, the stock should be protected.

It is possible, of course, that species extinction can proceed for some time at the current rate with no loss of unique medicinal or genetic value for humans. The remaining (millions) of species may provide an adequate resource base for developing medicines and biotechnologies on a sustained-yield basis. But they may not.

This example highlights another issue that arises in attempting to apply our sustainability criterion: the **uncertainty** of benefits flowing from natural capital. The genetic resources of the rain forest may yield tremendous improvements in health care and agricultural productivity, or they may prove relatively fruitless. (It is estimated, with substantial uncertainty, that around 1,400 rain-forest species contain anticancer properties.[10]) In the case of the rain forest, beyond the major loss of pharmaceutical material, the ultimate consequences of destroying so vast an ecosystem are essentially unknowable. Similarly, as we saw in the introductory chapter, the atmosphere may be able to absorb current emissions of greenhouse gases with minor changes in global temperature, but alternatively the real possibility exists of major catastrophe.

At the same time that there is substantial uncertainty about the potential yield of some natural capital, decisions to degrade capital stocks such as rain forests or the atmosphere are often **irreversible.** Once these resources are depleted, they can be restored if at all only at great cost. Uncertainty combined with irreversibility provide what is known as an option value to natural capital (discussed further in chapter 8). That is, preservation of the stock is valuable merely to keep our options open. The greater the uncertainty and the more severe the irreversibility, the more caution should be exercised in the exploitation of natural capital.

RENEWABLE RESOURCES AND THE SAFE MINIMUM STANDARD

One point worth stressing is that if the future benefits from preserving our options are truly unknown, then it is not just hard but *impossible* to make decisions about preservation on a benefit-cost basis. If we do not know, even within a large range what the benefits of preservation may be, then benefits cannot be usefully compared to costs. This fact has led some economists to advocate what is called a **safe minimum standard** (SMS) for resources with highly uncertain future value (Ciriacy-Wantrup [1968]; Bishop [1978]). Safe minimum standard advocates argue that unique resources should be preserved at levels that prevent their irreversible depletion, unless the costs of doing so are "unacceptably" high—with this limit determined by political support for preservation.[11]

Figure 7.2 illustrates the basic idea behind the SMS. The horizontal axis shows the

---

[10]Collins (1990: 32). The author also provides the 25% estimate for pharmaceutical content. For more detailed discussions of the economics of tropical deforestation, see chapters 22 and 23.

[11]Bishop (1978) introduced the "unreasonable cost" constraint. Both he and Ciriacy-Wantrup (1968) argue as well that the costs of preservation are, on a society-wide basis, likely to be low.

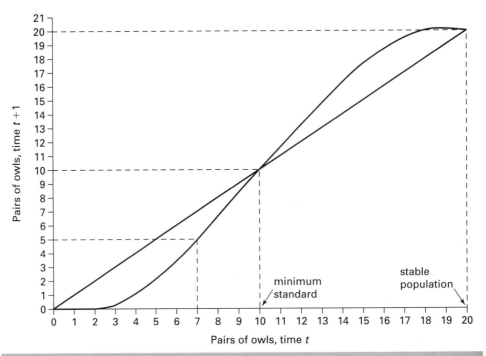

FIGURE 7.2 The Safe Minimum Standard

current stock of a renewable resource, in this case, mating pairs of spotted owls in a forested area. The *S*-shaped line relates the stock of owls alive today to the stock of owls around next year, graphed on the vertical axis. So, for example, if there are 7 pairs alive this year, there will be 5 pairs alive next year, implying that the natural death rate exceeds the birth rate. Carrying this logic further, if there are 5 pairs next year, there will be only 2.5 pairs the year after that, and so on, to extinction. Points on the 45-degree line reflect stable populations, because the number of owls in period $t+1$ is the same as in period t.

The point where the *S* curve first crosses the 45-degree line (10 pairs) is called the minimum standard (MS); any fewer owl pairs than the MS, and the species begins to decline in numbers, eventually slipping into extinction. With more pairs than the MS, however, the species will recover, since a given stock this period produces a larger stock next period, and so on. Eventually, the population size will stabilize at 20 pairs. (Extra credit question: Why does the *S* curve bend back down, and not keep rising?) The safe minimum standard lies a bit to the right of the MS—say 12 pairs—at the point where the resource can be guaranteed to recover on its own.

The safe minimum standard argument is often applied to endangered species. Each species has highly unique biological properties, with uncertain future genetic value; and, *Jurassic Park* aside, species extinction is irreversible. Moreover, endangered species often serve as **indicator species** for threatened ecosystems. Thus, saving the spotted owl in the Pacific Northwest means saving a complex and biodiverse old-growth forest ecosystem. Especially considering their role as indicators, endangered species clearly merit protection under a Daly Rule approach.

In fact, as we shall see in more detail in chapter 13, endangered species legislation is the one major national law currently on the books that reflects ecological sustainability as an underlying goal. The law states that natural capital in the form of species be protected from extinction regardless of the cost.

NONRENEWABLE RESOURCES

But what about resources less unique than species, which also have fairly certain future value—oil, for example? In the last chapter, we considered a neoclassical approach to the sustainable use of petroleum—Mr. Bill was acting sustainably so long as he invested and did not consume the resource rent from oil production. How do ecologicals approach this issue?

Currently, world petroleum consumption is around 20 billion barrels per year. Oil is a finite (nonrenewable) resource; while predictions are uncertain, oil supplies are sufficiently limited so that within the next fifty years, the price should rise to greatly curtail its use as a fuel for everyday transportation or electricity generation. Shell Oil predicts production to peak in 2030; the World Resources Institute sees a production peak between 2007 and 2014, all against a backdrop of much higher world demand.[12]

Ignoring the (major) environmental impact of oil consumption, are we penalizing our children's generation by depriving them of a more abundant oil supply? In fact, doesn't the use of any nonrenewable resource violate our sustainability criterion?

The answer is no if we as a society can somehow offset the reduction in natural capital through the use of created capital. In that case, oil is not really a unique resource. For example, solar technologies may power electric cars and provide cheap heat and electricity as oil stocks are depleted. Markets can act as one powerful social mechanism for replacing natural capital with created capital. As oil becomes increasingly scarce, its price will rise, inducing firms to search out and develop new technologies that serve similar functions or that use the existing oil with much greater efficiency.

The most important way of maintaining a sustained yield from natural capital is by developing ways of using that capital more efficiently or substituting services of comparable quality that do not rely on the natural capital. Efficiency and substitution opportunities are the keys to evaluating the appropriate level of exploitation of natural capital. But the bottom line remains: Are we running down the stock too fast?

This question can be rephrased in terms of oil prices. If we are overexploiting the resource, then current supplies are too large and current prices too low. Low prices, in turn, discourage investments in energy efficiency and the development of alternative technologies. Daly (1996: 83) in fact argues that for oil use to be sustainable, taxes should be high enough so that gas prices are equal to that of the *currently available* substitute (alcohol fuel from corn).

There is little evidence that oil prices today reflect any long-run scarcity. Figure 7.3 charts the inflation-adjusted price of automotive fuel over the last fifty-five years. As one can see, real prices today are almost as low today as they have been over the entire period.

The figure does reveal several big jumps in oil prices resulting from political-economic events. In 1974 and 1978, the OPEC oil cartel used its monopoly power to

---

[12]See Flavin (1985: 24–27); Romm and Curtis (1996), and MacKenzie (1997).

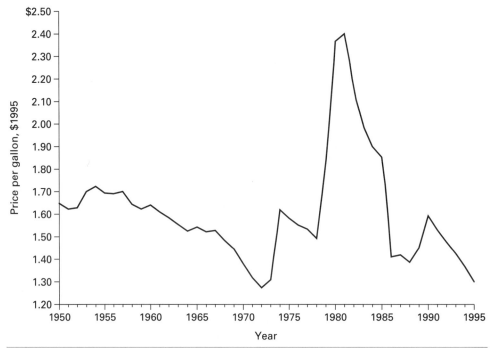

FIGURE 7.3 Inflation-Adjusted Gasoline Prices, 1950–1995 (1995 Dollars)

increase price, and in 1990, the Gulf War created great uncertainty about short-run oil supplies. The OPEC price increases did have their predicted impact on energy use. Overall oil consumption in developed nations declined dramatically during the early 1980s as firms and consumers adopted efficiency measures, but after 1985 consumption rose again and in the last decade has stabilized at mid-1970s levels.

Because there has been no long-run upswing in prices, private investors in the United States have not yet been involved on a large scale in developing or marketing alternative energy technologies, with the exception of government-subsidized nuclear power. However, in many other countries where, due to taxes, oil and gasoline prices are much higher, market forces are working more successfully to promote the development of substitute technologies. In addition, government R&D expenditures and tax credits have been important in promoting the development of energy alternatives —nuclear power, in particular—but also solar and renewable energy sources such as wind, biomass, and geothermal.

An optimistic assessment of renewable and solar alternatives is provided by Flavin and Lenssen (1990). The authors predict that improvements in existing technologies will generate renewable electricity from wind, geothermal, photovoltaic cells, and solar thermal sources at a cost comparable to or below current prices by the year 2030. The authors caution, however, that "the pace of deployment will be determined by energy prices and government policies," and they call for higher taxes on petroleum fuels as well as greater tax dollar support for renewable R&D.

From Flavin and Lenssen's perspective, petroleum is not unique; feasible substitutes can be developed over the medium term. And although exploitation is irreversible, there are no uncertain benefits at stake. Petroleum in the ground has no option value, so the argument for applying a safe minimum standard cannot be applied.

Yet current energy exploitation in the United States is still not following the Daly Rule. It is unsustainable, according to Flavin and Lenssen, since prices and government R&D funding levels are too low to encourage sufficiently rapid deployment of substitutes. Suppose that the full resource rent from petroleum production were being invested back into the economy, as a neoclassical approach demands. Ecologicals still argue that current rates of exploitation are likely to penalize future generations in the form of higher transport prices. Moreover, fossil fuel use poses long-term threats to the resilience of the regional and global ecosystems in the form of air and water pollution.

We will take a much closer look at U.S. energy policy in Chapter 20. For now, let us summarize: This section has explored the logic of managing our global stock of natural capital via the Daly Rule. The basic point is that depleting the natural capital stock is consistent with a broadened definition of sustainable yield, if and only if substitute services of comparable quality *will be* provided future users from created capital. How should this rule figure into development decisions? We have looked at two cases. Endangered species are unique renewable resources with uncertain future value, whose exploitation is also irreversible. Here, ecologicals advocate a safe minimum standard. For less unique resources, like oil, the pace of technological change must be weighed against the rate of resource depletion.

7.4 Markets, Governments, and the EIS

As a society, how could we implement the Daly Rule? Since many economic decisions are market-based, the first issue we need to explore is the degree to which unregulated market behavior promotes sustainability. Markets do provide incentives for sustainable use of privately owned natural capital. In this case, the owner has a strong economic interest in protecting the sustainability of the resource, either for her own profit or to maintain resale value. This will be true even if the resource currently has little value (say a stand of young timber), provided that the services it yields in the future will be sufficiently profitable. This phenomenon, which we discussed in the last chapter, is known as **profit-based conservation.**

Moreover, well-functioning markets have a built-in mechanism for promoting sustainability: As currently valued resources become scarce, their price rises, encouraging efficient use and the development of substitute products. Whether the price rise occurs early enough to allow for the development of substitutes is the issue highlighted in our discussion of the oil market above.

But even when markets are working well, sustainability is not guaranteed. In the agricultural sector, for example, in spite of private ownership, current rates of soil erosion and depletion of nonrenewable irrigation sources are not sustainable over the longer term, even ignoring population growth.[13] Here we again run into the "faulty telescopic faculty" of the current generation, which we expressed in the last chapter in the language of discounting.

As we saw in the hotel lighting example, individuals interested in maximizing their

---

[13]See the discussion in section 7.5 following.

profits from an investment should discount future benefits at the market rate of interest. However, because market interest rates are substantially higher than the rate of growth of NNW (5% to 10% versus 0% to 2%), rational private individuals will discount future benefits well above what we identified as the rate consistent with sustainability. Furthermore, there is mounting evidence that consumers, homeowners, and businesspeople implicitly discount at even higher rates for many investment decisions. For example, a payback period as short as four months, equivalent to a discount rate of 300%, has in the past not been sufficient to induce consumers to invest in energy-efficient appliances.[14]

Thus, even where property rights are well-defined and resources are currently profitable, **high market discount rates** work against sustainable use. In many cases, however, natural capital is a common property resource with free access: Here the public goods problem exacerbates overexploitation. One example we have already considered is overfishing off the New England coast. As a result of these factors, market systems do tend to diminish the stock of natural capital, both renewable and nonrenewable.

Ecological economists believe that markets, in the face of growing population and affluence, are not doing an adequate job to guarantee sustainability, due to excessive discounting, open access to common property, uniqueness of resources, uncertainty combined with irreversibility, or too low a pace of technological change. As a result, they argue for greater government involvement to promote sustainability by protecting natural capital.

Governments can rise to this challenge in many different ways; parts II to IV of this book explore issues ranging from pollution regulation to population control. The remainder of this section will consider direct regulation of development as one response.

In 1970, the U.S. Congress passed the National Environmental Policy Act (NEPA), mandating a modern version of the Iroquois "seventh-generation" approach to development decisions. One section of the act required that government agencies prepare an **Environmental Impact Statement (EIS)** for "legislation or other major federal actions significantly affecting the quality of the human environment." The statement must include:

i) Any adverse environmental effects which cannot be avoided should the proposal be implemented;

ii) Alternatives to the proposed action;

iii) The relationship between local short-term uses of man's environment and the maintenance and enhancement of long-term productivity; and

iv) Any irreversible and irretrievable commitments of resources which would be involved in the proposed action should it be implemented.[15]

The law also requires that public comments be solicited in the drafting of the impact statement. Over half the states have subsequently adopted their own version of the EIS to assist them in their decision making.

---

[14]This example is from Gately (1980); see also Ruderman et al. (1987).
[15]Section 102 of Title I, NEPA. Cited in Bear (1987a).

The EIS has forced every arm of the federal government to at least take notice of environmental considerations in its decision-making process. As one observer notes:

> The . . . process is applied, albeit unevenly, to the broadest range of federal activities of any environmental statute: highways and dams to be sure, but also to the formulation of programs, promulgation of regulations, development of new weapons systems, recommendations for Senate approval and consent to treaties, biotechnology experiments, even the abandonment of railroad tracks—the list extends as far as the federal government's reach. Major projects have been delayed, or in rare instances, cancelled, because of the information revealed through the analysis of environmental impact statements.

The basic philosophy behind the EIS is that the government should identify potential adverse environmental impacts of its actions and recommend superior alternatives. Further, by opening up the process to public comment, much broader perspectives on the likely effects can be incorporated into the decision-making process.

As a planning tool, the EIS has had its share of success stories. When it works well, it encourages agency officials to respond to the environmental concerns of the public—environmentalists, developers, workers, and citizens—and hammer out an ecologically sound compromise on development issues.[16]

However, even on its own terms, the process has its faults. The rather nebulous charge to identify adverse negative effects has lead to a situation in which "the usefulness of the NEPA process to decision makers often is weakened by a persistent tendency to overload NEPA documents with a voluminous amount of irrelevant or highly technical data. No one wants to read such documents: not public citizens, not members of public interest groups, not judges, and certainly not decision-makers." More importantly, there is no process by which post-project compliance with the recommended mitigation measures is assured.[17]

Finally, the EIS process imposes costs on both government and the private sector. From an industry perspective, the EIS provides an opportunity for environmentalists to drag out the permitting process, engaging in what is known as **paralysis by analysis.** Consider an extreme example. In October 1980, Occidental Petroleum filed an application to drill for oil in the Pacific Palisades area of Los Angeles. The project was highly controversial; the primary environmental concern centered around an unstable slope on an adjacent property. After (1) 20 public hearings, (2) a 788-page final Environmental Impact Review (California's EIS), (3) initial disapproval by the city, and (4) the preparation of a subsequent supplemental EIR incorporating recommended changes, the project was approved by a 10–4 vote of the city council in January 1985. However, a citizen's group then filed and won a suit challenging, among other points, the adequacy of the EIR. Occidental then appealed this decision. Finally, in 1989, a ballot initiative was introduced and passed, which prohibited drilling in the area.[18]

On the one hand, this example illustrates the positive aspects of the EIS process.

---

[16]Taylor (1984) provides a good overview of the EIS process.

[17]The quote is from Bear (1987b). For successes, see Sanderson (1987). On post-EIS monitoring, see Culhane (1987).

[18]Waterhouse (1987).

Substantial input by the affected public went into an important development decision, and final appeal to the courts insured that the process itself was fair. The initiative vote prohibiting drilling might be seen as ultimately validating the effort. On the other hand, the case highlights the potential pitfalls. Out of a ten-year EIS process, what appeared to be a politically acceptable compromise initially developed. Ultimately, however, the entire effort became entangled in a legal snare, focusing less on issues of substance than of procedure. Government regulatory efforts such as the EIS for promoting sustainability will invariably entail these types of costs and delays associated with bureaucratic decision making.

The EIS is one direct government regulation that seeks to implement the Daly Rule. In the past, the neoclassical assumption has held sway: that generally, the exploitation of natural capital would lead to increases in human welfare over time, with conservationists being forced to prove the reverse in order to slow the rate of resource depletion. Advocates of the EIS would shift the burden of proof to developers.

More radical governmental measures than the EIS have been proposed to protect natural capital. Back in the 1970s Herman Daly was arguing that the government should set **resource depletion quotas** (Daly [1991]). These would determine the maximum quantity of key resources that the country as a whole would be legally allowed to consume in a given year.

While this may sound utopian, Friends of the Earth in the Netherlands is pushing just such an approach, and the Danish government has accepted the idea of these kinds of resource consumption limits in principle.[19] Table 7.1 lists some of the targets that Friends of the Earth is proposing.

Closer to home, some of our environmental laws are beginning to look like resource depletion quotas—the 1990 Clean Air Act limits total emissions of SO_2 by power plants to 8.95 million tons per year. This in effect is a depletion quota for an environmental sink—the air. National ceilings on carbon dioxide emission limits would be another resource depletion quota of this type.

Clearly, applying the Daly Rule means augmenting market decisions. These can be rather tame governmental regulations such as the EIS; or much more aggressive measures, which from a conservative perspective begin to look like dreaded "ecoso-

TABLE 7.1   Proposed Resource Depletion Quotas for Europe

Resource	*Present* Annual Use per Capita	*Optimum* Annual Use per Capita	*Optimum* Change Needed (%)	*Interim* Target 2010 (%)
Energy CO_2 Emissions	7.3 tonnes	1.7 tonnes	−77	−26
Nonrenewable Raw Materials				
Cement	536 kg	80 kg	−85	−21
Pig Iron	273 kg	36 kg	−87	−22
Aluminum	12 kg	1.2 kg	−90	−23
Chlorine	23 kg	0 kg	−100	−25
Wood	0.66 m³	0.56 m³	−15	−15

Source: Friends of the Earth International, *Sustainable Europe Campaign Newsletter,* no. 2, August 1995.

---

[19]Friends of the Earth International, *Sustainable Europe Campaign Newsletter,* no. 2, August 1995.

cialism." The ecological economics view undoubtedly requires much stronger government intervention to promote sustainability than we are currently seeing.

Yet, government involvement has its own limitations. As we will discuss further in chapter 12, it is not clear to what extent government has the ability or the interest to promote sustainability. Beyond an increasingly short time horizon, the direction of technological progress is very hard to foresee. Thus, judgments made by government agencies or private researchers about the sustainability of any particular action, oil depletion, for example, will be just that—judgments subject to uncertain science and political influence.

On the one hand, detailed governmental involvement in *most* economic development decisions is undesirable on liberty grounds and would, in any case, likely be ineffective. Nevertheless, it is clear that, in a good many cases, unbridled exploitation of our natural capital will lead to a degradation in the quality of life for future generations. Regulations to promote sustainability will have the most impact on the welfare of the future generations if they are concentrated on instances where (1) natural capital delivers a unique flow of valuable resources, with no technological substitutes on the near horizon; (2) or future benefits are uncertain and depletion of the resource is irreversible.

7.5 The Ecological-Neoclassical Debate in Context

In many respects, the debate between ecologicals and neoclassicals over sustainability reflects the same underlying issues as the differences between the safety and efficiency camps. Both ecologicals and safety proponents view environmental protection as a special commodity that should not be traded off for more of "everything else."

Safety proponents privilege a clean environment on the grounds of individual liberty and the right to be free of assaults on the body; ecologicals argue that, in general, natural capital has no good substitutes for which it can be traded. Both groups reject benefit-cost analysis, arguing that the benefits of protection cannot be adequately captured, and both groups therefore rely on physical, not monetary, measures of their underlying goals: safety and sustainability.

Note that in advocating for strict standards, both safety proponents and ecologicals make utilitarian arguments: Environmental protection is *good for people* because the society-wide opportunity cost of protection is relatively low. Moreover, we have not to this point questioned the underlying assumption that more is better. If increasing material affluence in fact does not lead to greater well-being, a hypothesis we will explore in chapter 11, then the "low opportunity cost" case for the safety and ecological positions is strengthened.

Efficiency advocates and neoclassicals respond that the safety and ecological positions are too extreme. They insist there are trade-offs and that we can pay too much for a pristine environment. Resources and person power invested in reducing small cancer risks or preserving salmon streams, for example, are resources and people that then cannot be invested in schools or health care. Benefit-cost analysis is needed to obtain the right balance of investment between environmental protection and other goods and services. Moreover, in the sustainability debate, neoclassicals argue that history is on their side: Malthusian predictions have been discredited time and time again.

Indeed, in recent years, prominent natural scientists (though not economists) in the ecological economics community have made stunningly bad forecasts. Paul Ehrlich, who introduced the IPAT equation, also predicted in the 1960s that "the world is rapidly running out of food" (Ehrlich [1974: 12]). Ehrlich also bet neoclassical economist Julian Simon that the prices of half a dozen key minerals would rise during the 1980s: Ehrlich lost.[20] Finally, a well-known mid-1970s report called *Limits to Growth* (Meadows et al. [1972]) predicted (wrongly) that many natural resource supplies would begin to decline sharply in the mid-1980s.

The problem with all these early predictions, as with Malthus' original one, was that they dramatically underestimated the impacts of changing technologies. Looking just at the *P* and the *A,* and essentially ignoring the *T* (technology) in the IPAT relation, has not, in the past, proven to be justified. Neoclassicals point to these failed predictions to support their basic assumption that natural and created capital are indeed good substitutes—we are not "running out" of natural resources or waste sinks.

Ecologicals respond that history is not a good guide for the future. One hundred and fifty years after the beginning of the industrial revolution, the argument is that accumulating stresses have begun to fundamentally erode the resilience of local and global ecosystems upon which the economy ultimately depends. Indeed, ecologicals have largely shifted their 1970s concerns about running out of nonrenewable minerals and oil to other resources: biodiversity, freshwater, environmental waste sinks, productive agricultural land. While ecologicals stretching back to Malthus have indeed done their share of crying wolf, this does not, of course, mean the wolf won't yet come.

Let us end this chapter with an examination of an ongoing debate between ecological and neoclassical economists over the scarcity of one specific form of natural capital: topsoil. David Pimentel is an ecologist and prominent member of the Ecological Economics society. Along with several co-authors, he published an article in the journal *Science* in 1995 claiming that topsoil losses cost the United States some $27 billion per year in reduced agricultural productivity. This is a big number—about a quarter of total U.S. farm output.

In a stinging response, neoclassical economist Pierre Crosson (1995) accused Pimentel et al. (1995) of ignoring evidence contrary to their position. Crosson himself had earlier published an estimate of agricultural losses due to erosion at closer to $500 million per year, smaller than Pimentel's by a factor of 50. Two other studies ignored by the Pimentel et al. article backed Crosson's position.

So, are we running out of topsoil? Not being a soil scientist or even an agricultural economist, I am not going to settle this debate for you here. (A great term paper topic!) But one point to take away is this: The *I* in the IPAT equation—productivity declines from topsoil loss—arising from a given level of population, a given level of demand (affluence), and a given type of technology, can be quite hard to pin down. A second point. We do know that *unless* more environmentally friendly agricultural techniques are developed, this impact will quickly grow in the face of a doubling of *P,* and at least a doubling of *A.*

And indeed, this point is one that Crosson himself makes explicit. His position is that productivity declines due to topsoil erosion, while real, will be dwarfed by the expected three- to fourfold increase in world food demand over the next fifty years

---

[20]Tierney (1990).

(Toman and Crosson [1991: 19–25]). And in the area of world food supply, while there are some optimists, even many neoclassical economists are worried about the ability of the food system to cope, especially with problems of chronic undernourishment.[21] Even if we are not destroying our stock of topsoil as rapidly as Pimentel argues, the logic of IPAT, and the ghost of the Reverend Malthus nevertheless still hang over our shoulder when considering the world's food prospects.

7.6 Summary

This chapter examines the ecological economic view of sustainability. The basic theory resembles Malthus: geometric population growth bumping up against limited agricultural potential. But ecologicals stress problems arising from both population and consumption pressures on a much broader spectrum of natural capital—from freshwater, to planetary temperature, to biodiversity.

Ecological economists may have resurrected the dismal science, but the perspective is not without hope. Ecologicals challenge us to think about fundamentally redesigning our economy so that it restores rather than degrades natural systems; accrues, rather than depletes natural capital. Can it be done?

On a micro level, undoubtedly. One of the most interesting examples of ecological design is the so-called "living machine"—a series of pools supporting a complex artificial wetland that digests human waste, turning raw sewage into fresh drinking water. The ecological perspective seeks to expand this metaphor of the closed loop—where waste from one sector is food for another—to the macroeconomy at large.

But an economy that conforms to an ecological design will not emerge without major changes in government policy. Ecologicals see the need for widescale, far-reaching social initiatives to control population and consumption growth, and to promote clean technology. We will turn to the details of policy for achieving these goals in parts II to IV of the book.

In addition to the ecological perspective, in the last four chapters, we have laid out three other possible standards for environmental protection. The four are illustrated in Table 7.2: efficiency, safety, neoclassical sustainability, and ecological sustainability. We now want to ask, What tools does economics offer to help us identify real-world target levels of pollution cleanup or resource protection?

TABLE 7.2 Four Normative Standards for Environmental Quality

Standard	*Rule*	*Implementation*
1. EFFICIENCY	MB of reduction = MC of reduction	Benefit-cost analysis
2. SAFETY	Health risk < 1 in 1 million	Risk assessment
3. NEOCLASSICAL SUSTAINABILITY	Discount future at rate of growth of NNW; invest all resource rents	Benefit-cost analysis
4. ECOLOGICAL SUSTAINABILITY	Protect natural capital	Weigh resource stock against population and consumption growth

---

[21]See chapter 10 in World Resources Institute (1997).

As indicated in Table 7.2, implementing the efficiency and neoclassical sustainability standards requires a full accounting of the costs and benefits of environmental protection. And so, for these standards, clearly we need to know how to measure benefits and costs. But this is not true for the goals of safety and ecological sustainability. Safety is measured via a health-based standard, and sustainability by ecological measures of ecosystem resilience. If safety proponents and ecologicals reject benefit-cost analysis, what more can economics contribute toward defining their goal?

Advocates of the safety and ecological standards need to learn about benefit and cost estimation techniques, if only for defensive purposes. To paraphrase the famous economist Joan Robinson: "The purpose of studying economics is not to learn ready-made answers to economic questions. Rather, it is to learn how to avoid being fooled by (second-rate) economists." Learning the right way to measure costs and benefits is crucial for understanding neoclassical claims about how big the trade-offs between consumption and the environment really are.

Given this context, the next three chapters will explore the methods economists have developed for measuring the benefits of environmental protection and its costs, and for weighing one against the other.

APPLICATION 7.0

A Growth Parable[22]

Suppose that a bacterium lives in a test tube and the bacteria population doubles every minute, so that at the end of one minute there are two, at the end of two minutes there are four, and so on. Suppose also that at the end of fifteen minutes, the food supply runs out.

1. How many bacteria will be around at the end of fifteen minutes?
2. How many bacteria will be around at the end of fourteen minutes?
3. When will half of the food be used up?
4. What percentage of the food will be left at the end of thirteen minutes? Do you think that, after thirteen minutes, "Joe Average" bacterium would be easily persuaded that a food crisis was at hand?
5. Suppose, in spite of your answer to question 4, that at the beginning of the thirteenth minute the bacteria do get a wake-up call. They begin a crash scientific program, putting the best bacteria minds to work on growing more food. Success! By the beginning of the fourteenth minute, the bacteria manage to quadruple the remaining food supply. How much time do they buy themselves?
6. Is there a difference between these bacteria and people that might give us some hope for our long-run survival? If so, is it likely to work through P, A, or T?

Key Ideas in Each Section

7.0 Beginning with the **IPAT equation,** ecological economists argue that sustainability is threatened by geometric growth in both population and consumption per person (affluence). Ecologicals are dubious that technology can solve these problems because of two underlying assumptions. First, they argue that created capital cannot generally

---

[22]Thanks to Dennis Palmini for suggesting this problem, which he adopted from David Perry (1994), *Forest Ecosystems* (Washington, DC: Johns Hopkins University Press).

substitute for natural capital in production. Second, because the economy is embedded in what they believe is a rather "fragile" set of ecosystem relationships, accumulating stresses on natural ecosystems may lead to sudden large declines in human well-being.

7.1 Ecologicals' intellectual lineage can be traced back to Malthus, and his **population trap;** ecologicals are sometimes called **neomalthusians.** Through the mid 1980s, Malthus was "wrong," thanks in large measure to the Green Revolution in agriculture. However, gains from the Green Revolution have tapered off. Ecologicals share the Malthusian view that population (and consumption) pressures lead initially to steady and eventually to catastrophic declines in human welfare. Ecologicals differ from Malthus in that they rely on an ecological definition of sustainability: **ecosystem resilience.**

7.2 As with neoclassicals, the first task for an ecological economist is measurement. Ecologicals employ **physical measures of ecosystem resilience and resource stocks weighed against population and consumption pressure** as their measure of sustainability. If demand for resources without good substitutes is a large portion of current supply, then our use is unsustainable. If the absorbative capacity of environmental sinks is exceeded, leading to changes in ecosystems from stock pollutants, then our use of those sinks is unsustainable.

7.3 To achieve sustainability, ecologicals have proposed the **Daly Rule** for development decisions. In this framework, any reduction in the stock of natural capital must be compensated for by created capital capable of generating a comparable flow of services. Applying the rule to **unique** resources that also have **uncertain** future value and whose destruction is **irreversible** requires protection up to a **safe minimum standard.** Endangered species fit this bill, especially given their role as **indicator species.** For less unique resources, like oil, exploitation must be weighed against the pace of technological change.

7.4 Some features of well-functioning markets promote sustainability: Ownership rights encourage **profit-based conservation,** and rising prices in the face of resource scarcity encourage the increasingly efficient use and the development of substitute products. However, **high market discount rates** and the dominance of common property resources work against market achievement of sustainability. Given these problems, ecologicals see a much more aggressive role for government in protecting natural capital. As the **Environmental Impact Statement (EIS)** process illustrates, government efforts to promote sustainability have their own drawbacks, such as **paralysis by analysis,** and yet are essential in key areas. **Resource depletion quotas** are a more restrictive means of protecting natural capital.

7.5 Finally, the safety-efficiency debate over pollution standards is similar in nature to the ecological-neoclassical debate over natural resource exploitation. Both safety proponents and ecologicals argue that human society as a whole is best off protecting environmental quality at a high level *regardless of the trade-offs.* Ecologicals make this case by arguing that natural and created capital are not good substitutes in production. Neoclassicals counter that trade-offs are real, because perceived resource limits can be overcome via technology. The topsoil debate illustrates that these issues are not easy to resolve.

References

Arrow, Kenneth, Bert Bolin, Robert Costanza, Partha Dasgupta, Carl Folke, C. S. Holling, Bengt-Owe Jansson, Simon Levin, Karl-Goran Maler, Charles Perrings and David Pimentel (1995). "Economic Growth, Carrying Capacity and the Environment." *Science*, 268, April 28, 520–521.

Bear, Dinah (1987a). "The National Environmental Policy Act and the Council on Environmental Quality." *Environmental Impact Assessment,* ed. Nicholas A. Robinson. Albany, NY: NYS Bar Association.

Bear, Dinah (1987b). "Does NEPA Make a Difference?" *Environmental Impact Assessment,* ed. Nicholas A. Robinson. Albany, NY: NYS Bar Association.

Bishop, Richard C. (1978). "Endangered Species, Irreversibility, and Uncertainty: The Economics of a Safe Minimum Standard," *American Journal of Agricultural Economics,* 60, vol. 1, 10–18.

Brown, Lester R. and John E. Young (1990). "Feeding the World in the Nineties." In *State of the World,* 1990, ed. Lester R. Brown. New York: Norton.

Ciriacy-Wantrup, S. V. (1968). *Resource Conservation: Economics and Policies,* 3rd ed. Berkeley: University of California Press.

Collins, Mark (1990). *The Last Rainforests.* New York: Oxford University Press.

Common, Mick and Charles Perrings (1992). "Towards an Ecological Economics of Sustainability." *Ecological Economics,* 6, no. 1, 7–34.

Crosson, Pierre (1995). "Soil Erosion and Its On-Farm Productivity Consequences: What Do We Know?" *RFF Discussion Paper 95–29.* Washington, DC: Resources for the Future.

Culhane, Paul G. (1987). "Environmental Impact Statements and Post Decision Management: Theory and Practice." *Environmental Impact Assessment,* ed. Nicholas A. Robinson. Albany, NY: NYS Bar Association.

Daly, Herman (1996). *Beyond Growth: The Economics of Sustainable Development.* Boston: Beacon Press.

Daly, Herman (1991). *Steady State Economics,* 2nd ed. Washington, DC: Island Press.

Ehrlich, Paul R. (1974). *The Population Bomb.* Washington, DC: Sierra Club.

Ehrlich, Paul R. and John Holdren (1971). "Impact of Population Growth." *Science,* 171, no. 3977, 1212–1219.

Flavin, Christopher (1985). "World Oil: Coping with the Dangers of Success." *Worldwatch Paper,* 66 Washington, DC: Worldwatch Institute.

Flavin, Christopher and Nicholas Lenssen (1990). "Beyond the Petroleum Age: Designing a Solar Economy." *Worldwatch Paper,* 100. Washington, DC: Worldwatch Institute.

Gardner, Gary (1996). "Preserving Agricultural Resources." In *State of the World,* 1996, ed. Lester Brown. New York: Norton.

Gately, Dermot (1980). "Individual Discount Rates and the Purchase and Utilization of Energy-Using Durables: Comment," *Bell Journal of Economics,* 11, vol. 1, 373–374.

Goodman, David and Michael Redclift (1991). "The Machinery of Hunger: The Crisis of Latin American Food Systems." In *Environment and Development in Latin America,* eds. David Goodman and Michael Redclift. New York: Manchester University Press.

Mackenzie, James (1997). *Oil as a Finite Resource: When Is Global Production Likely to Peak?* Washington, DC: World Resources Institute.

Meadows, Donella, Dennis Meadows, Jorgen Randers and William Behrens (1972). *Limits to Growth.* New York: Universe Books.

Pimentel, D., C. Harvery, P. Resosudarmo, K. Sinclair, D. Kurz, M. Mcnair, S. Crist, L. Shpritz, L. Fitton, R. Saffourri and R. Blair (1995). "Environmental and Economic Costs of Soil Erosion and Conservation Benefits." *Science,* 267, no. 24, 1117–1123.

Postel, Sandra L. (1996). "Forging a Sustainable Water Strategy." In *State of the World, 1996*, ed. Lester Brown. New York: Norton.

Postel, Sandra L., Gretchen C. Daly and Paul R. Ehrlich (1996). "Human Appropriation of Renewable Fresh Water." *Science,* vol. 271, February 9, 785–788.

Rees, W. E., and M. Wackernagel (1994). "Ecological Footprints and Appropriated Carrying Capacity: Measuring the Natural Capital Requirement of the Human Economy." In *Investing in Natural Capital: The Ecological Approach to Sustainability,* eds. A. Jansson, M. Hammer, C. Folke and R. Costanza. Washington, DC: Island Press.

Romm, Joseph and Charles B. Curtis (1996). "Mideast Oil Forever?" *The Atlantic Monthly,* 277, no. 4, April, 57.

Ruderman, H., M. D. Levine and J. E. McMahon (1987). "The Behavior of the Market for Energy Efficiency in Residential Appliances Including Heating and Cooling Equipment," *The Energy Journal,* vol. 8, 101–124.

Sanderson, Richard (1987). "EPA and NEPA: Cases in Point." *Environmental Impact Assessment,* ed. Nicholas A. Robinson. Albany, NY: NYS Bar Association.

Sedjo, Roger A. (1991). "Forest Resources: Resilient and Serviceable." In *America's Renewable Resources,* eds. Kenneth D. Frederick and Roger A. Sedjo. Washington, DC: Resources for the Future.

Taylor, Serge (1984). *Making Bureaucracies Think: The EIS Strategy of Environmental Reform.* Palo Alto, CA: Stanford University Press.

Tierney, John (1990). "Betting the Planet." *New York Times Magazine,* December 2, 52.

Toman, Michael and Pierce Crosson (1991). "Economics and Sustainability: Balancing Trade-offs and Imperatives." *Discussion Paper ENR-91-05.* Washington, DC: Resources for the Future.

Waterhouse, William (1987). "California's Experience in Permitting Project Applicants to Prepare Environmental Impact Reports." In *Environmental Impact Assessment,* ed. Nicholas A. Robinson. Albany, NY: NYS Bar Association.

World Resources Institute (1997). *World Resources 1996-97.* Washington, DC: WRI.

Vitousek, P. M., P. R. Ehrlich, A. H. Ehrlich and P. Matson (1986). "Human Appropriation of the Products of Photosynthesis." *BioScience,* vol. 36, 328–373.

Measuring the Benefits of Environmental Protection

8.0 Introduction

The efficiency and neoclassical sustainability frameworks we have discussed in the last few chapters appear to give us a very precise answer to the question: Are we polluting too much? Yes, if the marginal benefits of reduced pollution (both today and in the future) exceed the marginal costs of reduction. However, determining the efficient pollution level requires that we first devise accurate measures of both the benefits and costs of decreased pollution.

The benefits of pollution control can be divided into two categories: **market benefits** and **nonmarket benefits**. For example, cleaning up a river may lead to increases in commercial fish harvests, greater use of tourist services, and fewer medical expenses and days lost at work due to waterborne diseases. Measuring these market benefits in dollar terms is a natural approach.

However, economists have also devised methods for measuring nonmarket benefits. In our example these would include increased recreational use of the river (boating, swimming, fishing), the enjoyment of greater species diversity in the river, and a reduction in premature death due to diseases contracted from bad water. Nonmarket benefits are measured by inferring how much money people *would be willing to pay* (or accept) for these benefits if a market for them did exist.

Complicating the measurement of nonmarket benefits is the need to estimate the *risk* associated with industrial pollutants. For example, consider the case of polychlorinated biphenyls (PCBs), industrial chemicals widely used until the late 1970s as lubricants, fluids in electric transformers, paints, inks, and paper coatings. PCB-contaminated waste dumps remain fairly widespread throughout the country today. PCB exposure is related to developmental abnormalities in people and causes cancer in laboratory animals. However, the risk to humans from exposure to low levels of

PCBs is not precisely known and can only be determined to lie within a probable range. The need to estimate, rather than directly measure, both nonmarket benefits and risk means that benefit measures for pollution reduction are necessarily fairly rough.

By a similar token, the direct costs of reducing pollution can be measured in terms of the increased expense associated with new pollution control measures and additional regulatory personnel required to insure compliance. However, indirect costs resulting from impacts on productivity and employment can only be inferred.

The next three chapters will take a close look at methods of measuring and comparing the benefits and costs of environmental cleanup. The principal conclusion is that benefit-cost analysis is far from a precise science. As a result, pinpointing the "efficient" pollution level can be achieved, if at all, only within broad boundaries.

This chapter will focus on direct, nonmarket benefits reaped from cleaner air, water, and land. However, an important *indirect* benefit of environmental protection is the development of new, internationally competitive industries, such as those manufacturing pollution control and cleanup equipment, as well as clean energy technologies in autos, lighting, motors, and alternative fuels. The Japanese, in fact, view the environmental field as so attractive that they have established a governmental-industry consortium targeting markets ranging from biodegradable plastics to carbon-digesting algae and solar power.[1]

8.1 Use, Option, and Existence Value: Types of Nonmarket Benefits

The nonmarket benefits of environmental protection fall into three categories: use, option, and existence values. **Use value** is just that—value in use. Returning to our river example, if people use a clean river more effectively for swimming, boating, drinking, or washing without paying for the services, then these are nonmarket use values.

We discussed the concept of **option value** in the previous chapter in connection with rain-forest preservation. An environmental resource will have option value if the future benefits it might yield are uncertain and depletion of the resource is effectively irreversible. In this case, one would be willing to pay something merely to preserve the option that the resource might prove valuable in the future. In certain cases option value may actually be negative; that is, people may value a resource today less than its expected future use value. However, in many important environmental applications, option value will be positive.[2]

Finally, economists have indirectly included moral concerns about environmental degradation, including empathy for other species, in their utilitarian framework under

---

[1]"In Japan, Environment Means an Opportunity for New Technologies," *Wall Street Journal,* June 3, 1992. See also Heaton et al. (1992).

[2]I focus here on option value arising from supply uncertainty, as in the rain-forest case, which seems most applicable to resource issues. Freeman (1985) shows that supply-side option value will be positive if supply is assured. If a project delivers supply only with a positive probability, a positive sign for option value will be more likely the greater is the uniqueness of the resource. But option value is usually brought up only in the context of unique resources. To illustrate a case in which supply-side option value will actually be negative, consider a resource with perfect substitutes, such as a dollar bill. A risk-averse individual would have to be paid to accept a fair lottery to preserve a dollar bill for possible future use.

the heading of **existence value.** For example, if a person believed that all creatures had a "right" to prosper on the planet, then they would obtain satisfaction from the protection of endangered species, such as the spotted owl or the right whale, even if these species had no use or option value. The desire to leave an unspoiled planet for one's descendants (a bequest motive) will also endow species or ecosystems with an existence value.

As an example of the potential importance of existence value, a survey-based study by Boyle and Bishop (1987) estimated that Wisconsin taxpayers were willing to pay $12 million annually to preserve the striped shiner, an endangered species of tiny minnow with virtually no use or option value. As we will see below, the results of this type of study must be interpreted with care. However, the Boyle and Bishop results do seem to indicate a substantial demand for the preservation of species for the sake of pure existence.

The **total value** of an environmental resource is the sum of these three components:

$$\text{Total Value} = \text{Use Value} + \text{Option Value} + \text{Existence Value}$$

8.2 Consumer Surplus, WTP, and WTA: Measuring Benefits

Having defined the types of benefits that nonmarket goods generate, the next step is measurement. The benefit measure for pollution reduction that economists employ is the increase in **consumer surplus** due to such a reduction. Consumer surplus is the difference between what one is willing to pay and what one actually has to pay for a service or product. A simple illustration: Suppose that it is a very hot day and you are thirsty. You walk into the nearest store perfectly willing to plunk down $1.50 for a small soft drink. However, you are pleasantly surprised to discover the price is only $.50. Your consumer surplus in this case is $1.00.

To illustrate how one would apply the consumer surplus concept to an environmental good, let us return to the example we employed in chapter 3, in which Mr. Peabody has a private demand for the preservation of a trout stream in Appalachia. This demand may be based on his expected use, option, or existence value or a combination of all three. His demand curve is illustrated in Figure 8.1.

Initially, ten acres of stream have been preserved. Assume Mr. Peabody did not pay for this public good. Nevertheless, he still benefits from it. His consumer surplus from the first acre preserved is his willingness to pay ($60), less the price ($0), or $60. We can portray this consumer surplus graphically as the area *A,* lying below the demand curve and above the price (zero) for the first unit. Similarly, for the second acre he is willing to pay around $59, which is also his consumer surplus since the good has a zero price. Consumer surplus from this unit is represented graphically as area *B.* Peabody's *total* consumer surplus from the ten initial acres is represented graphically by the entire area $A + B + C.$

Now suppose that a nature preservation society buys an extra acre of stream land. The benefits of this action for Peabody will be his increase in consumer surplus, area *D.* But this is just the price he is willing to pay for a one-acre increase! For small in-

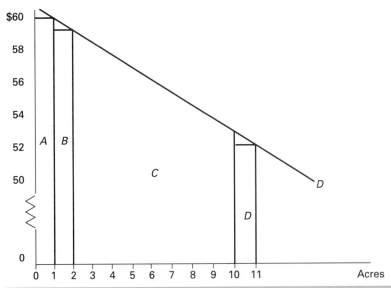

FIGURE 8.1 Consumer Surplus from Preservation

creases in the stock of a public good enjoyed at no charge by consumers—like trout streams, or clean air or water—*the price that people are willing to pay is a close approximation to the increase in consumer surplus that they enjoy.*

This analysis suggests that one can measure the benefits of environmental improvement simply by determining people's **willingness to pay** (WTP) for such improvement and adding up the results. However, WTP is not the only way to measure consumer surplus. An alternative approach would be to ask an individual his or her minimum **willingness-to-accept** (WTA) compensation in exchange for a degradation in environmental quality. In our example above, Peabody could be persuaded to give up the eleventh acre of stream in exchange for a little more than $52.[3]

In theory, WTP and WTA measures are both good approximations to the change in consumer surplus from a small change in a public good such as environmental quality. Economists predict that WTA will be a bit higher than consumer surplus, because individuals are actually made a bit richer when they are compensated for damage. On the other hand, WTP should be a bit lower than consumer surplus, since people will be made poorer if they actually have to pay for environmental improvement. However, the differences should not, in theory, be large since the income changes involved are not big.

To date, however, the evidence does not support this prediction. As can be seen in Table 8.1, reported WTA values are typically found to be from three to ten times as high as WTP. This discrepancy has persisted, even in studies such as Brookshire and

[3]In this example, I use WTP for improvement from the status quo and WTA for degradation to the status quo, where the status quo is ten acres. These are, respectively, compensating and equivalent variation measures. One can also use WTP for improvement to the status quo and WTA for degradation from the status quo. For a further discussion, see Freeman (1979).

TABLE 8.1	Disparities Between WTP and WTA (in year-of-study dollars)	
Study	*WTP*	*WTA*
Hammack and Brown (1974)	$247.00	$1,044.00
Banford et al. (1977)	43.00	120.00
	22.00	93.00
Sinclair (1976)	35.00	100.00
Bishop and Heberlein (1979)	21.00	101.00
Brookshire et al. (1980)	43.64	68.52
	54.07	142.60
	32.00	207.07
Rowe et al. (1980)	4.75	24.47
	6.54	71.44
	3.53	46.63
	6.85	113.68
Coursey et al. (1983)	2.50	9.50
	2.75	4.50
Knetsch and Sinden (1983)	1.28	5.18
Brookshire and Coursey (1987)	12.92	95.52

Sources: Ronald Cummings, David Brookshire, and William Schulze, eds. *Valuing Environmental Goods: An Assessment of the Contingent Valuation Method* (Lanham, MD: Rowman and Allenheld, 1986). Used with permission. And Brookshire and Coursey (1987).

Coursey (1987), where the researchers specifically attempted to control for factors that might lead to inflated WTA figures.[4]

How can we explain the divergence between WTP and WTA benefit measures? One possibility is that, for psychological reasons, people are more willing to sacrifice to maintain the existing quality of the environment than they are to improve environmental quality beyond what is already experienced. People may adopt the *status quo* as their reference point and demand higher compensation to allow environmental degradation than they are willing to pay for making improvements. If this hypothesis, known as **prospect theory,** is correct, it would reshape our marginal benefit curve for pollution reduction as illustrated in Figure 8.2.[5] Here, the marginal benefits of reduction rise dramatically just inside current levels of pollution.

A second explanation for the divergence between WTP and WTA is based on the degree of substitutability between environmental quality and other consumption goods.[6] Consider, for example, a case where people are asked their WTP and WTA to reduce the risk of cancer death for members of a community from air pollution. A substantial reduction in the risk of death is something that, for many people, has very few good substitutes. Nevertheless, a person whose income is limited will be able to pay only a certain amount for such a guarantee. On the other hand, because good sub-

---

[4]See the discussion in Knetsch (1990) and Mitchell and Carson (1989). The mean results from Brookshire and Coursey are presented in Table 8.1 for consistency with the other studies. However, their median WTA values also tended to exceed WTP by a substantial margin.

[5]See Kahneman and Tversky (1979).

[6]See Hanemann (1991).

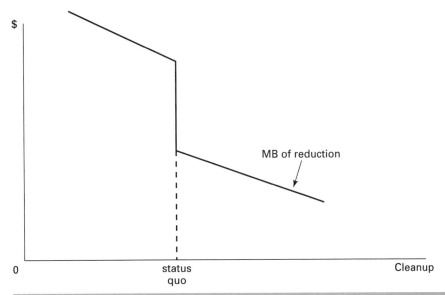

FIGURE 8.2 Prospect Theory and Marginal Benefits of Cleanup

stitutes for a reduced risk of death cannot be purchased, the compensation necessary for accepting such a risk might well be very large, even greater than the individual's entire income.

Some have argued that this "no good substitutes" argument is of limited value in explaining the measured discrepancy between WTP and WTA. Can it really be true, for example, that a stand of trees in a local park (the good in the Brookshire and Coursey study in Table 8.1) has no adequate substitute for people in the community? Chapter 11 takes up in more detail the degree to which environmental goods and more common consumption items might actually substitute for one another in the provision of utility. For now, however, we can note only that the divergence between WTP and WTA benefit measures is an unsolved problem in benefit-cost analysis.

Using WTP or WTA as benefit measures generates one additional concern. Rich people, by the simple virtue of their higher incomes, will be willing to pay more for environmental improvement and will require more to accept environmental degradation. In other words, using WTP or WTA to assess the benefits of identical pollution control steps in rich and poor areas will lead to a higher benefit value for the wealthy community. As we will see, the ethical dilemma posed by this measurement approach shows up strongest when comparing WTP and WTA for reduction in the risk of death or illnesses between rich and poor countries.

8.3 Risk: Assessment and Perception

The first step in actually measuring the benefits of pollution reduction is to assess the risks associated with the pollution. As noted in the introduction, this can be a difficult process. Information on health risks comes from two sources: epidemiological and animal studies. Epidemiological studies attempt to evaluate risk by examining past cases of human exposure to the pollutant in question. For example, in the case of PCBs, developmental abnormalities such as lower birth weights, smaller head circumference, and less developed cognitive and motor skills have been found in three separate communities of children whose mothers suffered substantial exposure. There is also limited evidence of a link between occupational exposure to PCBs and several types of cancer (Glenn et al. [1989]).

In animal studies, rats and mice are subjected to relatively high exposures of the pollutants and examined for carcinogenic effect. PCBs have been found to generate cancers in animal studies. The combined epidemiological and animal evidence has led the U.S. Environmental Protection Agency to label PCBs as probable human carcinogens.[7]

Due to concern about PCB (and other industrial pollutant) contamination of the Great Lakes, Glenn et al. (1989) undertook an evaluation of the risk of eating Lake Michigan sport fish. In this case, as in any risk assessment, it is necessary to estimate the number of cancers likely to happen from different levels of exposure. From animal studies, the number of extra tumors generated as a result of high exposure to PCBs is known. Translating this information to a human population requires two steps: First, the cancer incidence from high levels of exposure among animals must be used to predict the incidence from low levels; and, second, the cancer rate among animals must be used to predict the rate among people.

The assumptions made in moving from high-dose animal studies to low-dose human exposure constitute a **dose-response model.** A typical model might assume a linear relationship between exposure and the number of tumors, use a surface-area scaling factor to move from the test species to humans, and assume constant exposure for seventy years. Such a model would generate a much higher estimated risk of cancer for humans than if a different model were used: for example, if a safe threshold exposure to PCBs were assumed, if a scaling factor based on body weight were employed, or if exposure were assumed to be intermittent and short-lived.

The point here is that risk assessments, even those based on large numbers of animal studies, are far from precise. Because of this imprecision, researchers will often adopt a **conservative modeling** stance, meaning that every assumption made in the modeling process is likely to overstate the true risk. If all the model assumptions are conservative ones, then the final estimate represents the upper limit of the true risk of exposure to *the individual pollutant.* Even here, however, the health risk may be understated due to synergy effects. Certain pollutants are thought to do more damage when exposure to multiple toxic substances occurs.

Bearing this uncertainty in mind, the study by Glenn et al. estimated that, due to high levels of four industrial pollutants in the Great Lakes (PCBs, DDT, dieldrin, and chlordane), eating one meal per week of Lake Michigan brown trout would generate a conservative risk of cancer equal to almost 1 in 100. That is, for every 100 people consuming one meal per week of the fish, at most, one person would contract cancer from exposure to one of these four chemicals. The study concluded as well that high-consumption levels would likely lead to reproductive damage. There are, of course, hundreds of other potentially toxic pollutants in Lake Michigan waters. However, the risks from these other substances are not well-

---

[7]This discussion of PCBs is drawn from Glenn et al. (1989).

known. For comparison with the Glenn et al. study, Table 8.2 lists the assessed mortality risk associated with some other common pollutants and hazards, as well as the associated uncertainty.

The risk figures in Table 8.2 are the estimated number of annual deaths due to the activity, divided by the exposed population. Thus, at most, 2 out of every 10,000 people exposed to air pollution in the eastern United States will die from it each year. This is a conservative estimate, since the uncertainty, as much as twenty times, is primarily downward. Avid peanut butter fans will be disappointed to learn that it contains a naturally occurring carcinogen, aflatoxin. However, one would have to eat four tablespoons of peanut butter each day of one's life to raise the cancer risk by 8 in 1 million. This figure could be three times higher (24 out of 1 million) or three times lower (2 out of 1 million).

In 1990, the Scientific Advisory Committee of the Environmental Protection Agency attempted to rank environmental hazards in terms of the overall risk they present for the U.S. population. The committee's results are presented in Table 8.3.

The overall risk from a particular pollutant or environmental problem is equal to the product of the actual risk to exposed individuals, times the number of people exposed. Thus, topping the EPA's list are environmental problems likely to effect the entire U.S. population—global warming, ozone depletion, and loss of biodiversity. The relatively low-risk problems are often highly toxic—radionuclides, oil spills, and groundwater pollutants—but they affect a much more localized area.

Risks of equal magnitude do not necessarily evoke similar levels of concern. For example, although risks from exposure to air pollution in the eastern United States are somewhat smaller than risks from cigarette smoking, as a society we spend tens of billions of dollars each year controlling the former, devoting much less attention to the latter. Or, to take another example, airline safety is heavily monitored by the government and the press, even though air travel is much safer than car travel.

The acceptability of risk is influenced by the degree of control an individual feels he or she has over a situation. Air pollution and air safety are examples of situations in which risk is imposed upon an individual by others; by contrast, cigarette smoking and auto safety risks are accepted "voluntarily."

Other reasons that the public perception of risk may differ substantially from the

TABLE 8.2 Annual Mortality Risks with Associated Uncertainty

Action	*Annual Risk of Death*	*Uncertainty*
Drinking Water (EPA limit, chloroform)	6×10^{-7}	Factor of 10
Drinking Water (EPA limit, trichloroethylene)	2×10^{-9}	Factor of 10
Air Pollution (Eastern United States)	2×10^{-4}	Factor of 20, downward only
Peanut Butter (Four tablespoons per day)	8×10^{-6}	Factor of 3
Cigarette Smoking (One pack per day)	3.6×10^{-3}	Factor of 3
Motor Vehicle Accidents	2.4×10^{-4}	10%
Police Killed on Duty (By felons)	1.3×10^{-4}	10%

Source: Richard Wilson and E. A. C. Crouch. "Risk Assessment and Comparisons: An Introduction," *Science,* 236 (April 17, 1987), 267–270. Copyright 1987 by the AAAS. Used with permission.

TABLE 8.3 Relative Risks as Viewed by the EPA

Relatively High Risk
  Habitat alteration and destruction
  Species extinction and loss of biodiversity
  Stratospheric ozone depletion
  Global climate change
Relatively Medium Risk
  Herbicides/pesticides
  Toxics, nutrients, biochemical oxygen demand and turbidity in surface waters
  Acid deposition
  Airborne toxics
Relatively Low Risk
  Oil spills
  Groundwater pollution
  Radionuclides
  Acid runoff to surface waters
  Thermal pollution

Source: U.S. Environmental Protection Agency (1990).

actual assessed risk include lack of knowledge or distrust of experts. Given the uncertainty surrounding many estimates, the latter would not be surprising. Either of these factors may explain why the public demands extensive government action to clean up hazardous waste dumps (1,000 cancer cases per year) while little is done to reduce naturally occurring radon exposure in the home (5,000 to 20,000 cancer deaths per year).[8] The issue of imposed risk may also factor in here. However, to the extent that lack of knowledge drives public priorities for pollution control, education about risk is clearly an important component of environmental policy.[9]

Finally, economists do know that people, in general, are **risk averse;** that is, they dislike risky situations. Risk aversion explains, for example, why people buy auto theft insurance even though, on average, they will pay the insurance company more than the expected risk-adjusted replacement value of their vehicle. By purchasing insurance, people are paying a premium for the certain knowledge that they will not face an unexpected loss in the future. Risk aversion also partially underlies the option value placed on a natural resource.

If people are risk averse, then we should expect them to give extra weight to measures that avoid environmental disasters. Much of the concern over issues like global warming and nuclear power probably arises from risk aversion. It seems sensible to many people to take measures today to avoid the possibility of a catastrophe in the future, even if the worst-case scenario has a relatively low probability.

Indeed, if people are quite risk averse, this becomes another reason for choosing a safer rather than a more efficient standard for pollution cleanup, or an ecological rather than a neoclassical standard for protecting natural capital.[10]

---

[8]Gough (1989).

[9]For extended discussions of these issues, see Bromley and Segerson (1992) and Shrader-Frechette (1991).

[10]See Palmini (1996) for an elaboration on this point.

8.4 Measuring Benefits I: Contingent Valuation

With the risk of additional pollution established, the final step in estimating the benefits of changes in environmental quality is to obtain actual value measures. One might think that the most straightforward way of assessing benefits would be simply to ask people their WTP or WTA. Economists do use survey approaches for measuring the benefits of environmental protection, called **contingent valuations** (CVs), because the survey responses are "contingent" upon the questions asked. However, interpreting the results from CV studies is far from a straightforward process.

As with any survey, the answers given depend heavily on the way the questions are presented. This is especially true of surveys attempting to elicit true WTP or WTA for changes in environmental quality, since the respondents must be made to recognize the actual dollar cost associated with their answer. Contingent valuation researchers have identified at least four sources of possible error in their survey estimates: free riding, strategic bias, hypothetical bias, and embedding bias.

As we discussed in chapter 3, the potential for **free riding** exists when people are asked to pay for a public good. Mr. Peabody could decline to contribute to the preservation fund for the Appalachian trout stream in hopes that Mr. Massey would pick up the bill. In that case, the public good would be provided to Peabody without cost. Thus, Mr. Peabody has an incentive to understate his true WTP or WTA to CV researchers.[11]

Strategic bias arises if people really do not have to pay their stated WTP (or forego their WTA) for the good in question, say the preservation of the Wisconsin striped shiner. Under these circumstances, why not inflate one's WTP estimate? This would be a particularly good strategy if the respondent thought that larger WTP values in the survey results would lead to a higher likelihood of protection for the species. By contrast, the **hypothetical** nature of the question may lead respondents to provide hypothetical answers—poorly thought out or even meaningless.

Finally, the most serious problem with CV surveys is revealed by an observed **embedding bias.** Answers will be strongly affected by the amount of information provided about the issue at stake. This is particularly evident when valuation questions are "embedded" in a broader context. In the case of the striped shiner mentioned in the introduction to this chapter, Wisconsin residents may well have felt differently about the shiner if they had first been asked their WTP to protect the Higgins-eye pearly mussel, another endangered species. In this case, preservation of the one species is probably a good substitute for preservation of the other. That is, by stating, on average, a WTP of $4 to protect the shiner, Wisconsin residents may have been willing to commit those resources to preserving a species of "small water creatures."[12]

On the other hand, mightn't Wisconsinites, via their commitment to the shiner, be expressing a desire to preserve the broader environment or even to obtain the "warm glow" of giving to a worthy cause? Kahnemann and Knetsch (1992) maintain that the interpretation of CV responses is quite difficult in the face of this embedding bias. In one experiment they found that median WTP to improve rescue equipment decreased

---

[11]In small group experiments, free riding is less prevalent than most economists would have predicted. See Mitchell and Carson (1989).

[12]Bishop and Welsh (1992) make this point.

from $25 to $16 when respondents were first asked their WTP to improve disaster preparedness. When respondents were asked first their WTP for environmental services, then their WTP for disaster preparedness, their WTP for improving rescue equipment and personnel estimates fell to $1. Which of these estimates is the "true" WTP for rescue equipment?

Advocates of the CV method argue that carefully designed surveys can overcome much of the potential bias identified here, at least for eliciting WTP values. However, such studies can be expensive. A national survey studying the benefits of water quality improvement by Mitchell and Carson (1984) was administered by a professional survey organization and involved a forty-five-minute interview for each respondent. In addition, such ambitious efforts are relatively rare. In their generally favorable review of CV analyses, Mitchell and Carson (1989: 15) conclude that "it is still quite difficult to obtain data from CV surveys which are sufficiently reliable and valid to use for policy purposes, and that the dangers of attempting to draw conclusions from poorly conceived or executed studies are great." Most CV results must, therefore, be carefully reviewed for potential biases before they are accepted as reasonable estimates of true WTP or WTA.[13]

In spite of its problems, the CV approach is increasingly being used by economists, policy makers, and courts. This is because it provides the *only available means* for estimating nonmarket benefits based primarily on **existence value,** such as the benefits of preserving the striped shiner. These existence benefits are potentially quite large. In the case of the Exxon *Valdez* oil spill in Alaska in 1988, CV estimates of damages were on the order of $30 per household, for a total of $3 billion. This is roughly three times what Exxon actually paid out in damages.[14]

We now turn to two other methods for valuing nonmarket benefits. These methods are good for estimating use and option values but not pure existence values, since they impute a benefit to a resource based on its observed use.

8.5 Measuring Benefits II: Travel Cost

The first of these market-based approaches to estimating nonmarket values is known as the **travel-cost method.** This approach is used to measure the benefits associated with recreational resources, such as parks, rivers, or beaches. The basic idea is to measure the amount of money that people expend to use the resource (their "travel cost"). By relating differences in travel cost to differences in consumption, a demand curve for the resource can be derived and consumer surplus estimated.

One study on the recreational benefits of Florida beaches for tourists provides a good example. Bell and Leeworthy (1990) surveyed 826 tourists leaving Florida by plane or car and obtained information on days spent at the beach and expenses incurred to use the beach, including hotel/motel or campground fees, meals, travel to and from the beach, and access fees and other beach expenses. They also gathered data on initial travel costs in and out of the state, length of stay, age, income, and perception of the crowds and parking conditions at the beaches. Their basic hypothesis

---

[13]Mitchell and Carson (1989: 299) suggest a best practice standard for evaluating CV studies.
[14]"Value of Intangible Losses from Exxon *Valdez* Spill Put at $3 Billion," *The Washington Post,* March 20, 1991.

was that, holding all the other factors constant, lower beach expenses would lead tourists to spend a greater number of days at the beach. In other words, their plan of attack was to use the survey information to draw a demand curve such as the one illustrated in Figure 8.3.

Controlling for the initial investment in getting to Florida, length of the trip, income, age, and perceived beach quality, the quantity demanded of beach days by tourists should increase as the price of a day at the beach falls. If Bell and Leeworthy could use their data to draw a picture such as Figure 8.3, then by plugging in the average number of beach days consumed and calculating average beach expenses, they could calculate the total consumer surplus (the shaded area) for the average tourist.

Using a statistical technique called multiple regression analysis, the authors were able to control for all other factors and isolate the impact of beach expenses on consumption. They found that demand was price inelastic, with a 10% increase in "price" leading to only a 1.5% decrease in time on the beach, *ceteris paribus.* The average tourist spent 4.7 days on the beach, incurring an estimated daily expense of $85. With this information, Bell and Leeworthy estimated consumer surplus for all 4.7 days to be $179, for an average per day of $38. With 70 million tourist days per year, the authors calculated that Florida's beaches yield a flow of value to tourists equal to $2.37 billion annually.

Evaluating the reliability of a travel-cost study boils down to determining how good a job the authors have done controlling for "other factors" that might affect recreation demand. For example, the beach study has been criticized because Bell and Leeworthy did not control for the opportunity cost of the tourists' time. An extreme example shows why this might effect their result: Suppose an idle playboy and a heart surgeon, in all other respects identical, were two of the tourists surveyed. Suppose further that hotel prices were lower in the area visited by the playboy, and he was observed to stay longer in the area and visit the beach more frequently. The incorrect inference would be that

FIGURE 8.3 The Travel-Cost Method of Calculating Consumer Surplus

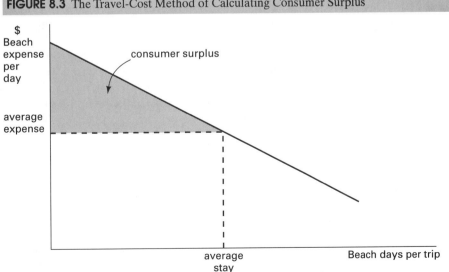

the lower prices caused the higher number of visits when, in fact, the surgeon simply could not afford to stay away from work.[15] Controlling for extraneous factors is a difficult yet essential task for inferring benefits from consumer activities.

8.6 Measuring Benefits III: Hedonic Regression

Like the travel-cost approach, the final method used for valuing nonmarket resources estimates benefits from observed market behavior. This method, **hedonic regression,** uses the change in prices of related (complementary) goods to infer a willingness to pay for a healthier environment. The word "hedonic" means "pertaining to pleasure"; a hedonic regression estimates the pleasure or utility associated with an improved environment. Regression techniques are used here as in the travel-cost method to hold factors constant that might be causing prices to change other than a degradation in environmental quality.

A good application of the hedonic regression method evaluates the damages arising from PCB contamination of sediments in the harbor of New Bedford, Massachusetts. The presence of PCBs was first made public in 1976; by 1983, about one-half the residents were aware of the pollution. Mendelsohn et al. (1992) attempt to measure the damage suffered in the community by examining the decline in real estate prices associated with the presence of this hazardous waste.

Their first step was to gather data on 780 single-family homes that had been sold more than once between 1969 and 1988. The authors' approach was to examine the relative decline in prices for those homes whose repeat sales spanned the pollution period, using regression techniques to control for home improvements, interest rates, the length of time between adjacent sales for the same property, property tax changes, and per capita income in New Bedford. Assuming that knowledge of the pollution was widespread by 1982, houses located closest to the most hazardous area, where lobstering, fishing, and swimming were prohibited, had their prices depressed by around $9,000 (1989 dollars), *ceteris paribus.* Homes in an area of secondary pollution, where bottom fishing and lobstering were restricted, experienced a relative decline in value of close to $7,000.

Multiplying these average damage figures by the number of homes affected, the authors conclude that total damages experienced by single-family homeowners were close to $36 million. This estimate does not include the impact on renters or on homeowners in rental neighborhoods. Based on the results from this and other studies, firms responsible for the pollution have since paid at least $20 million in natural resource damage claims.

As with the travel-cost method, the key challenge in a hedonic regression study lies in controlling for other factors that may affect the change in the price of the related good. The following section illustrates this difficulty when hedonic regression is used in its most controversial application: valuing human life.

8.7 The Value of Human Life

The most ethically charged aspect of benefit-cost analysis is its requirement that we put a **monetary value on human life.** I recall being shocked by the notion when I first

---

[15]See Shaw (1991). Hof and King (1992) point out that Bell and Leeworthy's model is not a "travel-cost study" but rather an "on-site cost study." They evaluate the relative merits of these two approaches.

learned of it in a college economics class. And, yet, when we analyze the value of environmental improvement, we clearly must include as one of the most important benefits reduction in human mortality. If we seek to apply benefit-cost analysis to determine the efficient pollution level, we have no choice but to place a monetary value on life. Alternatively, if we adopt a safety standard, we can merely note the number of lives an action saves (or costs) and avoid the direct problem of valuing life in money terms.

And, yet, because regulatory resources are limited, even the safety standard places an implicit value on human life. For example, U.S. courts have established that risks below 3 out of 10,000 may be "safe"; that is, such risks need not trigger regulatory action under a safety standard.[16] Yet, such risks could be reduced and often are at a cost. However, by ignoring some risks, regulatory agencies place a de facto value on human life. In 1988, the U.S. Department of Transportation was generally initiating regulatory actions in cases where the implicit value of life was $1 million or more, the Occupational Safety and Health Administration employed a cutoff of between $2 million and $5 million, while the Environmental Protection Agency used values ranging from $475,000 to $8.3 million.[17]

Courts also are in the business of valuing life when they award damages in the case of wrongful death. In the past, courts have often used the discounted future earnings that an individual expected to earn over her lifetime. This approach has some obvious flaws: It places a zero value on the life of a retired person, for example.

Efficiency proponents argue that the best value to put on life is the one people themselves choose in the marketplace. Hedonic regression can be used to estimate this value. By isolating the wage premium people are paid to accept especially risky jobs—police officer, firefighter, coal miner—it is possible to estimate a willingness to accept a reduction in the risk of death, and implicitly, the value of a life.

For example, we know from Table 8.2 that police officers face about a 1 in 10,000 higher risk of death of being killed by felons than the general population. Suppose that, holding factors such as age, work experience, education, race, and gender constant by means of regression analysis, it is found that police officers receive, on average, $500 more per year in salary than otherwise comparable individuals. Then we might infer that, collectively, police officers are willing to trade $5 million (10,000 police times $500 per officer) for one of their lives. We might then adopt this $5 million per life figure for use in estimating the environmental benefits of reducing risk and, thus, saving lives.

Note that this is not the value of a specific life. Most individuals would pay their entire income to save their own life or that of a loved one. Rather, the regression attempts to measure the amount of money the "average" individual in a society requires to accept a higher risk of death from, in our case, environmental degradation.[18] Yet, an overall increase in mortality risk *does* mean that human lives are, in fact, being exchanged for a higher level of material consumption.

Even on its own terms we can identify at least three problems with this measure.

---

[16]Travis et al. (1987). See also Glenn (1989: 23).

[17]"Putting a Price Tag on Life," *Newsweek,* January 11, 1988, p. 40.

[18]For this reason, some economists prefer to call the measure the "value of a statistical life" instead of the "value of a life." I use the latter term since the lives at stake are indeed quite real, even if they are selected from the population somewhat randomly.

The first is the question of *accurate information:* Do police recruits really know the increased odds of death? They might underestimate the dangers, assuming irrationally that it "won't happen to me." Or, given the prevalence of violent death on cop shows, they might actually overestimate the mortality risk. The second problem with this approach is *sample selection bias.* Individuals who become police officers are probably not representative of the "average" person regarding their preference toward risk. People attracted to police work are presumably more risk seeking than most.

A third problem with applying this measure to environmental pollution is the *involuntary nature of risk* that is generated. In labor markets, people may agree to shoulder a higher risk of death in exchange for wages; however, people may require higher compensation to accept the same risk imposed upon them without their implicit consent. Polluting the water we drink or the air we breathe is often discussed in terms of violating "rights"; rights are typically not for sale, while labor power is. We have explored the issue of a "right" to a clean environment already when we evaluated the safety standard in chapter 5.

Hedonic regression researchers have attempted to control for these factors as best they can. In a review of fifteen wage-risk studies conducted in the United States and the United Kingdom, Fisher et al. (1989) conclude that a value of between $1.9 million and $10 million (1990 dollars) is an appropriate estimate for the value of a statistical life.

Using hedonic measures to value life raises a basic question: To what extent are labor market choices to accept higher risk really "choices"? Consider the following recent description of twelve-year-old Vicente Guerrero's typical day at work in a modern athletic shoe factory in Mexico City:

> He spends most of his time on dirtier work: smearing glue onto the soles of shoes with his hands. The can of glue he dips his fingers into is marked "toxic substances . . . prolonged or repeated inhalation causes grave health damage; do not leave in the reach of minors." All the boys ignore the warning.[19]

Vicente works at his father's urging to supplement the family income with his wages of about $6 per day.

From one perspective, Vicente does choose to work in the factory. By doing so, he respects his father's wishes and raises the family standard of living. However, his alternatives are grim. Vicente's choices are between dying young from toxic poisoning or dying young from malnutrition. In important respects, Vicente's choices were made for him by the high levels of poverty and unemployment into which he was born.

Similarly, the "choice" that a worker in a First World country makes to accept higher risks will also be conditioned by general income levels and a whole variety of politically determined factors such as the unemployment rate and benefit levels, access to court or regulatory compensation for damages, the progressivity of the tax structure, social security, disability payments, food stamps and welfare payments, and access to public education and health-care services. All these social factors influence the workers' alternatives to accepting risky work. By utilizing a hedonic regression

---

[19]"Underage Workers Fill Mexican Factories, Stir U.S. Trade Debate," *Wall Street Journal,* April 8, 1991. Reprinted by permission of *The Wall Street Journal.* © 1992 Dow Jones & Co., Inc. All Rights Reserved Worldwide.

measure for the value of life, the analyst implicitly is either endorsing the existing political determinants of the income distribution or assuming that changes in these social factors will not affect the measure very much.

Valuing life by the "acceptance" of risk in exchange for higher wages reflects the income bias built into any market-based measure of environmental benefits. The hedonic regression method values Vicente's life much less than that of an American worker of any age simply because Vicente's family has a vastly lower income. Proponents of this approach would argue that it is appropriate, since it reflects the real differences in trade-offs faced by poor and rich people. We have already come across this issue when we discussed the siting of hazardous waste facilities in chapter 5. The point here is to recognize this core ethical dilemma posed by using hedonic regression to determine a value of life.

8.8 Summary

This chapter has discussed the methods that economists use for valuing the nonmarket benefits of environmental quality. The focus has been on problems with such measures. Consider the questions an analyst has to answer in the process of estimating, for example, the benefits of PCB cleanup:

1. Is consumer surplus a good measure of benefits, especially when valuing life?
2. Which measure should be used: WTP or WTA?
3. How reliable is the risk assessment?
4. How good are the benefit measures?
5. What discount rate is used to value future benefits?

There simply are no generally accepted answers to any of these questions. A good benefit analyst can only state clearly the assumptions made at every turn and invite the reader to judge how sensitive the estimates might be to alternative assumptions.

In spite of their many uncertainties, however, nonmarket estimates of environmental benefits are increasingly in demand by courts and policy makers. As environmental awareness has spread, claims for natural resource damages are finding their way into courts more and more frequently. One important decision confirmed the right to sue for nonuse-value damage to natural resources and explicitly endorsed the contingent valuation methodology as an appropriate tool for determining existence or option value.[20] In addition, policy makers require benefit estimates for various forms of benefit-cost analysis. As we will discuss further in chapter 10, since 1981, all new major federal regulations have been required to pass a benefit-cost test when such tests are not prohibited by law.

In a recent, very ambitious article in the journal *Nature,* an interdisciplinary group of scientists attempted to put a value on the sum total of global ecosystem services—ranging from waste treatment, to gas regulation, to nutrient cycling (Costanza et al. [1997]). They concluded, stressing the huge uncertainties involved, that ecosystems provide a flow of market and nonmarket use value greater than $33 trillion per year, as against planetary product (world GDP) of $18 trillion.

---

[20]Kopp, Portney, and Smith (1990).

The authors use many of the tools described in this chapter. In justifying their effort, they state: "although ecosystem valuation is certainly difficult and fraught with uncertainties, one choice we do not have is whether or not to do it. Rather, the decisions we make as a society about ecosystems imply valuations (although not necessarily in monetary terms). We can choose to make these valuations explicit or not . . . but as long as we are forced to make choices, we are going through the process of valuation."

Ultimately, economists defend benefit measures on pragmatic grounds. With all their flaws, the argument goes, they remain the best means for quantifying the immense advantages associated with a high-quality environment. The alternative, an impact statement like the EIS discussed in the previous chapter, identifies the physical benefits of preservation in great detail but fails to summarize the information in a consistent or usable form.

At this point, benefit analysis is a social science in its relative infancy, which, nevertheless, is being asked to tackle very difficult issues. Perhaps the wealth of research currently underway will lead to greater consensus on acceptable resolutions to the problems identified in this chapter.

APPLICATION 8.0

A Travel-Cost Example

Now it is time for your first consulting job as an environmental economist. The Forest Service would like to know whether they should set aside some national forest land, previously slated to be logged, for hiking. You are helping do a travel-cost analysis to estimate the benefits of the set-aside.

Survey data has been gathered from 500 hikers who visited a forest in a neighboring state. Using a statistical technique called regression analysis, you have controlled for differences in income, employment status, age, and other important factors that might affect the number of hiking trips taken. Taking these factors into account, you have developed the following relationship:

Cost to Get to Hiking Areas	# of Hiking Trips per Person per Year
$20	8
40	6
80	2

1. Graph the demand curve for hiking trips as a function of the "price"—the travel cost.

2. Based on demographic information about the people living in the vicinity of the proposed park, you have estimated that 50,000 people will take an average of four hiking trips per year. For the average person, calculate: (1) the consumer surplus for a single visit to the new park; (2) the total consumer surplus for an average visitor (*hint:* the area of a triangle is $1/2[B*H]$); and (3) the total expected consumer surplus per year from the proposed park.

APPLICATION 8.1

Moving from Mouse to Person

This problem is designed to illustrate some of the difficulties raised in doing scientific risk assessments. As a public health specialist for the Environmental Protection Agency, it is now your job to figure out the risk to the public of contracting cancer from exposure to ET-2, a chemical compound used in printing shops. You know from animal studies that mice, when exposed to airborne ET-2 at levels of 1 part per 10,000 for 8 hours a day, contract cancer at an elevated rate. In particular, 10 extra mice per 1,000 develop tumors when exposed to ET-2.

1. The mice have been exposed to ET-2 at a level of 1 part per 10,000. But since people are bigger than mice, exposure generating an equivalent effect in humans would have to be much larger. You can pick one of two "reasonable" approaches for adjusting the exposure to account for size differences:

   a. Body-weight scaling factor:
   Exposure per Human
      = Exposure per Mouse *
   (50 kgs per Human/.015 kg per Mouse)

   b. Surface-area scaling factor:
   Exposure per Human
      = Exposure per Mouse *
   (1.50 m^2 per Human/.01 m^2 per Mouse)
   Use the formulas to produce two different estimates of the exposure per human, measured in parts per thousand, required to generate 10 extra cancers per 1,000 people exposed for 8 hours per day.

2. Now you need to estimate the number of tumors likely to develop as a result of *real-world* exposure to ET-2. Engineers at your agency have estimated that, if ET-2 is unregulated, the typical airborne exposure will be 1 part per 100,000. Once again you have a choice of models.

a. If you choose a *linear* dose-response model, the number of tumors is strictly proportional to the actual exposure. That is, a 1% increase in the exposure level will lead to a 1% increase in the number of tumors. The formula is:
   # of tumors per 1,000 = (10) *
(actual exposure/exposure required to generate 10 tumors per 1,000)

b. If you choose a *threshold* model, you are assuming that exposure below some limit, say 1 part per 10,000, is "safe"—that is, not likely to cause any additional cancer.

   Use the linear dose-response formula in part (2a) to produce *two different* estimates of the number of additional cancers per 1,000 people exposed to ET-2 if it is unregulated. You will get two different estimates, depending on which scaling factor from part 1 you use. Under the threshold model, how many additional cancers are to be expected? Does it matter which scaling factor you use?

3. Which is the most *conservative* risk assessment? Why?

Key Ideas in Each Section

8.0 There are both **market and nonmarket benefits** to environmental protection. Market benefits are measured at their dollar value; a value for nonmarket benefits must be estimated using economic tools.

8.1 The **total value** of an environmental benefit can be broken down into three parts: **use, option,** and **existence values.**

8.2 Economists consider the benefits of environmental protection to be equal to the **consumer surplus** gained by individuals through such environmental measures. For a freely provided public good, like clean air or water, a consumer's **willingness to pay (WTP)** for a small increase in the good or **willingness to accept (WTA)** a small decrease should be good approximations to consumer surplus gained or lost. In actuality, however, measured WTA is almost always substantially greater than measured WTP. **Prospect theory** provides one explanation for the difference.

8.3 Environmental risks must be estimated by means of epidemiological or animal studies. The estimated risk to humans will vary depending upon such factors as the assumed **dose-response model.** The risk to the population at large from an environmental hazard depends upon both the toxicity of the pollutant and the number of people or animals exposed. Public perceptions of relative risk often differ from those based on scientific risk assessment. Among other factors, this may be due to a distrust of scientists, as well as **risk aversion.**

8.4 The first approach used for estimating nonmarket benefits is based on survey responses and is known as **contingent valuation (CV).** CV studies are controversial due to the possibility of **free riding,** and **strategic, hypothetical,** and **embedding biases.** However, CV is the only available approach for estimating benefits of environmental protection based primarily on **existence value.**

8.5 Another approach for estimating nonmarket benefits is the **travel-cost method,** used principally for valuing parks, lakes, and beaches. Researchers construct a demand curve for the resource by relating information about travel cost to the intensity of the resource use, holding all other factors constant.

8.6 The final method of measuring the nonmarket benefits of environmental protection is known as **hedonic regression.** This approach estimates the benefits of an increase in environmental quality by examining the change in the price of related goods, holding all other factors constant.

8.7 Hedonic regressions, which rely on the wage premium for risky jobs, are used to place a **value on human life.** This is often necessary if benefit-cost analysis is to be used for deciding the right amount of pollution. This is a gruesome task; yet, even if regulators do not explicitly put a dollar value on life, some value of life is implicitly chosen whenever a regulatory decision is made. As a market-based measure, hedonic regression will assign a higher value of life to wealthier people, since their WTP to avoid risks is higher. This poses an obvious **moral dilemma.**

References

Bell, Frederick and Vernon Leeworthy (1990). "Recreational Demand by Tourists for Saltwater Beach Days." *Journal of Environmental Economics and Management,* 18, no. 3, 189–205.

Bishop, Richard C. and Michael P. Welsh (1992). "Existence Value and Resource Evaluation." Unpublished paper.

Boyle, Kevin J. and Richard C. Bishop (1987). "Valuing Wildlife in Benefit-Cost

Analysis: A Case Study Involving Endangered Species." *Water Resources Research,* vol. 23, 942–950.

Bromley, Daniel W. and Kathleen Segerson (eds.) (1992). *The Social Response to Environmental Risk.* Boston: Kluwer.

Brookshire, David S. and Don L. Coursey (1987). "Measuring the Value of a Public Good: An Empirical Comparison of Elicitation Procedures." *American Economic Review,* 77, no. 4, 554–566.

Costanza, R, R. d'Arge, R. de Groot, S. Farber, M. Grasso, B. Hannon, K. Limburg, S. Naeem, R. V. O'Neill, J. Paruelo, R. G. Rakin, P. Sutton and M. van den Belt (1997). "The Value of the World's Ecosystem Services and Natural Capital." *Nature,* 387, no. 6630, 253–259.

Cummings, Ronald, David Brookshire and William Schulze (eds.) (1986). *Valuing Environmental Goods: An Assessment of the Contingent Valuation Method.* Lanham, MD: Rowman and Allenheld.

Fisher, Ann, Lauraine G. Chestnut and Daniel M. Violette (1989). "The Value of Reducing Risks of Death: A Note on New Evidence." *Journal of Policy Analysis and Management,* 8, no. 1, 88–100.

Freeman, A. Myrick III (1985). "Supply Uncertainty, Option Price, and Option Value." *Land Economics,* 61, no. 2, 176–181.

Freeman, A. Myrick III (1979). *The Benefits of Environmental Improvement.* Washington, DC: Johns Hopkins.

Glenn, Barbara S., J. A. Foran and Mark Van Putten (1989). *Summary of Quantitative Health Assessments for PCBs, DDT, Dieldrin and Chlordane.* Ann Arbor, MI: National Wildlife Federation.

Gough, Michael (1989). "Estimating Cancer Mortality." *Environmental Science and Technology,* 23, vol. 8, 925–930.

Hanemann, Michael (1991). "Willingness to Pay and Willingness to Accept: How Much Can They Differ?" *American Economic Review,* 81, no. 3, 635–647.

Heaton, George Jr., Robert Repetto and Rodney Sobin (1992). *Backs to the Future: U.S. Government Policy Toward Environmentally Critical Technology.* Washington, DC: World Resources Institute.

Hof, John G. and David A. King (1992). "Recreational Demand by Tourists for Saltwater Beach Days: Comment." *Journal of Environmental Economics and Management,* vol. 22, 281–291.

Kahneman, Daniel and Jack Knetsch (1992). "Valuing Public Goods: The Purchase of Moral Satisfaction." *Journal of Environmental Economics and Management,* 22, no. 1, 57–70.

Kahneman, Daniel and Amos Tversky (1979). "Prospect Theory: An Analysis of Decisions Under Risk." *Econometrica,* 47, no. 2, 263–291.

Knetsch, Jack (1990). "Environmental Policy Implications of Disparities Between Willingness to Pay and Compensation Demanded Measures of Values." *Journal of Environmental Economics and Management,* 18, no. 3, 227–237.

Kopp, Raymond J., Paul R. Portney and V. Kerry Smith (1990). "Natural Resource Damages: The Economics Have Shifted After *Ohio* v. *United States Department of the Interior.*" *Environmental Law Reporter,* vol. 20, 10127–10131.

Mendelsohn, Robert, Daniel Hellerstein, Michael Huguenin, Robert Unsworth and Richard Brazee (1992). "Measuring Hazardous Waste Damages with Panel Models." *Journal of Environmental Economics and Management,* 22, no. 3, 259–271.

Mitchell, Robert Cameron and Richard T. Carson (1989). *Using Surveys to Value Public Goods: The Contingent Valuation Method.* Washington, DC: Resources for the Future.

Mitchell, Robert Cameron and Richard T. Carson (1984). *A Contingent Valuation Estimate of National Freshwater Benefits: Technical Report to the U.S. Environmental Protection Agency.* Washington, DC: Resources for the Future.

Palmini, Dennis (1996). "Game Theroretic Foundations of a Safe Minimum Standard." *Working Paper.* Stevens Point, WI: University of Wisconsin.

Shaw, W. Douglas (1991). "Recreational Demand by Tourists for Saltwater Beach Days: Comment." *Journal of Environmental Economics and Management,* vol. 20, 284–289.

Shrader-Frechette, K. S. (1991). *Risk and Rationality: Philosophical Foundations for Populist Reform.* Berkeley, CA: University of California Press.

Travis, Curtis, S. A. Richter, E. A. Crouch, R. Wilson and E. Klema (1987). "Cancer Risk Management." *Environmental Science and Technology,* 21, no. 5, 415–420.

U.S. Environmental Protection Agency (1990). *Reducing Risk: Setting Priorities and Strategies for Environmental Protection.* Washington, DC: U.S. EPA.

Wilson, Richard and E. A. C. Crouch (1987). "Risk Assessment and Comparisons: An Introduction." *Science,* vol. 236, April 17, 267–270.

Measuring the Costs of Environmental Protection

9.0 Introduction

In the summer of 1997, the Environmental Protection Agency tightened the national air quality standard for smog—ground-level ozone. The agency developed official cost estimates for this regulation ranging from $600 million to $2.5 billion per year. Yet, some opponents of the regulation came up with much higher numbers: The U.S. Department of Defense, for example, put compliance costs for that agency alone at $1.36 billion annually.[1]

On the face of it, measuring the costs associated with environmental cleanup appears to be a substantially easier task than measuring benefits. One can simply add up all the expected expenditures by firms on pollution control equipment and personnel, plus local state and federal government expenditures on regulatory efforts, including the drafting, monitoring, and enforcing of regulations. This **engineering approach** to measuring cost is, by far, the most widespread method in use.

However, because engineering cost estimates are often *predicted* costs, they require making assumptions about future behavior. For example, cost estimates may assume full compliance with pollution laws or assume that firms will adopt a particular type of pollution control technology to meet the standards. To the extent that these assumptions fail to foresee the future accurately, engineering cost estimates may be misleading on their own terms. Indeed, in the early 1990s, the EPA overestimated the costs of sulfur dioxide control by a factor of 2 to 4; "credible" industry estimates were eight times too high (Burtraw [1996]).

Moreover, from the economic point of view, there are additional problems with the engineering approach. Economists employ a measure of cost known as **opportunity**

---

[1]"EPA Plans to Tighten Pollution Rules," *Wall Street Journal,* June 6, 1997, p. A16.

cost: the value of resources in their next best available use. To evaluate the opportunity cost of pollution control, we might consider the Clean Air Act amendments passed in 1990 and being enacted throughout the decade. Full compliance with these laws, designed to tackle the problems of acid rain, urban smog, and particulate pollution and toxic air pollutants, is expected by Portney (1990) to impose engineering costs of around $30 billion on the affected industries and government regulatory agencies. If as a society we were not devoting this $30 billion to pollution control, would we be able to afford just $30 billion in other goods and services? More? Less? The answer to this question provides the true measure of the cost of environmental protection.

Engineering cost estimates will overstate true social costs to the extent that government involvement (1) increases productivity either by increasing the efficiency with which available resources are used, forcing technological change, or improving worker health or ecosystem services; and/or (2) reduces structural unemployment.

On the other hand, engineering cost estimates will underestimate true social costs to the extent that government involvement (1) lowers productivity growth by diverting investment, and/or (2) induces structural unemployment, and/or (3) increases monopoly power in the economy. Finally, so-called "general equilibrium" effects of environmental regulation can either raise or lower the costs of regulation. This chapter will first examine recent EPA estimates of engineering cost and will then consider the degree to which these estimates overstate or understate the "true" costs of environmental protection.

9.1 Engineering Costs

Engineering cost estimates require the use of accounting conventions to "annualize" capital investments; in other words, to spread out the cost of investments in plant and equipment over their expected lifetimes. Table 9.1 provides EPA estimates of the current and historical "annualized" engineering costs of pollution control in the United States since the major federal programs were initiated in the early 1970s.

The figures in Table 9.1 for 1990 and 1995 are estimated and assume full compliance with pollution control regulations. Fixed capital costs for each year are determined by depreciating on a straight-line basis and assuming firms pay a 7% interest rate on funds borrowed to finance the investment.

The table shows historical and current annual pollution control expenditures for four categories of pollutant—air, water, land, and chemicals—as well as an "other" category including unassigned EPA administrative and research expenses. The costs listed here cover all direct compliance and regulatory expenses for pollution control, including investments in pollution control equipment and personnel, the construction of municipal water treatment plants, and the bill your family pays to your local garbage collector. (Note that these costs are not identical to the costs of environmental regulation: Even without regulations, the private sector would undertake some amount of sewage treatment and garbage disposal!)

As a nation, we have indeed been devoting increasing attention to pollution control. Over a period of twenty-five years, total spending has risen from $31 billion to over $161 billion, measured in 1990 dollars. Perhaps more significantly, pollution control as a percentage of GNP had been predicted to rise from less than 1% in 1972, to 2.1% in 1990, to over 2.5% by 1995, more than doubling its claim on the nation's re-

TABLE 9.1   U.S. Annualized Pollution Control Costs (1990 $billion)

Type of Pollutant	Year					
	1972	*1975*	*1980*	*1985*	*1990*	*1995*
AIR						
Air	9.2	12.7	20.6	27.3	32.3	42.7
Radiation	0.0	0.2	0.2	0.2	0.5	0.8
WATER						
Quality	10.6	16.4	26.7	35.6	45.4	56.3
Drinking	0.9	1.3	2.3	3.3	4.0	6.2
LAND						
Waste disposal	9.8	10.9	15.9	18.2	29.0	38.0
Superfund	0.0	0.0	0.0	0.4	2.0	5.5
CHEMICALS						
Toxics	0.0	0.0	0.5	0.4	0.7	1.3
Pesticides	0.1	0.2	0.6	0.6	1.2	1.6
OTHER	0.1	0.6	1.1	0.8	1.9	2.5
TOTAL	31.0	43.1	67.7	86.6	117.1	161.2
% of GNP	0.9	1.2	1.6	1.8	2.1	2.6

Source: Alan Carlin (1990). *Environmental Investments: The Cost of a Clean Environment,* Summary, Washington, DC: U.S. EPA, p. 16.

sources (Carlin, 1990). By comparison, in 1990, about 11.5% of GNP was spent on health care, while close to 0.9% was spent each on the categories of "sporting goods" and "travel abroad."

Chapter 12 is devoted to an overview of the current regulatory framework. At this point, however, it is useful to note some trends in the projected pollution control costs revealed by Table 9.1. The EPA predicts that air pollution expenses will rise by about $9 billion per year through the mid-1990s, primarily due to the passage of the 1990 Clean Air Act amendments. This is considerably below the Portney estimate of $30 billion per year cited in the introduction to this chapter. This is, in part, because the EPA estimates were made earlier than Portney's and are based on a less stringent version of the bill than actually passed. (In addition, the EPA predicts another $8 billion increase by 2000.)[2] However, the discrepancy does illustrate that engineering cost estimates are just that—estimates. Predicting the future is always an imperfect undertaking.

Table 9.1 also suggests that water costs will continue to rise as local governments spend more on wastewater treatment facilities and the private sector continues to invest in the control of industrial and agricultural discharges. Finally, of all categories, the cost of land disposal has been growing the fastest; it has been expected to more than double from $18.2 billion to $38.0 billion between 1985 and 1995. Much of this increase is due to more stringent requirements mandated during the 1980s for the disposal of solid and hazardous waste and the design of underground storage tanks, as well as the very rapid recent growth in the Superfund program. Superfund is the common name for the legislation requiring the cleanup of old hazardous waste sites.

---

[2]In addition, the smaller EPA figure may reflect some decline in expenditures not associated with the 1990 amendments.

Table 9.1 provides some idea of the direct expenses associated with pollution control in the United States. The question we seek to answer in the rest of this chapter is Do these engineering estimates understate or overstate the true social costs of environmental protection?

9.2 Productivity Impacts of Regulation

Undoubtedly, the biggest unknown when it comes to estimating the costs of environmental protection arises through its impact on *productivity*. Productivity, or output per worker, is a critical economic measure. Rising productivity means the economic pie per worker is growing. A growing pie, in turn, makes it easier for society to accommodate both the needs of a growing population and the desire for a higher material standard of living.

Since 1974, productivity growth in the Unites States has averaged only 1%, well below the 3% rate the American economy experienced in the 1950s and 1960s. Because growth is a cumulative process, such small changes in productivity can have dramatic long-run effects. Figure 9.1 illustrates the impact that the productivity slowdown has had on economic output.

If, rather than declining after 1974, productivity growth had continued at its 1950 to 1970 rate of 3%, GDP in 1990 "would have been" more than $2 trillion higher than it actually was! The productivity slowdown has been attributed to a variety of causes. Oil price shocks in the 1970s, the transition to a low-productivity service economy, in-

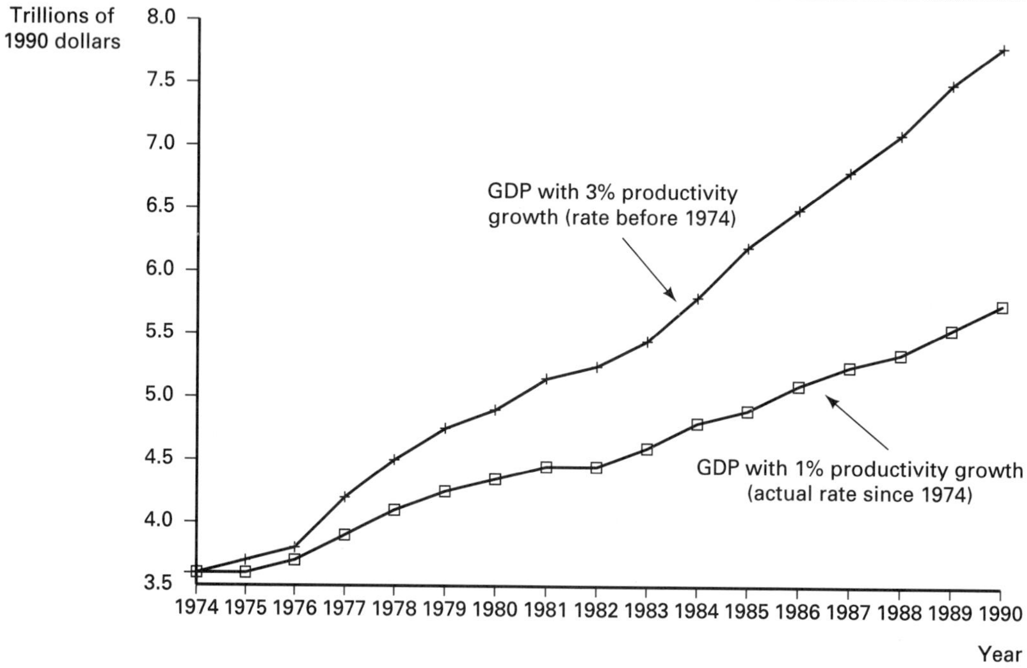

FIGURE 9.1 The Impact of Slow Productivity Growth on GDP

creasingly shortsighted American managers, poorly educated or motivated American workers, a resource drain into defense spending, lack of government spending on infrastructure, and a legal system that encourages excessive litigation and government regulation have all been labeled as suspects.[3]

Some have charged that environmental regulations specifically have been a major contributor to the productivity slowdown. By contrast, others have argued that pollution control efforts can *spur* productivity growth by forcing firms to become more efficient in their use of resources, and adopt new and cheaper production techniques. As we will see, this debate is far from settled. But because productivity growth compounds over time, the impact of regulations on productivity—whether positive or negative—is a critical factor in determining the "true" costs of environmental protection.

First, let us evaluate the pro-regulation arguments. Theoretically, regulation can improve productivity in three ways: (1) by improving the short-run efficiency of resource use; (2) by encouraging firms to invest more, or invest "smarter" for the long run; (3) by reducing health-care or firm level cleanup costs, which then frees up capital for long-run investment.

We ran into the short-run efficiency argument in our chapter 1 discussion of global warming. Some economists think tremendous cost savings are to be gained immediately if firms would only adopt already existing, energy-efficient technologies— more efficient lighting, cooling, heating, and mechanical systems. Indeed, we saw one study arguing that if firms would only do this, then greenhouse gases could actually be cut at a profit of over a trillion dollars!

However, most economists are suspicious that these so-called "free lunches" are actually widespread, arguing on theoretical grounds that "there ain't no such thing." Why would competitive firms ignore these huge cost-saving opportunities if they really existed? Chapter 20 is devoted to a discussion of energy policy and the free lunch argument. For now, recognize that should regulation force firms to use energy more cost-effectively, greater output from fewer inputs, and thus an increase in productivity, will result.

The second avenue by which regulation may increase productivity is by speeding up, or otherwise improving, the capital investment process. The so-called **Porter hypothesis,** named after Harvard Business School Professor Michael Porter, argues that regulation, while imposing short-run costs on firms, often enhances their long-run competitiveness (Porter and van der Linde [1995]; Goodstein [1997]). This can happen if regulation favors forward-looking firms, anticipates trends, speeds investment in modern production processes, encourages R&D, or promotes "outside-the-box," nonconventional thinking.

For example, rather than installing "end-of-the pipe" equipment to treat their emissions, some firms have developed new production methods to aggressively reduce waste, cutting both costs and pollution simultaneously.[4] In this case, regulation has played a **technology-forcing role,** encouraging firms to develop more productive manufacturing methods by setting standards they must achieve.

---

[3]See Baily and Chakrabarti (1988); Melman (1987); Bowles, Gordon, and Weisskopf (1991); and Aschauer (1990) for differing perspectives on this issue.

[4]See Barbera and McConnell (1990), as well as "Some Companies Cut Pollution by Altering Production Methods." *Wall Street Journal,* December 24, 1990.

Finally, the third positive impact of regulation on productivity flows from the health and ecosystem benefits that arise from environmental protection. In the absence of pollution control measures, the U.S. population would have experienced considerably higher rates of sickness and premature mortality. In addition, firms that rely on clean water or air for production processes would have faced their own internal cleanup costs. These factors would have reduced productivity directly and also indirectly as expenditures on health care and private cleanup would have risen dramatically. This spending, in turn, would have represented a drain on productive investment resources quite comparable to mandated expenditures on pollution control.

Productivity may also be dampened in a variety of ways. First, regulation imposes direct costs on regulated firms; these costs may crowd out investment in conventional capital. Second, a further slowdown in new investment may occur when regulation is more stringent for new sources of pollution, as it often is. Third, regulation will cause higher prices for important economy-wide inputs such as energy and waste disposal. These cost increases, in turn, will lead to reductions in capital investment in secondary industries directly unaffected by regulation; for example, the health and financial sectors of the economy.

Finally, regulation may frustrate entrepreneurial activity. Businesspeople complain frequently of the "regulatory burden" and "red tape" associated with regulation, including environmental regulation. Filling out forms, obtaining permits, and holding public hearings all add an additional "hassle" to business that may discourage some investment. In the last two decades, conservative Presidents Bush and Reagan have both acknowledged frustration among employers by imposing temporary moratoriums on new regulations issued by the federal government.

However, in spite of the chorus of voices attacking regulation as one of the main culprits in explaining low levels of recent American productivity growth, evidence for this position is not strong. A recent examination of five heavily regulated industries by Barbera and McConnell (1990) concluded that only 10% to 30% of the productivity decline in these industries could be accounted for by environmental regulation. Since most industries experienced substantially less regulation than the five examined in the study, the economy-wide effect would presumably be smaller.[5]

Nevertheless, because of the cumulative nature of economic growth, even productivity declines well under 1% have major effects over the long run. For example, Barbera and McConnell suggest that, on an economy-wide basis, less than 10% of the 2% productivity slowdown after 1970 can likely be attributed to environmental regulation. Assume for the purposes of illustration that federal environmental regulations depressed labor productivity growth from 1.1% to 1% beginning in 1974 (thus, accounting for 5% of the total slowdown). Then, in the absence of any federal pollution regulation, *GNP ceteris paribus* "would have been" over $90 billion larger in 1990.[6]

Hazilla and Kopp (1991) and Jorgenson and Wilcoxen (1990) undertake much more sophisticated counterfactual exercises and arrive at aggregate productivity impacts of $125 billion and $143 billion, respectively, for federal air and water pollution

---

[5]These results are consistent with a number of other industry-level studies finding small productivity effects. See the review in Goodstein (1994).

[6]GNP per civilian worker was $41,353 in 1974. Productivity growth of 1% would have raised that figure to $48,489 by 1990; growth of 1.1% would have increased productivity to $49,263. Given the civilian labor force in 1990, this translates into a GNP differential of $91 billion.

control efforts undertaken since 1970. These figures suggest that the indirect costs of existing pollution control efforts, measured roughly in foregone GNP, may be even larger than the direct engineering estimates.[7]

However, these figures are of only limited usefulness, since the *ceteris paribus* assumption does not hold. As the studies themselves acknowledge, they ignore all the important *positive* influences that regulation may have had on productivity growth. Repetto (1990) examined the positive effects (avoided costs) resulting from environmental expenditures on productivity in the electric utility industry, the sector most heavily impacted by regulation. He found that rough adjustments for reductions in emissions due to environmental regulation were large enough to offset the productivity declines found in earlier studies.

In summary, federal environmental regulations primarily put in place in the 1970s and 1980s have reduced measured productivity in heavily regulated industries somewhat; yet, such effects account for only a small portion of the total productivity slowdown. In addition, in the absence of regulation, productivity would have fallen anyway due to increased illness and the subsequent diversion of investment resources into the health-care field. Finally, there is scattered evidence for productivity improvements arising from regulation, following both the Porter hypothesis and the energy-efficiency lines of argument. Rolling back environmental laws to their 1970 status, even if this were possible, would, at best, make a small dent in the problem of reduced U.S. productivity and might easily make things worse.

Nevertheless, due to the large cumulative effects on output of even small reductions in productivity growth, minimizing potential negative productivity impacts is one of the most important aspects of sensibly designed regulatory policy. As we shall see in chapters 16 and 17, regulations can be structured to better encourage the introduction of more productive, and lower-cost, pollution control technologies.

9.3 Employment Impacts of Regulation

The second potential "hidden cost" of environmental protection is jobs. Here, however, political rhetoric on this issue has generated far more heat than light. In a 1990 *Wall Street Journal* poll, an astounding one third of the respondents thought it somewhat or very likely that their own job was threatened by environmental regulation.[8]

As will be made clear below, this assessment of the risk of job loss is dramatically overstated. Moreover, when the job creation aspects of pollution control policies are factored in, environmental protection, if anything, has probably led to a small net gain in U.S. employment. However, widespread fears of job loss need to be understood in the context of a "deindustrialization and downsizing" process that has become increasingly apparent to U.S. citizens during the 1980s and 1990s.

---

[7]Jorgenson and Wilcoxen estimate that regulations depress long-run GNP by 2.59%. This was $143 billion in 1990. The Hazilla and Kopp figure is from Table 3, "social cost" minus "EPA compliance cost" in 1990. Hazilla and Kopp attempt to measure cost as foregone consumer surplus. Because consumers and firms substitute away from higher priced goods, foregone GNP is not an accurate measure of lost welfare. They find that GNP is depressed by 5.85% in 1990, almost double the Jorgenson and Wilcoxen estimate. Both sets of authors use quite complex general equilibrium models to arrive at their conclusions. For a rather critical discussion of the Jorgenson-Wilcoxen model, see Joskow (1992). See the review in Goodstein (1994).

[8]"Americans Are Willing to Sacrifice to Reduce Pollution, They Say." *Wall Street Journal,* April 20, 1990.

Over the last couple of decades, the United States lost over 3 million manufacturing jobs, due primarily to increased import competition both from First World nations and the newly industrializing countries of Korea, Taiwan, and Brazil. At the same time, U.S. manufacturers increasingly began to "offshore" production, investing in manufacturing facilities in low-wage countries rather than at home. High-paying manufacturing jobs have traditionally been the backbone of the blue-collar middle class in the United States. The disappearance of these jobs has contributed to a decline in average real wages that has been occurring since 1973 and a shrinking middle class.[9] To what extent has environmental regulation contributed to this dramatic shift away from manufacturing and over to service employment?

Stringent pollution regulations might be expected to discourage investment in certain industries, mining and "dirty" manufacturing, in particular. This will contribute to **structural unemployment,** most of which will disappear in the long run as displaced workers find new jobs elsewhere in the economy. In essence, regulation cannot "create" long-run unemployment; instead, it will contribute to a shift in the types of jobs that the economy creates. Indeed, the one comprehensive estimate available suggests that, in 1992, just under 4 million jobs were directly or indirectly related to pollution abatement in the United States.[10]

This notion of job shifting should be familiar to you from the first week of your Econ 100 class, in which you undoubtedly saw a diagram that looked something like Figure 9.2. This production possibilities frontier (or transformation curve) shows how the economy has shifted from 1970 to 1995. If regulation were to have caused widespread unemployment, the economy would have moved from point A to point C.

However, again referring back to your Econ 100 class, you know that during the mid-1990s the U.S. economy was operating very close to full employment: at point B. Indeed, the Federal Reserve Board raised interest rates several times during this period to try to cool down the economy, by *raising* the unemployment rate. Clearly, the constraint on economy-wide job growth in recent years has been the inflationary fears of the Fed, not an economy devoting 2.6% of output to environmental protection.

What kind of jobs are generated by environmental spending? Somewhat surprisingly, environmental protection provides employment heavily weighted to the traditional blue-collar manufacturing, transport, communication, and utility sectors and away from services, both private and governmental. Figure 9.3 illustrates this point, providing an estimated breakdown of the composition of nonagricultural jobs directly

---

[9]Mishel (1989).

[10]By "directly and indirectly," I mean to include multiplier effects. For example, a complete accounting of jobs in the aluminum recycling industry needs to include workers in the steel industry who make the machines to recycle aluminum, as well as workers who make the equipment to make the steel to make the aluminum recycling machines, and so on. Economists use input-output models (see advanced topic chapter T3) to capture all these indirect effects.

The 4 million figure from Bezdek (1993) is based on Management Information Services' input-output model, described in Bezdek et al. (1989). To my knowledge, MIS is the only source that has generated I-O-based employment estimates for the EP sector. Nestor and Pasurka (1993) have developed an I-O model for the Environmental Protection Agency but have not published any employment figures.

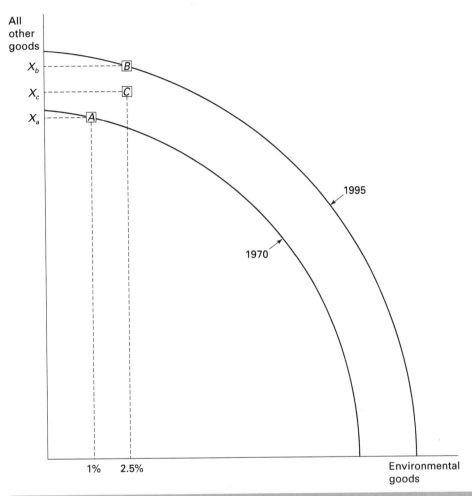

FIGURE 9.2 A Jobs-Environment Trade-off?

and indirectly dependent on environmental spending in 1991, with comparative figures for the economy as a whole.

While only 23% of all nonfarm jobs were in the manufacturing, transportation, communication, and utility sectors in 1991, 57% of employment generated by environmental spending fell in one of these categories. By contrast, only 22% of environment-dependent jobs were in wholesale and retail trade, finance, insurance, real estate, or services, compared to 55% for the economy as a whole. And in spite of criticisms that environmental regulation creates jobs only for pencil-pushing regulators, only 11% of environmental employment was governmental, as compared to an economy-wide government employment rate of 17%.

How can we account for these results? Environmental protection is an industrial business. In 1990, the private sector spent $18.4 billion on pollution control

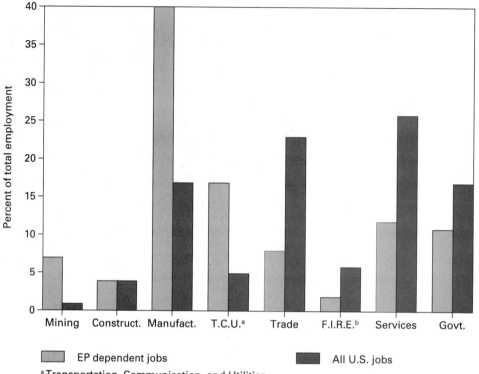

FIGURE 9.3 Jobs Dependent on Environmental Spending, 1991

Source: Environmental protection—dependent employment data are from Management Information Services (1991). Economy-wide data are from Employment and Earnings. Washington, DC: U.S. Department of Labor.

plant and equipment and $36.3 billion on pollution control operations, ranging from sewage and solid waste disposal to the purchase and maintenance of air pollution control devices on smokestacks and in vehicles. Federal, state, and local governments spent around $10.6 billion on the construction of municipal sewage facilities. In addition, only 2% of all environmental spending went to support the government's direct regulation and monitoring establishment.[11] The EPA's total budget was less than 4% of all spending. The bulk of environmental spending, thus, remains in the private sector generating a demand for workers disproportionately weighted to manufacturing, utilities, transport, and communications and away from services. This is not to say that environmental spending creates only high-quality, high-paying jobs. But it does support jobs in traditional blue-collar industries.

Of course, the 4 million jobs in the environmental industry in 1992 were not net jobs created. If the money had not been spent on environmental protection, it would

---

[11]This data is from Rutledge and Leonard (1992), with monetary values in 1990 dollars.

have been spent elsewhere—perhaps on health care, travel, imported goods, or investment in new plant and equipment. This spending, too, would have created jobs. In the long run, the level of economy-wide employment is determined by the interaction of business cycles and government fiscal and monetary policy. However, in the short run, and locally, where we spend our dollars does matter for employment. If, instead of spending $117 billion on the environment in 1990, we had spent only $100 billion, would there have been more or fewer jobs in the U.S. economy *that year* (in the short run)?

Clearly fewer if we had spent the $17 billion saved importing foreign-made goods. Perhaps more if we had spent the money on labor-intensive products made at home. As a rule, money spent on sectors that are both more labor-intensive (directly and indirectly) and have a higher domestic content (directly and indirectly) will generate more American jobs. Environmental spending is often either labor-intensive or has a high domestic content.

To illustrate, a study done for the Department of Sanitation in New York City found that boosting the percentage of waste that was recycled from 3% to 25%, while reducing the percentage incinerated from 76% to 57%, would result in a permanent net increase in local employment of around 400 jobs per year. This was true, even accounting for the higher taxes necessary to pay for the somewhat higher cost per ton for the recycling option. The increase in jobs arose first because recycling is labor- rather than capital-intensive, leading to a higher local payroll generating bigger indirect employment effects in the city. Second, New York City produces little of the equipment necessary to manufacture incinerators, so incineration had a low "domestic" content.[12]

At the national level, analyses of the employment impact of pollution control efforts have revealed a similar story. For example, Wendling and Bezdek (1989) found that some 95% of the direct expenditure on acid rain pollution control equipment products and processes would accrue to U.S. firms. As a result, a net increase in jobs was foreseen from the acid rain control policies they analyzed. Job losses in high-sulfur coal mining, electric utility, and electricity-intensive sectors would be more than balanced by pollution control jobs created from the expenditure of several billion dollars per year. Overall, Wendling and Bezdek predicted a net employment gain from acid rain control. The majority of macro-level studies of environmental protection have generated similar conclusions.[13]

Most of the time, if you hear a sentence that begins with "All economists agree," you should head for the door. But in this case, there is agreement that at the economy-wide level *there is simply no such thing* as a **jobs-environment trade-off.**

Of course, this knowledge will not be comforting to the manufacturing or mining worker who *has* lost his or her job due to regulation. Short-run, structural unemployment impacts from environmental regulation (or any other cause) should not be minimized. **Plant shutdowns** cause considerable suffering for workers and communities,

[12]Breslow et al. (1992). Because recycling also requires capital spending on "imported" equipment, the two options did not differ greatly in either their labor intensity or their "domestic" content. However, the differences were large enough to translate into an employment advantage for recycling.

[13]See Goodstein (1994; 1996). Environmental regulation can also boost net job growth somewhat because it provides an ongoing, recession-proof stimulus to aggregate demand.

particularly for older workers who find it difficult to retool. Moreover, the disappearance of high-wage manufacturing jobs is, indeed, cause for concern. Yet, fears of such effects from pollution control efforts are liable to be greatly overblown since industry officials can gain politically by blaming plant shutdowns due to normal business causes on environmental regulations.

Keeping this in mind, based on employer responses, the U.S. Department of Labor has collected information on the causes of mass (greater than 50 worker) layoffs. Table 9.2 presents this data, covering 75% of all layoffs at large employers and 57% of all manufacturing plants.

On average, *according to employers' own estimates,* environmental regulation accounted for less than one tenth of one percent of all mass layoffs nationwide. In the survey, *four plants per year* closed primarily as a result of environmental problems. If we double the figures to account for the remainder of manufacturing jobs, on average, 1,300 lost positions per year could be partially attributed to environmental regulation.

The number of actual layoffs due to environmental regulation is clearly much smaller than is generally believed. As noted above, one third of the entire U.S. workforce perceived a threat to their jobs from environmental protection measures! In reality, forty times more layoffs resulted from ownership changes than from environmental measures; IBM permanently laid off six times more workers in 1990 alone (over 18,000) than were identified by the Labor Department survey in four years as environmental protection layoffs.[14]

Here is a summary of the evidence so far: no job-environment trade-off at the economy-wide level and very small structural unemployment effects. However, rather than shutdowns, one might expect *new* investment to occur in poorer countries with less strict pollution regulations. How serious is this problem of flight to so-called **pollution havens?** A study by Leonard (1984) of the impact of the federal water and air pollution regulations of the 1970s suggests that such effects were localized to a very few industries. These included manufacturers of highly toxic substances such as asbestos and select pesticides and possibly a handful of organic chemicals.[15] These industries also tended to be facing declining demand and operating obsolescent facilities. In addition, occupational health standards seemed to be more important than environmental standards in the decision to shift investment overseas.

More recently, in their survey of twenty-five years of research on this issue, Jaffe et al. (1995) conclude: "Studies attempting to measure the effect of environmental regulation on net exports, overall trade-flows, and plant location decisions have produced estimates that are either small, statistically insignificant, or not robust to tests of model specification." In other words, in spite of looking hard, economists have found precious little evidence to suggest that the competitiveness of U.S. manufacturing firms has been hurt by environmental regulation.

Why have the effects not been greater? First, pollution control costs are a small portion of total business costs, and, second, costs are only one factor influencing busi-

---

[14]The Department of Labor figures presented here are consistent with a variety of other surveys covering the 1970s and early 1980s, including one that incorporated small businesses. See the discussion in Goodstein (1994).

[15]Leonard also argued that non-ferrous metal smelting had been negatively impacted by relocation to pollution havens; however, more recent data do not support this argument. See Goodstein (1997)

TABLE 9.2 Employer-Reported Reasons for Mass Layoffs, 1987–1990

	1987 Layoff Events	1987 Job Loss	1988 Layoff Events	1988 Job Loss	1989 Layoff Events	1989 Job Loss	1990 Layoff Events	1990 Job Loss	Average Layoff Events	Average Job Loss	Percent of Layoffs
Total, all reasons	2,020	406,887	2,322	450,300	2,764	572,570	3,078	586,690	2,546	504,112	
Automation	9	951	7	737	11	1,378	11	1,688	10	1,189	0.2
Bankruptcy	43	7,259	76	16,559	81	18,599	100	26,248	75	17,211	3.4
Business ownership change	88	30,955	92	18,973	82	19,147	78	16,989	85	21,516	4.3
Contract cancellation	25	4,168	32	3,894	26	5,824	48	8,532	33	5,605	1.1
Contract completion	147	27,696	178	50,822	225	50,971	201	40,167	188	42,414	8.4
Domestic relocation	49	10,877	68	12,816	68	1,138	114	18,512	75	10,836	2.1
Energy-related disruption	6	888	—	—	6	789	—	—	3	419	0.1
Environment related	4	511	4	388	5	1,304	4	390	4	648	0.1
Import competition	40	8,328	34	8,222	43	8,310	69	10,028	47	8,722	1.7
Labor-management dispute	43	12,592	26	2,824	47	40,387	—	—	29	13,951	2.8
Material shortages	11	1,872	20	2,169	24	4,318	20	5,859	19	3,555	0.7
Model changeover	17	16,441	21	7,186	17	9,089	15	3,039	18	8,939	1.8
Natural disaster	6	561	4	919	4	678	—	—	4	540	0.1
Overseas relocation	30	4,963	10	1,225	6	1,189	13	3,122	15	2,625	0.5
Plant or machine repairs	19	3,146	21	3,837	19	3,360	27	6,512	22	4,214	0.8
Seasonal work	516	101,168	710	144,522	889	175,970	884	167,287	750	147,237	29.2
Slack work	535	94,701	450	69,764	661	102,607	943	142,038	647	102,120	20.3
Vacation period	17	4,161	21	3,650	22	5,871	15	2,106	19	3,947	0.8
Weather-related curtailment	13	1,246	43	4,285	63	11,009	84	11,815	51	7,089	1.4
Other (including reorganization)	240	51,207	229	51,744	255	46,778	284	97,474	252	61,801	12.3
Not reported	162	23,826	276	45,764	210	53,604	168	24,704	204	36,975	7.3

Source: U.S. Department of Labor, *Mass Layoffs in (year).* Bureau of Labor Statistics *Bulletins* 2395, 2375, and 2310.

ness location decisions.[16] In addition to costs, factors as diverse as access to markets and the quality of life are important components of business location decisions. A recent study by Koechlin (1992) identified, in order of importance, market size, wages, tax rates, political stability, access to the European market, and distance to the United States as the primary determinants of U.S. investment abroad. Given these factors, most U.S. direct foreign investment continues to be in developed countries with environmental regulations comparable to our own.

A recent exception to this rule may, perhaps, be found in Mexico. Plants within one hundred kilometers of the U.S. border known as *maquiladoras* can import and export products freely. While these plants are required, in theory, to meet U.S. federal environmental standards, in practice, the underfunded Mexican government has not vigorously enforced the law. Due to its close proximity, low wages, and lax environmental enforcement, Mexico may attract investment that would otherwise occur in the United States.[17]

The most dramatic instance of plants moving South occurred in the wood furniture industry in the Los Angeles area. Based on rather sketchy evidence, it is estimated that four to five plants per year moved to the maquiladora region over the three-year period from 1988 to 1990, *partially* as a result of environmental regulations. This accounted for a loss of about 350 jobs per year.[18] The L.A. basin has the worst air pollution in the United States and some of the toughest emission control standards. Solvent-based coatings for wood furniture evaporate easily, contributing to smog; 1988 regulations in the Los Angeles area mandated the phase-in of expensive collection chambers to contain the solvent emissions. As of 1990, there were *no* regulations in the maquiladora region pertaining to emissions from solvents.

An added, if not primary, inducement for these firms to relocate was lower wages and benefits. The average hourly wage in L.A. was $8.92; across the border it was $0.77. In addition, as U.S. employers, the firms were required to pay $1.75 per hour in worker's compensation. The equivalent Mexican tax was only $0.13. For furniture makers, labor *and* environmental costs were clearly significant factors in the decision to locate in Mexico. More generally, a 1988 survey of 76 maquiladora plants found that 10% listed environmental factors as *among* the main reasons for locating in Mexico.[19]

However, a more comprehensive look at investment in the maquiladora region by Grossman and Krueger (1991) confirms the earlier Leonard (1984) insight that environmental factors are, in general, relatively unimportant. Industries with higher pollution abatement costs are not overrepresented in the maquiladora area, although those with higher labor costs are. At this point, we can conclude that the direct costs associated with pollution control have not been a major factor in influencing plant location decisions. Highly polluting industries are relocating to poor countries; the reason,

---

[16]On the relative importance of pollution control costs, see Dean (1992). For an interesting dissenting view, see Chapman (1991).

[17]"Border Boom's Dirty Residue Imperils U.S. Mexico Trade." *New York Times,* March 31, 1991.

[18]These mid-range estimates are from U.S. GAO (1991), based on 78% of employers reporting stringent air pollution controls as one reason for moving.

[19]See U.S. GAO (1991); and "A Warmer Climate for Furniture Makers," *Los Angeles Times,* May 14, 1990. The survey results are discussed in Sanchez (1990).

however, is low wages. Yet, as the furniture maker industry illustrates, in certain cases environmental control costs can rise sufficiently to become a dominant concern.[20] Moreover, as the Mexican case demonstrates, once having relocated, firms certainly take advantage of looser pollution standards.

As a final note on a possible jobs-environment trade-off in southern California, Berman and Bui (1997) conducted a detailed study comparing heavily regulated plants (of all types) in the region with similar plants in the rest of the country. They found no decrease in employment at existing California plants, and no effect on California jobs from increased bankruptcies or decreased investment.

This section has established that, first, economy-wide, net job loss has not resulted from environmental protection. As many, if not more, new jobs have been created than have been lost. At the national level, debates that assume a **jobs versus the environment** trade-off are, thus, based on pure myth. Second, gross job loss due to environmental protection has been surprisingly small. Something like 1,300 workers per year have been laid off in recent years, partially as a result of regulation. Finally, the flight of U.S. manufacturing capital overseas appears to be driven much more by wage differentials than stringent environmental rules. In spite of these facts, the fear of job loss remains widespread, as indicated by the poll results cited above. Much of the political resistance to environmental protection remains motivated by such fears.

Such concerns are understandable in a nation such as ours experiencing a dramatic and painful economic restructuring and where occasional plant shutdowns due to environmental regulation are highly publicized. In individual cases, such as the recent restrictions imposed on the timber industry to protect the old-growth forest in the Pacific Northwest or regulatory barriers faced by the Appalachian coal industry's high-sulfur coal, local unemployment has undoubtedly been exacerbated by environmental regulation.

Even in these two worst-case scenarios, however, job losses have been in the low thousands. Beyond numbers, of course, many of the jobs lost have been relatively "good" unionized, high-paying ones, and reemployment opportunities for some workers are quite limited. These negative effects should not be ignored and can be partially alleviated through job-retraining programs, conversion efforts, notification requirements for plant closing, and moving allowances for individuals displaced from pollu-

---

[20]Hettige, Lucas, and Wheeler (1992) report results that appear to contradict those of Leonard (1984) and Grossman and Krueger (1991). They find that in the 1960s "toxic intensity [in manufacturing] grew most quickly in the high-income economies. During the 1970s and 1980s, after the advent of strict OECD environmental regulation, this pattern was sharply reversed."

However, the authors find that "paradoxically . . . outward-oriented, high growth LDCs have slow-growing or even declining toxic intensity, while toxic intensity increases more rapidly in inward-oriented economies." It is presumably these outward-oriented, high-growth LDCs that should be attracting manufacturing capital from the developed world under the pollution-haven hypothesis.

In a more detailed paper, Lucas, Wheeler, and Hettige (1992) suggest that the results may be explained by "a shift toward a different global distribution [of production] without either direct investment or technology transfer." In other words, closed, high-growth economies may have deliberately fostered the domestic growth of polluting industries such as chemicals, and oil and mineral refining. The authors thus acknowledge that their findings do not support a capital flight argument.

Finally, there is some speculation that liability under the hazardous waste regulations passed during the 1980s may become significant enough to affect location decisions.

tion-intensive industries.[21] Both the 1990 Clean Air Act and President Clinton's spotted owl initiative included substantial funding for worker retraining. A small portion of the funds spent in the Northwest was targeted at retraining timber workers in forest restoration work.

9.4 Monopoly Costs

To this point, we have focused on two factors that might cause the social costs of regulation to be different than engineering cost estimates: impacts on productivity and employment. A third area of concern is the impact that regulation might have on the growth of monopoly power.

Complying with environmental regulations can impose substantial fixed costs on firms, such as purchasing control equipment, paying for permits, and hiring environmental lawyers, engineers, and scientists. Higher fixed costs in turn generate economies of scale, which can cause smaller firms to be squeezed out of business. Thus, one potential cost of environmental regulation is an increase in monopoly power in the economy.[22]

The best example of such a trend can perhaps be found in the solid and hazardous waste disposal industries. From a highly competitive market structure in the early 1970s, the industry has been transformed by regulation: Big firms like Waste Management and Browning Ferris now control over a 50% market share. This increased concentration, along with a number of landfill closings in the late 1980s, lead to a period of very high prices and profits.[23] Indeed, accord-ing to an acquaintance of mine who works in the solid waste business in Washington State, many small town officials are convinced that the strict landfill regulations were masterminded by the big waste haulers in order to reduce competition!

Of the two drawbacks to monopoly, the first relates to efficiency and the second to fairness. Because of lack of competition, monopolies may not produce efficiently (X-inefficiency); in addition, monopolies tend to sell goods at a price above production cost, thereby "artificially" restricting demand (allocative inefficiency). These inefficient practices both represent a real opportunity cost to society measured in terms of foregone goods and services.

Most public concern about monopoly, however, focuses on fairness issues: the ability of firms with market power to "rip off" consumers. In the waste management field, for example, one New York township discovered it was being overcharged some 50% by a major firm.[24] From an economist's point of view, however, such overcharging is not a true cost. Rather, high monopoly prices produce a (generally) unfair redistribution of wealth, from consumers to stockholders.

---

[21]For a closer look at the employment impact of protecting spotted owl habitat, as well as a more extended discussion of worker adjustment programs, see Goodstein (1994).

[22]See "Small Businesses Complain that Jungle of Regulations Jeopardize Their Futures," *Wall Street Journal,* June 11, 1992. But see also "Small Companies See Growth Potential in Preventing Environmental Problems," *Wall Street Journal,* June 1, 1992. For more systematic economic evidence of the impact of regulation on optimal scale, market power, and profitability, see Evans (1986), Pashigian (1984), Pittman (1981), and Hughes et al. (1986).

[23]See "Economics of Trash Shift as Cities Learn Dumps Aren't So Full," *Wall Street Journal,* June 2, 1992; and "Recycling: The Newest Wrinkle in Waste Management's Bag," *Business Week,* March 5, 1990.

[24]"Economics of Trash Shift as Cities Learn Dumps Aren't So Full," *Wall Street Journal,* June 2, 1992.

Might monopoly profits actually be a good thing? Some economic observers have defended monopolists' ability to earn high profits, *if* they are funneled back into investment in new plant and equipment or research and development. The *Wall Street Journal,* for example, credits Japan's impressive strides toward energy efficiency to an informal agreement between the nation's big firms and the government. Energy companies are allowed to keep prices high, "provided the windfalls are channeled into energy research."[25]

To sum up: An increase in market share for large firms is a likely consequence of environmental regulation. If this increase in market share also leads to increased monopoly power, the opportunity cost of environmental protection will probably exceed engineering cost estimates. How significant the costs arising from enhanced monopoly power really are is not known.

9.5 General Equilibrium Effects

The last important area in which there may be "hidden" costs (or benefits) of regulation lies in what economists call **general equilibrium (GE) effects.** These effects of regulation are felt throughout the economy, as opposed to effects felt in the specific regulated sector ("partial equilibrium" effects).

For example, if regulation raises the cost of waste disposal, and this raises the cost of hospital services, then the higher cost of hospitals will be one general equilibrium effect of regulation. On the other hand, when the price of hospital services rise, people tend to opt for more in-home care, thus mitigating the impact of the rise in hospital costs.

To make this issue concrete, suppose you were working at the EPA and trying to figure out the cost of a new air-quality regulation on coal-burning power plants. To simplify matters, first assume that there are 100 coal plants nationwide and each would install scrubbers, costing $100 million apiece. In that case, the estimated cost of the regulation would be $10 billion (100 plants * $100 million). Yet, even ignoring other compliance options (like switching to low-sulfur coal), this would be only a partial equilibrium estimate.

In fact, the higher cost for electricity would reduce electricity demand, as people conserved more. Hence, utilities would probably retire rather than retrofit some of the coal plants, leading to lower overall costs. Taking into account the general equilibrium effects in the electricity market, the real costs of the regulation would be lower than your partial equilibrium estimate. Of course, you would also want to calculate impacts throughout the economy of higher electricity prices.

Hazilla and Kopp (1991) undertook just such a study that broke the U.S. economy down into thirty-five sectors, finding that in the short run, engineering cost estimates tended to *overstate* economy-wide costs significantly—by as much as 50%. This is because engineering costs ignore the substitution opportunities (like energy efficiency) available to consumers as the price of regulated commodities rise.

While short-run substitution leads to lower than expected costs, general equilibrium effects can also raise costs indirectly by reducing labor supply. This impact has

[25]"How Japan Became So Energy Efficient: It Leaned On Industry," *Wall Street Journal,* September 10, 1990. The original theory is due to Schumpeter.

loomed large in a recent theoretical debate among economists over the so-called **double-dividend hypothesis.** In the early 1990s some economists (including myself, in the first edition of this book) were arguing that a shift to pollution taxes might be a good thing, and not just because it would reduce pollution. In addition, we claimed, if the revenues were used to cut taxes on labor or capital, pollution taxes might make the whole economy operate more efficiently, thus generating a "double dividend." The notion was that we should shift from taxing "goods" (work effort and investment) to taxing "bads" (pollution), leading to both less pollution and more output.

Unfortunately, this appealing idea of increased efficiency may not be true. (It does, however, remain the case that lower payroll taxes would promote low-skill job growth.) To see this, we need to delve a little more deeply into how economists measure costs. We saw in the previous chapter that environmental benefits were measured as the increase in consumer surplus when cleanup, a public good, was provided. Costs can be measured similarly, as the *decrease* in total surplus: consumer surplus plus producer surplus. Producer surplus is the difference between what a seller gets for a product and the minimum she would be willing to sell it for.[26] We add in producer surplus here, because regulations typically reduce private profits, and this reduction in profits is a cost to society.

Figure 9.4 illustrates a supply-and-demand diagram for corn; at price P, consumer surplus is equal to area a, while producer surplus is shown as area b—the difference between market price and the supply curve. (Recall from economics principles that the supply curve in a competitive market reflects the marginal costs of production.

FIGURE 9.4 Producer and Consumer Surplus

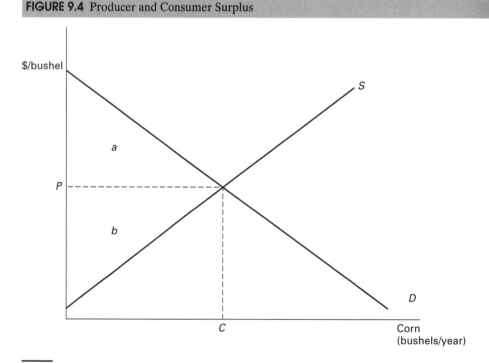

---

[26]Long-run producer surplus is another name for resource rent.

Thus, it illustrates the producer's minimum willingness to accept payment in exchange for its product.)

Now let us set up a simple general equilibrium economy in which there are three goods: corn (a private good), police protection (a public good), and water (a nonmarket good—people get it free from the stream). To provide the public good, there is a payroll tax per hour on labor, paid by employers. Finally, to round out our little economy, the production of corn leads to erosion, which pollutes the water.

We can illustrate the corn market in Figure 9.5. This figure looks just like the previous figure, except there are now two supply curves. S is the supply curve showing only private costs, while S' is the "true" supply curve, including both private and external social costs. Thus C' is the efficient level of corn production—where the true supply and demand curves intersect.

How do we know this? If the corn price is at P, instead of P', then people from C' to C are getting corn who are not willing to pay the full cost of production, including the externalities. The triangle h represents the costs to society of this overproduction and is known as the **deadweight loss** in total surplus from the unregulated pollution.

The way to see this social loss is to add up the total surplus at C and compare it to the surplus at C'. At C, total surplus is consumer surplus ($a + b + c + d$) plus pro-

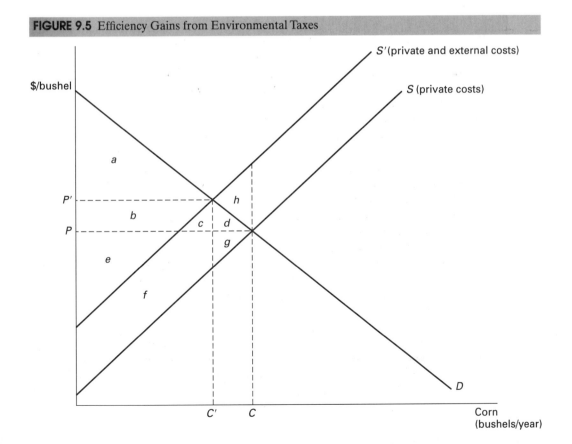

FIGURE 9.5 Efficiency Gains from Environmental Taxes

ducer surplus $(e + f + g)$ *minus externality costs* $(f + c + d + g + h)$, for a total of $(a + b + e - h)$. At C', with the externalities internalized, total surplus is just consumer plus producer surplus: $(a + b + e)$. Thus, the size of the pie—total surplus—is greater at C' than C'', by exactly the deadweight loss, area h.

So, the first point here is that taxing corn leads to efficiency gains of h, since it internalizes the pollution externality and eliminates the deadweight loss. Now, suppose we use the income from the pollution tax (area $f + c$) to reduce labor taxes? Won't this yield even more efficiency gains—a double dividend?

Figure 9.6A illustrates the labor market, with the nominal (money) wage on the vertical axis and the supply of hours (by workers) and the demand for hours (by firms) on the horizontal axis. This time there are two demand curves: D shows the labor demand without the tax; D' shows the lower demand with the tax. Note that the tax itself generates a deadweight loss equal to the hatched area. From L' to L, there are firms willing to pay the true (untaxed) cost of labor, but they are unable to do so because of the tax.

Why have the tax in the first place, then, if it creates deadweight loss? Because the efficiency gains from providing the public good of police protection—not shown here in a diagram—are greater than the losses from the tax.

To summarize: To this point we know that taxing pollution improves efficiency directly; we also have learned that the existing labor tax generates inefficiency in the labor market, but that this is the price we must pay to obtain a needed public good. Here is the question we still need to answer: What are the implications of reducing the payroll tax by using revenues from the pollution tax?

Figure 9.6B shows that there are two offsetting effects. On the one hand, the demand for labor shifts up to D'' as the payroll tax is cut. This effect led to initial optimism about a double dividend. On the other hand, and this is the hidden general equilibrium effect, the supply of labor also shifts up to S'. Why? Because as the price of corn rises due to the tax, an hour of work buys less corn. In other words, the real wage falls. As a result, people substitute labor for leisure, and work less.[27]

As I have drawn it, the reduction in supply outweighs the increase in demand, and the net effect is to increase, not decrease, inefficiency in the labor market—by the gray area. Of course, it could go the other way. The overall jury is still out on the double-dividend hypothesis, but some early research suggests that environmental taxes probably have on balance negative general equilibrium effects—that is, that the indirect costs are large and may even be large enough to offset the direct benefits![28]

Let's stop to summarize this rather complicated section: A first general equilibrium effect—substitution away from higher-priced products—leads engineering cost estimates to be too high. By contrast, when regulation raises prices and in turn reduces labor supply, costs will be higher than engineering estimates. Early research suggests that this latter impact is often big enough to offset any efficiency gains to be

---

[27]Only the substitution effect on labor supply is operable here because the tax shift is revenue neutral.

[28]The most accessible introduction to this topic is Oates (1995). Van Bovenberg and Goulder (1996) argue that in a GE framework, optimal carbon taxes may actually be negative—that is, we "should" be subsidizing global warming! Fullerton and Metcalf (1996) maintain that regulations that create rents, and thus raise product prices, have great distorting effects on labor (and/or) capital markets; this leads to the ironic conclusion that CAC regulation may be much more efficient (in the short run) than IB regulation (see chapter 16). Finally, Jaeger (1997) argues against the concensus view, maintaining that a proper specification of the pollution problem within a GE model reclaims the double dividend.

FIGURE 9.6 A Double Dividend in the Labor Market?

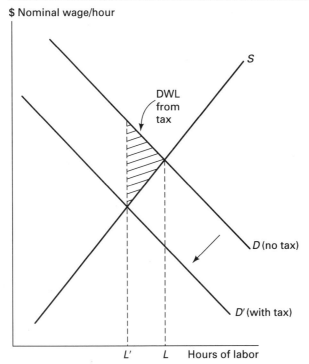

A: Efficiency Impact of a Payroll Tax

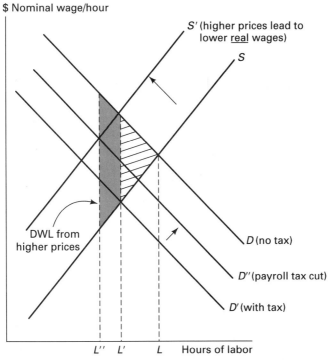

B: Efficiency Impact of Pollution Taxes

had from using pollution tax revenues to cut labor taxes. This means that the efficiency promise of the double-dividend hypothesis cannot generally be realized.

Unless you have taken intermediate microeconomic theory (and even then), upon your first reading of this section I suspect that you have only a vague idea what I have been talking about. General equilibrium effects are hard to comprehend because the interactions are quite complicated. And from a policy perspective, precisely because these general equilibrium costs (and benefits) are so deeply hidden, no one besides (a few) economists currently care much about them. Nevertheless, these indirect costs are just as real as the more obvious direct ones. The take-home message of this section is, again, that a careful reckoning of environmental protection costs can be as difficult as developing good benefit measures.

9.6 Summary

This chapter has explored different ways to evaluate the costs of environmental protection. Engineering cost data are much easier to obtain than nonmarket benefit information; as a result, the EPA has been able to put a 1995 price tag of $161 billion on our federal, state, and local pollution control efforts.

However, even on their own terms, engineering cost estimates are only as good as their predictions regarding, for example, compliance and control technologies. More significantly, engineering estimates do not generally incorporate indirect effects, such as negative or positive productivity impacts, negative or positive impacts on structural unemployment, monopoly costs, or general equilibrium effects.

A number of economic studies have found a small, negative impact on productivity growth from environmental regulation. However, none of these studies incorporates the positive effect (reduced costs) on productivity resulting from improved health and lower medical expenses, increased short-run efficiency of resource use, or long-run Porter hypothesis effects. Thus, the net impact on the productivity growth slowdown remains uncertain but is undoubtedly small. Nevertheless, small declines in productivity growth have big long-run effects and should be a primary concern of regulatory design.

On the employment front, environmental regulation has not lead to any net job loss in the economy; there is simply no evidence of a long-run "jobs versus the environment" trade-off. Instead, regulation has led to a shift in the types of jobs. Rather surprisingly, regulation-induced employment is heavily weighted to manufacturing and away from services. Gross job losses partially due to environmental protection in the late 1980s were on the order of 1,300 per year. Finally, there is little evidence to support widespread capital flight to "pollution havens."

Regarding monopoly power, an increase has likely resulted from regulation. However, the magnitude of this effect is not known. Finally, economists are only beginning to evaluate and quantify the general equilibrium impacts of regulation.

Due to these four different indirect effects, the "true" social cost of regulation (its opportunity cost) may vary widely from engineering cost estimates. This point again highlights the relative imprecision of benefit-cost analysis for determining the "efficient" pollution level. As noted in the introduction to this chapter, the official range of cost estimates for new ozone reduction regulations introduced in 1997 varied from

$600 million to $2.5 billion—a factor of 4. (In the heat of the political debate surrounding the regulatory proposal, some of President Clinton's business advisers were claiming that costs might reach $60 billion per year!) However, an imprecise tool can still be better than no tool at all. In the next chapter we will examine several recent applications of benefit-cost analysis.

In this chapter we have learned that the Clean Air Act amendments passed in 1990 and being implemented today, are predicted to cost, in engineering terms, around $30 billion per year. The meaning of a figure this large is very hard to comprehend. Considering the opportunity cost may make it a bit clearer. With $30 billion, we as a society could do one of the following: fully insure one third of the 37 million Americans who currently have no health insurance at all. Or, we could purchase for the richest one half of one percent of families in the country a new, fully loaded Cadillac STS sedan every year.

These two extreme examples suggest what could be done with the resources we are currently devoting to new efforts in air pollution control. They raise an interesting question: What are we really sacrificing to clean the environment? Basic necessities? Or luxury goods? As we noted, from an efficiency perspective, this issue is not important: Utility derived from luxury cars is equivalent to utility derived from better health or superior air quality. However, from the safety or ecological standpoint, spending money on environmental quality raises human welfare more than an equivalent sum spent on increased material consumption. From these perspectives, the opportunity cost of environmental quality is not adequately measured in dollars alone.

APPLICATION 9.0

The Importance of Productivity

Two well-known economists, William Baumol and Alan Blinder, have stated that, in the long run, "nothing contributes more to reduction of poverty, to increases in leisure, and to the country's ability to finance education, public health, environmental improvement and the arts" than the rate of growth of productivity.[29]

1. Define productivity.
2. See if you can verify Baumol and Blinder's very strong claim (*"nothing contributes more . . ."*) through the following exercise. Assume GNP in the United States is $5 trillion and that the labor force remains constant in size and fully employed. Estimate the value in GNP in one year's time if productivity growth is 3%. What if it were only 2%? How much will GNP fall in two years'

time if productivity growth remains at 2% rather than 3%? In three years?
3. Why might environmental regulation reduce productivity growth?
4. Why might it increase productivity growth?
5. Even if, on balance, environmental regulation has not reduced productivity growth, are negative productivity impacts from regulations something we should still worry about?

---

[29]Baumol and Blinder (1991: 356). *Macroeconomics: Principles and Policy* (New York: Harcourt Brace Jovanovich).

APPLICATION 9.1

Jobs and the Environment

In 1992, the United States was the odd country out at the Rio Earth Summit. President Bush chose not to sign an otherwise universally approved treaty on biodiversity, and his administration successfully weakened an agreement designed to curb carbon dioxide emissions thought likely to cause global warming. In both cases the President maintained he was, in the *Wall Street Journal's* paraphrase, "protecting American jobs from environmental extremists."[30]

1. Based on the information presented in this chapter, would signing the environmental treaties originally under consideration be likely to generate an economy-wide, net decrease in the number of U.S. jobs? Why or why not?

2. Is it likely that U.S. workers in particular industries might lose their jobs partially as a result of the treaties? If the impact of the treaties were comparable to current environmental regulations, how many workers per year might face layoffs? How might the blow to these workers be cushioned?

3. Suppose that people around the country felt it was unfair for workers to lose their jobs due to greenhouse gas regulation. Based on what you learned in the previous chapter on benefit estimation (chapter 8), how could we measure this moral concern, and include it as a cost of the regulation?

Key Ideas in Each Section

9.0 The standard method of estimating the costs of environmental protection, simply adding up direct compliance and regulatory expenses, is called an **engineering approach.** Economists, however, would like to measure the **opportunity cost:** the value of goods and services foregone by investing in environmental protection. Opportunity costs include four indirect effects: productivity impacts, employment impacts, the growth of monopoly power, and general equilibrium effects.

9.1 In 1995, the United States spent about $160 billion per year on pollution control measures, measured in engineering terms. Between 1970 and 1995, environmental protection expenditures jumped from less than 1% to over 2.5% of GNP, more than doubling their claim on the nation's resources.

9.2 The productivity slowdown of the 1970s has been partially blamed on environmental regulation. The main argument is that regulatory expenses divert investment from new plant and equipment. Several economic studies indicate that a small portion of the slowdown (less than 10%) may be due to environmental protection measures. However, this does not take into account possible positive impacts on productivity growth from more efficient resource use, **Porter hypothesis** effects, or a healthier population and resource base. One study that attempted to incorporate environmental benefits found no overall drop in productivity growth due to regulation. Nevertheless, even small negative effects on productivity growth can impose large costs in the long run.

---

[30]"President's Clumsy Handling of Earth Summit Results in a Public-Relations Disaster for Him," *Wall Street Journal,* June 15, 1992.

9.3 This section reviews the employment impact of environmental regulation and makes three main points. First, at the economy-wide level, environmental protection has *not* generated a **jobs-environment trade-off.** If anything, environmental protection appears to have boosted aggregate employment slightly. Second, extrapolating data from a large sample of employer responses, gross job loss from **plant shutdowns** due to environmental regulation was around 1,300 workers per year from 1987 to 1990. Therefore, little **structural unemployment** can be attributed to regulation. Finally, it appears that in only a few cases have U.S. firms invested in **pollution havens** to avoid environmental regulations.

9.4 Regulation can increase **monopoly power** by imposing high fixed costs on firms, which are more easily met by larger companies. Increases in monopoly power can generate costs in the form of inefficient production and pricing, and monopoly pricing is generally perceived to be unfair. Neither the extent nor the cost of a regulation-induced increase in market power is known.

9.5 General equilibrium (GE) effects work in two directions. Because people substitute away from products when regulation raises their price, engineering estimates tend to overstate the short-run costs of regulation. On the other hand, environmental taxes and marketable permit systems may be more costly than previously thought, because by raising product prices, they lower real wages and discourage work effort creating **deadweight loss.** GE studies have found this effect to be big, and thus provide little support for the **double-dividend hypothesis.**

References

Aschauer, David Alan (1990). *Public Investment and Private Sector Growth.* Washington, DC: Economic Policy Institute.

Baily, Martin N. and Alok K. Chakrabarti (1988). *Innovation and the Productivity Crisis.* Washington, DC: Brookings.

Barbera, Anthony J. and Virginia D. McConnell (1990). "The Impact of Environmental Regulations on Industry Productivity: Direct and Indirect Effects." *Journal of Environmental Economics and Management,* vol. 18, 50–65.

Baumol, William and Alan Blinder (1991). *Macroeconomics: Principles and Policy.* New York: Harcourt Brace Jovanovich.

Berman, Eli and Linda T. M. Bui (1997). *Clearing the Air: Implication of Environmental Regulation for the Economy and the Environment in the South Coast Air Basin.* Washington, DC: Economic Policy Institute.

Bezdek, Roger H. (1993). "Environment and Economy: What's the Bottom Line?" *Environment,* 35, no. 7, 7–32.

Bezdek, Roger H., Robert M. Wendling and Jonathan D. Jones (1989). "The Economic and Employment Effects of Investments in Pollution Abatement and Control Technologies." *Ambio,* 18, no. 5, 274–279.

Bowles, Samuel, David Gordon and Thomas Weisskopf (1991). *After the Wasteland.* Armonk, NY: Sharpe.

Breslow, Marc, John Stutz, Paul Lignon, Frank Ackerman, Nancy Ilgenfritz and Peter Murad (1992). *Socioeconomic Impacts of Solid Waste Scenarios for New York City: A Report to the New York City Department of Sanitation.* Boston: Tellus Institute.

Burtraw, Dallas (1996). "Trading Emissions to Clean the Air: Exchanges Few but Savings Many," *Resources,* Winter, no. 122, 3–6.

Carlin, Alan (1990). *Environmental Investments: The Cost of a Clean Environment, Summary.* Washington, DC: U.S. EPA.

Chapman, Duane (1991). "Environmental Standards and International Trade in Automobiles and Copper: The Case for a Social Tariff." *Natural Resources Journal,* 31, no. 3, 449–462.

Dean, Judith (1992). "Trade and the Environment: A Survey of the Literature." *Policy Research Working Paper WPS966.* Washington, DC: World Bank.

Evans, David B. (1986). "The Differential Effect of Regulation Across Plant Size: Comment on Pashigian." *The Journal of Law and Economics,* vol. 29, April, 187–200.

Fullerton, Don and Gilbert Metcalf (1996). "Environmental Controls, Scarcity Rents and Pre-existing Distortions." Paper presented at the American Economic Association Meetings, January 1997.

Goodstein, Eban (1997). *A New Look at Environmental Regulation and U.S. Competitiveness.* Washington, DC: Economic Policy Institute.

Goodstein, Eban (1996). "Jobs and the Environment: An Overview." *Environmental Management,* 20, no. 3, 313–321.

Goodstein, Eban (1994). *Jobs and the Environment: The Myth of a National Trade-off.* Washington, DC: Economic Policy Institute.

Grossman, Gene M. and Alan B. Krueger (1991). "Environmental Impacts of a North American Free Trade Agreement." *Working Paper 3914.* Cambridge, MA: National Bureau of Economic Research.

Hazilla, Michael and Raymond J. Kopp (1991). "Social Cost of Environmental Regulations: A General Equilibrium Analysis." *Journal of Political Economy,* 98-4.

Hettige, Hemamala, Robert E. B. Lucas and David Wheeler (1992). "The Toxic Intensity of Industrial Production: Global Patterns, Trends and Trade Policies." *American Economic Review,* 82, no. 2, 478–481.

Hughes, John S., Wesley Magat and William A. Ricks (1986). "The Economic Consequences of the OSHA Cotton Dust Standards: An Analysis of Stock Price Behavior." *The Journal of Law and Economics,* vol. 29, April, 29–59.

Jaeger, William (1997). "Optimal Environmental Taxation." *Working Paper.* Williamstown, MA: Williams College.

Jaffe, Adam B., Steven R. Peterson, Paul R. Portney and Robert N. Stavins (1995). "Environmental Regulation and the Competitiveness of U.S. Manufacturing: What Does the Evidence Tell Us?" *Journal of Economic Literature,* 33, no. 1, 132–163.

Jorgenson, Dale W. and Peter J. Wilcoxen (1990). "Environmental Regulation and U.S. Economic Growth." *Rand Journal of Economics,* 21, no. 2, 314–340.

Joskow, Paul (1992). "Carbon Taxes and Economic Welfare: Comment." *Brookings Papers on Economic Activity: Microeconomics 1992.* Washington, DC: Brookings.

Koechlin, Timothy (1992). "Determinants of the Location of U.S.A. Foreign Investment." *International Review of Applied Economics,* 6, no. 2, 203–216.

Leonard, H. Jeffrey (1984). *Are Environmental Regulations Driving U.S. Industry Overseas?* Washington, DC: The Conservation Foundation.

Lucas, Robert E. B., David Wheeler and Hemamala Hettige (1992). "Economic Development, Environmental Regulation, and the International Migration of Toxic Industrial Pollution 1960–1988." Washington, DC: World Bank.

Management Information Services, Inc. (1991). "U.S. Environmental Spending to Exceed National Defense Budget." Washington, DC: MIS, Inc.

Melman, Seymour (1987). *Profits Without Production.* Philadelphia, PA: University of Pennsylvania Press.

Mishel, Lawrence (1989). "The Late Great Debate on Deindustrialization." *Challenge,* 32, no. 1, 36–44.

Nestor, Deborah Vaughn and Carl A. Pasurka Jr. (1993). "The Environmental Protection Industry in an Input-Output Framework." Paper presented at the Eastern Economic Association Meetings.

Oates, Wallace E. (1995). "Green Taxes: Can We Protect the Environment and Improve the Tax System at the Same Time?" *Southern Economic Journal,* 61, no. 4, 915–922.

Pashigian, Peter B. (1984). "The Effects of Environmental Regulation on Optimal Plant Size and Factor Shares." *The Journal of Law and Economics,* vol. 28, April, 1–28.

Pittman, Russel W. (1981). "Issues in Pollution Control: Interplant Cost Differences and Economies of Scale." *Land Economics,* vol. 57, 1–17.

Porter, Michael and Claas van der Linde (1995). "Toward a New Conception of the Environment-Competitiveness Relationship." *Journal of Economic Perspectives,* 9, no. 4, 97–118.

Portney, Paul (1990). "Policy Watch: Economics and the Clean Air Act," *Journal of Economic Perspectives,* 4, no. 4, 173–182.

Repetto, Robert (1990). "Environmental Productivity and Why It Is So Important." *Challenge,* September, 33–38.

Rutledge, Gary L. and Mary L. Leonard (1992). "Pollution Abatement and Control Expenditures, 1972–1990." *Survey of Current Business,* 72, no. 6, 25–41.

Sanchez, Roberto A. (1990). "Health and Environmental Risks of the Maquiladora in Mexicali." *Natural Resources Journal,* 30, no. 1, 163–186.

U.S. GAO (1991). "Some U.S. Wood Furniture Firms Relocated from Los Angeles Area to Mexico," *GAO/NSIAD-91-191* Washington, DC: U.S. Government Accounting Office.

Van Bovenberg, A. Lans and Lawrence Goulder (1996). "Optimal Environmental Taxation in the Presence of other Taxes: General Equilibrium Analyses." *American Economic Review,* 86, no. 4, 985–999.

Wendling, Robert M. and Roger H. Bezdek (1989). "Acid Rain Abatement Legislation: Costs and Benefits." *OMEGA International Journal of Management Science,* 17, no. 3, 251–261.

CHAPTER 10

Benefit-Cost in Practice: Implementing the Efficiency Standard

10.0 Introduction

Our goal in this first part of the book has been to answer the normative question: "How much pollution is too much?" The first answer we considered was to reduce pollution to "the efficient level." From the efficiency perspective, pollution should be controlled until the additional costs of control just outweigh the additional benefits. Determining the efficient level first requires methods for calculating *all* the benefits and costs of environmental protection in dollar terms. Having spent the last two chapters developing tools to accomplish this, *albeit* imprecisely, we are now in a position to put the two sides together and attempt to pinpoint the efficient pollution level. This process is known as benefit-cost analysis.

Benefit-cost studies currently play an important, but not dominant, role in federal environmental regulation. Air, water, and hazardous waste are primarily regulated under a safety standard, with cost considerations playing a relatively minor role. For example, the Clean Air Act requires air standards that protect human health, while the Clean Water Act sets as its final goal zero discharge into navigable waters, with an intermediate target of "fishable and swimmable waters." In neither case are compliance costs mentioned.

And so, for example, in 1997 the EPA passed a regulation to tighten smog standards for which its own estimated costs ($600 million to $2.5 billion) exceeded the measurable benefits ($100 million to $1.5 billion). Why did it do this? On safety grounds. In spite of the negative benefit-cost picture, the regulations were expected to save lives and allow people to exercise safely outside.[1] In fact, the courts have ruled

---

[1] "Clintonites Debate Cost of a Bad Air Day," *Wall Street Journal,* June 9, 1997, p. A1.

that the air and water protection statutes, along with the national hazardous waste legislation, explicitly prohibit benefit-cost tests for new regulations.

On the other hand, pesticides, insecticides, and other toxic substances are regulated under an efficiency standard. Chemicals and pesticides cannot be banned unless the benefits of doing so are (roughly) shown to exceed the costs.

Even for the safety statutes, though, since 1981, the EPA has been required to conduct formal benefit-cost analyses of any new regulation expected to cost over $100 million. And during the Reagan and Bush years, the agency was explicitly required to adopt an efficiency standard where legal.

These benefit-cost studies, known as **Regulatory Impact Analyses (RIAs),** are prepared for new safety standard regulations, like the ozone tightening done in 1997, even though their results cannot legally determine the regulatory decision. Why do them then? Under a safety standard, the agency is still directed to select "the regulatory alternative maximizing net benefits from those alternatives within the scope of the law." In our terminology, the EPA is supposed to examine several different options and, among all the options that achieve a safety goal, pick the most efficient.[2]

Given that conservatives often push hardest for the use of benefit-cost tests, many environmentalists view benefit-cost analysis as merely a political tool for rolling back environmental gains, in part by burying the regulatory process under a mound of paperwork.[3] And at its worst, benefit-cost analysis is indeed used as an excuse to gloss over hard moral choices and provide a rubber stamp for preconceived notions about the right course of action. One EPA employee privately characterized the results of an RIA he had worked on as follows: "I wouldn't bet a week's salary on the results, but it justified the rule."

However, at its best, a benefit-cost study will clarify the decision-making process. As we will see in this chapter, a "good" benefit-cost study can highlight the trade-offs that regulators face when setting standards. What is meant by a **good benefit-cost study?** It will follow accepted procedures for estimating benefits and costs, provide a clear statement of all assumptions, point out uncertainties where they exist, and suggest realistic margins of error.

In this chapter, we will review two benefit-cost studies conducted by the EPA. The first focuses on a very detailed problem—exposure to the leachate from lead solder in water pipes (solder is the material used to fuse pipes together). In addition to the specificity of the problem, the benefits of reduced exposure to lead are fairly well-known. Nevertheless, even here, there is substantial uncertainty surrounding the benefit and cost estimates, casting some doubt over the usefulness of the final results.

The second RIA had a much broader mandate: to evaluate the benefits and costs of

---

[2]The two quotes from the executive order are cited in Fraas (1984). Presidents Reagan and Bush directed the EPA to simply maximize net benefits. President Clinton's executive order still directs the EPA to conduct a benefit-cost analysis for significant regulatory actions and select options that "maximize net benefits" to the extent permissible by law. But "net benefits" are now parenthetically qualified to include "potential economic, environmental, public health and safety, and other advantages; distributive impacts; and equity" (see Goodstein [1995]).

In my mind, Clinton's executive order is an improvement over Reagan's, since it explicitly recognizes a role for nonmonetary considerations in policy making. Yet, there is value to an economic accounting that keeps equity and efficiency issues distinct, and Clinton's order muddles them in an unfortunate way.

[3]Even some supporters of efficiency standards opposed the 1995 efficiency-based legislation, arguing that it was in fact a thinly disguised attempt to paralyze the regulatory process (Portney [1995]).

establishing design standards and performance regulations for the nation's 6,000 plus municipal solid waste landfills. Aside from the obvious difficulties associated with tackling such a vast problem, and in contrast to the lead case, the health and environmental benefits of stricter regulation for landfills are both highly uncertain and hard to quantify.

These two studies illustrate both the potential and limitations of benefit-cost analysis from a technical point of view. We will also evaluate the degree to which political interests can affect the benefit-cost process. Finally, we will consider the charge that, given its limitations, benefit-cost analysis is simply not up to the task of specifying the "right" level of pollution.

10.1 Doing Benefit Cost: Lead Standards

Under the Safe Drinking Water Act, the EPA is required to establish action standards for lead in drinking water. Lead concentrations from leachate higher than the action level would require remedial action—installation of pH control devices and inhibitors to reduce corrosion and/or public education campaigns to inform people how to reduce risks of lead in drinking water. Table 10.1 illustrates the three options the agency considered for lead leached from solder:

Option A is the most stringent, with action levels for both small ($<$ 50,000 people) and large ($>$50,000 people) systems occurring at 5 micrograms per liter. Option B loosens the standard for small systems to 15 μg/l. The rationale for this option is based on the increased per user expense associated with corrosion control in smaller systems. The high fixed costs of retrofitting such a system would be spread out over fewer users. Thus, they would have to pay higher water bills than large system users if option A, where the same protection level is afforded all users, were chosen. Option C relaxes both standards to 15 μg/l.

To estimate costs, the EPA first had to determine which of the over 63,000 systems nationwide would require remedial action and at what level to achieve the three different targets.[4] With this difficult feat accomplished, the next step was to establish engineering cost estimates for the different steps to be taken: water monitoring, conducting corrosion control studies, installing lime contactors to control pH, installing inhibitors, and mounting public education campaigns. After undertaking these two

TABLE 10.1	Proposed Action Levels for Lead Leached from Solder	
Option	*System Type*	*Action Level*
A	Small	5 μg/1
	Large	5 μg/1
B	Small	15 μg/1
	Large	5 μg/1
C	Small	15 μg/1
	Large	15 μg/1

Source: U.S. Environmetal Protection Agency (1991a).

---

[4]Some systems were expected not to be able to achieve the targets with the available control technology. These were expected to achieve reductions to 10 μg/l and to continue their public education campaigns.

tasks, the study gives a plus or minus 50% range for uncertainty in its cost estimates, due to factors such as "the effectiveness of treatment, current corrosion control practices, nationwide contaminant occurrence levels, as well as uncertainty regarding what specific actions will be required by the states in the implementation of this rule."[5]

On the benefits side, the agency had the luxury of dealing with a compound that is a well-established "bad actor." Lead drinking pipes, after all, have been given credit for the fall of the Roman Empire! Considerable research has been done documenting the negative effects of lead exposure. Table 10.2 lists the health costs associated with lead in drinking water. Items that the EPA was able to consider directly are marked with an *.

Of this long list, the EPA was able to quantify benefits only for hypertension, chronic heart disease, stroke, and death in adult males and reduced intelligence in children. (Feminists might speculate on the reasons for the lack of data on women!) Most of the other health effects of lead exposure fall into the category of suspected but not confirmed. As the RIA states: "Many categories of health effects from lead exposure cannot be quantified—credible dose-response functions are not yet available."[6] Finally, other nonwater benefits the RIA notes it does not consider are reduced lead content in sewage sludge, and longer pipe life and reduced water leakage from corrosion control.

The EPA tried to get at *some* of the benefits of lead reduction for children indirectly, by estimating the reduction in screening and subsequent mitigation costs due to the regulation. About 20% of American children are routinely screened for lead content in their blood; depending upon the lead level found, further screening and treatment are recommended. The agency estimated the savings from such testing and treatment resulting

---

TABLE 10.2 Health Costs of Lead Exposure

MEN (age group)
* a. Hypertension (adult)
* b. Heart disease, stroke, and death (ages 40–59)
   c. Possible item b. (ages 20–40; >59)
   d. Cancer

WOMEN
   e. Possible hypertension, heart disease, stroke, and death
   f. Fetal effects from maternal exposure, including diminished childhood IQ, decreased gestational age, and reduced birth weight
   g. Possible increases in infant mortality
   h. Cancer

CHILDREN
   i. Interference with growth
* j. Reduced intelligence
   k. Impaired hearing, behavioral changes
   l. Interference with PNS development
   m. Metabolic effects, impaired heme synthesis, anemia
   n. Cancer

*Items that the EPA was able to consider directly.
Source: U.S. Environmental Protection Agency (1991a).

---

[5]U.S. Environmental Protection Agency (1991a: 1–6).
[6]U.S. Environmental Protection Agency (1991a: 5–1).

from tighter regulation. The EPA included not only the direct costs but also the opportunity cost of the parents' time. (Stress and suffering costs were not included.) Ultimately, however, as we shall see below, these benefits proved to be very small.

The EPA also included as a benefit a reduction in the number of severely impacted children, those with an IQ of 70 or less. As a measure of the benefits, the agency used the expected reduction in compensatory education expenses. The authors of the study recognized this to be "a clear underestimate." Their preferred measure would have been parents' willingness to pay to avoid (or willingness to accept) a mentally handicapped child.

The direct effects of lead exposure to children were measured via a reduction in earnings resulting from lowered "intelligence." EPA again used the controversial IQ measure to measure general cognitive ability. It then used studies linking lead exposure to lower IQ, and lower IQ to lower earnings, to estimate the benefits of reduced exposure. The agency took into account three effects of lowered IQ on earnings: first, lowered innate "ability"; second, lowered educational attainment; and, third, lowered labor force participation rates.

For adult males, the EPA was able to quantify benefits associated with reduced hypertension, heart disease, stroke, and premature death. For hypertension, benefits included direct outlays for medical care and the value of lost workdays. Again, no estimates were included for pain and suffering. For heart disease and stroke, the agency relied on a more theoretically correct approach—willingness to pay to avoid risk of disease. However, the most closely related study available looked at chronic bronchitis, arriving at a figure of around $1 million per case. The EPA used this number, reasoning that the symptoms of the two former diseases are at least as severe as the latter. Finally, the EPA placed a value on deaths avoided of $2.5 million. Recall that this is at the low end of the range discussed in chapter 8.

Given all the assumptions and uncertainties associated with these estimates, the authors of the study "assume," based on "professional judgment," that the "true" benefit measure could be as much as two times as high, or 70% below, the actual value the estimation procedure generates. This "two-times" upper bound *does not* include all of the benefit categories identified in the discussion above that the EPA could not quantify. The authors, sensibly, could provide uncertainty ranges only for the estimates they did undertake.

Bearing in mind both the uncertainty and incomplete coverage, Table 10.3 provides the annual benefit estimates for the different categories of health effects. Option A, the strictest alternative, yields the highest total benefits; option C the lowest.

Table 10.3 illustrates in its boldest form the accounting procedure necessary for using benefit-cost analysis to determine the "right" amount of pollution. If you find it morally disturbing to see in print, "Number of deaths reduced: 672, Value: $1,680 million," rest assured that most people do and that this is a healthy sign. Whether you ultimately reject or accept the benefit-cost logic, it is important to keep in mind that people's lives and well-being, not dollars, are at stake in decisions about pollution levels. The dollars are placeholders for consumption items—ranging from better health care to luxury cars—that may make people happier and must be given up to reduce the risk of death from lead in drinking water.

The final step in the benefit-cost analysis is to compare the total costs and benefits of the different standards over the assumed twenty-year life of the existing lead-solder-based water delivery system. In this case, a discount rate of 3% was used. Table

TABLE 10.3   Annual Estimated Benefits of Reducing Lead in Drinking Water (1988 $million)

	Option		
	A	*B*	*C*
ADULT MALES			
Hypertension			
Cases reduced/yr	685,302	635,199	246,479
Value	$ 430	$ 399	$ 155
Heart Attack			
Cases reduced/yr	884	818	315
Value	$ 884	$ 818	$ 315
Stroke			
Cases reduced/yr	657	609	235
Value	$ 657	$ 609	$ 235
Death (Heart Disease)			
Cases reduced/yr	672	622	240
Value	$1,680	$1,555	$ 599
CHILDREN			
Treatment cost reduced	*	*	*
Additional education reduced	$ 2	$ 2	$ 2
Lowered IQ			
Children no longer affected	205,221	188,313	68,133
Value	$ 942	$ 864	$ 313
IQ < 70			
Children no longer affected	784	738	325
Value	$ 40	$ 38	$ 17
TOTAL	$4,635	$4,286	$1,635

*Less than $1 million.
Source: U.S. Environmental Protection Agency (1991a).

10.4 displays the guts of the benefit-cost study as it appears in the RIA: the total present discounted values of costs and benefits over the life of the project.

Now, having made it through many long and tedious chapters of this text to finally get to the point where you, as an informed economist, can read a benefit-cost analysis, use the information in Table 10.4 to see if you can answer the $64,000

TABLE 10.4   Summary Benefit-Cost Results, Lead Solder

	Option		
	A	*B*	*C*
Total Benefits	$68,957	$63,757	$24,325
Total Costs	$ 6,272	$ 4,156	$ 3,655
B/C Ratio	11.0	15.3	6.7
Marginal Benefits	$ 5,192	$39,400	$24,325
Marginal Costs	$ 2,117	$ 500	$ 3,655
Marginal B/C Ratio	2.5	78.8	6.67

Note figures are based on 20-year life, 3% discount rate, 1988 $million.
Source: U.S. Environmental Protection Agency (1991a).

PUZZLE

Which option is the most efficient?

SOLUTION

Let's see, this is multiple choice, so why not pick the one in the middle, right? Wrong. The correct answer is option

A

Why? The efficient option will maximize the size of the economic pie or the **net monetary benefits** to society. But this is just total benefits minus total costs. Unfortunately, there is no line in the Table 10.4 illustrating net monetary benefits, so we must do the math ourselves. Subtracting total costs from total benefits, we find net benefits for option A are estimated to be $62,685 m, for option B $59,509 m, and for option C $20,670 m.

   Another way to see that option A is the most efficient is to use marginal analysis: C is clearly a good buy, since marginal benefits ($24,325 m) exceed marginal costs ($3,655). Should we move from C to B? Yes, here the additional benefits ($39,440 m) are *much* larger than the additional costs ($500 m). Finally, should we move from B to A? Again the answer is yes. Marginal benefits ($5,192) still exceed marginal costs ($2,117 m), though not by as much as in the move from C to B. Figure 10.1 illustrates this using our familiar marginal benefit/marginal cost of cleanup diagram. Because the marginal benefits curve lies above the marginal cost curve, option A is more efficient than option B.

FIGURE 10.1 Estimated Benefits and Costs of Reducing Lead ($billion)

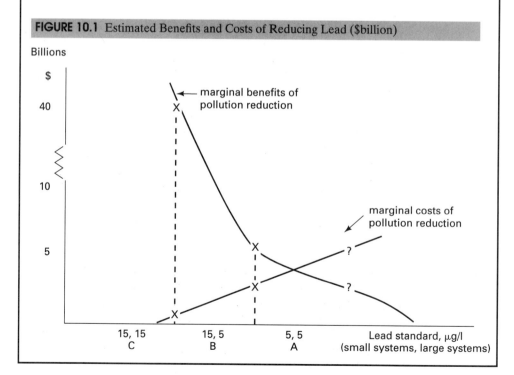

The summary in Table 10.4 (and Figure 10.1) gives us a very neat story. The numbers "speak for themselves." Option A is clearly the most efficient. The regulator can glance at the table, make the efficient decision, and go home. However, is the information in Table 10.4 the whole story? Well, of course not. We just spent a whole section stressing the uncertainty of both the cost and benefit estimates.

Figure 10.2 provides a somewhat more realistic and less neat way of looking at

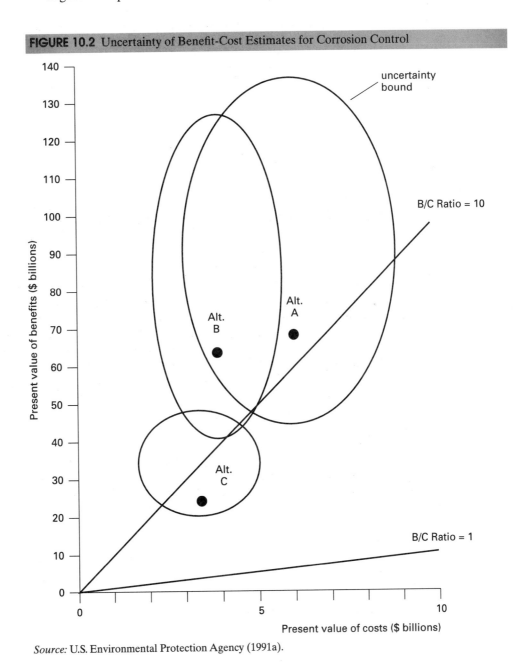

FIGURE 10.2 Uncertainty of Benefit-Cost Estimates for Corrosion Control

Source: U.S. Environmental Protection Agency (1991a).

the data. The graph shows benefits, measured in billions of dollars, on the vertical axis and costs, also measured in billions, on the horizontal axis.

First note that the estimates for options A, B, and C all lie above the line labeled "B/C Ratio = 1." The **benefit-cost ratio** is just the value of the benefits of the option divided by the costs. A B/C ratio greater than one means total benefits exceed total costs, while a B/C ratio that is a fraction means that total benefits are less than total costs. Because all three options have a ratio greater than one, all three options clearly pass a simple total benefits greater than total costs test.

The circles reflect the uncertainty bounds around the estimates discussed above. The fact that the circles for A and B overlap so substantially suggests that the differences between these options reported in Table 10.4 are essentially meaningless. For example, the $6 billion benefit difference between the two is swamped by an uncertainty of roughly $60 billion up to the top of each circle and $30 billion down to the bottom. Similarly, the costs of the two programs could, in reality, vary much more than the $2 billion difference that separates points A and B.

At the same time, however, option C can be clearly distinguished from options A and B. There is no overlap with A and only a bit with B. Even including the uncertainty, options A and B are more efficient than C.

Which option did EPA recommend? Interestingly, the EPA did not choose option A, the one its "best guess" identified as most efficient and which, in this case, is clearly the safest. In fact, the report *never acknowledged* that A is estimated to be the most efficient. Instead, the agency fell back on the uncertainty in the benefit estimates and opted for the less expensive option B. In the report's words: "The diagram [Figure 10.2] indicates that, when all uncertainties are weighed, the net benefits of corrosion control under alternative A may not be meaningfully different than those associated with alternative B."[7]

On the other hand, they may well be different; they may be dramatically larger! Figure 10.2 is rather deceptive. While appearing to be an example of "good" benefit cost by including "all" uncertainty, in fact, *most of the uncertainty is still left out* of the diagram. As was noted, many potential health and nonhealth benefits were ignored in the study since they could not be monetized.

Nevertheless, given the uncertainty illustrated in the graph, and the much larger uncertainty arising from omitted benefits, it is clear that the choice between A and B could not be made on benefit-cost grounds. Given also the general conservative, anti-regulation philosophy of the Bush administration in power at the time, the choice of the less costly option B was perhaps not surprising.

This case illustrates that, due to substantial uncertainty surrounding health effects and benefit measures for reducing even a well-studied compound like lead, benefit-cost analysis cannot discriminate between "relatively" close options. Ultimately, the choice between A and B could not be and was not made on efficiency grounds. On the other hand, benefit-cost analysis is capable of discerning "big differences" between policies. C is clearly inefficient relative to A or B. A critic would respond, of course, that we could save the time and money devoted to a benefit-cost study: A simple look at the lives saved in Table 10.3 makes it clear that C is an inferior policy.

As a final technical point, the major table in the EPA document, Table 10.4, relies

---

[7]U.S. Environmental Protection Agency (1991a).

on the B/C ratio to summarize the options. But note that B/C ratios have nothing to do with efficiency. Option A has a lower ratio (11) than option B (15.3), yet is more efficient. B/C ratios alone do not tell us very much. From an economist's point of view, Table 10.4 is missing the most important line: total net benefits. The option with the **maximum net benefits** is the most efficient, and it should be clearly identified in a summary table like 10.4.

10.2 Doing Benefit Cost: Landfill Regulation

If the lead case illustrates the pitfalls that emerge when working with a relatively well-defined problem, the second RIA highlights more common difficulties in benefit-cost analysis—poor data, long-time horizons, and hard-to-quantify benefits. The EPA, under the Resource Conservation and Recovery Act (RCRA), was directed to draft regulations for the siting, construction, and maintenance of municipal solid waste landfills. Originally, the agency evaluated five alternatives but ultimately focused on two. The first was a "pollute and cleanup" approach that imposed no design standards on landfills, requiring only groundwater monitoring and corrective action for any pollutants detected above the legal level defined in the Safe Drinking Water Act. This option reflected the minimal regulatory approach consistent with the RCRA law.

The second option took a preventive approach, requiring landfills designed to forestall any groundwater contamination. Depending upon site conditions, these designs might require soil compaction, clay or synthetic liners, leachate collection systems, and relatively impermeable covers. Both regulations imposed some location restrictions and required monitoring for a postclosure period of from ten to forty years.

EPA's engineers and economists faced a difficult problem in assessing the comparative costs and benefits associated with these options at over 6,000 landfill sites around the country. As a result, many simplifying assumptions went into the study. Of course, assumptions are necessary in any social scientific work; the question that an outside observer would ask is, will the results change substantially if other, equally plausible assumptions are used?

In this case, we have one indication of how important assumptions can be to the final results. The agency's approach was to compare the additional costs and benefits of each option to a "baseline" scenario, or continuation of current practice. The RIA was initiated in 1985; at the time, a reasonable baseline assumption was that most current landfills were unlined with vegetative covers. This assumption meant that achieving the EPA's preferred rule, which required liners and impermeable covers in many cases, would be quite costly. In 1990, the agency completed a two-volume RIA under this assumption.

Over the 1985–1990 time period, however, many states began requiring higher design standards, including liners and covers. After determining that these changes might substantially affect the results of the RIA, the agency obtained better information about state practices. EPA then issued a revised benefit-cost analysis assuming a baseline with more stringent existing regulations. While the benefits of both options were reduced under this assumption, the additional costs fell by a much larger margin—in the case of the "prevent" option, from $14.8 billion to $5.7 billion. Clearly, EPA's original assumption was outdated by the time the study was completed. Yet, benefit-cost analysts, without access to unlimited information and charged with producing numbers, are forced to make such assumptions. One can only speculate about the possibility of other sensitive assumptions buried in the two-volume study.

EPA's cost estimates, based on the engineering approach, include expenses associated with "land clearing, excavation, equipment, labor, liner materials and groundwater monitoring wells." Not surprisingly, the bulk of added costs over the baseline (70%) for the "pollute and cleanup" option were for corrective action, while for the prevention option, 50% of the added costs went for liners.

In the benefit category, EPA attempted two quantitative estimates: reduction in cancer risk and avoided cost of replacing damaged groundwater. Note that these are different measures of the same benefit—access to healthy drinking water—and thus cannot be added together. The health risk from solid waste landfills arises primarily from the presence of small quantities of hazardous household and industrial waste such as paints, oils, solvents, insecticides, and pesticides. These carcinogenic substances can be leached out of a landfill by rainfall and find their way into surrounding groundwaters.

On the cancer side, the EPA baseline estimate is low. Over the next 300 years the agency predicts 5.7 cancers nationwide would result from the drinking of contaminated groundwater under the current regulatory framework. This estimate suffers from the well-known uncertainties associated with assessing the cancer risk from hazardous waste, mentioned in chapter 8 and detailed in National Research Council (1991). In this case, the uncertainty is compounded by the need to model the highly uncertain process by which toxics leach out of the landfill and into groundwater, all over a very lengthy period.

The reason the risk estimate is so low is not because unregulated landfills are "safe." The EPA has estimated that 55% of existing landfills posed cancer risks from groundwater on the order of 10^{-4} to 10^{-5} for surrounding residents—above our 1 in 1,000,000 safety threshold. New, unregulated landfills are assumed by the agency to expose individuals to this risk level at about 6% of the sites.[8] (For comparison, police officers face a risk of about 10^{-4} of being killed by a felon while on duty.) Instead, cancer case estimates are low because the number of people who actually depend on groundwater from wells within one mile of a landfill, the agencies assumed cut off from contamination, is quite small. For example, over 50% of new landfills are assumed to have no wells at all within one mile, so the cancer risk was estimated to be zero. If the demand for groundwater increases as population grows, the estimated cancer figure would be higher.

Both regulatory options, pollute and cleanup, and prevent, reduced expected cancers by 2.4 over the 300-year period. These two estimates are identical, in part, because the EPA (unrealistically) assumes full compliance with groundwater monitoring laws and reporting and correction of all violations. However, the maximum estimated number of cancers reduced under either option would be only 5.7.

As an alternative measure to cancers avoided, the EPA estimated the cost of replacing damaged groundwater (dangerous or bad-tasting or foul-smelling) with an alternative supply. This approach probably overstates benefits: In effect, the estimate assumes society is willing to pay enough to insure 100% safety for affected residents

---

[8]Office of Technology Assessment (1989); and U.S. Environmental Protection Agency (1990).

nearby. Here, discounting plays a big role, due to the long-time horizon considered. A $1 million water supply built 250 years into the future and discounted at 3% (the rate used in the RIA) has a present discounted value of only $617! Table 10.5 reproduces the final net-benefit analysis:

Under the assumptions that (1) *all* benefits are captured by mitigating the effects on groundwater, and (2) the study's complex modeling process generates "precise" benefit and cost predictions, then by an efficiency standard, both policies are losers. Simply requiring landfills to monitor their discharges on an annual basis and comply with *existing* water laws costs $2.5 billion more than would simply supplying groundwater users with an uncontaminated supply. Moving to a pollution prevention strategy makes matters even worse.

Other benefits the EPA study mentions, but does not quantify, include reduced surface water contamination, avoidance of failures in groundwater monitoring and cleanup, existence value of groundwater, and increased public confidence in landfill siting. The latter could be quite important in the face of "Not in My Backyard" (NIMBY) movements opposing new landfill sites. The EPA study suggests an upper limit of $84 million per year in potential savings from expediting the site selection process.[9]

In addition to these unquantified benefits, the EPA further suggests that stricter regulation will have favorable equity implications. The EPA study is implicitly saying that *if* we set aside $270 million in the bank today as an **environmental bond,** we would have enough money to provide alternate water supplies for all those relying on water that becomes contaminated in the future. However, only this *potential* is revealed by the benefit-cost analysis. In actuality, no such payments are being proposed. Under these circumstances, a prevention strategy, first, avoids imposing high cleanup costs on future generations and, second, reduces the potential that a landfill will become a federal (taxpayers') burden. The authors, in effect, are suggesting that we weight the utility of (1) future victims and (2) taxpayers-at-large more heavily than the utility of local garbage producers alive today.

Of course, as in all moves toward efficiency, an alternative policy exists that could satisfy both equity and efficiency concerns: an environmental bond. One could tax solid waste disposal and set aside a fund equivalent to $270 million for building new water supplies. In this way, there would be no future victims, and federal dollars would not be committed to a cleanup. Additional money would still have to be spent for groundwater monitoring but none for cleanup.

TABLE 10.5   Marginal Analysis of Landfill Regulation (1988 $million)

Regulatory Scenario	*Total Cost Over Baseline*	*Groundwater Benefits Over Baseline*	*Net Benefits*
1. Pollute and Cleanup	$2,670	$120	−$2,550
2. Prevent Pollution	$5,770	$270	−$5,500

Note figures are based on one set of new landfills, 300-year period, 3% discount rate.
Source: U.S. Environmental Protection Agency (1991b).

[9]U.S. Environmental Protection Agency (1991b).

As a final point, the EPA study also makes a common double-counting error by suggesting the existence of another possible uncounted benefit of a stricter standard: limiting the impact on property values surrounding the landfill. Yet, property values fall due to perceived health concerns; this is the identical damage being measured by the cost of supplying an area with fresh water.

The two studies reviewed here are examples of "good" benefit-cost analysis. The authors work hard to clearly state and justify all assumptions; they also state what they view to be reasonable upper and lower bounds for their benefit and cost estimates. Nevertheless, in part because the EPA works with a limited budget, and in part because of the nature of benefit-cost analysis, it is still relatively easy to criticize the studies on their own terms.

Common pitfalls, even in sophisticated benefit-cost studies such as these, include double counting of either costs or benefits and reliance on benefit-cost ratios rather than maximum net benefits for project selection. More significantly, it is apparent that the precision presented by best-guess estimates such as those presented in Tables 10.4 and 10.5 is illusory. Given the unquantified benefits and the uncertainty associated with measuring both benefits and costs, dollar figures placed on net benefits or even the ranking of similar alternatives in terms of net benefits, are simply not reliable.

Most efficiency advocates accept this charge but still argue that efficiency as a goal makes sense and that benefit-cost analysis brings a useful light to bear on the policy decision-making process. Ultimately, what are the numbers in the lead and landfill studies telling us? In the case of lead, the EPA has identified many tangible benefits associated with restricting leachate from solder. A standard at least as stringent as option B is clearly justified following the efficiency logic. Sorting out A versus B is not really possible, but B relative to C is a good buy.

On the other hand, the EPA's recommended landfill rule or, indeed, requiring compliance with existing water laws, does not appear to be wise public policy *from an efficiency perspective.* The EPA analysts presumably thought hard about potential benefits of stricter landfill regulation. Clearly, some important benefits could not be quantified but, even if their benefit estimates were twenty times as large, the policy of relatively strict regulation would still be inefficient. When benefits outweigh costs by a margin large enough to subsume reasonable uncertainty, or *vice versa,* good benefit-cost studies can help us select the more efficient option if that, indeed, is our goal.

10.3 Political Influence in Benefit-Cost

One of the advantages of benefit-cost analysis, according to its advocates, is that it substantially reduces political influence in the policy arena. A naive claim in its favor is that benefit-cost analysis "allows the numbers to speak for themselves." In reality, as we have seen, if one tortures the numbers sufficiently, they will often confess to the analyst's viewpoint. The real advantage of benefit-cost analysis is that it places limits on the type of data torturing that can go on. For example, an economist may set out to prove that more stringent regulations of landfills are desirable on efficiency grounds. Within admittedly broad limits, however, her benefit and cost estimates are constrained by the methodology we have outlined in the last three chapters. It may well be that the numbers simply cannot credibly support her case.

How elastic are the bounds within which good benefit-cost studies must stay? This section will explore four ways in which political influence affects the benefit-cost process: through regulatory politics, agenda control, the hard numbers problem, and paralysis by analysis.

We can use the landfill RIA to examine how **regulatory politics** might influence the drafting of a benefit-cost study. The EPA's benefit-cost studies are reviewed by the Office of Management and Budget (OMB), which had an obvious deregulatory bias under the Reagan and Bush administrations. EPA administrators who were political appointees probably shared this general antiregulation conservative philosophy. Nevertheless, they presumably had no desire to forward regulatory proposals to OMB only to have them shot down. Therefore, the EPA benefit-cost analysts who actually prepared the report certainly faced some pressure, stated or unstated, from their superiors to generate numbers in support of their preferred rule. Yet such activities could not be done flagrantly since OMB, industry, and possibly environmental watchdog groups had their own economists reviewing the documents.

One might speculate on a political scenario underlying the landfill study. In the face of dramatic local public resistance to landfill siting, EPA officials probably felt originally that prevention-based regulation made sense. In its benefits analysis, EPA took the traditional cancers-reduced approach to measuring benefits; however, the results came out shockingly low. In the landfill report, the analysts chose *not* to monetize these benefits as they did for lead. The discounted benefits for the few lives saved by either policy option would have probably been under $10 million and would have looked downright silly against costs in the billions.

In what one might read as an attempt to boost the benefits, EPA took the somewhat unconventional step of measuring groundwater benefits in terms of replacement cost, in effect, assuming that society was interested in 100% safety. Still, the benefit numbers came out low. The final step was to (dramatically) reduce the cost estimates by revising the baseline assumptions (and reducing the regulatory requirements somewhat). Even here, as Table 10.5 shows, the numbers did not look good. After taking two not-unreasonable measures that improved the health-based net benefits measure, EPA still could not defend its preferred rule on a benefit-cost basis. Ultimately, the agency argued for the preferred rule based on the reasoning, not easily quantifiable, that a strict standard would lead to increased public confidence and facilitate the siting process and would be more equitable than a pollute and cleanup standard.

This purely speculative scenario suggests how regulatory politics might have influenced a benefit-cost process in subtle fashions. Another way that political decisions can affect a benefit-cost study is in its timing. The study may simply be put off until the important decisions have already been made. Thus, in spite of clear language direct from the U.S. President, which required the EPA to choose the most efficient option as identified by the RIA, it seems peculiar that in neither the lead nor the landfill case was this actually done. From an efficiency perspective, the lead decision generated "underregulation," in the landfill case "overregulation." In both cases, the estimated efficiency loss was around $3 billion.

According to one EPA source, the efficient outcome was not chosen, in part, because the benefit-cost process was not initiated until very late in the policy process. In other words, the timing of the benefit-cost studies insured that they did not have a major impact on the policy outcome.[10]

---

[10]Brett Snyder (personal communication).

Regulatory politics can clearly have an impact either on the underlying assumptions and presentation of an RIA or in the timing of the study. It is naive to believe that economists and engineers who work in regulatory agencies practice their craft in isolation from broader political forces. On the other hand, both the lead and landfill examples also make it clear that benefit-cost analysis is not wholly arbitrary. It is hard to justify the loose lead standard (option C) or *either* of the landfill options on efficiency grounds.

Given the fact that the "accepted methodology" puts some constraints on benefit-cost analysis, political influence shows up subtly in its impact on natural and social scientific debates. Corporate interests have used their resources to try and **control the scientific agenda** by funding conferences and targeting research in certain areas. For example, the American Paper Institute and the Chlorine Institute have aggressively promoted research downplaying the health effects of dioxin, a chemical used in these industries, while ignoring accumulating evidence to the contrary. The Chlorine Institute hosted a conference on dioxin, whose discussions it "then interpreted to suit its purposes," according to the *Wall Street Journal.*[11] Exxon sponsored a similar effort that many observers felt was aimed at discrediting the contingent valuation method of estimating existence value discussed in chapter 8. CV studies were being used to assess oil spill damages in the wake of the Exxon *Valdez* oil spill in 1989. And the Formaldehyde Institute has sponsored substantial research questioning the link between cancer in laboratory animals and in people.

The difference between the perspective of industry, government, and academic scientists is reflected in a poll showing that 80% of the first group, 63% of the second group, and only 40% of the last group believed that a threshold existed below which exposure to cancer-causing agents was risk-free.[12] Even academic scientists, however, must often obtain research funding from industry. In agriculture, for example, Curtis (1991) argues that industry funding sources dominate. Perhaps, for this reason, Cropper et al. (1991) report that academic scientists who commented on EPA pesticide benefit-cost studies generally supported the position of pesticide manufacturers.

In addition to regulatory politics and agenda control, benefit-cost studies have also been criticized for providing a false sense of precision to decision makers. This is known as the **hard numbers problem.** The apparently "hard" numbers in the summary tables for the two benefit-cost studies are really very soft when uncertainty and incomplete benefit coverage are factored in. Yet, decision makers are often not interested in "uncertainty" and incompleteness; they want an answer and often one that supports their particular political agenda. An appropriately crafted table like 10.4 or 10.5 fits this bill perfectly.

One EPA analyst revealed the kind of political pressure to produce hard numbers he faced when doing benefit-cost: "Recently, estimates of benefits and costs of alternative lead regulations were developed in order to promote one specific alternative. Discussions of the enormous uncertainties inherent in those estimates had no discernible

---

[11]"How Two Industries Created a Fresh Spin on the Dioxin Debate," *Wall Street Journal,* August 8, 1991.
[12]Greider (1992).

impact [on decision makers] until a graphical presentation was provided. While the presentation involved a degree of bureaucratic risk to the analyst, the significance of the uncertainty [was made apparent to decision makers]. . . . In passing, I note the risk to the analyst was realized [he was punished], but he slept better."[13]

Of course, plenty of "bad" benefit-cost studies step outside the accepted methodology. Washington, DC, is full of think tanks representing a variety of political viewpoints, all cranking out benefit-cost studies in support of their policy viewpoint. Many of these reports are poorly done, and yet, these hard numbers are widely reported and have an impact on policy decisions.

Finally, in the two cases we have considered here, regulators were not *required* to choose the option identified as most efficient by the benefit-cost analysis. In fact, in neither case did they do so. However, when an efficiency test is enshrined as law, opponents of regulation can resort to the legal system and exploit the uncertainty in the process to delay or block the implementation of regulations. This is known as **paralysis by analysis.**[14] Two major environmental statutes require regulations to pass an efficiency test—the Toxic Substances Control Act (TSCA) and the Federal Insecticide, Fungicide and Rodenticide Act (FIFRA).

Under TSCA, the EPA tried for over ten years to phase out the remaining uses of asbestos, a mineral product well-known to cause lung cancer. The two big uses left are in cement pipe and automobile brakes. In the early 1990s, an appeals court rejected EPA's proposed phaseout of these products on several grounds. Although EPA had in hand what it thought was a good benefit-cost study showing a substantial surplus of benefits over costs, the court ruled that EPA (1) had not adequately considered less costly alternatives, (2) had not adequately evaluated the environmental dangers of substitute products (non-asbestos brakes and piping), and (3) had not followed proper procedures for public comment on the dangers of asbestos.

Without dwelling on the merits of the case, it should be evident from this chapter that trying to "prove" in a court of law that any regulatory decision not only has positive net benefits but also is the *most* efficient option is a virtual impossibility. As a result of this decision, some have concluded that the provision for banning existing substances under TSCA is essentially unworkable.

In summary, politics clearly influences the benefit-cost process, just as it would any alternative decision-making tool. In spite of this, however, the benefit-cost methodology does provide a "consensus" framework for helping to judge the balance between measurable benefits and costs. There is such a thing as good benefit-cost. However, the only way to assure that the good benefit-cost is carried out is to assure adequate review of the study and opportunities for appeal by the affected parties. Given the technical nature of benefit-cost methodology, Campen (1986) has suggested that the government provide funds to community groups and others who seek to challenge government studies. Finally, legal standards that mandate efficiency are a poor idea on their own terms. Benefit-cost is just not capable of identifying efficient outcomes with a precision that can stand up in court.

---

[13]Schnare (1990: 151).
[14]Andrews (1984: 79).

10.4 Is Benefit-Cost Up to the Job?

In practice, benefit-cost analysis of pollution regulations should be evaluated on two grounds. First, given all its uncertainties and measurement problems, is it capable of identifying the efficient pollution level? Second, is efficiency (static or dynamic) in pollution control the right standard or are generally more stringent safety or ecological standards preferred? This section addresses the first question. We have already talked at length about the second.

Comparing costs and benefits when intangible factors such as human life and health dominate has been compared to the problem of "appraising the quality of a horse-and-rabbit stew, the [tiny] rabbit being cast as the consequences that can be measured and evaluated numerically, and the [gigantic] horse as the amalgam of external effects, social, emotional and psychological impacts and historical and aesthetic considerations that can be adjudged only roughly and subjectively. Since the horse [is] bound to dominate the flavor of the stew, meticulous evaluation of the rabbit would hardly seem worthwhile."[15]

One could argue that in the lead case analyzed above, where human life and health were indeed at stake, the RIA told us little that we did not already know. Given the well-known, adverse health impacts of lead alone, option C was not a realistic regulatory alternative. At the same time, promoting B over A was not a "scientific" decision, even within the logic of benefit-cost. The large "horse" of uncertainty in comparing these options was much bigger than the very small "rabbit" that could be assessed with any measure of scientific consensus.

On the other hand, the landfill RIA identified had surprisingly small health effects. As a result, a comparison of damaged groundwater with compliance costs appears to identify prevention-based or even pollute and cleanup regulation as inefficient. Even here, however, the study was unable to include a big part of the horse: difficult to measure benefits such as expedited landfill siting.

Clearly, benefit-cost analysis cannot pinpoint the efficient pollution level with the accuracy suggested by the diagrams in this book. Nevertheless, it does provide a framework for a general "balancing" of benefits against costs. In addition, and in particular, when the horse of intangible benefits does not become so large as to dominate the flavor of the benefit stew, benefit-cost analysis can be used to rank dissimilar proposals in terms of efficiency.

10.5 Summary

Lurking behind any benefit-cost study is the central question of this part of the book: Is the efficiency standard a good idea in environmental protection? We will return to this issue one more time in the next chapter. Let us here summarize the two cases just illustrated, focusing on a narrower question: Is benefit-cost a useful tool for identifying efficient outcomes?

In the lead case, option A was both the most efficient and safest of those considered. Here, a move in the direction of efficiency as identified by the benefit-cost study

---

[15]Cited in Dorfman (1965).

would also have been a move in the direction of safety and would, thus, have been good policy by both pollution standards considered in this book.

But the lead case also illustrates a serious bias that can arise in benefit-cost analysis: the tendency to ignore environmental benefits that cannot be monetized. In the lead RIA, the analysts themselves fell into the trap of believing that they had captured and were weighing "all" of the uncertainty in their summary diagram. In fact, most of the potential environmental benefits were not even considered in the final decision to choose option B. Ultimately, easy-to-measure costs weighed in more heavily than difficult-to-measure benefits.

Moving now to the landfill case, the practical effect of the RIA was to force EPA to think hard about the wisdom of requiring expensive preventive measures to attack very low-risk levels. In the initial stages of the RIA, more expensive options than the final rule were considered but rejected. Ultimately, the impact was to reduce the cost of the regulation for little, if any, sacrifice in benefits. In this case, the RIA generated movement from an extreme safety position in the direction of efficiency. However, due to uncertainty, unquantifiable benefits and equity concerns, the final option selected was much safer than efficiency. Paradoxically, in spite of the vastly greater complexity of the landfill problem, the RIA procedure was more useful in promoting a "balancing" of benefits and costs than in the narrowly defined lead case.

Is benefit-cost up to the job? Benefit-cost studies can identify more or less efficient options in a rough way, provided the differences in the net benefit figures are "big enough" to overcome all the associated uncertainty and incomplete coverage in the measurements.

APPLICATION 10.0

What's Wrong with This Picture?

As an aid to Governor Blabla, you are given the task of recommending whether or not the state should locate a low-level nuclear waste facility in a rural county. The nuclear industry provides you with a cost-benefit study it has conducted that gives you the following information:

COST-BENEFIT SUMMARY FOR PROPOSED WASTE FACILITY

Prepared by the Center for the Objective Study of Nuclear Issues

Conclusion: The project will result in net benefits of $3 billion, with a benefit-cost ratio of 13. While these figures, of course, depend on the assumptions of the study, the very large net benefit figure, along with the extraordinarily high benefit-cost ratio, both indicate that the project will remain attractive under most plausible assumptions. We, therefore, strongly recommend initiating the proposal.

Assumptions:

1. Discount rate of 10%.

2. Principal costs:
   a. worker exposure.
   b. risk of accidental exposure during transport.
   c. reduction to zero of the land value at the storage site.
   d. construction and maintenance.

3. Principal benefits:
   a. reduced exposure at current temporary storage sites.
   b. job creation—1,000 temporary, 200 permanent jobs.
   c. extends life of existing nuclear power plants by ten years.
      i. lower electricity costs for consumers
      ii. saves 7,000 jobs
   d. increased profits for local service industries.

Note: Benefits under point b. and cii. are given double weight, due to high unemployment in the county.

4. Risk Assessment:
   i. exposure/fatality assumptions from the U.S. Department of Energy.
   ii. probability of fatal exposure due to transport accident: 1/100,000,000 miles. Source: U.S. Department of Energy.
   iii. value of a statistical life: $1 million.

1. Do you believe the report?
2. See if you can find six separate problems with the study.

3. What further information you would like to have prior to making a recommendation to the governor?

Key Ideas in Each Section

10.0 To have a chance of identifying the efficient level of pollution, a **good benefit-cost study** is required. For major regulations, the EPA is required to do a benefit-cost study called a **Regulatory Impact Analyses (RIA),** though the results are not legally binding.

10.1 In the regulation of lead solder, many important potential health benefits of the regulation could not be quantified. In spite of this, **benefit-cost ratios** for all options were greater than one. However, the final choice of options could not be made on efficiency grounds, due to uncertainty. The lead case also illustrates that the most efficient option in a benefit-cost study will be the one maximizing **net monetary benefits.**

10.2 The landfill RIA highlights common difficulties in benefit-cost—**poor data, long-time horizons,** and **hard-to-quantify benefits.** In spite of this, because so few people are likely to be affected by contaminated groundwater in the vicinity of landfills, the measurable benefits of strict regulation are likely to be small. Nevertheless, the EPA chose to balance fairness to those likely to be affected, as well as to future taxpayers, against efficiency, and chose an inefficient, prevention-oriented strategy. Note that an **environmental bond** policy could have satisfied both fairness and efficiency concerns.

10.3 Benefit-cost is not immune from political influence. This section examined the impact of **regulatory politics, agenda control, the hard numbers problem,** and **paralysis by analysis.** However, any decision-making tool will be subject to political influence. The advantage of benefit-cost is that it sets up rules that define, in a more-or-less objective way, a good study.

10.4 Benefit-cost is most useful for identifying efficient options when hard-to-quantify benefits, such as lives lost or ecosystems destroyed, do not dominate the horse-and-rabbit stew of benefits. One example would be the landfill case. Under these circumstances, clear differences between options, based on net monetary gain, are most likely to emerge.

References

Andrews, Richard N. L. (1984). "Environmental Decisions, Past and Present." In *Environmental Policy Under Reagan's Executive Order,* ed. V. Kerry Smith. Chapel Hill, NC: University of North Carolina Press.

Campen, James (1986). *Benefit-Cost and Beyond.* Cambridge, MA: Ballinger.

Cropper, Maureen L., William N. Evans, Stephen J. Berardi, Maria M. Ducla-Soares and Paul R. Portney (1991). "The Determinants of Pesticide Regulation: A Statistical Analysis of EPA Decisionmaking." *Discussion Paper CRM 91-01.* Washington, DC: Resources for the Future.

Curtis, Jennifer (1991). *Harvest of Hope: The Potential of Alternative Agriculture to Reduce Pesticide Use.* San Francisco, CA: Natural Resources Defense Council.

Dorfman, Robert (ed.) (1978). *Measuring Benefits of Government Investments.* Washington, DC: Brookings.

Fraas, Arthur G. (1984). "Benefit-Cost Analysis for Environmental Regulation." In *Environmental Policy Under Reagan's Executive Order,* ed. V. Kerry Smith. Chapel Hill, NC: University of North Carolina Press.

Goodstein, Eban (1995). "Benefit-Cost at the EPA." *Journal of Social Economics,* 24, no. 2, 375–389.

Greider, William (1992). *Who Will Tell the People?* New York: Simon & Schuster.

National Research Council (1991). *Environmental Epidemiology: Public Health and Hazardous Wastes.* Washington, DC: National Academy Press.

Office of Technology Assessment (1989). *Facing America's Trash: What Next for Municipal Solid Waste?* Washington, DC: U.S. GPO.

Portney, Paul (1995) "Chain Saw Surgery." *The Washington Post,* January 15, 1995, p. C3.

Schnare, David W. (1990). "Raid on Sanity: Policy and Economic Analysis of Radionucleide Removal From Drinking Water." In *Radon, Radium and Uranium in Drinking Water,* eds. C. Richard Cothern and Paul Rebers. Chelsea, MI: Lewis Publishers.

U.S. Environmental Protection Agency (1991a). *Final Regulatory Impact Analysis of National Primary Drinking Water Regulations for Lead and Copper.* Washington, DC: U.S. EPA, Office of Drinking Water.

U.S. Environmental Protection Agency (1991b). *Addendum to the Regulatory Impact Analysis for the Final Criteria for Municipal Solid Waste Landfills.* Washington, DC: U.S. EPA, Regulatory Analysis Branch, Office of Solid Waste.

U.S. Environmental Protection Agency (1990). *Regulatory Impact Analysis for the Final Criteria for Municipal Solid Waste Landfills.* Washington, DC: U.S. EPA, Regulatory Analysis Branch, Office of Solid Waste.

11

Is More Really Better? Consumption and Welfare

11.0 Introduction

Item: The typical American family owns "twice as many cars, drives two-and-a-half times as far, uses 21 times as much plastic, and travels 25 times as far by air as did their parents in 1950."[1]

Progress, or overconsumption?

The last three chapters have explored the mechanics of measuring the benefits and costs of environmental protection, and of weighing the one against the other. Within this efficiency framework, there is simply no room for the concept of "overconsumption." The whole point of doing a benefit-cost study, after all, is to insure that we do not sacrifice too much consumption in pursuit of environmental quality. From an efficiency perspective, our generation's increase in consumption over what our parents enjoyed clearly reflects progress.

How then can overconsumption be viewed as an environmental problem? First, consumption (or affluence) crops up in the IPAT equation from chapter 7:

$$\text{environmental } \mathbf{I}\text{mpact} = \mathbf{P}\text{opulation} * \mathbf{A}\text{ffluence} * \mathbf{T}\text{echnology}$$

IPAT suggests that one of the three main causes of environmental decline is the growth in the consumption of material goods. Why? From an ecological perspective, pessimism is in order about the possibility for technological progress to keep up with the pace of consumption (and population) growth. Thus, for ecologicals, the fact that consumption levels are high and growing gets translated into overconsumption as a serious environmental problem. Efficiency advocates, by contrast, are technological optimists, and so do not view consumption itself as a serious issue.

[1]Durning (1991: 156–158).

If, as ecologicals believe, technological progress cannot offset the environmental impact of a quadrupling of consumption over the next fifty years, then this is one sense in which overconsumption is indeed a major environmental issue. But this chapter focuses on a second argument against high consumption. It does so by questioning a key assumption of the efficiency standard and benefit-cost analysis: "More is better."

Recall that our target of an efficient outcome was defined as one in which it is impossible to make one person better off without making someone else worse off. In practice, "better off" means "having more goods." We should remember that goods can include environmental amenities, like hikes in the mountains, nice views, or clean air, but these are considered by benefit-cost economists to simply be goods that are literally exchangeable for hair conditioners, air conditioners, or video games. They are exchangeable because having more of one of these goods means having less of another. This in turn means they can ultimately be valued in monetary terms, if only indirectly, along the lines spelled out in chapter 8.

But what if more isn't really better? If material gain in fact does not lead to greater happiness, then efficient outcomes do not really increase welfare. If more isn't better, then the trade-off identified by benefit-cost analysis—more environmental protection means less of all other stuff—loses much of its force, and safety or ecological sustainability goals make more sense. Finally, if more isn't better, then it is certainly fair to say that society is "overconsuming" resources.

11.1 Money and Happiness

One crude but accurate way to state the more is better assumption underlying benefit-cost analysis is that "Money buys happiness." Does it? According to Jesus, Poor Richard, and a recent fortune cookie, the answer is no. However, let's take a look at the more scientific findings of survey researchers (polltakers) on this issue.

For over two decades, researchers have been asking groups of people about the relationship between income and happiness in their lives. The results of many studies in America and western Europe reveal a strikingly similar conclusion: Money buys very little happiness, and it does so at a decreasing rate. Table 11.1 shows the results from a ten-nation European survey, including over 15,000 people between 1981 and 1983. These figures are typical of those found in most other studies and illustrate what has been called the **Easterlin paradox.**[2]

Rising income is clearly correlated with increased life satisfaction only up to around the median income, and the poorest people in a nation are only a bit less happy than the richest. About one in five poor people consider themselves very happy; this figure rises only to around one in four for the wealthiest 25% of the population. Living amongst riches rather than rags is by no means a guaranteed road to happiness.

Moreover, among western countries, people in wealthier nations often report being less happy than those in poorer ones. Ireland, for example, with one third of the per capita income of the United States, ranks consistently higher on the life satisfaction scale.[3]

---

[2]After his seminal article (1974).

[3]There are substantial intercountry differences. The French, for example, claim to be much less happy than the Belgians. Researchers conclude that this in part reflects social norms about reporting life satisfaction.

TABLE 11.1   Income and Reported Happiness

Income Quartile	Percent "Satisfied" or "Very Satisfied" with Life as a Whole	Percent "Very Happy"
Lowest Quartile	70%	19%
Second Quartile	78	22
Third Quartile	82	25
Highest Quartile	85	28
Income Refused or Don't Know	83	27

Source: Ronald Ingelhart and Jacques-Rene Rabier (1986:23), "Aspirations Adapt to Situations—But Why Are the Belgians So Much Happier than the French?" in *Research on the Quality of Life* (Ann Arbor: University of Michigan Press). Reprinted by permission.

Or, consider the same issue from another angle. As noted by psychologist Paul Wachtel, the 1960s are often remembered as a decade of relative affluence, while the 1970s are viewed in retrospect as a period of increasing economic hardship. And yet, from 1970 to 1979 there was an increase of "approximately 37% in the proportion of homes with air conditioners, a 62% increase in the proportion with dishwashers, a 38% increase for clothes dryers, a 43% increase for home freezers, a 24% increase for clothes washers, and an increase of 111% in the proportion of homes with color television sets."[4] The percentage of the U.S. population reporting themselves to be "very happy" has remained roughly constant since 1957, despite personal consumption expenditures per capita having roughly doubled.[5]

Why is it that money doesn't buy much happiness, and only does so up to a point? We will consider two answers to this question, the first rooted in the psychology of consumption, the second in the material realities of modern life.

11.2 Social Norms and the Rat Race

I have an eleven-year-old friend, who recently reported to his mother that he wanted a pair of brightly colored, baggy pants manufactured by a company called Skidz. These pants were retailing for $34, and so his mother was a bit reluctant to buy him the pants. She offered to make him a pair that looked and felt identical, figuring she could do that for as little as $10. "No way," said her son. The homemade pair would not have the Skidz label on the back and that was really what made them *cool.* She asked him if he really wanted her to spend $24 for a label, and he said without hesitation, "Yes."

In our affluent society, access to food and shelter sufficient for *basic* survival is widely, though not universally, available.[6] Under these circumstances, much consumption of goods and services takes on a profoundly "social" character. The utilitarian value of the Skidz pants—their warmth, comfort, and cheerfulness—was much less important to my friend than the fact that they were "way cool." Along the same lines, the pleasure felt by the owner of an expensive sports car lies not only in the excite-

[4]Wachtel (1983).
[5]The quote and statistical citation are from Durning (1991: 156–158).
[6]The increasing visibility of the homeless and the growth in demand at soup kitchens in our country reminds us of the severity of this problem.

ment of fast driving but also and perhaps more importantly in the image of a fast-driving man the car provides to both the owner and others.

The social norms that we satisfy through our consumption are established in the communities in which we seek membership and recognition. The type of community may range from a romantic community of two, to the nuclear or extended family, to a circle of friends, to a neighborhood, to a religious or ethnic group, to a union or professional organization, but the need to belong to at least one of these groups is a powerful motivating force. Critics of growth argue that much of our consumption—from the clothes we wear, to the food we eat, to the cars we drive—is geared not only or even primarily to attain physical warmth, nourishment, comfort, or transportation, but rather to attain membership and recognition in one of these communities.

The point here is *not* to pass a value judgment on this process in which we all participate. Rather, the idea of consumption norms simply explains the observation that money fails to buy much happiness. On the one hand, greater income increases access to intrinsically useful goods and services. On the other, as people grow wealthier the expectations of the community rise, and keeping up with social consumption norms becomes more costly.

One can divide the social motives for consumption into three rough categories: bandwagon, snob, and Veblen effects.[7] **Bandwagon effects** refer to a desire to consume something because others are as well, in order to conform to a social norm. Television commercials frequently play on the bandwagon effect. McDonald's recently ran a campaign advertising "Food, Folks and Fun." The message was clear: Come on down and join the party, and incidentally, you can eat here too.

At the same time, Burger King was trying to set itself off from the crowd with its slogan: "Sometimes, You Gotta Break the Rules." The appeal here was to the **snob effect**—the desire to do or consume something because others aren't. The snob effect is usually attributed to those buying expensive products to differentiate themselves from the common herd. But the sentiment may also be exploited, as in the Burger King case, to sell the humble hamburger. Or to take another example, it can be seen in the college professor who takes pride in driving a beat-up car to show that he, unlike the rest of the world, does not care about material goods. The desire for Skidz pants expressed by my friend's son showed both bandwagon and snob influences—they were cool both because cool people were wearing them and because uncool people were not.

The words "bandwagon" and "snob" are perhaps poorly chosen, because they have rather negative connotations. But the desire to join in and the desire to be different in fact reflect quite normal, universal, and important social drives. For example, the desire to "get ahead" in any pursuit—sport, music, science—reflects both the snob effect (get ahead of one's peer group) and the bandwagon effect (become like those who are already ahead).

The final social motive underlying consumption is named for Thorstein Veblen, an economist who argued that status could often be achieved in our society through the open display of wealth, what he termed "conspicuous consumption."[8] The **Veblen**

---

[7]Leibenstein (1950). Bagwell and Bernheim (1996) explore the microfoundations of Veblen-type consumption decisions in a signaling context.
[8]For a recent reformulation, see Bagwell and Bernheim (1996).

effect is the purchase of expensive goods in order to illustrate to the community that the owner is a person of "substance"—that is, someone with money and the power that money brings. Its purpose is to elicit envious statements like"He wears a Rolex" or "She drives a BMW" or "He belongs to the High Society Country Club." Part of the "coolness" of Skidz pants was certainly their high price—wearing them said to the rest of the kids in the class: "My parents have got the power to get me what I want, even if it costs a lot of money." While the Veblen effect is related to the snob effect, the two are not identical. Veblen goods hold appeal primarily because their expense denotes membership in a certain social class; as noted, the definition of a snob good varies from consumer to consumer and need not involve expensive goods.

To the extent that material consumption is not geared to utilitarian functions but is rather a means to an end of satisfying social needs for membership and status in a community, it is not surprising that attaining more material goods fails to increase happiness to any significant degree. Among both poor and rich, bandwagon and snob effects will greatly influence the degree of satisfaction obtained from consumption. Whether it is the right sound system to impress your friends, the right bike for joining a motorcycle gang, the right T-shirt to wear to a party, the right beer to serve at a cookout, the right restaurant to please your sweetheart, the right suit to keep your job, the right school for your children, or the right street address to get into a particular golf foursome, membership and recognition in the community is an important by-product of consumption. As people get wealthier, "basic" needs multiply; in other words, it costs more to satisfy social norms.

Having said that, it is clear that many people do *want* more material things. One of my early purchases out of graduate school was a dishwasher. I wanted it in part for its utilitarian nature—I'm lukewarm about washing dishes by hand. On the other hand, and more importantly, I needed it because of the increasing time pressure from my job. As a graduate student, I could take the time to wash the family dishes. The social need satisfied by the dishwasher was the "freedom" it gave me to work harder so as to maintain my status (and income) in the professorial world. The desire for more can thus be explained in part by the wish to "get ahead" in the social world. It may also be due to in part to the Veblen effect, the desire to possess the symbols of power in our society for their own sake. While I don't show my dishwasher off to friends, the fact that it is there in my kitchen brings me some satisfaction (or relief) that I've made it into the upper middle class.

And indeed, survey research reveals that "getting ahead" in terms of income is clearly correlated with increases in reported life satisfaction. While rich people are on average only a bit happier than poor people, people who have *recently* gotten richer are much more satisfied with their lives than people who have *recently* gotten poorer. Social satisfaction from consumption apparently requires not just keeping up but getting ahead of "the Joneses." *Exceeding* the consumption norms established by one's peer group, family, and personal expectations appears to be the material route to happiness.[9]

However, while "getting ahead" may make sense from the individual perspective, competitive consumption is a strategy that yields much smaller benefits to individuals when pursued at society-wide level. If everyone is racing for entry into the next highest social group, it becomes much harder to get there; and for every winner in the

---

[9]These ideas are developed further in Mishan (1968), Scitovsky (1986), Daly (1987), and Schor (1991).

race, there will be losers. Moreover, everyone now needs to run harder just to stay in the same place.

The common name for this kind of situation is a **rat race.** The two distinguishing features of a rat race are that (1) everyone would be better off if the race was canceled, and (2) given that everyone else is racing, each individual is better off trying to win.

This situation can be analyzed through the so-called **prisoner's dilemma** model. (Suggestion: Stall your class by asking your professor to explain the name "prisoner's dilemma.") Figure 11.1 illustrates the situation facing two students, Arnold and Maria, who have been asked to bring soft drinks to a party. Each student can choose to bring either Coca-Cola or budget cola. For the purposes of argument, assume that the quality of the products are identical—blindfolded, people on average don't prefer one to the other. (Suggestion: Stall your class by bringing in supplies for a demonstration taste test.) But Coke, given its large advertising budget, has developed some name recognition.

Suppose that the initial social norm among the students is to drink the budget brand. If both parties then go for the budget brand, nobody is embarrassed by bringing a product perceived to be cheap. As a result, the utility of both students is 10. This is clearly preferred to an outcome in which the social norm is to buy Coca-Cola— since the quality is the same, and the cost is higher. As a result, the Coke-Coke outcome yields utility of only 8 to each student.

But in this setup, it will be hard to maintain budget-budget choices as the social norm. Consider what happens if Arnold goes budget while Maria shells out for Coke. Maria receives (subtle) praise for exceeding the social norm, so her utility rises to 12, while Arnold is (quietly) shamed and finds his utility falling to 7. The same holds true in reverse if Maria buys budget while Arnold goes with Coke.

While both parties would prefer the budget-budget outcome, both have strong incentives to "cheat" on any informal agreement to maintain the budget-brand social norm. If on the one hand, Maria chooses budget, Arnold can gain at Maria's expense by exceeding the social norm and going for Coke. If on the other hand, Maria exceeds the norm, Arnold is better off defending himself by doing the same. Regardless of what choice Maria makes, Arnold is better off choosing Coca-Cola, and vice versa.

Landers et al. (1996) identify a real-world prisoner's dilemma operating in professional organizations. They find in a survey of legal firms that attorneys are "over-

FIGURE 11.1 The Rat Race as a Prisoner's Dilemma

		Maria	
		Coke	Budget
Arnold	Coke	$U_M = 8$ $U_A = 8$	$U_M = 7$ $U_A = 12$
	Budget	$U_M = 12$ $U_A = 7$	$U_M = 10$ $U_A = 10$

U_M = Maria's Utility
U_A = Arnold's Utility

worked" in the sense that they would like to trade increases in income for time off. But publicly, lawyers are afraid to admit their desire for shorter hours, fearing that this will signal to partners that they are unproductive (even if they are not). As a result, the social norm for hours worked is too high—everyone would be made better off if a lower-standard workweek could be agreed on and enforced. This change in norms would scale back the rat race, lowering both incomes and material consumption, while raising leisure time.[10]

By framing the rat race as a prisoner's dilemma, we can see how social consumption norms get ratcheted upward. A rat race will often emerge whenever people send social signals through their consumption or workplace behavior, and especially when bandwagon, snob, or Veblen effects dominate the motives underlying the desire for more material goods. And, if the social satisfaction obtained from material gain is indeed dependent on surpassing one's neighbors, economic growth simply cannot quench the social desires that people attempt to satisfy through increased consumption.

11.3 Positional Goods and Consumption Externalities

One reason that money does not seem to buy much happiness is because of the social psychology of consumption. However, another reason is rooted in the realities of modern-day growth. One of the paradoxes of our affluent society is that, even as we grow wealthier, access to certain goods becomes more and more difficult. Consider the widespread shortage of "affordable housing" in the United States. In the 1970s, when median family income was about the same in real terms as it is today, the average mortgage payment on a house was about 18% of family income. Now it is 30% or higher, effectively putting home ownership out of the reach of an increasing number of Americans.

Paradoxically, the housing shortage is occurring at the same time that many cities face massive vacancy rates: Boarded-up buildings are a common sight in many of our cities. The shortage is clearly not one of housing units but rather of units in "desirable" neighborhoods: ones that are prosperous and safe, and have good schools. However, housing in desirable neighborhoods is a good for which there is either a fixed or at least very inelastic long-run supply. Thus, one effect of the massive "suburbanization of America" that has been occurring over the last forty years has been to drive up the price of housing within the commuting shadow of all major cities. At the same time, these areas developed many of the urban problems that people were attempting to leave behind: increasing congestion, traffic jams, longer commuting time, higher crime rates, and in general a lower quality of life for residents. Simultaneously, citizens left behind in the inner city have seen their communities deteriorate drastically as members of the middle class fled to the suburbs, shrinking the tax base of the cities.

Driving this process has been increased private demand for "better housing."[11] While many individuals did get such housing, the social outcome was less positive. The limited supply of this good in the suburbs was rationed through both higher prices

---

[10]The authors frame their argument in a signaling context. The key assumptions are that the pool of professionals reap spillover benefits from having more productive team members, and that long hours are a signal for high productivity. For more on overwork, see Schor (1991) and Application 11.1 below.

[11]In the 1980s, this demand came primarily from those in the top 20% of the income distribution who did see large increases in family income over the period.

and increased congestion. Concurrently, property values in the cities plummeted, and the quality of life for many residents there has become increasingly desperate. Two economic concepts help explain this phenomenon: positional competition and consumption externalities.

Goods with a fixed or inelastic long-run supply, like uncrowded suburbs within an easy commute to the city, are referred to as **positional goods. Positional competition** is the competition for these goods. Some simple examples of positional goods are fifty-yard-line Super Bowl tickets, Rembrandt paintings, or spacious, seaside vacation homes. Less obvious examples include commuter highways, slots in prestigious four-year colleges, creative work, jobs with status and authority, green space in the city, accessible wilderness, and clean air and water.

As people grow wealthier, the demand for these positional goods increases. In the face of this growing demand, some rationing scheme is necessary. For privately owned goods, say football tickets, the price rises to eliminate the excess demand and clear the market. For many **public goods,** however, the price mechanism is ineffective. Here the rationing takes place through congestion, for example, as seen in traffic jams.

Higher relative prices for positional goods combined with increasing congestion in their consumption has generated a degradation in the quality of life for many people, at the same time that the per capita consumption of TVs, dishwashers, camcorders, private planes, fast-food outlets, computers, pain relievers, and a million other commodities has increased. To obtain access to many of the goods that people took for granted only a generation ago, we must either pay a higher proportion of our income or accept a degradation in quality. This is not to say that economic growth has been on the balance, negative. The point is that increased positional competition generates an important and often unrecognized cost of economic growth.

Hirsch (1976) likens positional competition to a concert hall, where the individuals in the front row stand up to get a better view, and then everyone in the entire arena has to stand. Eventually, everyone is uncomfortably up on their tiptoes, but no one can see any better than they could while sitting down! Once again, getting ahead makes sense from an individual perspective, but the social result is to leave everyone worse off.

Positional competition often generates **consumption externalities.** These are benefits and costs of consumption not borne by the consumer—in Hirsch's example, blocking a neighbor's view. Or consider the private decision to commute by car. Although it may save twenty minutes of the driver's time, it also reduces the speed at which others can get to work by contributing to traffic jams. More generally, the cumulative effect of thousands of private decisions to move to the suburbs is to introduce many of the problems of the city: increasingly depersonalized communities, deteriorating schools, rising crime rates, and environmental degradation.

Positive consumption externalities, on the other hand, play an important role in creating a livable neighborhood. For example, if a neighbor keeps up his house and yard in an attractive fashion, it increases the value of the surrounding property. Sociologist William Julius Wilson has argued that many of the problems facing inner-city minority teenagers, from unemployment to drug abuse, stem from the lack of a vital positive externality—middle-class role models among their neighbors.[12]

---

[12]Wilson (1987).

Consumption externalities are important in other markets beside housing. An individual's decision regarding educational attainment has important externalities, both positive and negative. On the one hand, there is such a clear social benefit to having a populace able to read and write that all agree the government must subsidize and indeed mandate a basic education. On the other hand, advanced education is in many respects a type of positional competition. One's decision to obtain a master's degree in business administration increases one's chance of getting a scarce "prestige" job, but at the same time decreases the chances of those without the degree. "Credentials inflation"—the competitive process by which degree requirements for entry into a given career are ratcheted upward—is a negative consumption externality.

Pure positional competition is what economists call a **zero-sum game.** For every person who gains access to a positional good, someone else must give it up. As positional goods become more important in our economy, increases in income channeled into this competition fail to be translated into overall increases in human welfare. This holds doubly true when consumption decisions bear important negative externalities, as in the cases of housing and advanced education.[13] These two factors help explain the paradox that although individuals act rationally to increase their wealth, collectively we fail to grow much happier.

11.4 Welfare with Social Consumption

It is useful to recast the arguments of the preceding section into our utility/social welfare function framework. To do so requires that we divide up each individual's consumption bundle into **competitive** and **noncompetitive** elements, X^c, X^{nc}. The former contains (1) rat race items—those that bring utility primarily because their consumption involves exceeding social norms; (2) positional goods; and (3) goods with significant negative consumption externalities. The noncompetitive bundle includes everything else: goods consumed primarily for their intrinsic utility (taste, warmth, relaxation); leisure time spent with family and friends; physically or intellectually challenging activities; and many environmental goods such as clean air, water, and health.

In practice, this competitive/noncompetitive distinction may be a difficult one to make. Under which category does bike riding fit? The biking experience itself is very noncompetitive, and yet some of the pleasure serious enthusiasts feel for the sport is driven by competitive social norms—wearing the latest clothing or owning the most up-to-date machine. Yet in principle it is possible to sort out the consumption components that are fashion- or status-driven from the consumption components of the sport itself.

By doing so, we can rewrite Aldo's utility function as:

$$U_A = U(\overset{+}{X_A^{nc}}, \overset{+}{X_A^c}, \overset{-}{X_{NA}^c})$$

The last term, X_{NA}^c, stands for the competitive consumption bundle of all people who are Not Aldo (*NA*); the negative sign above X_{NA}^c indicates that Aldo's happiness *decreases* as the social consumption of others goes up. Aldo still gets happier by increas-

---

[13]Of course, advanced education can have positive consumption externalities as well. Improvements in technology resulting from advanced training are the most obvious example.

ing his consumption of both noncompetitive X_A^{nc} and competitive goods X_A^c; more remains better for Aldo as an individual. But his overall happiness now depends on the consumption levels of his peer group.

There are two lessons to be learned from this form of the utility function. The first is that economic growth that increases the supply of competitive consumption goods need not increase happiness (though it may). Every time that one person gets ahead, a new standard is set for the community. Indeed, competitive consumption goods are often sold by making people who don't buy the product feel worse off! (Consider, for example, the typical deodorant campaign that exploits insecurities about being left out and unhappy.)

The second lesson is that, under this form of the utility function, increases in the stock of noncompetitive consumption goods unambiguously raise social welfare. Many if not most environmental "goods"—human health, appreciation of natural beauty, respect for both human and nonhuman life—are primarily noncompetitive. One person's enjoyment of his health does not "raise the standard" that others must aspire to. Similarly, land set aside for parks is land not available for private development as part of status-enhancing positional competition. Thus a case can be made for weighting these items more heavily than material consumption in a social welfare function.

What implications does this have for "efficient" pollution control? Howarth (1996) shows that when status effects are important in an economy, taxes on the consumption of status goods are efficient: That is, they increase overall well-being (by increasing time off from work). They also thereby reduce production and thus pollution.

To summarize: If social norms drive much material consumption, and positional goods and consumption externalities are relatively important in the economy, a strong utilitarian argument can be made for environmental protection. The happiness trade-off between environmental protection and economic growth is not as great as it seems.

As discussed in chapter 6, economists have in fact made several attempts to construct a social welfare index that reflects some of the disamenities of economic growth. The idea is to adjust our basic measure of economic growth—gross domestic product (GDP)—to better capture the "true" trend in social welfare over the last few decades. If you turn back to Table 6.3, you will find several different measures of the trend in net national welfare.

In Table 6.3, the Daly and Cobb study of the United States is unique because it does account for the negative consumption externalities arising from positional goods discussed in this chapter. For example, in addition to the conventional externality costs, the authors deduct from augmented GDP the costs of urbanization, increased commuting time, and auto accidents. They also subtract the rising price of land and a percentage of educational expense, viewing these as positional goods. Finally, the authors deduct the value of national advertising, arguing that it is essentially information-free, and thus not welfare enhancing.

Many assumptions go into constructing such an index, just as they do for the conventional growth measure, GDP. Yet Daly and Cobb argue that their measure does a better job illustrating what kind of progress we in fact are making. While recognizing that their results are tentative, the authors argue that since 1970, the growth rate in sustainable economic welfare has fallen dramatically and actually has become negative in recent years, even while GNP growth has been relatively constant.

Daly and Cobb arrive at this conclusion considering primarily the effects of externalities in production and consumption. For purposes of the index, they accept the conventional assumption that "more is better": "Our calculus of economic well-being has failed to take into account that happiness is apparently correlated with relative rather than absolute levels of wealth or consumption. Having more is less important than having more than the 'Joneses.' Yet in the absence of any way to quantify this sense of relative well-being, we have ignored this important finding in our index, just as others have."[14] If they had devised such a measure, it seems likely that net national welfare would have increased even less than they estimate over the past forty years, despite the tremendous growth in GDP.

11.5 Controlling the Impact of Consumption

A society in which consumption becomes the primary means of achieving social status is known as a **consumer culture.** The reasons for the advance of the consumer culture in rich countries are complex, ranging from factors as diverse as the increasing mobility of both workers and jobs and the subsequent breakdown in community, increasing exposure to television and advertising, and a decline in the moral influence of religion, which traditionally preached an antimaterialistic message.

Some people have argued that as environmental awareness spreads, people in wealthy countries can be persuaded to abandon their affluent lifestyles, and begin, for example, riding bikes to work. Yet, the advance of the consumer culture appears to be pervasive and very deep-seated. I see it best through a comparison of generational attitudes. I admit to being a bit shocked when I asked my six-year-old niece why she wouldn't let me cut the huge L.A. Gear tag off her new tennis shoes. "That's what makes them cool," she said. My young niece's strong brand identification—the shoes made her happy *because* of the label—was the result of a shift in marketing strategy by clothing firms. When I was small, firms marketed children's clothes to their parents, and the emphasis was on rugged and practical. Now Saturday morning cartoons are filled with clothing ads targeted directly at children, with the emphasis on beauty and status. My parents, of course, had much less exposure to marketing and find my attachment to many of our family gadgets a bit puzzling.

Thus, even if you believe that high levels of consumption in affluent countries are a major environmental threat, it is hard to imagine making much headway against the consumer culture via moral arguments alone. This section discusses two potential *economic* instruments for reducing consumption: **consumption taxes** and the **regulation of advertising.**

From the IPAT equation we know that the environmental impact of consumption can be reduced either by reducing consumption directly or by cleaning up the technology associated with producing and delivering consumption goods. The second strategy appears more attractive, both because it seems to entail less sacrifice and because it can accommodate the increasing demands of poor countries for a higher material standard of living. But in fact, as we shall see in this section, developing cleaner technologies also requires reducing consumption today in order to finance investment in research and development.

---

[14]Daly and Cobb (1989: 415).

Many economists have argued for nonenvironmental reasons that the U.S. consumption rate is too high, or equivalently, that the national savings and investment rate is too low. During the 1980s, national savings declined from around 8% to 2.4% of net national product, while the foreign debt skyrocketed. The argument is made that for the last decade and a half, we have been financing current consumption at the expense of investment in created capital, which in the words of economist William Nordhaus portends a "decline in living standards for the future."[15] Nordhaus makes, in effect, a nonenvironmental sustainability argument for reducing current consumption.

Nordhaus and others have called for an increase in taxes (income or sales) to reduce consumption and increase savings and investment. The ultimate purpose, however, is to *boost* consumption in the future. This is clearly not the policy goal proposed here. Yet, if the revenues from such a tax were invested in the generation of new, clean technologies, such as those discussed in chapters 18 and 19, this kind of policy could achieve the goal of reducing the environmental *impact* of consumption. This would be true despite the fact that consumption levels themselves had only temporarily declined.

Alternatively, taxes could be used to divert resources away from consumption in rich countries to sustainable development efforts in poor countries. Funds could be used for a variety of purposes, from debt relief, to family planning, to land reform or resource protection efforts, to transferring clean energy and manufacturing technologies to poor countries.

It is sometimes argued that high levels of consumption are necessary for a modern economy to operate, and that a reduction in consumption would lead to high levels of long-run unemployment. Does such a consumption-employment link exist? Not in the long run. For example, the Japanese have a much higher savings rate (lower consumption rate) than we do, and yet have had not major unemployment problems. How can this be true? As suggested above, reductions in consumption will be matched by increased spending elsewhere, which also employs people.

For example, assume the government raises $100 million in taxes to pay for condoms for use in the developing world. In this case, the $100 million fall in consumption is made up for by an increase in spending in the birth control industry. Intuitively, as jobs are lost in the tourism industry (consumption), they are added in the manufacturing of new birth control devices. While short-run unemployment may increase, in the long run workers will be able to find new jobs.[16]

The point here is that *consumption reductions* in rich countries need not imply *output or employment reductions*. Rather, the drop in consumption can be matched by an increase in consumption in poor countries, which can provide jobs in rich countries. (Such an increase in consumption in poor countries is desirable on environmental grounds for the reasons discussed in the last part of this book.) Or consumption reductions may be matched by an increase in savings and investment in rich countries, which also provide employment. If this investment is focused in the direction of developing clean technologies, then the goal of reducing the environmental impact of

[15]Nordhaus (1989). The existence of the savings rate decline has been challenged by, among others, Blecker (1990), who is nevertheless still worried about inadequate investment.

[16]For a more involved discussion of the business-cycle macroeconomic impacts of consumption-reducing tax increases, see Nordhaus (1989) and Moore (1990). The former concurs with this analysis; the latter presents a less optimistic, post-Keynesian rejoinder.

consumption will have been achieved, despite the fact that overall consumption in the affluent country declines only temporarily.

Finally, in rich countries, social consumption theory has a rather startling implication: Beyond an initial adjustment period, in which people lowered their expected consumption levels, a shift of resources from current consumption to investment or development assistance would not reduce overall social happiness or welfare.

Put in more practical terms, suppose that income taxes in the United States were raised gradually in a progressive fashion, so that ultimately the highest group faced a marginal tax rate of 50%, while poor Americans maintained the same tax rate. Suppose as well that the additional money raised was diverted to investment in environmental technology: to the training of scientists and engineers, and to research and development. Social consumption theory says that in the long run, on average, people would be just as content. (Incidentally, wealthy Americans did pay a 70% marginal tax rate or higher throughout the 1950s, 1960s, and 1970s.) The problem with this theory, of course, is that there is an initial adjustment period in which people are dissatisfied. Given this, the political prospects for new taxes to promote sustainability—either environmental or economic—are not favorable. For example, President Clinton's energy tax proposal of 1993, which targeted deficit reduction, was watered down to a small increase in the gasoline tax. Even then, it passed by a very narrow margin.

Beyond taxes, a second possible strategy for controlling consumption is to regulate advertising. For such a strategy to make sense, one must first make the case that advertising in fact raises aggregate consumption levels. It is possible that advertising merely causes people to switch brands, leading to no overall increase in consumption. On the other hand, in the United States, we receive massive exposure to advertising. Indeed, TV might be thought of as the church of the late twentieth century. By the time the typical American reaches college, he or she will have spent three to four hours a week watching TV ads, about 100,000 of them in all.[17] These advertisements all preach a variation of the same underlying social message: satisfaction through purchase. Such a constant propaganda barrage may well induce us to consume more than we otherwise would.

Assuming that advertising does have a major positive impact on overall consumption, effective regulation of advertising remains a difficult task. From an economic point of view, advertising plays a very important function—fostering competition by providing consumers information about the availability, quality, or price of a product.[18] Advertising can be thought of as a useful product itself, whose production generates a negative externality, in the same way that paper production generates water pollution. Regulation should focus on controlling the negative externality—the promotion of consumer culture—rather than the product itself.

One way this has been traditionally accomplished is through the regulation of advertising on children's television. The government sets limits on the number of minutes per hour that can be devoted to advertising and has in the past prohibited the mixing of advertisements and entertainment. These regulations were dramatically loosened in the early 1980s under the banner of deregulation by the conservative Reagan administration but were tightened up somewhat in the early 1990s.[19]

---

[17]Durning (1991).

[18]For a discussion of the economic costs and benefits of advertising, see Scherer (1980).

[19]Durning (1991).

Another way to try and sort out "good" commercials from "bad" ones is by medium. Ads in the print and radio media have a harder time exploiting emotional weaknesses to develop brand identification than does television advertising. They thus tend to provide much more useful information about price, quality, and availability. Local and trade-specific advertising also tend to be more information-intensive than national advertising does. Perhaps reflecting the limited economic usefulness of national television advertising, many European countries have commercial-free television. (They finance the production of TV programs with tax dollars.)

In the United States, one possible policy measure would be to institute a "pollution tax" on national TV advertising. As with any tax, such a measure would cause firms to shift resources away from television to other media, or out of advertising altogether.

In the long run, any successful attempt to rein in the growth of per capita consumption in rich countries will require a broad social movement that challenges the consumer culture and its values head on, a discussion well beyond the scope of this book.[20] Economic analysis does provide us with some useful insights, however. First, policies of shared sacrifice may in fact lead to little reduction in overall welfare, if the happiness derived from consumption is relative. If this view is widely held, it suggests people will more likely accept a tax increase to reduce their consumption for a "good cause," like their children's welfare. Second, reducing consumption in rich countries need not lead to an increase in unemployment. Rather, labor and other resources can shift into production of goods for consumption in poor countries or into investment in clean technologies. Finally, a common proposal to restrict the advance of consumer culture, regulation of advertising, must be approached carefully because of the economic benefit—information—that advertising can generate.

11.6 Summary

The central metaphor behind benefit-cost analysis and the efficiency standard is a perceived environment-growth trade-off. More environmental protection in the form of regulations, bans, and red tape means higher costs and ultimately fewer "goods" for consumers. Princeton economist Alan Blinder asks, "Why should everyone be required to have a Cadillac environment, 'regardless of the cost'?"[21]

Overconsumption critics respond in two ways. First, ecological economists argue that technology is increasingly less capable of providing substitutes for natural capital, and that the long-run costs of "business as usual consumerism" are much higher than efficiency advocates envision.

Second, some economists have questioned the fundamental assumption that more is better, which underlies Blinder's defense of efficiency. Because much of the satisfaction derived from consumption is social rather than intrinsic in nature, and because of the negative externalities in the competition for positional goods that growth engenders, the benefits of economic growth are much smaller than conventionally measured.

If the more is better assumption underlying efficiency analysis is often simply

---

[20]See for example, Durning (1991), Daly and Cobb (1989), Wachtel (1983), or Schor (1991).
[21]Blinder (1987).

wrong, then the case for pursuing safety or ecological sustainability instead is strengthened. When more isn't better, "efficient" outcomes aren't really efficient, that is, welfare enhancing. As a result, stricter safety or ecological sustainability standards *may actually be more efficient* than an approach grounded in conventional benefit-cost analysis.

The global impact of consumption growth is becoming larger as more and more people look to material consumption to satisfy social needs for membership and status in a community—the advance of consumer culture. Two policies were explored for controlling the growth of consumption. The first was a tax, with the proceeds going to finance either investment in clean technology or increased consumption in poor countries. An important point is that declines in consumption in rich countries need not reduce overall employment; instead, they can represent a shift of resources including labor into other productive sectors. However, as social consumption theory predicts, tax policies lower utility in the short run, and are thus very difficult to sell politically.

The second policy involved regulating advertising, on the grounds that it promotes the growth of an unsustainable consumer culture. The danger here is that advertising plays a useful economic function, providing information and promoting competition. One possibility would be a "pollution tax" on national television advertising, which tends to be heavy on emotional appeal and low on information content.

This chapter concludes the first part of the book, and our discussion of "How much pollution is too much?" At one end of the spectrum we have considered efficiency as a target. In learning about the efficiency standard, we explored the tools that economists have developed to measure environmental protection benefits and costs, and the use of benefit-cost analysis. We have also examined the logic of promoting efficiency over time (dynamic efficiency) through discounting, granting the neoclassical assumption that technological progress will offset all resource shortages, and that as a consequence, human welfare will continue to rise.

At the other end of the spectrum, we have considered two stricter standards: safety and ecological sustainability. Both these approaches reject benefit-cost analyses and argue for protecting the environment "regardless of the cost." But in evaluating these approaches we learned that there really is no such thing as a free lunch; ultimately trade-offs do emerge, even if they are not as severe as neoclassicals believe.

So, how much is too much? This ultimately is a values question and cannot be resolved by economics alone, but the goal of the last eleven chapters has been to provide the information and analytical tools you need to better resolve the question in your own mind. In the next presidential election, global warming is likely to be an important issue. Whether you support a candidate speaking for an efficiency, a safety, or an ecological sustainability standard for carbon dioxide emissions, you now have a better understanding of the issues at stake in your decision.

APPLICATION 11.0

Overworked Americans

In the United States, the flip side of increasing consumption over the last thirty years has been increasing hours of work. Schor (1991) calculates that on average, full-time employees worked an additional 163 hours per year more in 1987 than they did in

1969. For men, the increase was about 98 hours, for women, 305. The increase has arisen because of both longer hours per week and more weeks worked. (At the same time, the number of unemployed individuals has risen.)

The increase in hours of work is surprising first because it goes against historical trends: Until 1940, the length of the workday fell continuously, and workers gained additional vacation time. This forward progress has continued in most European countries, which have strong unions. U.S. manufacturing employees work almost two months per year longer than their German or French counterparts.

The increase in work hours is also surprising because economists assume that leisure is a normal good: As people get richer they should consume more of it. Instead, leisure appears to be an inferior good. Since 1948 U.S. output per worker has more than doubled: In other words, we could consume at the level of our parents in early adulthood, and *take every other year off.* Instead, we work a little harder and consume more than twice as much.

1. Schor identifies two chief culprits behind the increased workweek: hiring incentives and the lack of a strong union movement to push for shorter hours. As far as incentives go, in spite of the fact that employers must, by law, pay time and a half for overtime, they seem to prefer this to hiring new employees. Why do you think this might be?

2. Among salaried and professional employees, Schor argues that increased competition has led to a natural upward progression in hours spent at the office. The monster workweek experienced by young doctors is becoming common for corporate lawyers, accountants, architects, and other professionals. In an increasingly competitive environment, "'enough' is defined not by some pre-existing standard like the length of the workday, but by the limits of human endurance."[22] Some economists respond: There is nothing wrong with this lengthening of the workweek. If people didn't like it, they could just quit and choose less demanding jobs, with more leisure and less consumption. Do you agree?

Key Ideas in Each Section

11.1 This chapter considers arguments that economic growth in affluent countries fails to deliver increases in welfare. **The Easterlin paradox** refers to survey data showing that increases in income boost reported happiness only slightly, and only to about the median income level.

11.2 One way to explain the Easterlin paradox is that satisfaction from consumption depends on one's consumption relative to social norms. Social consumption patterns are influenced by **bandwagon, snob,** and **Veblen effects.** When people attempt to obtain happiness by competing in consumption levels, the process often degenerates into a self-defeating **rat race,** which can be modeled as a **prisoner's dilemma.**

11.3 Positional competition is competition over goods with a limited long-run supply, or **positional goods.** Private positional goods are rationed by their increasingly high price; **public goods** are rationed by congestion. Competition over pure positional goods is a **zero-sum game.** Negative **consumption externalities** are often generated through positional competition.

---
[22]Schor (1991: 70), citing Kanter.

11.4 This section illustrates how the utility function changes in the presence of social consumption and positional goods. Goods must be divided up into **competitive and noncompetitive consumption** bundles. While more of everything is still better at the individual level, externalities generated by other's consumption now depress each individual's utility. It is thus no longer true that increases in society-wide consumption must increase happiness.

11.5 A **consumer culture** is one in which the primary means of achieving social status is via material consumption. Two economic policies for reducing the spread of consumer culture are **consumption-reducing taxes** and the **regulation of advertising.** However, economic tools can change attitudes only if they are part of a much broader cultural movement.

References

Bagwell, Laurie Simon and Douglas Bernheim (1996). "Veblen Effects in a Theory of Conspicuous Consumption." *American Economic Review,* 86, no. 3, 329–348.

Blecker, Robert A. (1990). "The Consumption Binge Is a Myth." *Challenge,* 33, no. 3, 22–30.

Blinder, Alan (1987). *Hard Heads, Soft Hearts.* New York: Addison-Wesley.

Daly, Herman E. (1987). "The Economic Growth Debate: What Some Economists Have Learned but Many Have Not." *Journal of Environmental Economics and Management,* 14, no. 4.

Daly, Herman E. and John J. Cobb, Jr. (1989). *For the Common Good.* Boston: Beacon Press.

Durning, Alan (1991). "Asking How Much Is Enough." In *State of the World,* 1991, ed. Lester R. Brown. New York: W. W. Norton.

Easterlin, Richard (1974). "Does Economic Growth Improve the Human Lot: Some Empirical Evidence." In *Nations and Households in Economic Growth.* New York: Academic Press.

Hirsch, Fred (1976). *Social Limits to Growth.* Cambridge, MA: Harvard University Press.

Howarth, Richard B. (1996). "Status Effects and Environmental Externalities." *Ecological Economics,* 16, no. 1, 25–34.

Ingelhart, Ronald and Jacques-Rene Rabier (1986). "Aspirations Adapt to Situations—

But Why Are the Belgians So Much Happier than the French?" In *Research on the Quality of Life.* Ann Arbor: University of Michigan Press.

Landers, Renee, James B. Rebitzer and Lowell J. Taylor (1996). "Rat Race Redux: Adverse Selection in the Determination of Work Hours in Law Firms." *American Economic Review,* 86, no. 3, 349–372.

Leibenstein, Harvey (1950). "Bandwagon, Snob and Veblen Effects in the Theory of Consumers' Demand." *Quarterly Journal of Economics,* vol. 64, 183–207.

Mishan, E. J. (1968). *The Costs of Economic Growth.* London: Staples Press.

Moore, Basil J. (1990). "Why Investment Determines Savings." *Challenge,* 33, no. 3, 54.

Nordhaus, William (1989). "What's Wrong with a Declining National Savings Rate?" *Challenge,* 32, no. 4, 22–26.

Scherer, F. M. (1980). *Industrial Market Structure and Economic Performance.* Chicago: Rand McNally.

Schor, Juliet B. (1991). *The Overworked American.* New York: Basic Books.

Scitovsky, Tibor (1986). *Human Desire and Economic Satisfaction.* New York: New York University Press.

Wachtel, Paul (1983). *The Poverty of Affluence.* London: Free Press.

Wilson, William Julius (1987). *The Truly Disadvantaged.* Chicago: University of Chicago.

PART II

IS GOVERNMENT UP TO THE JOB?

The first part of this book focused on an explicitly normative question: How much pollution is too much? We analyzed several possible answers to that question—efficiency, safety, and ecological sustainability—from both ethical and practical points of view. Having set a goal, at least in our own minds, we can now consider how to get there. As it turns out, we have only one vehicle: government. From chapter 3, we know that private markets generate too much pollution from *both* efficiency and safety perspectives. Thus, it is up to government to devise policies that modify market behavior and reduce pollution.

Government has a variety of tools at its command to attack the pollution problem, ranging from regulations and bans, to pollution taxes and marketable permit systems, to subsidy policies and infrastructure and R&D investments. But, before discussing policy details, we first need to consider a more central question: Is government up to the job?

In recent years, many people have become skeptical of government's ability to accomplish positive goals. In the early 1960s, less than one third of Americans agreed with the statement "The government is pretty much run by a few big interests looking out for themselves." By the 1980s, that figure had risen to over two thirds of those surveyed.[1] This increased distrust may well have been fueled by the rising number and severity of problems we now expect government to resolve: shoring up disintegrating families, tackling increasingly violent crime and drug abuse, reducing unemployment, poverty, homelessness and hunger, controlling inflation, providing worker training and retraining, insuring the safety of consumers and workers, *and* protecting the environment. As we

---

[1]Herbert Gans (1988: 39), *Middle American Individualism.* New York: Free Press.

have demanded more from government, we have perhaps become more aware of its limitations.

This part of the book provides an overview of governmental efforts to control pollution. Chapter 12 begins by developing a theory of government action that highlights two primary issues: the information-intensive nature of environmental regulation and the potential for political influence in the regulatory process. In light of this theory, chapter 13 reviews the major environmental legislation and chapter 14 evaluates regulatory accomplishments and constraints. Finally, chapter 15 deals with a vital, yet often overlooked, component of environmental regulation: enforcement and compliance.

The conclusions reached in this part of the book may seem harsh. At their best, regulators marshal the available information about environmental impacts and control costs and lurch in a steady, yet cumbersome, fashion to define and achieve an environmental goal: "efficiency," "safety," or "sustainability." At their worst, regulators become partners in a corrupt process where back-door deals are struck with disregard for environmental consequences. More generally, legislating, drafting, and enforcing regulations is a complex, tedious affair whose outcome bears the stamp of the various organized interests likely to be affected. In general, interests with more resources have more influence.

Just as markets fail to deliver many desirable social goals, including a clean environment, so too does government have its own failings. It would be naive to think otherwise. The point of this section is to isolate and identify these problems so that government policies to promote a cleaner planet can become more successful. Is government up to the job of protecting the environment? This is really a rhetorical question. If it is not, we had better make it so. It is the principal tool we have.

CHAPTER 12

The Political Economy of Environmental Regulation

12.0 Introduction

In 1970, the U.S. Congress passed the Clean Air Act, declaring it the law of the land that the air breathed by Americans should provide "an adequate margin of safety . . . requisite to protect the public health." Yet in the mid-1990s, some tens of millions of people were still exposed on occasion to ground-level ozone (smog) concentrations considered dangerous; air toxic emissions at some industrial facilities still remained high enough to impose cancer risks greater than 1 in 1,000 to surrounding residents.

Is this evidence for government failure? Some would turn these figures around, saying instead, look how far we have come. Several cities now meet the ozone standard that didn't in 1970; more significantly, consider how many *would* be failing today if we had not taken the measures we have. We shall look in more detail at the overall impact of regulation, which can be viewed as a glass half-empty or half-full, in the next few chapters. However, many would argue that twenty-five years is a long time to wait for a law to be enforced.

What lay behind this slow progress? Scientific uncertainty as to an "adequate margin of safety"? High compliance costs? Other priority areas at the Environmental Protection Agency (EPA)? Insufficient funds allocated to the EPA by Congress? Industry influence over legislators and regulators? All of these factors have played a role. The point here, however, is simply to illustrate that passing a law is only the first step in the long process of changing market behavior.

Economists have identified two main obstacles that stand in the way of effective government action to control pollution. The first is the highly **imperfect information** that regulators possess. To begin with, regulators are never given a clear-cut goal. For most pollutants, it is difficult, if not impossible, to define "safe" emission levels in purely scientific terms. Thus, a political definition of safety, based on technical information, must be worked out. More generally, the available risk assessments give only rough, if any, indications of health risks, while cost estimates can be equally unreliable. Moreover, regulators must often turn for information to the very sources they seek to regulate. Thus, as we shall see, many economists have focused on improving regulators' access to information as a crucial strategy for improving regulation.

However, ultimate uncertainty about the "facts" means that any decision to promote safety or efficiency, while informed by the technical merits of the case, will also leave substantial room for bureaucratic discretion. With the opportunity for discretion comes the opportunity for **political influence.** Government officials clearly have motivations other than fulfilling the letter of the law: career building or satisfying ideological preferences, for example. Given the existence of bureaucratic discretion, industry and environmental groups deploy substantial resources to affect elections, government legislation, and regulatory decisions.

This chapter will begin by detailing the generic process of environmental regulation and then go on to explore, in some detail, the obstacles presented by poor information and political influence. Finally, we consider briefly what lessons the disastrous environmental policies followed by the former Soviet Union hold for western, market-oriented democracies. Chapter 13 will then provide a more detailed overview of the major environmental laws now in effect.

12.1 The Process of Environmental Regulation

Today, the level of ozone concentration in the air (known as the ambient pollution level) officially designated by the government as providing an "adequate margin of safety" is 0.08 parts per million (ppm). Where did this particular environmental regulation, and thousands of others like it, come from? The history of a regulation such as ozone control is a three-step process.

STEP 1. U.S. CONGRESS PASSES BILL

Of course, step 1 doesn't come out of nowhere. First, there must be a generally perceived environmental problem. Next, some enterprising congressperson or congressional aide decides to make the problem a top issue. Then, legislation is drafted, and industry and environmental lobbyists line up support for and against and try to insert friendly amendments. Finally, legislation is passed, and the President signs on.

Even though this first step takes several years, the legislation is usually not very specific. Because of compromises struck between various parties, the language of the bill is often purposefully vague or even contradictory. All this leads to:

STEP 2. EPA DRAFTS REGULATIONS

Congress usually delegates to the EPA the hard work of figuring out exactly the meanings of terms like "safety," "prudent," and "reasonable balance." The EPA tries to translate the bill's language into actual regulations, specifying either allowable levels of emissions or of ambient pollution.

As we saw in chapter 10, the process of creating a major new regulation requires the EPA to generate a Regulatory Impact Analysis, a technical document that includes extensive documentation of both the scientific basis for its decision as well as its likely economic impact, including compliance costs. Yet the EPA most often has only limited information about the environmental impacts of pollutants and the technologies available for their control. Thus, during the process of drafting regulations, the agency will ask for comments from industry and environmental groups. Before the regulations can become law, they must also officially go through several rounds of public comment, to which the agency is legally required to respond. Thus, interest groups are formally incorporated into the decision-making process.

Part of this is self-defense on the EPA's part—many decisions the agency makes will be appealed or one side or the other will sue. Former EPA administrator William Ruckelshaus estimated that 80% of the EPA's rules were subsequently challenged in court.[1] For example, in the late 1970s the ozone standard mentioned above was revised upward from 0.08 ppm to 0.12 ppm under the threat of industry lawsuits, and this revision itself was challenged in court by both industry and environmentalists. In 1997, after again being sued by environmentalists and in the light of new scientific evidence, the EPA tightened the standard back to the original 0.08 ppm.

This information-gathering and public-comment phase can take a couple of years when it proceeds smoothly. Generally, however, Congress fails to appropriate enough money for the EPA to do all its tasks, and certain regulations get put on the back burner. Finally, the President's staff in the Office of Management and Budget reviews the new regulation and may send it back to the EPA with recommended revisions.

Typically, the EPA regulations will provide general guidelines for industries and municipalities to follow. However, the implementation details are left to:

STEP 3. STATE GOVERNMENTS IMPLEMENT AND ENFORCE REGULATIONS

The EPA often requires state governments to submit plans detailing how they intend to achieve the agency's goals. In the ozone case, for example, the state agency would need to tell the EPA what measures it intended to take to control emissions from vehicle tailpipes and stationary sources like petroleum refineries in order to come into compliance with the 0.08 ppm ambient air standard. Failure to do so would, theoretically, result in the EPA mandating certain measures, although it might just result in more delay. Thus, the hard economic choices are often left to state officials. Enforcement, too, is primarily a state function, although the EPA does have its own enforcement division to supplement state efforts.

There are three major points to be taken from this brief review of the legal process. First, even when it operates on schedule, drafting regulations is a cumbersome and time-consuming process. Because information about benefits and costs is highly imperfect and not widely available, legislators and regulators have provided many opportunities for affected parties to explain their position.

In this process, the United States has adopted a **judicial model of regulation.** The EPA is expected to adhere to strict procedural guidelines for accepting and addressing comments and must build a quasi-legal case for each major regulation it issues. Even under ideal circumstances, regulators gather their information in a forum where both sides are doing their best to obscure, rather than clarify, the underlying issues. This process tends to exaggerate differences over scientific and economic issues, rather than generate a consensus position the agency can accept as the "truth."

[1]Bryner (1987:117).

Moreover, those interested in stalling regulations have ample opportunity to do so merely by flooding regulators with extraneous information. For example, about seven feet of shelf space was required to hold over 4,000 comments, all of which required responses, that the EPA received on a single proposal.[2] "Paralysis by analysis" is a frequent outcome.

Finally, the regulatory process can be influenced at dozens of points. The following provides only a partial list of opportunities for interested parties to shape the final outcome: drafting of initial laws or insertion of amendments; discussions with high EPA officials or mid-level technicians involved in the agency's day-to-day work; formal and informal public comments; limiting or enlarging the budget that Congress and state legislators provide for regulatory agencies to do their work; meeting with the President's oversight agency in the Office of Management and Budget; influencing state implementation plans and state enforcement mechanisms; suing in court for changes once regulations have finally been put into place; and, finally, bargaining with enforcement officials over compliance.

Given the complex nature of the regulatory task, regulators *must* turn to industry and private groups for information about the potential benefits and costs of regulation. Moreover, since Congress itself has no way of knowing whether the EPA is making wise decisions, following our familiar system of checks and balances, the regulatory process itself has been consciously opened up to all interested parties. A complex, legally binding, decision-making process (the judicial model) has been put in place to prevent abuse of power by regulatory bureaucrats. Yet, the politics of information gathering itself has often yielded regulatory gridlock.

12.2 Regulation under Imperfect Information

The Environmental Protection Agency was founded in 1970 as an independent agency within the executive branch of government. It now employs over 16,000 people in 10 regional offices and Washington, DC, with an annual budget of more than $6 billion. The agency is required to develop, implement, and enforce regulations under dozens of different laws. Table 12.1 gives an idea of the complexity of the task, listing only the *major* jobs that the EPA was expected by Congress to undertake in 1988.

In addition to this list, the EPA has many other ongoing projects and responsibilities, including the regulation of tens of thousands of water pollution sources and hazardous waste dumps, hundreds of thousands of stationary air pollution sources, millions of automobiles, and hundreds of new chemicals and pesticides introduced each year.[3]

To accomplish these tasks, the EPA is obviously provided only limited resources. Thus, the agency has to determine priorities—not all of its regulatory functions can be performed adequately without spreading personnel too thin. As a result, in virtually all of its decisions, the agency gathers or generates less than full information about the problem before acting.

The extent of this information gap was revealed by a joint EPA-Amoco study of benzene air pollution at an Amoco oil refinery in Virginia. In 1990, the agency issued regulations to control benzene emissions from wastewater ponds at refineries.

---

[2]Bryner (1987: 115).
[3]Bryner (1987: 94).

TABLE 12.1   Significant Regulatory Actions for the EPA in 1988

1. Review of the National Ambient Air Quality Standards for Carbon Monoxide
2. Review of the National Ambient Air Quality Standard for Lead
3. Decisions on Regulating Various Air Pollutants
4. Benefits Analysis in Support of Air Regulatory Decisions
5. Review of the National Ambient Air Quality Standard for Nitrogen Dioxide
6. New Source Performance Standards: Municipal Waste Combustion
7. Environmental Radiation Protection Standards for Low-Level Radioactive Waste— Management and Disposal
8. Review of the National Ambient Air Quality Standard for Ozone
9. Residual Radioactivity Criteria
10. Fuels and Fuel Additives: Lead Phasedown (BAN)
11. Federal Promulgation of State Implementation Plans to Protect Visibility
12. Revised Hydrocarbon Emission Standards for Light-Duty Trucks
13. Resource Conservation and Recovery Act: Air Emissions from Hazardous Waste Treatment, Storage, and Disposal Facilities
14. National Emission Standards for Hazardous Air Pollutants (NESHAP)—10 Compounds
15. Diesel Fuel Quality
16. Strategy for Control of Gasoline Refueling Emissions
17. Trading and Banking of Heavy-Duty Engine NO_x and PM Emission Credits
18. Prevention of Significant Deterioration (PSD) Increments for Particulate Matter—10 Micrometer (PM10)
19. Emission Standards for Sources Emitting Radionuclides to Air NESHAPS: Radionuclides
20. Federal Radiation Protection Guidance for Public Exposure to Radiofrequency Radiation
21. Development of the EPA's Stratospheric Ozone Protection Plan
22. Review of National Ambient Air Quality Standards for Sulfur Oxides
23. Development of a Strategy for Expeditious Attainment of the National Ambient Air Quality Standard for Ozone and Carbon Monoxide
24. Groundwater Protection Standards for Inactive Uranium Tailing Sites
25. Prevention of Significant Deterioration (PSD) Increments for Nitrogen Oxides (NO_x)
26. Alternative Rural Fugitive Dust Policies for PM10
27. NESHAP: Benzene Reconsideration
28. Pesticide Inert Ingredient Strategy
29. Environmental Protection Agency Response to the National Academy of Sciences Study *Regulating Pesticides in Food*
30. Pesticides in Groundwater Strategy
31. Nitrosamines in Metalworking Fluids
32. Regulatory Investigation of Formaldehyde
33. Regulatory Investigation of Chlorinated Solvents
34. Restricted-Use Classification for Groundwater-Contaminating Pesticides
35. Rule Making Concerning Certain Microbial Products ("Biotechnology")
36. Pesticide Special Reviews
37. Sara Section 110 Test Rules
38. Manifesting and Notification of Polychlorinated Biphenyl (PCB) Wastes
39. Worker Protection Standards for Agricultural Pesticides (Revision)
40. Toxic Substances Control Act Section 8(a) Comprehensive Assessment Information Rule

Continued

TABLE 12.1   (cont.)

41. Action Concerning Commercial and Industrial Use of Asbestos
42. Labeling Requirements for Pesticides and Devices (Revision)
43. Procedural Rule for Expedited New Chemical Follow-up
44. Management of Used Oil
45. Determination on Wastes from the Combustion of Coal by Electric Utility Power Plants
46. Determination on Solid Waste from Selected Metallic Ore-Processing Operations
47. Restriction of Land Disposal of Certain Hazardous Wastes
48. Reportable Quantities for Releases of Hazardous Substances
49. National Oil and Hazardous Substances Pollution Contingency Plan
50. National Priorities List for Uncontrolled Hazardous Waste Sites
51. Groundwater Monitoring at Hazardous Waste Facilities
52. Solid Waste Disposal Facility Criteria
53. List of Hazardous Constituents for Groundwater Monitoring
54. Location Standards for Hazardous Waste Facilities
55. Hazard Ranking System for Uncontrolled Hazardous Substance Releases
56. Mining Waste Management Under RCRA Subtitle D
57. Corrective Action for Solid Waste Management Units at Hazardous Waste Management Facilities
58. Landfill, Surface Impoundment, and Waste Pile Closures for Hazardous Waste Management Facilities
59. Emergency and Hazardous Chemical Inventory Forms and Community Right-to-Know Reporting Requirements Threshold Amendment
60. Emission Controls for Hazardous Waste Incinerators
61. Statistical Methods for Evaluating Groundwater Monitoring Data from Hazardous Waste Facilities
62. Air Toxicity Characteristics
63. Municipal Waste Combustor Ash Management
64. Concentration-Based Hazardous Waste Listings
65. Corrective Action for Releases to Groundwater from Regulated Hazardous Waste Units
66. Wood Preserving and Surface Protection Waste Listings
67. No Migration Variance for Restricted Hazardous Waste Land Disposal
68. Planning and Implementing Superfund Off-Site Response Actions
69. Disposal of Containerized Liquids in Hazardous Waste Landfills
70. Burning of Hazardous Waste in Boilers and Industrial Furnaces
71. Liners and Leak Detection for Hazardous Waste Land Disposal Units
72. Identification of Hazardous Wastes by Toxicity Characteristic and Listing of Additional Organic Toxicants
73. Underground Storage Tanks—Technical Requirements
74. Petroleum Refinery Primary Treatment Sludge Listing
75. Double Liner and Leachate Collection Systems for Hazardous Waste Land Disposal Units
76. Permitting Mobile Hazardous Waste Treatment Units
77. Permit Modifications for Hazardous Waste Management Facilities
78. Future Effluent Guidelines—Standards Initiatives
79. Denial or Restriction of Disposal Sites in U.S. Waters
80. National Primary Drinking Water Regulations: Synthetic Organic Chemicals and Inorganic Chemicals, Monitoring

TABLE 12.1   (cont.)

81. Ocean Incineration Regulation (Revision)
82. Sewage Sludge Use and Disposal Regulations
83. Comprehensive Revisions to Ocean Dumping Regulations
84. Current Effluent Guidelines
85. National Primary Drinking Water Regulations: Radionuclides
86. National Primary Drinking Water Regulations: Disinfection, Disinfectants, and Disinfection By-products (Revision)
87. General Pretreatment Regulations for Existing and New Sources
88. Underground Injection Control Program: Hazardous Waste Disposal Injection Restrictions
89. Required SDWA Indian Regulations
90. Required Clean Water Act Indian Regulations
91. Regulation of Corrosion By-products in Drinking Water (Lead and Copper)
92. National Pollutant Discharge Elimination System Sewage Sludge Permit Regulations State Sludge Management Program Requirements
93. Guidelines for Classifying Groundwater Under the EPA Groundwater Protection Strategy
94. Criteria for Identifying Critical Aquifer Protection Areas
95. National Primary Drinking Water Regulations: Filtration and Disinfection, Turbidity, Giardia Lamblia, Viruses, Total Coliform, Legionella, and Heterotrophic Bacteria

Source: U.S. Office of Management and Budget (1988).

These regulations, based on research done in 1959, proved dramatically far off base. When the joint research project was completed in 1993, ponds were discovered to be polluting at a level twenty times lower than predicted, while the real benzene pollution problem arose on the loading docks where fuel was pumped into barges.

Amoco eventually constructed a $41 million treatment system to deal with pollution from the ponds, while much more extensive pollution from the loading docks, which could have been controlled for $6 million, went unregulated and unabated.[4] How could such a situation develop? In general, prior to writing a regulation, the EPA has neither the staff nor the legal right to conduct the kind of intensive examination of an industrial facility as it eventually did in the Amoco case. Usually, the agency can sponsor only limited research of its own; as a result it must turn to industry, environmental groups, or university researchers for much of its data.

In addition to relying on outdated or poor information, the EPA must also contend with a **reporting bias** when it turns to industry for information about compliance costs. To illustrate the problem, suppose the EPA seeks to regulate a pesticide thought to contaminate groundwater. The agency is considering a ban on the use of a pesticide in high-risk counties. As is discussed in the next chapter, pesticides are regulated under an efficiency standard—Congress has directed the EPA to weigh benefits against costs in this case. Figure 12.1 illustrates our efficiency standard diagram.

---

[4]The EPA refused to grant Amoco a waiver based on the study's results. The agency says that loading dock regulations will be forthcoming in the mid-1990s. See "What Really Pollutes? Study of a Refinery Proves an Eye-Opener," *Wall Street Journal,* March 29, 1993.

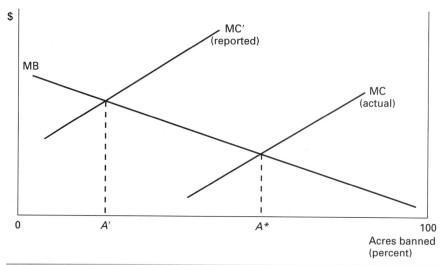

FIGURE 12.1 Regulation with Imperfect Information

The true marginal benefits and costs of the ban are reflected by the curves labeled MB and MC. If the EPA had access to this information, efficiency would require a ban applying to A^* acres. However, suppose the EPA must rely on agrichemical company sources for information about how much it will cost farmers to switch over to alternative pest control methods. Industry has a clear incentive to lie and overstate the cost (MC'). If the industry does so and the EPA uses the industry estimates, the agency will ban A' acres, an inefficiently low number.

There are two responses to this reporting bias problem. The first is to improve the **in-house analytic capability** of the agency. While the EPA will never have the resources to fund all the research it needs, concentrating on training and retaining technical personnel is a basic aspect of improved regulation. Unfortunately, two political developments in the 1980s worked against this goal. In the early years of the anti-regulation Reagan administration, the EPA's budget was cut severely, and morale was undermined by official hostility to the agency's mission. As a result, almost 40% of the agency workforce resigned or was fired in 1980 and 1981.[5]

More subtly, following the general trend toward privatization of services, much of the EPA's technical work over the last decade or so has been contracted out to private consulting firms. The ostensible motive has been to save money (a goal that, in fact, proved elusive), but the net result was to reduce the agency's technical capabilities. Reliance on contractors has reached the point, according to some critics, that the agency cannot even evaluate whether contract work is being performed well.[6] Moreover, many of the consulting firms also depend for their livelihoods on contracts from industries regulated by the EPA. Reducing outside contracting would help build up the EPA's technical expertise and reduce conflicts of interest.

---

[5]Landy et al. (1990).

[6]See the congressional testimony of Joel Hirschorn, quoted in "Cleaning Up," *The Atlantic,* October 1990; and "U.S. Says Lack of Supervision Encouraged Waste and Fraud in Contracts: Billions Misspent in Last Decade Auditor Finds," *New York Times,* December 2, 1992.

The second approach to the information problem is to rely on so-called **incentive-compatible regulation.** Regulation designed to elicit truthful information is called incentive-compatible because the *incentive* for the regulated party is *compatible* with the regulatory goal. Using the mix of tools at their command, regulators can, in fact, do better than is illustrated in Figure 12.1. As we will discuss more fully in advanced topic chapter T4, it turns out that if regulators were to control pesticide use by taxing rather than banning it, then firms would have an incentive to *understate* rather than overstate their control costs. In chapter T4 we also find that an appropriate mix of taxes and marketable permit systems (discussed more fully in chapters 16 and 17) can help provide just the right incentives for truth telling.

12.3 Bureaucratic Discretion and Political Influence

Regardless of the degree to which the EPA is able to hone its information-gathering and evaluation abilities, regulatory issues will never be resolved in a clear-cut fashion. The ambiguous and often contradictory goals provided by Congress, as well as the underlying uncertainty in scientific and economic analyses, insure that bureaucrats will retain substantial **discretion** in regulatory decision making. Because regulatory decisions impose substantial costs on affected industries, businesses will devote resources to influence the discretion that regulators exercise (in ethical, questionably ethical, and unethical manners) just as they devote resources to minimizing labor or energy costs.

In addition, simply because a business lobbies for regulatory relief does not mean that the relief is unjustified. It remains true that industry has the best knowledge about the likely impact of regulation and that bureaucrats have the power to arbitrarily impose substantial burdens on firms for reasons that are not obvious. Thus, the ability of industry (and environmental groups) to lobby regulators is not necessarily a bad thing. The problem is that legitimate access can become transformed into undue influence. This section will consider factors that motivate bureaucrats to stray from "doing their job." The next section will look into a related question: Who has more undue influence in the regulatory process, industry or environmentalists?

Environmental regulators are expected by the public to pursue their congressionally mandated goals: efficiency or safety in pollution control. However, like all other people, they have personal interests to consider. To the extent that they are able, bureaucrats are likely to use their position to satisfy three types of goals: agency building, external career building, and job satisfaction.

Many observers of bureaucracy (both governmental and corporate) have argued that a primary goal of managers is **agency growth.** Protecting and enlarging the agency budget, of course, can make the agency more effective in doing its primary job, but it also provides more prerequisites (new computers, travel, opportunities for promotion, etc.) and prestige for agency personnel. A bias toward unwarranted growth may lead to "over-regulation" (especially from an efficiency point of view) as the agency personnel engage in new activities to justify greater funding. On the other hand, it may just lead to wasted money.

The second factor that regulators keep in mind is **external career building.** A few years ago I interviewed for a job in the Antitrust Division of the U.S. Justice Department. The typical career track, I was told, involved working at Justice for five years, at which point one's salary topped out. Most people then went on to work for law firms or economic consulting firms that *defended* companies from antitrust suits. This so-called **revolving door** between industry and its regulators is widespread. EPA employees need to keep in mind future career options when making tough regulatory decisions.

While there are some jobs in environmental organizations or academic institutions, most private-sector jobs for people with experience in the EPA, and virtually all the high-paying ones, are in private industry. Table 12.2 provides a partial listing of the EPA's top administrators who have subsequently worked for industries in the field of hazardous waste management *only*. (The administrator is the EPA chief.)

Table 12.2 provides only a partial view through the revolving door, since it focuses on a single industry and only on top administrators. Indeed, one could point to a few top EPA administrators with environmental credentials.[7] The fact that the individuals listed in Table 12.2 went on to work for industries that they previously regu-

TABLE 12.2 The Revolving Door: EPA and the Hazardous Waste Industry

Name	Government Position	Industry Position
William Ruckelshaus	Administrator, EPA	Director of Weyerhauser[a], Monsanto[a], CEO of Browning Ferris[b]
Douglas Costle	Administrator, EPA	Chairman, Metcalf and Eddy[c]
Lee Thomas	Administrator, EPA	CEO, Law Environmental[c]
Walt Barber	Acting Administrator, EPA	VP, Chemical Waste Management[b]
Al Alm	Deputy Administrator, EPA	VP, SAIC[c]
Joan Bernstein	General Counsel, EPA	VP, Chemical Waste Management[b]
Chris Beck	Assistant Administrator, EPA	CEO, Air & Water Technologies[c]
Rita Lavelle	Assistant Administrator, EPA	Consultant to waste industry
Jack Ravan	Regional Administrator, EPA	Pres., Rollins Env. Services[b]
Jack Schram	Regional Administrator, EPA	Dir., Govt. Affairs, Waste Management[b]
Marcia Williams	Director, EPA Office of Solid Waste	Washington Rep., Browning Ferris[b]
James Sanderson	Policy Advisor, EPA	Attorney, Chemical Waste Management[b]
Gary Dietrich	Director, EPA Office of Solid Waste	VP, Consulting Firm doing work for Waste Management[b]
Brian Malloy	Enforcement Attorney, EPA	Attorney, Chemical Waste Management[b]
Jeff Miller	Enforcement Task Force, EPA	Attorney, Chemical Waste Management[b]
Susan Vogt	Deputy Asst. Administrator, EPA	Washington Rep., Law Environmental[c]

[a]Resource or chemical corporations regulated by the EPA.
[b]Hazardous waste firms.
[c]Superfund (waste cleanup) contractors or consultants.
Source: William Sanjour (1992: Appendix B), *What EPA Is Like and What Can Be Done About It* (Washington, DC: Environmental Research Foundation). Used with permission.

[7]David Gardener, an assistant administrator under President Clinton, was a Sierra Club employee. William Reilly, Bush's EPA administrator, served as head of the (conservative) environmental group the Conservation Foundation. Tom Jorling and David Hawkins, deputy administrators under the Carter administration, respectively directed the Center for Environmental Studies at Williams College and worked for the Natural Resources Defense Council.

lated does not necessarily mean that they were unable to set aside private interests to serve their public mission. However, the potential for conflict of interest clearly exists. More significantly, in the struggle to define exactly what the public interest really is, top policy makers are clearly aware of the industry position since they are on intimate terms with many from that side of the aisle. They may be less aware of what it is like to live next to a hazardous waste dump.

This leads us to the third bureaucratic motivation that might influence regulatory policy: **job satisfaction.** Are bureaucrats likely to use their discretion to draft and enforce aggressive or meek laws? Three factors come to play here: **ideology, power,** and **the quiet life.** First, regulators with either an environmental or free-market ideological bent may satisfy their own personal preferences for more or less regulation. Second, regulators may impose harsh restrictions on industry because it provides them with power and authority. Conservatives have often charged that the EPA is staffed by power-hungry, environmental zealots. And on the face of it, it seems more likely that persons attracted to a job in the EPA would be sympathetic to environmental concerns.

While this claim is hard to evaluate in general, one can point to counterexamples. As noted above, almost half of the staff of the EPA from the more liberal Carter era quit or were fired in the early 1980s. Moreover, some of the staff within the EPA came from agencies with "pro-business" traditions. For example, Landy et al. (1990: 181) note that the EPA's Office of Pesticide Programs was transferred intact from the Department of Agriculture, where it had favored "expeditiously licensing new pesticides."

One factor that would mitigate against environmental activism within the agency is the contrasting desire for "a quiet life." The road to advancement within a bureaucracy is often to avoid antagonizing outside interests and to proceed with caution when doing so. The outcome is an emphasis on procedure over substance. Stalon (1990) argues that this generates a substantial bias towards the *status quo.*

One of the most outspoken environmental critics of the EPA is William Sanjour, an agency employee whose job has been protected by the U.S. Congress under a whistle-blower provision. (Between 1989 and 1992, Sanjour, while still officially employed, was given no assignments in the agency.) Sanjour (1992) argues that EPA employees are more interested in keeping their heads low than in sticking their necks out. Because industry is highly concerned with the process of drafting the details of regulations, mid-level bureaucrats often find themselves in day-to-day contact with industry officials. Here, "in addition to real and hinted at job opportunities," EPA officials become aware that "people who cooperate with the lobbyists find that the lobbyist will lobby for their advancement with upper management. Those who don't cooperate will find the lobbyists lobbying for their heads."

This section has identified three potential goals beyond their legislative mandate which bureaucrats might pursue: agency growth, external career building, and job satisfaction. Growth suggests, if anything, a tendency toward over-regulation; career building would lead to underregulation; and job satisfaction might generate either. As a result, it is not possible to identify an *a priori* bureaucratic bias. However, it is worth keeping in mind that bureaucrats are people too. Like anyone else, they take pride in a job well-done—serving the public interest as they see it.

12.4 Who Wins the Influence Game?

The answer to this question, of course, depends upon whom you ask. Environmentalists would point to twenty or thirty years of delay in enforcing the Clean Air Act; industry would respond that the laws themselves make unrealistic demands. Rather than answer this question outright, we can identify the resources available to the two sides and the arenas in which the parties tend to prevail.[8]

The two types of resources in the political world are **votes** and **dollars.** In general, environmentalists are better at martialing voting support, while industry has greater monetary resources at its command. Tough environmental laws command broad public support in the polls, even when the opportunity cost of higher prices is explicitly factored in. Thus, environmentalists have a large natural political constituency. Moreover, environmentalists are a more trusted source of information about environmental issues among the public than either industry or government officials.[9]

This advantage is translated into influence in the crafting of national environmental protection legislation. Ten major national environmental organizations (Sierra Club, National Wildlife Federation, National Audubon Society, Environmental Defense Fund, Natural Resources Defense Council, Wilderness Society, Nature Conservancy, Greenpeace, Ducks Unlimited, and World Wildlife Fund) represent around 12 million members. These groups hire experts to analyze the benefits and costs of new policies, lobbyists to spread this information and promote environmental legislation, and lawyers to sue government agencies. The combined annual policy analysis, lobbying, and legal budgets of these groups runs well into the millions of dollars, a substantial sum, but much less than the resources that industry can bring to bear. However, environmental dollars often have greater leverage among many legislators due to the votes they represent, as well as a higher perceived level of credibility.

It is probably fair to say that environmentalists win more often than they lose in drafting and passing national environmental protection laws. This is reflected in the general tendency of environmental laws to set safety rather than efficiency standards for pollution control, as well as the passage of substantial environmental legislation under conservative Presidents Bush and Reagan.

Due to their ability to mobilize voters, grassroots environmental movements have also done well at the local level, particularly in blocking the siting of new facilities (power plants, landfills, incinerators) and, in some cases, promoting alternatives such as recycling. Environmentalists have also had some success leveraging their voting power at the state level (California, Wisconsin, New York) but have also faced severe challenges in states traditionally dominated by particular industries (Louisiana, oil, gas, and chemicals; and Kentucky, coal).

If environmentalists have the edge in votes, industry has a clear-cut dollar advantage. The Chemical Manufacturers Association (CMA), for example, has a $48 million annual budget. The Sierra Club, by contrast, has a budget of about $20 million, but at least a fifth of that goes to fund-raising. The Sierra Club, in addition, focuses on a wide variety of environmental issues ranging from wilderness protection, to natural resource management, to pollution control. The CMA by contrast is more focused on

---

[8]For a more formal approach based on information asymmetry, see Selden and Terrones (1993). Consistent with the observations below, their model predicts strong laws and weak enforcement.
[9]McCallum and Covello (1989).

the environmental regulatory process. Moreover, the CMA borrows most of its scientific expertise (toxicologists, epidemeologists, economists) from its member companies while the Sierra Club must keep them on staff.

A few of the dozens of other major industry trade groups with a strong lobbying presence in Washington include the American Petroleum Institute, the Fertilizer Institute, the American Paper Institute, and the Chlorine Institute. In addition, most of the large chemical, petroleum, and manufacturing firms maintain their own Washington staffs, and/or hire DC law firms to lobby on their behalf.[10]

Dollars can be used to buy a number of things useful for influencing the regulatory debate: technical studies, lobbying staff, the promise of future jobs, access to legislators and regulators and votes (through advertising).

As I have stressed, control over information is a crucial aspect of regulation. Thus, the ability to hire "experts" to conduct **technical studies** of benefits and costs is an important channel of influence. Grieder (1990) describes a "full court press" launched by industry against the EPA's proposed technological standard for injection of hazardous wastes into deep wells. The Chemical Manufacturers Association, along with many of its members—Monsanto, CYRO Industries, Dow, Dupont, BP Chemicals, Celanese, Cynamid, and ARCO—met repeatedly with mid-level EPA officials in 1989, providing them with data about the cost of the new proposals as well as warnings of plant shutdowns. Some of the lobbyists threatened political repercussions if the agency did not respond. According to one EPA official: "We were attacked on a technical basis— the kind of case they felt they could make in a lawsuit if we didn't yield. Industry argued there would be huge costs if we went forward with the proposed rule. Depending on who you listened to, it was the end of the world."[11]

The EPA's final rule was ultimately watered down substantially. The point here is not, were the company's claims correct, which they may have been. Rather, in the information war surrounding the impact of the regulation, environmentalists did not have the resources to bring much expert testimony to bear. Moreover, even if they had access to information about costs, environmental groups did not have the **staff** capacity of the chemical companies. Dozens of industry lobbyists repeatedly delivered the same message to mid-level EPA officials, as well as to President Bush's staff. In this particular case, Grieder (1990) provides some evidence that pressure from a close Bush adviser influenced the final EPA decision.[12]

Money buys information, lobbying and legal staff, and **access** to politicians and regulators. Out-and-out bribery—I'll contribute $5,000 to your campaign if you vote against bill X—is not common in the United States, though it is not unknown. Instead, the more money one contributes to a political campaign (or party), the more often one gets to meet with the politician or his or her appointees at the EPA to make one's case known. In an information war, where all sides can make a "reasonable" case on the surface, access is easily translated into influence. For example, an EPA official would be unlikely to refuse to meet with the representatives of the Sunshine Chemical company if they had contributed several thousand dollars to his boss's po-

---

[10]See "Doing More with Less: Trade Groups Feel Recession's Pinch," *Chemical Week,* June 10, 1992; and "Earth Day Plus 20 and Counting," *Smithsonian* (1992) 21, no. 1, 46.

[11]Grieder (1990: 138).

[12]Grieder (1990: 140).

litical party. He would, however, be more likely to shunt off a meeting with a grass-roots environmental group from Sunshine's hometown to someone lower down in the agency hierarchy. The more often he hears Sunshine's case, the more reasonable it is likely to seem.

Finally, dollars can buy votes through advertising. Good examples are found in California, where many laws are passed directly by the voters through ballot initiatives. An ambitious 1990 proposal put forward by environmentalists, dubbed "Big Green," was defeated after industry spent $16.5 million in opposition, more than four times what supporters could muster.[13] However, buying votes is not easy. A nuclear industry TV campaign in Nevada actually increased opposition to the siting of a waste facility in the state.[14] And just before writing this chapter, I witnessed an election in Washington State in which a former timber industry lobbyist raised almost $600,000, outspending her environmental opponent by 3–1, in a race for commissioner of public lands. The industry candidate blanketed the airwaves with what I thought were quite effective commercials, but ultimately still lost.

Industry has not been able to translate its dollar advantage into many clear-cut victories at the legislative level. Tough environmental laws continue to be passed. However, industry is much more effective in using its resources to dilute the impact of these laws. Through the revolving door, domination of information generation and delivery, large legal staffs, and superior access to politicians and political appointees, industry probably wins more often than it loses in all of the steps subsequent to the passage of laws. From the public comment phase in the drafting of regulations by the EPA, through the implementation and enforcement of these laws by state officials, through the budgeting of resources to these agencies, through the opportunity for court challenges, through bargaining over compliance, industry has many opportunities to influence how the ultimate regulatory process will work.

Washington lawyer Lloyd Cutler, whose firm has represented many corporate clients, put it this way: "It would be wrong to think that corporations are on top or ahead. They feel very put upon or defeated. It's true that they manage to survive and deal and push things off—they feel the added costs of regulation exceed the benefits [editor's note: an efficiency perspective!]—but they would say the notion that they now control or dominate the health and safety agencies is just crazy." Still, Cutler explained, "It's harder to pass a law than to stop one. On the whole, I would say the professional lobbyists and lawyers prefer to live in this world where there are so many buttons to push, so many other places to go if you lose your fight."[15]

Given this balance of power—environmentalists with the edge in the national legislative arena, business dominant in the regulatory sphere—an unfortunate dynamic develops. Environmentalists, anticipating that laws will be weakened upon implementation, try to push through Congress very stringent, sometimes unachievable goals. Industry, galvanized by this threat, pours more resources into mitigating the regulatory impact.

One of the big losers in this regulatory bazaar is public respect for the law. As noted in the introduction to this section, Americans increasingly believe that govern-

---

[13]"Environmental Initiative Rejected in California," *Wall Street Journal,* November 4, 1990.

[14]"Nevadans Dump Dump Ads," *Bulletin of Atomic Scientists,* 48, no. 4, May 1992.

[15]Greider (1990: 134).

ment has been captured by "a few big interests" who are able to mold the law as they see fit. While, in fact, neither side fully dominates the entire process, the mere fact that so many aspects of regulation are open to negotiation invites scandal and public suspicion. If public belief in the ability of government to solve problems further diminishes, this in itself will pose a difficult challenge to resolving environmental problems.

There are many potential solutions to the problem of bureaucratic discretion and political influence; several will be explored later in this book. At this point we shall focus on the potential for political reform of the regulatory process itself.

12.5 Political Reform of Regulation

Efforts at gaining political influence are often a form of the positional competition discussed in the last chapter. In such a zero-sum game, the gains of one party can only come at the expense of another. Under these circumstances, a natural tendency is to overinvest resources in unproductive competition. This situation can be analyzed through the prisoner's dilemma model, last seen in our chapter 11 discussion of the rat race. Figure 12.2 illustrates the situation in a hypothetical regulatory decision about an emissions standard.

Each side must decide how many lobbyists to deploy. If neither group lobbies, then a standard of 4 parts per million (ppm) will be set. Note that an identical result will occur if both sides send a lobbyist—the extra efforts cancel one another out. If environmentalists don't lobby and industry does, then a loose standard of 6 ppm will result. If, on the other hand, industry doesn't lobby and environmentalists do, a strict standard of 2 ppm will emerge.

What will be the likely outcome of this kind of setup? If there is no agreement to restrict lobbying, environmentalists must assume that industry will lobby (and vice versa for industry). Thus, each side will choose a lobbying strategy for defensive purposes, even though the same outcome could be achieved at lower cost. Moreover, the process is likely to escalate into a full-blown "lobby race" as each side tries to forestall the other from gaining an advantage.

An agreement to limit lobbying seems in the interests of both parties. If cheating on such an agreement were easily observable, the agreement would be self-enforcing: If industry observed environmentalists cheating, it could simply retaliate by sending in its own lobbyist. However, if cheating is not easily detectable, as is the case in lob-

FIGURE 12.2 A Zero-Sum Lobbying Competition

Environmentalists

		Don't Lobby	Lobby
Industry	Don't Lobby	4 ppm	2 ppm
	Lobby	6 ppm	4 ppm

bying, the agreement will break down as each side cheats to protect itself from the possibility that the other will cheat!

The prisoner's dilemma model implies that cooperation rather than competition might be in everyone's best interest. How might this insight actually be applied in the regulatory arena? One approach is to adopt a **corporatist model of regulation.** Here, regulations would be explicitly decided in a bargaining context between representatives of "corporate" groups—the EPA, private firms, and environmental organizations.[16] In exchange for being included at the table, all the groups would have to agree to abide by and support the final outcome. The EPA would, thus, be given much more flexibility in determining policy and be insulated from subsequent lawsuits. In essence, the corporatist model accepts that "a few big interests" determine the details of government environmental policy and provides a more efficient forum for them to do so.

European countries have adopted a more corporatist approach to regulation than we have in the United States. The fruits of corporatism can be seen in efforts by the Netherlands; since 1989 the Dutch government has instituted a series of "environmental covenants" with different industries. These covenants are voluntary agreements among government regulators and industry to reduce specific pollutants by specified amounts, which, once signed, have the force of a contract under civil law.[17]

However, it is not clear how well corporatist regulation really works, nor whether it can be successfully translated to the United States.[18] Corporatism requires trimming back general public access to decision makers and is often perceived as a restriction of democracy. Who, for example, gets a seat at the table? Indeed, some believe that the environmental movement has already been split between the "conservative" DC-based national groups and more "radical" grassroots organizations, with the latter accusing the former of selling out to industrial interests.[19] Moreover, the national groups have few members from working-class or minority communities, which have their own environmental interests.

Unlike European countries (and Canada), the United States does not have a strong labor or social-democratic political party to counterbalance the political influence of business. Partly for this reason, Americans have been much more distrustful of placing discretionary decision-making power in the hands of government bureaucrats than have Europeans. In the United States, it is not clear that the national environmental groups—unaccountable to the voters—or indeed the EPA, have the power to represent and enforce the public's general interest in environmental protection. Thus, many people would oppose trading in the restrictions imposed on bureaucratic discretion under the current judicial regulatory model for a more goal-oriented, but less open, corporatist model.

If excess resources are indeed being devoted to influencing the political process, a straightforward economic response would be tax lobbying. A more feasible proposal would perhaps be to eliminate the status that lobbying now holds as a **tax-deductible business expense.** More generally, **campaign finance reform,** including restrictions on the now-unlimited contributions of so-called "soft money" to the political parties,

---

[16]Bryner (1987) presents the conventional arguments for corporatist regulation. Landy et al. (1990) attack corporatism as "managed pluralism" but defend a stronger leadership role for the EPA.

[17]See Bryner (1987); and Ministry of VROM (1994).

[18]For a harsh critique of Finnish corporatism, see Hukkinen (1995).

[19]See "War Among the Greens," *Newsweek,* May 4, 1992.

could serve to reduce efforts by all sides to gain advantage. Unfortunately, given the benefits to incumbent politicians of the existing system, genuine campaign finance reform has proven quite difficult to achieve.

Finally, moving more responsibility for regulation to the state level, known as **environmental federalism,** would both bring issues closer to those affected and reduce the influence of Washington-based interests. Ironically, business ascendancy over the national environmental agenda during the Reagan years probably prompted the renewal of activism at the state level observed in the late 1980s and early 1990s.[20] The case against such environmental federalism is that competition between states for business will lead to lower overall levels of environmental protection. The seriousness of this latter problem remains unclear.[21]

Political reform of the regulatory process might occur through a move away from a judicial to a corporatist model—by reducing the role of money in politics through a tax on lobbying or campaign finance reform—or through decentralization. However, while potentially helpful, none of these reforms would fundamentally challenge the underlying issues of imperfect information and political influence in the regulatory process. Indeed, these two issues have lead some to despair of government's ability to stem the process of environmental decline. As an extreme example of government failure, we turn briefly to the experience in the former Communist nations.

12.6 Lessons from Communism

Since the fall of the Berlin Wall in 1989, an increasingly frightening portrait of environmental conditions in the former Communist regimes has begun to emerge. Driven to industrialize at all costs and in spite of official laws mandating strict environmental protection, officials in the state-owned industries proceeded to raise the level of poison in the land, water, and air to fatal degrees. Commenting on the widespread use of highly toxic pesticides like DDT; the contamination and exhaustion of agricultural water resources; urban centers with air pollutants typically five times above legal levels; rivers and seas filled with untreated agricultural, industrial, and human waste; and death and disease from the Chernobyl nuclear accident and military nuclear wastes, one set of authors concluded: "When historians finally conduct an autopsy on the Soviet Union and Soviet Communism, they may reach the verdict of death by ecocide."[22]

What lessons can we learn from this story? Traditional conservatives have argued that the lesson is a simple one: "free-market economics, good; government involvement in the economy, bad." Yet, with the Soviet model of a centrally planned economy discredited, the environmental problems the globe faces are now generated primarily by market economies and market-driven growth. Thus, the traditional conservative lesson provides us with only limited guidance. Clearly, governments can create environmental disasters that rival, if not exceed, those generated by private economic actors. Yet, in capitalist countries, government *is not* the primary source of environmental problems.

Instead, with the world population and economic activity expected to at least

---

[20]Portney et al. (1991) suggest this line of argument.
[21]See the discussion in Cropper and Oates (1992).
[22]Fesbach and Friendly (1992: 1).

double in the next fifty years, the Soviet story is best viewed as a cautionary tale: Without an *effective* governmental process forcing economic actors to pay for the externalities they impose on others, ecocide is a future that may await many countries, if not the entire globe.

Most economic comparisons between communism and capitalism have focused on the market versus private ownership distinction. Yet, in capitalist countries, environmental degradation is the result of factors *external* to market transactions. A **demand for environmental protection** can be expressed only through government action. Thus, the key issue is the responsiveness of the political system to this kind of demand.

Given this, the political distinction between western countries and the former USSR—democracy versus totalitarianism—is probably more relevant to environmental concerns than the market/state ownership distinction. When scientists or environmentalists in the Soviet Union attempted to bring information forward, they did so only at personal risk and generally found themselves cut off from any effective means of communication. Whenever economic decision makers can insulate themselves from those exposed to pollution—either through control over information or suppression of dissent—externalities are unlikely to be accounted for by the political system.

For example, one need not look to the Soviet Union to find governmental abuses of the environment. Many of the worst hazardous waste sites in our country resulted from U.S. military programs, shrouded in cold war secrecy. At the Hanford nuclear site in eastern Washington, for example, the U.S. Department of Energy has created a gargantuan waste problem, the extent of which is only now becoming clear after fifty years of tight information control.[23] The cleanup at Hanford, if indeed it goes through, is expected to cost at least $60 billion—more than the entire Superfund program directed at civilian dumps. In the United States, however, the potential for this kind of environmental abuse by the government has been largely reigned in by mandated public scrutiny of major decisions: the Environmental Impact Statement process described in Chapter 7.

Consider another example: Agricultural workers in many poor market-oriented countries employ the same environmentally destructive agricultural techniques so decried in the Soviet Union. These include the widespread use of pesticides like DDT that have been banned in developed countries.[24] Farmworkers and their families who bear the brunt of the environmental costs in these countries have neither access to information about alternatives nor sufficient political power to challenge the marketing efforts of the firms who profit from the sale of these chemicals. (Indeed, farmworkers in our own country have much less influence over environmental policy than suburban professionals who provide the core support for major environmental groups.)

Both **access to information** and the practice of **effective and widespread democracy** are, thus, necessary ingredients for successful environmental policy. Without them, citizens will be unable to translate their demand for environmental protection into a reality. Absent substantial pressure from those affected, government will have

---

[23]One obstacle the Department of Energy faces in its cleanup efforts is a widely acknowledged "credibility" problem, due to its history of providing inaccurate or misleading statements to the public regarding the extent of the health and environmental hazards at weapons facilities. See Office of Technology Assessment (1991).

[24]See, for example, Murray and Hoppin (1992).

neither the power nor the inclination to force economic decision makers—whether state bureaucrats, managers of private corporations, or ordinary citizens—to internalize the external environmental costs generated by their actions.

Part IV of this book will explore how this prescription of knowledge and power might be applied in poor countries, to address problems ranging from population growth to conservation. Here in the United States a general trend toward accountability has been embodied in environmental law, ranging from the EIS, to requirements for public hearings in the regulatory process, to more recent innovations such as the **Toxics Release Inventory.** In 1986, after a chemical factory in Bhopal, India, exploded, killing and maiming thousands, the U.S. Congress passed the Emergency Planning and Right-to-Know Act. The act required companies to report on their releases of 450 chemicals suspected or known to be toxic, many of them unregulated.

The Toxics Release Inventory provides self-reported data on chemical releases on a plant-by-plant basis across the country. It has a variety of goals, but an important one has been to make industry decision makers more accountable to the communities in which they operate. The TRI has spawned a variety of community-based, non-regulatory efforts to reduce chemical emissions. It provides a good example of how expanded information and effective democracy can serve to internalize externalities associated with economic production. (For more on the TRI, see chapters 13 and 14.)[25]

What, then, are the environmental lessons from communism? Given that government action is needed to force market actors to account for external costs, the experience of the former USSR teaches that "*unaccountable* government intervention is bad." When government uses its authority to silence its critics or distort and control information flows, or when those on the receiving end of environmental externalities have little real power, government failure in the environmental arena is likely. Strict environmental laws, without a vigilant, informed citizenry, are hollow laws.

12.7 Summary

This chapter has provided an introduction to the political economy of regulation. The regulatory process begins with national legislation. The EPA then translates the law into specific regulations. Finally, state governments implement and enforce the guidelines developed by the EPA. The United States has adopted a judicial model of regulation in which the EPA is required to go through a formal and elaborate process of information gathering and public hearings and must establish a quasi-legal basis for its major regulatory actions. The judicial model is designed to limit abuse of authority by regulatory bureaucrats but can be easily exploited to generate regulatory gridlock.

From an economic point of view, the primary obstacle to effective regulation is imperfect information. Regulators have only limited resources with which to gather information on the costs and benefits of a proposed rule, and so must often turn to the very sources they regulate for information about the problem. This sets up a reporting bias problem: How can regulators be sure the information they receive is correct? One way is to train and retain qualified technical personnel within the regulatory

---

[25]Sarokin and Schulkin (1991) and Hadden (1989). The impact of the TRI on emissions is discussed in detail in chapter 19.

agency. Another way is to design regulatory policy to minimize incentives for distortion.

Regardless of how much good information the agency collects, however, bureaucrats will still be left with substantial discretion in interpreting how environmental laws are to be implemented. Consideration of bureaucratic interests—agency building, personal career building, and job satisfaction—reveal no necessary bias toward over- or underregulation. Yet discretion raises the problem of political influence.

Who wins and who loses in the influence game? This question is difficult to answer in an objective fashion. I argue that due to their superior ability to mobilize votes, environmentalists tend to win more often than they lose in the legislative arena, while given their monetary advantage, industry tends to come out ahead in the regulatory process. The big loser from this adversarial structure is public faith in the rule of law. Public disenchantment with the EPA is a serious problem since an effective and respected regulatory agency is the principal tool we now have for controlling market externalities.

The prisoner's dilemma model suggests that competition between environmentalists and industry to influence bureaucrats leads to an inefficiently high level of lobbying and lawsuits. One suggested response to this problem has been to replace the judicial model of regulation, which imposes many legal restrictions on the EPA's behavior, with a corporatist model, giving the EPA much more discretion. Corporatism could potentially foster a more cooperative spirit between industry and environmentalists and is more widespread in Europe. Critics of corporatism argue, however, that in the U.S. context, where the government bureaucracy is relatively weak, corporatism amounts to a sellout to industry interests.

More straightforward ways of reducing lobbying include eliminating its tax-exempt status and instituting campaign finance reform. Environmental federalism would also help reduce the influence of Washington, DC–based interests but might lead to interstate competition to weaken standards.

Many have argued that the collapse of the Soviet Union demonstrates the ecological superiority of market-based economic systems over centrally planned systems. Environmental disaster in the former USSR certainly confirms that state socialism is not the answer to environmental problems. But the problem remains: Market-based economic systems have the potential to ultimately generate ecocide on a level comparable to that of communism.

The relevant lesson from the former USSR is that a lack of effective democracy will doom well-meaning government environmental initiatives to failure. Economic decision makers—whether state planners or private managers—will only take external environmental costs into account (internalize them) if those who bear the costs have the political power to force internalization. Nurturing effective democracy, in turn, requires both empowering citizens and providing access to information. The Toxics Release Inventory provides a good example of this in the United States.

This chapter has focused on the obstacles that the information-intensive regulatory process has encountered in attempts to achieve its legislative target—efficiency, safety, or sustainability in pollution control. The potential solutions discussed here have focused on procedural or political reforms such as better information gathering, a move to corporatism, campaign finance reform, and right-to-know laws.

By contrast, Part III of this book will focus on economic reforms of the pollution control process. Chapters 16 and 17 explore one option: a system of regulation that relies on *economic incentives,* requiring less information and fewer bureaucratic decisions. A second possibility is discussed in chapters 18 through 20. Rather than reform the regulatory process itself, instead refocus government pollution control policy on the promotion of clean technology, which reduces pollution in the first place. A final, and more optimistic view is that, in spite of the many problems with the regulatory process, overall it has worked surprisingly well. We will take up this line of argument in the next two chapters.

APPLICATION 12.0

Corporatist Solutions?[26]

To implement portions of the 1990 Clean Air Act, the EPA adopted a distinctly corporatist approach—negotiating the regulatory details with representatives from industry, the states, and big environmental groups. Agreement was reached by representatives of these generally hostile groups on regulations designed to encourage the use of so-called "clean" fuels. Industry benefited by having gasoline content standards set on an average basis rather than for every gallon of fuel. This provision reduced costs substantially. Environmentalists won a favorable resolution of an ambiguity that Congress had left in the law about the maximum allowable vapor pressure for fuels.

1. As the price for participation, all of the parties to the agreement pledged not to sue the EPA over its final clean fuel regulations. Assume the agreement to sue is not legally binding. What incentives do the parties at the table have to abide by their promise not to sue?

2. The *New York Times* reports that all parties involved were happy with the clean fuels decision, calling it a "win-win" solution. Relabel the prisoner's dilemma diagram in Section 12.5, using the strategies "negotiate" and "negotiate and sue," and the payoffs "average gas content" or "per gallon gas content" (for industry) and "strict vapor emissions" or "lax vapor emissions" (for environmentalists). Does the diagram illustrate, in principle, that all parties can be made better off by making an enforceable pledge not to sue?

3. In spite of the apparent success of the clean fuels negotiations, the EPA has made little headway in encouraging other corporatist endeavors. The Consensus and Dispute Resolution Staff at the agency has succeeded in getting agreements in only 12 out of 600 cases. Why might corporatist strategies be hard to implement in the United States?

4. In fact, not everyone was happy with the agreement. One critic of the corporatist approach, Stephen Viederman, put it this way: "'Where you stand,' according to Miles Law, 'depends on where you sit.' Who comes to the table is undeniably central to what is decided at the table. . . . The good news [about the clean fuels decision] was a broader participation in rule-making, with the views of business and industry balanced by other groups."[27] Based on the criticisms of corporatism discussed in Section 12.5, what do you think Viederman's bad news might be?

---

[26]This problem is drawn from information reported in "U.S. Agencies Use Negotiations to Pre-empt Lawsuits Over Rules," *New York Times,* September 23, 1991.

[27]"Who Comes to the Table?" (New York: Jessie Smith Noyes Foundation, 1991).

Key Ideas in Each Section

12.0 This chapter discusses two primary obstacles to effective government regulation of pollution: **imperfect information** and the opportunity for **political influence.**

12.1 The "generic" regulatory process has three steps: (1) passage of a law by Congress and the President, (2) drafting of regulations by the EPA, and (3) implementation and enforcement by state officials. The United States currently relies on a **judicial model of regulation,** which reduces bureaucratic discretion but also can lead to regulatory gridlock.

12.2 The first obstacle facing regulators is highly imperfect information. Because the agency has so many tasks, it often drafts rules based on inadequate or poor data. In addition, the agency must deal with a **reporting bias** when it turns to outside groups for information. Two ways to address this problem are to improve i**n-house analysis** and rely on **incentive-compatible regulation.**

12.3 Imperfect information gives rise to **bureaucratic discretion** in drafting and enforcing regulations. Bureaucratic motivations include **agency building, external career building** (influenced by the **revolving door**), and **job satisfaction.** Job satisfaction, in turn, can depend on **ideology,** the exercise of **power,** and the maintenance of a **quiet life.**

12.4 Where there is bureaucratic discretion, there is the opportunity for political influence. Political resources wielded by environmental groups and industry include **votes** and **dollars.** Dollars are useful for buying (1) **technical studies,** (2) lobbying **staff,** (3) **access** to decision makers, and (4) votes. This book argues that environmentalists win more often at the legislative stage of the regulatory process, while industry wins more often at all subsequent stages.

12.5 The prisoner's dilemma model suggests that competition for political influence is a zero-sum **game,** leading to an overinvestment in lobbying. Political reforms that might reduce this wasted effort include adopting a **corporatist model of regulation,** moving toward more **environmental federalism, campaign finance reform,** and eliminating the **tax-deductible status** of lobbying. The first two policies, however, are not without costs, while the latter two have proven politically quite difficult.

12.6 The Communist experience illustrates the potential for massive government failure in the regulatory process. Such failure is most likely when citizens are unable to express their political **demand for environmental regulation.** Doing so requires both **access to information** and **effective and widespread democracy.** The **Toxics Release Inventory** provides a good example of government action to encourage such trends in the United States.

References

Bryner, Gary C. (1987). *Bureaucratic Discretion.* New York: Pergammon.

Cropper, Maureen and Wallace Oates (1992). "Environmental Economics: A Survey." *The Journal of Economic Literature,* 30, no. 2, 675–740.

Feshbach, Murray and Alfred Friendly Jr. (1992). *Ecocide in the USSR.* New York: Basic Books.

Greider, William (1990). *Who Will Tell The People? The Betrayal of American Democracy.* New York: Simon & Schuster.

Hadden, Susan (1989). "Right-To-Know: What It Can Mean for Citizens." *The EPA Journal,* May–June.

Hukinnen, J. (1995). "Corporatism as an Impediment to Ecological Sustenance: The Case of Finnish Waste Management." *Ecological Economics,* 15, no. 1, 59–76.

Landy, Marc, Marc Roberts and Stephen R. Thomas (1990). *The Environmental Protection Agency: Asking the Wrong Questions.* New York: Oxford University Press.

McCallum, David B. and Vincent T. Covello (1989). "What the Public Thinks About Environmental Data." *EPA Journal,* May/June.

Ministry of VROM (1994). *Towards a Sustainable Netherlands.* The Hague: VROM.

Murray, D. L. and P. Hoppin (1992). "Recurring Contradictions in Agrarian Development: Pesticide Problems in Caribbean Basin Non-Traditional Agriculture." *World Development,* 20, no. 4, 597–606.

Office of Technology Assessment (1991). *Complex Clean-up: The Environmental Legacy of Nuclear Weapons Production.* Washington, DC: U.S. GPO.

Portney, Paul, Katherine Probst and Adam Finkel (1991). "The EPA at Thirtysomething." *Discussion Paper CRM 91-03.* Washington, DC: Resources for the Future.

Sanjour, William (1992). *What EPA Is Like and What Can Be Done About It.* Washington, DC: Environmental Research Foundation.

Sarokin, David and Jay Schulkin (1991). "Environmentalism and the Right-To-Know: Expanding the Practice of Democracy." *Ecological Economics,* vol. 4, 175–189.

Selden, Thomas M. and Marcoe E. Terrones (1993). "Environmental Legislation and Enforcement: A Voting Model with Asymmetric Information." *Journal of Environmental Economics and Management,* 24, no. 3, 212–228.

Stalon, George (1990). "Is Regulation What Regulators Do?" *Discussion Paper ENR90-05.* Washington, DC: Resources for the Future.

U.S. Office of Management and Budget (1988). *Regulatory Program of the United States Government.* Washington, DC: U.S. GPO.

CHAPTER 13

An Overview of Environmental Legislation

13.0 Introduction

Perhaps the most striking aspect of the U.S. national environmental regulation is its brief history. As recently as thirty years ago, the United States had *no* major federal legislation controlling the discharge of pollutants into the air and water, *no* national regulations covering the disposal of hazardous waste onto land, *no* process for reviewing new chemicals, only a limited procedure for registering new pesticides, and no protection for endangered species.

Prior to 1970, the states had sole responsibility for pollution control activities, but even at the state level, serious efforts at environmental protection have only a short history. Oregon initiated the first statewide air pollution control effort in 1952; only California had mandated tailpipe emission standards for cars by 1970. In the late 1950s and 1960s, as national attention began focusing on environmental problems, the federal government passed a variety of laws encouraging such decentralized efforts to regulate air and water pollution. These laws sponsored research on the health effects of pollution, provided resources for technical assistance and mechanisms for resolving cross-boundary disputes, and put informal pressure on U.S. automakers to reduce vehicle emissions.

On April 20, 1970, Americans celebrated Earth Day for the first time. Also that year, motivated by increasing public awareness, dissatisfaction with slow state regulatory efforts, and little improvement in the pollution performance of U.S. cars, the U.S. Congress struck out on a different, centralized environmental road. The Clean Air Act amendments of 1970 embraced a new philosophy in which minimum standards for air pollution control for the entire nation would be set in Washington. During the remainder of the decade, a similar approach was adopted for water pollution, solid and hazardous waste disposal, and chemical and pesticide registration.

By historical standards, environmental protection efforts are still in their early childhood, if not infancy. Nevertheless, environmental protection is growing up fast. As is detailed in chapter 9, the share of national output devoted to the environment has increased from about 1% to 2.5% over the last twenty years. This chapter provides an overview of national legislation in five areas: air pollution, water pollution, hazardous waste, toxic substances, and endangered species.

With this background laid, in the next chapter we will then move on to consider the actual accomplishments of this legislation, criticisms of regulation, and an evaluation of the prospects for future regulatory success.

13.1 Cleaning the Air

The original **Clean Air Act** (CAA), passed in 1963, focused on federal assistance to the states. Major amendments to the CAA occurred in 1970, 1977, and 1990, and have shaped the national regulatory framework.[1] The CAA (as amended) mandates a safety standard. Standards are to be set to "provide an **adequate margin of safety** . . . to protect the public . . . from any known or anticipated adverse effects associated with such air pollutants in the ambient air." Congress explicitly ruled out a consideration of costs and benefits in the attainment of this goal. Yet, as we saw in chapter 5, completely safe levels of many pollutants, short of zero discharge, do not exist. One of the difficulties the EPA has had in implementing the CAA has been in hammering out a politically acceptable definition of safety.

The CAA distinguishes two types of air pollutants. First are the so-called **criteria (or common) air pollutants:** particulates, sulfur dioxide, carbon monoxide, nitrogen oxide, ground-level ozone (smog), and lead. All these pollutants generate a variety of respiratory and heart-related problems, some contribute to cancer, and lead also causes neurological diseases. Ground-level ozone, better known as smog, should not to be confused with ozone in the upper atmosphere. Ground-level ozone is a harmful pollutant, while the ozone layer surrounding the earth provides a shield protecting us from dangerous ultraviolet rays. Similarly, carbon monoxide (CO)—the fatal gas that accumulates in a closed garage when the car is running—should not be confused with carbon dioxide (CO_2). Carbon dioxide, which is the major contributor to global warming, is also emitted from cars but is not now regulated by the government.

In addition to the criteria pollutants, Congress was also concerned about other less common air pollutants, which are also carcinogenic or interfere with reproductive, immune, or neurological systems. These pollutants, now called **hazardous air pollutants or air toxics,** are also regulated under a safety standard, but in a different fashion than the criteria pollutants.

For the criteria pollutants, Congress directed the EPA to develop **National Ambient Air Quality Standards (NAAQS). Ambient air quality** refers to the average quality of the air in a particular region. Each criteria pollutant was to be given a primary standard designed to protect human health, and a secondary standard focused on protecting wildlife, visibility, and ecological systems. Table 13.1 lists the primary NAAQS for the six criteria pollutants.[2]

---

[1]Portney (1990) provides a good detailed discussion of air pollution policy. For details on the 1990 Clean Air Act amendments, I relied on Robinson and Pease (1991) and Milkanovich (1992).

[2]Only sulfur dioxide has a secondary standard tighter than the primary standard. Carbon monoxide has no secondary standard; for particulates, nitrogen oxide, ozone, and lead, the secondary standard is identical to the primary standard. See Portney (1990: 35).

TABLE 13.1   Primary NAAQS for Criteria Air Pollutants, 1997

Pollutant	Averaging Time	Concentration Level ppm	Concentration Level μg/m³
Particulate Matter (PM10)	Annual	—	50.0
	24-Hour	—	150.0
Particulate Matter (PM2.5)	Annual	—	15.0
	24-Hour	—	65.0
Sulfur Dioxide	Annual	0.030	80.0
	24-Hour	0.140	365.0
Carbon Monoxide	8-Hour	9.000	10.0
	1-Hour	35.000	40.0
Nitrogen Oxide	Annual	0.053	100.0
Ozone	8-Hour	0.008	—
Lead	Max Quarterly	—	1.5

Source: Portney (1990: Table 3-2), who cites as his source The Office of Planning and Standards (1987), *National Air Quality and Emissions Trend Report,* 1987 (Research Triangle Park, NC: U.S. EPA. The particulate standards for PM2.5 were introduced in 1997 (but will not be binding for several years) at the same time that the ozone standard was tightened; see "Clinton Sharply Tightens Air Pollution Regulations," New York Times, June 26, 1997, p. A1.

The NAAQS are minimum standards, uniform around the country. In other words, regardless of the variation in compliance costs, all regions are expected to meet the NAAQ levels of air quality. If they desire, states are allowed to impose stricter standards.

What about areas already cleaner than the NAAQS? The 1977 CAA amendments set up a three-tiered system designed to prevent the significant deterioration of air quality. National parks and other scenic areas were designated Class I, in which air quality was to be maintained at the current level. Most areas were put into Class II, in which some deterioration was allowed. In the remaining areas, Class III, air quality was allowed to fall to the level of the NAAQS, but not below.

Once the NAAQs were set, each state was required to develop a **state implementation plan** detailing how emissions from both **stationary sources** (factories, power plants) and **mobile sources** (cars, trucks, airplanes) would be controlled in order to meet the ambient standards. To do this, state environmental officials first had to divide up their territory into so-called **air quality control regions,** geographic areas sharing similar air pollution problems. The plan would then provide an implementation strategy for each region.

For stationary sources, the EPA requires states to use what is known as **technology-based regulation.** For all new sources, the states must mandate the type of pollution technology required for new plants. These New Source Performance Standards (NSPS) require firms to install the "best technological system of emissions reduction" commercially available at the time the standards are set. Note that NSPS technology may not be sufficient to achieve the NAAQ standard; it is simply supposed to represent a serious effort to get there.

State regulators are also supposed to define even more stringent technology-based regulation for sources wishing to locate in areas that have not achieved the NAAQ standards (**non-attainment areas**). Such firms must use the lowest achievable emission rate (LAER) technology. Those wishing to locate in Class I (pristine) areas are theoretically required to achieve yet another standard, the best available control technology (BACT). In practice, there is often little difference between NSPS, LAER, and BACT.

Until 1990, states were not required to impose technology-based regulations on existing sources. However, the 1990 Clean Air Act amendments require the states to define and impose RACT, reasonably available control technology, on existing sources in non-attainment areas. RACT, BACT, LAER, NSPS—these acronyms seem bewildering upon introduction, but in fact, the actual regulatory process is much more tortured. The legal struggle to define what these different terms mean for individual industries has been one of the primary battlegrounds in the information war discussed in the last chapter.

There are two major, ongoing exceptions to the technology-based regulation of stationary sources common under the CAA. Authorities in the Los Angeles area are experimenting with an incentive-based program designed to provide firms with substantial flexibility in achieving targets for emissions of criteria pollutants. The 1990 CAA amendments also provide for a similar flexible system to control acid rain. This alternative incentive-based approach will be explored in detail in chapters 16 and 17.

To control emissions of criteria pollutants from mobile sources, the CAA has put most of the burden on auto manufacturers, requiring several rounds of reductions in vehicle emissions for new cars. This policy, however, has been criticized as a cost-ineffective strategy for achieving the NAAQS, because it builds in equally high costs for auto consumers in both clean and dirty areas. In other words, rural residents wind up paying for cleanup they may not need in the form of higher-priced cars. The EPA has also required non-attainment areas to use more closely targeted programs, including vehicle inspection programs and since 1990 the sale of reformulated (lower-polluting) fuels. In addition, as we will discuss further in chapter 20, California has implemented an electric vehicles program in an attempt to meet the NAAQ standard.

To summarize: For the criteria pollutants the regulatory process is now well advanced and progress has been made on several fronts, though problems remain. By contrast, the air toxics case illustrates regulatory gridlock at its extreme. Under the 1970 CAA statute, the EPA was instructed to identify and regulate hazardous air pollutants, defined as substances "which may reasonably be anticipated to result in an increase in mortality or an increase in serious, irreversible, or incapacitating reversible, illness."[3] As with the criteria pollutants, the CAA established "an ample margin of safety" as the regulatory target.

Over the next twenty years, the process went into a deep stall. The EPA argued that a literal interpretation of the CAA's safety mandate would require a zero-discharge standard, effectively banning dozens of valuable industrial chemicals. Unwilling to take such a severe step, the agency chose to ignore the problem, regulating only a couple of air toxics during the 1970s. Environmentalists sued the agency, arguing that bans were not necessary; instead, high levels of (expensive) controls should be

---

[3]This discussion of the air toxics program draws from Robinson and Pease (1991), who also provide the quote from the 1970 CAA.

imposed on products without substitutes. A compromise along these lines was developing in the late 1970s but collapsed with the election of President Reagan in 1980, who had campaigned on a deregulatory agenda.

During the first half of the decade, the EPA chose to "study the problem." However, by the late 1980s, pressure was building for action: The 1984 explosion of a chemical plant in Bhopal, India, and the congressionally mandated release of plant-by-plant chemical emissions (the TRI discussed in the last chapter), prodded the EPA into a study revealing that cancer risks from air toxics in 205 communities around the country exceeded 1 in 1,000.

The impasse was finally addressed in the 1990 Clean Air Act. The 1990 amendments adopt technology-based regulation, requiring the EPA to specify MACT (maximum achievable control technology) for different sources emitting 189 air pollutants presumed to be hazardous. The EPA can add or delete substances from this list. MACT is not suppose to achieve an "ample margin of safety" immediately, since Congress mandated that it be selected with some consideration of attainment cost. However, once MACT has been put in place (theoretically in 1996), additional control measures will be required to reduce any residual cancer risk down to a level of at least 1 in 10,000 for the most exposed population, with an ultimate risk target of 1 in 1 million for the population at large.

FIGURE 13.1 Outline of the Clean Air Act as Amended

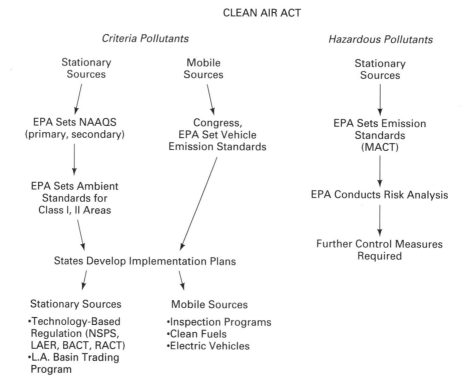

Thus, after twenty years of stalled progress and contentious litigation, policy makers finally took the bull by the horns and defined more clearly what was meant by an "ample margin of safety." The process of regulating air toxics can now get underway. The 1990 CAA amendments, however, address only stationary sources of hazardous air pollutants. Portney (1990) reports that only 20% of air toxics are in fact emitted by stationary sources that fall under the purview of the amendments. Thus, air toxic emissions from small and mobile sources remain uncontrolled under current legislation.

Figure 13.1 provides a general outline of the Clean Air Act amendments. To summarize: The CAA sets a general goal of "safety" for the two categories of criteria and hazardous pollutants. Emissions of the criteria pollutants are regulated with the intent to achieve an ambient air quality standard within each air quality control region. By contrast, hazardous pollutants must meet emission standards ultimately designed to reduce cancer risks to the most exposed to *at least* 1 in 10,000. Finally, both programs are technology-based. With a few exceptions, regulators decide on particular pollution control technologies that firms are then required to adopt.

13.2 Fishable and Swimmable Waters

The first national water pollution law was passed in 1899. Its simple intent was to prevent industries from disrupting navigation by literally clogging rivers and streams with sludge, sawdust, or fiber. There was little national activity beyond this until the 1950s and 1960s when the federal government began assisting and encouraging states to develop their own pollution standards. In 1972, however, Congress opted for a centralized strategy with the passage of the **Federal Water Pollution Control Act** (FWPCA). In combination with the **Clean Water Act** of 1977, this legislation provides our basic water pollution framework.[4]

FWPCA laid out an ambitious safety-based goal: the achievement of **fishable and swimmable waters** by 1983. However, the legislation set its sight beyond this charge, which we might consider a reasonable safety standard as defined in chapter 10 (the elimination of "significant" risk). FWPCA, in fact, calls for the elimination of all risk — zero discharge of pollutants into navigable waters by 1985. Needless to say, this last goal has not been met. Finally, the act prohibits the discharge of "toxic materials in toxic amounts," another ambiguous phrase that has provided grist for the regulatory lawyers' mill.

Individual states are left to draft their own water quality emissions guidelines. For consistency with the FWPCA, they must be sufficiently strict to allow swimming and some types of fishing. However, states are free to draft stricter regulation, for example, to protect water habitat or undeveloped rivers.

The approach used to achieve state water quality targets is in many ways similar to the regulation of air toxics described in the previous section. In 1972, the Congress envisioned two initial rounds of technology-based controls. The EPA was directed to determine the best practical technology (BPT) and a more stringent best available technology (BAT) so that all industrial dischargers could have the technologies installed by 1977 and 1983, respectively. The timetable proved too stringent, however, and was amended in 1977.[5] It took until 1988 for the EPA to issue all (save one) of its

---

[4]The next few paragraphs are based on the more detailed discussion in Freeman (1990).

[5]An additional technology category, best conventional technology, was also added here (Freeman [1990]).

BAT regulations. With BAT regulations issued, it will take many more years until the tens of thousands of sources nationwide have adopted the technology. Once BAT is in place, the EPA has the authority to impose a third round of even more stringent (better than the best!) technology-based controls on sources contributing to the pollution of lakes or streams that have yet to achieve state ambient quality standards.

In addition to installing BPT and then BAT (or BAT alone for newcomers), each discharger must hold a permit that specifies his or her legal pollution emission level. State agencies are by and large responsible for the permitting process and for enforcing compliance.

One of the major sources of water pollution is improperly treated sewage. As a result, a principal component of federal clean water legislation has been the provision of **grants to municipalities** for the construction of sewage facilities. From 1973 to 1983, Freeman (1990) reports that $34 billion in federal dollars was committed for this purpose, with several billions more allocated since that time. While the increased federal spending has displaced spending by state and local authorities, overall federal aid *has accelerated* the pace of sewage treatment. In addition, financing sewer projects with federal tax dollars has proven less regressive than local financing. However, because the federal aid has come in the form of large grants, local incentives to carefully monitor construction costs have been reduced and costs inflated.

Finally, federal clean water legislation has focused primarily on stationary point sources of pollution (factories and sewage plants). However, **non-point water pollution** (runoff from storm sewers in urban areas, and from farms and construction sites) has always been an important source of water pollution. Siltation and nutrient loading from agricultural runoff are the primary pollution sources affecting the nation's streams, rivers, and lakes.[6] The rapid destruction of the nation's wetlands from pollution and drainage has also become a major environmental concern.

The federal clean water legislation puts responsibility for regulating non-point pollution on the states; the 1987 Water Quality Act requires states to develop so-called "best-management practices" to control runoff from industrial and agricultural sites. Progress in this area has been slow because the diverse nature of the non-point problem makes centralized, technology-based regulation infeasible.

Two ways to control non-point water pollution are to (1) reduce runoff and (2) reduce the volume of pollutants available to be mobilized, a "pollution-prevention" strategy. As an example of the latter, farmers have begun adopting so-called conservation-tillage practices, which leave stubble in fields to reduce runoff. In addition, a variety of measures have been introduced that reduce overall pesticide use.[7] We will look more closely at some of these steps in chapter 19.

13.3 Hazardous Waste Disposal on Land

The 1970s were the decade of air and water pollution legislation. In the 1980s, concern shifted to land disposal of hazardous waste. Although the initial law covering hazardous waste disposal, the **Resource Conservation and Recovery Act** (RCRA, pro-

---

[6]Griffin (1991). The primary problem for estuaries is still a point source: municipal water treatment facilities.
[7]For a further discussion, see Griffin (1991).

nounced *ricra*), was passed in 1976, actual regulation did not get underway until 1980 and accelerated when the law was amended by Congress in 1984.[8] RCRA is concerned with current disposal practices. By contrast, the second major piece of hazardous waste legislation deals with abandoned dump sites. The Comprehensive Environmental Response, Compensation and Liability Act (CERCLA, better known as **Superfund**) was passed in 1980 and amended in 1986.

What exactly is hazardous waste? One inclusive definition is any substance that poses a potential, substantial threat to human health or the environment. However, resolving what this means has proved a thorny problem. The EPA has developed a **RCRA list** of about 450 substances and waste flows deemed to be hazardous, based on criteria of ignitability, corrosivity, reactivity, and toxicity. However, certain materials—oil-drilling muds, mine tailings, and ash from solid waste incinerators and coal-fired utilities—were granted immunity from hazardous waste regulation under RCRA. Some states, such as California and Washington, have instituted more stringent definitions that effectively double the volume of substances regulated as hazardous.[9]

A typical hazardous waste dump will include many substances known or suspected to be either carcinogenic or to have adverse effects on reproductive, immune, or neurological systems. While hazardous waste thus clearly poses a potential threat to human health and the environment, what are the actual risks? This is a very contentious topic. Most exposure to waste occurs when chemicals leach out of dumps in rainwater or into the air in vaporous form. However, because the numbers of people living in close proximity to the dumps is small, and because residents come and go, it is difficult to establish whether elevated levels of disease sometimes found by such dumps occur by chance or as a result of exposure to waste. Moreover, because many wastes are quite long-lived, long-term effects that are difficult to predict must be factored in.

Love Canal, a one-time suburb of Niagara Falls, New York, is the best-known example of a hazardous waste dump. From 1942 to 1953, the Hooker Chemical and Plastics Corporation (now Occidental Chemical) buried millions of pounds of chemical wastes encased in metal drums in the abandoned canal. Hooker then sold the site to the city for $1 as a possible location for an elementary school. A suburban housing development soon grew up around the area. However, the drums rusted, and liquid waste began to pool on the surface and seep into people's basements. In 1978, after growing concern by residents over reported health effects—ranging from the loss of fur on pets to birth defects and breast cancer—and the detection of high levels of chemicals in some homes, the state of New York ordered the area immediately around the dump evacuated.

Love Canal is probably the most extensively studied hazardous waste site in the world, yet many questions remain about possible health effects. Two early studies of elevated cancer rates and chromosomal defects among Love Canal residents—which sparked a second round of evacuations—have since been discredited. However, the New York State Department of Health did find roughly double the expected rate of

---

[8]RCRA also authorizes the EPA to regulate a variety of nonhazardous wastes. These include wastes at municipal landfills (discussed in chapter 10), as well as hazardous industrial wastes exempted from official designation as "RCRA hazardous wastes," for example, oil-drilling muds or incinerator ash.
[9]Office of Technology Assessment (1992).

low birth-weight babies in a low-lying area adjacent to the dump during the period of active dumping, as well as a statistically significant increase in babies born with birth defects after the chemicals were dumped.[10] Paigen et al. (1987) found that children who had lived in the canal area were shorter and weighed less than a control group.

The Love Canal case illustrates first that improperly handled hazardous waste can pose a real health threat. Second, establishing the full nature of extent of adverse health effects is quite difficult. A recent government-sponsored scientific review panel, charged with assessing public concern that hazardous waste poses a serious threat to public health, concluded only that such concern could be neither confirmed nor refuted.[11]

Nevertheless, because of the limited routes of exposure, and the small numbers of people living in the close vicinity of dumps, many have argued that hazardous waste is unlikely to pose a national health threat comparable to that of air and water pollution.[12] Following this line of reasoning, the EPA's Science Advisory Panel did not list hazardous waste as a primary concern for ecological, welfare, or health risks (see Table 8.3). At Love Canal, after the dump had been capped with a layer of clay, the streams cleaned up, and other remedial action taken, the New York State Department of Health Commissioner concluded in 1989 that some homes in the area could be safely reoccupied.[13]

However, in spite of official assessments that downplay the overall risk from hazardous waste, the public remains quite concerned. Partly, this has to do with a disagreement over the normative goal of environmental policy. Under a safety standard, the fact that the numbers at risk of exposure are small does not lessen concern. Concern over hazardous waste also has to do with the visibility of victims. While tracing a birth defect directly to a neighboring waste dump is difficult, it is easier than linking it to smokestack emissions a hundred miles away. Finally, the public remains wary of scientific risk assessment; given the current state of knowledge about possible effects of hazardous waste, such skepticism might be warranted.

The volume of hazardous waste is significant. Each year, American industry and households generate around 700 million tons, under the EPA definition. In 1986–1987, the EPA estimated that around 238 million tons fell under RCRA regulation; much of the remainder was disposed of through liquid discharges regulated by the Clean Water Act.[14] Household hazardous wastes takes the form of used motor oil, house paint, pesticides, and batteries. However, the bulk of waste is produced by industry. Shapiro (1990) reports that, in 1985, although there were over 650,000 generators of hazardous waste, around 2% of these produce 95% of the total.

What happens to all this waste? Common disposal methods include surface impoundment, landfilling, injection into deep underground wells, direct or indirect discharge into surface waters, incineration, and treatment. However, under the presumption that disposal on land posed the greatest long-term environmental threat from hazardous waste (and given that discharge into water and air was already regulated),

---

[10]See Vianna and Polan (1984), and the discussion in Brown (1989).

[11]National Research Council (1991: 1).

[12]Four million people live within one mile, and 40 million within four miles, of a Superfund site (National Research Council [1991]).

[13]Brown (1989).

[14]Office of Technology Assessment (1992).

the 1984 RCRA amendments built in a strong **bias against land disposal.** The legislation essentially puts the burden of proof on firms to demonstrate that the disposal method is indeed safe.[15] Incineration, recycling, and water discharge are thus likely to become the most common disposal methods in the future.

The regulatory framework for hazardous waste disposal under RCRA has a three-part focus. First, as noted above, the EPA has been required to designate which substances are to be deemed hazardous. RCRA than requires cradle-to-grave tracking of such wastes. When hazardous waste is shipped it must be accompanied by a manifest, stating its origin and intermediate stops. This manifest system was designed to discourage illegal dumping, though its effect on this process is unclear.[16]

Finally, RCRA requires that facilities that treat, store, or dispose of hazardous wastes are to be regulated under a safety standard. To accomplish this goal, RCRA imposes location restrictions and requires personnel training, groundwater monitoring, closure and post-closure plans, and adequate insurance coverage. Under RCRA, facilities can also be forced to clean up old dump sites under their jurisdiction in order to receive a permit.[17] However, the stringency of regulations vary from program to program. As we saw in chapter 12, the EPA's final regulatory standards for deep-well injection of wastes (finalized in 1989) were successfully challenged as too onerous by the chemical industry.

RCRA governs the current disposal of wastes. By contrast, CERCLA, or Superfund, provides a mechanism for cleaning up abandoned dump sites. Superfund takes its name from a pool of money collected by the government in the form of taxes on the chemical and petroleum industries, a general corporate environmental tax, and personal income tax revenues—about $1.5 billion per year in 1990—to finance dump cleanups.

However, Superfund also provides a more controversial funding mechanism. Any party who disposed of waste in a particular dump, legally or not, can be sued by the government to finance the entire cost of the cleanup. This system, known as **strict, joint, and several liability,** was put in place as a way to fund cleanups without spending additional government dollars. If the government could find one responsible party, the theory went, that party would then have the incentive to uncover other dumpers. However, the system has developed into a legal morass. Rather than bear what are potentially tremendous cleanup costs, firms have devoted resources to suing one another and the government over who will pay what share. Detroit automakers, for example, sued over 200 parties, including the Girl Scouts, to contribute to one Michigan cleanup.[18]

Given this situation, the legal costs of Superfund have begun to mount. Although data are limited, the best study available estimates that, as a percentage of cleanup costs, legal fees and other transaction expenses range from 7% to 41%.[19] Probst and Portney (1992), using a "speculative" legal fees percentage of 20%, estimate that around $8 billion could be saved from currently designated Superfund sites if retroactive liability provisions were eliminated and cleanup was financed solely out of the trust fund.

---

[15]Wagner (1991).

[16]Shapiro (1990) notes that most waste (95%) never officially leaves the site at which it is generated; moreover, incentives for illegal dumping, bypassing the manifest system altogether, still exist.

[17]Wagner (1991).

[18]"The Toxics Mess Called Superfund," *Business Week,* May 11, 1992.

[19]These results are from a 1989 RAND study, summarized in Probst and Portney (1992).

The liability system under Superfund does have one attractive efficiency feature: The fact that waste *generators,* not just disposal facility operators, are held strictly responsible for the ultimate fate of their waste clearly provides a powerful incentive for careful management practices today. **Fear of future liability** under Superfund has spurred manufacturers both to seek methods for reducing their use of hazardous chemicals and to take greater care in their disposal practices. (For more on this point, see chapter 19.) Moreover, Superfund liability applies to a broader spectrum of potentially hazardous materials than does RCRA regulation.

In addition, some fear that weakening the retroactive liability provisions under Superfund in order to reduce legal costs may send the wrong signal to industry about government's future intent to force polluters to pay. Retroactive liability also encourages private parties to initiate cleanups of non-Superfund sites.[20]

Beyond high legal costs, Superfund has been bedeviled by other problems, including site selection, costly cleanup efforts and resolving the "How clean is clean?" issue. By 1995, from a universe of some 30,000 dump sites nationwide, the EPA had designated 1372 as high-priority Superfund sites. Figure 13.2 shows the status of these sites: A total of 346 sites had been cleaned up to varying degrees.[21] Average per site cleanup cost estimates range from $27 million to $50 million.[22] Total cleanup costs for the currently designated sites alone will thus run to at least $33 billion. Given these problems, Congress has long considered major changes to the Superfund program; as of mid-1997, however, no revision had been undertaken.

Superfund also authorizes the EPA to conduct emergency action at sites where immediate risks to the public or the environment are present. By 1991 the agency had undertaken remedial emergency action at over 1,600 sites. Over 20,000 people were evacuated from their homes, with close to 90% eventually returning. Alternative water supplies had been supplied to 267,000 people.[23]

FIGURE 13.2 Status of Superfund Sites on the NPL, 1995

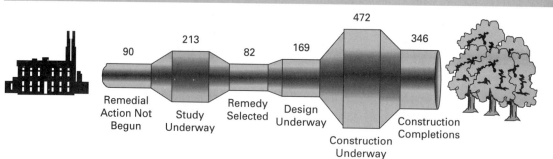

Note: The Remedial Action Not Begun Category figure includes sites with Removal Actions.

Source: http://www.epa.gov/superfund/oerr/whatissf/mgmtrpt.htm.

---

[20]For an extensive discussion, see Probst and Portney (1992). The authors point out that, on the surface, prospective rather than retroactive liability is all that is necessary to effect current management practices. However, Superfund's retroactive structure has clearly underscored to firms what strict liability will mean.

[21]"The Toxics Mess Called Superfund," *Business Week,* May 11, 1992.

[22]Probst and Portney (1992).

[23]U.S. EPA (1991).

13.4 Chemicals and Pesticides

So far, this chapter has given a brief review of the legislation governing the disposal of wastes into the air and water, and onto the land. The government has also passed two laws that share the ostensible goal of restricting the use of environmentally dangerous products in the first place. The Federal Insecticide, Fungicide and Rodenticide Act (**FIFRA**) and the Toxic Substances Control Act (**TSCA,** pronounced tosca) provide a mechanism for the EPA to review both new and currently marketed pesticides and chemicals, respectively, for their environmental impact. The agency can then recommend restrictions on such products, *if* they can be justified on a benefit-cost basis. Thus, unlike the other major pollution statutes described above, FIFRA and TSCA direct the EPA to pursue an explicit balancing of costs and benefits in the regulatory process. **Efficiency** rather than safety is the intended goal.

FIFRA was originally passed by Congress in 1947 to protect farmers from fraudulent claims by pesticide manufacturers. Amendments in 1964, 1972, 1978, and 1988 have provided the legislation with an environmental mandate. Under FIFRA, all new pesticides must be registered with the EPA; to obtain approval for major new ingredients, manufacturers must conduct and submit scientific studies of an agent's toxicity. This can be an expensive and time-consuming process. According to an industry source, registering a major new ingredient will cost between $5 million and $7 million in scientific studies, and take up to five years.[24] The EPA is then expected to weigh the benefits of approving the new pesticide (lower costs to farmers and, ultimately, food prices for consumers) against the environmental costs.

If evidence accumulates that an *existing* pesticide is harmful, the EPA can institute a benefit-cost analysis of the product and, depending upon the findings, limit or restrict its use. This so-called **special review** process entails a lengthy, trial-like procedure. Finally, under the 1972 amendments, the EPA was required to reregister hundreds of existing pesticides that had already been registered without environmental analysis. However, until 1988, when it was forced to do so by Congress, the EPA took no action on this front.

The EPA's cost-benefit analyses under FIFRA have been subject to criticism, primarily on the benefits side. In theory, pesticide benefits should be measured as the net increase in consumer surplus from lower food prices, plus any change in growers' and manufacturers' profits. Ironically, if pesticides boost yields, farmers as a group may be worse off since crop prices fall and demand is unresponsive to price decreases (inelastic). In the agricultural case, one also needs to subtract additional subsidy payments to farmers resulting from an increase in yields. To do this properly, one would need good estimates of the pesticide's effectiveness relative to the next best alternative, as well as the price responsiveness of demand (elasticity) for different crops in question, and good input and output price data.[25]

This information is generally hard to get. In fact, for pesticide registration, the EPA does no benefits estimation at all. Instead the agency relies on the manufacturer's willingness to expend money on the registration process as evidence that the project will yield some benefit. The EPA in fact does not even require any evi-

---

[24]R. Sherref, quoted in Shapiro (1990).
[25]For a discussion of the issues involved in pesticide benefit estimation, see Gianessi et al. (1989).

dence that the pesticide is effective; thus it cannot even begin a formal benefit analysis. As a result, the process for new pesticides looks only at risks and is essentially a "loose" safety standard.[26]

Under the special review process for existing pesticides, the agency does engage in benefits analysis, but there are no formal guidelines for conducting such an assessment. In addition, available information is often poor. Thus the quality of the benefits assessment will vary from study to study. Cropper et al. (1991) find that numerical benefit estimates were available for only 167 of the 245 food use decisions they studied in the special review process.

In an interesting look at the political economy of the special review process, Cropper et al. found that regulators did in fact respond to the information presented in the benefit-cost analyses. Pesticide uses were more likely to be canceled the greater the associated health and environmental risks. At the same time, higher estimated costs of cancellation reduced the likelihood that such an action would be taken.

Cropper et al. also find substantial evidence for political influence. Comments by environmentalists (often concerned about protecting marine life) dramatically increased the likelihood of restriction, while comments by growers and academics (primarily representing industry) had the opposite effect. Environmentalists commented on 49% of the decisions, while growers and academics commented on 38% of the decisions. On any particular decision, the combined influence of the latter group outweighed that of the former. Of course the influence of the pesticide manufacturer, involved throughout the process, was also very important but could not be independently identified. In addition, during the early years of the deregulatory Reagan administration, environmentalists did not participate at all in the public comment process, although the influence of growers increased.

This brief discussion of the benefit-cost process under FIFRA highlights several of the points made in chapter 12. First, information about the benefits and costs of regulation is not easy to obtain. Second, regulators must often turn to regulated firms to obtain access to the information that is available. Third, lobbying resources and political orientations matter; special review decisions were clearly affected by the presence of industry and environmental advocates. Finally, lobbying is not the only thing that matters. Controlling for the presence of industry and environmental advocates, regulators did respond to their legislative mandate to weigh costs against benefits.

The legislation governing toxic chemicals, TSCA, was passed in 1976. In a fashion similar to FIFRA, TSCA requires the EPA to *review all new chemicals* and provides the agency with the *authority to restrict the use of existing chemicals.* However, TSCA gives the government much less leverage than does FIFRA. Under TSCA, the EPA must be notified ninety days before the manufacture of a new chemical. However, no scientific data need be included with the notification. The agency then uses the premanufacture period to review the chemical. Since most of the new chemicals will not be accompanied by substantial test data, the EPA must rely on toxicity comparisons with similar compounds. Even here, however, information is quite slim. One study which examined a subsample of the 65,000 plus chemicals regulated by the EPA in

---

[26]See Shistar (1992) for a fuller discussion. Cropper et al. (1991) report maximum accepted risks in the special review process of 1.1 in 100 for applicators, 3.1 in 100,000 for mixers, and 1.7 in 10,000 for mixers.

1977 estimated that, for 78% of chemicals with production in excess of 1 million pounds, no toxicity data existed.[27]

As a pointed example of how little we know about chemical toxicity, in 1996, Theo Colborn, a scientist at the World Wildlife Fund, published a book called *Our Stolen Future.* She linked evidence of declining sperm counts and a rising reported incidence of breast cancer to so-called "endocrine disruptors"—fairly common synthetic chemicals whose structure mimics that of natural hormones. At this writing Colborn's thesis about human health impacts remains controversial—for example, human sperm count declines appear to be geographically isolated. But there is clear evidence that wildlife populations have been damaged by exposure to these chemicals.

If the EPA determines that the new product may pose an unreasonable health risk, the agency can prohibit manufacture of the chemical until the manufacturer provides sufficient data to make a final decision on the product. Otherwise, the product is presumed safe. The EPA currently reviews over 2,000 new chemicals each year. In fiscal year 1984, 84% of the new chemicals submitted passed the EPA's screen, 4% were withdrawn by manufacturers, and 7% were subject to regulation.[28] By 1987, the EPA had prohibited or restricted the manufacture, distribution, or use of 553 new chemicals.[29]

For existing chemicals, the EPA must go through a formal legal procedure, which can easily take more than two years, merely to require testing. A similar legal process is then necessary to justify, on a benefit-cost basis, any proposed restrictions on the chemical. As of 1986, the EPA had requested tests on only thirteen groups of chemicals and had regulated just one: ozone-depleting chlorofluorocarbons from aerosol cans in the late 1970s. (For more on the ozone hole problem, see chapter 23.) As discussed in chapter 10, the EPA's ten-year effort to restrict asbestos use under TSCA was thrown out by the courts in 1991 for failing to meet a rigorous efficiency standard. Because TSCA places a much higher legal burden of proof on the EPA than does FIFRA, there has been substantially less regulatory activity under the former statute.

While TSCA regulates the *use* of chemicals, an information-based law appears to have had a much bigger impact on U.S. chemical *emissions.* In 1986, after a chemical factory in Bhopal, India, exploded, killing and maiming thousands, the U.S. Congress passed the Emergency Planning and Right-to-Know Act. The act required companies to report on their releases of 450 chemicals suspected or known to be toxic, many of them unregulated at the time. The so-called **Toxics Release Inventory (TRI),** mentioned briefly at the end of chapter 12, provides self-reported data on chemical releases on a plant-by-plant basis across the country.

The TRI data first went public in 1989 and proved to be startling: Industry was emitting nearly 5 billion pounds of chemicals of various toxicities, mostly substances that were either unregulated or under legal limits. In the face of public relations pressures generated by the TRI list, many big chemical firms adopted pollution prevention programs.

The TRI numbers provide evidence of success. Overall, releases of the seventeen most toxic chemicals fell by 51% from 1988 to 1994.[30] Arora and Cason (1996) pro-

[27]This result is from a National Academy of Sciences study, reviewed in Shapiro (1990).
[28]Shapiro (1990). An additional 2% were in suspended status.
[29]Carlin (1990).
[30]Davies and Mazurek (1997).

vide evidence that firms with more public exposure reduced emissions the most. Unlike all the other laws discussed in this chapter, the TRI did not mandate emission reductions or indeed have any particular goal other than informing the public about emissions. Its success suggests that preventing pollution at industrial plants, either through recycling or source reduction—discussed further in chapter 19—is relatively inexpensive.

13.5 Endangered Species Protection

The **Endangered Species Act (ESA)** is our one piece of ecologically motivated environmental legislation. The law, passed in 1973, requires protection of a certain type of natural capital—species—regardless of the cost. The rationale for the law is strictly anthropocentric: "these species . . . are of aesthetic, ecological, educational, historical, recreational and scientific value to the Nation and its people."[31]

The strict implications of the law became apparent in the mid-1970s, when a University of Tennessee law school student filed suit and successfully halted the construction of a nearly completed $110 million dam. The reason? A new species of fish called the snail darter had been discovered downriver. Upset by the successful lawsuit, Congress created the so-called "God Squad"—an appointed committee with the authority to overrule ESA decisions on efficiency grounds.

Ironically, the God Squad concluded that the dam in fact didn't make sense even on benefit-cost terms. Finally, Congress overrode the God Squad and authorized construction by a special act of legislation. A new population of snail darters, meanwhile, had been discovered elsewhere, and in 1984 the status of the fish was upgraded from "endangered" to "threatened."

Under the ESA, federal agencies are required to list animals and plant species considered to be **endangered** or **threatened** (likely to become endangered). Recovery plans for these organisms must be developed and then **critical habitat** designated. Once this has been done, both public and private actors must refrain from damaging this habitat. (Technically, the act prohibits "taking" of a listed species, and the Supreme Court has ruled that this includes damaging their habitat.) Both the listing and habitat designation decisions are supposed to be purely scientific, with no consideration of economic costs or benefits.

In 1996, there were 955 listed species, 753 endangered and 206 threatened. Some 4,000 other species are potential candidates for listing (Jost [1996], Easter-Pilcher [1996]). The scientific basis for deciding which critters and plants to list is far from precise; Metrick and Weitzman (1996) find that both larger and perceived "higher" life forms are more liable to get listed, while Easter Pilcher (1996) finds little consistency in the scientific justifications across listings. In 1990, ten feathered or fuzzy species (eight birds, one bear, one panther) accounted for over half of all federal expenditures on recovery.

These expenditures are not large: In 1995 the government spent around $80 million in total on listing and recovery, about the cost of two miles of interstate highway (Jost [1996]). However, the ESA has been embroiled in controversy because, its critics

---

[31]Cited in Jost (1996).

allege, it imposes large economic costs on private landholders. Recall that the statute prohibits all actors—public and private—from disturbing the critical habitat of a listed species. This means, in practice, that should an endangered animal be discovered on your property, then you might not be able to develop it—no matter how much you paid for it.

Now, from an economic perspective, markets should be able to adapt readily to this kind of situation. If such surprise discoveries happened often, then people would begin to pay attention to them. One might even expect potential property buyers to demand an "ESA survey" before they bought a piece of land. Indeed, such surveys are routine now for uncovering the presence of hazardous waste. The fact that we don't see a market for ESA surveys suggests the problem is fairly isolated. And the data bear this out. From 1987 to 1991, the U.S. Fish and Wildlife Service engaged in 2,000 formal consultations on development proposals under the ESA; 18, less than 1%, were blocked.[32]

Nevertheless, the ESA like all regulations, imposes costs on the private sector, and in certain cases, these have been large and dramatic. Perhaps the best-known case involves protection of the spotted owl in the old-growth forests of the Pacific Northwest. While a far cry from the disaster predicted by critics, owl protection beginning in 1994 has meant that a few thousand timber jobs lost in the 1990 recession have not reappeared. (As noted in chapter 9, this case, along with high-sulfur coal mining, represent by far the most severe local jobs-environment trade-offs found in the United States.)

However, the overall Pacific Northwest economy has been performing quite well in recent years, with very low unemployment rates. Many area economists (Power [1996]) attribute the robust growth of the non-timber economy to be due in good measure to the high quality of life—including protected forests—found there. Finally one benefit-cost study found that the nationwide WTP for owl preservation exceeded the costs, implying that owl preservation met the standard not only of ecological sustainability but also of efficiency (Hagen et al. [1992]).

Beyond high and/or unfairly distributed compliance costs, the ESA has received two other types of criticism. The first is economic. The ESA is all stick and no carrot; in its current format it gives landowners no incentive to go beyond the letter of the law. (Indeed, some have argued that it provides an opposite, very perverse incentive. Upon discovering an endangered critter, landowners might be tempted to "shoot, shovel, and shut up." True, but the penalties if caught are very high!)

The second criticism is biological. The ESA's focus on species rather than ecosystems distracts attention from the primary task—preserving biodiversity. Too much energy can be devoted to saving a single species while a rich ecosystem goes down the tubes. (This is similar to the criticism that the safety standard provides no guide to cost-effectiveness.) As a result, interest has turned to the identification and preservation of so-called "hot spots"—ecosystems rich in threatened or endangered biodiversity. In spite of these criticisms, however, a 1995 National Academy of Sciences review of the ESA was generally favorable (National Research Council [1995]).

---

[32]Schlickeisen (1996),

TABLE 13.2   Principal Resource Protection Laws

Resource or Pollutant	Major Legislation	Standard
Air	Clean Air Act (Amended, 1990)	safety
Water	FWPCA; Clean Water Act	safety
Land	RCRA: new sites; CERCLA (Superfund): old sites	safety
Pesticides	FIFRA	efficiency
Chemicals	TSCA	efficiency
Species	ESA	ecological sustainability

13.6 Summary

This chapter has provided a brief look at the existing structure of national environmental protection legislation. Table 13.2 provides a summary. The three statutes governing disposal on land and in the air and water have as their goal the achievement a safe and clean environment, irrespective of the cost. In fact, costs do enter through the back door, in decisions about the resources the EPA can devote to each area and in the specific regulations that emerge to implement the laws. However, the clear intent of the legislation is to target environmental cleanup at a level much higher than efficiency would dictate.

By contrast, the two statutes governing the introduction of new pesticides and chemicals seek explicitly to balance the costs and benefits of environmental protection, in an attempt to achieve something like efficient regulation. (Chemical *emissions* have also been affected by the public relations pressure generated from the TRI.) Finally, the Endangered Species Act is our only major statute that explicitly seeks ecological sustainability as a goal.

Given this background, we turn now to an evaluation of the successes and failures of this impressive, if young, regulatory structure.

APPLICATION 13.0

Time to Regurgitate

1. Give some examples of technology-based regulation.

2. Give some examples to show how safety-based legislation can be inefficient. Give some examples to show how efficiency–based legislation can be unsafe. Give an example in which ecological sustainability-based legislation also happens to lead to an efficient outcome.

Key Ideas in Each Section

13.0 This chapter reviews the major federal environmental laws and their accomplishments in five areas: waste disposal (1) in the air, (2) in the water, and (3) on land, (4) the regulation of new and existing pesticides and chemicals, and (5) protection of endangered species.

13.1 The **Clean Air Act** and its amendments require regulation to achieve an **adequate margin of safety.** Two types of pollutants, **criteria (common)** and **hazardous air pollutants (air toxics),** are regulated differently. The EPA sets **National Ambient Air Quality Standards (NAAQS)** for criteria pollutants and a health-based standard for air toxics. States must develop **implementation plans** to bring both **stationary** and **mobile sources** into compliance with standards. **Non-attainment areas** face special requirements. In all cases, the EPA relies on **technology-based regulation,** specifying particular types of technology firms must use; for example, NSPS, LAER, BACT, RACT, and MACT.

13.2 Water quality regulation, under the **Federal Water Pollution Control Act** and the **Clean Water Act,** also has safety as its target, mandating **fishable and swimmable waters.** Technology-based regulation (BPT, BAT) is employed. The government has invested directly through **grants to municipalities,** for sewage treatment plants. Difficult to regulate **non-point sources** are now the major contributors to water pollution.

13.3 Two statutes deal with hazardous waste disposal on land, both requiring a **safety standard.** The **Resource Conservation and Recovery Act (RCRA)** has created the **RCRA list:** a variety of substances which must be disposed of in a controlled fashion. RCRA has a built-in **bias against land disposal** of hazardous waste. Assessing the actual health risks from hazardous waste dumps like the one at **Love Canal** is difficult. Nevertheless, in contrast to popular opinion, the EPA's science advisory board currently views hazardous waste as a **relatively low priority** environmental problem. **Superfund** is the second hazardous waste statute, dealing with existing dumps. Cleanups are financed through a trust fund and by means of **strict, joint, and several liability.** While the latter has led to high legal costs, **fear of future liability** may have had a positive effect on current disposal practices. Superfund has been bedeviled by **high costs, uncertain benefits,** and **slow progress.**

13.4 The statutes regulating new and existing pesticides (**FIFRA**) and chemicals (**TSCA**) are based on an **efficiency standard.** Both laws have a registration and screening process for new substances, and both provide for **special review** of existing substances. Benefit-cost analysis to support efficient regulation under these laws is often sketchy to nonexistent. Many more regulatory actions have been taken under FIFRA than TSCA because the burden of proof under the former lies more with industry and less with the EPA. The **Toxic Release Inventory (TRI),** taking an information-based approach, has proved an effective weapon to promote the reduction of chemical emissions.

13.5 The **Endangered Species Act (ESA)** seeks ecological sustainability—the protection of natural capital—as its goal. The act requires listing of **endangered** and **threatened** species on a scientific basis and prevents activities that disturb **critical habitats.** The ESA has been criticized because of the costs it imposes on a small number of landholders and rural workers, lack of incentives for participation, and a focus on species instead of ecosystems.

References

Arora, Seema and Timothy N. Cason (1996). "Why Do Firms Volunteer to Exceed Environmental Regulations? Understanding Participation in the EPA's 33/50 Program." *Land Economics,* 72, no. 4, 413–32.

Brown, Michael H. (1989). "A Toxic Ghost Town." *Atlantic,* July.

Carlin, Alan (1990). *Environmental Investments: The Cost of a Clean Environment, Summary.* Washington, DC: U.S. EPA.

Colborn, Theo, Diane Dumanaski and John Peterson Myers (1996). *Our Stolen Future.* New York: Penguin.

Council on Environmental Quality (1991). *Environmental Quality.* Washington, DC: U.S. GPO.

Cropper, Maureen L., William N. Evans, Stephen J. Berardi, Maria M. Ducla-Soares and Paul R. Portney (1991). "The Determinants of Pesticide Regulation: A Statistical Analysis of EPA Decisionmaking." *Discussion Paper CRM 91–01.* Washington, DC: Resources for the Future.

Davies, Terry and Jan Mazurek (1997). *Industry Incentives for Environmental Improvement: Evaluation of U.S. Federal Initiatives.* Washington, DC: Global Environmental Management Initiative.

Dower, Roger C. (1990). "Hazardous Wastes." In *Public Policies for Environmental Protection,* ed. Paul Portney. Washington, DC: Resources for the Future.

Easter-Pilcher, Andrea (1996). "Implementing the Endangered Species Act." *BioScience,* 46, no. 5, 355–362.

Freeman, A. Myrick III (1990). "Water Pollution Policy." In *Public Policies for Environmental Protection,* ed. Paul Portney. Washington, DC: Resources for the Future.

Gianessi, Leonard P., Raymond J. Kopp and Cynthia A. Puffer (1989). "Regulating Pesticide Use: Social Costs, Policy Targeting and Economic Incentives." *Discussion Paper QE89-21.* Washington, DC: Resources for the Future.

Griffin, Robert Jr. (1991). "Introducing NPS Water Pollution." *EPA Journal,* December, 6–9.

Haigne, Daniel A., James W. Vincent and Patrick G. Welle (1992). "Benefits of Preserving Old-Growth Forests and the Spotted Owl." *Contemporary Policy Issues,* 10, no. 1, 13–26.

Jost, Kenneth (1996). "Protecting Endangered Species." *CQ Researcher,* 6, no. 15, 339–357.

Metrick, Andrew and Martin L. Weitzman (1996). "Patterns of Behavior in Endangered Species Preservation." *Land Economics,* 72, no. 1, 1–16.

Milkanovich, Valerie (1992). "Clean Air Act Amendments." *Memorandum.* Albany: New York State Energy Office.

National Research Council (1995). *Science and the Endangered Species Act.* Washington DC: National Academy Press.

National Research Council (1991). *Environmental Epidemiology: Public Health and Hazardous Wastes.* Washington, DC: National Academy Press.

Office of Technology Assessment (1992). *Managing Industrial Solid Wastes.* Washington, DC: U.S. GPO.

Paigen, Beverly, Lynn R. Goldmann, Mary M. Magnant, Joseph Highland and A. T. Steegman, Jr. (1987). "Growth of Children Living Near the Hazardous Waste Site, Love Canal." *Human Biology,* 59, no. 3, 489–508.

Portney, Paul R. (1990). "Air Pollution Policy." In *Public Policies for Environmental Protection,* ed. Paul Portney. Washington, DC: Resources for the Future.

Power, Thomas M. (ed.) (1996). *Economic Well-Being and Environmental Protection in the Pacific Northwest.* Missoula: University of Montana.

Probst, Katherine N. and Paul R. Portney (1992). *Assigning Liability for Superfund Cleanups.* Washington, DC: Resources for the Future.

Robinson, James C. and William S. Pease (1991). "From Health-Based to Technology-Based Standards for Hazardous Air Pollutants." *American Journal of Public Health,* 81, no. 11, 1518–1522.

Schlickeisen, Roger (1996). "Should the Endangered Species Act Be Re-enacted Without Major Changes? Yes." *CQ Researcher,* 6, no. 15, 339–357.

Shapiro, Michael (1990). "Toxic Substances Policy." In *Public Policies for Environmental Protection,* ed. Paul Portney. Washington, DC: Resources for the Future.

Shistar, Terry, Susan Cooper and Jay Feldman (1992). *Unnecessary Risks: The Benefit Side of the Pesticide Risk-Benefit Equation.* Washington, DC: National Coalition Against the Misuse of Pesticides.

U.S. Environmental Protection Agency (1991). *Superfund: Environmental Progress.* Washington, DC: U.S. EPA.

Vianna, Nicholas J. and Adele K. Polan (1984). "Incidence of Low Birth Weight Among Love Canal Residents." *Science,* 226, no. 4679, 1217–1219.

Wagner, Travis (1991). *The Complete Guide to Hazardous Waste Regulations.* New York: Van Nostrand Reinhold.

CHAPTER 14

The Regulatory Record: Achievements and Obstacles

14.0 Introduction

The last chapter provided an overview of the major environmental legislation in the United States. What has twenty-five years of regulation actually accomplished? Beyond that, how can the regulatory process be improved?

Two lines of criticism have been leveled at the current regulatory approach. First, from a normative perspective, efficiency advocates have charged that current legislation often buys relatively small environmental benefits at a substantial cost. Second, regardless of whether the pollution control target chosen is efficiency, safety, or ecological sustainability, the existing regulatory system is more expensive than it need be. By building in greater flexibility and harnessing economic incentives, many economists argue that we could buy our current level of environmental quality at a substantially lower cost.

However, assuming we can improve the regulatory process in this way, a final question remains. By their very nature, regulatory approaches are limited to control of narrowly defined pollutants, and work best for stationary and "point" sources; moreover regulatory gains may be swamped by economic growth. In order to achieve sustainability, does government need to move beyond internalizing externalities through regulation, and directly promote the development of clean technology?

14.1 Accomplishments of Environmental Regulation

After more than two full decades of extensive environmental regulation and the expenditure of several hundred billion dollars on pollution control, where do we now stand? The record is clearest for air pollution. As Table 14.1 reveals, in absolute terms, ambient concentrations of all of the criteria air pollutants declined over the period 1978–1990. Declines were largest for lead at 93%, due largely to a phaseout of leaded gasoline, beginning in 1984. Over the period, sulfur dioxide concentrations dropped by 39%, carbon monoxide by 42%, and particulates by 24%. Comparable progress has been made in reducing concentrations of nitrogen oxides (down 24%) and ground-level ozone (down 27%). (Recall that ground-level ozone, or smog, is created from a mixture of nitrogen oxides [NOx], volatile organic compounds [VOCs], and sunlight.)

However, for particulates, nitrogen oxides, and ozone, three quarters of the total reduction in pollution concentrations was already achieved by 1982. Forward momentum in these areas has slowed substantially since that date.[1] The second column shows that, especially for nitrogen oxides and ozone, progress has essentially stalled out. However, for ozone (and also particulates) air quality may begin to show further improvement since the EPA tightened both standards substantially in 1997.

Progress on NOx (an ozone component) will be tougher—unlike all the other criteria pollutants, which showed reductions in *emissions* over the period 1970–1994 paralleling the Table 14.1 improvements in air quality, nitrogen oxide emissions actually increased—by some 14%.[2] At the same time, NOx air quality did improve somewhat, indicating that the new source growth—mostly autos—was occurring in less polluted areas.

While headway toward reducing absolute concentrations of the criteria air pollutants has been made, with the exception of lead, it has not been spectacular. Yet, *relative to where we would have been without regulation,* our achievements are more substantial. The third column of Table 14.1 shows the reduction in air pollution in 1988 from what it is estimated to have been in the absence of controls. In other words, actual concentrations of volatile organic compounds (chemicals that along with nitrogen oxide react to form ozone) were 42% below what they would have been with no federal regulation. Regulation has thus had a much bigger effect on the national smog problem than the 26% reduction in actual ozone concentrations suggest.

With the exception of ozone, between 75% and 90% of all the sites sampled had achieved attainment of the NAAQS by the late 1980s.[3] In many areas, however, some of the NAAQs are violated at least during parts of the year, with the biggest offender being ozone. As Figure 14.1 illustrates, in 1995, 77 million people lived in counties where the NAAQ was violated at some time over the course of the year. Greater CO compliance is expected as a result of the 1990 Clean Air Act and the use of reformulated automobile fuels; Table 14.1 picks up a significant improvement through the mid-1990s.

Ozone is likely to remain as a stubborn and serious air pollution problem, affecting roughly one third of the population to varying degrees, as long as cities remain dependent upon private gasoline-powered autos for transportation. (Indeed, after the

---

[1]Ozone concentrations actually increased during the 1980s, but fell substantially in 1989, 1990, and 1991. Some of this progress may have simply reflected cooler summers.

[2]*The Statistical Abstract of the United States, 1996,* Table 374.

[3]Carlin (1990); for EPA compliance stats, see http://www.epa.gov/oar/oaqps/greenbk/onsuml.html.

Table 14.1 Progress in Reducing Air Pollution (AVERAGE NATIONWIDE AMBIENT CONCENTRATIONS)

PERCENTAGE REDUCTION IN AVERAGE AMBIENT CONCENTRATIONS

| | *Actual* | | *Estimated Assuming 1970 Control Levels* |
Period	*1978–1990*	*1990–1994*	*1970–1988*
Particulates	24	11	70
Sulfur Dioxide	39	12	42
Nitrogen Oxides	24	0	28
Carbon Monoxide	42	14	57
Lead	93	50	97
Ozone	27	4	—
Volatile Organic Compounds	—	—	42

Sources: Actual reductions are from Council on Environmental Quality (1991: Table 38), and *The Statistical Abstract of the United States, 1996*, Table 373. The 1988 estimated pollution levels are from Carlin (1990).

FIGURE 14.1 People Living in Non-attainment Counties, 1995

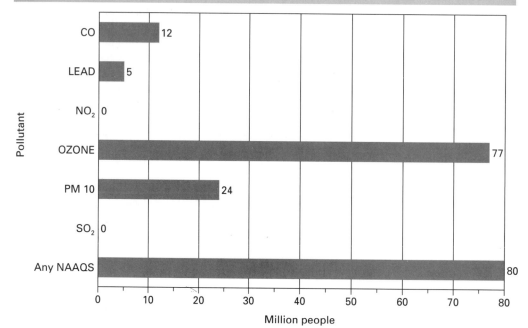

tightening of the ozone standard in 1997, many more areas will begin failing to meet the new, more stringent NAAQ.)

Air toxic regulation mandated in the 1990 CAA amendments is only now getting underway. However, as noted in the last chapter, since 1986 companies have had to report their chemical emissions in the Toxics Release Inventory publicly, and public pressure has led to substantial *voluntary* progress in the reduction of chemical emissions—on the order of 50% for seventeen chemicals targeted by the EPA. Most of these reductions were of airborne emissions; the firms would have been required to make these particular reductions by the late 1990s under the CAA amendments (Davies and Mazurek [1997]). It appears that the twin hammers of public pressure along with a looming regulatory deadline have had a significant impact on air toxic emissions.

Turning now to water quality, forward progress is less apparent. Freeman (1990), reviewing a variety of sources, concludes that in absolute terms little overall improvement in surface water quality can be seen through the early 1980s. More recent data confirm this picture. Some streams, rivers, and lakes have shown improvement although others have deteriorated. A study of trends in stream water quality from 1978 to 1987 at close to 400 locations nationwide found that overall, average water quality had improved at about 14%, deteriorated at 9%, and remained the same at 76% of the measuring stations.[4]

According to the EPA, absolute levels of water quality have failed to improve in large measure because increases in non-point water pollution, particularly agricultural runoff, have offset regulatory gains.[5] Of course, as in the case of air pollution, the achievements of the regulatory program would look better compared to where we would have been in the absence of federal controls, but no comprehensive estimates are available.

Regulation *has* had a major effect on point sources of water pollution. Industrial discharges of two conventional water pollutants (suspended solids and dissolved oxygen) declined by over 90% from 1982 to 1987. This improvement resulted from the installation of BPT and BAT technologies, as well as the diversion of substantial industrial effluent to municipal waste facilities for treatment. In part because of this latter phenomenon and in part due to population growth, the substantial government investment in sewage treatment over the last two decades has merely held the line on water pollution. By 1988, municipal discharges of suspended solids and dissolved oxygen were comparable to mid-1960 levels, though below the peak discharges recorded in 1973.[6]

There is little available data on trends in toxic emissions into surface water, yet toxic pollutants pose a serious obstacle to achieving a goal of "fishable and swimmable" waters. A 1992 EPA report identified 46 sites nationwide where estimated cancer risks from occasional fish consumption (one or two meals per month) were significant—on the order of 1 in 10,000. People who depend more heavily on fish from inland waters—including some Native American and rural populations—

[4]Council on Environmental Quality (1991: 261). The composite quality figures reported here average trends in fifteen different pollutants. See also Carlin (1990).
[5]Carlin (1990).
[6]Carlin (1990).

face substantial additional risk. Over 4,000 health bans or advisories are in effect around the country.[7] Finally, groundwater pollution from pesticides and hazardous waste dumps, a topic addressed in chapter 19, has begun to emerge as an increasing environmental problem.

Evaluating the impact of hazardous waste legislation is difficult. The ostensible goal of RCRA (and Superfund liability) has been to prevent future Love Canals. Relatively strict regulations governing land disposal may begin to increase waste recovery, treatment, and incineration in coming years; on the other hand, it may increase illegal dumping. At this point, it is too early to tell.[8] In addition, as is discussed further in chapter 19, there is some evidence that rising disposal costs are encouraging firms to reduce toxic chemical use in the first place, though the extent of this activity is still relatively limited.

The cleanup of old dump sites has proceeded at a slow pace; as noted only 346 sites have been cleaned up. However, as Probst and Portney (1992) detail, it is not clear how much of the limited progress is due to the nature of the beast (the need for careful evaluation and consideration of options) and how much is due to excessive litigation or bureaucratic foot-dragging.

On the pesticide front, Cropper et al. (1991) find that the estimated value of a life saved under the pesticide review process was $35 million. They thus imply that pesticide regulation has been inefficiently strict; that is, that marginal costs have outweighed marginal benefits. In addition, recent reforms have speeded the review process for older, more dangerous pesticides. (For more on the pesticide issue, see chapter 19.)

New chemicals were being introduced at a substantially higher rate during the mid-1980s than during the 1970s. Given the limited information on the potential toxicity of these compounds, whether the EPA's screen for new chemicals successfully achieves its stated goal of efficient regulation, is difficult to assess. However, many chemicals known to be toxic at high doses have accumulated at low levels in the body fat of the American population.[9]

Finally, of the 955 species listed as either threatened or endangered, 41% are stable or improving, 35% are declining, 23% face an uncertain future, and 1%—seven species—have gone extinct. Only five species have been delisted after a successful recovery, and eleven upgraded from endangered to threatened.

What are we to make of this record? Let us for the moment take an optimistic view. In spite of the fact that economic activity almost doubled from 1970 to 1990, the general criteria air pollution picture has actually improved somewhat, dramatically for lead. In addition, large reductions in air toxics have been recorded over the last decade. Industrial emissions of some waterborne pollutants have dropped dramatically and, overall, water quality has probably not deteriorated beyond 1970 levels. Regulation of hazardous waste *is* likely to prevent the development of future "Love Canals." And the rising cost of disposal, along with the "right-to-know" TRI regulation and the potential for Superfund liability, is beginning to focus corporate attention on reducing waste through pollution prevention. Particularly nasty new pesticides are

[7]Environmental Defense Fund (1992).

[8]From 1983 to 1987, the share of waste headed to landfills (and incinerators) actually increased. Carlin (1990).

[9]Commoner (1990).

not likely to make it through the EPA's initial screen, and under prodding from Congress the agency will restrict the use of the worst of the existing pesticides by the end of the century. Finally, only a few listed species have slipped into extinction.

The fact that regulation has managed to hold the line against economic growth is in itself an impressive accomplishment. Can this success continue? At the end of the chapter, we will turn to a somewhat darker view of the prospects for continued regulatory accomplishment. First, however, we will look at more specific criticisms of the current regulatory structure.

14.2 Normative Criticisms of Regulation

The national laws covering pollution into the air and water and onto land are governed by a safety standard. We have seen that defining safety has posed a difficult problem. In practice, pursuing a safety standard generally involves buying the highest level of protection possible given the political constraints on regulatory authority and the available dollars allocated by the political process. On the other hand, laws governing the use of toxic substances require regulatory actions to meet an efficiency standard. Here, the government weighs costs and benefits in a more or less crude fashion, depending upon the information available.

Not surprisingly, efficiency advocates attack the pursuit of safety as inefficient; safety advocates counter that efficiency standards provide the public with an inadequate level of environmental protection. Economists, perhaps due to their professional training, tend to be efficiency advocates, so one will often find economists leveling normative criticisms at safety-based environmental protection laws. For example, Portney (1990) is critical both of the uniformity of standards and the high level of protection afforded to remote areas under the Clean Air Act. Uniformity fails to account for the fact that the benefits and costs of control may vary between sites, and Portney finds it "hard to see why the allowable degradation should be the same in all [Class I] areas, since they are not equally endowed with resources or amenities."

Economists are not wrong to level efficiency criticisms at safety standard environmental legislation; in some cases, particularly when marginal benefits are very close to zero, the argument may be quite convincing. It is, however, important to remember that economists have no special authority when it comes to proscribing what the appropriate target of pollution control *should be*.[10]

As usual, efficiency criticisms are most persuasive when they suggest that an *actual* improvement in environmental quality will result from a move from safety to efficiency. Cropper et al. (1991), for example, in the pesticide study discussed above argue: "Since there are a variety of public policy measures, both environmental and otherwise, which are capable of preventing cancer at much lower costs [than the $35 million per life saved from pesticide regulation], we might be able to reduce the cancer rate through a reallocation of resources."

The problem with this line of reasoning is that the resources freed up from less stringent pesticide regulation, to the extent they are properly estimated, would reemerge as higher profits for pesticide manufacturers and lower food prices for consumers. They would not likely be channeled into other "public policy measures" to im-

---

[10]Bromley (1990) makes an argument along these lines.

prove environmental health.[11] Thus, only a potential and not an actual Pareto improvement would emerge by relaxing pesticide regulations to achieve efficiency gains.

14.3 Cost-Effectiveness Criticisms of Regulation

In contrast to normative questions of goal setting, an area that economists do have special authority in is cost-effectiveness analysis. **Cost-effectiveness** in environmental protection means achieving a desired goal—whether it is safety or efficiency—at the lowest possible cost. Part III of this book will be devoted to an extended discussion of cost-effectiveness; at this point, it is useful to outline the basic criticisms of existing policy.

As you probably learned when you were about three years old, one of the best ways to discredit someone is to call them a name. Economists have coined a not-very-flattering label for the current regulatory approach: **command-and-control (CAC)** regulation. CAC involves two parts. The first is the **uniform emission standards** typically mandated under the Clean Air and Water acts, and under RCRA. All similar sources are "commanded" to meet identical emission levels. The problem with uniform emission standards (from a cost-effectiveness point of view) is that they fail to take advantage of differences in costs between firms.

To use a simple illustration, consider two neighboring oil refineries. Refinery A, which has the ability to reduce emissions of say, nitrogen oxides, at very low cost, is nevertheless expected to meet the same standard as next-door refinery B, a firm with very high costs of reduction. The reason this is not cost-effective is simple: The same overall emission reduction (and local air quality) could be achieved at lower cost by having the low-cost firm meet a tighter emission standard, while relaxing the standard for the neighboring high-cost firm. Chapters 16 and 17 will review a variety of mechanisms—collectively known as *incentive-based regulation*—that harness market incentives to achieve this kind of **cost-saving, pollution-neutral** result.

However, there is one area in which current legislation does not require uniform standards: New sources and old sources are generally treated much differently. The Clean Air Act requires more stringent control technologies for new sources (the New Source Performance Standards); RCRA allows for regulations to differ between existing and new hazardous waste facilities; FIFRA and TSCA regulate the introduction of new pesticides and chemicals on a preemptive basis but challenge existing substances only on case-by-case review.

The reason for this type of grandfathering (providing special protection for existing sources) is not hard to understand. It is politically much easier to pass pollution control laws that have their largest impact on firms not currently around to object. However, regulating new sources more stringently introduces a **new source bias.** Because higher costs are now attached to new investment, firm managers and consumers will hold on to their old, polluting technologies longer than they otherwise would. For example, rather than build new, cleaner electric generating facilities, firms may stretch out the lives of older, dirtier ones.[12] Similar effects have been observed for new cars.[13]

---

[11]Only if the EPA shifted its internal resources away from pesticide regulation toward other priority areas would a very small portion of these net benefits serve other "public policy measures."

[12]Maloney and Brady (1988).

[13]Greene and Duleep (1992) provide estimates of elasticities of scrappage with respect to price of around -1 for automobiles.

Or, to consider another case, some new pesticides that have been denied registration are actually safer than substitutes already approved for use on the market.

A new source bias reduces the cost-effectiveness of a given policy in both the short and long run. In the *short run*, regulators impose tougher standards on new sources that are likely to be cleaner already, ignoring existing and potentially more severe problems. For example, in some places, one cost-effective way of reducing urban air pollution may be buying up and junking old, highly polluting cars.[14] The *long-run* cost effect, however, is probably more severe. By slowing down investment in new technology, the pace of technological change itself slows down. With less technological progress, long-run pollution control costs fall slower than they otherwise would.

To review, the first aspect of CAC regulation is the emission standards which the government "commands": uniform for all similar areas and sources, with the often perverse exception that new sources are more stringently regulated than old ones. Both uniformity and the new source bias serve to reduce the cost-effectiveness of regulation.

The second, "control" part of the name refers to the **technology-based regulatory approach** employed by much current regulation. NSPS, BACT, RACT, MACT, LAER, BPT, BAT: Defining all these acronyms involves regulators in a highly detailed process of specifying precisely which technologies firms will employ. There are two cost-effectiveness problems here. First, in the short run, a uniform technological mandate is unlikely to provide the cheapest pollution control solution for different firms all over the country. This lack of flexibility inherent in centralized, technology-based regulation raises costs.

Again, however, long-run cost effects are probably more important. Technology-based regulation works against technological improvements in several ways. First, once a firm has installed BACT, for example, it has no incentive to do better. Second, the firm actually has a positive incentive *not* to do better. If, for example, it discovered a better technique for pollution reduction, and the EPA then decided to deem this new technology BACT, the firm might legally be required to upgrade its pollution control technology at other new facilities. Firms have a distinct incentive to keep the agency from upgrading the state-of-the-art technological standard. Finally, if in spite of these obstacles, firms do seek an innovative, non-BACT approach, they must first obtain regulatory clearance to do so.

What would be an alternative to technology-based regulation? Again, we will explore this issue further in chapters 16 and 17, but in essence, the regulator might simply specify a pollution goal for each firm and then let the firms achieve it as they see fit. Provided that *monitoring and enforcement resources were adequate* to insure that firms were complying, such a flexible system could result in the same emission levels at much lower cost in the short run, and provide substantially better incentives for cost-reducing technological progress in pollution control in the long run.

To summarize: Many economists would argue that the current command-and-control regulatory strategy is cost-ineffective. That is, we could achieve the same goals—whether safety, efficiency, or ecological sustainability—at much lower cost, by shifting to more flexible, incentive-based approaches.

---

[14] Old cars are very polluting. Whether a purchase program is cost-effective depends upon (1) whether the cars purchased are heavily driven *and* are not likely to be soon retired anyway, and (2) the purchase price. Economists are currently studying these issues. See, for example, Alberini et al. (1993).

Incentive-based regulation, however, is still regulation. Firms must be punished for exceeding allowable emissions of pollutants. Some have argued that this kind of "stick" strategy of forcing firms and consumers to internalize externalities—no matter how flexibly it is designed—will face an increasingly difficult task holding the line on environmental quality.

14.4 Beyond Regulation? Promoting Clean Technology

As documented above, regulation has scored substantial successes. First, there has been some real improvement, most noticeably in air quality for millions of people. Second, environmental quality elsewhere is being held roughly constant in the face of increasing economic growth.

However, some hold a darker view of the prospects for future regulatory success. This pessimistic outlook rests on three assumptions. First, economic growth can eventually swamp the regulatory process. As noted, since 1982 relatively little progress has been made in reducing smog, nitrogen oxide emissions, or particulates.[15] In spite of tremendous investment in sewage treatment facilities, emissions from these sources have improved marginally if at all. And while regulation may forestall particularly egregious insults like Love Canal, the fact remains that as the economy grows, industry continues to generate more and more hazardous wastes and toxic chemicals, and *these must go somewhere.* Even if stored according to best practice, it is argued that general exposure levels must ultimately increase.

Second, regulation has already picked off the "easy" targets—stationary air pollution sources and point water pollution sources. In fact, urban smog is due largely to automobiles, while non-point pollution has become the dominant water quality problem. Regulating these diffuse sources will prove much more difficult. In economic terms, the marginal costs of a regulatory approach to controlling pollution are likely to rise significantly for the next generation of problems.

We can see how these two issues interact using the IPAT equation from chapter 7. Increases in growth (A) increase environmental impacts, unless offset by improvements in technology (T). The argument is that if the marginal costs of pollution control are rising, then this will undercut the ability of new technology to counterbalance an ever-growing increase in material affluence.

As a final point, even if regulation is successful in one media, say improved air quality, the "reduced" pollution is likely to squeeze out somewhere else. For example, coal power plants reduce sulfur dioxide by "scrubbing" the sulfur out of the gaseous emissions. However, this process produces a hazardous sulfur sludge, which must be disposed of on land. Or, limits on industrial discharge of water pollutants have caused an increase in discharge through municipal sewage facilities. Or, RCRA's tough regulations for land disposal, focused on a handful of sites, are likely to increase the rate of on-site incineration of hazardous waste. This will occur at thousands of points across the country, spawning an additional regulatory headache.

Economists call this the **piecemeal problem**. Regulating the environment a piece at a time will lead firms to seek out substitute media for disposal. Under these circum-

---

[15]Some additional progress is likely on nitrogen oxide via the 1990 Clean Air Act.

stances, regulation ultimately boils down to channeling dangerous substances into areas where they do the least environmental harm.

However, by focusing on improvements in air quality or water quality or land disposal practices, one loses sight of the bigger picture: Is overall environmental quality being affected by regulation? Reviewing much of the evidence presented in this chapter, the noted ecologist Barry Commoner (1990: 40) concludes: "there is inescapable evidence that the massive national effort to restore the quality of the environment has failed."

Nevertheless, our twenty-year experience with regulation has not been futile. While we may not have achieved our ambitious target of creating a safe and clean environment, and in spite of the many political-economic obstacles faced, regulation has made a major difference in the environmental quality experienced by Americans. The real question is, Can regulation continue to at least hold the line against continued economic growth and even begin to improve the state of the environment?

Economic growth clearly requires increasingly strict emission standards in order to maintain the same level of environmental quality. If (1) tightening regulation leads to ever-rising marginal costs of reduction, or if (2) the pollution "reduced" squeezes out elsewhere, regulatory strategies will clearly fail over the long run.

Is there a way out of this trap? Yes. Our standard assumption is that firms reduce pollution using an **end-of-the-pipe** strategy. That is, faced with a regulation requiring lowered emissions, firms make small adjustments to their production process: say, adding on a scrubber to the "end of the pipe" or switching to a cleaner and more expensive fuel.

Consider an example of a firm trying to reduce particulate emissions, measured in parts per million (ppm). Under these circumstances, the marginal cost of reduction curve takes on the familiar look of Figure 14.2A: That is, it becomes increasingly difficult (expensive) to clean up emissions as the standard tightens from 100 ppm to 0 ppm.

However, one effect of regulation might be to induce firms to seek out whole new

FIGURE 14.2 Two Technologies for Particulate Control

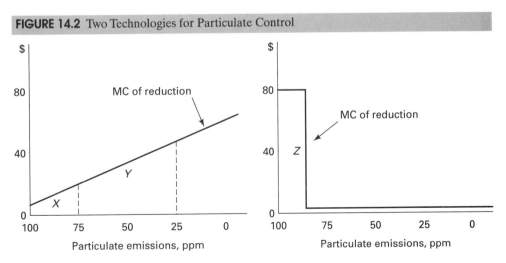

A: "End-of-the-Pipe" Control

B: Pollution Prevention

technologies that avoid emitting the pollutant of concern in the first place—a **pollution prevention** strategy. In this case, the marginal cost curve takes on the shape of Figure 14.2B. Here, if the firm bears an initial expense to significantly alter its production process (Z), the marginal costs of reduction, and consequently pollution emissions, go to zero. Because the firm no longer emits the pollutant in question, there are no marginal costs of reduction below a level of 90 ppm. Note that *once the new technology is in place*, both the piecemeal problem and the problem of rising marginal cost disappear.

Which technology will the firm adopt? That depends on a comparison of the total costs of the two options. In this simple example, the firm will go with an end-of-the-pipe solution if the area under the marginal cost curve is smaller for Figure 14.2A, as opposed to Figure 14.2B. This is true for a standard of 75 parts per million ($X < Z$), but as the required cleanup increases to 25 parts per million, the pollution prevention technology becomes the cheaper approach ($X + Y > Z$).

Unfortunately, the story is not this simple. The real-world problem is that firms have little incentive to invest in developing the pollution prevention technology in the first place until regulatory costs become very high, especially because regulations are easier to fight politically as they become more stringent and costly. Investment in the cleaner technology, of course, would have led to reductions in cost—through research and development, "learning by doing," and economies of scale.

But a lack of investment means that the cleaner technology seldom exists as an easy, reliable, or low-cost alternative. A chicken-and-egg problem thus emerges: Stricter emission standards are too costly (not politically feasible) using end-of-the-pipe approaches, but new pollution prevention technologies will not be developed by industry until stricter emission standards are required. This in turn implies that the "stick" of regulation—no matter how flexible—may never be strong enough to prod firms into investing in pollution prevention strategies.

In chapter 18 we will explore further why normal market processes tend not to generate clean technologies of this type—which involve major rather than marginal changes in production processes. But as a preview: To achieve sustainability it may be necessary to supplement the stick of regulation with the carrot of direct government investment in, and promotion of, clean technologies.

The take-home message of this section is that, unless regulation induces major technological change, we cannot escape the logic of IPAT. That is, if the marginal costs of control continue to rise, then technology simply cannot offset the impact of increased growth. This means that the quality of the environment must deteriorate over time. The key issue then becomes: Can regulation alone drive technological innovation, or must the government take a more active role investing in clean technology?

14.5 Summary

This chapter has looked back at our twenty-five-year pollution control record. In summary, it is probably fair to say that regulation has managed to hold the line against economic growth. It is of course possible to view this accomplishment either as a cup that is half full or half empty.

Normative criticisms of the existing laws have been directed both at safety standards (too costly) and efficiency standards (insufficiently safe). These criticisms are

important and were dealt with at length in the first part of this book. However, we now want to leave our discussion of the goals of environmental policy behind and begin to consider more effective implementation. The question we will move on to address in part III of the book is: How can we improve the cost-effectiveness of environmental protection?

Whether our goal is safety, efficiency, or ecological sustainability, this chapter has identified three features of the current command-and-control regulatory system that tend to work against cost-effectiveness: uniform emission standards, a new source bias, and a technology-based approach. By contrast, we will argue in chapters 16 and 17 that much more flexibility could be built into the regulatory process and incentives harnessed to improve overall cost-effectiveness. However, for a more flexible approach to succeed, careful emissions monitoring will be required, and adequate enforcement resources must be available. The next chapter will explore the monitoring and enforcement record to date and provide some suggestions for doing better.

Finally, while a switch to more flexible regulation is in many cases a good idea, more flexible regulation is still regulation, facing three obstacles to continued success. First, economic growth is a real challenge to effective regulation. As the volume of activity increases, so does the volume of harmful externalities. Second, non-point, mobile, and other widely dispersed sources, difficult to regulate by traditional methods, have all become more important players in the pollution story. Finally, the piecemeal problem—in which pollution regulated in one media squeezes out into another—places a limit on the level of overall environmental cleanup that regulation can ultimately provide. These factors imply that beyond regulation, the direct promotion of clean technology is another important role for government. How to do this wisely will be addressed in chapters 18 to 20.

APPLICATION 14.0

Regulating Nukes

In an interesting article, England and Mitchell (1990) report on the progress of regulation in the nuclear power industry.

1. The first civilian nuclear reactor began operation in 1957. Yet the agency in charge of overseeing the nuclear industry "had fewer than a dozen active regulations in 1970. . . ." One explanation for fairly lax safety regulation was the (mistaken) belief that a threshold existed below which exposure to radiation was safe. Why did this belief persist? One reason was that "centralized [government] funding of radiation research . . . encouraged a methodological inbreeding which underestimated the scope of nuclear hazards."

Use the concepts of the *revolving door* and *agenda control*, both explained in chapter 12, to explain how the regulatory establishment could persistently underestimate health risks from exposure to radiation.

2. In the 1970s, the laissez-faire regulatory attitude shifted. From a hands-off approach in 1970, "there were several dozen [active regulations] by 1972, and several hundred by 1977." Is this burst of regulatory activity in the 1970s consistent with the pattern we saw in other areas? What do you think explains it?

3. In the nuclear area, it is possible to view regulatory achievements in either a positive or gloomy light. From 1974 to

1984, reported emissions of four out of the six radioactive elements studied by England and Mitchell either declined or remained stable, in spite of a tripling of electrical output from the nuclear industry over the period. However, in spite of constant or declining emission levels, the *total amount* of these four radioactive materials in the environment was substantially higher in the mid-1980s than the mid-1970s. How can you explain this?

Key Ideas in Each Section

14.1 This section provides a progress report. There has been some success in reducing criteria air pollutants. Forward movement in several areas had stalled out. However, tighter regulation for particulates and ozone may lead to more improvement over the next decade. On the air toxic front, large emission reductions have been driven by a combination of regulation and bad publicity from the TRI. Gains in water quality from point-source regulation have been balanced by increases in non-point pollution. The impact of regulation on land disposal of waste and chemical safety is hard to evaluate. Finally, one study indicates that pesticide regulation is inefficiently strict, though not strict enough to be safe. Finally the ESA has also had mixed success—generally preventing extinction, but failing to promote recovery.

14.2 Efficiency advocates, some of whom are economists, often criticize the current safety-based laws from a normative perspective. They argue that the air, water, and land disposal statutes often have marginal benefits well below marginal costs and *should* thus be weakened. Safety proponents respond that many of the statutes are insufficiently strict. Economists, of course, have no special authority to decide what the right level of pollution ought to be.

14.3 The current regulatory approach, dubbed **command-and-control (CAC)**, is not **cost-effective**. **Uniform emission standards** and a **new source bias** (the "command" aspects) along with **technology-based regulation** (the "control" aspect), mean that the regulatory system has little flexibility to adapt to local conditions. Provided that monitoring and enforcement are adequate, increased flexibility can allow firms to pursue **cost-saving**, **pollution-neutral** measures. In addition, the CAC system discourages technological innovation in pollution control technology.

14.4 Is regulation alone sufficient? Obstacles to further regulatory progress include economic growth, the increasing importance of non-point and mobile pollution sources, and the **piecemeal problem**. These three factors imply that the marginal cost of **end-of-the-pipe** regulation will rise; unless regulation induces rapid technological change, leading to **pollution prevention**, the quality of the environment must deteriorate. But the "chicken-and-egg" relationship between regulation and new technology development suggests a critical role for the direct government promotion of clean technology.

References

Alberini, Anna, Winston Harrington and Virginia McConnell (1993). "Determinants of Participation in Accelerated Vehicle Retirement Programs," Paper presented at the Eastern Economic Association Meetings.

Bromley, Daniel (1990). "The Ideology of Efficiency: Searching for a Theory of Policy Analysis," *Journal of Environmental Economics and Management*, 19, no. 1.

Carlin, Alan (1990). *Environmental Investments: The Cost of a Clean Environment, Summary*. Washington, DC: U.S. EPA.

Commoner, Barry (1990). *Making Peace with the Planet*. New York: Pantheon.

Council on Environmental Quality (1991). *Environmental Quality*. Washington, DC: U.S. GPO.

Cropper, Maureen L., William N. Evans, Stephen J. Berardi, Maria M. Ducla-Soares and Paul R. Portney (1991). "The Determinants of Pesticide Regulation: A Statistical Analysis of EPA Decisionmaking," *Discussion Paper CRM 91-01*. Washington, DC: Resources for the Future.

Davies, Terry and Jan Mazurek (1997). *Industry Incentives for Environmental Improvement: Evaluation of US Federal Initiatives*. Washington, DC: Global Environmental Management Initiative.

Dower, Roger C. (1990). "Hazardous Wastes." In *Public Policies for Environmental Protection*, ed. Paul Portney. Washington, DC: Resources for the Future.

England, Richard and Eric P. Mitchell (1990). "Federal Regulation and Environmental Impact of the US Nuclear Industry." *Natural Resources Journal*, 30, 537–559.

Environmental Defense Fund (1992). *The Contamination of Our Natural Waters: A Report on State Fish Advisories and Bans in the United States*. Washington, DC: EDF.

Freeman, A. Myrick, III (1990). "Water Pollution Policy." In *Public Policies for Environmental Protection*, ed. Paul Portney. Washington, DC: Resources for the Future.

Greene, David and Kili Duleep (1992). "Costs and Benefits of Automotive Fuel Economy Improvement: A Partial Analysis," *ORNL-6704*. Oak Ridge, TN: Oak Ridge National Laboratory.

Griffin, Robert Jr. (1991). "Introducing NPS Water Pollution." *EPA Journal*, December, 6–9.

Maloney, Michael T. and Gordon L. Brady (1988). "Capital Turnover and Marketable Pollution Rights." *Journal of Law and Economics*, 31, no. 1, 203–226.

Office of Technology Assessment (1992). *Managing Industrial Solid Wastes*. Washington, DC: U.S. GPO.

Portney, Paul R. (1990). "Air Pollution Policy." In *Public Policies for Environmental Protection*, ed. Paul Portney. Washington, DC: Resources for the Future.

Portney, Paul R. (1989). "Policy Watch: Economics and the Clean Air Act." *The Journal of Economic Perspectives*, 4, no. 4, 173–182.

Probst, Katherine N. and Paul R. Portney (1992). *Assigning Liability for Superfund Cleanups*. Washington, DC: Resources for the Future.

Robinson, James C. and William S. Pease (1991). "From Health-Based to Technology-Based Standards for Hazardous Air Pollutants." *American Journal of Public Health*, 81, no. 11, 1518–1522.

Shapiro, Michael (1990). "Toxic Substances Policy." In *Public Policies for Environmental Protection*, ed. Paul Portney. Washington, DC: Resources for the Future.

The Statistical Abstract of the United States, 1996, Table 374.

U.S. Environmental Protection Agency (1991). *Superfund: Environmental Progress*. Washington, DC: U.S. EPA.

Monitoring and Enforcement

15.0 Introduction

OK, so the law is on the books, the EPA has written its regulations, states have developed their implementation plans and permitting processes: Now one last step remains. Monitoring for violations and enforcing the law is, as they say, a dirty job, but one that is essential to the entire regulatory process. Tough environmental regulations mean little if society does not have the resources or willpower to back them up. Monitoring and enforcement are particularly important, as we shall see in chapters 16 and 17, when firms are allowed to have greater flexibility in pursuing innovative—and cost-saving—pollution reduction options.

This chapter begins with a look at the economics of crime and punishment. With this background, we move on to examine the degree to which firms appear to comply with environmental laws. We then consider some of the political-economic pressures faced by enforcement officials; private enforcement of environmental law through citizen suits; and ways in which the EPA might restructure the enforcement process to achieve more cost-effective compliance. The bottom line is that the monitoring and enforcement process is much less effective than it could and should be.

15.1 The Economics of Crime

Economists tend to view the decision by an individual to comply with an environmental law in terms of economic motivations. While good citizenship—obeying the law simply because it is the law—certainly plays a role in affecting behavior, it is also useful to analyze compliance decisions in terms of benefits and costs.

The benefits that come from complying with environmental laws are essentially the avoided costs of punishment: monetary costs (fines and penalties), a damaged reputation (both for corporations and individuals), and the fear of jail terms. The expected benefits depend upon two factors: the magnitude of the punishment if imposed and the likelihood of getting caught and convicted. The costs of compliance, on the other hand, are simply the additional outlays needed to install, service, and maintain pollution control equipment, and complete the relevant paperwork.

Figure 15.1 illustrates a hypothetical marginal cost, marginal benefit analysis for a manager in a coal-fired power plant who has to decide what percentage of the time she plans to be in compliance with the sulfur dioxide emission standards on her state permit. The marginal benefits of compliance start out high, because with a low compliance rate the probability of a detectable air quality violation—and subsequent punishment—rises. However, at higher compliance levels, the probability of getting caught declines, and so the marginal benefits (MB) of compliance also fall.

What are some of the costs of compliance? Let us assume that the major cost is maintaining the scrubbers that remove sulfur dioxide from the plant's gaseous emissions. The marginal costs of maintenance are initially low because the manager can divert engineers from other tasks to work on the scrubbers at relatively low cost. However, as engineers spend more time inspecting and repairing scrubbers, the other tasks they neglect become more and more important. Thus the costs of additional maintenance time begin to rise. As usual, X marks the spot: The manager will choose a C^* compliance level. At higher levels, the additional costs of compliance outweigh the additional benefits, and vice versa for lower levels.

The basic insight of this model is that compliance with the law will increase as the marginal benefits of compliance rise or the marginal costs fall. There are two basic ways to increase the marginal benefits of compliance. First, increase the severity of punishment. Raising fines or prison terms or the public exposure of offenders will tend to improve environmental performance by shifting the MB curve up and to the right.

However, the benefits of compliance depend on not only the magnitude of the punishment but also the probability of getting caught and convicted. Increased monitoring activity by enforcement officials will have an effect similar to increased punishment levels. In a study of water pollution enforcement, for example, Magat and Viscusi (1990) found that pulp and paper firms were much more likely to be in compliance with their discharge permits after an inspection by state or EPA officials.

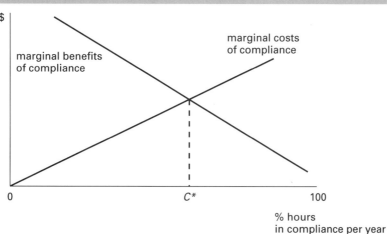

Figure 15.1 The Private Compliance Decision

This ability of punishment levels and the probability of detection and conviction to substitute for one another—known as the **punishment-detection trade-off**—can be useful to regulators. In theory, higher penalties can always substitute for lowered enforcement efforts. In the extreme, if the EPA could enforce the death penalty for any violation of sulfur dioxide emission standards, the agency could probably get by with one inspector for the entire country, saving taxpayers a lot of money! In reality, the law (and common norms of justice) place limits on total fines that can be levied, as well as the severity of criminal sanctions. In addition, firms cannot pay unlimited fines. Bankruptcy always looms in the background as a constraint on overly high monetary penalties. Given these limitations on penalties, increased detection becomes an attractive strategy.

A cost-effective way to increase monitoring efforts is to focus regulatory attention on **repeat offenders**. Thus, if enforcement officials could commit to a policy of increased inspections for any firm found in violation, then firms would have substantially greater incentive to obey the regulations. Russell (1990) recommends that the EPA "sentence" firms who have violated the law twice in a row to frequent audits for an extended period.

Alternatively, a greater use of electronic **continuous emissions monitors**, instead of physical on-site inspections, would have a similar effect. In 1990, about 1,065 facilities, only 11% of the 10,000 air pollution sources for which they were technically and economically feasible, had such automatic monitoring devices. EPA officials estimate that such electronic monitors are about ten times as likely to detect a violation as will an on-site inspection.[1]

Raising the marginal benefits of compliance through more certain or more severe punishment will thus lead to fewer violations. Lowering the marginal costs of compliance will have a similar effect. If regulators can force polluters to install a pollution control technology with very low *marginal costs* of operation (regardless of the upfront, fixed cost), then once that technology is in place, the polluter has little incentive not to comply with the law. In the extreme, if a control technology automatically insures compliance, then the marginal cost line in Figure 15.1 shifts down to become a straight line at zero dollars, and the manager chooses full compliance. In this case (zero marginal costs), the EPA need only check that the equipment has been properly installed.

Indeed, this argument provides some of the rationale behind the command-and-control regulatory approach, discussed in the last chapter, that dominates current legislation. The notion was that, once a firm had installed BAT or NSPS or BPT, the marginal costs of meeting the regulations would be sufficiently low to insure high compliance rates. As we will see below, however, this theory has not proven correct, and the need for ongoing monitoring to insure compliance remains.[2]

A principal reason that technology-based regulation has not provided automatic compliance is that the performance of control equipment tends to deteriorate over time. For example, catalytic converters on cars are automatic pollution control devices with zero marginal costs of operation. Unfortunately, they rapidly lose their effective-

---

[1] U.S. Government Accounting Office (1990).

[2] Tietenberg (1985) points out that the high initial cost of technology-based regulation raised incentives for not installing pollution control technology in the first place. However, as we shall see, so-called initial compliance rates have been fairly good.

ness. A 1984 study revealed that up to 25,000 miles of use, 45% of the cars meet the carbon dioxide standard; with more than 50,000 miles, only 10% of vehicles do so.[3] As a result, the EPA has mandated emission control inspection and maintenance programs for automobiles in many areas.

However, current inspection procedures themselves, mostly done at auto repair shops, are themselves highly imperfect. One EPA study found that 69% of facilities passed vehicles that were intentionally designed to fail the test. As a result, the agency is considering requiring testers to use more expensive, more reliable equipment. This technology—with high up-front costs but lower marginal costs for a proper test— presumably will increase compliance among private-sector inspectors who are supposed to be increasing compliance by auto owners! For this strategy to succeed, however, the new testing equipment must remain reliable over time.[4]

15.2 The Economics of Punishment

In addition to developing a marginal benefit/marginal cost framework for analyzing decisions to commit crimes, economists have also focused attention on punishment issues. On an economic basis, which punishments are preferred, **jail terms** or **fines**? Table 15.1 provides a listing of the costs and benefits associated with each option.

Fines have two principal benefits over incarceration. First, they have much lower administrative and other social costs. Jail terms entail not only prisons and guards but also the lost tax revenues and output from the jailed individual. Second, to impose jail terms prosecutors must prove guilt "beyond a reasonable doubt"; fines can be levied under a much lower standard of evidence.[5]

On the other hand, fines also have drawbacks. Principal among these is the ability to **shift fines**: Typically, a corporation will pay only a portion of the monetary penalty it is assessed. Other parties will pick up some of the tab, including insurance companies; taxpayers (firms can write off cleanup efforts or damage payments but not actual fines); and/or consumers, as firms pass on fines in the form of higher prices. For example, Exxon's total bill for the 1989 *Valdez* oil spill in Alaska's Prince William Sound was something over $3 billion—$2 billion in cleanup costs and just over $1 billion in penalties and fines. Of this total, however, insurers paid about $400 million;[6] assuming a 30% corporate income tax, Exxon benefited by paying at least $500 million in

TABLE 15.1	Fines versus Jail Terms	
	Fines	*Jail Terms*
Benefits	Low social costs; lower level of proof.	Cannot be shifted; large reputation effect.
Costs	Can be shifted; often too small for deterrence.	High social costs; high level of proof.

[3]Council on Environmental Quality (1984: 71).

[4]Harrington and McConnell (1993).

[5]Segerson and Tietenberg (1992).

[6]Goodstein (1992). The author also discusses the degree to which insurance companies can shift some of these costs back to the insured firm by increasing their premiums; this will depend upon their ability to monitor the behavior of the insured firm.

reduced income taxes; finally, the oil companies capitalized on the accident by boosting gas prices substantially.[7]

The penalties assessed in the *Valdez* case were truly spectacular. More commonly, however, the magnitude of fines are limited by statute and often bargained down by corporate attorneys. Fines are often criticized as only a **slap on the wrist**, that is, providing no real deterrent. From 1985 to 1992, Weyerhaeuser—a major international paper company—racked up 122 penalized violations at its three Washington State plants, paying $721,000 in fines, bargained down from an initial $1 million. "In many cases, Weyerhaeuser continued over the years to illegally discharge the same pollutant into the same waterway . . . paying the fine with little protest."[8] The fines in this case were not trivial—averaging around $6,000 per incident and $100,000 per year—but at the same time they had little immediate deterrent effect.

The Weyerhaeuser fines were about double the state average of $3,220 for violations that were actually penalized. However, many other violations were detected but not punished, and still others went undetected. Table 15.2 provides a somewhat

TABLE 15.2   State Enforcement Activity

State	Notice of Violations (Nov) Issued	Penalties Issued	Average Penalty Size	Average Penalty Per Nov
Colorado	124	1	$ 120	1
Connecticut	800	22	363	10
Indiana	59	21	4,050	1,440
Kentucky	194	5	2,520	68
Massachusetts	NA	0	0	0
Minnesota	41	10	10,900	2,660
Nebraska	59	1	200	0
New Jersey	1,167	350	1,430	428
Oregon	197	31	705	110
Pennsylvania	NA	176	1,480	NA
Rhode Island	5	0	0	0
South Carolina	68	2	24,250	785
South Dakota	17	1	1,000	20
Tennessee	193	0	0	0
Virginia	161	3	200	4
Wisconsin	81	8	7,951	760

Source: Clifford S. Russell (1990), "Monitoring and Enforcement," in *Public Policies for Environmental Protection*, ed. Paul Portney (Washington, DC: Resources for the Future). Figures have been rounded; notes detailing compilation methods are included in the original source. Reprinted by permission.

[7]"Gasoline Prices Post a Sharp Rise," *New York Times*, April 13, 1989. While market fundamentals may have underlain the increase in prices, the accident provided an opportunity for a swift, substantial, and profitable increase. See "Bad Times for Exxon, Good Times for the Other Major Oils," *Fortune,* May 8, 1989.

[8]"Penalties Aren't Stopping Land, Water Pollution," Associated Press Story reported in the Spokane *Spokesman-Review,* December 12, 1992.

broader look at the average enforcement activity and average fine levels in seventeen states from 1978 to 1983.

New Jersey had the highest annual activity level, issuing an average of 1,167 notices of violation (NOVs) and assessing 350 penalties averaging $1,430 each. However, the average penalty per NOV was only one-third as large, $428. By contrast, Rhode Island enforcement officials issued just 5 NOVs per year and levied no fines. The overall probability of actually being fined if caught ranged from a high of 36% in Indiana, to less than 1% in Colorado, and averaged around 10% across the states.

State enforcement activity has probably increased since the early 1980s, the period covered by Table 15.2. For example, between 1985 and 1992, Washington State levied an average of 210 penalties per year, well above the average listed in the table. Nationwide, in 1988 and 1989, the probability of being fined if caught for a significant air quality violation nationwide was 46%.[9] Nevertheless, in 1989 the EPA's inspector general was posed the following question by a U.S. senator: "Is it your testimony that the EPA's enforcement policies are so weak that it frequently pays polluters to keep polluting and pay the EPA's small fines rather than clean up their act?" "Absolutely," was the official response. " . . . We have found that over and over again."[10]

In theory, the EPA's official policy is to set the size of the fine equal to the economic benefit gained from noncompliance. However, by and large, the states have not adopted the EPA's philosophy, and fines are typically much lower. State inspectors, more sensitive to local economic and political issues and needing to maintain a working relationship with the industries they regulate, tend to use penalties only as a last resort. Their goal is to "achieve compliance by working cooperatively with facility owners." Penalties need be large enough only to "get the attention of management." Thus, state officials tend to reject the **deterrent feature of large fines** highlighted by our economic analysis of crime and punishment.[11]

When financial penalties are limited by either statute, fear of bankruptcy, or political realities, or when their impact is blunted by the ability of firms to shift the burden either to insurance companies, taxpayers, or consumers, a role for more costly jail terms emerges.[12]

However, because of the high cost of jail terms, the difficulty in establishing guilt (as well as the fact that corporate officials donate a lot of money to the political system?), criminal prosecutions for environmental crimes remain an infrequently used option. While criminal prosecutions increased during the 1980s, so did the overall level of enforcement. Criminal cases remained constant at about 1% to 2% of the total.[13] However, the average sentence for a convicted defendant did increase from two

---

[9]U.S. Government Accounting Office (1990).

[10]Testimony of John C. Martin, EPA Inspector General, before Senator John Glenn in "Serious Management Problems in the U.S. Government," Senate Government Affairs Committee, September 28, 1989.

[11]This paragraph and the quotes are drawn from U.S. Government Accounting Office (1990: 33–37). Gray and Deily (1991) present evidence that in counties with high unemployment rates, enforcement officials reduced the number of inspections for plants in the steel industry with a high probability of closing.

[12]Segerson and Tietenberg (1992) discuss the issues of inefficiency (over-deterrence) and fairness (jail terms for nonnegligent offenders) in criminal prosecution when fines are limited. They conclude that negligence-based prosecutions will generally be efficient; if reputational costs are large, a strict liability rule can also induce efficient levels of compliance.

[13]Segerson and Tietenberg (1992) make this point.

months to fourteen months from 1985 to 1990, while actual time served increased from one month to about four months.[14]

Most of the executives who do go to jail are from small companies. Examining a sample of 116 cases representing over 75% of all firms sentenced for environmental crimes in federal court from 1984 to 1990, Cohen (1992) reports the results in Table 15.3.

Considering just the raw numbers, 93 out of the 116 successful cases (80%) were brought against small firms—those with sales of less than $1 million or fewer than 50 employees. Of these, individuals were sentenced to prison in 23 cases, while fines were levied in the remainder. Compare this with 2 jail terms out of the 23 total cases brought against large firms. On the face of it, not only were small firms prosecuted more often, but the likelihood of jail time once convicted appears much higher.

However, Cohen notes that small firms were more likely to be involved in additional criminal behavior beyond violating pollution laws (perjury, grand jury tampering, bribery, or conspiracy), while larger firms were more likely to be brought up on charges involving accidental discharge or activity by employees that occurred in clear violation of company policy. Disregarding these observations, Cohen finds that individuals from large and small firms face roughly the same probability of jail time once convicted.

Yet even when contrasting "comparable" cases, it still remained true that thirteen out of fifteen individuals in Cohen's sample who served time for environmental crimes over the period were from small companies. This imbalance resulted from the prosecutorial focus on small firms. From 1984 to 1988, only 15% to 20% of federal criminal prosecutions for environmental crimes involved firms with annual sales greater than $1 million.[15]

Several possible reasons exist for the disproportionate criminal focus on smaller firms. First, of course, there are more small firms than large firms. Second, it may be the case that small firms, with thinner profit margins, are less able to comply with the relevant laws or, alternatively, command the legal and/or political resources necessary to avoid criminal prosecution. Third, it is easier for prosecutors to pinpoint responsibility in small firms. Moreover, small firms are less able to pay large fines, so in some instances, jail time may be all that the prosecutor can get. Or perhaps, as an EPA offi-

TABLE 15.3   Jail Terms by Firm Size

	Small Firms[a]	*Large Firms*
Number of Cases	93	23
Sentences with Jail Terms	23	2
Simple Incarceration Rate	25%	9%

[a]Less than $1 million in sales or fewer than 50 employees.

Source: Data from Mark A. Cohen (1992), "Environmental Crime and Punishment: Legal/Economic Theory and Empirical Evidence on Enforcement of Environmental Statutes," *The Journal of Criminal Law and Criminology,* 82, no. 4, p. 1092 (footnote 124).

[14]U.S. Environmental Protection Agency (1991a).
[15]Cohen (1992).

cial told the *Wall Street Journal*: "'judges don't feel as comfortable' sending a Fortune 500 executive to prison."[16]

The last two sections have focused on the economic theory of crime and punishment. To some extent, the EPA's official enforcement strategy follows the guidelines laid out here. The agency in fact does look at compliance history in targeting its enforcement efforts, although it falls short of sentencing firms to extensive future audits. In principle, the EPA endorses the greater use of continuous emissions monitoring. The agency also provides publicity about settled cases to insure that negative reputation effects are maximized. Finally, the EPA has officially adopted a policy of tying fine size to the economic benefit of noncompliance, but many states have not yet accepted this approach.

Yet, as suggested by the data on the imposition of fines and the ability of firms to bargain over them, as well as the skewed distribution of criminal prosecutions, the agency can fail in insuring swift, evenhanded, and certain punishment when violations are detected. Given this background, we now turn to the record of industry compliance.

15.3 The Compliance Record

With technology-based regulation, there are two types of compliance to consider: **initial compliance** and **continuous compliance**. Initial compliance simply requires the installation of the required pollution control technology (BAT, BACT, etc.), and is easy to confirm. Continuous compliance, more difficult to insure, can be checked in two ways. First, inspectors can examine the control technology and determine if it has been maintained and operated properly. Most inspections follow this route.[17] An alternate approach, generally more difficult and expensive, involves sampling emissions to see if they meet the standards specified on a firm's operating permit, if one has been issued.

Some laws, notably the Clean Water Act, the 1990 Clean Air Act amendments, and the enabling legislation for the Toxics Release Inventory, require firms to monitor and self-report their emissions. Falsifying such reports is usually prosecuted as a criminal case. While the EPA has in the past been reluctant to use self-reported emissions as the basis for a violation, private groups have used this information in so-called "citizen suits" discussed in Section 15.5 below.

While initial compliance performance has been reasonably good, the more important environmental issue is continuous compliance: how well do firms meet the emission standards that are written into their operating permits? Given the vast resources devoted to pollution control efforts in the United States over the last twenty years, it is surprising how little we know about the continuous compliance record of U.S. industrial and municipal pollution sources. There are simply no comprehensive estimates of the degree to which firms and cities comply with relevant environmental laws.

Some data are available. In 1988, 14% of the 30,000 plus major stationary air pollution sources had permit or initial noncompliance violations; 30% of these (1,404 in total) were in violation one or more times each month during the year. On the face of

---

[16]"Few Big Firms Get Jail Time for Polluting," *Wall Street Journal*, December 9, 1991.

[17]Russel (1990) reports that in 1979, only 3% of sources deemed to be out of compliance were so-judged on the basis of emissions tests.

it, this appears to be a reasonably good record: Eighty-six percent of the sources passed inspection. Yet, this figure almost surely overstates the true rate of continuance compliance with air pollution regulations. Studies from the late 1970s, when the EPA was also reporting 90% compliance rates based on on-site inspections, found actual rates of continuous compliance to be much lower, around 45%.[18] Why the disparity?

The EPA most commonly relies on announced, on-site inspections, thus giving firms a chance to tune up and repair their equipment. Major sources are inspected on average only once a year, and the inspection process, characterized by the EPA as "hit-or-miss," lasts only two to four hours. Inspectors focus attention on insuring that equipment is working properly; actual emissions are rarely tested. Finally, inspections are often hampered by cumbersome or unreliable testing equipment. In one case, for example, although "visible emissions from a major stationary source appeared to be about 60 to 80 percent capacity—well in excess of the 20% limit," the inspector could not perform his test because of the angle of the sun, and no violation was recorded. Given these limitations, the EPA itself has characterized its on-site inspection process as indicating only "whether a source is capable of being in compliance, rather than whether it is in compliance in its day-to-day operations."[19]

Some comfort can be taken from the fact that of the several thousand Clean Air Act violations uncovered by the inspection process each year, the EPA considers only about 500 or so to represent **significant noncompliance**. Significant noncompliance includes violations of state implementation plans in non-attainment areas and Class I (prevention of significant deterioration) areas, violations of toxic air pollutant standards, and failure to meet initial compliance requirements for new sources. At the beginning of fiscal year 1990, the EPA and the states had identified 459 facilities in significant noncompliance. By the end of the year, 537 more were added to this list, while 584 of the total either were brought into compliance, were placed on a compliance schedule, or had become the subject of an enforcement action.[20]

In some areas, notably surface water pollution, the EPA has had more compliance success. This is in part because firms are required to monitor and report their own discharges on a monthly basis. The EPA inspectors can thus focus their visits on ensuring that the self-reporting process is working as it should. Self-reported data from the pulp and paper industry in the early to mid-1980s revealed continuous compliance rates of from 75% to 82%, with significant noncompliance of 6%.[21] As noted in the last chapter, industrial discharges of two conventional water pollutants (suspended solids and dissolved oxygen) declined by over 90% from 1982 to 1987.

Little data are available on compliance rates for hazardous waste, pesticide, and chemical regulation. However, a review of RCRA enforcement actions from 1984 to 1988 revealed that in 80% of the cases, no clear evidence of compliance with enforcement orders was available.[22]

---

[18]Russel (1990) summarizes these studies.

[19]This paragraph, as well as quotes from the EPA's *1984 Compliance Monitoring Strategy for Major Stationary Sources*, is drawn primarily from U.S. Government Accounting Office (1990).

[20]U.S. Environmental Protection Agency (1991b: 6-1).

[21]Magat and Viscusi (1990).

[22]Testimony of Martin, before Senator John Glenn in "Serious Management Problems in the U.S. Government."

One acknowledged problem for the EPA has been enforcing regulations at government facilities. The federal government alone manages 27,000 industrial facilities. In fiscal year 1990, Congress budgeted $1.74 billion for pollution control and abatement. However, this is simply not enough money to insure compliance at federal facilities. The EPA conducted 930 federal inspections in 1990, finding compliance rates of 90% for Clean Air Act regulations, 91% for Clean Water Act regulations, 41% for RCRA, and 66% for TSCA. The 90% figure for air and water violations is roughly comparable to the overall picture reported above.

This section has reviewed the compliance record of the private and public sectors in the United States. On the surface, the figures for air and water pollution look encouraging. However, when one digs a bit deeper, it seems probable that official compliance rates overstate the actual degree of continuous compliance in these areas, probably by a substantial margin for air pollution. Little is known about private-sector compliance rates in the areas of hazardous waste, pesticides, and chemicals, but the government record is not encouraging. In short, and consistent with the economic model developed in the first section of this chapter, compliance with environmental regulations cannot be taken for granted. Indeed, in many areas, violations appear to be fairly widespread.

15.4 The Political Economy of Enforcement

The states have the primary responsibility for enforcing most environmental law. For example, state officials conducted 91% of the 37,716 inspections of stationary air pollution sources in 1988.[23] The EPA's role, as characterized by former agency administrator William Ruckelshaus, is to be the "gorilla in the closet," available to back up state efforts.[24] The gorilla's efforts, however, have waxed and waned with the political winds. As indicated in Figure 15.2, civil and criminal enforcement efforts climbed steadily during the 1970s but took a dramatic dip during the early 1980s. During this period, under President Reagan's conservative strategy to reduce the overall size of government, the EPA's budget was cut by close to 30%, while the number of staff enforcement attorneys at the agency fell from 200 to 30.[25]

Environmental protection, however, remained quite popular politically. By 1983, the Reagan administration was unable to maintain its attack on the EPA budget. By 1985, overall enforcement activity was back up to the level experienced under President Carter and has continued to climb since then. However, all of the increased enforcement activity has been due to the new regulations controlling land disposal of wastes that came into force in the mid-1980s. The number of air and water enforcement actions have not increased over late 1970 levels; the budget for stationary air pollution compliance was actually 35% lower in real dollars in 1990 than in 1979.[26]

Figure 15.2 clearly illustrates the sensitivity of enforcement efforts to the political climate and **budget pressures**. Because the bulk of enforcement occurs at the state

---

[23]U.S. Government Accounting Office (1990).

[24]Testimony of Martin, before Senator John Glenn in "Serious Management Problems in the U.S. Government," Senate Government Affairs Committee, September 28, 1989.

[25]These figures are reported in Naysnerski and Tietenberg (1992).

[26]For a breakdown of enforcement activity by sector see, U.S. Environmental Protection Agency (1991b). The budget figures are from U.S. Government Accounting Office (1990: 27).

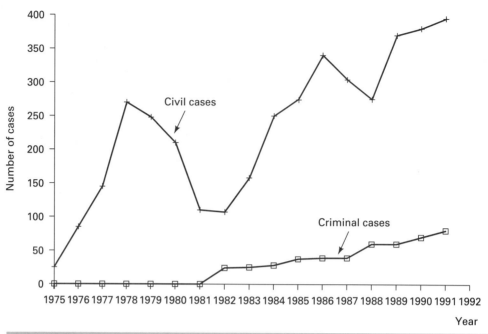

Figure 15.2 Trends in Federal Enforcement, 1975–1991 (EPA'S Civil and Criminal Referrals)

Source: United States Environmental Protection Agency (1991b).

level, as is illustrated in Table 15.2, variations in enforcement activity across state lines can be substantial. Political struggles between industry and environmental advocates over the size of the environmental agency budget are an annual event in states across the country.

When the EPA gorilla does swing into action, it can impose punishment at three levels. The agency can take an **administrative action** and impose fines directly. These can then be appealed through a quasi-judicial process within the EPA known as administrative review. This approach is by far the most common and accounts for around 90% of the penalties imposed. In 1990, the agency took 3,804 such administrative actions, while the states initiated an additional 10,105.[27] The EPA can also refer cases to the Department of Justice for prosecution as either a **civil case**, where fines can be levied, or a **criminal case**, where a combination of monetary sanctions and incarceration can be obtained. As one moves up the chain, both the standards of proof required for conviction and the available penalties become higher.

Even at the administrative level of punishment, however, the EPA inspectors are not empowered to impose fines as if they were parking tickets. Typically, a complex process of reporting, documentation, and review will be put in place prior to any penalty being assessed; once assessed, penalties are typically reduced on appeal or in a bargaining process. Figure 15.3 illustrates the steps in the **enforcement procedure** necessary to impose a penalty, once an inspector has uncovered a RCRA violation at a hazardous waste facility.

---

[27]U.S. Environmental Protection Agency (1991b).

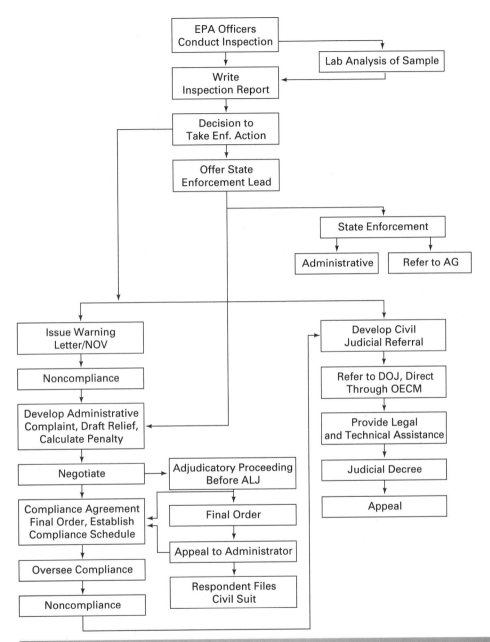

Figure 15.3 The RCRA Enforcement Process

Source: William Sanjour (1992), *What EPA is Like and What Can Be Done About It* (Washington, DC: Environmental Research Foundation). Used with permission.

From inspection (at the top), the most common enforcement path (administrative action) proceeds down the left side of the chart. After several steps, one arrives at a box labeled "Compliance Agreement Final Order, Establish Compliance Schedule." At this point a monetary penalty may be assessed, although the final order might just as easily include only a timetable for compliance. Yet the ballgame is still not over, since the alleged violator can make an appeal to the EPA administrator and, failing that, to civil court. In the event of further noncompliance, the agency might refer the case to the Department of Justice (DOJ) for prosecution as a civil or criminal case.

Part of the haggling over penalties arises from the fact that regulations are not always written so that violations are clear-cut. A recent EPA report called for "field-testing" regulations prior to implementation to insure that they could actually be enforced.[28]

A final political-economic constraint on enforcement is the motivation, training, and experience of the EPA's inspectors. The EPA admits that **turnover** is a serious problem in its regional offices and in state enforcement agencies.[29] EPA employee and harsh critic William Sanjour provides a particularly blunt assessment of the hazardous waste enforcement program: "The job of inspecting hazardous waste facilities in EPA regions is a dead end job that nobody wants. Turnover is high, training is poor and morale is low. Just as in EPA headquarters, young inspectors soon learn that you don't become a hero by finding major violations in hazardous waste management facilities regulated by EPA. [Due to the revolving door among EPA management and the industry,] It's like the young cop busting the whore house that has been paying off the mayor. As a result, inspectors engage in trivial "bean-counting" exercises while looking for another job."[30]

Sanjour's characterization of the enforcement process as essentially corrupt is, I believe, an overstatement. Most agency officials work hard under difficult conditions to try to get a tough job done. Nevertheless, on occasion, political favoritism in the enforcement process is exposed to public view. In 1992, two regional chief inspectors for the Office of Surface Mining, Reclamation and Enforcement (a non-EPA regulatory agency) charged that the office director had "ordered them to end investigations, reduce fines, eliminate penalties, divert prosecutions and prevent inspections." In one instance, after a two-year effort to get a strip-mine company to comply with water pollution regulations, a work-stoppage order was rescinded by superiors in Washington after having been in effect for only three days.[31]

Like any other aspect of the regulatory process, enforcement is subject to **political influence**. This can take the form of budgetary restraints, regulations that are either unenforceable or highly cumbersome, or pressures (informal or direct) placed on field workers to take a "nonconfrontational" approach to their work. The point of this section is *not* to suggest that the EPA and state enforcement agencies are corrupt organizations. In fact, the EPA has focused substantial attention over the last few years on more effectively addressing one of its hardest tasks.[32] Rather, the point is merely to recognize the real-world constraints under which the enforcement process operates.

---

[28]U.S. Environmental Protection Agency (1991a).

[29]U.S. Environmental Protection Agency (1991a).

[30]Sanjour (1992: 11).

[31]"U.S. Mine Inspectors Charge interference by Agency Director," *New York Times*, December 21, 1992.

[32]For a discussion of some of these initiatives, see Wasserman (1992).

15.5 Citizen Enforcement

When writing most of the major environmental statutes, Congress recognized that public enforcement efforts might well prove inadequate to insure full compliance with the new laws. As a result, a provision in most of the statutes allows private citizens to take violators to court. As can be seen in Figure 15.4, these **citizen suits** became an increasingly important mechanism for enforcing environmental laws in the 1980s. Only 25 suits were filed in 1979. However, the declining federal enforcement efforts of the early 1980s (noted in Figure 15.2 above) sparked a growth in private actions to 266 in 1986.

Congress limited the enforcement powers of citizens in a variety of ways. Citizens are required to give the alleged violator a sixty-day-notice period, providing an opportunity to come into compliance. Any settlements must be reviewed by the EPA and the Justice Department, and citizens cannot sue if public officials are already pursuing a "diligent" enforcement effort.

However, citizen suits do have real teeth. Citizens can sue not only to force firms into compliance but also for damage restoration and often the imposition of penalties. Out-of-court settlements increasingly involve corporate financing of so-called environmentally beneficial expenditures—"donations" to organizations like the Nature Conservancy, which buy up land for preservation purposes, or the financing of cleanups or environmental studies. Finally, private groups can recover court costs for successful suits.[33]

Given these incentives, why aren't private environmental groups more active in filing suits? The primary problem lies in the difficulty of monitoring emissions and **proving a violation**. The great majority of citizen suits (67%) have been filed under the Clean Water Act, where self-reporting of emissions is required. Environmental groups have been able to obtain these self-reported records (at some expense). Prov-

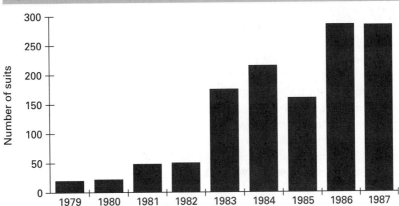

Figure 15.4 The Growth in Citizen Suits

Source: Wendy Naysnerski and Tom Tietenberg (1992), "Private Enforcement of Federal Environmental Law," *Land Economics*, 68, no. 1, 28–48. Reprinted by permission of The University of Wisconsin Press, Madison, WI.

---

[33]This paragraph is based on Mann (1991).

ing a violation has thus been as simple as checking emission records against a firm's permit.

Hazardous waste violations make up most of the remainder (30%) of citizen suits.[34] While violations under RCRA and Superfund are not as easy to prove as Clean Water Act violations, Naysnerski and Tietenberg (1992) point out that the water and hazardous waste statutes are the only ones that allow citizens to sue for the courts to impose **penalties** on violators. These are thus the statutes most likely to attract citizen attention.

To date, very few suits have been brought under the Clean Air Act, since firms have by-and-large not been required to report their emissions or hold permits specifying legal emissions, and because penalties have not been an available remedy. However, recognizing the importance of citizen suits, the Clean Air Act amendments of 1990 expanded permitting and self-reporting requirements to most stationary air pollution sources. In addition, the act authorizes the imposition of penalties for violations established under citizen suits. Thus, we will likely see a major increase in citizen enforcement of the Clean Air Act in this decade.[35]

Finally, citizen enforcement can serve a particularly important role in enforcing compliance at government-owned facilities. If EPA or state officials are reluctant to pursue a government polluter for political reasons, citizen suits provide a fallback.

15.6 Cost-Effective Enforcement

Because the states and the EPA will never be provided sufficient resources to insure 100% compliance with all environmental laws, the enforcement agencies must make short-run decisions about how to best allocate their budgeted resources. The EPA's current strategy is to **target areas** for "maximum environmental results," while still maintaining some presence in all areas.[36] In practice, this may mean paying less attention to hazardous waste enforcement (where health and ecosystem risks are currently thought to be "low"), and more attention to controlling airborne ozone or sulfate pollution, where environmental risks are thought to be higher.

In the long run, however, reducing bureaucratic discretion in the enforcement process appears to provide the best hope for reducing enforcement costs and, thus, increasing compliance rates overall. Three strategies can be recommended. First, require states to establish a penalty formula in which violations will lead to fines with a high probability. Fines need not be large and, indeed, must be low enough to be credibly imposed without bankrupting the violator, but they must be imposed with a high degree of certainty. By recognizing the deterrent value of fines, enforcement officials can get much greater compliance for the enforcement dollar.

Second, write regulations in which violations are clear and easily detected. For example, under the Clean Water Act, violations can be demonstrated merely by comparing self-reported emissions with allowable emissions of a firm's permit. By contrast, until the 1990 amendments kick in, proving a violation under the Clean Air Act has proven difficult for the EPA and virtually impossible for private citizens.

[34]The percentages are calculated from data provided in Naysnerski and Tietenberg (1992).
[35]Buente (1991).
[36]U.S. Environmental Protection Agency (1991a: 10).

Finally, rely more heavily on **continuous emissions monitoring,** rather than inspections, for establishing violations. Continuous monitoring greatly increases the probability that a violation will be detected, thus increases the benefits of compliance.

Similar recommendations have been made before. After making his own suggestions for improvement, Russel (1990: 270) speculates that better compliance may in fact not be the real goal of policy. Instead he raises the possibility that "legislation and accompanying regulations are meant to give the *appearance* of strictness while the reality is reflected by a lack of commitment to monitoring and enforcement." While there are obviously powerful political pressures that have shaped the "enforceability" (or lack thereof) of the current regulatory system, the reforms suggested here could help improve the long-run cost-effectiveness of the enforcement process.

15.7 Summary

In the real world, compliance with environmental protection laws is not automatic. To explain noncompliance, economists argue that polluters weigh the marginal benefits of compliance against its marginal costs. If the latter outweigh the former, firms choose to ignore regulations. Given this framework, one way regulators can increase compliance rates is by increasing the marginal benefits of compliance—imposing stiffer fines or prison terms, or more frequent inspection rates for violators.

Alternatively, regulators can in principle lower the marginal costs of compliance by requiring firms to install low marginal cost abatement technology. However, this latter strategy, which provided an argument for command-and-control regulation, has proven less successful than proponents had hoped. In fact, most control technologies lose their effectiveness over time without proper maintenance.

Regulators have two different punishment tools, fines and incarceration. Fines have two advantages: They impose lower social costs (prisons, jailers, and foregone productivity) and require a lower standard of proof. However, the magnitude of fines that can be imposed are limited by bankruptcy constraints as well as political practice. Moreover, firms can shift portions of some types of monetary penalties to insurers, taxpayers, and customers. Neither jail terms nor fines are imposed in a consistent fashion. Most violators receive no fines, fines are often reduced on appeal, and there is wide variation between states. Small companies face the bulk of criminal prosecution for environmental crimes.

The actual compliance record by firms and government agencies is far from perfect. While initial compliance—the installation of required equipment—has been forthcoming, continuous compliance is both harder to monitor and less often achieved. The highest compliance rates are probably achieved by private firms subject to the Clean Water Act, around 75% to 82%, where self-reported emissions monitoring is required.

Turning to political-economic considerations, enforcement activities are hampered by tight budgets, difficult to detect violations, cumbersome inspection procedures, poorly written regulations, complex mechanisms for punishing violators, high turnover among inspectors, and political influence. If legislators and regulators were so motivated, the enforcement process could be made much more effective by recognizing the deterrent value of "certain" punishment, writing enforceable regulations, and relying more heavily on continuous emissions monitoring. The latter two would also encourage private enforcement of regulations through the citizen suits. Recently, there have been initiatives and reforms in these directions, particularly at the national EPA level.

Overall, enforcement is probably the weakest link in the environmental protection chain. This insight will be particularly important in part IV of this book, where we turn our attention to international issues. If enforcement is difficult in developed countries, it becomes even more challenging in poor countries. In a developing nation, the problems of underpaid and inadequately trained inspectors, combined with very weak governmental authority, can lead quickly to a corrupt and ineffective enforcement process. For these reasons, it is unlikely that a regulatory strategy can be pursued with great effectiveness in many poor countries. This provides a strong rationale for government policy to focus on the development of "clean technology," discussed in chapters 18 to 20, which reduces the need for regulation in the first place.

A second application of the enforcement lesson relates to international pollution control agreements, the topic of chapter 23. Such agreements are also only as strong as the underlying enforcement mechanism. If it is difficult for EPA officials to insure compliance with national water quality laws in, say, Ohio or Montana, the problem will be compounded when the agency is forced to consider compliance with carbon dioxide emission limitations in, say, France or Angola. Here the question of credible sanctions emerges. What penalties can be imposed on countries (or firms within countries) that violate an agreement and how will compliance be monitored?

The last four chapters of this book have focused on the question: Is Government Up to the Job? Along the way, we have examined a portrait of the policy process that some might characterize as cynical, others overly optimistic. The main point is that government intervention in the economy to promote environmental goals does not automatically follow any "rational" process—for example, cost-minimization or risk reduction. Instead, it is inherently political.

This does not mean that government intervention is necessarily bad, useless, or self-defeating. It simply means that we need to go into it with our eyes wide open. The challenge for environmental economists is to recommend policy reforms that are (1) politically feasible and (2) still effective when implemented in a politically compromised form. The next part of this book will examine two general economic strategies for improving governmental performance in the environmental arena—incentive-based regulation and the promotion of clean technology.

APPLICATION 15.0

Enforcing Auto Emission Limits

Noncompliance with auto emission limits is fairly widespread; as I noted in the text, some 69% of test facilities passed cars that were designed to fail. In a review of the issues faced, Harrington and McConnell (1993) cited faulty testing equipment, exemptions in some states for old (and highly polluting) cars, and poor enforcement. The response of the EPA and Congress to this situation has been to call for improved testing equipment, to restrict exemptions, and to centralize the testing procedure in state-run centers, rather than have the tests done in gas stations. While the last step should improve compliance by testers, it also increases costs to consumers, who will now have to travel farther to get tested.

Figure 15.5 provides Harrington and McConnell's estimates of the marginal costs of reducing volatile organic compounds (VOCs), based on three types of testing equipment the EPA may require. (VOCs are chemical compounds that contribute to ozone pollution or smog.)

The 2500 idle test is the current technology that measures emissions only at the tailpipe; the pressure and purge tests pick up currently unmeasured VOCs that escape from the car's emission recycling system. The IM240 test is a more effective (and expensive) version of the 2500 idle test of tailpipe emissions and has been proposed as a replacement.

1. The horizontal axis measures tons of emission reduction per thousand cars inspected. How much extra per ton does it cost to increase emission reductions from around 2.7 tons (achieved with the 2500 idle test) to around 4.9 tons (with a pressure test added)? Does the graph indicate that it is actually cheaper for testing centers to have both a 2500 idle and a pressure test available, rather than just a 2500 idle test?

2. Up to the point where the purge system is installed, the MC of reduction curve slopes downward. Is this the usual shape for a MC of reduction curve? (Refer to chapter 4.) If not, can you tell a story about technological progress and compliance rates that might explain the downward slope?

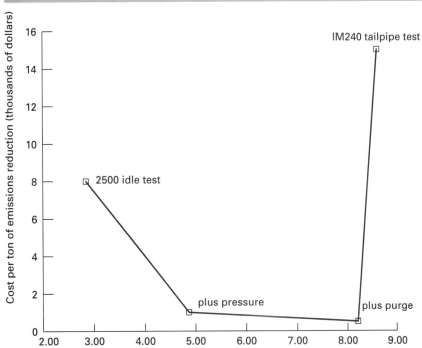

Figure 15.5 Marginal Costs of Reducing VOCs Through Improved Enforcement

Source: Winston Harrington and Virginia D. McConnell (1993), "Vehicle Emissions Inspection and Maintenance: Where Do We Go from Here?" *Resources,* vol. 110 (Winter), 11–15. Reprinted by permission.

3. How much extra does it cost per ton of VOCs reduced to go from an emission reduction of around 8.2 (with the 2500, pressure and purge tests) to around 8.7 (with the pressure and purge tests, and the IM240 replacing the 2500)? What does this say about the relative importance of VOC emissions from the tailpipe versus the recycling system? Does this mean that, from an efficiency point of view, the IM240 test is a bad idea?

APPLICATION 15.1

Fun with Graphs

It was stated in this chapter that the EPA officially supports a policy of setting fines to eliminate all monetary gain from noncompliance with regulations. (The states have generally not adopted this policy, opting for smaller fines.)

1. Assume that any violation by a firm will be detected with certainty. In this case, try and figure out what the MB curve of compliance in Figure 15.1 looks like under the EPA's recommended policy. (The MC curve stays the same.) Will the plant manager choose full compliance?

2. In the real world, detection does not occur with certainty. In this case, will the manager choose full compliance under the EPA policy?

Key Ideas in Each Section

15.0 Enforcement is the bottom line in environmental regulation. Without an effective commitment to enforcement, significant and widespread noncompliance will develop.

15.1 In an economic model of environmental crime, economic decision makers weigh the marginal benefits of compliance against the marginal costs. Regulators can **trade-off punishment for detection** to raise the marginal benefits of compliance; detection can be increased via use of **continuous emissions monitors** or a focus on **repeat offenders**. Low marginal compliance costs have been used to justify CAC regulation, but this argument fails if control technology breaks down over time.

15.2 Fines are used much more often than **jail terms** because the standard of proof and the cost to the state are lower. However, state enforcement officials tend *not* to impose high enough fines for **deterrent purposes**. In addition, fines are often **shifted** and reduced through bargaining. Incarceration rates are also not uniform, being much higher for small firm managers.

15.3 There are two types of compliance: **initial compliance**, which has been fairly good, and **continuous compliance**. Data on continuous compliance with environmental laws are not good, but the available evidence suggests **significant noncompliance** in both the private and public sectors. This is due in part to the unreliability and infrequency of on-site inspections.

15.4 Most enforcement is done by the states. The principal political constraint on enforcement is **budgetary pressure**. Enforcement measures take the form of **administrative action** (by far the most common) or can proceed as **civil or criminal cases**. **Enforcement procedures** are lengthy and complex. There is also high **turnover** among inspectors and some evidence of **political influence** in the enforcement process.

15.5 Citizen suits to enforce environmental laws became increasingly important in 1980s. Suits are most common where it is easiest to **prove a violation** and where a **penalty** can be imposed on violators.

15.6 One way to improve the cost-effectiveness of enforcement efforts is to **target violations** that pose high levels of risk. In the long run, cost-effective regulation can be achieved by designing regulations which are **easy to enforce, insure punishment** with a high probability, and rely on **continuous emissions monitoring,** rather than inspection, to prove a violation.

References

Buente, David T. (1991). "Citizen Suits and the Clean Air Act Amendments of 1990: Closing the Enforcement Loop." *Environmental Law*, vol. 21, 2233–2253.

Cohen, Mark A. (1992). "Environmental Crime and Punishment: Legal/Economic Theory and Empirical Evidence on Enforcement of Environmental Statutes." *The Journal of Criminal Law and Criminology*, 82, no. 4, 1053–1108.

Council on Environmental Quality (1984). *Environmental Quality*. Washington, DC: U.S. GPO.

Goodstein, Eban (1992). "Saturday Effects in Tanker Oil Spills." *Journal of Environmental Economics and Management*, vol. 23, 276–288.

Gray, Wayne and Mary E. Deily (1991). "Enforcement of Pollution Regulations in a Declining Industry." Clark University *Working Paper 89–8* Worcester, MA: Clark University.

Harrington, Winston and Virginia D. McConnell (1993). "Vehicle Emissions Inspection and Maintenance: Where Do We Go from Here?" *Resources,* vol. 110 (Winter), 11–15.

Magat, Wesley A. and W. Kip Viscusi (1990). "Effectiveness of the EPA's Regulatory Enforcement: The Case of Industrial Effluents." *Journal of Law and Economics*, 33, no. 2, 331–360.

Mann, David S. (1991). "Polluter-Financed Environmentally Beneficial Expenditures: Effective use or Improper Abuse of Citizen Suits Under the Clean Water Act?" *Environmental Law*, 21, no. 175, 175–211.

Naysnerski, Wendy and Tom Tietenberg (1992). "Private Enforcement of Federal Environmental Law." *Land Economics*, 68, no. 1, 28–48.

Russel, Clifford S. (1990). "Monitoring and Enforcement." In *Public Policies for Environmental Protection*, ed. Paul Portney. Washington, DC: Resources for the Future.

Sanjour, William (1992). *What EPA Is Like and What Can Be Done About It.* Washington, DC: Environmental Research Foundation.

Segerson, Kathleen and Tom Tietenberg (1992). "The Structure of Penalties in Environmental Enforcement: An Economic Analysis." In *Innovation in Environmental Policy*, ed. Tom Tietenberg. Brookfield, VT: Edward Elgar.

Tietenberg, Tom (1985). *Emissions Trading: An Exercise in Reforming Pollution Policy.* Washington, DC: Resources for the Future.

U.S. Environmental Protection Agency (1991a). *Enhanced Environmental Enforcement for the 1990s.* Washington, DC: U.S. EPA.

U.S. Environmental Protection Agency (1991b). *Enforcement Accomplishments Report, FY1990.* Washington, DC: U.S. EPA.

U.S. Government Accounting Office (1990). *Air Pollution: Improvements Needed in Detecting and Preventing Violations.* Washington, DC: U.S. GAO.

Wasserman, Cheryl (1992). "Federal Enforcement: Theory and Practice." In *Innovation in Environmental Policy*, ed. Tom Tietenberg. Brookfield, VT: Edward Elgar.

PART III

HOW CAN WE DO BETTER?

In part II of this book, we reviewed the current regulatory picture, and discovered that after more than two decades of dedicated national efforts to control pollution and expenditures of hundreds of billions of dollars, our accomplishments are decidedly mixed. With a few exceptions, regulation has essentially held the line against economic and population growth, yet it has failed to achieve its stated objective of substantially reducing most pollutant concentrations to "safe" levels.

We also identified three main obstacles to successful government action to control pollution. First, hampered by imperfect information and motivated by either material gain, peer approval, or ideological commitment, regulators may pursue policies that deviate from their legislative mandate—whether that mandate is safety or efficiency. Second, the current command-and-control (CAC) regulatory structure often discourages cost-effective pollution control in the short run and innovation in new technology in the long run. Finally, the difficult yet vital job of monitoring and enforcing compliance with regulations is often underfunded.

Given this background, part III will explore the question "How can we do better?" Doing better is defined as achieving a specified pollution goal at lower cost and with greater certainty.

Incentive-Based
Regulation: Theory

16.0 Introduction

In the late 1960s when major new environmental legislation was being contemplated, economists had a bit of advice to offer: Why not harness market incentives to control pollution? The basic idea was twofold. First, make polluting an expensive activity. This would both reduce pollution directly and induce a search for less polluting substitutes. Second, lower the costs of pollution control by leaving decisions about how specifically to reduce pollution up to firms and individuals.

Two schemes were widely discussed. The first was a **pollution tax** (also known as an *effluent or emission charge*). For example, to reduce the acid rain caused by sulfur dioxide emissions from power plants, one could institute a tax on emissions of, say, $600 per ton of SO_2. Alternatively, one might achieve a rollback through a **marketable permit system.** Here permits would be issued only up to a certain target level of emissions. These permits could then be bought and sold, again putting a price tag on pollution. These two regulatory approaches—pollution taxes and marketable permit systems—are referred to as **incentive-based (IB) regulation** since they rely on market incentives to both reduce pollution and minimize control costs.

As we saw in chapter 13, the recommendations of economists were largely ignored in the drafting of the major environmental legislation of the early 1970s. Instead, the nation opted for what we have called the command-and-control (CAC) approach to regulation, requiring uniform emissions across sources and mandating the adoption of particular pollution control technologies. Since that time, economists have maintained a steady drum beat of support for the more flexible incentive-based approach. Twenty-five years later, the mid-1990s will see the first wide-scale test of this type of regulation in air pollution control. Since 1995, sulfur dioxide emission credits have been traded among 110 coal-burning electric facilities, mostly in the East and Midwest. At the same time, a tradeable permits system is being introduced in the Los

Angeles basin, covering three urban air pollutants: sulfur oxide, nitrogen oxide, and volatile organic compounds.

From a theoretical perspective, incentive-based systems offer several advantages over a CAC approach. First, IB systems will promote more cost-effective regulation in the short run. (Recall that cost-effectiveness is defined as achieving a given pollution target at the lowest possible cost.) Perhaps more importantly, over the long run IB systems provide incentives for firms to seek out new technologies to lower pollution control costs. Finally, in theory, an IB approach reduces the costly burden of information gathering for regulatory bureaucrats—rather than having to choose which technology is to be deemed BACT or BAT or LAER, regulators need only specify the tax level or the number of permits and then let private incentives take over. Because, as we saw in chapter 12, control over information is a primary means of political influence, IB approaches can reduce such influence in the regulatory process.

However, IB approaches are not without their theoretical drawbacks, including among others, problems of monitoring and enforcement, hot spots (high local concentrations of pollutants), thin markets, and the possible exercise of market power. Overcoming these obstacles to realize the potential of IB regulation is the challenge facing policy makers today.

This chapter examines in some detail the theoretical advantages and disadvantages of IB regulation. Chapter 17 will then take a closer look at the lessons to be learned from our limited practical experience with IB systems and the way that potential problems with the IB approach are being dealt with in the ongoing acid rain case.

16.1 The Cost-Effectiveness Rule

One defining aspect of the stereotypical CAC regulatory approach is its prescription of *uniform standards* for all pollution sources. Economists have widely criticized this requirement, since it essentially blocks any effort to achieve cost-effective pollution control.[1] To see why, we need to understand a:

> **Cost-effectiveness rule.** Cost-effectiveness is achieved if and only if the marginal cost of reduction is equal for each pollution source.

It is easy to show that this is true. Consider a town called Grimeville, hosting an oil refinery, A, and a coal plant, B. The Grimeville City Council wants to control total emissions of harmful gunk at 20 tons per day and is considering a uniform standard of 10 tons per day for each plant. Suppose that when refinery A emits 10 tons of gunk, it has marginal reduction costs of $10 per ton, while at an emission level of 10 tons, coal plant B has marginal reduction costs of only $2 per ton. Here's the

---

[1]Uniform standards are also typically inefficient. For example, they mandate the same level of protection for densely and sparsely populated areas. However, uniform standards are easier to defend on safety grounds.

PUZZLE

If the Grimeville City Council imposes a uniform, 10 ton per plant standard, will it be achieving its pollution target cost-effectively?[2]

SOLUTION

No, because there is a less expensive way of keeping pollution at 20 units total in Grimeville. Suppose that plant B decreased its pollution level from 10 tons to 9 tons. This would cost $2. If plant A then increased its pollution from 10 tons to 11 tons, it would save $10. Overall, industry in Grimeville would save $8.

Whenever the marginal cost of pollution reduction at one source is greater than that at another, overall costs can be reduced *without changing the pollution level* by decreasing pollution at the low-cost site and increasing it at the high-cost site. Thus, cost-effectiveness is achieved *only* when the marginal costs of reduction are equal at all sites.

Let us expand the Grimeville example to illustrate how the city council might identify the cost-effective method of reducing pollution to 20 tons. Table 16.1 below lists the complete marginal reduction cost schedules for the two plants.

Table 16.1 reveals that it will cost $1 for plant A to reduce pollution from 20 tons to 19 tons per day, $2 to move from 19 to 18, and so forth. Marginal reduction costs thus rise as pollution falls. Plant B, on the other hand, faces zero marginal reduction costs all the way back to 10 units of gunk. Below 10 units, however, pollution reduction becomes increasingly costly for plant B as well. Of the two, plant B clearly has lower overall emission reduction costs.

The council has a two-part problem to solve: Choose pollution levels at the two plants so that total pollution equals 20 tons, and marginal reduction costs are (roughly) equal. We already know that cost-effectiveness will require plant A to pollute more than 10 tons, while plant B pollutes less. The simple way to identify the cheapest solution is to try a few combinations.[3] Table 16.2 rearranges the information in Table 16.1 to examine pollutant combinations that add up to a total of 20 tons per day.

We can use the table to find the cost-effective regulatory option. We have already discovered that moving from (10, 10) to (11, 9) lowers total costs by $8. Similarly, moving

---

[2]This is a purely illustrative example. As we learned in chapter 14, most environmental standards are set at the federal level, with state governments responsible for implementation.

[3]A more general approach is to use algebra. The equations for the marginal reduction costs for plants A and B are, respectively: $MC_a = 20 - x_a$, and $MC_b = 20 - 2x_b$. For cost-effectiveness, these two MC equations should be set equal to each other. We also have the constraint that total pollution must equal 20: $x_a2 + x_b = 20$. With three equations and two unknowns, we can solve the system to get $x_a = 13.333$ and $x_b = 6.666$.

TABLE 16.1   Marginal Cost of Gunk Reduction in Grimeville

Pollution at Each Plant (tons/day)	MC of Reduction ($/ton) Plant A	MC of Reduction ($/ton) Plant B
20		
	1	0
19		
	2	0
18		
	3	0
17		
	4	0
16		
	5	0
15		
	6	0
14		
	7	0
13		
	8	0
12		
	9	0
11		
	10	0
10		
	11	2
9		
	12	4
8		
	13	6
7		
	14	8
6		
	15	10
5		
	16	12
4		
	17	14
3		
	18	16
2		
	19	18
1		
	20	20
0		

on to (12, 8) generates savings of $9 at a cost of only $4. Finally, moving to (13, 7) saves an additional $2 ($8–$6). However, the (14, 6) option increases net costs by $1, since the additional savings ($7) are less than the additional costs ($8). Moving on to (15, 5) is an even worse idea, since the savings are only $6 for an additional expense of $12. Thus, the cheapest regulatory option that achieves total pollution of 20 is plant A: 13, plant B: 7. Note, as our rule predicts, at this point marginal reduction costs are roughly equal.

TABLE 16.2   Identifying the Cost-Effective Option

Plant A — Pollution (tons of gunk/day)	Plant A — Marginal Savings as Pollution Rises	Plant B — Pollution (tons of gunk/day)	Plant B — Marginal Cost as Pollution Falls
10		10	
	$10		$ 2
11		9	
	$ 9		$ 4
12		8	
	$ 8		$ 6
13		7	
	$ 7		$ 8
14		6	
	$ 6		$10
15		5	

We can compare total costs at the uniform standard option (10, 10) and the cost-effective option (13, 7) to see how much money we save from the latter choice. Total costs can be calculated as just the sum of all the marginal costs, so total costs at (10, 10) are $1 + 2 + 3 + 4 + 5 + 6 + 7 + 8 + 9 + 10 = 55$. Total costs at (13, 7) are $1 + 2 + 3 + 4 + 5 + 6 + 7 + 2 + 4 + 6 = 40$, for a net savings of $55 - 40 = 15$.

This example illustrates a principal reason why, in general, CAC systems that require uniform standards do not achieve cost-effectiveness. Since both high- and low-cost plants must meet the same standard, in our example 10 tons per day, opportunities for reducing overall costs are ignored. But why are uniform standards set in the first place? Couldn't the Grimeville City Council achieve a cost-effective solution by going through the above exercise and choosing (13, 7) in the first place?

In general, the answer is no. In the real world, the council might well founder on a lack of information, what economists refer to as **imperfect information.**[4] Only the firms have access to the pollution control cost information in Table 16.1, and they would be unwilling to share this data with the public. Of course, the regulators might still recognize in a qualitative way that refinery A has higher reduction costs than coal plant B, and, thus, incorporate some concern for cost savings into their regulatory design. As we shall see below, some CAC systems do just this.

Yet, such a rough approach would not capture all cost savings. In addition, in the political arena, plant B's owners and residents around plant A might argue against such a move on the grounds of equity or safety. The next section illustrates that, in theory, incentive-based regulation will achieve cost-effectiveness "automatically" through a market mechanism.

16.2 IB Regulation and Cost-Effectiveness

Back in the Grimeville City Council offices, the village economist proposes a tax system for controlling pollution and claims that the tax will deliver cost-effective pollution control. To prove her point, she draws graphs of the two marginal cost of reduction curves, reproduced in Figure 16.1. (Note that she has switched the direction of the horizontal axis—it now shows *increasing* pollution rather than pollution reduction.)[5] She then proclaims, "Consider, if you will, the effect of a tax on gunk emissions of $7.50 per ton on the pollution situation in our fair city. Faced with such a tax, plant A will reduce its pollution level from 20 to 13 units. It won't go below 13 tons because for these units it is cheaper for it to pollute and pay the tax than it is to reduce pollution. By a similar logic, plant B will reduce pollution down to 7 tons per day. Because at the final pollution levels (13, 7) the marginal cost of reduction for both firms will be just less than the tax and thus equal to each other, my plan will be cost-effective.

"Moreover," the economist continues, "since pollution now has a 'price,' every day they pollute the firms will pay for the privilege, $20 * \$7.50$, or $150 in all (areas *W* and *X* in the figure). This will provide them with a tremendous long-run incentive to search out new, less polluting ways of doing business. But best of all, Grimeville will be rich! We'll earn tax revenue from the 20 units of pollution equal to $150 per day!"

---

[4]See advanced topic chapter T4 for a discussion of regulation under imperfect information.

[5]The reason for this is that it is easier to illustrate cleanup costs and tax revenues when the marginal cost of reduction curve is drawn sloping downward.

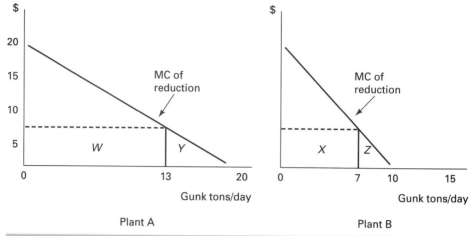

FIGURE 16.1 Pollution Taxes Are Cost-Effective

For a moment, the audience is awed by the overwhelming clarity and logic of the economist's argument. But only for a moment. "Wait a minute," objects the oil refinery lobbyist. "Grimeville won't earn a dime. Those steep taxes will drive both plants out of business. Not only are you making industry pay to reduce pollution from current levels back to 20 units (areas *Y* and *Z*), but now you're imposing additional taxes as well!"

"Hmmmm," mumbles the village economist. "We can solve this problem. You'll still have to pay the pollution tax, but we'll give the industry an income tax rebate based on the average pollution tax to make the whole thing 'revenue neutral.' [So much for Grimeville's tax windfall!] As long as the size of the rebate is not connected to your individual firm's efforts to reduce pollution, the pollution tax will still give you an incentive for further reductions."

"But, how will we know where to set the tax?" the village environmentalist demands. "If we set it too low, gunk pollution will be more than 20 tons per day. Then we'll have to adjust the tax upward, and he," pointing at the refinery lobbyist, "is bound to complain about taxes being raised again. Besides, inflation will erode the value of the tax. And even if the tax is inflation-adjusted, pollution levels will keep going up as population and production levels grow."

"Valid points," the economist concedes. "But here's another idea. Suppose, instead of the pollution tax, we institute a marketable permit system."

"A what?" asks the mayor.

"A marketable permit system. Let me explain. We're interested in reducing total pollution to 20 tons per day, correct? Suppose we give each firm 10 one-ton permits allowing them to pollute, but we also allow the firms to buy or sell these permits. What will be the outcome?"

"I'm all ears," says the mayor.

"Plant A, facing high marginal reduction costs, would dearly love to have an eleventh permit. In fact, from Table 16.2 we know it would be willing to pay up to $10 per day to get its hands on one. Plant B, on the other hand, would be willing to sell one permit, reducing to 9, for anything over $2 per day. Thus, a deal will be made. By a similar logic, A would be willing to pay up to $9 for a twelfth permit, and B would sell another for anything over $4. Finally, A would buy the thirteenth for a price of up to $8, while B would part with an additional permit for a price greater than $6. However, the firms would stop there. Plant A would be willing to pay only $7 for the fourteenth permit, while B would have to be paid $8 to reduce down to 6 permits. So, *voila!* Market incentives will generate trade in permits until a cost-effective solution (13, 7) is reached.

"Note that the final price for a permit in this bargaining scenario is between $6 and $8 per day, which is very close to our $7.50 tax. As in the tax case, pollution now has a 'price,' giving firms long-run incentives to develop new, less pollution-intensive techniques, so that they can sell their excess permits. Moreover, if new firms enter the area, they can do so only by buying existing permits. Total pollution will be *fixed* at 20 units."

"Wait a minute," objects the environmentalist. "Why should we give away the 'right to pollute'?"

"Well," says the economist, "we do that already whenever we set legal pollution standards. But one alternative would be for the government to sell the permits, instead of giving them away. A price of $7.50 or so would clear the market—since at that price plant A would demand 13, and plant B would demand 7. [Take a minute to check this]. Certain types of auctions would in fact generate such a price. But if you think about it, government sale of permits is really identical to a tax system! Selling permits to pollute one unit at $7.50 per day is the same thing as charging a tax of $7.50 per day for any units of gunk emitted."

"Which is exactly why we oppose permit sales by the government," pipes in the oil refinery lobbyist. "Once again you're asking industry to cough up areas *W* and *X* in taxes, in addition to paying areas *Y* and *Z* in cleanup costs. But this permit giveaway idea sounds interesting. . . ."

Now the conversation in Grimeville went on well into the night, but at this point I would like to interrupt and summarize the main points. First, both tax systems and marketable permit systems will achieve cost-effective pollution control "automatically," at least on the chalkboard. In either case, *government regulators do not need to know anything about control costs at different sources.* In the case of a tax, regulators merely specify a tax level, observe the market response, and if the induced pollution reduction is too little (or too great), adjust the tax upward (or downward). In the permit case, the government merely specifies the number of permits desired and distributes them by either sale or giveaway.

The discussion also highlights one of the political drawbacks of taxes (and permit sale systems). Polluters, whether firms or consumers, object strenuously to having to pay the government for the right to pollute up to the legal limit, in addition to the cleanup costs they face. For example, if the government were to impose a CAC standard of 13 units for plant A, the firm would have to pay area *Y* in Figure 16.1 to cleanup from 20 tons back to 13 tons. Under a $7.50 per ton tax (or permit-sale system), the firm would have to pay, in addition to these cleanup costs, 13 * $7.50 = $97.50, or area *W*. Such additional costs might in fact drive a firm out of business and, thus, they impose a **bankruptcy constraint** on the imposition of tax or permit policies.

In principle, pollution taxes or permit sales can be made **revenue neutral** by rebating the revenues back to the affected firms or individuals in the form of income tax cuts. Parties paying the tax would not receive a rebate exactly equal to their pollution tax, since that would negate its effect. Instead, each polluter would receive an 'average' rebate. In this way, average incomes remain the same, but the price of pollution still rises. Such income tax rebates have been widely discussed as a way to reduce both the political opposition to and the regressive impact from any substantial carbon tax imposed to combat global warming.

In addition, substituting pollution tax revenues for a tax on labor (the income tax) would enhance **labor market efficiency,** because in this particular case, people would work harder if they faced lower income taxes. Indeed, recent work on the general equilibrium effects of pollution taxes and marketable permits has shown that if tax or permit sale revenues *are not* recycled, then the short-run costs of the regulation (working through the impact that higher product prices have on labor supply) become much more significant. For more detail on this point, see chapter 9.[6]

Finally, because pollution taxes on their own are regressive, any widespread scheme to introduce them should also be part of a package that is at least **non-regressive.** That is, the regressive impact of pollution taxes should be offset by cutting income taxes for poor and working-class people more than for wealthier individuals.

In the case of marketable permits, rather than permit sales by government, permit giveaways substantially reduce the cost to, and political opposition from, industry. In the example above, where each firm was endowed with ten permits, plant A ultimately had to pay for only three of its thirteen permits, while plant B actually reaped a windfall from the giveaway policy.

The Grimeville discussion of the permit system also demonstrates that, in theory, *the final outcome doesn't depend on whether the permits are sold or distributed free of charge;* in either case a cost-effective solution will be achieved, though who pays how much to whom will vary. This is an important application of the Coase theorem discussed in chapter 4.

A **Coase theorem corollary** can be stated as follows:

> In a well-functioning market, a cost-effective outcome will be achieved by a marketable permit system *regardless* of the initial ownership of the permits.

Take a minute to convince yourself that even if all 20 permits are initially given to plant A, the cost-effective solution (13, 7) will ultimately result. (Since we have only two firms, market power may be present. You have to assume that plant A isn't interested in driving plant B out of business by refusing to sell any permits!)

Having convinced the Grimeville City Council that, at least in theory, incentive-based systems achieve short-run cost-effectiveness, a final question to the

---

[6]In addition to the references cited in chapter 9, see Goulder et al. (1996). In general, lower income taxes need not induce more work effort. People may work harder when taxes are lowered, substituting work for leisure. Economists call this the substitution effect of an income tax cut. On the other hand, people may work less hard because their after-tax income has gone up. Because they are richer, they "buy" more leisure. This is the income effect of a tax cut. Which effect wins out is not clear. However, in this particular case, the income effect is eliminated by the increase in pollution taxes.

village economist might be, "So what?" How much could we, as a society, really save from a shift to an IB approach? At least a dozen studies have been done comparing the compliance costs of CAC regulation with the costs of a hypothetical cost-effective approach. These studies provide a median CAC cost that is four times as high as the least-cost approach.[7] Does this mean that we should expect overall savings of around 300% from a shift to IB regulation?

The answer is no. In practice IB systems have not performed as well as they do on paper. For a variety of reasons discussed below, real-world pollution tax or tradeable permit approaches do not achieve truly cost-effective regulation. What the studies cited above suggest is that in some markets it is technically feasible to reduce pollution control costs to a quarter of their current level and substantially further in other markets. Thus there is clearly room for doing better. Yet while an IB approach is likely to reduce compliance costs for the reasons discussed above, they will not operate perfectly and capture 100% of the potential cost savings.

Taken as a whole, the studies also suggest that the IB cost advantage diminishes as the pollution standard tightens. At the extreme, Hahn and Noll (1982) estimate that the CAC approach to controlling sulfate pollution in Los Angeles is essentially cost-effective. This is because all sources are already so tightly controlled that there is little flexibility left in the system from which pollution traders can take advantage.[8]

16.3 IB Regulation and Technological Progress

The magnitude of short-run cost savings from incentive-based regulation, while uncertain, is probably substantial. However, potentially more important are the cost savings from long-run technological improvements in pollution control and waste reduction induced by the IB approach.

Taxes and permits generate important incentives for **long-run technological progress** in pollution control. Both systems put a "price" on pollution, so that every unit of pollution emitted represents a cost to the firm or individual. In the tax case, the cost is direct: Less pollution would mean lower taxes. In the permit case, pollution bears an *opportunity cost* since less pollution would free up permits for sale. In both cases, since pollution is now costly to firms, they are provided with the motivation to continuously seek out new ways of reducing pollution.

Figure 16.2 illustrates the benefits of introducing new pollution control technology for a firm under an IB approach. The improved pollution control system lowers the MC of reduction curve to MC', generating savings in two areas. First, the firm pays less for the units it was already cleaning up, area A. Second, the firm also pays less in taxes (or earns money from the sale of permits) by reducing pollution from P_1 down to P_2, area B.

Compare these savings with those achievable under our stereotypical command-and-control system. First, the CAC systems are standard-based. Once the firm has achieved the delegated emission standard (P_1), it gains relatively little by improving

---

[7]See Tietenberg (1990).
[8]Also, the CAC system in California was designed with some concern for promoting cost-effectiveness. See Tietenberg (1992) and Oates et al. (1989) for a further discussion.

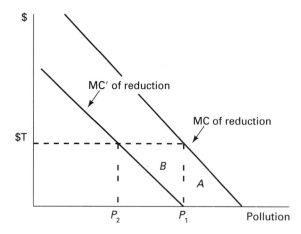

FIGURE 16.2 Incentives for New Technology Under 1B and CAC

pollution control technology. Introducing an improved system gains the firm only area *A,* since there is no incentive to reduce pollution below P_1.[9]

In addition, because the CAC approach specifies individual technologies as BACT, LAER, and the like, firms face regulatory obstacles in experimenting with new processes. In order to do so, they must convince regulators that the new process will be superior to the industry standard, something the firm may not be able to demonstrate before installing the technology. In addition, firms may be reluctant to raise the industry standard by introducing new technologies that may then become the new BACT. This would force them to adopt the new technology in any new construction.[10]

Finally, the CAC system dampens incentives for innovation due to the new source bias discussed in chapter 14. By regulating new sources more stringently than old ones, the CAC system encourages firms and individuals to concentrate their energies on making old, high-pollution technologies last longer, rather than developing new, less pollution-intensive substitutes. For example, Maloney and Brady (1988) report that in 1979, the average age of electrical generating capacity in the states with nine of the highest environmental enforcement budgets was 16.5 years to 15 years, as against 11.5 years for the rest of the states. It is difficult to sort out how much of the age increase was in fact due to higher regulation, because most of the nine were also "rustbelt" states, hit with declining demand for electrical generation in the same period. Yet some of the increase is undoubtedly due to a heightened new source bias.[11]

By putting a price on every unit of pollution, by reducing specific technology re-

---

[9]Maleug (1989) shows that in the marketable permits case, incentives for adopting new technology exist only for firms that are permit sellers. Firms that are permit buyers will actually face lower incentives under an IB than a CAC scheme, because the availability of a permit or tax option gives them a "low-cost" out. For a discussion including diffusion and control agency response to innovation, see Milliman and Prince (1989). The authors conclude that auctioned permits and tax systems are superior to permit giveaways (as well as CAC) in encouraging technological innovation. Under the giveaway system, the innovator will face increased costs if the control agency responds to the innovation by tightening controls.

[10]See Bohm and Russell (1985) for a further discussion.

[11]Maloney and Brady (1988) try to account for demand effects on capacity age in a regression context, but their demand variables both are poor proxies for expected growth and fail to perform well. Thus, I am unconvinced by their principal result, that pollution was actually higher in high enforcement states due to the new source bias effect.

quirements, and by leveling the playing field between new and old sources, IB regulation on paper appears to do a better job of promoting long-run investment in new pollution control technologies and waste reduction than does the CAC system. How important are these potential cost savings? This would depend on how fast the pace of technological innovation was accelerated by a switch to IB, a difficult effect to forecast. However, as we saw in chapter 9, small changes in productivity have large long-run effects on costs, due to the cumulative nature of economic growth. Thus it is safe to say that heightened incentives for technological progress in pollution control generated by IB regulation are probably more important than the short-run savings available from achieving cost-effectiveness.

16.4 Potential Problems with IB Regulation

There are several potential problems with implementing IB regulation. This section will look at six different issues raised by IB critics. The first two, hot spots and monitoring and enforcement, apply to both tax and permit systems.[12] The last four, thin markets, market power, relocation incentives, and permit life, apply only to marketable permit schemes.

PROBLEMS WITH IB IN GENERAL

Turning our attention first to potential problems associated with both marketable permits and pollution taxes, Grimeville can be used to illustrate the **hot-spot** issue. Hot spots are high local concentrations of pollutants. The IB system would indeed keep total pollution in Grimeville at twenty tons per day. However, residents living near plant A, which would pollute thirteen tons per day under either a tax or a marketable permit scheme, would view the IB system as unacceptable *if* the higher levels of emission translated into a higher health risk.

Different pollutants display a different relationship between the sites at which emissions and damages occur. To illustrate this principle, suppose that Grimeville was divided into two air quality regions, one containing plant A, the other plant B. If gunk were a **uniformly mixed pollutant,** one ton of emissions from either plant would translate into an even concentration of gunk, and its associated health risk, across the two areas. By contrast, if gunk were a **concentrated pollutant,** all the damage done by emissions from plant A would occur in the area adjacent to A. The more general case is that of a **nonuniformly mixed pollutant,** where the bulk of the damage is done locally, but effects do drift into other areas.

IB approaches work best for uniformly mixed pollutants, those evenly dispersed over fairly broad areas. Two examples are chlorofluorocarbons, which deplete the ozone layer, and carbon dioxide, which contributes to global warming. An IB approach would clearly not work for a concentrated pollutant like nuclear waste, where uniform safety standards are demanded on equity grounds. To deal with the hot-spot problem in the intermediate case of nonuniformly mixed pollutants, economists have

---

[12]A final disadvantage of IB systems in real-world applications is that they can result in higher pollution levels. Because CAC systems typically result in *overcontrol* relative to the desired standard, they generate more pollution reduction than do IB schemes. Oates et al. (1989) illustrate this for the case of total suspended particulates in the Baltimore atmosphere.

recommended trades (or taxes) based on the contribution of emissions to *ambient* air or water quality. (Recall from chapter 13 that ambient air quality is the concentration of pollutants actually in the air.)

Implementing such a scheme requires a means of estimating the impact of emissions from specific plants on regional air or water quality. Consider the hypothetical situation in Grimeville illustrated in Figure 16.3. Suppose that due to prevailing wind patterns, one ton of gunk emissions from plant A pollutes 70% in area *A* and 30% in area *B*. On the other hand, emissions from plant B are split 50/50 between the two areas. At the (13, 7) solution, a hot spot will indeed emerge in area *A*. In numerical terms, residents in *A* will face ambient pollution of $13 * .7 + 7 * .5 = 12.6$ tons, while residents in area *B* will face ambient pollution of $13 * .3 + 7 * .5 = 7.4$ tons.

In this case, the Grimeville authorities would need to impose an ambient air quality standard (like the NAAQS discussed in chapter 13) of 10 tons for each region, and then control emissions in the two regions to meet the ambient standards. To do so using a tax approach would require higher pollution taxes in area *A* than in area *B*. Alternatively, if marketable permits were to be used, a given permit would allow lower emissions in area *A* than in area *B*.

Carrying this idea beyond Grimeville, taxes would also have to be higher (or the emissions value of a permit lower) in already polluted areas where new sources are more likely to result in a violation of ambient standards. The exact tax levels, or terms of trade for permits between areas, can be determined as long as the relationship between emissions and ambient standards is known.[13]

As we will see in chapter 17, trades of this type do occur under the EPA's "bubble" policy for air pollution control. However, if hot-spot problems proliferate, tax or permit systems can quickly become quite complex and, thus, lose their primary advantage to regulators—simplicity. In addition, the transactions costs for firms are raised if they need to employ complicated air quality models to demonstrate that emission trades will not violate ambient standards.[14]

Beyond hot spots, the next and potentially quite serious problem with IB regulation arises in the area of **monitoring and compliance.** As we saw in chapter 15, one of the primary monitoring techniques used under the CAC system is simply to insure that firms have actually installed the required abatement technology. For example, in about twenty states, cars are required to have catalytic converters yet not to pass

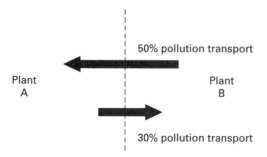

FIGURE 16.3 Nonuniformly Mixed Pollutants in Grimeville

---

[13]See Tietenberg (1992).
[14]See Atkinson and Tietenberg (1991).

emissions tests. This monitoring system is clearly imperfect since the control equipment may break down and actual emissions are not checked. It does, however, provide regulators with a relatively straightforward tool for insuring at least initial compliance.

Unlike the CAC case, however, IB regulation does not specify particular pollution control technologies with known abatement impacts. Thus regulators must rely even more heavily on (currently inadequate) monitoring of emissions to insure compliance with permits or to collect taxes. As was illustrated in chapter 15, monitoring budgets are a soft political target for regulated industries. Thus, for an IB system of regulation to achieve its potential of reducing pollution at lower cost, a commitment to strict monitoring and stiff enforcement that is insulated from the budgetary axe must be made.

Los Angeles is attempting to deal with this problem via technology: "individual smokestack monitors that relay emissions information to [regulator's] computers and supermarket-style computer bar codes to track the movement of cans of vapor-emitting solutions . . ." such as oils, paints and solvents. Critics, however, remain skeptical of the bar-coding system.[15]

From the enforcement perspective, taxes have an advantage over permit systems because they generate a revenue stream for the government based on emissions. Thus, regulators have an economic incentive to monitor emissions closely to insure maximum government revenues. Brown and Johnson (1984) report that the introduction of taxes on water pollutants in Germany has led government to require better monitoring technologies and to become more aggressive in enforcement.

PROBLEMS WITH PERMIT SYSTEMS

The major problem unique to the marketable permits approach is that many proposed users face **thin markets**—markets with only a few buyers and sellers. The thin market problem is essentially this: Why go to the trouble of "going to the market" when due to the small number of traders there is a low probability of getting a good deal? In the Grimeville case, in order to trade permits, plants A and B would have to go to considerable trouble and expense to calculate with some precision their respective marginal cost of reduction curves, then employ brokers to engage in a face-to-face bargaining process. Is it worth the bother if there is only one other plant in town, which may well not have anything to offer?

As the Grimeville case illustrated, CAC regulation is seldom cost-effective since regulators do not have access to the control cost information necessary to impose least-cost regulation. In thin markets where trades are infrequent and prices not easily defined, IB systems are also hampered by **imperfect information.** Under such conditions, private firms know little about potential permit trades and face large transactions costs in completing such deals. As we shall see in the next chapter, many of the small-scale experiments with permit systems in the United States have foundered on the thin market problem. By contrast, acid rain pollution permits are traded on the futures markets in Chicago. Plant managers can read in the newspaper the going price for an SO_2 credit, greatly reducing informational barriers to trade.

---

[15]See "New Rules Harness Power of Free Markets to Curb Air Pollution," *Wall Street Journal,* April 14, 1992; and "Monitoring Pollution at Its Source," *New York Times,* April 8, 1992.

A second problem with permits is the potential for the development of **market power.** Concerns here typically focus on access to permits as a barrier to entry. What if existing firms refuse to sell to new entrants in the market as a way to limit competition? Misiolek and Elder (1989) suggest that this may be a problem when both of the following circumstances hold: (1) New firms are forced to buy permits from direct competitors, and (2) a single dominant firm faces new entrants with higher pollution control costs.

Condition (1) does not generally hold. Under the new acid rain program, for example, SO_2 trades will be nationwide; thus a utility in Massachusetts would have a hard time blocking the entry of new power producer that could purchase credits from a noncompetitor in Ohio. Why is condition (2) necessary? If there are several existing large firms in the industry, the benefits of excluding new rivals to any given firm are lower. Moreover, the existing firms must maintain an informal agreement not to sell. As the price of permits new entrants are willing to pay rise, each firm will have an incentive to cheat on this agreement.

Economists disagree on how significant this market power problem is.[16] However, few would argue that the problem is big enough to seriously undermine the appeal of IB regulation. Indeed, the CAC approach has its own entry barriers associated with high cost of compliance for new sources. Nevertheless, concern should be focused on designing IB systems to minimize these problems. In particular, permit giveaways that endow large firms with a substantial share of the permits should be avoided.

A third potential problem with permit systems has been raised in the Los Angeles basin case. The basin plan involves a permit giveaway. By endowing firms with wealth in the form of pollution rights, the permit systems will provide an extra incentive for firms to "sell out" and relocate to a region with less stringent regulation, in this case, Mexico. But supporters of the program have countered that the extra investment resulting from lowered compliance costs would balance any job loss effect from this **relocation effect.**[17]

A fourth possible problem with permits relates to **permit life.** Suppose that the Grimeville City Council issued twenty permits but in five years decided that pollution levels needed to be reduced to ten tons per day. Would the council then have to buy back ten permits from the firms? Here it is important to keep a distinction between "pollution rights," granted forever, and "pollution permits," which can be issued with a limited life.

However, permits with lives that are too short quickly lose their value and are not worth trading. Moreover, to gain the most from permit markets, firms must be allowed to **bank** their permits—that is, if a reduction is made in one year, the permit can be saved, or banked, for trade in a later year. If permits have a limited life, firms will take a use-it-or-lose-it attitude to reducing pollution and banking their permits. Thus, a potential need for further reduction in pollution must be balanced against the negative impact that limited permit lives introduce into permit markets. A different solution to

[16]See Misiolek and Elder (1989) and Tietenberg (1985). The latter source also offers a discussion of another form of market power—attempts to manipulate the permit price itself in order to minimize control costs.
[17]The relocation incentive emerges under a marketable permit system relative to CAC regulation. The roughly equivalent effect for a pollution tax is the bankruptcy constraint discussed in Section 16.2.

this problem is being pursued in the Los Angeles basin, where permits will shrink over time—8% annually for nitrogen oxides and 6% annually for volatile organic compounds.[18]

A related objection has been raised by many environmentalists, that granting pollution permits "legalizes" pollution and thus takes the social stigma away from pollution as an activity. (An analogy here could be made to the legalization of recreational drugs.) This, it is argued, will lead to a long-run increase in pollution as individual moral codes against polluting weaken. One might counter that existing regulations already mandate some level of pollution as acceptable. Perhaps more importantly, the formal legal status of pollution is probably not one of the primary determinants of social attitudes toward pollution.

To conclude this section, it is useful to point out that although economic theory is very useful in thinking through environmental problems, the real world is always messier than our theory. Indeed, CAC and IB systems are seldom found in their pure forms, and their advantages and disadvantages must be weighed in the context of each specific situation. For example, in a close look at CAC regulation of particulate air pollution in Baltimore, Oates et al. (1989) discovered that the CAC approach is often not as clumsy as it is made out to be by the economist's stereotype.

In Baltimore, regulators specified different uniform standards for different categories of sources—"industrial coal-fired boilers, grain shipping facilities, etc.," so that all areas in the city achieved a standard of at least 100 ppm. Thus, while CAC regulators did impose uniform standards across categories of sources and mandated the use of specific abatement technologies, they also cast "at least one eye on cost savings." This was reflected in their decision to regulate low-cost categories of sources more stringently than high-cost source categories.

This attention to cost greatly reduced any possible benefits from moving away from CAC and toward an IB system. Oates et al. conclude: "a carefully designed and implemented CAC system may stack up reasonably well relative to a feasible IB counterpart."

In their twenty-five-year struggle to influence the pollution control debate, economists originally concentrated on singing the praises of a chalkboard form of IB regulation, as against an equally theoretical enemy characterized as CAC. In the process we have somewhat oversold our product. This section has focused on problems that real-world IB regulation either has faced or is likely to face in its implementation.

The existence of these problems, however, does not mean that the shift to IB regulation is a bad idea. On the contrary, pollution taxes and marketable permit systems have an important role to play in reducing short-run compliance costs, and especially in encouraging long-run innovation in pollution control and waste reduction. The policy challenge is to capture this potential in the face of real-world constraints.

16.5 Summary

As a partial answer to the question "How can we do better?" this chapter has focused on the theoretical arguments in favor of shifting to an IB system of pollution regulation. The economic advantages are twofold: (1) a reduction in the short-run costs of

---

[18]See "Trying a Market Approach to Smog," *New York Times,* March 25, 1992.

complying with regulations, and (2) greater incentives for long-run cost savings and pollution reduction through technological progress. There is also a political-economic argument to be made in favor of IB schemes. By reducing the information necessary for regulators to make intelligent decisions, IB approaches reduce the influence that political actors can wield in the process.

Incentive-based approaches work by putting a price on every unit of pollution produced by a firm. Short-run cost-effectiveness (equality of marginal reduction costs across all sources) is then achieved "automatically," as firms cut back (or increase) pollution levels until marginal reduction costs are just less than the tax or price of a permit. Because all firms do this, marginal costs of reduction equalize across the economy. Moreover, since any level of pollution costs the firm money, the pollution price also generates a long-run incentive for further pollution reduction through technological innovation.

Although taxes and tradeable permit systems are quite similar in many respects, there are also important differences, summarized in Table 16.3.[19] When permit systems are initiated through permit giveaways, they are much less costly than pollution taxes for the affected firms. Permits also generate a much more certain level of pollution control than taxes and do not need to be adjusted for inflation or population increases and economic growth. However, permit systems have the drawbacks associated with market power, thin markets, the determination of permit life, and relocation incentives. In addition, taxes generate strong incentives for monitoring and enforcement, and, if used to replace income taxes, can increase labor market efficiency. Of course, revenues from government permit sales could serve these same two functions.

Other potential problems with both types of IB systems include the generation of hot spots and greater reliance on direct performance monitoring to insure compliance. In spite of these potential problems, IB approaches deserve and are receiving broader attention as mechanisms for reducing pollution control costs and pollution at the same time. The next chapter reviews the record on IB systems to date and discusses some of the challenges in implementation faced in the ongoing acid rain experiment.

TABLE 16.3 Taxes and Marketable Permits Compared

Advantages of Permits	*Advantages of Taxes*
If permits are given away, lower cost to firms.	Issues of thin markets, market power, relocation incentives, and permit life are avoided.
More certain pollutant level.	If revenues are used to cut income taxes, labor market efficiency will be improved.
No need for adjustment to account for economic growth or inflation.	If revenues are partially retained by enforcement agencies, enforcement incentives are strengthened.

---

[19]Taxes and permits also differ in their effects when there is cost or benefit uncertainty. This discussion is deferred to advanced topics chapter T2.

APPLICATION 16.0

Cost-effective Gunk Control

Two plants are emitting a uniformly mixed pollutant called gunk into the beautiful sky over Tourist-Town. The city government decides it can tolerate total emissions of no more than 100 kgs of gunk per day. Plant G has marginal reduction costs of $100 - 4x$ and is currently polluting at a level of 25, while plant K has marginal reduction costs of $150 - y$ and currently pollutes at a level of 150 (x and y are the level of emissions at each plant).

1. What is the cost-effective pollution level for each plant if total pollution must equal 100? Suppose the city government knows marginal reduction costs at the two plants. In this case could the city obtain cost-effective pollution reduction using a CAC approach? If so, how?

2. In reality, why might the city have a hard time getting this information? What are the two "incentive-based" policies that could be used to get a cost-effective reduction of pollution to 100 units, without knowing the MC of the two firms? Be specific. Discuss two advantages each method has over the other.

3. Suppose the authorities are considering a tradeable emission permit system in which they give half the permits to each firm, or a tax system. If both systems work perfectly, how much will the firms have to pay, in total, for pollution reduction under the two schemes? (Assume permits are bought and sold by firms at a price equal to the tax.) Could

this explain why Tourist-Town would be more likely to adopt a permit giveaway system?

4. Several theoretical studies have shown that incentive-based policies might generate huge cost savings with the IB approach being as much as twenty-two times cheaper as a CAC approach. Discuss at least three reasons why Tourist-Town might not get such substantial savings in moving from CAC regulation to a marketable permit system.

5. Would a CAC system in Tourist-Town generate benefits in the form of a reduction in hot spots, relative to an incentive-based approach?

6. **(Review of Efficiency)** Suppose the marginal benefits of pollution reduction in Tourist-Town are constant and equal to $64. (Each unit of pollution reduction brings in one more tourist, who spends $64.) Is 100 units of pollution, obtained cost-effectively, an efficient level? If not, will efficiency be achieved through more or less pollution? Why?

Key Ideas in Each Section

16.0 Economists have argued that **incentive-based (IB) regulation** can both lower the short-run costs of pollution control and provide better incentives for long-run technological improvements than the current CAC approach. The two types of IB regulation are **pollution taxes** and **marketable permit systems.**

16.1 This section illustrates that **cost-effective pollution control** can only be achieved when the marginal costs of reduction at each source are equal. Due to **imperfect information,** regulators have a hard time mandating cost-effectiveness.

16.2 The Grimeville City Council meeting is used to illustrate how IB regulation can help achieve cost-effective pollution control "automatically." Three additional points are stressed. (1) Pollution taxes, if used to replace taxes on labor, would increase **labor market efficiency.** (2) Although pollution taxes can be made **revenue neutral** (and **non-regressive**) in theory, in practice they seldom are, so firms prefer permit give-aways. (3) The **Coase theorem corollary** indicates that, in a well-functioning market, cost-effectiveness can be achieved regardless of the initial distribution of permits.

16.3 More important than short-run cost-effectiveness, IB regulation provides better incentives than CAC does for **long-run technological progress** in pollution control.

16.4 This section discusses some of the disadvantages of IB regulation. Disadvantages of both systems include **hot spot**s for the case of **nonuniformly mixed** and **concentrated pollutants,** and **monitoring** and **compliance** problems. Disadvantages specific to permits include **thin markets, market power, relocation incentives,** and **permit life.** Disadvantages specific to taxes include **bankruptcy constraints.**

References

Atkinson, Scott and T. H. Tietenberg (1991). "Market Failure in Incentive-Based Regulation: The Case of Emission Trading." *Journal of Environmental Economics,* vol. 21, 17–31.

Bohm, Peter and Clifford Russell (1985). "Comparative Analysis of Alternative Policy Instruments." In *Handbook of Natural Resource and Energy Economics,* Vol. 1, eds. Allan V. Kneese and James L. Sweeney, 395–460. Amsterdam: North Holland.

Brown, Gardener W. Jr. and Ralph W. Johnson (1984). "Pollution Control by Effluent Charges: It Works in the Federal Republic of Germany, Why Not in the U.S.?" *Natural Resources Journal,* vol. 24, 929–966.

Goulder, Lawrence, Ian Parry and Dallas Burtraw (1996). "Revenue Raising versus Other Approaches to Environmental Protection: The Critical Significance of Pre-Existing Distortions." *RFF Discussion Paper 96-24.* Washington, DC: Resources for the Future.

Hahn, R. and R. Noll (1982). "Designing a Market for Tradeable Emissions Permits." In *Reform of Environmental Regulation,* ed. W. Megat. Cambridge: Ballinger.

Lee, Dwight and W. S. Misiolek (1986). "Substituting Pollution Taxation for General Taxation: Some Implications for Efficiency in Pollution Taxation." *Journal of Environmental Economics and Management,* 13, no. 4, 338–347.

Maleug, David A. (1989). "Emission Trading and the Incentive to Adopt New Pollution Abatement Technology." *Journal of Environmental Economics and Management,* vol. 16, 52–57.

Maloney, Michael T. and Gordon L. Brady (1988). "Capital Turnover and Marketable Pollution Rights." *Journal of Law and Economics,* 31, no. 1, 203–226.

Milliman, S. R. and R. Prince (1989). "Firm Incentives to Promote Technological Change in Pollution Control." *Journal of Environmental Economics and Management,* vol. 17, 247–265.

Misiolek, W. S. and H. W. Elder (1989). "Exclusionary Manipulation of Markets for Pollution Rights." *Journal of Environmental Economics and Management,* vol. 16, 156–66.

Oates, Wallace E., Paul R. Portney and Albert M. McGartland (1989). "The Net Benefits of Environmental Regulation." *American Economic Review,* 79, no. 5, 1233–1242.

Tietenberg, T. H. (1992). *Environmental and Natural Resource Economics.* New York: Harper Collins.

Tietenberg, T. H. (1990). "Economic Instruments for Environmental Regulation." *Oxford Review of Economic Policy,* vol. 6.

Tietenberg, T. H. (1985). *Emissions Trading: An Exercise in Reforming Pollution Policy.* Washington, DC: Resources for the Future.

Incentive-Based
Regulation: Practice

17.0 Introduction

We are only now beginning to gain experience with incentive-based regulation in the United States. Marketable permits have seen one major success in lead trading and at least one relative disappointment in the EPA's Emissions Trading Program. The sulfur dioxide (acid rain) program got underway only in 1995; early reports are quite favorable. Finally, permit trading in the Los Angeles basin has, as of this writing, just been launched.

Pollution taxes, or charges tied to emissions, are used very little in the United States, the exceptions being fees levied on wastewater (sewage) and solid and hazardous waste (pay-by-the-bag garbage fees, tipping fees at landfills). We also have some fee-based programs to control pollution, such as the bottle deposits and mining bonds discussed in chapter 6. Finally, state utility regulators in the United States have also recently begun to incorporate environmental externality costs in decisions about new electric power sources.

By contrast, several European countries have had broader experience with emission taxes, though, as we will see, none relies on them as an exclusive means of pollution control. European nations historically also have had much higher taxes on energy—electricity, oil, and gasoline. Although energy taxes are not pollution taxes because they do not tax emissions directly, they reduce many important pollutants indirectly.

This chapter will review the record of IB regulation, with an eye toward uncovering the obstacles to its successful implementation. With policy makers already envisioning grand schemes for global carbon taxes or tradeable permits to control global warming, it is doubly important that we learn all we can from the existing track record.

17.1 Lead Banking

As was discussed in chapter 10, lead is a particularly nasty pollutant, generating developmental problems in children and heart disease and stroke in adults. Lead in gasoline becomes airborne when the fuel is burned in an automobile engine. Unleaded gas

313

is required for most new cars, because lead also damages the catalytic converters used to control other auto pollutants. However, in the mid-1980s, leaded gas was still widely used in older vehicles. Early in 1985, the EPA initiated a phase-in of lower lead standards for leaded gasoline, from an existing 1.1 grams per gallon standard, to .5 grams per gallon by July 1985, to .1 grams per gallon by January 1986. To ease the $3.5 billion compliance costs associated with such a rapid changeover, the EPA instituted its lead banking program.

Under this program, gasoline refiners who reduced the lead content in their gasoline by more than the applicable standard for a given quarter of the year were allowed to bank the difference in the form of lead credits. These credits could then be used or sold in any subsequent quarter. In addition, the lead credits had a limited life, because the program ended on schedule at the end of 1987, with all refiners required to meet the new standard.

In spite of its short life, the program proved quite successful. Over 50% of refiners participated in trading, 15% of all credits were traded, and about 35% were banked for future trading or use.[1] Hahn (1989) suggests that cost savings from the program may well have been in excess of $228 million, the EPA's estimate of potential cost savings from a less ambitious program. If this estimate is correct, lead trading reduced costs by less than 10% over a CAC approach. While important, such cost savings from even a successful trading program are substantially below the 400% predicted by some theoretical studies of other markets discussed in the previous chapter.

Lead trading encouraged low-cost firms to accelerate their compliance with the new regulations in order to obtain lead credits for sale. At the same time, firms who had greater problems retrofitting their equipment could pay for an extension by buying lead credits in the market. In this way, the program helped achieve the more stringent lead standards cost-effectively. However, because of the short life of the program, it is unlikely that it had much relative impact on improving pollution control technology in the industry.

What factors underlay the success of lead trading? First, because all refiners were granted permits based on their performance, market power did not emerge as an issue. (In addition, new entrant access was not a problem in this declining market.) Markets were not thin, since trading was nationwide, and firms were already required to develop considerable information about their lead content. Because the permits were shrinking, the issue of permit life did not emerge, and hot spots, although they might have developed on a temporary basis, could not persist. Finally, monitoring and enforcement did not suffer, since the lead content in gasoline was already reported by refiners on a regular basis. In one instance the agency fined a company $40 million for spiking 800 gallons of gas with excess lead.[2] Thus, none of the theoretical bugaboos identified in chapter 16 were present in the lead trading market.

In 1988, the EPA introduced a scheme similar to the lead trading program for chlorofluorocarbons (CFCs), which contribute both to depletion of the earth's protective ozone shield and to global warming. Like lead in gasoline, CFCs are also being

---

[1] Hahn (1989: 102).
[2] "Trades to Remember: The Lead Phasedown," EPA Journal, 18, no. 2 (May 1992).

phased out, this time globally, as is discussed further in chapter 23. The interesting wrinkle in this case is that, as the number of permits in existence shrink, their value will rise dramatically, conferring windfall profits on the firms who received permits in the initial giveaway phase. The expectation of such a price rise may indeed cause firms to hoard permits and further drive up the price.

To capture some of these profits and discourage speculation, Congress imposed a tax on all ozone-depleting chemicals used or sold by producers or commercial users of these chemicals. The tax rate was set at $1.37 per pound in 1990, rising to $4.90 per pound by the end of the decade. By increasing the price of the final product, the tax will also encourage consumers to switch to substitute products.[3]

17.2 The Emissions Trading Program

Aside from lead banking and the new CFC program, a second major experiment with marketable permits in the United States has been the EPA's **Emissions Trading Program.** While the program does appear to have resulted in savings of several billion dollars over its lifetime, relative both to initial expectations and the success of the lead banking program, emissions trading has been a disappointment. Less than 1% of the potential trades appear to have been consummated.[4]

The Emissions Trading Program, initiated in 1976, allows limited trading of **emission reduction credits** for five of the criteria air pollutants: VOCs, carbon monoxide, sulfur dioxide, particulates, and nitrogen oxides. Credits can be earned whenever a source controls emissions to a degree higher than legally required. Regulators certify which credits, can then be used in one of the program's three trading schemes or banked for later use. The degree of banking allowed varies from state to state.

The three trading programs are the offset, bubble, and netting policies. **Offsets** are designed to accommodate the siting of new pollution sources in non-attainment areas. Under the offset policy, new sources may locate in such regions if, depending upon the severity of existing pollution, they buy between 1.1 and 1.5 pollution credits from existing sources for each unit they anticipate emitting. For example, in 1992, The *Wall Street Journal* reported that the March Air Force Base near Los Angeles absorbed the staff and equipment of another base that was closing. The March Base anticipated doubling its pollution emissions from power and heat generation, and aircraft operation and maintenance.

> March recruited pollution-credit brokers that acted as middlemen in trades between polluters. Officers also scoured local newspapers and hunted for potential sellers among public documents of previous pollution-credit trades. They made cold calls to refineries and utilities. . . . Eventually, March managed to buy the credits it needed from five sellers, for a total of $1.2 million. They even found a bargain or two, including the right to emit 24

---

[3]"Congress Rests; Taxpayers Won't," *Chemical Week,* 145, no. 23, 6 (December 6, 1989).

[4]Hahn (1989: 102). The author also describes another disappointing application of marketable permits: in water pollutants along the Fox River in Wisconsin. This program appeared to founder on the thin markets problem, as well as limitations on permit life.

pounds of nitrogen oxide and six pounds of carbon monoxide a day for the rock-bottom price of $975 a pound—from a machinery company that got the credits by closing down a plant. "This company didn't know what it had," says Air Force Lt. Col. Bruce Knapp.[5]

The offset policy was designed to accommodate the conflict between economic growth and pollution control, not to achieve cost-effectiveness. Over almost twenty years, thousands of offset trades have occurred but, as suggested by the above example, the markets still do not function smoothly. High transactions costs remain a serious obstacle to new firms seeking offsets to locate in a non-attainment area. This is reflected in the fact that around 90% of offset transactions have involved trades within a single firm.

The **netting policy** also focuses on accommodating economic growth and has had a significant impact on compliance costs. This program allows old sources that are expanding their plant or modifying equipment to avoid the technological requirements for pollution control (the new source performance standards discussed in chapter 13) if any increase in pollution above the standard is offset by emission reduction credits from within the plant. As of the early 1980s, Hahn (1989) estimates that between 5,000 and 12,000 netting transactions had occurred. He also argues the program had saved industry between $.5 billion and $12 billion in reduced permitting costs and emission control savings, while having little if any negative impact on air quality. The netting program has been the most successful of the three, primarily because it has involved only internal trades.

In contrast to the offset and netting trades, the **bubble policy** was designed primarily to generate cost savings and, of the three programs, is most similar to the theoretical marketable permits model discussed in chapter 16. "Bubbles" are localized air quality regions with several emission sources; a bubble may include only a single plant or may be extended to include several sources within a broader region. Under the bubble policy, emission reduction credits can be traded within the bubble. In its simplest form, a firm may violate air quality emission standards at one smokestack, provided it makes up the difference at another. Of course, trades between plants within a regional bubble can occur as well.

Bubbles were introduced in 1979, three years after offsets, with high expectations of cost savings. One study, for example, predicted that the cost of nitrogen dioxide control in Baltimore might fall by 96%.[6] However, by the early 1980s, Hahn (1989) reports that nationwide only 129 bubble trades had actually occurred, with estimated cumulative savings of less than $.5 billion. Only two of these trades were estimated to have involved external transactions.

Why this disappointing performance? Some analysts have pointed to restrictions placed by states on trading. Many states have not yet allowed banking of permits. Others institute a two- or three-year life on banked credits. The latter policy, while di-

[5]"New Rules Harness Power of Free Markets to Curb Air Pollution," *Wall Street Journal,* April 14, 1992. Reprinted by permission of The Wall Street Journal. © 1992 Dow Jones & Co., Inc. All Rights Reserved Worldwide.
[6]Krupnick (1986).

rectly reducing some pollutants, also discourages firms from taking full advantage of banking and trading opportunities.

Dudek and Palimasano (1988) argue that opposition to the trading concept itself by regulators and environmentalists was one reason for the relatively poor performance of the bubble program. They maintain that regulators resisted giving up the "freedom to be arbitrary"—their power to mandate particular technologies—leading to slow implementation of trading regulations. Environmentalists, who objected to firms making money off of pollution sales, increased uncertainty over bubble trades by threatening lawsuits.

Atkinson and Tietenberg (1991) stress the role of imperfect information and thin markets to explain the relative failure of the EPA's bubble policy. Because of the difficulty in locating potential deals, most firms simply did not participate. Also, each individual trade between firms must satisfy the constraint of no increase in pollution. This results in much less activity than traditional models of IB regulation, which unrealistically assume that the constant pollution constraint is met as all feasible deals are consummated simultaneously.

Finally, Atkinson and Tietenberg argue that the lack of inter-firm trading can be explained in part by the non-uniformly mixed nature of the pollutants. Since the NAAQ standards relate to ambient air quality, not emissions, trades of such emission permits require firms to demonstrate through (costly) air quality modeling that ambient standards will not be violated by the trade.

In short, many economists underestimated real-world complications associated with designing permit markets when they generated rosy predictions for emissions trading. Of the theoretical issues discussed in chapter 16, the problems of thin markets and limited permit life greatly reduced the effectiveness of emissions trading. In addition, the hot-spot problem with non-uniformly mixed pollutants has been vexing. The technical complications involved in demonstrating that emissions trades will not affect ambient air quality substantially raised the transactions costs for firms engaged in external trades under the bubble program.

Overcoming this latter problem in the new Los Angeles basin trading scheme will be a substantial challenge, although the existence of a sophisticated technical infrastructure, as well as scale economies, may lower transactions costs. As one observer has put it: "Previous emission trading programs . . . are like playing checkers. What they're doing in California is more like elevating it to chess."[7]

Of course, a tempting regulatory response is just to ignore the local hot-spot problem, in an attempt to capture greater cost savings. The offset program takes this approach. For example, in southern California, Mobil Oil's Torrance refinery recently purchased pollution credits originally owned by a General Motors factory in a neighboring city that had shut down. The *Wall Street Journal* quotes a retiree who lives in the shadow of the plant and is trying to sell his house: "It's hurting this area."[8]

---

[7]Joseph Goffman, cited in "New Rules Harness Power of Free Markets to Curb Air Pollution."
[8]"New Rules Harness Power of Free Markets to Curb Air Pollution."

Although allowing local hot spots may reduce compliance costs, such a policy is clearly inconsistent with a safety standard. And, as is often pointed out in such a debate, economists and regulators who advocate such cost savings are generally wealthy enough to avoid living down wind from a local hot spot.

17.3 Marketable Permits and Acid Rain

In the mid-1960s, freshwater fishermen in Sweden, Norway, Canada, and the Adirondack Mountains of New York State began to notice a decline in the fishery stocks of mountain lakes. By the late 1980s, Sweden was reporting 14,000 lakes unable to support sensitive aquatic life, with 2,200 virtually dead. In Norway, lakes covering 13,000 square kilometers had lost fish species. In Canada, over 14,000 lakes were strongly acidified, while in the Adirondacks over 180 lakes had lost the ability to support most native fish.[9]

In the late 1970s, German foresters noted a rapid decline in the health of their resource; by 1985, over half the forests in the country were damaged in what was termed simply *waldsterben* or forest death. Similar, though less dramatic, reports of retarded forest growth came from North America, with particular concern about sugar maples and high-elevation red spruce in Canada and the Northeast, and pines in the Southeast and California.[10]

Acid rain was the suspected culprit in the damage to both water and forest resources. **Acid rain** is formed when sulfur dioxide, primarily released when coal is burned, and nitrogen oxide, emitted from any kind of fossil fuel combustion, are transformed while in the atmosphere into sulfuric and nitric acids. These acids return to the earth attached to raindrops or in some cases dry dust particles. Researchers have established that acid rain is guilty on the charge of acidification of lakes and streams. In the case of forest death, no widespread link has yet been established. However, ground-level ozone (produced by the transformation of nitrogen oxides), possibly in combination with acid rain, has been shown to reduce forest and agricultural productivity.

Acid deposition harms fish and plant life directly and also can cause indirect damage by leaching and mobilizing harmful metals like aluminum and lead out of soil. The impact of acid rain on ecosystem health varies from region to region, depending upon the base rocks underlying the area. Naturally occurring limestone or other alkaline rocks can neutralize much of the direct impact of the acid. Such rocks are not found in the primarily igneous terrain of the Adirondack Mountains in New York State, southeastern Canada, or northern Europe. This has led some economists, concerned primarily about lost fishing opportunities, to recommend liming lakes sterilized by acid rain as a relatively inexpensive way to deal with the problem.[11]

---

[9]French (1990).

[10]French (1990).

[11]On the economics of liming, see Mullen and Menz (1985). Olem (1991) provides a review of the scientific literature. Since the passage of the Clean Air Act of 1990, some environmentalists have supported liming as a complementary strategy to emissions reduction; see, for example, Lechner (1991).

In addition to damaging water and forest resources, the acids also erode buildings, bridges, and statues. Suspended sulfate particles can also dramatically reduce visibility. Finally, they contribute to sickness and premature death in humans.[12]

Pollution from sulfur dioxide was at one time concentrated around power plants and metal refineries. The area around Copper Hill, Tennessee, for example, is so denuded of vegetation from now-closed copper-smelting operations that the underlying red clay soil of the region is clearly visible from outer space.[13] In an attempt to deal with these local problems, and with the encouragement of the ambient standards mandated by the Clean Air Act of 1970, smokestacks were built higher. And yet, dilution proved not to be a complete pollution solution. Sulfur and nitric oxides were picked up by the wind and transported hundreds of miles only to be redeposited as acid rain. The acid rain problem in the northeastern United States and Canada can, thus, be blamed on regional polluters—coal-fired utilities and nitrogen oxide emitters ranging from the Midwest to the Eastern seaboard. Similarly, Germany's forest death and acidified lakes in Sweden and Norway require a European-wide solution.

The fact that polluters and victims are in different parts of the country, or even different countries, has made resolving regional pollution problems difficult. The Helsinki Protocol, signed in 1985, committed twenty-one European nations to a sulfur dioxide emissions target of 70% of 1980 levels by 1993. Thirteen European countries, including Spain and the UK, did not sign the protocol. Prevailing westerly winds meant that these countries export around 70% of their SO_2 emissions, while importing relatively little. Subsequently, the UK has reduced sulfur and nitrogen oxide emissions as a requirement of membership in the European Community.[14]

In the United States, progress on acid rain legislation through the late 1980s was stymied both by opposition from conservative President Reagan and by the fact that several thousand high-sulfur coal jobs were likely to be lost in Pennsylvania, Indiana, Ohio, and Illinois, as utilities switched to lower-sulfur coal mined in other regions. Of course, many new jobs would be created by the legislation as well, some in the mining of low-sulfur coal, others in the manufacture of scrubbers to remove sulfur prior to its emission, still others in the development of new "cleaner" coal technologies. One study predicted that, on net, the legislation would lead to an overall increase in employment.[15] The environmental benefits of the legislation, meanwhile, were expected to be reaped in New York, Vermont, New Hampshire, Maine, and Canada.

Canadian benefits, of course, count little in U.S. politics but, in addition, a major ten-year government study released in 1990 suggested that the impact of acid rain on

---

[12]One frequently cited government study maintained that up to 50,000 premature deaths per year might be attributed to sulfate pollution in the United States (Office of Technology Assessment [1984: 47]). Even using much more conservative estimates, however, the health effects are significant (Burtraw et al. [1997]). Technically, the offending pollutants are suspended acidic aerosols of several types. Acidic sulfates appear to dominate these aerosol mixes. See NAPAP (1991:132).

[13]See also the description in Firor (1989).

[14]World Bank (1992: 155); French(1990).

[15]Wendling and Bezdek (1989).

domestic ecosystems, though serious, was not as widespread as had been feared. Although some of the findings remain preliminary and controversial, the report drew conclusions in the following areas:[16]

1. *Water quality.* Fourteen percent of lakes in the Adirondack Mountains (180) were so acidified as to be unable to support many fish species. Although 23% of lakes in Florida were also highly acidic, local fish species were more acid-tolerant. A third area of concern for lakes was found in the Upper Peninsula of Michigan. In addition, some 21% of mountain streams in the eastern highlands were acidified. In the rest of the eastern United States, less than 5% of lakes were seriously acidified. However, about three times as many lakes in the region experience acid pulses associated with rainstorms or snow melt.

Continued deposition at 1980 levels was predicted to increase serious acidification by roughly one third. About 75% of acidification in lakes and 50% in streams is accounted for by acid rain. The remainder results from acid mine drainage (especially for streams) and natural sources.

2. *Forest health.* Although the majority of American forests show no damage, acid rain could affect the soil chemistry with an unknown impact in the lower midwestern and southeastern United States over the next 50 to 100 years. Acid rain, in combination with ozone, is currently exacerbating natural stress (disease, insects) faced by red spruce and possibly other trees in high altitude areas of the eastern United States.

3. *Agricultural productivity.* No impact was found on agricultural productivity.

4. *Visibility.* Sulfates are the dominant source of light extinction in the eastern United States. A decrease in ambient sulfate levels of 40% would improve visibility by around 30%. Several contingent valuation studies suggest that people value visibility substantially, particularly in national parks, forests, and recreational areas.

5. *Human-made structures.* Acid rain has increased the rate of deterioration of galvanized steel, bronze, marble, and limestone structures and statues and carbonate-based paints.

These environmental concerns, along with the large health risks from sulfate pollution discussed above, finally led to action on acid rain in the 1990 Clean Air Act. The legislation requires a 10-million-ton reduction of sulfur dioxide emissions from 1980 levels, down to an annual average of 8.95 million tons per year, and a 2.5-million-ton reduction of nitrogen oxide emissions by the year 2000.[17] Some scientists consider the reduction in SO_2 emissions to be sufficient to protect most aquatic ecosystems. If this judgment is correct, the policy is roughly consistent with a safety standard.[18] In addi-

[16]See NAPAP (1991), especially Table 6-1. In contrast to conclusion 2 below, many Canadian researchers also believe that acid rain is responsible for the sugar maple population's decline in their country. See "Acid Test," *Scientific American* (April 1990), 262, no. 4, 18. For an interesting discussion of the politics of NAPAP, see "Learning from an Acid Rain Program," *Science,* 251, no. 4999, (March 15, 1990), 1302–1304. In addition, because the acid rain problem is fairly new, scientists have only begun to scratch the surface of possible effects. See, for example, Fanning (1989), and Drent and Woldendorp (1989).

[17]NOx control will be by means of technologically based, uniform emission standards, that is, a CAC approach.

[18]According to NAPAP (1991), a 50% reduction in emissions should be sufficient to "deacidify" all affected water systems, save 3% of lakes in the Adirondacks. Also see Firor (1989: 24).

tion, recent research has shown that, largely due to health and visibility benefits, the measurable benefits far exceed the costs (Burtraw et al. [1997]). Thus, while possibly meeting a safety standard, the acid rain policy clearly passes an efficiency test.

The first stage of the SO_2 rollback was achieved by issuing a first round of marketable permits to 110 of the nation's largest coal-burning utilities, mostly in the East and Midwest; the second stage will impose tighter restrictions and include another 2,400 sources owned by 1,000 other power companies in the country. To reduce the financial burden on, and political opposition from, utilities and rate payers, most of the permits are not sold by the government. Instead, beginning in 1995, utilities were simply given permits based on their emission levels ten years earlier. When the program is fully phased in, each utility will receive permits equivalent to 30% to 50% of their 1986 pollution.[19]

Trading is nationwide, although state legislators and utility regulators do have the authority, legal or informal, to restrict permit sales. Given such a broad market, a utility in, say Ohio, will have little power to prevent a competitor from setting up shop in the neighborhood, merely by refusing to sell permits. Such a firm could simply go shopping in Texas.

To combat possible problems of speculation and the potential market power problems arising if new entrants are forced to buy permits from incumbent competitors, the government distributes 2.8% of the permits by auction and sale. Most of the permits are sold at auction, though some were available on a first-come, first-serve basis for a price of $1,500 per ton—well above the current market clearing price of around $125.

Because sulfur dioxide and nitrogen oxides emitted from the tall stacks of power plants are more or less uniformly mixed on a regional basis (and because midwestern plants are likely to be net sellers), major geographical hot spots are not likely to emerge from the acid rain program.[20]

The program envisions an 8.9-million-ton cap on SO_2 emissions from power plants after the year 2000. However, Congress has the authority to reduce the number of permits even further without buying them back from the firms. The states' authority to impose tighter regulations has also not been affected. Thus, the permits confer no tangible property rights, although firms can certainly expect at least a decade's trading before the emission cap is reconsidered.

On the enforcement front, the acid rain program mandates the installation of continuous monitoring equipment, which is required to be operative 90% of the time and to be accurate to within 10% to 15% of a benchmark technology. The EPA certifies the monitors at each plant; thus, the monitoring process itself retains a CAC fla-

---

[19]A good discussion of the mechanics of the program can be found in Claussen (1991).
[20]See NAPAP (1991: 447), and Bohi et al. (1990). However, Kriz (1993) reports some opposition to trading from local environmental groups concerned about potential hot spots from specific trades. Kriz also discusses the early trades.

In addition, the possibility of a *temporal* hot spot exists. Because firms are allowed to bank their permits, the 8.9-million-ton sulfur dioxide limit might easily be exceeded in a given year, if many firms should choose to use their banked permits simultaneously. However, if as Bohi et al. (1990) argue, permit prices are not likely to rise substantially, there will be little incentive to bank, and thus this problem will be minimal.

vor. Once a plant's monitoring units are certified, the EPA records all trades and then checks allowances against emissions on an annual basis to insure compliance. One key to success of the program will depend upon the ultimate long-run accuracy and performance of the monitoring technology.[21]

Violators face a $2,000-per-ton fine for excess emissions and must offset those emissions the following year. The fine level was set substantially above the expected market price and yet not so high as to be unenforceable. Thus, it represents a very credible threat to firms. In addition, once a violation is established, the fine is nondiscretionary. These factors should lead to more certain enforcement and better compliance. In fact, we have seen 100% compliance as of mid-1997 (Bohi and Burtraw [1997]).

As a last note, the acid rain legislation contained measures to compensate high-sulfur coal miners and others who lost their jobs. Funding for support while in job retraining programs was authorized at a level of up to $50 million for five years. Job loss estimates through the mid-1990s were on the order of 3,000 to 5,000 in total, almost all of them eastern coal miners.[22]

Before the program was introduced, economists were optimistic that the legislated acid rain trading program, expected to cost around $4 billion annually, would result in savings of between 15% and 25% over a stereotypical CAC option.[23] This optimism arose because the theoretical objections to an IB approach raised in the last chapter, some of which contributed to the disappointing performance of bubbles, did not appear likely to emerge in this case.

To begin with, the existence of a national market with hundreds of participants (including the Chicago Board of Trade) minimizes transactions costs and the thin market problem. Because of the approximately uniformly mixed nature of the pollutants, major hot spots are unlikely to emerge. The potential exercise of market power and speculative behavior has been mitigated by the set-aside and auction of a limited number of permits. The issue of permit life has been settled by providing firms with an indefinite guarantee—a cap of 8.9 million tons in 2000 with Congress holding the authority to restrict emissions further. And finally, an up-front commitment to better monitoring technology and streamlined enforcement has been made.

From an economic point of view, the acid rain program was one of the best laid of regulatory plans. Nevertheless, to paraphrase Shakespeare, reality often reveals more complications than are dreamt of in our philosophy. This experiment will be worth monitoring closely as it unfolds; to date, the results have been quite pleasant, if somewhat surprising.

The first benefit has been cost savings: Utilities are set to achieve the cutbacks spending roughly half to one third what a traditional command-and-control system would probably have cost—savings on the order of $1 billion to $2 billion per year when the program is fully phased in. There have been two surprises: The first is that these cost savings were substantially bigger than anyone anticipated. Most analysts thought that marginal control costs (and thus permit prices) for SO_2 would settle in at

---

[21]Claussen (1991); details on monitoring specifications were obtained from David Hawkins of the NRDC.
[22]"Aiding Displaced Workers," *Congressional Quarterly,* October 27, 1990. See also Goodstein (1997).
[23]NAPAP (1991: 510).

between \$750 and \$1,500 per ton. Instead, permits are selling for between \$100 and \$150 per ton.[24]

The second surprise has been that in the first two years of the program, relatively few trades between different firms have actually occurred; in 1995, less than 5% of the permits in circulation traded hands. Both of these surprises—lower costs and fewer trades—can be explained in retrospect by the increased flexibility that firms were given under the acid rain program. Rather than install expensive scrubbers (or buy extra permits), most firms have met their SO_2 targets by switching to low-sulfur coal or developing new fuel blending techniques. Railroad deregulation led to an unexpected decline in low sulfur coal prices. And with the increased competition from coal, scrubber prices fell by half from 1990 to 1995.

Recall that a stereotypical CAC regulation has two features that raise costs: uniform standards (which block short-run cost-reducing trades) and technology-based regulations (which discourage long-run cost savings by restricting firm-level compliance options). In the acid rain case, almost all of the initial cost savings came from increased flexibility *within* the individual firm. This includes the ability to engage in intra-firm trading (so that any single firm's different plants don't face uniform standards), as well as the ability to use a mix of control technologies.

Unlike in the offset and bubble cases, which were hobbled by thin markets, the lack of external trades for the acid rain program partially reflects marginal compliance costs across firms that are now relatively similar: Almost everybody has switched to substantial reliance on (unexpectedly) cheap low-sulfur coal.

But significant marginal cost differences exist among some players in the industry, and external trades have been picking up over the last year (1997). Bohi and Burtraw (1997) argue that environmental managers at utilities have taken a while to exhaust internal cost savings from trade and are just now beginning to look outward.[25] Thus, we can look forward to even greater cost savings as inter-firm trading accelerates.

17.4 Pollution Taxes in the United States and Europe

As was noted in the introduction to this chapter, the primary American experience with pollution taxes has been in the area of waste disposal. Homeowners typically pay by the gallon for sewage disposal, and waste haulers pay by the ton to dispose of hazardous and solid waste. These closely resemble textbook pollution fees, which, in theory, should result in conservation measures as disposal costs rise.

However, at least in the case of solid waste, this has not been the general result because the incentives for waste reduction are not passed on to consumers. The vast majority of residential and most commercial and industrial municipal solid waste disposal is financed through a lump sum fee. Thus, residential consumers may pay, say \$10 per week, for garbage service regardless of how much garbage they produce. In some com-

---

[24]Not all of these price differences reflect "real" cost savings: Permit prices are lower than anticipated because early bonus allowances added to the near-term supply, thus driving down price (Bohi and Burtraw [1997]). Real cost savings have been on the order of four to eight times greater than predicted, not four to fifteen.

[25]The last five paragraphs have been drawn from Burtraw (1996).

munities, city government handles waste disposal, and the fee is included in property taxes; in others, private firms charge for disposal on a weekly or monthly basis.

This presents us with a curious

PUZZLE

Why don't private garbage haulers provide their customers with a unit pricing option? **Unit pricing** refers to paying for garbage disposal by the bag rather than in a lump sum. The lump sum pricing system, in effect, generates a subsidy from small to large garbage producers. A "smart" garbage firm could offer a unit pricing scheme to small garbage producers. By getting rid of (dumping?) its large garbage customers, the firm could service more customers per trip to the landfill and generate a higher profit margin.

SOLUTION

Sorry, I'm not a garbage hauler, so I don't know the answer to this one. However, it might have to do with the higher transactions costs associated with unit pricing. To implement this approach, a garbage firm might face a considerable challenge marketing its idea, then would have to sell bags to its customers and finally keep track of the number of bags used per customer per week. Perhaps these added costs are enough to offset the extra profit opportunity that a unit-pricing scheme offers. Some evidence to support this view comes from Morris and Byrd (1990), who find that, in fifteen of seventeen communities with unit pricing, collection was organized as a municipal monopoly, and, in one of the exceptional cases, unit pricing was legally mandated. At any rate, this example again reminds us that markets that emerge on a chalkboard sometimes have a harder time in the real world.

In the past, solid waste disposal fees have been relatively low. However, as landfills around the country close and political resistance to new construction has arisen, solid waste disposal costs have been rising rapidly. This has led some municipalities to experiment with unit pricing, often in combination with curbside recycling programs, as a way to reduce waste flows.

In a study of unit pricing in suburban Perkasie, Pennsylvania, semi-rural Ilion, New York, and urban Seattle, Washington, Morris and Byrd (1990) found that the introduction of unit pricing in the first two communities in 1988 reduced waste actually generated by 10% or more, while the flow to the landfill was reduced by more than 30%. In addition, these two communities reduced their waste management costs by 10% or more, with the savings passed on to households through reduced fees. At the same time unit pricing was adopted, both of these communities also introduced or expanded curbside recycling.

By contrast, Morris and Byrd also looked at Seattle's program from 1985 to 1987, *prior* to the introduction of curbside recycling in the late 1980s. Seattle had a unit-pricing system in place since 1961 but raised the rates per can substantially over the three years of the study. The response among Seattle residents to the rising rates was to increase trash compaction (locals call it the "Seattle Stomp"), slightly increase recycling rates, and, ultimately, to slightly reduce overall waste generated. The study suggests that in the absence of a good substitute (curbside recycling), waste disposal is fairly insensitive to price increases; that is, it is price inelastic.

Of course, a pollution tax will always drive people to look for unintended substitutes. In the Perkasie case, the shift to unit pricing led to an increase in trash burning, which was subsequently banned, and to an increase in out-of-town disposal. However, the town found no increase in sewage disposal of waste. Seattle reported some increase in illegal dumping. Comparable results have been reported in more recent research by Fullerton and Kinnaman (1996).

POLLUTION TAXES IN EUROPE

In contrast to the United States' limited experience with pollution taxes, Germany, France, and the Netherlands have all instituted effluent charges for water pollutants.[26] While the taxes are highest in the Netherlands, in no case are they the sole instrument used to control water quality. Rather, effluent systems are grafted on to CAC systems, which mandate standards and control technologies.

What lessons can be learned from the European experience? First, in all cases, taxes were introduced at low levels and then slowly raised. The real value of taxes has, thus, *not* been eroded by inflation. However, a tax high enough to be a primary determinant of pollution levels appears to be politically unfeasible in most cases. This point is quite relevant to proposals to employ carbon taxes as a means of controlling global warming. Although theoretically appealing, many analysts have questioned whether a tax that doubles the price of gasoline—even if accompanied by an offsetting income tax cut—is politically feasible.

Interestingly, as an apparent means of increasing the political acceptability of pollution taxes, the European countries typically direct the funds raised from the pollution taxes into government-financed investments in improved water quality. Thus, the taxes tend to serve a dual environmental purpose, both encouraging reduction by polluters and subsidizing cleanup efforts by third parties. In practice, it seems, taxes often function like the environmental bond systems discussed in chapter 6. Finally, as noted in the previous chapter, the German tax system seems to have generated greater monitoring and enforcement efforts by regulators.

17.5 Indirect Pollution Taxes: The Case of Energy

Two weeks before writing this section, I returned from a trip to Denmark, where I was visiting my cousins. They had borrowed a friend's house for us to stay in, and when we departed, my cousins left a little envelope with some money in it. "To pay for the electricity," they said. This was a little surprising to me, since in America we are used to thinking of electricity as a virtually free good. But due to high taxes on energy, Danes pay about twice as much as we do for electricity. As a result, they think about their energy use more carefully than we do.

---

[26]This discussion is drawn from Hahn (1989); see also Morgenstern (1996).

	TABLE 17.1 Energy Consumption, Prices, and CO_2 Emissions		
Country	*1990 Energy Comsumption Per Capita (kgs of oil equivalent)*	*1989 CO_2 Emissions Per Capita (tons)*	*1989 Gasoline Price ($/gallon)*
United States	7,822	5.34	$1.28
Japan	3,563	2.31	$2.55
Germany	3,491	2.82	$2.53

Sources: World Bank (1992), *World Development Report* (Oxford: Oxford University Press); and New York State Energy Office (1992), *New York State Energy Plan, Volume II* (Albany, NY: NYSEO).

The production of energy, via the burning of carbon-based fuels or the fissioning of radioactive material, is a highly polluting process. Most of the criteria air pollutants are generated through the former activity, while nuclear waste results from the latter. As Table 17.1 illustrates, for uncontrolled pollutants like carbon dioxide, the relationship between energy use and pollution is fairly clear-cut. The United States, with high per capita energy use, also has the highest per capita carbon dioxide emissions. The table also illustrates a strong negative relationship between energy prices and energy consumption. High prices promote low consumption and vice versa. Thus, one strategy to reduce pollution is to *tax it indirectly* by taxing energy use.

However, indirect pollution taxes can generate counterproductive results. Suppose, for example, a gasoline tax were instituted to reduce the emission of greenhouse gases. This might provide an impetus for electric-powered cars. However, to the extent that batteries were charged from electricity produced by coal-fired power plants, CO_2 emissions would rise. Thus, by taxing the fuel instead of its pollution content, one could wind up promoting another, perhaps dirtier, fuel. Moreover, taxing gasoline instead of its carbon content directly discourages innovation designed to generate "low-carbon" gas.

The potential for unintended "perverse effects" means that a direct pollution tax is clearly preferred to an indirect energy tax, since the former taxes all sources based on their pollution contribution and promotes a search for all types of cleaner energy sources. Nevertheless, energy taxes do have the advantage of being administratively simpler, particularly if there is no easy formula for assigning pollutant emissions to energy sources.

In 1993, President Clinton proposed a U.S. energy tax based on the energy content (BTU) of different fuels. The main purpose of the tax was deficit reduction, but it was also recognized to have significant environmental advantages. However, the energy tax, expected to raise about $23 billion per year, was strongly opposed by a coalition of energy-intensive industries. As a result, the proposal was dumped in favor of a modest 4.3-cent-per-gallon increase in the gasoline tax. Such a small increase in gas prices had little impact on gasoline use.

Although the gas tax was expected to raise only $5 billion per year, it met fierce opposition in Congress, passing the House of Representatives by two votes and the Senate by one, before the President signed it into law in 1993. And still the issue wouldn't die, returning as a political football in the 1996 presidential election. The point: Pollution taxes, whether direct or indirect, may be theoretically appealing but are politically quite difficult to enact.

17.6 Environmental Adders and Electric Power

One interesting attempt to introduce something like a pollution tax in the electricity industry has recently gained momentum in the United States. These "taxes," called **adders,** are used only in the project selection phase and are never actually collected. Adders reflect the external social costs associated with different types of power production and are "added" on to private cost estimates when firms bid to supply electricity to a utility's distribution grid. Thus, cleaner power sources are provided an advantage at the bidding stage. State utility regulators in at least twenty-nine states are either using adders or considering this option.[27]

To achieve efficiency, the adders should reflect the marginal social cost of adopting the technology. Under the most common form of regulation, command and control, this question can be rephrased: How much additional environmental damage will one kWh of, for example, coal electricity inflict on the environment? The efficient approach is to determine pollutant levels per kWh of coal power and then estimate, using the techniques of risk analysis and benefit estimation discussed in chapter 8, the marginal damage from each pollutant.[28]

Table 17.2 shows the actual adders used in New York State in the early 1990s. A

TABLE 17.2	Electricity Adders in New York State (based on cost-of-control estimates)
Externality	*Cents/kWh*
Sulphur oxides	.25
Nitrogen oxides	.55
Carbon dioxide	.10
Particulates	.10
Water discharges	.10
Land use impacts	.40
Total Externality Costs	1.40

Sources: Richard L. Ottinger et al. 1990, *Environmental Costs of Electricity* (New York: Oceana Publications).

---

[27]For an overview, see Energy Information Administration (1995).

[28]Adders equal to marginal damages will lead to more efficient pollution control under CAC regulation only. Under a well-functioning marketable permit system, adders are not necessary to achieve efficiency. Why? First, any new source will have to purchase permits from existing firms. Thus, there is no net increase in pollution from a new source and no overall increase in environmental damage. Further, built into a firm's electricity bid will be the price of the permits it has to purchase, which include, in turn, the additional pollution control costs undertaken by the firm who sold the permits. Thus, all additional social costs of the technology will *already* be reflected in the bid, meaning the appropriate adder is zero. Of course, if a hot spot is expected to emerge at the new source, an adder could be justified on safety (and possibly efficiency) grounds. See Burtraw et al. (1992).

The authors also show that in the case of emissions taxes, an efficient adder will reflect the difference between marginal damage and the tax level. This means that in the case of a tax that results in inefficiently stringent pollution controls, the efficient adder will actually be negative. However, as our review of pollution taxes suggests, this situation is quite rare in practice.

clean source could gain at most a 1.4 cent/kWh advantage over a dirty competitor in the bidding process.

However, these numbers are not based on the theoretical ideal sketched in the previous paragraph. Rather than considering the marginal damage done by the additional pollutants (equivalently, the marginal benefit of cleanup), regulators used adder values equal to the additional *cost* of controlling those pollutants. A look at our standard pollution reduction diagram (Figure 17.1 below) reveals that the two will be equal only under the unlikely case when pollution is controlled at the efficient level.[29]

Joskow (1992) argues that in fact marginal control costs for many pollutants are much higher than marginal damages; that is, they are overcontrolled from an efficiency perspective. If efficiency, rather than safety, is our normative goal, using high marginal control costs as adders overly penalizes the polluting technologies.

Recognizing this possibility, New York developed a method for calculating the marginal damages caused by the pollutants on a site-specific basis; these adders turned out to be much smaller than the cost-of-control values.[30] As of 1997, New York was sticking with the higher values in Table 17.2, at least until the impact of increased competition in the power generation industry could be assessed.

One potential disadvantage of using adders is that, since they raise the delivered price of electricity, consumers have an incentive to search for other energy sources. This may lead firms to generate their own (dirty) electricity or to locate in states with-

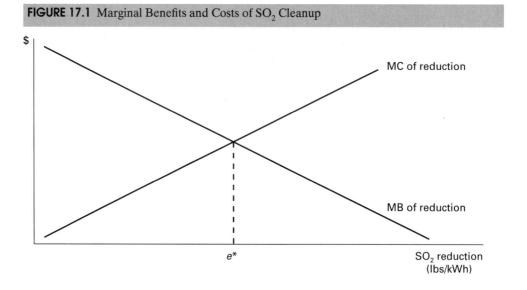

FIGURE 17.1 Marginal Benefits and Costs of SO_2 Cleanup

---

[29]One argument for using cost-of-control estimates instead of damage estimates is that, because regulators require firms to bear these costs to reduce pollution to the legal limit, society has indicated a "revealed preference" for such a price. However, one could as easily argue that our revealed preference for a price on pollution below the legal threshold is in fact zero, since it is unregulated. A better argument for cost-of-control measures is that they represent a relatively easy-to-measure interim standard, acknowledging that residual pollution damage should not be valued at zero.

[30]For a harsh criticism of the New York damages study, see Ottinger (1995); Hohmeyer et al. (1995) provide a good collection of papers on adders.

out adder policies. A case for coordinating a utility adder policy nationwide can, thus, be made. In addition, if utilities do not impose adders on proposals to extend the life of existing facilities, a new source bias may emerge: The adder policy may lead firms to extend the life of old facilities rather than build new ones.[31]

Under the adder system, some unusual players have been attracted to the electrical generation business. In fact, Skidmore College (where I used to teach) put in a bid in conjunction with a private firm to build a natural gas plant. The plan was for Skidmore to use the heat generated by the relatively clean new gas plant; the plant would, thus, *cogenerate* heat and electricity. This would allow us to shut down our own oil-based heating system, which, in spite of meeting environmental standards, remained relatively dirty (and expensive). The project scored very well on the environmental front. Unfortunately, high production costs for such a small-scale operation meant that our project bid still was not low enough to win.

During the same bidding round, however, analysts working in a New York State Energy office did enter a winning bid. This group is now "producing" power through increased energy efficiency in several state prisons and college campuses. It offered the utility 1.8 MW of peak summer power and 12,000 GWh of overall energy reduction at a competitive price, with dramatic environmental benefits.[32]

17.7 Summary

This chapter has reviewed our experience with incentive-based regulation. The primary lesson from the existing marketable permit systems is that a permit market can be a delicate thing. The fact that markets initially have few players can easily discourage potential traders from participating, thus prolonging the thin market problem. Market designers should strive to minimize transactions costs by providing clear, simple trading rules. Banking provisions should also be clarified at the outset.

Because of hot-spot problems, permit systems in practice work best for uniformly mixed pollutants. For non-uniformly mixed pollutants, permit designers face a trade-off between insuring uniform pollution exposure and achieving a workable permit system. In practice, some compromise of safety seems necessary if a permit system is to be successfully implemented for these types of pollutants. Otherwise, transactions costs will rise and choke off trades.

The main lesson to be learned from our experience with pollution taxes is that they are very hard, if not impossible, to implement at levels high enough to function as a sole means of pollution control. This was clearly illustrated by the fierce opposition to President Clinton's modest gasoline tax proposal of 1993. Thus, taxes should be viewed as a complement to, not a substitute for, conventional command-and-control regulation. One example of this is the environmental adder used to influence technology choice in the electricity field.

In practice, pollution taxes also tend to provide a source of revenues for improved pollution control technology. Finally, indirect pollution taxes such as gasoline or en-

---

[31]Palmer and Dowlatabadi (1991). Palmer (1992) also points out that, because demand-side management programs (discussed in chapter 20) extend the life of existing facilities, they may also increase pollution in the short run.
[32]Barnes et al. (1992).

ergy taxes are often a compromise solution when direct pollution taxes prove politically unfeasible or are too hard to administer. In Europe and Japan, high energy taxes originally imposed as energy security measures, have also functioned to reduce pollution in those countries.

Any type of regulation requires a strong commitment to enforcement to be effective. This is especially true of IB regulation, where no special technology is mandated. In the U.S. context, the two most recent marketable permit initiatives (acid rain and the Los Angeles basin) have featured an up-front commitment to better monitoring technology. Whether this technology will ultimately generate better enforcement and compliance remains to be seen.

APPLICATION 17.0

Taxing Hazardous Wastes

In 1989, thirty states had instituted taxes on the disposal of hazardous wastes, either at landfills, incinerators, or both. At the same time, federal legislation (RCRA) discussed in chapter 12 was making land disposal of hazardous waste much more difficult for firms. Sigman (1992) conducted an interesting study in which she looked at the variation in tax rates across the states to address two questions:

1. What impact did the taxes have on the quantity of waste generated?

2. What impact did the taxes have on the choice of disposal method by firms?

Sigman looked at a class of compounds called chlorinated solvents, used primarily for cleaning metals. Some of the data provided in her study are reproduced below.

1. Based on the data in Table 17.3, do you think the taxes would be more likely to discourage incineration or land disposal?

2. Suppose it was found that overall chlorinated solvent waste production was, on average, lower at plants in Vermont than in Tennessee. Could we simply

TABLE 17.3 Data on Chlorinated Solvent Wastes		
Selected States	*Tax Rate On Land Disposal (1989 $/ton)*	*Tax Rate On Incineration (1989 $/ton)*
California	$170.69	$ .00
Connecticut	15.00	15.00
Idaho	21.00	1.00
Tennessee	5.00	2.50
Wisconsin	.50	.00
Vermont	112.00	56.00
Average (30 States)	26.95	10.73
Percent of Waste Disposed (1987–1988)	2%	25%

Sources: Hillary Sigman (1992: Table 1), "The Effects of Hazardous Waste Taxes on Generation and Disposal of Chlorinated Solvent Waste," paper presented at the American Economic Association Meetings, January 1993. Tax rates are for waste generated in-state. Used with permission.

TABLE 17.4	Disposal Costs for Selected Hazardous Wastes (1987, $/ton)
Land Disposal	$ 97–166
Incineration	320–700
Treatment	625–285
Recovery	95–237

Sources: Hillary Sigman (1992: Table 3 and P. 14), "The Effects of Hazardous Waste Taxes on Generation and Disposal of Chlorinated Solid Waste," paper presented at the American Economic Association Meetings, January 1993. Used with permission.

conclude that the higher taxes were responsible? If not, what other factors would you want to control for to find out the true effect of taxes on waste production?

3. Sigman's most optimistic estimate was that the hazardous waste taxes in place in 1988 reduced overall waste generation by about 10%. (This was presumably made possible by an increase in recycling and/or a reduction in chemical use.) Based on the data in the tables above, is such a relatively small effect surprising?

4. Suppose that the tax rates in Table 17.3 were tripled or quadrupled. If government monitoring and enforcement capabilities were inadequate, is it possible that such a move might generate worse hazardous waste pollution problems than we currently have? How?

Key Ideas in Each Section

17.0 This chapter discusses several real-world applications of incentive-based regulation: marketable permits and direct and indirect pollution taxes.

17.1 Perhaps the most successful example of a marketable permit system has been the **lead banking** program, because none of the obstacles identified in the last chapter proved to be significant. A similar trading scheme is now underway for ozone-depleting CFCs.

17.2 In contrast to the lead case, the **Emissions Trading Program** has been disappointing relative to initial expectations. **Emission reduction credits** for criteria air pollutants are traded in the **offset, netting** and **bubble** programs. Bubbles, in particular, have performed poorly due to imperfect information, thin markets, high transactions costs for non-uniformly mixed pollutants, and unclear permit banking rules.

17.3 A major ongoing experiment in marketable permits can be found in current efforts to control sulfur dioxide emissions, which cause **acid rain.** This section discusses acid rain's environmental impact, as well as potential obstacles to successfully controlling SO_2 emissions from power plants via trading. From a theoretical perspective, things look pretty good; initial results show higher cost savings and fewer trades than expected.

17.4 Pollution taxes are not widely used in the United States. Major examples are fees for the disposal of solid and liquid waste, both hazardous and nonhazardous. Although disposal costs have risen sharply in recent years, **unit pricing** for disposal is not always employed, and thus, incentives for waste reduction have been diluted. In the absence of recycling or some other substitute for waste disposal, demand is inelastic. Finally, effluent fees are more common in Europe but are still typically used in conjunction with CAC regulation.

17.5 When direct pollution taxes are not feasible, indirect pollution taxes such as energy or gasoline taxes can also help to reduce pollution. The theoretical problem with an indirect tax is that it may have an unintended and counterproductive effect on other behavior. The U.S. gasoline tax hike of 1993 was too small to generate significant environmental benefits.

17.6 The final example of something like a pollution tax in the United States is the environmental **adder** used in the selection of electric-generating technology. One environmental problem with adders applied only to new sources is a potential for new source bias. From an efficiency perspective, adders should be based on marginal damages rather than marginal control costs.

References

Atkinson, Scott and Tom Tietenberg (1991). "Market Failure in Incentive-Based Regulation: The Case of Emission Trading." *Journal of Environmental Economics and Management,* 21, no. 1, 17–31.

Barnes, Patricia, Paul A. Decotis and Brian Platt (1992). "A State Government Bidder's Experience and Perspective." In *DSM Bidding: Status and Results.* Bala Cynwyd, PA: Synergic Resources Corporation.

Bohi, Douglas R. and Dallas Burtraw (1997). "SO$_2$ Allowance Trading: How Do Expectations and Experience Stack Up?" *The Electricity Journal,* August–September, 67–75.

Bohi, Douglas R. and Dallas Burtraw (1991). "Avoiding Regulatory Gridlock in the Acid Rain Program." *Journal of Policy Analysis and Management,* 10, no. 4, 676–684.

Bohi, Douglas R., Dallas Burtraw, Alan J. Krupnick and Charles G. Stalon (1990). "Emissions Trading in the Electric Utility Industry." *Discussion Paper QE90-15.* Washington, DC: Resources for the Future.

Burtaw, Dallas (1996). "Trading Emissions to Clean the Air: Exchanges Few but Savings Many." *Resources,* vol. 122 (Winter), 3–6.

Burtraw, Dallas, Winston Harrington, A. Myrick Freeman III and Alan J. Krupnick (1992). "Some Simple Analytics of Social Costing in a Regulated Industry." *Discussion Paper QE93-13-REV.* Washington, DC: Resources for the Future.

Burtraw, Dallas, Alan Krupnick, Erin Mansur, David Austin and Dierdre Farrell (1997). "The Costs and Benefits of Title IV." *RFF Working Paper.* Washington, DC: Resources for the Future.

Claussen, Eileen (1991). "Acid Rain: The Strategy." *EPA Journal,* 17, no. 1, 21–23.

Drent, P. J. and J. W. Woldendorp (1989). "Acid Rain and Eggshells." *Nature,* 339, no. 6224, 3.

Dudek, D. J. and J. Palamisano, (1988). "Emissions Trading: Why Is This Thoroughbred Hobbled?" *Columbia Journal of Environmental Law,* vol. 13, 217–256.

Energy Information Administration (1995). *Electricity Generation and Environmental Externalities, DOE/EIA-0598.* Washington, DC: U. S. Department of Energy.

Fanning, Kent A. (1989). "Influence of Atmospheric Pollution on Nutrient Limitation in the Ocean." *Nature,* 339, no. 6224, 460–464.

Firor, John (1989). *The Changing Atmosphere.* New Haven, CT: Yale University Press.

French, Hillary (1990). "Clearing the Air." In *State of the World* 1990, ed. Lester R. Brown New York: Norton.

Fullerton, Don and Thomas Kinnaman (1996). "Household Response to Pricing Garbage by the Bag." *American Economic Review,* 86, no. 4, 971–984.

Goodstein, Eban (1997). "Does Preserving the Earth Threaten Jobs?" *Dollars and Sense,* 3, no. 2, 95–114.

Hahn, Robert W. (1989). "Economic Prescriptions for Environmental Problems: How the Patient Followed the Doctor's Orders." *Journal of Economic Perspectives,* 3, no. 2, 95–114.

Hohnmeyer, O., R. L. Ottinger, and K. Rennings (1995). *Social Costs and Sustainability: Valuation and Implementation in the Energy and Transport Sectors.* Berlin: Springer-Verlag.

Joskow, Paul (1992). "Weighing Environmental Externalities: Let's Do It Right." *The Electricity Journal,* May.

Kriz, Margaret (1993). "Emission Control." *National Journal,* July 3, 1696–1701.

Krupnik, Alan J. (1986). "Costs of Alternative Policies for the Control of Nitrogen Dioxide in Baltimore." *Journal of Environmental Economics and Management,* 13, no. 2.

Lechner, Sheryl (1991). "Liming Acid Lakes: Industry and Environmentalists Have Switched Sides." *Audubon,* 94, no. 3, 26.

Morgenstern, Richard (1996). "Is There a Double-Dividend?" *Environment,* 38, no. 2, 16–34.

Morris, Glenn E. and Denise C. Byrd (1990). "Charging Households for Waste Collection and Disposal." *EPA 530-SW-90-047.* Washington, DC: U.S. EPA.

Mullen, John K. and Frederic C. Menz (1985). "The Effect of Acidification Damages on the Economic Value of the Adirondack Fishery to New York Anglers." *American Journal of Agricultural Economics,* vol. 67, 112–119.

NAPAP (1991). *National Acid Precipitation Program, 1990 Integrated Assessment Report.* Washington, DC: National Acid Precipitation Program.

New York State Energy Office (1992). *New York State Energy Plan, Volume II.* Albany, NY: NYSEO.

Office of Technology Assessment (1984). *Acid Rain and Transported Air Pollutants: Implications for Public Policy.* Washington, DC: U.S. GPO.

Olem, Harvey (1991). "Liming Acidic Surface Waters." In *Acidic Deposition: State of Science and Technology,* ed. Patricia Irving. Washington, DC: National Acid Precipitation Program.

Ottinger, Richard L. (1995). "Have Recent Studies Rendered Environmental Externality Valuation Irrelevant?" In *Social Costs and Sustainability: Valuation and Implementation in the Energy and Transport Sectors,* eds. O. Hohnmeyer, R. L. Ottinger, and K. Rennings. Berlin: Springer-Verlag.

Ottinger, Richard L. et al. (1990). *Environmental Costs of Electricity.* New York: Oceana Publications.

Palmer, Karen (1992). "Social Costing of Electricity and the Benefits of Demand-Side Management." *Discussion Paper QE92-19.* Washington, DC: Resources for the Future.

Palmer, Karen and Hadi Dowlatabadi (1991). "Implementing Environmental Costing in the Electric Utility Industry." *Discussion Paper QE91-13-REV.* Washington, DC: Resources for the Future.

Portney, Paul (1989). "Policy Watch: Economics and the Clean Air Act." *Journal of Economic Perspectives,* 4, no. 4, 173–182.

Sigman, Hillary (1992). "The Effects of Hazardous Waste Taxes on Generation and Disposal of Chlorinated Solvent Waste." Paper presented at the American Economic Association Meetings, January 1993.

Wendling, R. M. and Bezdek R. H. (1989). "Acid Rain Abatement Legislation—Costs and Benefits." *OMEGA International Journal of Management Science,* 17, no. 3, 251–261.

World Bank (1992). *World Development Report 1992.* Washington, DC: World Bank.

CHAPTER 18

Promoting Clean Technology: Theory

18.0 Introduction

As we have seen in the last two chapters, many environmental economists spent the last couple of decades preparing a theoretical case for and advocating the adoption of incentive-based regulation. Their response to the question "How can we do better?" was to say, "We can achieve the same pollution reduction at less cost."

While IB advocates prescribe better regulatory design for our environmental problems, a more fundamental criticism is increasingly being leveled at *any* regulatory approach to pollution control, including *both* CAC and IB. As was discussed at the end of chapter 14, regulation faces three generic problems: (1) rapid economic growth, (2) rising marginal costs of control (the "easy" point and stationary sources are already controlled), and (3) the piecemeal problem (pollution regulated in one medium squeezing out elsewhere). As a result, regulation alone, even when incentive-based, may not be sufficient to achieve environmental goals.

Moreover, regulation is highly susceptible to political influence, due to its information-intensive nature. Thus, industry spends tens of millions of dollars to influence and defuse the process, and yet still finds itself saddled with burdensome and seemingly irrational regulatory requirements mandated by a frustrated Congress. At the same time, environmentalists charge that the actual regulations have no teeth and are enforced only erratically. As one observer put it, "the classical sense of law is lost in sliding scales of targets and goals, accepted tolerances and negotiated exceptions, discretionary enforcement and discretionary compliance."[1]

As indicated in chapter 14, the regulatory approach taken over the last twenty-five years *has* made a difference. Pollution levels are well below what they would have been in the absence of regulation, although relative to the initial goal of a "clean and safe" environment, the results have been disappointing. Nevertheless, the widespread

---

[1]Greider (1992: 109).

perception is that the effectiveness of the regulatory approach is limited by the complexity of the issues at stake and the related opportunities available for political influence. In addition, there is no doubt that the regulatory approach, with its associated need for detailed bureaucratic decision making, has been costly.

Recent interest has focused on the development of clean technologies as a complementary strategy to regulation. Rather than rely solely on controlling pollutants at the "end of the pipe," advocates of this approach argue that government should promote the use of technologies that *reduce polluting inputs and processes in the first place.*

Waste reduction in manufacturing, recycling of wastes, low-input agriculture, energy and water efficiency, renewable resource use, and renewable energy production are often cited as candidates for governmental promotion on environmental grounds. Collectively they may be referred to as **clean technologies (CTs).**

However, this simple formulation begs at least three questions: (1) How can we identify a clean technology? (2) If the technology is so clearly superior, why isn't the market adopting it in the first place? (3) If the market is failing to develop the CT rapidly, how can the government successfully "pick winners" and promote certain types of technologies over others? This chapter explores in more detail the theory of clean technology, focusing on these three questions. Chapter 19 will then consider recent efforts to promote three types of alternative technology: waste reduction in manufacturing, less chemical intensive, alternative agriculture, and solid waste recycling. Chapter 20 concludes the CT discussion with a comprehensive look at energy policy.

18.1 Path Dependence and Clean Technology

An early and influential book arguing for the clean technology approach appeared in 1977. *Soft Energy Paths: Towards a Durable Peace,* was written by American physicist Amory Lovins.[2] Lovins viewed the United States as being at a crossroads, from which two paths diverged. The first was the road then being followed—a society based on the promotion and production of cheap electricity, via an increased reliance on coal, oil, and nuclear power. Lovins termed this the "hard" path. By contrast, the "soft" path involved a conscious governmental effort to redirect the economy toward efficient use of energy and the promotion of renewable energy technologies, especially solar power.

Because the soft path depends on decentralized power production and greater reliance on locally available resources, it promised many social benefits: "A soft path simultaneously offers jobs for the unemployed, capital for businesspeople, environmental protection for conservationists, enhanced national security for the military, opportunities for small business to innovate and for big business to recycle itself. . . ."[3] But best of all, according to Lovins, it was cheaper.

From a theoretical point of view, government efforts to influence the direction of technological progress can be justified by what economists call **path dependence.**[4]

---

[2]Lovins acknowledges his debt to another author, E. F. Schumacher, whose equally influential book, *Small Is Beautiful: Economics As If People Mattered,* appeared in 1973. Lovins, however, redirected the debate away from a philosophical commitment to issues of scale and toward questions of economic transition.

[3]Lovins (1977: 23).

[4]For an accessible introduction to path dependence theory, see Arthur (1991).

This theory maintains that current production technologies—for example, U.S. reliance on private automobiles for urban transportation—represent only one possible path of development. A potentially cost-competitive alternative in this case might be mass transit, dominant in many European and Japanese cities.

The path a society chooses depends on a variety of factors, including the relative political strength of the conflicting interests, chance historical circumstance, and of course consumer preferences and relative production costs. In the auto example, the government's decision to construct the interstate highway system beginning after World War II, which in turn promoted suburban development, provided the decisive advantage to private transport.

However, once a path has been chosen, other paths are closed off; this happens for three reasons. First, infrastructure and R&D investments are increasingly directed toward supporting the chosen technology and diverted from the competing path. Second, the chosen technology is able to exploit economies of scale to consolidate its cost advantage. Third, complementary technologies develop that are tailored to the chosen path, further disadvantaging the competing path. In the transportation example, this would include the sprawling retail and housing patterns of U.S. cities, which now virtually require a private vehicle for access.

Path dependence theory suggests that once a path is chosen, there is no easy way to switch tracks. However, in retrospect, we can see that technological choices have social consequences—the adoption of private transport, for example, has borne a substantial environmental cost. Thus, the role of government is to try and influence the current market-driven process of technological development toward a path consistent with a sustainable future. Note that this theory assumes that governments in modern capitalist societies already necessarily play a major role in shaping technological change through infrastructure decisions and subsidy policies; the key here is to insure that role is a positive one.

18.2 Clean Technology Defined

For the purposes of this book, clean technology has four characteristics:

1. It is not speculative.
2. It generates services of similar quality to existing technologies.
3. It has minimum long-run *private* marginal costs comparable to existing technologies.
4. It is environmentally less destructive than existing technologies.

1. *CTs are not speculative.* Point one requires commercial development and application of the technology to be within a few years' reach. Although there certainly is a role for "pure" government sponsored research, if clean technology is intended as a method of environmental improvement, it must be readily available.

2. *CTs provide comparable quality services.* Judging quality can be a difficult task. For example, in sunny climates a cost-saving and convenient way to preheat water for a dishwasher is to install a fifty-gallon drum painted black on the roof. However, early attempts to market such a simple and cost-effective technology foundered on consumer resistance—the barrels looked ugly to most people. (On the other hand, some

consumers were proud to have an energy saving barrel on their roof.)[5] Judgments about "similar quality" are necessarily subjective. Nevertheless, a governmental decision to promote one certain technology over another requires some judgment about the relative quality of service. Bad choices will ultimately be rejected by consumers, leading to failure of the CT policy.

3. *CTs are cost-competitive on a market basis.* Cost comparisons between technologies should be made on the basis of long-run *private* marginal costs, including taxes and regulatory costs. Why not include external social costs in the comparison? A comparison of private plus social costs does indeed provide the true measure of which technology is theoretically "better." However, *if CTs cannot compete on the basis of private costs,* then they will not be adopted, regardless of government efforts to promote them.

For example, consider photovoltaic or solar electricity. In 1990, photovoltaic (PV) electricity production cost about $.25 per kilowatt hour (kWh). The cost of *peak power* (on a hot summer day when all the air conditioners are running) in New England was as high as $.20 per kWh, because utilities have to operate oil-fired generators for only short periods of time to satisfy this demand. However, if one includes all the subsidies and externality costs associated with conventional power, it is possible to make a case that PVs were already the "cheaper" technology. Table 18.1 reproduces one such effort.

The information in the table suggests that in 1990, PVs may *have already been* the socially preferred technology. Yet if PV prices cannot be brought down to levels competitive in the private market within a few years' time (and many believe they can), their use will not spread rapidly, regardless of governmental efforts to promote them.[6] Clean technologies must be competitive in the marketplace to succeed.

TABLE 18.1   Social and Private Costs of Peak Power

	Photovoltaics	*Fuel Oil*
Private Costs	$.25	$.20
Externality Costs	.00–$.02	.08
Total Costs	.25–$.27	.28

Sources: Externality costs are from Richard L. Ottinger, et al. (1990–31), *Environmental Costs of Electricity* (New York: Oceana). Private cost estimates are from Ken Zweibel (1990), *Harnessing Solar Power: The Photovoltaics Challenge* (New York: Plenum Press).

---

[5]Thanks to Dallas Burtraw for this example.

[6]There is one exception to the rule that cost comparisons should be based on private, not private plus social costs. This is when the government has a virtual monopoly on the provision of the service in question and can thus unilaterally decide which technology society will adopt. We have already looked at one such example in the last chapter: electricity production. By using adders, state utility regulators do in fact make choices between technologies based on social plus private costs. However, even here the "bypass" problem emerges. Firms can decide to locate in areas where social costs are not included in electricity generation decisions.

What is meant by **long-run marginal costs?** Simply the cost of producing an additional unit once the technology is mature. CTs can be divided into two categories, based on whether or not they require high-volume production to achieve their long-run minimum marginal cost. **Small-scale CTs** are cost-competitive with existing technologies at low-volume production. Examples would include the installation of housing insulation or low-flow showerheads, the on-farm adoption of less chemical-intensive pest control, or "housekeeping" measures by manufacturing firms to reduce the generation of hazardous waste. While small-scale CTs are by definition currently cost-competitive, they may still experience economies of scale through marketing.

Large-scale CTs, by contrast, require high-production volumes to achieve minimum long-run costs. Examples would include newspaper recycling, photovoltaic or solar thermal electricity production, and the manufacture of energy-efficient consumer durables, such as cars, refrigerators, lights, and air conditioners.

Figure 18.1 illustrates an estimated long-run average cost curve for electricity produced by photovoltaic cells in the United States. PV electricity costs are predicted to fall rapidly, from the 1990 price of around \$.25 per kWh, to close to \$.05 per kWh when a market size of 160 GW is achieved. (Costs have already plummeted from around \$30.00 per kWh when PV cells were being produced for the space program in 1970.)

Per unit costs fall for three reasons. First, as the firms invest in research and development (R&D) and gain experience, they generate new and lower-cost methods of organization and production. Second, as the market size increases, firms can take advantage of **economies of scale:** lower-cost production arising from the ability to use

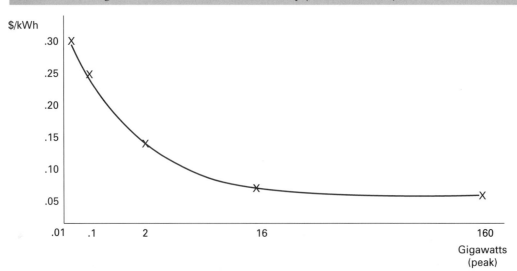

FIGURE 18.1 Long-Run Costs of Photovoltaic Electricity (Estimated \$1990)

Source: Adapted from Ken Zweibel (1990), *Harnessing Solar Power: The Photovoltaics Challenge* (New York: Plenum Press), Table 18-1 and Figure 48. These cost estimates assume policy makers give PV a \$.02 per kWh premium over other electric sources to stimulate its development.

specialized machinery and personnel at high volumes. Third, as complementary industries and markets develop, input costs fall.[7]

As drawn, the average cost curve eventually flattens out as opportunities for technological advancement and specialization are exhausted. This portion of the curve is the minimum long-run average cost, and since the average is constant, marginal cost as well. This long-run cost, to the degree it can be estimated, should be the baseline for a comparison between two technologies, for example, photovoltaics and oil-powered electricity.

The history of cost forecasting is replete with major disasters, such as the famous prediction that nuclear power would one day be "too cheap to meter." Thus credible forecasts stay as far away as possible from scenarios relying on unproven or speculative technologies, and depend instead on the expected costs of implementing known production methods within a relatively short time frame.

4. *CTs are environmentally superior.* Point four in the definition of clean technology insures that it is indeed clean, which is in fact more difficult to establish than it appears. First, it is necessary to account, at least in a rough way, for all of the major environmental impacts of a technology: in manufacturing, use, and disposal. This kind of cradle-to-grave approach is known as **life-cycle analysis.** A second problem arises because different technologies have various types of environmental impacts. This leads to an **adding-up problem,** in which the superiority of one technology over the other may not be clear-cut.

The recent "diaper wars" debate illustrates both the life-cycle and adding-up problems. Each year, American babies use around 17 billion disposable diapers made of paper and plastic. These diapers account for between 1% and 2% of material entering the solid waste stream, ultimately winding up in landfills or incinerators. In the early 1990s, many argued that cloth diapers, provided through diaper services, offered a clean alternative—comparable in quality of service (including convenience) and price, and better for the environment. With consumer demand spurred by this "green" marketing claim, the diaper service business was booming.

However, as a counter to the solid waste concern, Procter & Gamble (maker of Pampers and Luvs) sponsored a study and related PR campaign, which maintained that reusable cloth diapers generate substantially more water pollution in the washing process than throwaways do in manufacturing. In response, the National Association of Diaper Services sponsored its own research, which undertook a life-cycle analysis of the environmental impact of the two products. The authors of this study found that, in general, liquid effluent from the manufacturing process was less harmful for cotton than disposable diapers, and that the overall water pollution advantage of disposables did not hold for cotton diapers laundered commercially.

At this point, it appears that cotton diapers have an edge in areas with solid waste problems, and overall in terms of manufacturing effluents, although disposables may

[7]You may recall from an earlier course that short-run average costs also fall as firms spread out their fixed costs. Initial investments in plant and equipment, advertising, and service and sales networks do mean that for a given plant size, costs per unit are high at low output levels. However, in the long run, average fixed costs need not fall as an industry grows, since overhead expenses may grow proportionately.

In addition, decreasing returns to scale, resulting from managerial breakdown, may set in at some point, causing long-run average costs to actually rise.

be preferable in areas where municipal water treatment facilities are overloaded or inadequate. However, the scientific details have not mattered much in the marketplace. Thanks in some large measure to P&G's ad campaign, cloth diaper services have lost their environmental luster and were virtually eliminated as a competitive threat by 1997. In the New York City area, for example, there are now no cloth diaper services; the National Association of Diaper Services has less than half the members it had in 1991.[8]

Life-cycle accounting of environmental impacts is an emerging science that, in certain cases, is capable of identifying the relative pollution impact of different technologies with more or less precision. However, as the diaper case illustrates, a given technology need not dominate another in all pollution areas, and depending upon how the life-cycle boundaries are drawn, conflicting results may arise.[9] At this point, a policy commitment to support one technology over another often must rely on "common-sense" judgments. This in turn means that "close calls," like cloth diapers, should *not* be considered candidates for governmental promotion as clean technologies.

A natural way to solve the adding-up problem and compare two technologies is to monetize and total the expected life-cycle environmental damages from each source. This would generate an "adder" of the type discussed in the last chapter for energy technologies. Such an adder could be used to compare the social costs of the two technologies, as is done in Table 18.1 for electricity generation from coal and solar power. Note that the clean technology, photovoltaics, does impose some externality costs on society. However, the pollution generated in the manufacture of PVs does substantially less damage than that arising from the burning of oil. Through the use of adders, a CT's environmental superiority can be judged. However, as discussed in point three above, adders should not generally be used in an assessment of a CT's *cost*-competitiveness.

This section has provided a working definition of clean technology. We have found that both small- and large-scale technologies can qualify; there is no up-front bias toward "small is beautiful." However, all of the clean technology candidates discussed in this chapter and the next—photovoltaics and other renewable energy technologies, energy efficiency, diaper services (in some areas), recycling, waste reduction and alternative agriculture—achieve their environmental advantage by being relatively labor-intensive and/or relying to a greater extent on locally produced resources. As a result, they often tend to favor smaller-scale technologies, which can also generate higher *local* employment levels.

18.3 If You're So Smart, Why Aren't You Rich?

The first objection raised to the clean technology approach is this: If these technologies are close to commercial development, generate a quality of service and have long-run production costs comparable to existing technologies, *and* are environmen-

---

[8]See "In the Diaper Wars, Cloth Has Just About Folded," *New York Times,* February 9, 1997, p. D1; A. D. Little (1990); Hershkowitz (1990); and Lehrberger et al. (1991).

[9]For another example, comparing paper and plastic cups, see Hocking (1991). A theoretical problem with life-cycle accounting emerges when indirect effects (see chapter 19) are taken into account. Because indirect pollution may be bigger than direct pollution, a technology that appears clean in a life-cycle framework may in fact have lots of dirty processes lurking in the input-output matrix. At this point, indirect effects must be assumed to cancel each other out. This point is explored further in advanced topics chapter T3.

tally superior, why aren't private entrepreneurs developing them in the first place? In other words, if CT advocates are so smart, why aren't they rich?

The first response is that, in some cases, they are. For example, tens of thousands of American farmers have adopted various forms of low-input farming; recycling has emerged as an economic form of waste disposal in many communities; service corporations that identify cost-effective energy savings for firms and households are growing rapidly. Thus, market forces do provide some support for clean technologies. Yet, the market share for each of these CTs, while growing, remains tiny.

A variety of obstacles can discourage the market deployment of environmentally superior, cost-effective technologies. Table 18.2 provides a summary. The principal market obstacle is the **lack of a substantial profit advantage** for CTs. There is little incentive for private firms to undertake the marketing efforts necessary to overcome marketplace barriers to rapid diffusion: poor information, thin resale markets, poor access to capital, and high discount rates.[10]

A second substantial barrier arises from current governmental policy: subsidies tilted in favor of existing competitor technologies. These subsidies range from R&D funding, to price supports, to tax credits, to efforts on behalf of industry by state and federal agency personnel. Finally, of course, market prices for the competitor technology fail to reflect externality costs.

MARKET OBSTACLES FACING CTS

Simply because CTs are potentially cost-competitive does not mean they are *more* profitable than existing technologies. Entrepreneurs tend to introduce products to fill a "market niche" and provide at least temporary monopoly profits. Clean technologies, by contrast, generally are not offering a new product; rather they go head-to-head with an existing, well-established technology in a mature industry. Thus, they must enter an already competitive field, where only normal profits can be expected. The only clear-cut advantage CTs have is in their environmental impact. While this may provide some marketing leverage, it generally will not guarantee high profitability.

Under normal market circumstances, new technologies often take substantial time to develop a widespread following. This is due to consumers' lack of knowledge (again, imperfect information) about the advantages of the new technology, as well as differences in consumer needs. The transition to any new technology requires a *mar-*

TABLE 18.2 Obstacles to the Rapid Diffusion of CTs

Market Obstacles	*Government Obstacles*
Lack of profit advantage to overcome:	Subsidy policies favoring dirty technologies
*Poor information	Failure of regulation to internalize all externalities
*Thin resale markets	
*Limited access to capital	
*High discount rates	

---

[10]Sullivan (1991) points out, that, with the exception of imperfect information, these are not market "failures" in the classic sense. For a discussion of the diffusion literature, see Jaffe and Stavins (1991).

keting commitment to overcome this lack of information. Marketing expenses are **sunk costs,** those that cannot be recovered if an investment fails. The higher the sunk costs associated with an investment, the riskier it becomes.[11]

Clean technologies face particularly high sunk costs (and thus high risk) because they do not "market themselves" by offering a service consumers do not already have. Instead, CTs need to woo consumers from the use of the existing technology. While CTs offer comparable services, they also tend to require users to learn new consumption habits. This requires a big investment in marketing, which cannot be recovered if the business fails.

Moreover, existing firms do not take inroads into their markets lightly. Witness, for example, Procter & Gamble's ongoing and massive public relations effort to convince consumers that the disposable diaper is not environmentally inferior to cotton. This type of counter-marketing campaign from powerful incumbent firms can make large-scale entry into a CT market even more risky or deter it entirely.

As we saw in the case of marketable permits, imperfect information also generates a **thin market problem.** For example, a homeowner may be reluctant to shoulder the high up-front costs of outfitting her home with energy- and money-saving compact fluorescent lightbulbs because most prospective home buyers know little about them. Thus, she would probably not be able to recoup her initial investment if she decided to sell the house within a few years. Thin markets for durable technologies (those with resale value) tend to dampen the rate of adoption.

Access to capital is a problem for both small- and large-scale technologies. Small-scale CTs often entail an initial up-front investment, which is compensated for by lower operating costs. Returning to our homeowner, a bank might extend her a home-improvement loan to purchase energy-efficient lightbulbs, although such loans are certainly not common; however, the interest rate charged would be much higher than a utility faces when it borrows several hundred million dollars to build a new power plant. The bank would justify its differential lending practices on the basis of increased transactions costs associated with small loans, and, perhaps, increased risk.

At the other extreme, clean technologies with major scale economies, for example, in solar electric power, require large amounts of capital for research and development, production, marketing, and service efforts. They also need a pool of specialized human capital—management and technical expertise familiar with the market. In the solar field, the "natural" organizations with access to this kind of capital and expertise are the large corporations in the energy and utility fields. Why, by and large, do these companies ignore clean technologies?

As we learned in chapter 6, private discount rates are often higher than socially appropriate for environmental investments. **High discount rates** mean that profits made in the future are less valuable than profits earned today. And, as was stressed above, because CTs compete with mature, conventional technologies, a major invest-

---

[11]From the finance theory point of view, marketing costs tend to be systematic risks; that is, risks that cannot be diversified away. They require a higher rate of return. Sullivan (1991) points out that the risk associated with actually installing energy-efficient equipment tends to be unsystematic, in principle requiring no profit premium. However, consumers and small businesses generally face imperfect capital markets and must absorb much of this risk personally.

ment in CTs is not likely to be a profit center in the near term—say a decade or more. Yet, a 20% before-tax rate of return, a common requirement in many U.S. industries, implies roughly a five-year payback on any investment.[12]

This central fact has kept interest in solar, wind, and renewables on the back burner for most large energy and utility corporations; few have interest in R&D investments with long-term payoffs. In addition, these tend to be the very firms with a strong vested interest in the status quo. Why develop products that will compete with already profitable electricity and fuel sales? (German and Japanese businesses, facing higher conventional fuel prices, are naturally more interested in energy CTs. There is also some evidence that German and Japanese firms engage in longer term planning than do American companies.)[13]

In the absence of commitments to technologies like solar electricity by large firms, small firms enter to serve niche markets. However, neither substantial R&D nor economies of scale in production cannot be achieved by these firms. Thus, costs remain high, and the market widens only slowly.

Finally, consumers also appear to require high rates of return for investments in durable CTs. As discussed in chapter 6, observed discount rates of 50% to 100% are not uncommon for the purchase of energy-efficient air conditioners, refrigerators, or lightbulbs. This unwillingness to commit funds to highly profitable investments reflects a combination of poor information, restricted access to capital, risk aversion, and thin resale markets.

GOVERNMENT OBSTACLES TO CTS

In addition to market barriers, CTs are often disadvantaged by government action in the form of **direct or indirect subsidies** to highly polluting competitors. Consider agriculture, for example. As you may have learned in an introductory economics course, due to the high variability in agricultural prices, the government has historically provided farmers with a guaranteed price floor. If the market price falls below the price floor, say $2.80 per bushel for corn, the government makes up the difference. However, as illustrated in Figure 18.2, the price floor also guarantees an excess supply of corn (q_d to q_s) that the government must stockpile.

One consequence of the surplus production is of course greater pesticide use. The Conservation Foundation estimates that the *surplus* wheat and corn grown in 1986 required the application of 7.3 billion pounds of fertilizer and 110 million pounds of pesticides.

In addition to promoting excess pesticide use, however, subsidy programs can directly penalize cleaner agricultural practices. Until recently, price supports were pri-

---

[12]Scherer (1988) found median after-tax hurdle rates to be around 15% in 1983. He also discusses the argument that during the 1980s fear of takeovers induced managers in large corporations to reduce overhead costs, including substantial cutbacks in research and development funding.

[13]Through the late 1980s, the biggest U.S. solar company and the world leader in photovoltaic sales was owned by the oil company ARCO. ARCO purchased the solar company in the late 1970s as a hedge against rising oil prices; in 1986, with oil prices flat, ARCO decided to sell its solar unit. The solar company was purchased by a German electronics firm, Siemens, in 1989, the year it turned its first profit. The exceptional U.S. firm is Enron; see the discussion of its solar and wind investments in chapter 20. See also Zweibel (1990), Scherer (1988), and the review article by Porter (1992).

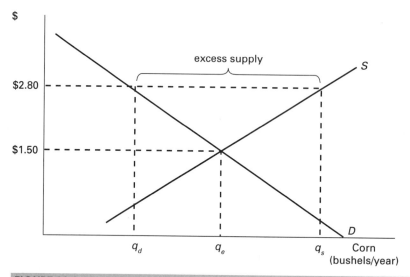

FIGURE 18.2 The Impact of Agricultural Subsidies

marily available for a limited number of crops, and these crops (coincidentally?) were very high users of chemical fertilizers and pesticides. Moreover, the subsidy payments for a given year were based on past yields of the crop in question, effectively tying farmers to the production of subsidy crops. During the 1980s, a farmer desiring to adopt a CT based on diversification into less chemical-intensive crops, and crop rotation as a method of fertilization, and weed, pest, and erosion control was, thus, doubly damned. Not only would she lose her subsidy this year, but subsidies for any future program crops she grew would also be reduced.[14]

Overall, the farm subsidy programs have been substantial. Between 1985 and 1990, federal farm program expenditures were $71 billion.[15] However, in the mid-1990s many of the farm subsidy programs began to be scaled back.

While farm subsidies provide a very visible example, most CTs face competitor technologies that receive important governmental aid, direct or indirect. As we discussed in the last chapter, for example, solid waste disposal is often paid for through lump sum tax payments, not by unit pricing. This provides a subsidy for large garbage producers, disadvantaging recycling. Recycling is also placed at some disadvantage through a variety of subsidies to raw materials producers.[16] Chapter 20 will focus on subsidies for polluting technologies in the energy field.

The next section suggests a method by which government policy makers can in fact select and promote CTs in the most cost-effective manner.

---

[14]Crosswhite and Sandretto (1991); and Curtis (1991).

[15]See Office of Technology Assessment (1991). Curtis (1991) cites the Conservation Foundation study.

[16]Office of Technology Assessment (1989). The OTA suggests that such subsidies are probably not a major barrier to increased recycling in general. Nestor (1991) draws a similar conclusion for newspapers.

18.4 Picking the Winning Path

While I was driving to my in-laws' house yesterday, a prominent environmentalist and forest service critic was on the radio. He made the argument that many of the environmental problems in the western United States could be traced directly to bad government decisions reflecting industry's influence: subsidies for ranchers leading to overgrazing; subsidies for timber companies leading to clear-cuts; subsidies for mining companies leading to water contamination and the destruction of wilderness areas; and radiation leaks and releases from government-owned, -leased or -subsidized nuclear facilities.[17]

There are two responses to these governmental efforts at industrial promotion. One is to despair of government's ability to intervene rationally in economic affairs. Traditional conservatives would adopt this position and argue that, in spite of possible market obstacles to the rapid adoption of clean technology, the only thing government should do is to level the playing field by eliminating all subsidies.

Progressives adopt an alternative response. While acknowledging government failures, they also point to environmental success stories, such as weatherization and soil conservation programs, improvements in fuel efficiency, and the creation of wilderness areas. They argue that a blanket call for the elimination of subsidies is naive: After all, a decade of conservative government in the 1980s saw at best only marginal reduction in the subsidy levels for industry.[18] The challenge is thus to recognize the limitations of government intervention and, taking this into account, implement policies to promote CTs.

How can bureaucratic errors and political influence be minimized in this process? A three-step procedure should be followed.

1. *Level the playing field.* To the extent possible, subsidies for dirty technologies should be eliminated, and their external costs should be internalized, preferably through IB regulation. (As we saw in chapter 16, IB regulation is superior to a command-and-control approach for promoting technological change within a regulated industry.[19]) "Leveling the playing field" by reducing subsidies and internalizing social costs may provide clean technologies with the edge needed to succeed.[20]

2. *Promote only clear environmental winners.* Given the uncertainty associated with assessing the actual environmental impacts of different technologies, only CTs with a clear environmental advantage should be considered for promotion.

---

[17]For a scholarly analysis along these lines, see Stavins and Jaffe (1990).

[18]The major conservative victory on the subsidy front was the tax reform of 1986; yet even this bill retained benefits for the oil and gas industry. Lucke and Toder (1987). See also Koplow (1993). As discussed below, the Reagan and Bush administrations did substantially reduce R&D in the energy sector but in doing so, disproportionately favored the "hard path."

[19]CAC regulation does promote substitution *away* from the products or services produced by the regulated industry. As we shall see in the next chapter, by raising the production costs for products such as pesticides and landfill disposal, CAC regulation has led to the development and adoption of cleaner technologies *outside* of the regulated industry.

In addition, under a CT strategy, pollution taxes (or permits) are not viewed primarily as a means to achieve a pollution standard. Rather, they play the role of encouraging the adoption of CTs. Thus, the precise tax level is not as critical in the CT strategy as it is under IB regulation; any level of pollution tax will provide for accelerated diffusion of the CT, with higher taxes leading to faster diffusion.

[20]Larson and Knudson (1991) make this point forcefully for agricultural technologies.

3. *Tie subsidies to least-cost performance.* When the government does decide to promote a technology actively, subsidies should be directed only to projects that either are *already* cost-effective, or promise to deliver cost-effective services within a relatively short period of time, say a decade or less. Subsidies to the latter category should be conditioned on observable cost reductions. In sum, government planners should focus attention on **least-cost** technology options, subject to an environmental screen.

This least-cost approach is consistent with path dependence theory; the government is looking for environmentally friendly "infant" industries that need only time-limited support to attain a sufficiently large scale to be self-supporting. The rationale for government subsidies under path dependence theory is to jump-start an industry for its environmental benefit, not provide indefinite promotion efforts.[21]

Least-cost planning of this type achieves two goals. First, government's objective is to speed up, not replace, the market process of adoption of CTs. Market forces will naturally spread technologies with a greater profit advantage faster. The faster the technology spreads, the greater the environmental benefits society reaps.

Second, by using a least-cost approach, bureaucrats can avoid making expensive commitments to technological white elephants. A good example of such a poor choice is nuclear fusion. Fusion is an approach to energy production based on fusing two atomic nuclei together. By contrast, commercial reactors today generate power through fission, the splitting apart of particles. The government commitment to fusion research began in 1952 and continued rising steadily until 1984 when it peaked at around $440 million per year. Today, after four decades of federal funding, even fusion optimists concede that commercial power generation would require comparable R&D subsidies for at least another fifty years.[22]

How can we explain the continued flow of substantial funds to this ill-fated project? The allure of fusion has always been its promise of an energy source with limitless fuel and, relative to fission, low-waste production. The initial commitment to fusion was made during the Cold War, with the fear that the Russians would gain a competitive edge. The steady flow of dollars then generated a "fusion community"—physicists and engineers at university and federal laboratories, and Department of Energy bureaucrats—dependent for their livelihood on federal subsidies. This fusion community maintained and developed allies in Congress and the White House; fusion funding remained high through the 1970s because of energy security concerns. Finally, within the fusion community, until 1983 there was a tacit agreement to avoid public debate of the economic viability of the technology.[23]

In contrast to the open-ended support of fusion, path dependence theory suggests that a CT program can and should focus on technologies with a clear environmental advantage that will stand on their own relatively quickly. Government can then make only time-limited or performance-based commitments to the technology, and thus avoid the development of vested political interests attached to a particular technology. Fusion would neither have passed an environmental screen nor survived subsidies conditioned on rapid cost reductions.

---

[21]Development economists call this the "infant industry" argument for subsidies; here, however, the government motivation is for the environmental benefit provided by the new technology.

[22]See Hafele (1991) for example.

[23]For a sympathetic look at the fusion community, see Herman (1990).

One recent triumph of least-cost planning occurred in New York State. In 1988, the state power authority had made an initial commitment to purchase 1800 MW of electricity from a massive hydroelectric project being planned by the Quebec Provincial Government in northern Canada. The James Bay project was expected to have a major environmental impact, flooding 2,700 square miles of sub-arctic tundra used for subsistence hunting by Cree and Inuit native peoples.

In a review of the project, motivated in part by environmental concerns, New York State concluded that aggressive government and utility promotion of energy-efficiency measures would forestall the need for new capacity through the year 2006. The State Energy Office estimated that reductions in energy demand sufficient to offset the hydro project could be obtained at a cost of 2.5 cents per kWh, while James Bay power came in at 5.35 cents per kWh.[24]

Following a least-cost strategy insures that policy concentrates on "picking the low-hanging fruit." Doing this gets more environmental protection for a lower investment, with less risk, and a lowered probability of prolonged government involvement.

18.5 Promoting Small-Scale CTs

It is useful to divide clean technologies into small- and large-scale groupings, since the market obstacles they face are somewhat different. Small-scale technologies, by definition, do not require large markets to reach their minimum long-run production costs; thus, they are already cost-competitive with existing technologies. The barriers these technologies face to rapid diffusion are related to imperfect information and higher capital costs. Large-scale technologies, by contrast, require assistance in achieving high-volume production before they can be cost-competitive with existing technologies.

Consumer and business resistance to small-scale CTs reflects a natural inclination to stick with "what works," rather than adopt an unknown and possibly risky alternative. As we have seen, the relatively low profit advantage of many CTs discourages private-sector marketing initiatives to overcome this resistance. Government policy should thus be directed at providing information to consumers and reducing perceived risks of adoption. Informational barriers can be dealt with through (1) product labeling requirements, (2) flexible design standards, (3) the reorientation of utility regulation, and (4) technical assistance programs. A program of (5) subsidies for consumers also can attack the information problem, as well as compensate for higher capital costs.

Product Labeling   The simplest policy step is to require product labeling. For example, the EPA has developed a standard method for testing the miles per gallon that automobiles can achieve and requires firms to publicly report this information. Similar energy-efficiency reporting is required for consumer durables like refrigerators and air conditioners, and most recently computers, under the EPA's "green star" program. This list could be expanded to lamps, motors, and other durables. Product labeling requirements provide consumers with ready access to information on the environmental consequences of their purchase.

Poll results indicate that people are willing to pay a small premium for environ-

---

[24]New York State Energy Office (1992).

mentally friendly products. However, the rush to green marketing widely anticipated in the early 1990s has not materialized. Commenting on the "wilting" of this market, the *Wall Street Journal* cited consumer distrust of manufacturers' claims.[25] Federal regulations governing environmental or green marketing emerged only in 1992, with Federal Trade Commission guidelines governing claims such as "biodegradable," "recyclable," and "ozone safe."[26]

Beyond the regulation of marketing terminology, whole products can be certified as "environmentally friendly." In Germany and Canada, the government runs such a certification program. In the United States, Green Seal and Scientific Certification Systems, two private organizations, have been working since 1990 to develop this kind of labeling scheme.[27] The U.S. programs have had a hard time getting underway because of the complexity of identifying clean products in a life-cycle framework. Green Seal has opted for identifying the major environmental impacts of a given product, then publishing a draft standard for review and comment by affected industries. As of 1997, Green Seal had developed certification standards for twenty-eight products, including tissue and writing paper, rerefined engine oil, compact fluorescent lighting, and water-efficient fixtures.[28]

Minimum Design Standards   Product labeling programs leave some choice in consumer hands. However, in markets where complex purchases are made infrequently, consumers have a hard time judging the relative merits of available technologies. Here *flexible* design standards, requiring a minimum level of environmental performance, can be introduced. The most well-known example of a design standard is a building code; many local governments have established energy-efficiency requirements for new homes.

The purchase price for an energy-efficient house is typically more than for a leaky alternative. Because consumers are reluctant to absorb larger loans and because banks are hesitant to make them, people naturally opt for the energy-inefficient choice. However, the savings in monthly heating bills from energy efficiency will quickly cover the initial up-front expense, and homeowners will save money in the long run. Thus, from an economic point of view, banks should provide and consumers should shoulder larger loans for an energy-efficient house.

However, neither banks nor consumers are particularly well-equipped to evaluate energy cost-saving opportunities on a case-by-case basis. By mandating minimum design standards, government closes off the option of the leaky alternative. The risk to all parties of opting for the CT is thus reduced. Banks will soon learn that, due to lower utility bills, they can offer higher loans on new houses, and all parties, including the environment, are better off in the long run.

---

[25]"Green Product Sales Seem to be Wilting," *Wall Street Journal,* May 18, 1992.

[26]"State Your Claim," *EPA Journal,* July–August 1992.

[27]Green Seal is a nonprofit organization; Scientific Certification Systems (formerly Green Cross) has applied for nonprofit status. See "Seals Slow to Sprout," *Advertising Age,* April 20, 1992. The Environmental Defense Fund has been highly critical of Green Cross, accusing it of engaging in a variety of questionable certification practices. See Smith and Dennison (1991). EDF has also criticized Green Cross's life-cycle approach to certification. For a discussion of European and Canadian labeling programs, see OECD (1991).

[28]See the Green Seal web site at http:\\www.crest.org\environment\GreenSeal\whatisGS.html; and Green Seal (1992).

Energy-efficiency requirements are included in many local building codes. In addition, federal law now requires banks to offer lower-rate, energy-efficiency mortgages, though this regulation is not well-known. Several cities and counties in the United States, including San Francisco and Ithaca, New York, now have retrofit energy standards that must be met for old buildings whenever they are sold, leased, or renovated. The increased cost is passed on to the buyer, who can then qualify for an energy-efficient mortgage.[29]

The key to the success of a design standard is flexibility. Thus, governments should state efficiency targets and stay away from requiring builders to install a list of particular conservation measures. Otherwise, the standard problems with a command-and-control approach emerge: a lock-in of one technology, stifling the deployment of superior approaches. One interesting example of a bad design standard involved a building code requiring a furnace or other conventional heating system. Solar builders in the community apparently circulated an electric baseboard heater that could be plugged in to pass the inspection and was later removed.[30]

Design standards have also been suggested for lighting, appliances, and electric motors, as a way to promote adoption of these CTs. Design standards provide a "free lunch" when the product's quality is quite generally perceived to be comparable to the conventional technology and its long-run private cost is less. In this case, government is simply mandating the choice that the majority of people would make on their own if given the information. However, design standards become more costly if individual opinion differs substantially as to the CT's quality, or if its cost rises above that of the conventional technology. Nevertheless, even in this case, design standards may still be justifiable as a cost-effective way to control pollution.

Utility Marketing   Another approach to the marketing problem facing small-scale CTs is to have the technologies marketed by large firms, with lower-cost access to both financial and human capital. In the energy field, many states have restructured their regulation of utilities so that the firms can earn a profit on energy conservation. Until recently, utilities had no incentive to promote efficiency—every kilowatt saved was a reduction in their revenue. However, the new regulations recognize that energy saved is also energy freed up for other uses. Thus, investments in energy efficiency are increasingly treated like investments in new generating plants, on which firms are allowed to make a normal profit.

The last few years have seen an increasing level of utility marketing for energy-efficiency efforts. For example, in 1989, my local utility retrofitted our house's water heater, gave us a low-flow showerhead and some pipe and outlet insulation, and conducted an energy audit, all free upon request. Utilities have also been involved in rebate programs for lightbulbs and appliances, and "refrigerator roundups" where the utility buys up and then junks ancient energy-hog refrigerators. These services are paid for through higher electricity bills. From both an economic and environmental point of view, these are all good investments, because by freeing up electricity, they allow the utility to avoid having to build expensive, polluting power plants.

---

[29]Geller et al. (1991).
[30]Lovins et al. (1986).

Technical Assistance Programs   A fourth approach to marketing small-scale CTs is a direct one. Here, government technicians provide advice to firms interested in undertaking CT investments. As we shall see in the next chapter, this direct approach is advocated to promote waste-reducing, clean technologies in manufacturing. It also is the logical way to promote CTs in agriculture, since the government already has a technical assistance program—the state agricultural schools and extension services— in place.

Consumer Subsidies   Efforts to provide consumers with information through labeling, standards, utility marketing, and technical assistance can be supplemented by subsidies for CTs. The presence of subsidies provides consumers with an incentive to educate themselves about the product; they also can overcome obstacles to rapid diffusion associated with higher capital costs. For example, the New York State government, using a pool of funds obtained in a court settlement with oil companies overcharging, provides matching grants to public and nonprofit institutions interested in energy-efficiency projects. The projects must have payback periods of no more than 10 to 15 years. By the early 1990s, the programs had saved around 2,000 GWh of electricity.[31]

Subsidies can take several forms: **tax credits, low-interest loans,** or **grants.** To encourage small-scale CTs, loans and grants are preferable because they are easier to target. Loan applications and grants require groups to justify their investment, discouraging non-serious applicants, and they also provide government officials a means to allocate funds on a least-cost basis.

In addition, a problem with any subsidy program is that it may provide "windfalls" for people planning to adopt the technology anyway (free riders). A study of a tax credit for residential energy savings provided in the late 1970s found that only 8% of the 15 million claimants would definitely or probably not have undertaken the investment without the credit. To deal with this problem, loans and grants can be targeted to working- and middle-class individuals, small businesses, and nonprofit corporations.[32] These groups, being resource-constrained, are least likely to adopt the CTs in the first place. Finally, tax credits are typically used by wealthier individuals and corporations and, thus, skew the benefits of the policy in a regressive direction. If tax credits are used, one way to avoid promoting windfalls and tax cuts for the wealthy is to put an income limit on the claim.

18.6 Promoting Large-Scale CTs

In contrast to small-scale technologies, the primary barrier facing large-scale CTs is achieving high-volume production. As illustrated in Figure 18.1, this lowers per unit costs through R&D, learning-by-doing, and scale economies. The key policy issue is to provide some incentive for existing or new firms to enter these markets. This section discusses four policies to encourage such interest: (1) research and development fund-

---

[31]New York State Energy Office (1992).

[32]Hirst et al. (1982). The tax credit program was also criticized for promoting expensive, rather than effective, energy-efficiency measures. To solve this problem, tax credits could be offered based on energy saved, rather than capital invested.

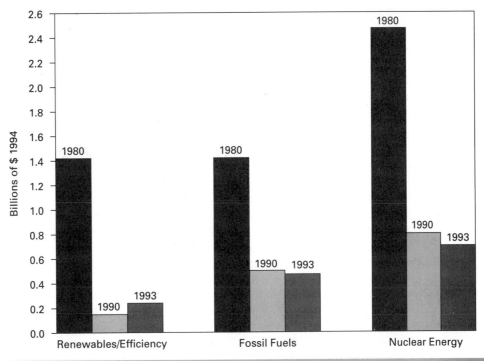

FIGURE 18.3 Department of Energy R & D Expenditures (1980, 1990, 1993)

Source: Department of Energy, Office of the Secretary. Figures for 1993 are estimated.

ing, (2) producer subsidies, (3) technology-forcing standards, and (4) infrastructure investment.

Research and Development Funding   The first step to promote large-scale CTs lies in adequate government funding of R&D. Figure 18.3 illustrates government funding levels for research in different energy sources in 1980, 1990, and 1993.

First note that overall funding levels fell dramatically from 1980 to 1990—the influence of conservative administrations, philosophically opposed to government involvement in economic affairs, especially commercial research. But renewables and conservation research were particularly hard hit. Under the last year of the Carter administration, 1980, renewables and conservation received a share of funding comparable to fossil fuels. Government policy during the decade clearly moved in the direction of a commitment to the hard path. By 1990, fossil fuels received two-and-one-half times as much support as did conservation and renewables, while the nuclear research budget was more than three times as large.

Clinton's election in 1992 brought about a reversal in these trends. Following up on election commitments to boost funding for clean technology, spending on fossil fuel research declined in the first year of the administration, with a (roughly) offsetting increase in research dollars directed to solar and renewable energy. By 1994 the renewables budget was $344 million—three times the level in 1990—but still less than half of 1980 spending (Berman and O'Connor [1996]).

Producer Subsidies   Another approach to encouraging commercial development is to provide subsidies to producers—tax credits, loans, grants, or purchase guarantees. One form of purchase guarantee is a **price preference.** Many state governments will pay a premium of up to 5% or 10% for recycled products. Government **procurement contracts** are another way of providing infant CT industries with guaranteed markets. We will look more closely at subsidy issues in our discussion of energy policy in chapter 20.

Technology-Forcing Standards   Beyond the carrots of R&D funding and producer subsidies, government policy makers can also employ sticks. The primary tool here is to make access to the market subject to meeting a **technology-forcing standard.** In contrast to the building energy codes or lighting efficiency standards discussed above for small-scale CTs, technology-forcing standards set a deadline for firms to deliver technology that is *not yet* marketed.

Perhaps the best-known technology-forcing standards are the Corporate Average Fuel Economy, or **CAFE,** standards. In 1975, Congress mandated that car companies had to achieve an average of 18 miles per gallon by the 1978 model year, and 27.5 miles per gallon by the model year 1985. Stiff fines were to be levied on corporations that failed to comply, although a one-year "carryover" was permitted. Firms that exceeded the standard in one year could credit the excess MPG savings for the next year.[33]

From the point of view of increasing vehicle mileage, the CAFE has been a success—average fleet mileage did increase to around 28 miles per gallon, with little additional progress after 1987. The first round of CAFE appears to have been much more important than increasing gas prices (from 1974 to 1982) in achieving these mileage improvements.[34]

We will defer a more detailed discussion of the costs and benefits of the CAFE to chapter 20, which focuses on energy policy. For now, it is worth pointing out the principal theoretical drawback of any technology-forcing standard: inefficiency. If the CAFE standards are intended primarily to reduce urban air pollution, they do so at a substantial cost to rural residents who face few air pollution problems. The latter group must sacrifice vehicle size and possibly safety for little benefit.

Inefficiency associated with technology-forcing standards can be reduced when the standards are imposed locally. Thus, California did the rest of the nation a service by imposing technology-forcing energy standards for refrigerators beginning in the 1970s. The California standard tightened from about 1,500 to 1,000 kWh per year between 1978 and 1988; access to California's market was important enough to manufacturers to spur significant progress. The average new refrigerator cost $64 less per year to run in 1990 than it did in 1970. The federal government adopted appliance standards in 1988; by 1995 average energy use for refrigerators dropped to no more than 700 kWh per year.[35]

---

[33]One-year "carrybacks" were allowed as well.

[34]Greene (1990). An earlier study, Crandall et al. (1986) arrived at the opposite conclusion. However, three years later, Crandall had apparently changed his mind, (Crandall and Graham [1989]) because he attributed increased highway deaths from car downsizing to the CAFE. For more on the safety issue, see chapter 20.

[35]Fickett, et al. (1990).

From a theoretical perspective, sufficiently high pollution taxes can always achieve the same result as technology-forcing standards, with the inefficiencies reduced due to greater consumer and manufacturer flexibility.[36] However, as in many other cases, technology-forcing standards appear to be easier to legislate than do high taxes.

Infrastructure Investment   The final tool available to government to influence the adoption of CTs is perhaps the most powerful. As we noted in the introduction to this chapter, the overwhelming dominance of the automobile in American life has much to do with the government-funded interstate highway system. Recognizing this, New Jersey is trying to deal with problems of traffic congestion and air pollution by pursuing a novel approach: cut highway spending. Beginning in 1992, the state planned to double its investment in mass transit, while it has canceled $1.2 billion in new highway projects.[37]

Table 18.3 provides a summary of policy tools that government can use to promote CTs and suggests CTs for which their use may be appropriate. Of course, all these tools can be abused; a successful CT program will require that government policy focus on promoting only cost-effective, environmentally superior technologies. In particular, as was argued in Section 18.3 above, government subsidies should support only (1) cost-effective small scale technologies and/or (2) large-scale technologies that demonstrate substantial progress toward competitive pricing.

TABLE 18.3   Policy Tools for Promoting CTs

Small-scale CTs

Policy	*CTs*
Product Labeling	Energy and Water Efficiency, Recycling, Alternative Agriculture
Design Standards	Energy and Water Efficiency
Utility Marketing	Energy Efficiency
Technical Assistance	Waste Reduction in Manufacturing, Alternative Agriculture, Passive Solar, Wind Power
Consumer Subsidies: grants, loans, tax credits	Energy and Water Efficiency, Recycling, Passive Solar

Large-scale CTs

Policy	*CTs*
R&D	Solar Electric, Wind Power, Electric Vehicles, Biomass Fuels, Hydrogen Fuels, Alternative Agriculture, Waste Reduction in Manufacturing
Producer Subsidies: price preferences, procurement contracts	Solar Electric, Electric Vehicles, Alternative Agriculture, Waste Reduction in Manufacturing
Technology-Forcing Standards	Energy Efficiency, Electric Vehicles, Recycling
Infrastructure Investment	Mass Transit, Recycling

[36]Bold (1987).

[37]"States Try New Tactic to Curb Auto Traffic: Cut Highway Spending," *Wall Street Journal,* April 8, 1992.

18.7 Summary

This chapter identifies government promotion of CTs as a potentially attractive alternative to regulation for controlling pollution. At a basic level, the two strategies are complements, not substitutes. By internalizing social costs, regulation provides a more level playing field on which clean technologies can compete. Yet, with the easy "point and stationary source" regulatory gains already achieved, and in the face of constant pressures from population and economic growth, rapid development and diffusion of CTs will become an increasingly important means of improving environmental quality.

Regulating waste once it is produced exacerbates short-run conflicts between economic growth and environmental quality. While in the long-run, environmental regulation spawns new technologies and creates new industries and jobs, "in the long run," as the economist John Maynard Keynes once said, "we are all dead." As a supplement to the stick of pollution taxes (or other IB regulation), the CT approach offers a carrot of government-promoted, substitute technology. Thus, the short-run trade-off between material well-being and the environment becomes much less stark.

Moreover, path dependence theory suggests that a continued exclusive government focus on end-of-the-pipe regulation of pollutants will lead to technological progress in end-of-the-pipe waste management, rather than in waste-reducing CTs. Concerned primarily with regulatory compliance, and provided with the funding to do so, environmental managers in industry and government will continue to develop expertise in emissions monitoring and enforcement, risk analysis, and benefit-cost analysis; engineers will focus on cheaper ways of scrubbing and filtering emissions, and safer ways of incinerating or burying wastes. While these skills and technologies are important for making regulation work better, they are not primarily the skills and techniques needed for a transition to CTs.

Finally, in practice, we have seen that regulation is an adversarial process in which environmentalists and industry compete in an information-intensive conflict over the drafting and enforcing of standards. A regulatory approach in one sense sets government up to fail, since the affected parties have many opportunities, and much to gain, from influencing the process. The political economy of a CT approach promises to reduce both the day-to-day conflict between regulators and firms, and limit the opportunities for political influence.

Promoting CTs, of course, is certain to have its own bureaucratic problems associated with implementation. Conservative critics would charge that the "light-handed" planning process described here, while nice in theory, would dissolve as soon as a CT agency were established. Once provided a budget, CT promotion would devolve into "heavy-handed" restrictions on industries arbitrarily judged to be "dirty" by environmentally motivated bureaucrats, coupled with expensive crash programs to develop completely ludicrous technologies, located in the districts of powerful members of Congress.

Yet, a case can be made that a CT strategy would be an effective complement to regulation, reducing both costs and regulatory conflict with industry. Because a CT strategy would not involve rule making at the level of individual pollutants, or extensive monitoring and enforcement, informational requirements would be diminished. As the need for information falls, so do opportunities for political influence, delay, and indecision. Once funded, technology subsidies are a "win-win" situation; firms are rewarded for reducing pollution, rather than punished for not doing so.[38] Thus, CTs can transform an adversarial relationship into a partnership. Finally, path dependence theory suggests that government subsidy commitments can and should be time-limited and/or performance-based, thus reducing the probability of both picking losers and the development of vested interests.

APPLICATION 18.0

Path Dependence and QWERTY[39]

One of the best examples illustrating path dependent technological development is the arrangement of the letters on the computer keyboard. Next time you sit down to write a paper, notice that the top six keys on the left-hand side spell QWERTY. The standard keyboard, widely used in English-speaking countries, is thus called QWERTY. How did QWERTY develop?

Not on the basis of efficiency. Other keyboard arrangements lead to much faster typing. Instead, QWERTY was designed in the 1870s as a way to prevent typewriter keys from clashing and sticking together on the upstroke.

1. Use the theory of path dependence to explain why the inefficient QWERTY design still has a monopoly on the market for computer keyboards today.

2. A U.S. Navy study done in the 1940s indicated that the increased efficiency due to a switch from QWERTY to a keyboard with a superior key arrangement would pay for the retraining of a group of typists in ten days. If this is true, why do you think firms do not retrain their typists to use superior keyboards?

3. Suppose, for the sake of argument, that a new keyboard arrangement called BETTER, equally efficient as QWERTY, allowed computer makers to reduce energy use by 20%. BETTER would thus qualify as a clean technology. Should the government be involved in promoting a transition from QWERTY to BETTER? If it did, what steps might you recommend?

APPLICATION 18.1

Designing Subsidies

Governor Blabla has decided that, rather than build a new nuclear power plant to service power needs, the state should save an equivalent amount of energy. As one component of an efficiency plan, he has turned to you, his top aide, to design a policy to encourage adoption of compact fluorescent (CF) lightbulbs. Recall from chapter 6 that although CFs save a tremendous amount of money (and energy) over their lifetime, they are quite expensive initially ($20 or so per bulb in 1993). In addition, they give off a slightly bluer light than normal bulbs, are generally somewhat larger, and cannot be used with dimmer switches. You've thought up three possibilities:

---

[38]You may recall that in chapter 4, it was claimed that subsidies for emission reductions were a bad idea, because in the long run this would simply draw other polluters into the business. By contrast, CT subsidies are for better technologies, not for reductions in emissions.

[39]This application is based on David (1985).

Utility Rebates Have publicly regulated electric companies provide "rebates" of 75% of the purchase price to consumers who install CF bulbs. Allow utilities to cover the cost of the program through higher electricity rates.

Government Procurement Contract Have the state government agree to purchase, using general tax revenues, a large quantity of bulbs from an in-state supplier (at competitive rates). The bulbs would be used to retrofit government buildings.

R&D Subsidies Provide funds from general tax revenues to in-state firms to develop CF bulbs that can be sold at lower cost and/or are more comparable to standard incandescent bulbs. Continued receipt of such subsidies should be conditional on cost reductions or performance enhancements.

1. For each of the three plans, answer the following questions:
a. How expensive will the policy be for the state (i.e., taxpayers)?
b. What obstacles to successful implementation might arise?
c. If you had to pick one policy to push for, which would it be? Why?

Key Ideas In Each Section

18.1 This chapter focuses on government efforts to promote so-called clean technology as an alternative to regulation. Government intervention in the early stages of technology development and promotion may be justified to achieve environmental goals under a theory known as **path dependence.**

18.2 Clean technology (CT) is defined as having four components. (1) CTs are not speculative. CTs must (2) deliver services of a comparable quality and (3) do so with **long-run marginal costs** comparable to existing dirty technologies. (**Large-scale CTs** must achieve **economies of scale** before low-price production can be achieved.) Finally, CTs must (4) be environmentally superior to existing options. Determining this requires considering all major **life-cycle** impacts and addressing the **adding-up problem.**

18.3 Two general obstacles to rapid diffusion of CTs are (1) a **lack of substantial profit advantage** in the marketplace and (2) government **direct or indirect subsidies to competitors.** The lack of high profits means there is little private pull to overcome barriers such as high **sunk costs** (R&D and marketing), **thin markets, access to capital,** and **high discount rates.**

18.4 Government can help pick winners if it (1) levels the playing field. This entails removing subsidies for competitor technologies and internalizing social costs, preferably through IB regulation. (2) Focuses on environmentally superior options only. And (3) engages in **least-cost planning.** Under a least-cost approach, all subsidies are either time-limited or conditioned on cost-reducing performance.

18.5 This section discusses tools for promoting small-scale CTs. These include (1) product labeling, (2) flexible design standards, (3) utility marketing of energy efficiency, (4) technical assistance programs, and (5) consumer subsidies. Subsidy programs must be carefully designed to avoid **free riders.**

18.6 Large-scale CTs can be promoted by (1) R&D funding, (2) producer subsidies such as **price preferences** and **procurement contracts,** (3) **technology-forcing standards** like the **CAFE,** and (4) infrastructure investment.

References

A. D. Little, Inc. (1990). *Disposable Versus Reusable Diapers: Health, Environmental and Economic Comparisons.* Washington, DC: A. D. Little.

Arthur, Brian W. (1991). "Positive Feedbacks in the Economy." *Scientific American,* February, 92–99.

Berman, Daniel and John O'Connor (1996). *Who Owns the Sun?* White River Junction, VT: Chelsea Green.

Bold, Frederick (1987). "Responses to Energy Efficiency Regulations." *Energy Journal,* 8, no. 2, 111–123.

Crandall, R. and John D. Graham (1989). "The Effects of Fuel Economy Standards on Automobile Safety." *Journal of Law and Economics,* 32, no. 1, 97–118.

Crandall, R., H. K. Greunsprecht, T. E. Keeler, and L. B. Lave (1986). *Regulating the Automobile.* Washington, DC: Brookings.

Crosswhite, William M. and Carmen L. Sandretto (1991). "Trends in Resource Protection Policies in Agriculture." *Agricultural Resources: Cropland, Water and Conservation Situation and Outlook AR-23.* September. Washington, DC: U.S. Department of Agriculture.

Curtis, Jennifer (1991). *Harvest of Hope: The Potential of Alternative Agriculture to Reduce Pesticide Use.* San Francisco: Natural Resources Defense Council.

David, Paul (1985). "Clio and the Economics of QWERTY." *American Economic Review,* 75, no. 2, 332–337.

Fickett, Arnold P., Clark W. Gellings and Amory B. Lovins (1990). "Efficient Use of Electricity." In *Readings From Scientific American.* New York: W. H. Freeman.

Geller, Howard, Daniel Lashoff, Alden Meyer and Mary Beth Zimmerman (eds.) (1991). *America's Energy Choices: Investing in a Strong Economy and a Clean Environment.* Cambridge: Union of Concerned Scientists.

Greene, David (1990). "CAFE or Price?" *The Energy Journal,* 11, no. 3, 37–57.

Green Seal (1992). *Green Seal Environmental Standards.* Washington, DC: Green Seal.

Greider, William (1992). *Who Will Tell the People?* New York: Simon and Schuster.

Hafele, Wolf (1991). "Energy from Nuclear Power." *Energy for Planet Earth.* New York: W. H. Freeman.

Herman, Robin (1990). *Fusion: The Search for Endless Energy.* Cambridge: Cambridge University Press.

Hershkowitz, Allen (1990). "NRDC Diaper Letter." New York: Natural Resources Defense Council.

Hirst, Eric et al. (1982). "Household Retrofit Expenditures and the Federal Residential Energy Conservation Credit." *ORNL/CON-95.* Oak Ridge, TN: Oak Ridge National Laboratories.

Hocking, Martin B. (1991). "Paper versus Polystyrene: A Complex Choice." *Science,* vol. 251, 504–505.

Holdren, John P. (1991). "Energy in Transition." *Energy for Planet Earth.* New York: W. H. Freeman.

Jaffe, Adam B. and Robert N. Stavins (1991). "The Energy Paradox and the Diffusion of Conservation Technology." Paper presented at NBER Conference on Economics of the Environment.

Koplow, Douglas (1993). *Federal Energy Subsidies: Energy, Environmental and Fiscal Impacts.* Washington, DC: Alliance to Save Energy.

Larson, Bruce A. and Mary K. Knudson (1991). "Whose Price Wins: Institutional and Technical Change in Agriculture." *Land Economics,* 67, no. 2, 213–224.

Lehrburger, Carl, Jocelyn Mullen and C. V. Jones, (1991). *Diapers: Environmental Impacts and Lifecycle Analysis.* (Philadelphia: National Association of Diaper Services.

Lotker, M. (1991). "Barriers to Commercialization of Large-Scale Solar Electricity:

Lessons Learned from the LUZ Experience." Washington, DC: National Technical Information Service. Sandia National Laboratory.

Lovins, Amory (1977). *Soft Energy Paths: Towards a Durable Peace.* New York: Harper-Collins.

Lovins, Amory B., L. Hunter Lovins and Seth Zuckerman (1986). *Energy Unbound: A Fable for America's Future.* San Francisco: Sierra Club Books.

Lucke, Robert and Eric Toder (1987). "Assessing the U.S. Federal Tax Burden on Oil and Gas Extraction." *The Energy Journal,* 8, no. 4, 51–65.

New York State Energy Office (1992). *Hydro-Quebec Economic Study, Draft Report.* Albany: NYSEO.

New York State Energy Office (1991). *Draft New York State Energy Plan, 1991 Biennial Update.* Albany: NYSEO.

Nestor, Deborah V. (1991). "Partial Static Equilibrium Model of Newsprint Recycling." *Applied Economics,* vol. 24, 411–417.

OECD (1991). *Environmental Labelling in OECD Countries.* Paris: OECD.

Office of Technology Assessment (1991). *Beneath the Bottom Line: Agricultural Approaches to Reduce Groundwater Contamination.* Washington, DC: U.S. GPO.

Office of Technology Assessment (1989). *Facing America's Trash: What's Next for Municipal Solid Waste?* Washington, DC: U.S. GPO.

Ottinger, Richard, et al. (1990). *Environmental Costs of Electricity.* New York: Oceana.

Porter, Michael (1992). "Capital Disadvantage: America's Failing Capital Investment System." *Harvard Business Review,* September–October, 65–82.

Scherer, F. M. (1988). "Corporate Takeovers: The Efficiency Arguments." *The Journal of Economic Perspectives,* 2, no. 1, 69–82.

Smith, R. Justin and Richard A. Denison (1991). At Cross Purposes? *A Critical Examination of Green Cross's Environmental Record.* New York: Environmental Defense Fund.

Stavins, Robert N. and Adam B. Jaffe (1990). "Unintended Impacts of Public Investments on Private Decisions: The Depletion of Forested Wetlands." *American Economic Review,* vol. 80, 337–352.

Sullivan, Ronald J. (1991). "Market Barriers to Energy Efficiency Investments." *The Energy Journal,* 12, no. 3, 15–34.

Zweibel, Ken (1990). *Harnessing Solar Power: The Photovoltaics Challenge.* New York: Plenum Press.

Promoting Clean Technology: Practice

19.0 Introduction

In the previous chapter, we defined what was meant by clean technologies and looked in a general way at both the obstacles to and opportunities for their rapid diffusion. This chapter takes a detailed look at three clean technologies: waste reduction in manufacturing; less chemical-intensive, alternative agriculture; and solid waste recycling. The discussion will follow the theoretical outline in the last chapter, considering the following questions: Are these technologies really CTs? What, if any, are the market barriers to diffusion? Has government successfully promoted these technologies? Finally, have the resources devoted to promotion been adequate or excessive?

Before plunging in, however, we need to address a general point about the environmental benefits of potential CTs. The advantages of reducing waste or minimizing the use of toxic inputs can be divided into two categories: direct and indirect. For example, if a farmer finds she can cut pesticide use by 10% through more careful timing of application, the **direct environmental benefit** is less pesticide contamination of surface or ground water. The **indirect benefits** encompass all of the "upstream" effects of a reduction in pesticide production: less pollution and environmental damage at the factory, in the extraction of the petroleum needed to produce the pesticide, in the production of equipment and fuel necessary to manufacture and transport the pesticides, and so forth. Any one direct polluting activity has lurking behind it a whole web of indirect polluting activities.

Indirect pollution from consumption is quite significant. A study by Bingham et al. (1987) examined the breakdown between the direct and indirect contributions of overall personal consumption to air pollution. (See advanced topic chapter T3 for a discussion of how this can be done.) Table 19.1 illustrates their results.

For air pollutants, overall the authors find that the direct contribution from consumption is a little over 50% of the total, ranging to a low of 10% for particulates. The direct contribution of consumption to other negative externalities, water pollution, habitat destruction, scenic impacts, would certainly be lower than 50%, because con-

TABLE 19.1 Air Pollutant Discharges Due to Consumption, 1972 (10^6 mg/yr)

	Direct	*Indirect*	*Percent of Total Indirect*
Particulates	0.7	6.3	90%
Sulfur oxides	1.0	14.7	93
Nitrogen oxides	4.7	9.7	67
Hydrocarbons	10.4	8.4	44
Carbon monoxide	52.7	26.5	33
Total pollutants	69.5	65.6	48

Source: Taylor H. Bingham, Donald W. Anderson, and Phillip C. Cooley (1987), "Distribution of the Generation of Air Pollution," *Journal of Environmental Economics and Management,* vol. 14, 30–40. Used with permission.

sumers produce substantial direct air pollution via the automobile, home heating, and electricity. As a result, indirect pollution probably accounts for well over 50% of the total pollution generated in consumption.

Bingham et al. also find that total pollution in 1972 rose roughly on a one-to-one basis with increased consumption. Thus, they found that the wealthiest 10% of American families generated four to six times as much air pollution as did the poorest 10%. (At the same time, as we discussed in chapter 5, poorer families are more likely to suffer from air pollution exposure.) Much of the recent interest behind recycling and waste reduction technologies has been driven by a desire to capture these "global," indirect environmental benefits.

Indirect environmental benefits are largest for technologies that strictly *reduce* input use. Most potential clean technologies, however, involve substituting one technology for another. The substitute resources employed have their own direct and indirect environmental costs. For example, solid waste recycling requires the purchase and use of (polluting) trucks for collection and transport of materials to recycling mills, as well as (polluting) capital equipment needed to process and remanufacture the recyclables.

As a result of these greater indirect environmental costs, a **recycling** technology will generally be more polluting than a technology involving **reuse,** and a reuse technology will generally be more polluting than one that strictly **reduces** input use. For example, recycling grocery store paper bags is preferable to throwing them away, reusing them is preferable to recycling them, and not using them at all (for small loads) is preferred to both. Clean technology candidates are, thus, ranked in a general order of environmental preference by the **three R's**: *reduce, reuse, recycle.*

19.1 Waste Reduction in Manufacturing

One widely touted, but as of yet undeveloped CT, is waste reduction in manufacturing and retailing. **Waste reduction** (or **pollution prevention**) refers to cutting the generation of waste at the source, to avoid its handling, treatment, or disposal. Waste reduction does not include technologies such as recycling and incineration, which reduce the volume of waste after it is produced. Waste reduction often provides a cost advantage to firms because it involves directly reducing the use of inputs. Let us begin by considering two private-sector initiatives in waste reduction, illustrating both the potential and problems that this CT faces in the marketplace.

The acknowledged leader in waste reduction is the 3M Company. Beginning in the 1970s, 3M began a corporate campaign to reduce waste in its production processes as a way to cut costs and improve its environmental performance. Between 1977 and 1987, the company achieved a 50% reduction in its generation of hazardous waste and was shooting for an additional 30% by 1992. The company saved over $1 billion in the process.[1]

However, few major manufacturing or chemical firms followed 3M's lead until 1986. That year Congress created the annual **Toxics Release Inventory**, in which firms were required to report publicly their air, land, and waterborne emissions of 450 chemicals. In the face of public relations pressures generated by the TRI list, many big chemical firms adopted pollution prevention programs. Several companies announced numerical reduction targets on the order of 10% to 40%. By 1992, roughly 70% of the members of the Chemical Manufacturers Association had made at least a token commitment to waste reduction.

Moving from manufacturing to retailing, in the late 1980s McDonald's made a decision to pursue a similar waste reduction strategy. The company had come under public fire for its continued use of polystyrene foam "clamshells" for packaging its sandwiches. The clamshells kept sandwiches warm but, relative to a paper-based wrap, were resource-intensive in their production and took up a lot of landfill space.

McDonald's initial response was to try and collect the used clamshells and turn them into recycled plastic. However, this effort foundered on impracticality and consumer resistance. In the face of increasing public pressure, including polystyrene bans in some communities, McDonald's sought outside help. In 1990, the company signed an agreement with the Environmental Defense Fund (EDF), a nonprofit environmental group, to provide technical advice on improving the company's environmental performance. To avoid charges of a "sell-out," EDF took no money from the company.

On EDF's recommendation, McDonald's abandoned the clamshell for a quilted wrap of paper and polyethylene. (This CT had been tested in communities that had banned the clamshell.) The polystyrene industry then launched a counterattack, based on a consultant's report comparing the environmental impact of cardboard containers with polystyrene, which showed the clamshell coming out ahead. However, a fuller life-cycle analysis by the same consultants later confirmed the superiority of the wrap.

The EDF group promoted the three R's in order of priority: reduce, reuse, recycle. On the reduction front, McDonald's provided thinner straws and smaller napkins. Following the complaints of milkshake customers, straws were restored to their former size, though the smaller napkins remained. The company balked at EDF's suggestion to shift to reusable dishes, arguing this was incompatible with fast-food service. However, the company did begin shipping products like ketchup in reusable crates.

While technically not a waste reduction effort, the most significant achievement

---

[1]Office of Technology Assessment (1987); Porter (1991). For other examples of waste reduction in the private sector, see Hirschorn (1990).

the company could make would be in composting. With roughly half of its waste composed of food scraps and paper, large-scale composting for fertilizer would dramatically reduce McDonald's waste flows. The company is experimenting in this field.

What lessons can be learned about waste reduction from 3M and McDonald's? The chemical industry response to TRI suggests that substantial industrial waste reduction is economically feasible; in 3M's case it has also been shown to be cost-effective. With the help of EDF, McDonald's found that it could reduce its waste generation substantially. Overall, the Office of Technology Assessment (1987) has argued that a 10% per year reduction in hazardous waste is an achievable goal for many industries. However, both the chemical industry and McDonald's cases illustrate that waste reduction will not materialize without a major corporate commitment to developing or hiring the expertise necessary to implement the technology.

Is waste reduction a CT? From an environmental perspective, if inputs are simply reduced, then by definition, waste reduction has an edge over its competitors. If a process change generates a greater reliance, for example, on paper, then environmental gains from reduced clamshell use must be balanced against externalities associated with paper production and use.

On the cost front, private-sector waste reduction initiatives to date have been cost-effective. In addition, a handful of case studies suggest appearance of a lot of "low-hanging fruit." In an EPA-funded pilot project operating out of Colorado State and the University of Tennessee, engineering faculty and graduate students conducted waste minimization assessments of twelve medium-sized manufacturing plants. Overall, the teams recommended waste-reducing measures expected to generate cost savings of $1.28 million per year. Table 19.2 provides a breakdown of the measures for two plants, the first a paint factory and the second a factory producing oil coolers for heavy equipment.

TABLE 19.2   Waste Reduction in Two Manufacturing Plants

Plant	Problem	Recommendation	Annual Waste Reduced	Annual Savings ($1,000/yr)	Payback Period (yrs)
1	Pipe rinse water	Use foam plugs for dry wipe	1,780 gal/yr	11	0.2
1	Solvent disposal	Recycling	3,300 gal/yr	5	0.9
1	Mercury in bactericide	Use organic substitute	3,100 gal/yr	6	0.0
2	Vapors from degreaser	Install cover or use ultrasonic cleaning	50% 99%	17 20	0.0 2.4
2	Recycling contaminants	Reduce lubricants	20%	1	0.3
2	Sludge from salt baths	Use mechanical method or use vacuum method	4% 80%	20 203	2.1 3.5
2	Paint-contaminated cardboard	Reduce paint loss with air jets	22%	4	0.6
2	Paint-contaminated filters	Electrostatic spray control	36%	11	1.2

Source: William F. Kirsch and Gwen P. Looby (1990). "Waste Minimization Assessment Centers," in *The Environmental Challenge of the 1990s: Proceedings of the International Conference on Pollution Prevention* (Washington, DC: U.S. EPA), Tables 2 and 3.

The engineering teams' recommendations ranged from simple "housekeeping" measures, such as putting a lid on a degreasing tank, to more complex process innovations, such as switching from a solvent-based to a vacuum cleaning method. For the two plants, waste reduction ranged from 4% to 99%, while the average payback period was well under one year. The biggest waste reducers also generate the largest annual savings—for example, using ultrasonic degreasing in plant 2. And in spite of the fact that such measures have the longest payback periods, they are probably the most profitable investments due to the large cost savings. The evident cost-effectiveness of these pilot projects in Colorado and Tennessee have been supported by other case studies.[2]

Having established that waste reduction is indeed a CT, are market forces sufficient to drive major private-sector initiatives in waste reduction? Judging from the limited data available, the answer is probably not. While companies have indeed aggressively reduced emissions found on the Toxics Release Inventory, most of these reductions have come through end-of-the-pipe treatment, recycling, or energy recovery, rather than waste reduction (Davies and Mazurek [1997]). In a recent report, the EPA identified twenty-four companies with ongoing waste reduction programs at the corporate level. While the report stresses that the list is by no means complete, it suggests that private-sector involvement in waste reduction is still at an early stage and primarily confined to large manufacturing companies.[3]

Why the slow private-sector response? First, such efforts do not provide much of a marketing edge. While McDonald's originally undertook the initiative under the threat of consumer pressure, in spite of its highly publicized efforts, none of its major competitors have announced similar programs. The anecdotal evidence of waste reduction efforts available suggest that the handful of industrial companies with a serious commitment to waste reduction, like 3M, also appear to be exceptions that prove the rule.

On the other hand, waste disposal costs are rising, thanks in large measure to citizen protests over the citing of waste facilities, the NIMBY phenomenon discussed in Chapter 5. Lois Gibbs, a former resident of Love Canal (the community hit by the chemical dumping incident discussed in chapter 13), has in fact expressed increasing the cost of disposal as a goal of the grassroots environmental movement: "Our overall strategy is to plug up the toilet. If we can stop unsafe facilities from being built, the waste will back up on the corporation's own property, the few remaining waste dumps will charge an arm and a leg, and since all they know is profit and loss, they'll stop producing wastes or reclaim them."[4]

Yet not all the toilets are stopped up. A government study suggests that rather than waste reduction, a more likely private-sector response to rising off-site disposal costs will be on-site incineration, noncompliance, or illegal dumping. Waste reduction, as is common with CTs, simply does not have enough of a cost advantage over its competitors to redirect corporate thinking away from traditional proven approaches, with known risks. To underscore this point, although McDonald's paper-based wrap is

---

[2]See, for example, Richardson (1990) and Bridges (1990). For details on industry programs at twenty-nine chemical plants, see Dorfman et al. (1991).
[3]U.S. EPA (1991a).
[4]"Earth Image 1990," *In These Times,* April 18, 1990.

cheaper to buy and dispose of than the clamshell (it takes up about one-tenth the space in landfills), as of 1992 the company had made the switch in only a few of its major markets outside of the United States.

Within the waste reduction field, one can identify both large- and small-scale technologies. Small-scale approaches include "reducing wastewater from cleaning operations involving toxic chemicals, covering vessels containing volatile chemicals, improving inventory controls to eliminate outdated chemicals that become hazardous waste, reusing off-specification products, and replacing water or solvent cleaning of equipment with other methods."[5] Exploiting these housekeeping or commonsense opportunities nevertheless requires technical expertise.

On the other hand, adoption of a large-scale waste reduction strategy requires a substantial up-front expense, including a commitment to hiring a waste auditing firm, and researching and implementing subsequent changes in production processes. For example, a jewelry company in North Providence, Rhode Island, hired a consulting firm to design and install an untested water recycling system to prevent the discharge of heavy metals into Narragansett Bay. The risk of recycling lay in the possibility of contamination problems, leading to a poor product quality. In this case, the problems did not materialize, and the firm saved money through reduced water use, water quality monitoring, and regulatory expense.[6]

While experiences like those at the jewelry firm suggest that waste reduction investments can be profitable, such an undertaking is risky. And particularly for small businesses, pollution prevention must compete for capital with more traditional investments in plant and equipment, product development, and sales.

The market has thus been slow to adopt waste reduction for the reasons identified in the last chapter: lack of a profit advantage large enough to overcome the barriers of poor information and limited capital resources. In addition, corporate environmental managers have limited flexibility to experiment with waste reduction and still remain in compliance with existing regulations.[7]

Given the slow rate of market adoption, what is the role for government in promoting this CT? Hirschorn (1990) suggests many of the policy options discussed in the last chapter, including information collection and distribution, on-site technical assistance, tax credits and small business loans, support for R&D, and technology-forcing standards.

Of these options, information distribution and technical assistance are the route that the federal government has pursued to date. The EPA's Division of Pollution Prevention operates an information clearinghouse, describing waste reduction technologies introduced by firms across the country. In addition, between 1989 and 1992, the agency dispersed roughly $25 million in matching grants to state governments for technical assistance to help firms reduce waste. State agencies are essentially offering on a broader scale the services that EDF provided to McDonald's.

The EPA's most ambitious pollution prevention effort, launched in 1991, was called the 33/50 program. EPA attempted to focus industry attention on waste reduc-

---

[5]Hirschorn (1990).

[6]Uva (1989).

[7]See Hirschorn (1990) for a more detailed discussion.

tion, by seeking voluntary reductions of emissions of 17 priority chemicals from the 1988 TRI baseline emissions of 1.46 billion pounds. The program goal was 33% reduction by 1992 and 50% reduction by 1995, which explains the program title. EPA provided technical assistance and recognition to program participants.

By 1994 the 50% goal had in fact been met, with program participants reducing about 19% more than those not in the program. Given the voluntary nature of the program, the size and speed of the reduction suggests that chemical emission reduction has indeed been relatively cheap. However, most of the reduction did not come from source reduction, but rather from end-of-the-pipe and other more conventional means. Yet, program participants did reduce their production-related waste slightly, while nonprogram participants increased their waste by 9%—indicating the program had some impact on waste reduction (Davies and Mazurek [1997]).

Beyond the carrot of technical assistance and voluntary initiatives to encourage waste reduction, many states have been using a stick of mandatory waste reduction plans. Such legislation's intent is presumably to focus industry's attention on economically attractive investments in waste reduction. However, the measures may do little to confront the underlying problems of poor information, risk, and access to capital. As Levin (1990) puts it: "mandatory waste management plans turn on companies' good-faith execution of waste management audits, could promote risky substitutes because they cover only a small segment of the hazardous waste universe, and seem likely to generate a flood of paperwork seldom reviewed."

Levin (1991) goes on to suggest an IB approach to forcing waste reduction: The EPA could issue tradeable permits to landfills (solid or hazardous waste) that mandate a 2% reduction in volume received each year for ten years, over and above a 25% recycling goal. Municipalities or private operators exceeding the 2% goal could sell their additional permits to areas having difficulty achieving source reductions. Funds raised from permit sales could then be used to fund further reductions through more aggressive recycling or waste reduction efforts.

Such an approach would avoid much of the "wasted energy" likely to be expended in developing waste reduction plans. However, in the absence of federal action, states have been moving ahead with requiring such plans. The EPA also has begun requiring environmental audits as part of its enforcement and compliance efforts.[8] This kind of targeted effort seems likely to have a higher payoff.

Waste reduction efforts in the manufacturing and retail sectors show substantial promise but are only just getting underway. By contrast, as the next section illustrates, waste reduction CTs in the agricultural sector have received attention on and off for many years and have recently gathered greater support at the federal level.

19.2 Alternative Agriculture and Pesticides

Farming interest in clean technology has arisen in response to the heavy reliance of modern agriculture on petrochemical pesticides, herbicides, and fertilizers, as well as production methods that promote soil erosion. Beginning in the 1940s, American agriculture experienced a technological revolution based on mechanization, petrochemi-

---

[8]U.S. EPA (1991b).

cal inputs, and genetically engineered high-yielding seed varieties. These new technologies yielded impressive productivity gains: Between 1950 and 1980, U.S. crop production doubled, while cultivated land increased only 5% and the number of farmworkers fell by 63%. The success of these new technologies led to the abandonment of traditional methods of weed and pest control, and husbanding of soil fertility, as farmers boosted yields by planting the same crop "fence-row to fence-row," year after year.

However, these productivity gains have leveled off over the last decade and have left some farmers in an increasingly difficult position. On the economic front, dependence on off-farm resources has increased dramatically, requiring farmers to resort more heavily to credit. Hence, smaller farms, with higher cost access to capital, are at a disadvantage. In addition, loss of soil fertility and increasing pesticide resistance sometimes require larger and larger doses of fertilizer and pesticide to maintain yields.

In the environmental arena, farm communities themselves are the most vulnerable to environmental hazards—nitrate pollution from fertilizer in groundwater, and pesticide exposure in water supplies or on the farm. A 1992 National Cancer Institute Study report found that farm cancer rates were substantially above the national average. Although no official explanation for the results were given, one of the authors speculated that pesticide use was primarily responsible.[9] Curtis (1991) provides an estimate that 130,000 rural Iowa residents drink well water that exceeds EPA's legal standard for nitrates, while 5,400 residents in rural Iowa are consuming drinking water with pesticide levels above EPA's advisory standards. An additional 90,000 are estimated to be exposed to pesticide at levels below the EPA threshold.

In the face of these problems, farmers have increasingly been experimenting with waste reduction technologies. CTs in agriculture stress biological methods of promoting soil fertility and reducing pests and disease. These include crop rotation to disrupt pest cycles, biological and mechanical weed control and fertilization, reducing pesticide use through scouting, use of resistant species, use of natural predators, and control over planting time. While building on traditional methods, the techniques are thoroughly modern, often computer-assisted, and management-intensive. Collectively known as "low-input," "sustainable," or simply **alternative agriculture,** these techniques all share a reduced reliance on chemical fertilizers and pesticides.[10]

A review of current pesticide regulation will suggest why promoting alternative agriculture is viewed by some as an attractive supplement to regulation. Each year, American farmworkers, landscapers, and homeowners apply around one billion pounds of pesticides to crops, fields, lawns, and gardens. Specifically designed to be toxic to insects and other pests, these chemicals unfortunately affect the broader environment as well. Pesticides show up as residue in foods, harm wildlife, contaminate groundwater, and are a significant non-point source of surface water pollution in the United States today.

---

[9]"Farmers May Be Getting Cancer from Pesticides," Associated Press story reported in Spokane *Spokesman-Review*, September 23, 1992. The potential of alternative agriculture to reduce nitrate pollution is unclear, because nitrates also occur in manure. See Crosson and Ekey (1988) and Curtis (1991).

[10]For a further discussion, see National Research Council (1989).

PESTICIDE RESIDUES ON FOOD

Around 300 different pesticides are used on food in the United States. Of these, at least 63 are classified by the EPA as probable or possible human carcinogens. Others are known to be reproductive toxins. Still others are suspected to have a negative impact on human and animal immune systems. In addition, another 200 or so pesticides are widely used in other parts of the world. Developing countries still employ pesticides, such as DDT, which were banned for use in this country in the early 1970s; lack of clean water and sanitation compounds the impact of pesticide exposure abroad.[11]

In 1987 the EPA estimated, with substantial uncertainty, the number of U.S. cancer deaths from pesticide food residue at about 3,000 per year, with an additional 250 arising from pesticide application and other exposure. In addition, occasional news reports of acute pesticide poisonings make food safety one of the public's primary environmental concerns. In its 1987 report, EPA ranked pesticides in food as one of the nation's most serious environmental problems. In a 1990 update, however, the agency had backed off from this characterization. Although pesticide residue exposure was still considered a potentially serious health problem due to the numbers exposed, the agency viewed data on its effect to be insufficiently "robust" to draw any firm conclusions.[12]

One should not conclude from this information that eating fresh fruits and vegetables is, on balance, bad for you. Even while recognizing the risk from pesticide residues in food, a report by the National Academy of Sciences study urged greater consumption of these products. In fact, health risks from other dietary sources—primarily fat and cholesterol—are much greater than the risks from pesticide residue in food. However, this does not mean that fruits and vegetables should not necessarily be made safer.

As was discussed in chapter 13, pesticides are currently regulated under the Federal Insecticide, Fungicide and Rodenticide Act (FIFRA). In theory, consumers are further protected by a safety standard; the EPA is directed to establish "tolerances" for pesticide residues on food designed to eliminate significant health risks.[13] The Food and Drug Administration (FDA) has the responsibility for testing and enforcing these tolerances for fruits, grains, vegetables, and animal feed.[14]

However, as suggested by the EPA's 1987 ranking, the process is not working as planned. One possible reason relates to the tolerance levels. Prior to 1996, critics charged that the EPA's tolerances often reflected outdated or inadequate scientific information on health risks, were based on outdated consumption habits (Americans have been eating more fresh fruits and vegetables lately), and did not adequately protect children, who consume proportionately more food than adults. On the other hand, industry scientists have criticized the tolerances set for raw crops as being unrealistically strict, since pesticide residues are often, but not always, reduced during pro-

---

[11]Repetto and Baliga (1996) detail the health risks from pesticides and focus on the problem in developing countries.

[12]Cancer cases, as well as the ranking, are from U.S. EPA (1987). See also U.S. EPA (1990).

[13]The standards are based on animal studies. Prior to 1996, the EPA commonly used a 1 in 1 million standard for carcinogens and a "no observable effects" standard for neurotoxicity and reproductive effects (Moore [1989]). However, according to Hathaway (1991) the 1 in 1 million standard was sometimes waived. In 1996, the Congress passed the Food Quality Protection Act, which mandated a single minimum standard. However, it also allowed pesticide benefits to be considered when setting tolerance levels for carcinogenic effects.

[14]The USDA enforces tolerances for meat, poultry, and eggs.

cessing, food preparation, and cooking. Some of these concerns were addressed by Congress in the 1996 Food Quality Protection Act.[15]

In addition, FDA's monitoring and enforcement efforts have been criticized as inadequate. FDA necessarily monitors only a small fraction of the nation's food supply. In 1989, less than 1% of the food sampled had pesticide residues in excess of legal limits; 61% had no detectable pesticides.[16] However, due to slow processing of test results, food with illegal residues is often consumed before the FDA can seize it. A government review of the program found that in 60% of the cases in which domestic food contained illegal residues, the sale of food was not prevented. In no case were penalties levied by FDA against growers.[17] Thus, it appears that the FDA does not compensate for its low-monitoring rate with certain and harsh penalties. The monitoring-penalty trade-off discussed in chapter 15 is not being used here. Again, in response to these problems, enforcement penalties were beefed up by Congress in 1996.

Perhaps more significantly, as of the late 1980s, the methods that FDA used to screen food could detect only 41% of the 496 pesticides potentially used on food. Of the 81 pesticides identified by FDA as requiring high-priority monitoring, 33 could not be identified by routine surveillance methods.[18]

PESTICIDES IN GROUNDWATER

While consumers, in theory, are shielded from pesticide exposure by a safety standard, farmworkers, homeowners, surface and groundwater, and wildlife are protected, again, on paper, by a looser efficiency standard. **Groundwater** protection is an important concern, since around 75 million Americans rely on this source for drinking water. Manufacturers of pesticides containing new active ingredients are required to submit test data demonstrating that their product does not impose an "unreasonable risk"; that is, that the benefits to manufacturers, growers, and consumers outweigh the health risk to people and the environment.[19]

However, as noted in chapter 13, the EPA's benefit-cost studies for new pesticides, or old ones that have been challenged, are generally of poor quality, and decision making is subject to political influence. Another aspect of the benefits estimation process has been criticized by the National Research Council (1989). EPA neglects to assess the potential for the use of nonchemical alternatives. The standard practice in a special review is to select the second most commonly used pesticide as the fallback technology, although a variety of CTs already in use may be more profitable. For example, in the alachlor case, the EPA assumed metalachlor was the likely substitute; this compound is both more expensive and is also somewhat toxic to corn. Yet, in the face of cancellation, some farmers would be likely to adopt CT methods, which in at least one Iowa demonstration generated better yields for corn and soybean than the state average. By neglecting CTs, the benefits process tends to overstate pesticide benefits.[20]

---

[15]See Mott and Snyder (1987), Whyatt and Nicholson (1991), and McCarthy (1991).
[16]Carneval et al. (1991).
[17]U.S. GAO (1986).
[18]Taylor (1988).
[19]Mott and Snyder (1987: 136) note that in the case of one private laboratory, studies supporting the registration of over 200 pesticides were later found to be poorly done and in some cases fraudulent.
[20]See Shistar et al. (1992); National Research Council (1989: 218).

Finally, several hundred pesticides were registered many years before current scientific and legal standards were established. For these old chemicals, the EPA was directed in 1972 to begin a reregistration process. For a variety of reasons, including lack of funding, the agency had taken no action on reregistration by 1988. That year Congress amended FIFRA, directing the agency to complete the task within nine years.[21] The grandfathering of pesticides also generated a new source bias: The EPA has denied registrations for some new pesticides safer than older pesticides in current use.[22]

Beyond the registration process, pesticide levels in groundwater are subject to either legally binding maximum standards under the Safe Drinking Water Act (SDWA) or advisory standards under the Federal Insecticide, Fungicide and Rodenticide Act. However, these statutes provide little additional protection. The EPA has yet to set standards for many pesticides under the SDWA, and violations typically require public notification, not remediation. Under FIFRA, the EPA has handled violations on a case-by-case basis as they have been uncovered. However, groundwater monitoring for pesticide contamination is quite limited. Thus, those exposed to pesticide contamination from drinking water are generally not aware of it.

The pesticide issue reflects many of the problems of end-of-the-pipe regulation that have led to increasing frustration with the regulatory system. First, the informational requirements are daunting. Registering a new pesticide is currently an expensive process, costing in 1985 from $5 million to $7 million and taking from one to five years.[23] Outside of pharmaceutical drugs, pesticide registration imposes the most comprehensive scientific reporting requirements on manufacturers of any new product.

Second, in spite of these efforts, setting a safety standard remains difficult because of remaining substantial data gaps. These in turn arise from the potential multiple avenues of toxicity represented by each new pesticide. An efficiency standard, theoretically required in the registration process, introduces the further complications of monetizing improvements in health and environmental quality, as well as pesticide benefits, of uncertain magnitude. In part because the informational requirements are so burdensome, and in spite of a clear legislative mandate requiring a risk-benefit balancing for initial registration, this process has been adopted only for special review. Even here, political factors weigh in as heavily as does the benefit-cost analysis.

Finally, once the standards have been set, enforcement is impeded by the inability to monitor pesticide levels adequately in a timely fashion. Technical obstacles arise in tracking pesticide residues on food, and widespread groundwater monitoring is prohibitively expensive. In addition, as we have seen elsewhere, regulators have evidenced a reluctance to punish violators.

Given the multiple uncertainties, environmentalists and industry are locked into a never-ending and costly battle over the evaluation of risks and exposure, the registration of new pesticides and the reregistration of old ones, and the degree to which pesticide laws will in fact be enforced. The National Agricultural Chemicals Association, for example, has a $7 million annual budget, while the Agricultural Council of Amer-

---

[21]Ironically, the EPA's recent commitment of resources to the reregistration of old pesticides has stalled the registration of new, biologically based pest control methods. See Curtis (1991).
[22]Benbrook (1991).
[23]Shapiro (1990).

ica launched a $50 million effort in 1989 to "restore public confidence in the safety of the food supply."[24] Citizens, and many farmers and farmworkers, meanwhile, continue to feel that the protection of food and water is inadequate. In response, Congress passed new legislation in 1996.[25]

However, even if the reforms succeed, pesticides will remain difficult to regulate for two primary reasons. First, in spite of increased toxicological information, risk assessments will remain poor due to **imperfect information.** Second, the **non-point source** nature of the pollutant imposes a costly burden on regulators seeking to monitor and enforce regulations.

THE CLEAN TECHNOLOGY APPROACH

The first step in the clean technology approach to the pesticide problem, and related problems of chemical fertilizer pollution as well as soil erosion, is to ask, are there alternatives? The answer appears to be yes. Over a decade of documented field experience suggests that farmers can successfully reduce pesticide use and still remain profitable. While adoption of alternative agricultural methods may reduce yields (though it need not), it also reduces costs. The cost reduction is generally sufficient to offset any lost production.[26]

Indeed, Cowan and Gunby (1996) specifically invoke the theory of path dependence to explain how different areas chose between chemical-intensive agriculture and cost-competitive alternative methods beginning in the 1940s. They argue that alternative agriculture has several sources of increasing returns, or positive feedback mechanisms: Biological pest control has high fixed costs associated with machinery and predator rearing; farmers experience substantial "learning-by-doing"; and farmers also depend on "network externalities"—information gained from fellow farmers and extension agents. Finally, if neighboring farmers are spraying pesticides, this will also kill off natural predators.

These factors make it hard for individual farmers to adapt alternative technologies if their neighbors are not also doing so, while chemical pesticide use faced no such hurdles. However, the Israeli citrus industry was one region that stuck with, and thrived on, biological pest controls. And in Texas, growers successfully shifted back to alternative pest control methods after cotton developed insecticide resistance in the late 1960s. In both cases, government infrastructure and legislative support were critical. The Mexican cotton industry, with no comparable support to that in Texas, simply died out after chemical controls failed.

In addition to being cost-competitive in the long run, alternative farming is generally a CT; that is, environmentally superior to conventional agriculture. Critics have

[24]Shistar et al. (1992).

[25]For a pre-1996 discussion, see Malloy et al. (1991), and Shapiro (1990). Gianessi et al. (1989) find that limited bans of pesticides in areas where groundwater contamination is likely, or pollution taxes, are preferable from a cost point of view to EPA's general policy of a total ban. The new law is described in "Highlights of the Food Quality Act of 1996," on the Web at www//epa.gov/.

[26]For an annotated bibliography on this issue, see Morris et al. (1992). See also National Research Council (1989). Crosson and Ekey (1988) conclude that "organic" agriculture, a subset of alternative agriculture, is not as profitable as conventional agriculture, primarily because crop rotation requires keeping considerable acreage in low-value crops. However, the authors still conclude that environmental benefits from alternative agriculture deserve its promotion by the USDA.

pointed out, however, that some of the practices that fall under the alternative heading may, on occasion, lead to greater environmental hazards. For example, Gianessi (1991) notes that scouting for pests on peanut crops in Alabama led to increased fungicide use, as previously undiscovered problems were found. In addition, organic growers use large quantities of sulfur, a naturally occurring compound, to control diseases on grapes. Yet, little is known about the potential impact of exposure to sulfur residues. Thus, some care must be taken in promoting alternative agriculture as a cure to the pesticide problem.

What degree of protection of environmental protection do CTs offer? A recent study by the Natural Resources Defense Council examined twelve crops grown in California and Iowa. Based on techniques currently being employed in alternative agriculture, NRDC estimated that potential pesticide reductions for these crops ranged from 25% to 80%.[27]

Having argued that alternative agriculture is a CT based on our definition in the previous chapter, what obstacles stand in the way of its widespread adoption? The primary barrier is a low-profit advantage coupled with substantial **adjustment costs.**

A successful transition from conventional chemical-intensive farming is a complex and risky undertaking for an individual farmer. To begin with, farmers need to invest substantial resources in learning new techniques. In addition, successful techniques are highly region-specific. Finally, a period of two or three years may be necessary to convert a field worked with conventional methods into a productive alternative field.[28] These factors mean that a substantial up-front investment is necessary to redirect a farm onto an alternate path. And while such a farm may experience comparable profitability to a chemical-intensive one, in the highly competitive agricultural field, it is unlikely to be substantially more profitable.

The "organic" label lends only a small advantage. The industry has largely been restricted to specialty health-food stores. A few supermarket chains have begun testing their produce and advertising it as "pesticide free." However, this "green marketing" movement is as yet minor, possibly due to consumer distrust of the retailers' claims. Perhaps more significantly, the *Wall Street Journal* reports that the large food-processing firms who control most supermarket shelf space are not yet interested in organic products. "Big Foods fear [is] that launching a no-chemical brand would prompt consumers to look askance at their conventional brands, whose ingredients are grown with everything from synthetic fertilizer to antibiotics."[29]

Alternative agriculture illustrates perfectly the CT dilemma. On the one hand, we appear to have available a technology capable of holding its own in the market, once adjustment costs have been overcome, with clear environmental benefit. On the other, adoption of the technology is slow due primarily to lack of a profit advantage sufficient to overcome costs associated with a transition. What is to be done?

Following our outline in the last chapter, the first step is to identify the agricultural CTs with clear environmental benefits and those with the greatest cost advan-

---

[27]Curtis (1991).

[28]Reganald et al. (1990); Cowan and Gunby (1996).

[29]"Major Companies in the Food industry Have Little Taste for Organic Products," *Wall Street Journal,* January 10, 1992.

tage. On the environmental front, this suggests a focus on reducing chemical pesticide use overall through a switch to biological and mechanical methods, and argues against an approach relying principally on substituting pesticides currently thought to be less dangerous for those currently thought to be more dangerous. On the cost front, given the complexity of the transition, it suggests a go slow approach: Avoid a crash program urging farmers to go 100% organic.

The second part of a CT strategy is to attack inappropriate subsidies and begin to internalize environmental costs, preferably through IB regulation. As was discussed in the last chapter, price supports for chemical-intensive crops have been an important obstacle to the spread of CTs. Access to water subsidies also has encouraged pollution-intensive agriculture, since agricultural chemicals and water tend to be complements in production. The farm sector also has traditionally been subject to very light environmental regulation of the CAC variety.[30]

The third component is to promote CTs directly. Here, agriculture is unique among American businesses in that the government already is deeply involved in the pace and direction of technological change in the industry. Because farming is highly competitive and, thus, a low-profit industry, government has traditionally financed much of the research and development in the field. In addition to this R&D function, the government has also taken a leading role in disseminating information about new techniques through the state-funded agricultural colleges and agricultural extension services.

However, the agrichemical industries have become increasingly important players in the research and development field, as well as in technical assistance. For obvious reasons, these companies tend not to fund research into less chemical-intensive farming. At the same time, academic agricultural researchers must be sensitive to corporate needs since the probability of getting federal funding for any given project is quite low. Cropper et al. (1991) conclude that academic researchers who comment during special reviews of pesticides tend to support the industry position.

In addition to agrichemical influence in research, in recent years the government's extension service has focused less and less on on-farm assistance, and more on laboratory research and teaching. Many farmers receive the bulk of their information about farming techniques from fertilizer and pesticide dealers.[31]

Hence, a sensible CT strategy would be first to increase government R&D funding for region-specific strategies to reduce pesticide use. The second step would be to increase the budget for technical assistance, to promote the diffusion of these technologies. Increases in these funds could be financed either through reductions in research on conventional farming techniques, which the private sector now covers adequately, or by modest taxes on agricultural chemicals.

Because of the diverse nature of the possible CT options, direct subsidy programs, such as tax credits or loans to encourage a transition, would be hard to implement without facing a large windfall problem, or actual fraud. However, grants could be channeled to private farmers' groups seeking to do their own CT extension work. In the absence of significant government effort, such groups now provide a primary in-

---

[30]See Larson and Knudson (1991).

[31]Curtis (1991), Office of Technology Assessment (1991).

formation source for farmers seeking to reduce chemical inputs. In addition, the relative profitability of CTs can be boosted by revising subsidy policies. Crop rotation and natural fertilization methods should not be penalized, and water subsidies should be reduced.[32]

Recent federal legislation includes some movement on all the fronts just identified. However, the government has by no means adopted a CT approach wholeheartedly. R&D funding for on-farm research into alternative agriculture remains at less than 2% of the Department of Agriculture's research and development budget, and extension services in alternate alternative agriculture have not been expanded. Subsidy policies are changing slowly—one interesting reform has been to condition crop subsidies on the adoption of so-called conservation tillage measures (see Application 19.0). Finally, the EPA's focus remains on pesticide regulation. Overall, the percentage of acreage treated with herbicides and insecticides showed little, if any, downward movement in the 1980s, although there may have been some reduction in the volume of chemical use due to greater targeting.[33]

Given the lack of federal pesticide protection for groundwater resources noted above, state governments have been attempting to fill in the gap. Two contrasting experiments are worth noting. California has opted for a regulatory strategy, in 1985 passing the Pesticide Contamination Prevention Act. The act requires a state agency to identify pesticides liable to leach into groundwater and to monitor for their presence. Critics have charged that the act, while tough on paper, has been difficult to implement effectively, for the reasons discussed above. By 1992, the state was monitoring for only a single pesticide.[34]

On the other hand, Iowa has been most aggressive in implementing a CT approach to protect groundwater. Rather than opt for further regulation, since 1987 the state has funded public research and education centers through taxes levied on commercial fertilizers, pesticides, hazardous household materials, and landfills. The Office of Technology Assistance (1991: 215) provides the following description of one aspect of Iowa's program:

> The Butler County Integrated Crop Management Project . . . provides cost-share assistance to 50 farmer-cooperators for implementing agrichemical related [reforms]. . . . In the first year, farmers are provided with services free-of-charge by six field scouts trained by the Cooperative Extension Service. The farmer-cooperators are expected to pay $1.50 and $3.00 per acre

---

[32]Office of Technology Assessment (1991) and Curtis (1991) provide a more comprehensive discussion of policies to promote alternative agriculture. Both focus additional attention on Federal Agricultural Marketing Boards, which enforce cosmetic grading standards for fruits and vegetables destined for "fresh markets." Economists have long been critical of these standards as barriers to entry. See, for example, Salant and Goodstein (1990).

[33]See Curtis (1991) for a review of current policy. According to O'Conell (1991), $11 million was devoted to whole-farm research in alternative agriculture, while an additional $83 million was spent on research related to components of alternative agriculture. Given the systems nature of alternative approaches, the National Research Council (1989) stresses that the former have much greater utility for promoting a transition to CTs. Finally, USDA (1991a: 87) shows an encouraging drop in insecticide use on corn, matched, however, by increased use on cotton from 1986 to 1990. Overall herbicide use was essentially unchanged over the period. Gianessi (1991) reports on reduction in herbicide volumes.

[34]Curtis (1991).

for scout services in the second and third years, respectively, and then take over full payment for scout services when the project is over. In 1989, the total cost of the services was estimated at $4.50 per acre, with farmers saving about $20 per acre in agrichemical costs. That year, the 50 cooperators reduced nitrogen applications by about 26,000 pounds and improved their net income by a total of $500,000. One farmer-cooperator reported avoiding a loss of $42,000 due to timely treatment of cutworms, while another saved $15,000 in additional fertilizer costs when soil tests showed that he did not have to add phosphorus and potassium.

This kind of cost-effective technical assistance should form the heart of a governmental effort to promote CTs in agriculture.

19.3 Recycling Solid Waste

In contrast to waste reduction in manufacturing and agriculture, the CT of recycling solid waste has recently received widespread governmental promotion. The number of curbside collection programs grew from 600 in 1989 to over 7,200 in 1994, serving 40% of U.S. households;[35] the EPA set an official goal of 25% recycling of solid waste by 1992; and the 1990 Federal Pollution Prevention Act declares that recycling is to have precedence over waste disposal as a matter of national policy. In spite of these efforts, however, recycling still often receives less governmental assistance than its principal competitor—incineration.

Americans generate over 195 million tons of garbage each year. Depending upon your perspective, that is (1) enough garbage to fill a fleet of trucks stretching half of the way to the moon, or alternatively, (2) garbage that can be landfilled in a space equivalent to less than .00001% of the continental United States (but preferably not in my backyard). On a per person basis, it works out to around three quarters of a ton, twice as much per capita as many European countries. The per capita rate has also been rising, in the 1980s at 1.8% per year.[36]

Figure 19.1 illustrates the composition of the nation's garbage.[37] Newspapers and telephone books are the biggest items in the household garbage bag. Plastics pose more of a relative disposal problem than suggested by the table, since they take up 20% by volume of the nation's landfill space.

Although the extent of recycling is difficult to measure, in the early 1990s U.S. citizens recycled or composted around 21% of our household waste, up from around 5%

---

[35]"As Recycling Surges, Market for Materials Is Slow to Develop," *Wall Street Journal,* January 17, 1992; and "The State of Garbage in America," *Biocycle,* April–May 1996. Long-run average costs per ton for recycling fall as the volume of waste processed increases. One of the sources of scale economies in recycling is in collection—denser collection routes mean that per ton collection costs fall. This is one of the reasons that cost-effective curbside recycling programs are often mandatory and at the least require marketing efforts to insure high-participation rates. However, incineration can be as "mandatory" as recycling—communities with incinerators often have flow control ordinances to insure that the incinerators receive enough waste to operate at close to capacity.

[36]This is down from the 1970s per capita rate increase of 2.3%. Data are from Franklin and Franklin (1992). Both the "alarmist" and "don't worry" characterizations of the solid waste problem appeared in *The EPA Journal.* See "A Strategy to Control the Garbage Glut," and "Will the U.S. Recycling Approach Work?" July–August 1992.

[37]Office of Technology Assessment (1989).

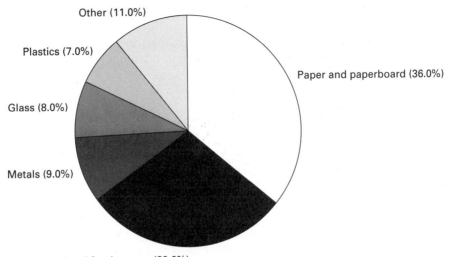

FIGURE 19.1 Composition of Municipal Solid Waste, Estimated by Weight

Source: Office of Technology Assessment (1989).

to 7% in 1970 (Ackerman [1996]). Incineration accounted for an additional 10% to 15%, while the remaining garbage was landfilled.

Both recycling and incineration have seen rapid growth in their share of waste management over the last twenty years, as landfill costs rose under increasingly tight regulation and as citizen opposition to the siting of new landfills escalated. Tipping fees at landfills have risen from around $5 per ton in the early 1970s, to anywhere from $30 to well over $100 per ton today. The dramatic price rise leveled off in the early 1990s, under the impact of increased recycling and incineration, the opening of several large new landfills, and the economic recession.[38]

Through the early 1990s incineration remained a preferred option among government waste management officials. A 1989 survey of 18 midwestern and northeastern states found planned expenditure through 1995 on incineration of around $7 billion, as compared to less than $1 billion on recycling.[39] Incineration was favored by government policies throughout the 1970s and 1980s because of one of its by-products— energy. Around 120 of the 170 or so incinerators in operation are waste-to-energy facilities, although collectively they account for only a small portion of the nation's electricity supply, around one tenth of one percent.[40] Incinerators have received a variety of subsidies, ranging from purchase guarantees for their electric power at above market rates, to tax-free municipal financing, to governmental land grants. In addition, as discussed in chapter 17, the failure of municipalities to use **unit pricing**—charging for garbage by-the-bag—subsidizes large garbage producers and promotes disposal over recycling.

---

[38]"Economics of Trash Shift as Cities learn Dumps Aren't So Full," *Wall Street Journal,* June 2, 1992.
[39]A Northeast-Midwest Institute survey, cited in Denison and Ruston (1990).
[40]Based on figures in Office of Technology Assessment (1989).

Beyond government subsidies, Denison and Ruston (1990) attribute the continuing enthusiasm for incineration on the part of waste management professionals and local officials to the option's "prepackaged" nature. Incinerator vendors have considerable financial and service expertise, and offer municipalities a familiar waste disposal method. Prepackaged options for recycling are only beginning to develop; the nation's two big waste management firms entered the recycling industry in the mid- to late 1980s, and have not yet made a lot of money off of recycling services. With high prices, profits in landfilling and incineration have been much higher.[41]

In spite of continued interest in incineration, recycling has made substantial headway in recent years. Recycling has always been supported by environmentalists but has been boosted tremendously by the rising costs of alternative options. Incinerator costs have risen for identical reasons to those of landfills: increased regulation and citizen opposition to facility siting. A survey of twelve incinerators by Clarke et al. (1991) found tipping fees in the late 1980s ranging as high as $100 per ton for materials requiring special handling, and averaging about $30. At least thirty planned or proposed incineration facilities were canceled or postponed in the latter half of the 1980s, while two new facilities surveyed in a government study reported expected tipping fees of $75 to $80 per ton.[42] In response to these rising costs, as well as citizen concern over resource waste, local governments across the country have been adopting recycling programs.

Solid waste recycling yields two types of environmental benefits. The most obvious is a **direct benefit:** cleaner waste disposal. Since recycled products are not sent to landfills or incinerators, they do not pose environmental problems in the disposal process. Recall that environmental hazards from state-of-the-art landfills are not as great as from many other pollution sources, primarily because the only significant exposure route is local, via groundwater. Nevertheless, hazards from leachate do exist.

New incinerators, although generally complying with most air pollution regulations, still generate residual hazards from regulated pollutants, as well as some that are still unregulated.[43] Incinerator ash must be disposed of. If this is done via landfilling, the ash also presents a leachate problem.

Beyond direct benefits, the second environmental plus arising from recycling are indirect benefits. Table 19.3 compares the production cycle for products made from recycled and virgin materials.

The recycling process is of course not pollution-free. In all production stages, recycling generates significant pollution. Unique recycling wastes, for example de-inking sludge from paper recycling, also pose serious disposal problems.[44] However, relative to production from virgin material, recycling often yields two important indirect environmental benefits: **energy savings** and **upstream pollution** avoided.

Because secondary materials are already "pre-processed," it generally takes much

---

[41]"Recycling: The Newest Wrinkle in Waste Management's Bag," *Business Week,* March 5, 1990.

[42]Office of Technology Assessment (1989).

[43]Office of Technology Assessment (1989) and Ottinger et al. (1990) discuss the health impacts of both landfilling and incineration. In addition to conventional pollutants, incinerators emit dioxins and heavy metals. Concern about dioxin has recently focused on contamination of milk in cows; see also the discussion of dioxin in chapter 10.

[44]Office of Technology Assessment (1989: 191).

TABLE 19.3 Production from Recycled and Virgin Materials	
Virgin	*Recycling*
1. Raw material production	1. Collection/processing
2. Transport	2. Transport
3. Manufacturing	3. Manufacturing
4. Distribution	4. Distribution

less energy to convert them into finished products. Energy savings in turn often translate into significant environmental benefits. Figure 19.2 shows the energy requirements needed to produce a variety of products from both virgin and recycled materials. Particularly for plastics, the energy savings are impressive, with recycled plastic requiring only about one-fourth the energy of plastic made from virgin material.

FIGURE 19.2 Energy Consumption in Manufacturing: Virgin Versus Recycled Raw Materials

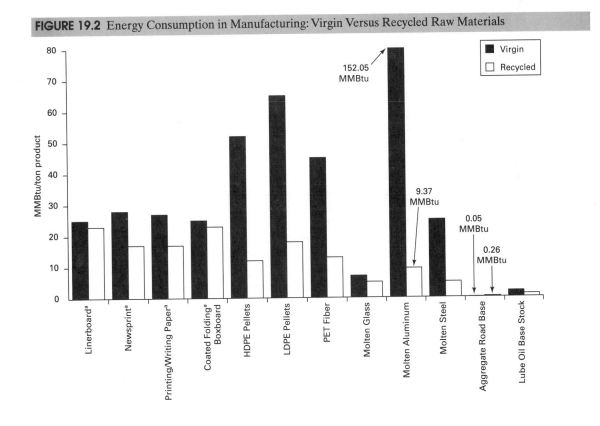

[a]Using recycled feedstock in paper production while reducing total energy use can actually increase use of purchased (generally nonrenewable) energy, since production from virgin materials uses waste wood to produce energy.

Source: New York State Energy Authority (1994: Figure 3–5), *Energy Implications of Integrated Solid Waste Management Systems* (Albany, NY: NYSERDA). For similar results, see Morris and Canzoneri (1992).

In addition to energy savings, the collection and processing of recycled materials can be less environmentally damaging than the production and transport of raw materials from virgin sources. In a life-cycle analysis of five products that monetized environmental costs, Schall (1992) found overall that virgin materials inflicted damages that ranged from 104% (steel) to 618% (aluminum) of damages from using recycled materials. Schall also found that *all* of the advantage accruing to recyclables took the form of indirect benefits.[45]

Such indirect benefits from recycling programs are more likely to be reaped when: (1) recycled goods replace products made from nonrenewable resources, for example, old-growth forest or petroleum; (2) goods can be recycled repeatedly; (3) the collection of recycled materials displaces garbage collection, producing little additional pollution; and (4) recycled materials are available closer to manufacturing centers, making transport of recycled materials substantially less pollution-intensive than the transport of raw materials.

Some critics have argued that recycling of old newspapers fit few of these criteria. First, much pulpwood used in the United States is grown on tree plantations, not in old-growth forest. Second, newspaper cannot be repeatedly recycled. Third, recycling systems cannot displace garbage collection completely, and they, thus, add to urban air pollution. Finally, much of the new recycled mill capacity is being built as expansions to existing mills, close to forests and away from cities, which are the source of the raw materials.[46]

Defenders of the indirect benefits of newspaper recycling respond that growing and clear-cutting pulp plantations is itself a polluting process, that even limited recycling of newspapers is desirable since it uses less energy in manufacturing than does virgin fiber, and that transport of materials is in fact being reduced.[47] In his life-cycle analysis, Schall (1992) argues that newspaper production from virgin materials results in damages between 143% and 200% of those for production from recycled material.

Whatever the final resolution to this debate, it illustrates the general point made in the introduction, that input-reducing technologies have larger indirect benefits than input-substituting technologies (like recycling). Using recycled products cannot eliminate all indirect pollution, since the recycling process itself requires resources. However, to the extent that recycling satisfies the four criteria outlined above, it does have the potential to yield large indirect benefits by reducing upstream economic activity. Reduced upstream activity in turn lowers overall demands on the planet's resource base: habitat, energy, and the stock of clean air and water.

---

[45]Schall used marginal abatement cost estimates to monetize damages. As discussed in chapter 17, a preferred, though generally unavailable measure, would be marginal damage estimates. If regulation is inefficiently strict, Schall's absolute dollar estimates would overstate true damages. However, the ratio figures reported here are less subject to bias.

[46]Wiseman (1990) makes many of these arguments; for a more polemical view, see Tierney (1996). Pulp plantations are common in the Southeast and on private lands in the Northwest. However, timber from the rain forests in southeast Alaska has been used to manufacture paper diapers.

[47]Denison and Ruston (1990) argue that when old newspapers are shipped to mills they displace otherwise "empty backhauls." Regarding displacement, they report that an efficient recycling system displaces one garbage collection trip for every two recycling trips.

Recycling can thus have local (direct waste management) and global (indirect) benefits. From an environmental point of view, global benefits have often been thought to dwarf the local benefits. As a result, the latter attribute has motivated popular enthusiasm for recycling. "Think globally, act locally" was the slogan adopted by community groups who first promoted recycling in the 1960s. In its early days, recycling was urged as an environmental duty, and even today most of its political impetus derives from broad support for a cleaner environment. In addition, some of its cost advantage lies in voluntary citizen efforts to sort and/or collect recyclable material. However, recycling did not take off until the local advantages of recycling as a *cost-competitive* waste management strategy became apparent in the late 1980s.

Is recycling cost competitive? Yes, up to a point. Communities developing a waste management plan have to decide on a mix of disposal options, including recycling (and composting), incineration, and landfilling. Thus, a community needs to choose a recycling target, and an incinerator or landfill of the appropriate size to minimize disposal costs. Committing to an incinerator or landfill with large-volume requirements can discourage otherwise cost-effective recycling. Careful analysis is necessary before deciding on the appropriate mix.

Denison and Ruston (1990) working for the Environmental Defense Fund have recently published a guide to determining cost-effective investment in the different options, based on the present discounted value method laid out in chapter 6 of this book. When discounting is used, the high up-front cost, and relatively slow startup times for incineration and landfilling, favor recycling. Because much of the expenditure for recycling is for ongoing operations, it occurs in the future and, thus, has a lower present discounted value.[48]

Consider this

PUZZLE

Suppose that a new recycling program is expected to cost GarbageTown $50 per ton, but GarbageTown's existing landfill covers its costs charging only $30 per ton. Could introducing the recycling program actually save the town money?

SOLUTION

Maybe. By extending the life of the existing landfill, a recycling program would forestall expensive new landfill construction in the future. Whether this factor would justify a recycling program could be answered for a specific case using the present discounted value framework. What this puzzle illustrates is that comparing simple per ton disposal costs on a year-to-year basis does not tell us which option is to be preferred.

---

[48]The Tellus Institute has also developed a software package called WastePlan for modeling waste disposal costs, which can be adapted to local conditions.

Per ton disposal costs for each method will in fact vary from site to site and over time, as regulations change and the prices for recycled goods fluctuate. The latter can have an important impact on the viability of a recycling program. Figure 19.3 illustrates the growth in supply of old newspapers, the recent increase in the capacity of recycling mills to process the paper (demand), and the overall impact on prices.

Used newspapers were fetching good prices on the East Coast through 1987 but collapsed in 1988 as supply increased and export demand dropped. Prices remained low as supply surged in the early 1990s but suggest some recovery in 1993, as paper companies began completing the construction of new processing mills. Indeed, by 1995, most recycling programs were turning a small profit.[49] West Coast prices (not shown) were less volatile over the period, generally averaging around $20 to $30 per ton, due to the existence of major export markets in the Far East.

The uncertainty associated with the prices for recycled goods appears to favor other disposal options; however, if prices rise for recyclables, then incinerators or landfills may find themselves coming up short on waste, leading to higher tipping fees to make up for lost volume. However, the explosive growth in recycling in the early 1990s has generally kept prices down, as new supplies have outstripped the growth in end-use markets.[50] Volatile prices in end-use markets mean that recycling programs will "pay" some years and require operating subsidies in others. Ackerman (1996) calculates that the typical recycling program raised disposal costs by $21 per household in 1993 (when prices were low) and saved $5 per household in 1995 (when prices were high).

Due to pressure from citizen groups, municipalities considering incineration options are increasingly undertaking head-to-head economic comparisons with recycling. The city of Seattle concluded in the late 1980s that an aggressive recycling program—60% by 1998—would be cheaper than incineration at any level. As a result, the city canceled its proposed incinerator project.

On the eastern side of Washington State, Spokane proceeded with both an incinerator and an aggressive recycling plan. Recycling rates rose from 5% to 22% from 1984 to 1989, and were targeted to rise further in the early 1990s. (Washington has established a statewide recycling goal of 50% by 1995.) The incinerator, however, has proven to be much more expensive to operate than was originally estimated.[51]

In New York City, the Environmental Defense Fund sponsored a series of studies in the 1980s, which concluded that recycling would provide lower-cost disposal than incineration; as of 1992, the city was going ahead with a major incineration project but had also announced an ambitious recycling scheme.[52]

[49]"Deinked Pulp Floods the Market but Appears to Find a Home: More to Come," *Pulp and Paper Week,* 15, no. 7 (February 7–15, 1993); see also Ackerman (1996).

[50]"As Recycling Surges, Market for Materials Is Slow to Develop," *Wall Street Journal,* January 17, 1992.

[51]See Parametrix, Inc. (1990); and "Incinerator Cost Higher Than Expected," Spokane *Spokesman Review,* December 27, 1992.

[52]Denison and Ruston (1990); and "Dinkins Offers Changes in Solid Waste Disposal," *New York Times,* March 31, 1992.

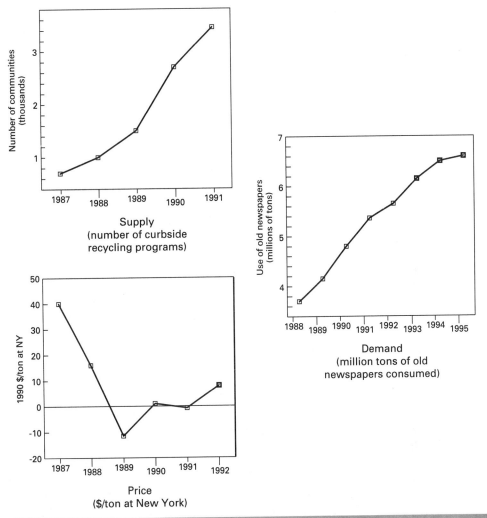

FIGURE 19.3 Supply, Demand, and Price for Old Newsprint, 1987–1992

Source: Supply is from Marcia Berss, "No One Wants to Shoot Snow White," *Forbes,* October 14, 1991, p. 42. (Berss cites *Biocycle* as her source.) Demand is "Total Domestic Use of ONP," from *Recovered Paper Statistical Highlights, 1992* (Washington, DC: American Forests and Paper Association). Figures for 1993–1995 are based on a capacity survey. Prices are from *Pulp and Paper Week,* various issues.

Of course, city managers' decisions to adopt waste management options are motivated as much by political as economic concerns. The recent rush to recycling has been driven by politics, though boosted by economics. In addition, economic studies forecasting the relative cost-effectiveness of different disposal options are merely educated guesses. A given community planning to adopt a curbside recycling scheme in 1989 could hardly have foreseen a 700% growth in supply of recyclables over the next three years and the subsequent collapse of prices in the secondary market. Thus, recycling economics were unfavorable in 1992 in the Minneapolis area, where haulers were dumping or burning recyclables they could not dispose of. At the same time, few would have foreseen the relatively rapid growth in end-user applications and markets in the mid-1990s. At this point, it is difficult to assess whether states and communities in general are overinvesting in recycling on purely economic grounds.

The key to the long-term success of recycling has been and will be the development of end-user markets. Of course, the mere existence of cheap sources of junk will inspire entrepreneurs to dream up things to do with it. In recent years, old newspapers have been shredded and turned into animal bedding, while glass has been ground up to use for "glassphalt" road bed.

However, state and local government actions have been very effective at technology-forcing. For example, the paper industry has felt sufficiently encouraged by the increase in mandatory recycling, recycled content laws, and government purchase programs to increase investment dramatically in recycled mill capacity.[53] Chemical manufacturers, responding in part to actual and threatened local bans on plastics, have been working hard to develop recyclable products and create end-user-markets. Technology-forcing has worked well here because of the wide diversity of location of these initiatives. Under such circumstances, industry was better off meeting the technology challenge than fighting it. Moreover, as discussed in the last chapter, local technology-forcing regulations reduce any inefficiencies that such laws may generate.

Recent popular enthusiasm has thus pushed recycling to the edge of being a dominant, long-term waste management option. According to William Ruckelshaus, former head of the EPA and now chairman of Browning-Ferris, a major garbage disposal firm, "If the infrastructure gets put into place, with collection systems, processing centers and end-user markets, then it will not matter if the current 'feel good' attitude subsides. Economics will take over and the system will be self-sustaining."[54]

Recycling is an example of a successfully promoted CT. As federal regulation (of the command-and-control variety) internalized the environmental costs associated with landfills and incineration, these options became more expensive, and recycling became cost-competitive. At the same time, popular support for recycling at the local level was sufficient to overcome a natural tendency on the part of municipal officials to stick with proven technologies. In addition, carrots in the form of market guarantees, as well as sticks in the form of product bans and content laws, both emerging simultaneously in dozens of locales, have generated substantial investment by the private sector in developing end-use markets for recycled products.

---

[53]Jacques and Ince (1992) maintain that between 15% and 20% of the increase in recycled capacity resulted from state-level recycled content legislation, with the rest resulting from lower prices driven by the surge in local collection programs. The authors strangely refer to the latter phenomenon as a "free-market" phenomenon. The authors also argue that recycled content legislation has led to an inefficient regional distribution of de-inking plants.

[54]Quoted in "In Solid Waste, It's the Breakdown That Counts," *New York Times,* March 31, 1991.

19.4 Summary

This chapter has reviewed the current state of three clean technologies: waste reduction in manufacturing, alternative agriculture, and recycling of municipal solid waste. In all three cases, the first task was to establish that the technologies were in fact CTs: cleaner (in general) than the conventional technologies, and potentially at least as profitable.

The obstacle to rapid diffusion of all the technologies could be boiled down to this: lack of sufficient profit advantage to overcome poor information and risk associated with the CT. Consider, for example, the paint factory in Table 19.2. State advisers were able to recommend savings of $23,000 per year—nothing to sneeze at, certainly, but probably insufficient to justify hiring a waste assessment firm, of unknown reliability, which might ultimately have come up with nothing. And because of thin markets, waste assessment firms are few and far between, meaning that the paint firm probably did not have an easy option to hire one in the first place.

For farmers, the risk associated with CTs is even higher. Rather than purchasing a new piece of equipment, farmers must sink investments in new management skills and face adjustment costs as alternative methods are introduced. On the other hand, because some of the environmental costs of conventional farming are borne by farmers directly, they do have a natural interest in switching. Finally, in the recycling case, the profit advantage alone is insufficient to overcome one of the chief attractions of incineration for municipal authorities—its relative management simplicity.

Has government successfully promoted these technologies? On the waste reduction front, the most successful government action to date has been a product-labeling effort, the Toxic Release Inventory. The TRI and the EPA's 33/50 program have focused public and industry attention on toxic releases on a plant-by-plant basis and have motivated some companies to begin serious waste reduction efforts. A second strong incentive for waste reduction (as well as on-site incineration and illegal dumping) has been the increase in hazardous waste disposal costs brought on by regulation. Technical assistance programs, though promising, are currently funded at a low level. Mandatory waste reduction plans, less promising, have also been introduced by some states.

In agriculture, rising pesticide costs due to regulation (and decisions by companies not to reregister some old pesticides) may have induced some movement in the direction of CTs. However, because of the difficulty associated with such a transition and the availability of other chemical alternatives, the stick of rising costs may have only limited effect in encouraging movement toward CTs. Government technical assistance and R&D, while increasing, remain at low levels, while subsidy policies continue to discourage alternative agriculture.

In the recycling case, a combination of regulation-induced rising costs for alternatives as well as aggressive local promotion has led to tremendous growth in this CT over the last decade. Particularly important has been the development of the recycling infrastructure—processing technologies and end-use markets necessary to support the industry.

The final issue: Are we spending too much promoting these CTs? The evidence suggests that technical assistance programs in industry and agriculture can be quite cost-effective; once established they should be able to recover their own operating costs through fees. This will be increasingly true if costs for hazardous waste disposal and pesticides continue to rise. In addition, a further shift in agricultural R&D funding from conventional to alternative agriculture makes sense, given the presence of private-sector R&D in the former field, financed by agrochemical companies. Finally, with the tremendous flux in markets for recycled goods, it is difficult to tell "on average" whether state and local governments' actions to promote recycling make sense on purely economic grounds.

Ultimately, however, efforts to promote CTs need not all be free lunches. Just as with environmental regulation, CT promotion should be judged on a comparison of economic costs against environmental benefits, however broadly defined. Let us look at a specific example: community bans on nonrecyclable plastic containers, such as that in force in Minneapolis–Saint Paul in the early 1990s.

The local environmental benefits of such an effort are unlikely to be substantial; some reductions in certain toxic emissions from the local incinerator, perhaps made up for by greater emissions from burning paper. The local costs? Perhaps some increase in expense on packaging, certainly a decrease in convenience: Glass breaks easier and is heavier, a special burden for older people.

However, we have already established that broad public support for recycling is based on a belief in global benefits. Here we step into the unknown; very little work has been done detailing how large the global pollution reduction—both direct and indirect—from using recycled materials really is.

Beyond the indirect benefits from using recycled materials, the plastics ban in Minneapolis–Saint Paul, and other communities, has provided impetus to private-sector initiatives to develop recyclable plastics and end-use markets. The tremendous growth in the recycling industry in the early 1990s is quite consistent with the theory of path dependence sketched out in the beginning of the previous chapter. Without aggressive government action, recycling would have remained a limited waste management option, as waste managers stuck with conventional disposal technologies. However, due to public pressure, both public and private infrastructure investment has been undertaken, economies of scale have been realized, and complementary industries developed. Eventually, in Ruckelshaus' words, "Economics takes over," and the nation locks in on a recycling path.

In the long run, nothing is more important to a sustainable economic future than the development of clean technologies. With the earth's population expected to reach at least twice its current level before stabilizing, less environmentally destructive means of satisfying human needs must be found and pursued. The delicate task facing government is to channel creative market forces in a clean direction, without unintentionally stifling the very progress it seeks.

APPLICATION 19.0

The Conservation Tillage Program

In 1985, the U.S. Congress changed the rules governing the crop subsidy program. Farmers operating on highly erodible land were required to implement a soil conservation plan (developed in consultation with the extension service of the Department of Agriculture) by 1995 or risk losing their subsidies. Erosion not only lowers the long-run productivity of the farm but also is a major source of surface water pollution.

As chapter 13 pointed out, agricultural runoff of herbicides, insecticides, and fertilizers is the primary source of water pollution nationwide.

A key feature of most soil conservation efforts are so-called *conservation tillage* systems. Conventional tillage systems leave bare dirt fields after the harvest in order to minimize the growth of weeds; by contrast, conservation tillage leaves a minimum of 30% of the soil surface covered with crop residue. The increased residue reduces soil erosion.

Farmers can control weeds in a conservation-tilled field by tilling the surface clear just prior to planting. However, weed problems may still be more severe under conservation tillage, requiring greater use of herbicides. Conservation plans require scrutiny of chemical use and encourage crop rotations to reduce pesticide use.

On the economic front, savings in labor, machinery, and fuel costs from reduced tilling must be balanced against a need for more careful timing of tillage for maximum weed control. Timing of chemical use must also be improved if pesticide and herbicide use is not to grow. By 1993, around 100 million acres, or 36% of U.S. cropland, was planted under some type of conservation tillage system. In 1989, the comparable figure was 25%.[55]

1. Can you tell if conservation tillage is a clean technology, as defined in chapter 18? Why or why not?

2. What tools is the government using to promote conservation tillage?

Key Ideas in Each Section

19.0 This chapter looks at efforts to promote clean technology. Clean technologies yield both **direct** and **indirect environmental benefits.** Indirect benefits from input-reducing technologies are larger than those from input-substituting technologies. As a result CTs are listed in a general order of preference by the **three R's: reduce, reuse, recycle.**

19.1 Waste reduction or pollution prevention involves reducing the generation of pollution at the source. Because it often reduces the use of inputs as well, pollution prevention efforts can be profitable and thus qualify as a CT. This section reviews private-sector efforts at pollution prevention, motivated in the chemical industry case by the **Toxics Release Inventory.** The most promising governmental promotion efforts center around technical assistance programs.

19.2 Alternative agriculture includes a variety of practices designed to reduce the use of chemical pesticides and fertilizers. This section emphasizes the difficulties regulators face, due to (1) **imperfect information** and (2) the **non-point source** nature of farm pollutants, in regulating pesticide residues on food and in groundwater. Major obstacles to alternative agriculture include **high adjustment costs** for individual farmers. Government efforts should focus on reforming subsidy policy and expanding alternative R&D and technical assistance programs.

---

[55]Midwest Plan Service (1992); U.S. Department of Agriculture (1993).

19.3 Recycling of solid waste yields primarily indirect, rather than **direct, environmental benefits,** because it yields **energy savings** relative to manufacture from virgin materials and can reduce **upstream pollution.** Recycling has been discouraged by subsidies for incineration, and the lack of **unit pricing** for garbage. Recycling economics are more favorable when a high discount rate is used. Recycling can only spread as fast as end-use markets for secondary materials are developed. Finally, the recent success of government efforts to promote recycling illustrates the theory of path dependence in technological development.

References

Ackerman, Frank (1996). *Why Recycle? Markets, Values and Public Policy.* Covela, CA: Island Press.

Arora, Seema and Timothy N. Cason (1996). "Why Do Firms Volunteer to Exceed Environmental Regulations? Understanding Participation in EPA's 33/50 Program." *Land Economics,* 72, no. 4, 413–432.

Benbrook, Charles M. (1991). "What We Know, Don't Know and Need to Know about Pesticide Residues in Food." In *Pesticide Residues and Food Safety: A Harvest of Viewpoints,* eds. B. G. Tweedy et al. Washington, DC: American Chemical Society.

Bingham, Taylor H., Donald W. Anderson and Phillip C. Cooley (1987). "Distribution of the Generation of Air Pollution." *Journal of Environmental Economics and Management,* vol. 14, 30–40.

Bridges, James S. (1990). "Waste Minimization Assessments at Selected DOD Facilities." In *The Environmental Challenge of the 1990s: Proceedings of the International Conference on Pollution Prevention, 1990.* Washington, DC: U.S. EPA.

Carnevale, Richard A., Wesley A. Johnson, Craig A. Reed and Alan Post (1991). "Agricultural Chemical Residues in Food: Evaluating the Risks." In *Agriculture and the Environment: The 1991 Yearbook of Agriculture.* Washington, DC: USDA.

Clarke, Marjorie J., Maarten de Kadt and David Saphire (1991). *Burning Garbage in the U.S.* New York: Inform.

Cowan, Robin and Philip Gunby (1996). "Sprayed to Death: Path Dependence and Lock-in and Pest Control Strategies." *The Economic Journal,* vol. 106, 521–542.

Cropper, Maureen L., William N. Evans, Stephen J. Berardi, Maria M. Ducla-Soares and Paul R. Portney (1991). "The Determinants of Pesticide Regulation: A Statistical Analysis of EPA Decisionmaking." *Discussion Paper CRM 91-01.* Washington, DC: Resources for the Future.

Crosson, Pierre and Janet Ekey (1988). "Alternative Agriculture: A Review and Assessment of the Literature." *Discussion Paper ENR88-01.* Washington, DC: Resources for the Future.

Curtis, Jennifer (1991). *Harvest of Hope: The Potential of Alternative Agriculture to Reduce Pesticide Use.* San Francisco: Natural Resources Defense Council.

Davies, Terry and Jan Mazurek (1997). *Industry Incentives for Environmental Improvement: Evaluation of U.S. Federal Initiatives.* Washington, DC: Global Environmental Management Initiative.

Denison, Richard and John Ruston (1990). *Recycling and Incineration.* Washington, DC: Island Press.

Dorfman M., C. G. Miller and W. M. Muir (1991). *Cutting Chemical Wastes — Update.* New York: INFORM.

Franklin, William E. and Marjorie A. Franklin (1992). "Putting the Crusade into Perspective." *EPA Journal,* 18, no. 3, 7–14.

Gianessi, Leonard P. (1991). "Use of Pesticides in the United States." In *Pesticide Residues and Food Safety: A Harvest of Viewpoints,* eds. B. G. Tweedy et al. Washington, DC: American Chemical Society.

Gianessi, Leonard P., Raymond J. Kopp and Cynthia A. Puffer (1989). "Regulating Pesticide Use: Social Costs, Policy Targeting and Economic Incentives." *Discussion Paper QE89-21.* Washington, DC: Resources for the Future.

Hathaway, Janet S. (1991). "Why Isn't the

EPA Reducing Pesticide Risks?" In *Pesticide Residues and Food Safety: A Harvest of Viewpoints,* eds. B. G. Tweedy et al. Washington, DC: American Chemical Society.

Hirschorn, Joel S. (1990). "Preventing Industry Waste." *The EPA Journal,* January–February, 36–39.

Jacques, Romain and Peter Ince (1992). "The Economic Impact of State Legislation on Mandatory Recycled Fibre Content: An Application of the North American Pulp and Paper Model." Paper presented at the IUFRO conference, Berlin.

Kirsch, William F. and Gwen P. Looby (1990). "Waste Minimization Assessment Centers." In *The Environmental Challenge of the 1990s: Proceedings of the International Conference on Pollution Prevention.* Washington, DC: U.S. EPA.

Larson, Bruce A. and Mary K. Knudson (1991). "Whose Price Wins: Institutional and Technical Change in Agriculture." *Land Economics,* 67, no. 2, 213–224.

Levin, Michael H. (1990). "Implementing Incentives: Experience and Expectations." In *The Environmental Challenge of the 1990s: Proceedings of the International Conference on Pollution Prevention.* Washington, DC: U.S. EPA.

Malloy, Edward et al. (1991). "A Harvest of Questions: Chemical in the Food Chain." In *Pesticide Residues and Food Safety: A Harvest of Viewpoints,* eds. B. G. Tweedy et al. Washington, DC: American Chemical Society.

McCarthy, John F. (1991). "Average Residues versus Tolerances." In *Pesticide Residues and Food Safety: A Harvest of Viewpoints,* eds. B. G. Tweedy et al. Washington, DC: American Chemical Society.

Midwest Plan Service (1992). *Conservation Tillage Systems and Management.* Ames, IA: Iowa State University.

Moore, John A. (1989). "Speaking of Data: The Alar Controversy." *The EPA Journal,* May–June.

Morris, Jeffrey and Diana Canzoneri (1992). "Comparative Lifecycle Energy Analysis: Theory and Practice." *Resource Recycling,* November, 25–31.

Mott, Laurie and Karen Snyder (1987). *Pesticide Alert: A Guide to Pesticides in Fruits and Vegetables.* San Francisco: Sierra Club Books.

National Research Council (1989). *Alternative Agriculture.* Washington, DC: National Academy Press.

O'Conell, Paul F. (1991). "Sustainable Agriculture." In *Agriculture and the Environment: The 1991 Yearbook of Agriculture.* Washington, DC: U.S. GPO.

Office of Technology Assessment (1992). *Managing Industrial Solid Wastes.* Washington, DC: U.S. GPO.

Office of Technology Assessment (1991). *Beneath the Bottom Line: Agricultural Approaches to Reduce Groundwater Contamination.* Washington, DC: U.S. GPO.

Office of Technology Assessment (1989). *Facing America's Trash: What Next for Municipal Solid Waste?* Washington, DC: U.S. GPO.

Office of Technology Assessment (1987). *From Pollution to Prevention: A Progress Report on Waste Reduction.* Washington, DC: U.S. GPO.

Ottinger, Richard L., et al. (1990). *Environmental Costs of Electricity.* New York: Oceana Publications.

Parametrix, Inc. (1990). *Spokane County Comprehensive Solid Waste Management Plan Update and Draft Environmental Impact Statement.* Spokane, WA: Spokane Regional Solid Waste Disposal Project.

Porter, Michael E. (1991). "America's Green Strategy." *Scientific American,* April.

Reganald, John P., Robert I. Paperclick, and James F. Parr (1990). "Sustainable Agriculture." *Scientific American,* June, 112–120.

Repetto, Robert and Sanjay Baliga (1996). *Pesticides and the Immune System: The Public Health Risks.* Washington, DC: World Resources Institute.

Richardson, Stephanie (1990). "Pollution Prevention in Textile Wet Processing: An Approach and Case Studies." In *The Environmental Challenge of the 1990s: Proceedings of the International Conference on Pollution Prevention.* Washington, DC: U.S. EPA.

Salant, Stephen and Eban Goodstein (1990).

"Predicting Committee Behavior in Majority-Rule Experiments." *The Rand Journal of Economics,* 21, no. 2, Summer 1990.

Schall, John (1992). "Does the Solid Waste Hierarchy Make Sense?" *Program on Solid Waste Policy, Working Paper 1.* New Haven: Yale University Press.

Shapiro, Michael (1990). "Toxic Substances Policy." In *Public Policies for Environmental Protection,* ed. Paul Portney. Washington, DC: Resources for the Future.

Shistar, Terry, Susan Cooper and Jay Feldman (1992). *Unnecessary Risks: The Benefit Side of the Pesticide Risk-Benefit Equation.* Washington, DC: National Coalition Against the Misuse of Pesticides.

Tierney, John (1996). "Recycling Is Garbage." *New York Times Magazine,* June 30.

Taylor, Sarah (1988). "Developing Pesticide Analytical Methods for Food: Considerations for Federal Policy Formulation." In *Pesticide Residues in Food.* Washington, DC: Office of Technology Assessment.

U.S. Department of Agriculture (1993). "Farmers Expand Use of Crop Residue Management." *Agricultural Resources: Cropland, Water and Conservation Situation and Outlook,* AR-30, May.

U.S. Department of Agriculture (1991a). *1990 Fact Book of Agriculture.* Washington, DC: USDA.

U.S. Department of Agriculture (1991b). *Agricultural Statistics 1991.* Washington, DC: USDA.

U.S. Environmental Protection Agency (1993). *EPA's 33/50 Program Third Progress Update.* Washington, DC: U.S. EPA, Office of Pollution Prevention.

U.S. Environmental Protection Agency (1991a). *Enhanced Environmental Enforcement for the 1990s.* Washington, DC: U.S. EPA.

U.S. Environmental Protection Agency (1991b). *Pollution Prevention 1991.* Washington, DC: U.S. EPA.

U.S. Environmental Protection Agency (1990). *Reducing Risk: Setting Priorities and Strategies for Environmental Protection.* Washington, DC: U.S. EPA.

U.S. Environmental Protection Agency (1987). *Unfinished Business: A Comparative Assessment of Environmental Problems.* Washington, DC: U.S. GPO.

U.S. Government Accounting Office (1986). *Pesticides: Need to Enhance FDA's Ability to Protect the Public From Illegal Residues.* Washington, DC: U.S. GPO.

Uva, Thomas (1989). "Eliminating Those Regulatory Headaches." *EPA Journal,* November–December.

Whyatt, Robin M. and William J. Nicholson (1991). "Conducting Risk Assessments for Preschooler's Dietary Exposure." In *Pesticide Residues and Food Safety: A Harvest of Viewpoints,* eds. B. G. Tweedy et al. Washington, DC: American Chemical Society.

Wiseman, A. Clark (1990). "U.S. Wastepaper Recycling Policies: Issues and Effects." *Discussion Paper ENR 90-14.* Washington, DC: Resources for the Future.

CHAPTER 20

Energy Policy and the Environment

20.0 Introduction

Item: On the morning of March 24, 1989, the Exxon Valdez ran aground in Alaska's Prince William Sound, spilling 11 million gallons of crude oil. Three years later scientists reported a continued decline in the sea otter population, as well as the disappearance of a significant number of killer whales. In addition, the social structure of the whale pods was effected by the spill, with some mothers abandoning their calves.[1]

Item: Americans consume two times as much gas per capita as the world's second-largest consumer, Sweden.[2]

Of all economic activities, energy production and use present the biggest challenge to the quality of the environment. This book began with an extended discussion of the problem of global warming, due to the release of carbon dioxide from the combustion of fossil fuels. But beyond global warming, energy production and use also yield as by-products acid rain and sulfate pollution, urban air pollution and traffic jams, oil spills, oil drilling and strip mining in sensitive habitat, acid mine drainage, hazardous mine tailings and oil drilling muds, occupational diseases such as black lung, and exposure to radioactivity in the mining, transport, and disposal of nuclear fuel and waste. Our three main energy sources—oil, coal, and nuclear—each have their own environmental drawbacks.

Yet reliable access to reasonably priced energy is the lifeblood of any economic system, and as the quote above suggests, the American economy relies more heavily on it than most. This chapter presents an overview of the current energy picture and then considers the prospects for a cleaner energy path, one based on a combination of

---

[1]"Valdez Spill Toll Is Now Called Far Worse," *New York Times,* April 18, 1992.
[2]MacKenzie and Walsh (1992).

renewable energy (solar, wind, and biomass fuels) and energy efficiency. The basic message is that the future is up for grabs. Depending upon the interaction of technology, economics, and government policy, the energy system could follow the current fossil fuels path or switch to either a renewable/efficiency path or, less likely, a high nuclear path.

How costly is a clean energy path likely to be? As was suggested in the introductory chapter on global warming, there is substantial disagreement among economists about the economic impact of pursuing the different options. Some argue that combating global warming will be quite expensive, while others have maintained that, through aggressive energy-efficiency measures, we might actually be able to reduce global warming at a profit. This chapter will look more closely at these arguments.

20.1 The Current Energy Picture

Each year, Americans consume around 82 quadrillion British Thermal Units (BTUs) of energy, the equivalent of 6.5 gallons of oil per day for each man, woman, and child in the country. Figure 20.1 shows an index of per capita energy consumption in the United States from 1973 to 1994, with 1973 consumption set equal to 1.

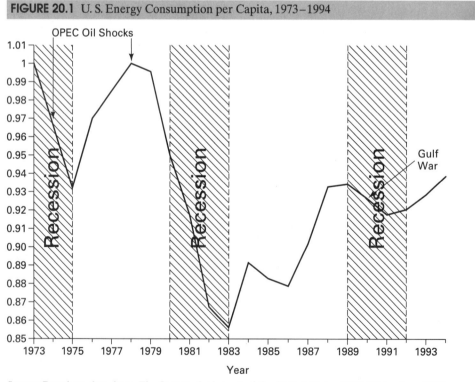

FIGURE 20.1 U. S. Energy Consumption per Capita, 1973–1994

Source: Based on data from *The Statistical Abstract of the United States,* 1996, Tables 2 and 916. Reported energy use after 1991 is adjusted downward by 2.5 quads, to maintain consistency with earlier data.

Energy use has varied widely over time, depending both on economic conditions and oil prices. In 1974, and again in 1978, the **Organization of Petroleum Exporting Countries (OPEC)** quadrupled the price of oil. Over the period, prices rose from around $3 to $40 per barrel. Both of these oil shocks contributed to subsequent recessions, a short one from 1974 to 1975, and a much deeper one from 1980 to 1983. Figure 20.1 reveals that in the face of the 1974 oil price hike and recession, energy use declined rapidly. However, as the economy recovered in the mid-1970s, energy use began rising again. During this period, American industry and consumers were still dependent on highly energy-inefficient technology.

Energy use plunged again after the second oil price shock, and the deep recession of the early 1980s. By this time, under the long-term pressure of higher prices and government-mandated efficiency measures, the technological base in the country had become much more energy-efficient. Because energy use stayed flat while the economy continued to grow, the ratio of economic output to energy use also grew. Between 1973 and 1985, *energy use per dollar of GNP produced fell by more than one quarter.*

However, after 1983, oil prices collapsed to under $20 per barrel, and the U.S. economy experienced steady, if unspectacular, growth through 1989. Figure 20.1 shows that, beginning in 1983, under the influence of low energy prices, a reduced governmental commitment to energy efficiency, and steady economic growth, per capita energy use began to climb again. This growth finally leveled out in the face of the recession of the early 1990s, but resumed after 1991. Overall the combined effect of oil shocks, growth, and increased efficiency meant that in 1994, Americans were consuming about 6% less energy on a per person basis than they had twenty years before.[3]

How do Americans stack up against the rest of the world in energy use? Unfortunately, as Figure 20.2 illustrates, we are close to the top of the heap among wealthy countries.

What explains the wide variation in international demand for energy illustrated in the figure? National income, of course, but in addition, climate, population density, energy prices, transportation infrastructure, and government conservation policy are all important factors. Canada loses on all fronts—cold climate, low population density, low energy prices, a transport system geared to the automobile and a government with a relatively laissez-faire attitude, by international standards, toward energy conservation. Electric power in Norway is also cheap, due to abundant hydropower.

Germany, Japan, and Belgium, each of which uses less than half as much energy per capita than we do in the United States, have comparable climates. However, all three are much more densely populated and have urban and interurban transport systems designed heavily around mass transit. Of the three, Japan has pursued energy efficiency most aggressively. Before the first oil shock in 1974, Japan already had one of the most energy-efficient economies; since then, the nation has improved its efficiency by one third, compared to a 25% improvement in other industrial countries.

The *Wall Street Journal* cites two successful government policies: (1) Japanese factories are required to have at least one energy conservation engineer on site who must

---

[3]Energy use per dollar of GNP remained roughly constant at 1985 levels throughout the early 1990s.

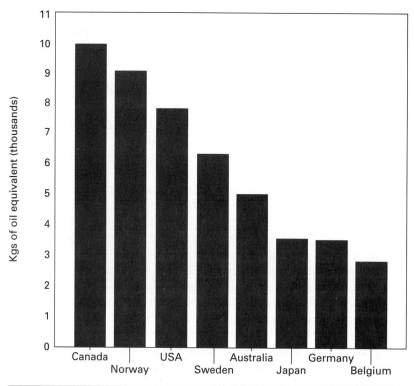

FIGURE 20.2 1990 Energy Consumption per Capita, Eight Countries

Source: From *World Development Report 1992* by The World Bank. Copyright © 1992 by The International Bank for Reconstruction and Development/The World Bank. Reprinted by permission of Oxford University Press, Inc.

pass a rigorous national test. (2) Japanese companies are allowed to keep energy prices high, provided they channel profits into R&D into energy research. These governmental measures have lead to dramatic improvements in Japan's energy efficiency.[4]

This section has provided a brief overview of the U.S. energy picture. The three primary uses of energy are for electricity, heat, and transportation. The next few sections will provide a more detailed look at the major energy technologies available in these sectors and will discuss policies designed to promote a cleaner energy future.

20.2 Technology Options: Electricity and Heat

Options for attacking energy needs for electricity and heat exist on both the demand and supply sides. **Demand-side management (DSM)** involves promoting technologies that use energy more efficiently. Note that many conservation mea-

---

[4]"How Japan Became So Energy Efficient: It Leaned on Industry," *Wall Street Journal,* September 10, 1990.

sures, such as turning down the thermostat from 68 to 65 degrees or driving 55 mph on the highway, are not efficiency measures since they involve some sacrifice in consumption. By energy efficiency we mean technologies that generate a comparable quality of service using less energy. Such DSM measures "produce" energy by freeing up supply.

In earlier chapters, we have discussed many DSM options: compact fluorescent lighting (chapter 6), energy-efficient building codes, and standards for refrigeration and lighting (chapter 18). Other DSM measures include using waste energy from electricity production to heat buildings (cogeneration), as well as adoption of energy-efficient industrial motors and cooking and cleaning appliances.

The potential for cost-effective DSM is substantial. Figure 20.3 shows two estimates of the potential for reduced electricity consumption.

The Electric Research Power Institute maintains that electricity use could be reduced about 25% at a cost of less than $.06 per kWh (roughly the cost of power from a new coal plant). More optimistically, the Rocky Mountain Institute argues that, at that price, we could reduce consumption by 75%. Both estimates suggest that many DSM measures qualify as clean technologies by being cost competitive and environmentally superior.

Moving on to the supply side of the market, half a dozen major options exist for producing heat and electricity. Coal is currently the primary fuel source for producing electric power in the United States (54%), with nuclear second (21%), hydroelectric power third (10%), natural gas fourth (9%), petroleum fifth (6%), and other renewables last (less than 1%). Natural gas, oil, and passive solar technologies are also used to generate heat. Each option has its own environmental and/or economic problems; each also has promising technologies that supporters maintain are capable of addressing those problems.

The dominance of coal in electric power generation to date has been due to one primary factor—a reliable, low-priced fuel source. The technology for producing electricity from coal is well-developed, and because domestic coal resources are abundant, the supply of fuel is not subject to the disruption and price fluctuations associated with oil.

On the other hand, coal's environmental and social problems are well known. In addition to problems of acid rain and criteria air pollutants discussed in chapter 13, underground mining for coal is quite dangerous, while strip mining disturbs natural ecosystems. Both can generate acid drainage problems. Coal transport also has a major impact on the nation's roads.

Looking to the future, coal-burning power plants have recently faced tighter regulation of their sulfur dioxide and nitrogen oxide emissions, in order to control acid rain. However, new **clean coal technologies,** developed as part of a government-industry research consortium, could dramatically reduce the emission of these air pollutants from new coal plants. The Office of Technology Assessment (1990) expects commercial application of some of these technologies to begin in the late 1990s. Coal's long-run outlook hinges most on the progress of global warming. Electric power contributes about 33% of America's carbon dioxide emissions, mostly from coal. Any serious effort to control the greenhouse effect will require that coal-burning power production be restricted.

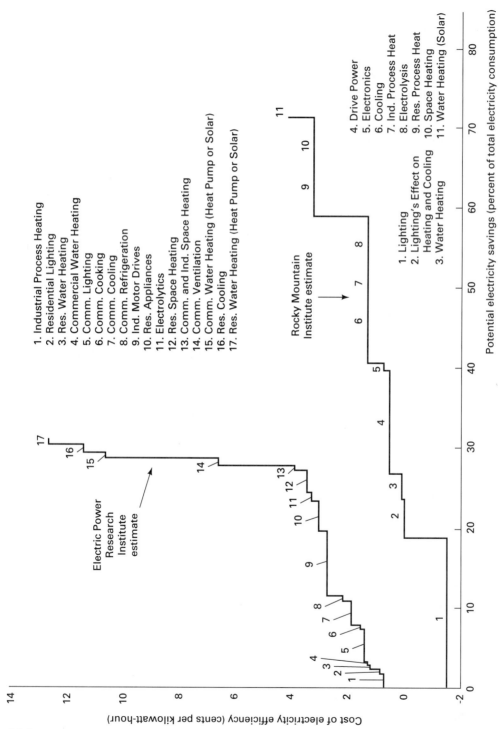

FIGURE 20.3 Potential for Electricity Savings Through DSM

Source: "Efficient Use of Electricity," in *Readings From Scientific American*, Arnold P. Fickett, Clark W. Gellings, and Amory B. Lovins. Copyright © 1990 by Scientific American, Inc. All rights reserved. Used with permission.

Nuclear power faces both economic and environmental challenges. There are currently around 110 plants operating in the United States, though no new plants have been ordered since the mid-1970s. Due to mounting costs resulting from increased regulation and construction costs, nuclear electric power from new U.S. plants would currently be cost-competitive only if siting and permitting procedures were dramatically streamlined. Given the historical record of construction delays, a new nuclear facility would probably deliver power at around $.12 to $.16 per kilowatt hour, more than twice the cost of power from coal.[5] The nuclear slowdown has been worldwide. Even in countries more nuclear-dependent than the United States, such as France and Japan, new facility orders have dropped dramatically.

A primary factor leading to rising costs has been construction delays from opposition to the siting and permitting of production and waste disposal facilities. There has been much debate about the safety of nuclear facilities, with most concern focused on a Chernobyl-type core failure, or meltdown. In 1985, the Nuclear Regulatory Commission estimated the probability of a severe core meltdown at 45% over the next twenty years at one of 109 U.S. reactors.[6] Estimates of cancer-induced fatalities from meltdowns have ranged from zero (Three Mile Island) to as high as 500,000 for Chernobyl, though most fatality estimates for Chernobyl are much lower. A 1982 Nuclear Regulatory Commission study predicted that a worst-case disaster in a populous area of the United States might generate around 100,000 deaths. Based on this figure, the *worst-case* fatality estimate for a meltdown is 45,000 over the next twenty years.

Recall that in chapter 17 we learned that sulfate pollution from coal-fired power plants may be responsible for as many as 50,000 premature deaths *each year*. Comparing worst cases on a risk-assessment basis, nuclear power production currently stacks up favorably compared to coal. Bear in mind, though, that improved coal technologies as well as the 1990 Clean Air Act are expected to cut sulfate emissions substantially. In addition, risks to those living close by a nuclear power plant will be higher, perhaps explaining intense local opposition to siting.

Moreover, a risk assessment looks only at the relative probability of death, without assessing the magnitude of the potential disaster—whole communities destroyed overnight. As we noted in chapter 8, people will buy insurance to avoid very risky situations that occur with low probability. Stronger opposition to nuclear power facilities may, thus, reflect simple risk aversion.

---

[5]The cost of power from a new nuclear unit is very difficult to estimate, because none have been ordered in the United States since the 1970s. Much of the uncertainty in costs is due to political factors: A good portion of nuclear's expense has resulted from construction delays and unanticipated retrofits required to meet new regulatory requirements (Cantor and Hewlett [1988]). Reducing costs in the nuclear industry would thus require a dramatic streamlining of the permitting and siting process. However, in the face of intense public concern about safety, such an outcome seems highly unlikely.

Flavin (1987) provides a 1985 cost estimate, based on industry sources of $.12 per kWh. Hall (1990) puts private costs at between $.14 and $.16 per kWh. These estimates seem reasonable, given the fact that the political opposition to any new plant is likely to be substantial.

Nuclear optimists see the technology as cost-competitive. Westinghouse, for example, maintains that its new modular reactors could generate power for as low as $.042 per kWh, given timely permitting and construction. (It is not clear whether this estimate assumes scale economies from mass-producing the modular units.) Manne and Richels (1990b) and The New York State Energy Office (1991) also view new nuclear plants as a relatively low-cost option.

[6]Ottinger et al. (1990).

Finally, public distrust of scientific risk assessment in the nuclear field—whether by government or industry officials—is very high. (Witness *The Simpsons!*) In part, this is due to the widespread perception that the Nuclear Regulatory Commission (NRC), which enforces safety standards for nuclear power, has been captured by the industry.[7] In part, it is due to uncertainty in the science. Official estimates of "safe" exposure to radiation have been repeatedly lowered.[8]

The other major environmental issue facing the nuclear industry is waste disposal.[9] Nuclear waste is divided into two categories: high-level and low-level waste. **High-level waste** consists of spent fuel rods and waste from weapons production; it remains toxic for hundreds of thousands of years. **Low-level waste** includes contaminated clothing and equipment from nuclear power plants and defense establishments, and wastes from medical and pharmaceutical facilities. Nuclear power accounts for about 80% of the radioactivity found in low-level civilian waste. The radioactive elements in most low-level waste decay to levels the NRC considers harmless within one hundred years, although about 3% of this waste needs to be isolated for longer periods.[10]

Currently, there are no operating permanent waste storage facilities for high-level waste in the United States, although a facility for defense waste is being built in Carlsbad, New Mexico, and one is planned for civilian waste at Yucca Mountain in Nevada. However, recent public opinion polls in Nevada put opposition to the plant at 4–1.[11]

There are currently three commercial waste facilities for low-level waste, although these sites are increasingly reluctant to accept out-of-state waste. In 1985 Congress directed each state to come up with a site for disposing of its low-level waste. However, the law was ruled unconstitutional by the Supreme Court in 1992, putting the ball back into the hands of the federal government and electric utilities.[12] As a result of the unresolved storage question, both high- and low-level waste have been piling up in temporary facilities at commercial power plants and government installations. Regardless of the future of nuclear power, solving the waste disposal problem should be a major environmental priority.

The main waste disposal options are burial in geologically stable formations, or above-ground storage. Given the extraordinarily long-term nature of the waste's toxicity, the scientific community is divided on the safety of various permanent waste disposal options.[13] Regardless of the technical issues at stake, however, political opposition to the siting of waste facilities has essentially put a brake on nuclear power. Solving the disposal problems—technical and political—for existing waste is essential before we move on to produce more of it.

---

[7] Flavin (1987: 44) quotes "dissident" NRC commissioner James Asseltine as saying, "This commission believes its job is to protect the industry and not the public. . . . There's a misplaced sense of optimism, even to the point of ignoring the messages we're getting from the operating experiences of the plants."

[8] Ottinger et al. (1990: 370).

[9] Other issues include worker safety, both for uranium miners and plant operators, as well as problems associated with decommissioning old plants. See Ottinger et al. (1990).

[10] Office of Technology Assessment (1990).

[11] See "Nevadans Dump Dump Ads," *Bulletin of Atomic Scientists,* 48, no. 4, (May 1992) 3; and Lenssen (1991).

[12] "High Court Eases State Obligation Over Toxic Waste, *New York Times,* June 20, 1992.

[13] Carter (1987) argues that from a technical point of view, waste management is probably the least risky aspect of nuclear power. He provides an overview of the debate.

Unlike most other energy sources, production of nuclear power inherently requires ongoing government involvement. First, the possibility of nuclear terrorism has meant that government must closely monitor shipments of fuel and waste. Some nuclear supporters even envision the need for an international solution to the waste problem to avoid nuclear terrorism.[14] Second, the need for intense regulation of reactor safety has led to extensive bureaucratic involvement in reactor design, operation, and maintenance. Finally, public opposition to siting, as well as the long-lived nature of waste, has meant that government has taken over the responsibility for trying to solve the disposal problem.

Nuclear power is a significant player in the energy field today as a result of ongoing government support. As we will see in our discussion of subsidy policy below, nuclear power in the United States has been aggressively supported by government funds. In France, the country with the world's biggest commitment to nuclear power, the industry is state-owned and heavily subsidized.[15]

Yet this remains nuclear power's principal advantage—thanks to the substantial investment of public funds it is today a proven source of large-scale electricity production, albeit somewhat expensive. Nuclear's best hope in the United States is that global warming quickly proves itself to be a serious environmental threat, requiring an immediate reduction in coal-fired power production. Only then will intense local opposition to facility siting, leading to construction delays and high costs, have a significant chance of being overcome.

Natural gas, composed primarily of methane, is the cleanest of fossil fuels: It has a low-sulfur content and yields about 70% more energy for each unit of CO_2 emitted than does coal. As a result, it is likely to increase its share of the electric power and heating markets over the next few years. However, from an economic point of view, natural gas has two primary drawbacks—a supply that is relatively small and unevenly distributed geographically. If natural gas were to be substituted for coal in all applications, the world's supply of known and estimated undiscovered reserves might be exhausted in as little as fifty-five years. Any major shift to natural gas in the United States would also increase dependence on foreign suppliers. Both of these factors mean that the price of natural gas is likely both to be volatile and to rise over time.[16]

In addition, methane itself is a greenhouse gas. Thus, if a switch from coal to natural gas is undertaken to avoid global warming, careful controls must be implemented to prevent the release of methane into the atmosphere during production or transport. This, too, will raise the price of energy generated by natural gas.

The final major energy category is renewables: primarily hydroelectric, solar, and wind energy.[17] **Hydroelectric power** currently contributes about 10% of the nation's

---

[14]Hafele (1990).

[15]Flavin (1987). In the United States, one of the biggest subsidies is a federal cap on liability for accidents at nuclear power plants. Because nuclear plants would otherwise be unable to obtain private insurance, the Price-Anderson Act limits liability for nuclear accidents. From 1959 to 1988, the limit was set at $560 million; in 1988 it was raised to $7 billion. Dubin and Rothwell (1990) estimate the value of this subsidy to have been $60 million per reactor per year prior to 1988, and $22 million per reactor per year after 1988.

[16]Fulkerson et al. (1990).

[17]Other renewable sources of energy with less near-term economic potential include geothermal, tidal, and wood.

electricity. About half of the nation's potential hydro sites have been developed. Although, from a pollution perspective, hydroelectric energy is relatively clean, dam projects can have significant environmental impacts, ranging from the flooding of ecologically valuable lands to negative impacts on aquatic life.

Solar energy is divided into two categories: **active solar,** which produces electric power (and heat as a by-product), and **passive solar,** which produces heat. The major use of passive solar is for heating water for direct use, but it can also be used to heat and cool homes.

The two principal active solar technologies are **photovoltaic** power, produced directly from solar cells, and **solar thermal** power, produced by focusing the sun's energy to heat a fluid, which is then used to create electricity. Although commercial solar thermal plants in California today deliver power at less than \$.10 per kWh, solar thermal is limited to sunny climates. However, for such areas, including much of the developing world, solar thermal has substantial potential.

Photovoltaic cells (PVs) potentially face no such geographic limitations. In fact, one of the first widespread applications of PVs is expected to be in the Northeast, where it costs utilities around \$.20 per kWh to service peak summertime demand.

Commercial applications of PVs are currently concentrated in remote areas where hookup to conventional power systems is expensive. Although PV costs in the early 1990s were high, at \$.20 to \$.30 per kWh, a history of very rapid technological progress provides optimism that PVs will be cost-competitive as a major baseload technology within the next ten to twenty years. By 2030, Zweibel (1990) argues that PVs could be producing over one third of today's electrical output at competitive rates.

Photovoltaic systems are very low-risk projects: Fuel sources are assured at a constant (zero) price, and there is no danger of increased environmental regulation in the future. For this reason, Lotker (1991) argues that utilities should require a lower rate of return from solar projects than others. The discount rate used to evaluate a PV project matters, because PV systems have very high up-front investment costs and very low operating and maintenance costs. Thus, Zweibel (1990) points out that, with access to low-interest loans (3%), PV electricity could have been delivered in 1990 at \$.10 per kWh, competitive in some markets.

In 1997, with substantial U.S. government support, the Amoco/Enron Solar company began construction of a 10 MW plant in the Nevada desert. The company has already been building a larger facility in India and is negotiating to construct a smaller unit for Hawaiian Electric. The Nevada facility, originally proposed as a much larger, 100 MW facility, was targeting a \$.055 kWh price.[18]

PVs hold out the lure of clean, low-cost power. (Most of the negative environmental effects of PVs can be traced to the manufacture of silicon chips.)[19] PV supporters envision a decentralized power system, with PV roofing tiles producing independent power for each household. Low-cost PVs would certainly be one important

---

[18]"Solar Power for Earthly Prices," *New York Times,* November 15, 1994, p. D2; and "Amoco Enron to Build 10 MW in Nevada," *PR Newswire,* http:\\www.entek.chalmers.se/pvflash12.html.

[19]See Ottinger et al. (1990) for a discussion of the environmental impact of photovoltaics.

link in the technological chain necessary to promote sustainable development in poor countries.

The other promising renewable electric technology is **wind power.** In 1989, U.S. wind power plants generated 2 billion kWh of electricity, at costs ranging from $.05 to $.08 kWh. Costs are expected to drop to around $.035 per kWh for sites with only moderate wind potential. In 1997, Amoco/Enron Solar contracted to build the largest wind facility in the world in Iowa, with an expected price of $.045 per kWh.[20]

The major economic obstacle to wind energy is site evaluation; customized wind analysis must be performed prior to locating a wind farm. The major environmental impact is noise and aesthetics, though the former problem has been reduced in modern designs. Twelve states, mostly in the Midwest, contain 90% of the nation's wind potential.[21]

While in theory, wind production could satisfy all U.S. electricity needs, in practice, there is one major obstacle: storage and transport. Both wind and active solar technologies produce power on an intermittent basis when the wind blows or the sun shines. Thus, effective long-run development of these resources will require **storage.** The current solution is to use the electricity grid; PV and wind power now supply electricity to the existing system for distribution. However, because electricity is lost in the transmission process, grid storage and transport are limited. A variety of technologies are being explored, primarily improved batteries. Other options include using electricity to pump water behind a dam or compress air or to create hydrogen, all to be used for future power production.[22]

20.3 Policy Options: Electricity and Heat

In a recent report, Congress's Office of Technology Assessment (1991a) described three possible energy futures: a baseline scenario, in which current trends remained unchanged, and two different scenarios motivated by concerns over global warming: high nuclear and high renewables/efficiency. Figure 20.4 illustrates how the different energy sectors are expected to evolve under the three paths by 2015.

The baseline, or business-as-usual, scenario envisions substantial growth in coal power to 34 quadrillion BTUs (up from 19 quads in 1989). Renewable energy use will also increase noticeably under the baseline, but without government support the nuclear industry is actually expected to decline as old plants are retired and not replaced. By contrast, emphasis on either renewables/efficiency or nuclear power by the government leads to an actual reduction in coal use from 1989 levels, to about 15 quads. In addition, both alternative options dramatically slow the rate of growth of total energy consumption through an emphasis on energy efficiency. Oil and natural gas use (not shown here) are also slightly reduced under both the renewables/efficiency and the nuclear options.

---

[20]"Blowing in the Wind," *New York Times,* March 23, 1997.
[21]Weinberg and Williams (1990).
[22]See Zweibel (1990) for a further discussion. Storage technologies will reduce the cost of fossil electric power as well, since inexpensive power could be produced at night and sold during times of peak demand. Thus, storage R&D is likely to proceed independent of renewable development.

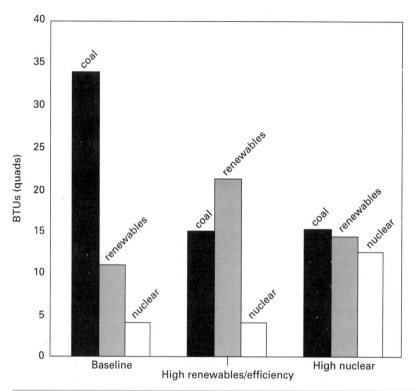

FIGURE 20.4 Three Energy-Use Futures, 2015

Source: Office of Technology Assessment (1991a).

Given these three possible paths our nation might take, how do we proceed? Chapter 16 provided a three-part approach for evaluating decisions like this:

1. Pick the clean, low-cost technology.
2. Increase CT profitability by eliminating subsidies and/or internalizing social costs for competitor technologies, preferably through IB regulation.
3. Promote the technology directly.

Step 1—Picking Winners. On the environmental scale, efficiency comes in first, wind power second, solar power third, natural gas fourth, with nuclear power and coal vying for last place. Ranked in terms of current costs, efficiency measures appear cheapest, with coal second, wind power third, natural gas fourth, nuclear fifth, and solar last. However, ranked in terms of feasible, long-run average costs, photovoltaics have a reasonable shot at being competitive with coal.

The low-hanging fruit in this case are clearly efficiency and wind power; photovoltaics, though risky, present a good bet.[23] Is there a case for aggressive promotion of

---

[23]Hydro and solar thermal electricity are also attractive technologies on economic and environmental grounds. However, they have somewhat limited long-run potential in the United States.

nuclear? Probably not at this point. While nuclear plants can undoubtedly be made safe, few feel that nuclear costs in the United States can be substantially reduced below their current range of over \$.12 per kWh range and still provide a politically acceptable margin of safety.[24] Photovoltaics offer a feasible, cleaner, cheaper option than nuclear to fossil fuels. However, if PVs do not pan out and global warming emerges as a serious environmental threat, then nuclear technology remains available as a fallback, provided the waste disposal problem is resolved.

Step 2—Level the Playing Field. The current U.S. energy market is far from the ideal of a free market; government intervention is widespread through both regulation and subsidy. For 1989, estimates of federal subsidies by Koplow (1993) ranged from a high of \$36 billion to a low of \$21 billion.[25] The author identified two main categories of subsidies: tax breaks and expenditures supporting industry by federal agencies.

To provide a feel for the type of expenditure undertaken by government agencies, Table 20.1 details the agencies involved in supporting just the exploration phase of oil production. One of the biggest agency subsidies to the oil industry, not quantified in the Koplow report, is spending by the military to protect Persian Gulf oil fields. Hall (1992) estimated that defense spending to protect oil imports in 1985 was \$14.8 billion. Hall's estimate did not include the cost of the Desert Storm war.

Who wins and who loses from federal subsidies? Table 20.2 and Figure 20.5 break down the subsidies between the major energy sources. Efficiency and non-hydro renewables, the two clean technologies identified above, receive only 5.4% of the total. The major beneficiaries of subsidy policies are clearly the conventional fuel sources—nuclear and fossil fuels receive 88.5% of all energy subsidies.

TABLE 20.1 Federal Agency Subsidies for Oil Exploration

Support Activity	*Agency Involvement*
Procurement	U.S. Geological Survey, National Oceanic and Atmospheric Administration, and Bureau of Indian Affairs all provide survey, mapping, and development support.
Technological Development	Department of Energy finances R & D on oil extraction.
Industry Infrastructure	Bureau of Land Management provides low-cost access to leases.
Risk Reduction	Fish and Wildlife Service conducts environmental impact assessment of Arctic drilling.

Source: Douglas Koplow (1993: Appendix A–2), *Federal Energy Subsidies: Energy, Environmental and Fiscal Impacts* (Washington, DC: Alliance to Save Energy), p. 46 Used with permission.

---

[24]Regarding costs, see footnote 5. On the safety issue, see "A Comeback for Nuclear Power?" *National Geographic,* August 1991, as well as Office of Technology Assessment (1990).

[25]The high-end estimate measures the value of the subsidy to industry; the low end measures the accounting cost to government. To illustrate why the two may vary, suppose a government agency provides \$1,000 in free services to a company. A company paying a 30% corporate income tax would have to earn \$1,300 to purchase equivalent services in the marketplace. Of course, the opportunity cost to government is in fact \$1,300, since it loses the \$300 in tax revenue by subsidizing the company's activity. High- and low-end estimates also incorporate other uncertainties. See Koplow (1993) for further elaboration.

	TABLE 20.2 Federal Energy Subsidies by Sector, 1989[a]	
Energy Source	***Subsity Level (1989 $Million)***	***Percent of Total Subsity***
Fossil	17,125	59.8
Coal	6,800	23.7
Oil	7,114	24.8
Natural Gas	3,212	11.2
Mixed Oil and Gas	0	0.0
Nuclear	8,223	28.7
Fission	7,809	27.3
Fusion	414	1.4
Hydroelectric	500	1.7
Emerging Renewables	769	2.7
Nonethanol Biomass	321	1.1
Solar	167	0.6
Wind	51	0.2
Geothermal	206	0.7
Other	24	0.1
Other Supply Sources	1,260	4.4
Ethanol	707	2.5
Waste to Energy	339	1.2
Mixed Supply	46	0.2
Supply Efficiency	169	0.6
Demand-side Efficiency	775	2.7
TOTAL	28,652	100.0

[a]These are the mid-range estimates calculated from Koplow (1993: Table 6). See footnote 25 for a more detailed discussion of Koplow's "high" and "low" estimation methodology.
Source: Douglas Koplow (1993), *Federal Energy Subsidies: Energy, Environmental and Fiscal Impacts* (Washington, DC: Alliance to Save Energy), p. 16. Used with permission.

The fact that coal, oil, and fission (nuclear) technologies receive the bulk of subsidies is not surprising; they also supply the bulk of the country's power (and have important political constituencies). In addition, if global warming proves to be less serious than currently thought, coal will likely remain our major electric fuel. Thus, R&D to support reducing conventional pollutants from coal plants is certainly reasonable. However, even on an energy-adjusted basis, coal and nuclear fission received the highest subsidies calculable, with efficiency coming in last.[26]

This discussion of subsidy policy highlights two points. First, energy markets are not free markets; government intervention to promote technologies has been and continues to be substantial. Thus, the baseline scenario sketched above, in which coal dominates the energy future, is not a "natural" outcome of market forces. Coal receives the bulk of federal subsidies today, including large R&D expenditures to develop cleaner coal technologies, which will allow the industry to expand. Second, federal policy currently tilts the playing field heavily against renewables and energy

---

[26]Koplow (1993: Table 11).

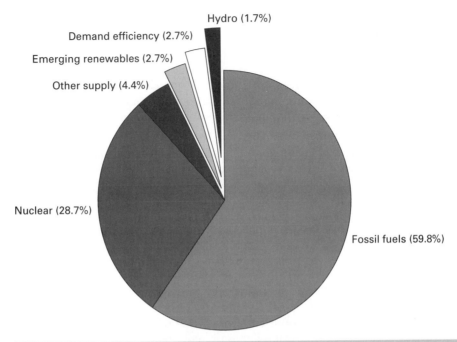

FIGURE 20.5 Federal Energy Subsidies by Sector, 1989

Source: Data taken from Douglas Koplow (1993), *Federal Energy Subsidies: Energy, Environmental and Fiscal Impacts* (Washington, DC: Alliance to Save Energy), p. 16.

efficiency. The government's substantial support of conventional technology works against market penetration of inherently clean alternatives.

Reducing the subsidies for conventional options, or at least leveling the playing field by boosting subsidies for clean technologies, is necessary for their promotion. What about internalizing externalities associated with conventional fuels? The major externalities associated with fossil fuels used for heat and electricity are urban air pollution, acid rain, and global warming. Regulations covering the first two have recently been tightened under the Clean Air Act of 1990.

Ultimately, these regulations may have a significant impact on the price of coal-fired electricity from existing facilities in some regions; more relevant from a competitive point of view will be impact on the price of electricity from new coal-fired plants. Bohi et al. (1990) argue that such plants will probably adopt the "clean coal" technologies discussed above and, as a result, not face the full cost increases associated with installing scrubbers, using low-sulfur coal, or purchasing SO_2 permits. In addition to the Clean Air Act, state utility adder policies (discussed in chapter 17) may ultimately tack on an additional penny or two to the cost of a coal-fired kWh, depending upon whether global warming effects are factored in.

A tax on the carbon content of fuels has been widely discussed as a means of combating global warming. A carbon tax of $100 per ton is thought to be sufficient to freeze emissions at 1990 levels; such a tax would raise the price of oil and coal by around 90% and natural gas by about 50%.[27] While such a tax is unlikely in the near term, it would certainly hasten the development of clean alternatives.

Nuclear advocates often maintain that, on safety grounds, the industry is over-regulated, which explains its cost disadvantage. Given public opposition to facility siting, regulation may well need to tighten if new nuclear facilities are built. Realistic assessments of waste disposal costs and decommissioning expenses (no one has yet disposed of an abandoned nuclear facility) should also be built into cost per kWh estimates for any new facilities.

Step 3—Direct Promotion of CTs. Here we will proceed by example, considering government policy to directly promote small-scale (energy efficiency) and large-scale (solar) technologies. The basic message is that, to avoid waste and counterproductive incentives as well as to insure equity, subsidies should be carefully targeted. Begin with a

---

PUZZLE

Suppose that Octopus Power is considering providing a weatherization service to about a quarter of its customers "free of charge." Why? Because, by reducing energy demand, it will be able to avoid building a new power plant. However, since there is no such thing as a free lunch, the utility will pay for the weatherization by charging higher electricity rates for all its customers. Is the weatherization subsidy a good idea?

SOLUTION

Probably not. The problems with the plan highlight a variety of pitfalls facing all efforts to promote energy efficiency: These include equity issues, strategic behavior, free riding and rebound effects.

Here is the **equity issue.** By providing the weatherization service free of charge, Octopus would provide dramatic benefits to a quarter of its clients at the expense of the rest. While the company and ratepayers will save money in total, most of Octopus's clients will be worse off than if the power plant were built.

Another possible problem is **strategic behavior;** by subsidizing one portion of the population, Octopus may inadvertently discourage others from weatherizing on their own. This group may hold back until more subsidies become available. Octopus may also be paying more than it needs to for conservation due to the potential for **free riding;** some who would have otherwise weatherized on their own may take advantage of the subsidy.

Finally, there is the problem of **rebound effects.** Because electric bills for weatherized homes are now lower, residents will spend some of their increased income on

---

[27]Pearce (1991).

keeping their house warmer or buying new appliances, which uses more electricity. The size of the rebound effect in the electricity field is the subject of current debate.[28]

An alternative plan helps resolve all these issues: Have the residents whose buildings are weatherized pay the bill. Consider a house with pre-weatherization electricity use of 12,000 kWh per year; weatherization reduces it to 10,000 kWh. The residents could, thus, afford a substantial rate increase (from $.05 up to $.06 per kWh for example) and still come out with a lower overall electricity bill ($.06 per kWh * 10,000 kWh = $600; $.05 per kWh * 12,000 kWh = $600).

If energy-efficiency measures are truly cost-effective, then in theory it will always be possible to design a financing mechanism where *the recipient ultimately pays* for a substantial portion of the service *and still comes out ahead.* That is, cost-effective efficiency investments can be designed to generate something close to a Pareto improving situation.

In practice, the government or utility ratepayers at large may still need to absorb the risk and marketing costs necessary to overcome poor information and access to capital on the part of its clientele. For example, one utility found that requiring participants to pay for insulation to cover hot-water heaters, *even though the clients would save money at zero risk,* reduced program participation substantially. Lowered participation, in turn, increased the cost per kWh saved by 350% due to scale economies in operating the program.[29]

Yet, *minimizing* the subsidy level by requiring recipients to pay at least a portion of the cost will reduce problems of inequity, strategic behavior, free riding, and rebound effects. This general rule will be true for any subsidy policy designed to encourage small-scale CTs.

Efforts to promote large-scale solar power through subsidies should be crafted with a similar eye toward the potential for waste. In the photovoltaic field, the challenge is to reduce PV costs. As discussed in chapter 18, there are essentially two ways to do this: (1) Develop better technology through R&D and (2) Capture cost savings through economies of scale and learning by doing. In the early 1980s, government policy makers prematurely took the latter route, funding flashy but uneconomic solar demonstration projects at the expense of basic R&D. At the same time, tax credits for the purchase of solar units were instituted to encourage the purchase of PVs; however, because PV was still not a competitive technology, when the credits expired in 1986, the PV market collapsed.[30]

Through the mid-1990s, PVs will remain at the stage where the bulk of cost savings will come through R&D. Zweibel (1990) argues that boosting federal funding for photovoltaic R&D from its mid-1980s level of around $35 million to closer to $100 million would be sufficient to achieve rapid cost reductions. (In fact, by 1994, the PV research budget was up to $78 million.)[31] In order to keep commercialization of the technology at the forefront of policy, Zweibel suggests that R&D funds should be

---

[28]Hobbs (1991) develops a "most-value" test, which incorporates all these factors for determining when DSM measures are efficient. He also discusses the rebound issue. On this point, see also Geller et al. (1992).

[29]This example is cited in Hobbs (1991). One way to boost participation rates would be to penalize nonparticipants by charging them extra for the energy they refused to save. See Katz (1989).

[30]See Walton and Hall (1990) and Zweibel (1990).

[31]Department of Energy, Office of the Secretary.

channeled to private U.S. firms already engaged in PV research, rather than concentrated in government labs.

By the late 1990s, assuming R&D funding is forthcoming, PV costs are expected to fall in the $.05 to $.10 range, making them competitive in some major markets. At this stage, government could begin to promote cost reductions by stimulating PV markets. In 1997, the U.S. government was pursuing a modest course along these lines, providing a purchase guarantee and tax-free construction bonds for a 10 MW facility in Nevada to be built by Amoco/Enron Solar. The danger here is to avoid paying for "yesterday's technology." Path dependence theory tells us that access to such funds should be conditional on demonstrating tangible progress in cost reduction; at the time of this writing, no details were available on the contract, but Amoco/Enron originally promised $.055 per kWh.[32]

In addition to supply-side subsidies targeted at firms, in the late 1990s, demand-side subsidies should be considered as well. One possibility would be tax credits for solar consumers; while such programs have proved effective in the past by encouraging adoption of solar technologies, they are expensive (since they are not targeted) and run the danger of subsidizing obsolete technology.[33] Zweibel (1990) argues that a cost-effective way to stimulate the industry might be through infrastructure policy. Government could support a major PV project to encourage clean transportation in a heavily polluted urban area—electric rail in Denver or electric cars in Los Angeles.

Photovoltaic power is so attractive that, in the long run, it is likely to be developed by private industry regardless of U.S. government policy. The question really is when and by whom? Path dependence theory tells us that, if PV arrives later rather than sooner, in the interim, we will continue to invest in long-lived infrastructure to support our fossil fuel economy. Thus, attempts to capture environmental benefits through a transition to PV will become more difficult. The "who" question is also important from an economic point of view. Our European and Asian competitors are currently showing the most interest in photovoltaics—not surprising, given their higher energy costs. This is in spite of the fact that most of the important basic PV research has been done in America.

To summarize this subsection: CT-promoting subsidies need to be carefully tailored. Consumer subsidies need to minimize pitfalls such as equity problems, strategic behavior, rebound effects, and free riding. Subsidies targeted at large-scale technologies should strike an appropriate balance between research and development and market building.

20.4 Technology Options: Transport

Our transportation system relies almost exclusively on oil and accounts for the bulk of petroleum use. The United States currently consumes around 17 million barrels of oil (around 3 gallons per person) per day, about 45% imported. Close to 26% of U.S. imports come from the Persian Gulf, a figure likely to rise in coming years. The Orga-

---

[32]"Solar Power for Earthly Prices," *New York Times,* December 15, 1997, p. D2.

[33]Durham et al. (1988) find that state tax credits significantly increased the rate of adoption of solar water systems.

nization of Petroleum Exporting Countries (OPEC), whose members are primarily Middle Eastern nations, control three quarters of the world's proven oil reserves.

The social costs of oil use fall into three categories: (1) taxpayer subsidies (discussed in Section 20.3 above), (2) environmental externalities, and (3) energy security. In developed countries, motor vehicles are a major source of urban air pollution, accounting for half of the nitrogen oxide (NOx) and volatile organic compound (VOC) emissions, and nearly two thirds of the carbon monoxide (CO) emissions. (Recall from chapter 13 that nitrogen oxide causes airborne acid pollution and, in combination with VOCs, ground-level ozone. CO reduces the oxygen content of the blood.) While autos contribute to local pollution problems, they are also a major source of carbon dioxide, the principal greenhouse gas. Worldwide, autos account for 14% of CO_2 emissions from fossil fuels, and this figure rises to 24% in the United States.[34]

The **energy security** issue arises from the impact that dramatic oil price swings have had on the U.S. economy over the last twenty years. Oil price shocks, the latest from the Persian Gulf War, have been associated with and have deepened our last three economic recessions. In addition, such price shocks substantially boost inflation. Estimates of the economic costs of dependence on oil have ranged from $1 to $20 a barrel.[35]

Related to the energy security issue is the fact that high U.S. demand (25% of world consumption in 1989) for oil props up the price. As a result of our major presence in the market, we have what economists call **monopsony power** over the price; a unilateral cut in U.S. demand would lower oil prices around the world. Greene and Duleep (1992) estimate that a decline in U.S. demand of 1 million barrels per day would translate into a price drop of between $.45 and $.80 per barrel of oil.

Unlike the case for electricity and heat, few clean technologies as defined in chapter 18 appear in the transport field. All options that offer environmental improvements over oil come at some price, either in private costs or convenience. However, because of the social costs associated with petroleum use, an economic case can certainly be made for promoting alternative technologies.

The major technology options can be divided into two categories. The first includes those options compatible with continued reliance on private auto transportation: increased fuel efficiency and switching to cleaner fuels. The second involves a switch to alternative transportation modes: urban mass transit, intercity and long-haul rail, car pooling, and even bicycling and walking.

FUEL EFFICIENCY

Of all the options, increased fuel efficiency comes closest to being a CT. Few doubt that substantial increases in fuel efficiency are possible. Congress' Office of Technology Assessment (1991b) sees an increase in the fleet average from 28 mpg to 38 mpg over the 1990s as a feasible goal. In addition, while fuel-efficient cars cost more to manufacture, Greene and Duleep (1992) argue that within the range up to 36 mpg to 37 mpg, the fuel savings tend to offset this cost. Thus, on the economic front, consumers wind up roughly even.

---

[34]MacKenzie and Walsh (1992).
[35]Greene and Duleep (1992).

More radical efficiency gains are imaginable; Amory Lovins (1995) of the Rocky Mountain Institute has been an advocate of ultralight, aerodynamic vehicles he calls "hypercars." He argues that complete redesign and reengineering—rather than the marginal modifications now pursued by automakers—could boost fuel efficiency by a factor of 10, with no compromise in safety or performance.

However, conventional efficiency improvements have faced both of these objections: safety and (Pareto) efficiency losses. One way to achieve better fuel performance is through "downsizing"—building smaller, lighter cars. However, in the past, lighter cars have been more prone to rollovers and proven less safe in a collision with a heavier vehicle. Based on these factors, the National Highway Traffic Safety Administration has estimated that the fleet downsizing since 1975—due both to rising oil prices and federal standards—has led to an increase of as many as 2,000 traffic fatalities per year.

Critics have charged that this is a substantial overestimate, because it fails to take into account that smaller cars pose less danger to others, as well as the fact that the disparities between car sizes—another factor in accidents—have shrunk as the fleet downsized. Moreover, small cars have become safer in recent years, as engineers have focused increasing attention on rollover and crash problems. The true impact on safety of increased fuel performance could be zero. Nevertheless, to the extent that fuel efficiency is achieved through downsizing (and it need not be), there is likely to be some safety impact.[36]

The Pareto efficiency issue relates to auto performance. American consumers have a taste for many energy-intensive features: large size, air-conditioning, four-wheel drive, rapid acceleration. Increased fuel efficiency requires giving some of this back. These performance costs of fuel efficiency may well exceed the local environmental benefits for residents where the air quality is currently adequate, making increased fuel efficiency inefficient in economists' terms. Indeed, stringent standards, by lowering the perceived quality of new cars, probably cause people to keep their dirtier cars longer—a new source bias. On the other hand, to the extent that widespread benefits like energy security or global warming are targeted by fuel performance, efficiency is less of a concern.

In addition to safety and efficiency concerns associated with improved fuel economy, increased fuel efficiency in the long run can be swamped by other factors. The first is increased driving. Total vehicle miles travelled increased at a rapid rate of 3.3% per year between 1970 and 1988. Miles per vehicle traveled remained relatively constant at 10,000; thus, total miles have been increasing as the number of cars per family increases.

There is also the possibility of a rebound effect—better fuel efficiency will lead to savings, some of which will be spent on increased driving. Estimates of the rebound effect in auto transport are in the 10% range.[37] Finally, American drivers have been shifting from cars to light trucks, which get much poorer mileage. As a result of these factors, total U.S. fuel consumption by cars, trucks, and buses actually grew by 40% between 1970 and 1988.[38]

---

[36]Office of Technology Assessment (1991b); Greene and Duleep (1992).

[37]Office of Technology Assessment (1991b); Greene and Duleep (1992).

[38]Mackenzie and Walsh (1992).

FUEL SWITCHING

The second transport option is fuel switching. Unlike fuel efficiency, which could tackle both local and global pollution problems at little net dollar cost to consumers, fuel switching is likely both to be expensive and to yield mixed environmental benefits. The major near-term fuel contenders are methanol, natural gas, ethanol, and electricity. Of these four, all but electricity are already in use as commercial vehicle fuels in different parts of the world. (Over the long run, many see promise in vehicles fueled by hydrogen fuel cells, whose major by-product is water!)[39]

On the cost front, all the major options appear likely to be more expensive than gasoline in the near term, though all are potentially competitive in the long run. Yet, the long-run cost estimates for these new technologies are highly unreliable; all depend on uncertain estimates of raw material prices, infrastructure investment, technological progress, and economies of scale. Thus, any one of the technologies could prove to be cheaper or much more expensive than gasoline.

Table 20.3 provides a list of the major near-term competitors and their environmental advantages and disadvantages vis à vis gasoline.

TABLE 20.3   The Environmental Effects of Alternative Fuels

Fuel	Advantages	Disadvantages
Methanol	Reduced emission of ozone precursors Reduced emission of most toxics Moderate reduction in greenhouse emissions if made from natural gas	Increased emission of formaldehyde Increased greenhouse emissions if made from coal
Natural Gas	Reduces most toxic and criteria pollutants Moderate reduction in greenhouse emissions	Increased nitrogen oxide emission
Ethanol	Reduced greenhouse emissions (potential) Reduced emission of ozone precursors Reduced emission of most toxics	Impacts from growing harvesting, and distilling biomass
Electricity (Battery)	Zero emissions in urban areas Reduced greenhouse emissions if made from solar or nuclear	Export of pollution to electricity facility Increased greenhouse emissions if made from coal Lead in batteries

Source: Office of Technology Assessment (1990). Not included in this list are hydrogen fuels and reformulated gasoline.

---

[39]For a good overview, see MacKenzie (1994).

Methanol, a liquid fuel made from natural gas, is the closest to being cost-competitive with gasoline. In the near term, methanol could compete with gas at a price of around $1.50; in the long run, after a substantial commitment to building a methanol infrastructure, some analysts feel methanol costs might fall as low as the equivalent of $1.00 per gallon. Methanol's primary environmental advantage is that it lowers emissions of ozone precursors—nitrogen oxide and volatile organic compounds.

Cars can also be run off of **natural gas** directly, either in liquified or compressed form. Natural gas is one of the cleanest of the alternative fuels, but even mass-produced natural gas vehicles would cost several hundred to a thousand dollars more than a conventionally fueled vehicle. The fuel itself is potentially cost-competitive with petroleum in the $1.00 to $2.00 per gallon range, although a major supply and distribution network would have to be constructed.

Ethanol is a liquid fuel—alcohol distilled from **biomass** or vegetable matter. The primary source for ethanol today is corn. Ethanol is not cost-competitive with gasoline; in the early 1990s, it was being heavily subsidized ($.60 per gallon) by the federal government as a way to reduce direct subsidy payments to farmers. Government researchers are trying to get wholesale ethanol costs from wood wastes down to less than $1.00 per gallon within the next decade.

Because biomass is a renewable resource, ethanol has the potential to reduce greenhouse emissions substantially. Carbon dioxide emissions from burning ethanol could be matched by the growth of new biomass. Currently, however, ethanol production provides less CO_2 relief than might be imagined since the energy used to harvest the corn and distill the ethanol releases nearly as much CO_2 as is trapped by the subsequent planting of more corn.[40] Greenhouse benefits would increase substantially if ethanol could be made from waste wood and/or if the distilling process were powered by renewable energy sources.

The final fuel option is electricity in the form of battery-powered cars. A precondition for **electric vehicles (EVs)** to make global environmental sense is the development of clean electricity. Otherwise, use of EVs will result in little overall reduction in pollutants. Moreover, there is concern that the use of lead-based batteries will generate significant environmental problems (Lave et al. [1995]).

However, because they have essentially zero on-site emissions, cars powered by batteries charged from coal, oil-fired, or nuclear plants could be used to improve urban air quality. In effect, the pollution could be exported to the vicinity of the electric generating facility.

Estimates of the potential cost-competitiveness of battery-powered cars range widely. Electric cars will cost more than conventional vehicles but have lower maintenance and fuel costs and last longer. The biggest concern is performance; EVs now on the drawing board will have relatively short cruising ranges. Thus, EVs will see their first widespread use as urban commuting vehicles, provided that improvements in battery technology are forthcoming.

To summarize: There are no obvious winners among the alternative fuels, either on environmental or cost grounds. Methanol and ethanol have the advantage of pro-

---

[40]Office of Technology Assessment (1990). Ethanol is still probably preferable to gasoline on this score, which also generates CO_2 emissions in the extraction, transport, and refining phases.

viding a familiar liquid alternative; cars can even be designed to run on either fuel or conventional gasoline, thus smoothing any transition. By contrast, both natural gas and electric vehicles are unfamiliar technologies and will require a larger upfront investment. On the other hand, methanol and natural gas depend on the development of a natural gas infrastructure. Finally, ethanol and EVs are currently not cost-competitive, and the full environmental benefits from either cannot be obtained unless new technologies are forthcoming.

MODE SWITCHING

Urban mass transit—rail or bus—has considerable environmental advantages over private transport. First, because these options are more energy-efficient, they reduce both local and global air pollution problems. For example, a busload of 40 commuters on a 10-mile trip to work emit 1140 pounds less of carbon dioxide than if they had driven their cars to work.[41]

In addition to increased efficiency for a given passenger-mile-traveled, mass transit helps slow the growth in total miles traveled. Holtzclaw (1991) estimates that cities with well-developed mass transit systems experience substantially lower rates of miles traveled per person. In a comparison of two San Francisco suburbs with similar histories, households living in the neighborhood served by transit since 1975 traveled only two-thirds as many miles by car in 1988; one mile on the transit system appeared to reduce total vehicle miles traveled by four. In other words, even when people used their cars, they traveled shorter distances, because the greater residential and retail densities that developed along with the mass transit system reduced the need for auto travel.

America's high reliance on private auto transport clearly illustrates the importance of **path dependence** in technological development, discussed in chapter 18. Why do some cities depend heavily on cars while others have well-developed transit systems? Adler (1991) describes a twenty-year political battle over transport options beginning in Los Angeles in the late 1920s. Downtown business interests favored an electric rail system to funnel shoppers into the central city; outlying business interests argued for freeways. Ultimately, the latter group triumphed and, in the late 1940s, the state and federal government began a massive spending program to construct the highway system that has subsequently shaped southern California. Without *comparable* governmental support, the mass transit system in the area collapsed.

By contrast, Toronto has North America's best public transportation system. Here, central city interests triumphed in municipal government; a key victory involved the defeat of a major freeway project in 1971. The Toronto city government has also kept mass transit a viable long-run option through zoning laws. These encourage relatively dense residential neighborhoods, as well as business development, in the area of mass transit stations.[42]

However, the dominance of private auto transport is not based solely on accidents of history. Cars clearly have an edge in convenience and greater mobility. Thus, as incomes have risen in developed countries, people have tended to opt for auto

---

[41]Mackenzie and Walsh (1992).
[42]Frisken (1991).

travel. Even in a supportive environment like Toronto, mass transit accounted for only 26% of all trips in 1987, down from 41% in 1961. However, mass transit's share of peak period travel in and out of the city remained constant at 70% over the period. The decline of mass transit has occurred in spite of the fact that in the United States, private transport—including vehicle purchase, finance charges, insurance, and fuel— costs the average commuter about twice as much as using public transport.[43]

The suburban sprawl that now characterizes most American cities means that private transport is a virtual necessity for shopping, getting to work and school, and for recreation. In addition, many residents of developed countries have shown an evident preference for auto travel. Thus, any rapid switch to mass transit will be difficult. Nevertheless, given the potential environmental benefits from mass transit—greater efficiency and reduced passenger-miles traveled—a gradual transition to this mode could be promoted where economically feasible.

A more attractive short-run form of mode switching may involve inter-urban travel; roughly one third of air travel involves trips of fewer than 600 miles. **High- speed rail** is a potentially attractive alternative for this market in terms of convenience and cost. From an environmental perspective, rail can use as little as one-third the energy as air travel.[44]

20.5 Policy Options: Transport

What is the case against petroleum-based automobile transport? The primary concerns are urban air pollution, global warming, and energy security. To this list, we should add congestion, oil spills, and oil drilling in sensitive habitat. What kind of a technology promotion response do these externalities justify? Section 20.4 suggested that there are no completely clean technologies in transport; as a result, any one of the three options we have discussed—fuel efficiency, fuel switching, or mode switching—will be relatively costly.

POLICY OPTIONS FOR FUEL EFFICIENCY

Fuel efficiency appears to be closest to a CT. In fact, under a variety of scenarios, achieving greater fuel efficiency standards through technology-forcing regulation passes a benefit-cost test. Greene and Duleep (1992) analyze the impact of raising the **Corporate Average Fuel Economy (CAFE)** standards to 36.5 mpg for passenger cars and 27.5 mpg for light trucks by 2001. They find that under favorable assumptions, the present value of net benefits equals $286 billion; under unfavorable conditions, raising standards would generate a net cost of $11 billion. Table 20.4 summarizes their cost-benefit findings for a set of "moderate" assumptions.

Greene and Duleep include as costs of the CAFE increased vehicle price, reductions in performance, and reductions in safety; however, fuel savings tend to largely offset these costs, at least for the CAFE increases under consideration. The major benefits of tightening the CAFE standards arise from carbon dioxide control and improved energy security, including the monopsony effect discussed above. By contrast,

---

[43]Frisken (1991); Lowe (1991).
[44]Geller et al. (1992).

TABLE 20.4 Benefits and Costs of Increasing the CAFE for Cars[a] (1989 $billion)

	Benefit (Cost)
Vehicle Cost (including value of reduced performance)	− 63.2
Safety	− 3.3
Fuel Savings (adjusted for reduced fleet turnover)	+ 69.7
Oil Costs (monopsony)	+ 15.6
Energy Security	+ 5.8
Global Warming	+ 6.6
Urban Air Pollution	+ 1.3
Total	+ 32.5

[a]For ease of exposition, this table omits the categories of consumer surplus (very small), and wealth transfer to oil producers; the latter is a "fairness" adjustment of the type discussed in chapter 2. The authors, while recognizing that damage estimates are preferred, use mitigation cost estimates for volatile organic compounds and CO_2 (see the discussion in chapter 17 on adders). However, they do examine the robustness of the their result to different CO_2 estimates.

Source: David L. Greene and K. G. Duleep (1992: 5–8), "Costs and Benefits of Automotive Fuel Economy Improvement: A Partial Analysis," *ORNL-6704* (Oak Ridge, TN: Oak Ridge National Laboratory).

control of urban air pollutants provides relatively small benefits. Because most of the benefits from a tighter CAFE are global, rather than local, the standards are not as inefficient as one might have suspected.

As always, benefit-cost analyses are subject to substantial uncertainty; Greene and Duleep identify several important factors, which lead to the wide swings in their result. Much of the benefit from fuel efficiency comes from fuel-cost savings and lower oil prices due to the reduction in U.S. demand. Thus, the CAFE standards look worse if oil prices fall in the future, a high discount rate is used, and/or the oil price is assumed to be insensitive to changes in demand (elastic supply). Nevertheless, under most scenarios, increased CAFE standards pass a benefit-cost test.

Having argued that tighter CAFE standards could probably be justified on efficiency grounds, is there a better way to achieve fuel efficiency? Two types of pollution taxes might be considered: **gas taxes** and taxes on gas-guzzling cars. Gas taxes have the advantage of simultaneously forcing fuel-efficiency improvements and attacking the growth in vehicle miles. CAFE standards, by contrast, probably increase the growth in vehicle miles through the rebound effect.

The problem with gas taxes is that they would have to be very high to force efficiency improvements on the order of 10 mpg, a 30% to 35% increase over the current level of 28 mpg. As casual evidence, European cars are about as efficient as American cars though gas prices are at least double and, in some cases, four times as high. Greene (1990) estimates a maximum price elasticity of mpg of .21, meaning that a 1% increase in price leads to a 0.21% increase in fuel economy. This suggests that prices would have to rise from $1.36 per gallon to $2.15 per gallon to achieve only a 10% increase in mpg.[45]

---

[45]Greene (1990) also finds that even during the period of rapidly escalating gas prices, the CAFE standards were much more important than gas prices in driving fuel efficiency up.

Another widely discussed possibility has earned the nickname **feebates.**[46] Feebates combine a fee on gas-guzzling cars with a rebate on fuel-efficient cars. A feebate policy would, thus, be revenue-neutral in an obvious way, have the politically attractive feature of punishing evildoers and rewarding the good, and probably not be regressive, since poor folks would opt for the subsidy. Davis (1991) estimated that a feebate proposal in California, DRIVE+, would achieve around a 10% reduction in both emissions and fuel use. The United States currently does have a gas-guzzler tax on vehicles achieving less than 22.5 mpg, though no rebates. In 1986, the tax level ranged from $500 to $3,850.[47]

Feebates appear to be a better alternative to high gas taxes for encouraging a market-driven shift to fuel efficiency. However, by lowering the cost of fuel-efficient automobiles, feebates might increase the growth in vehicle miles. In addition, setting the right feebate schedule to get precisely a 10 mpg increase in fuel efficiency would require some experimentation.

As was documented in chapter 17, taxes have seldom proven adequate on their own to achieve pollution control targets. Ultimately, some mixture of CAFE standards, gas taxes, and feebates will provide the best feasible mechanism for increasing fuel efficiency and dealing with the growth in vehicle miles.

POLICY OPTIONS FOR FUEL SWITCHING

Applying our method for evaluating clean technologies to fuel switching suggests that the opportunities for successful government promotion in this field are essentially limited to R&D, subsidy elimination, and some targeted technology-forcing regulation. Because there are no clear environmental winners with the potential for near-term cost-competitiveness, aggressive government action to promote one fuel over another, at this point, is as likely to foreclose as to open up attractive development paths.

Fuel switching yields potential local and global environmental benefits. The local benefits are reductions in urban air pollution, particularly ozone precursors (VOCs and NOx) and carbon monoxide. About 70 to 100 urban areas still violate ozone standards, with a similar number of communities violating CO standards. However, the EPA expects more communities to come into compliance with CO regulations as old cars are replaced.

Ranking our alternative fuels in terms of improving urban air pollution, EVs come in first, natural gas second, methanol third, and ethanol last. The Clean Air Act of 1990 includes a provision that 10% of all cars sold in California by 2003 must be "zero-emission" vehicles. This technology-forcing regulation clearly favors EVs, consistent with our ranking.

Unfortunately, there is little economic logic behind the federal government's ongoing subsidy for ethanol produced from corn. Any effort to promote fuel switching on a *nationwide* basis to tackle *local* problems is bound to be highly (Pareto) inefficient; why encourage rural residents to switch to costlier vehicles or fuels when their local air quality is already safe?

---

[46]I believe this term originated with the Rocky Mountain Institute.
[47]MacKenzie and Walsh (1992).

But the ethanol case goes well beyond simple inefficiency. Ethanol is the worst of the alternative fuels in terms of improving urban air pollution, and yet receives a very large, ongoing production subsidy. The $707 million subsidy in 1989 almost equaled government spending to promote other renewable technologies. Moreover, the subsidy is completely untargeted. Ethanol use is highest in the Midwest, a region with only moderate air pollution problems. Finally, in spite of receiving subsidies since 1978, ethanol is nowhere near competitive with gasoline in price.

The ethanol subsidy is an example of bad government policy directed toward noble ends: energy security, higher farm incomes, and, more recently, positive environmental effects. Yet *noble ends are not sufficient to justify government promotion.* Our CT test requires clear-cut and substantial environmental benefits, as well as long-run cost-competitiveness. Ethanol from corn provides neither. In part because the subsidy was not conditional on improved cost performance, the ethanol subsidy, like those for conventional fuels, is now deeply entrenched. To shore up this support, the principal producer of ethanol in the United States, Archer Midland Daniels, along with the company C.E.O., contributed $900,000 to the Republican party in 1991 and 1992. In 1993, pushed by Democratic farm-state legislators, Clinton's EPA proposed an expansion of mandated ethanol use.[48]

As in the ethanol case, large-scale programs to promote methanol cannot be justified as a way to improve urban air quality. The fuel's local environmental benefits are simply not large enough to compensate for its higher costs. This conclusion has been borne out by a number of benefit-cost studies.[49]

How can we deal with urban air pollution if not through subsidized fuel switching? Fuel switching can be encouraged via an incentive-based approach in a variety of ways. One interesting proposal is for an **auto emissions tax.** When cars go in for their annual inspection, owners could be required to pay a tax based on their total emissions: the product of emission per mile and yearly mileage. This would have the effect both of encouraging cleaner fuels (based on market criteria) and reducing miles driven.[50] The tax could be tailored to suit regional needs.

In addition, a variety of command-and-control methods are available for attacking urban air pollution. These include reducing the volatility of gasoline, applying stricter controls to hazardous waste facilities, and improving vapor-trapping devices on gasoline nozzles. Congress's Office of Technology Assessment (1990) maintains that such measures could bring two thirds of the non-attainment areas into compliance with ozone standards.

What about the global benefits from fuel switching, reduced emissions of carbon dioxide? Here the fuels rank in the following order: EVs (from solar or nuclear), ethanol (from wood waste), natural gas, and methanol. California's zero-emission auto market is probably sufficient to kickstart industry interest in EV production. One side benefit of this technology-forcing regulation will be heightened private-sector R&D in battery storage, a precondition for the successful spread of solar-

[48]Associated Press, "Northwest Airlines Contribution Questioned," Spokane *Spokesman-Review,* December 6, 1992; and "Ethanol Fuel on Horizon, Clinton Says," Albany *Times Union,* December 15, 1993.

[49]Walls and Krupnick (1990); Lareau (1990). On the economics of ethanol, see Walls et al. (1989).

[50]Collinge and Stevens (1990) discuss such an approach.

powered electricity. Finally, due to the potential of ethanol from wood waste to both reduce CO_2 emissions and be cost-competitive in the near term, government R&D in this field should be supported.

POLICY OPTIONS FOR MODE SWITCHING

Mass transit is often viewed as a highly subsidized, noncompetitive option vis à vis private transport. Indeed, transit does receive substantial government subsidies. The systems in Toronto and New York, for example, cover about two thirds of their costs through fees, while fares in Seattle recover only 30% of costs.[51] Less often recognized is that private auto transport also receives public subsidies that can rival those of transit systems. Table 20.5 provides estimates of some of these subsidies on a per vehicle basis.

The table does not contain estimates of hard-to-measure benefits related to defending Persian Gulf Oil supplies or the external costs of congestion, which would add significantly to the total. Nor does the table include the urban air pollution and greenhouse costs of auto travel. Nevertheless, even omitting these items, private vehicle owners directly cover only about 72% of the measurable costs associated with vehicle use. The rest of the bill is footed by taxpayers or nonauto insurance premiums.

In addition, the marginal cost of constructing new highways can be quite high. Goldstein (1991) compares the capital expenses of the BART system in San Francisco with the costs of a comparable freeway system (including vehicles) and finds that BART was a good buy. Transit systems can win out in terms of the cost-effective delivery of new transport.

As noted above, the primary advantage of transit is the way that it "naturally" reshapes urban and suburban densities. With denser living patterns, transit does

TABLE 20.5 Selected Subsidies for Private Auto Transport

Source of Social Cost	Annual Cost Not Borne by Drivers ($ per car)
Roadway Construction	69
Roadway Maintenance	42
Highway Services (ambulance, fire, police)	360
Parking	589
Accidents (pedestrians, cyclists)	291
Total Subsidy per Car	1,352
Total Private Cost per Car (fuel, taxes, depreciation, insurance, and so on)	3,820
Subsidy/total cost	0.26

Source: MacKenzie, Dower, and Chen (1992) provide gross subsidy levels. I convert them to a per vehicle basis using figures of 144 million cars (parking) and 188 million total vehicles (other costs) found in *The Statistical Abstract of the United States,* 1991. The figure for private costs, based on 10,000 miles per year, is also obtained from this source.

---

[51]Frisken (1991).

much more than simply replace auto trips in and out of the city. It also substantially reduces vehicle transport for shopping and entertainment. At the same time, cities dominated by urban and suburban sprawl have a hard time providing competitive mass transit. Thus, zoning laws are needed to lay the groundwork for a successful transit system.

Most economists have focused on promoting mode switching by removing subsidies for private transport (for example, tax-free, employer-provided parking) and internalizing externalities, particularly those associated with congestion. Congestion generates a variety of problems: wasted commuting time, increases in vehicle operating costs, pollution and accident rates, lowered productivity through worker fatigue and stress, and slowed delivery of products. While most of these costs are borne by vehicle travelers as a group, the commuting decision is a classic open access problem (discussed in chapter 3).

The individual commuter may recognize that, by taking her car to work, she will slow down average traffic by fifteen seconds. This is a small amount of time to her and a cost she is willing to bear. But fifteen seconds times several thousand commuters quickly adds up to large social costs. With each commuter viewing the problem in the same way, the result is a "Tragedy of the Commons" quite similar to an overfished ocean.

With the highways being common property, some kind of rationing system is necessary. One rationing system is price: Many economists have advocated toll systems to internalize congestion externalities. These systems can be quite sophisticated, with sensors in the road bed monitoring passing traffic equipped with electronic identification, and generating monthly bills. One way to attack congestion is **congestion or peak-load pricing:** charging higher tolls for travel during congested hours. However, this may have the effect of shifting work habits and commuting times without reducing overall vehicle use. While this may be useful for reducing certain urban air pollutants, it would not have much impact on greenhouse gases. Congestion pricing would tend also to be regressive unless the funds raised were used to compensate for this problem.

A non–price rationing scheme involves **dedicated traffic lanes.** These lanes are reserved for (or dedicated to) buses and multi-occupant vehicles and effectively lower the price of car pooling or bus travel. Dedicated lanes offer a carrot to those interested in mode switching, which could be combined with the stick of congestion pricing and higher parking fees. In addition, since poorer people tend to take the bus, the overall income impact of dedicated lanes would be progressive.

20.6 Slowing Global Warming at a Profit?

Having provided a review of energy technology choices and policy options, we can now return to an important question posed in the introduction to this book: How much will it cost to slow down and eventually halt global warming? Recall that estimates ranged from a high of $3.6 trillion in costs to possible net benefits from increased efficiency of $2.3 trillion.

By now you should have developed a healthy degree of skepticism about the ability of any economist to predict the future with reliability. As one participant in the economic debate over the greenhouse effect put it: "Everybody knows that nobody knows what will happen." Having said that, there is substantial agreement among economists on a number of points.[52]

First, the costs of reducing greenhouse gases depend upon how effective government policy can be in two key areas: (1) promoting energy efficiency above and beyond what will be achieved through rising energy prices, and (2) promoting the development of cheap non-carbon energy sources.

Optimists see the government moving in a rational manner to implement cost-effective demand-side measures, while funding R&D in renewable energy sources to bring their costs down to a level competitive with coal and gasoline by early in the twenty-first century. Optimists are not overly concerned about government failure because of the existence of very obvious "low-hanging fruit," especially in the heat and electricity field and possibly in ethanol-fueled or electric vehicles for transport. Because they see these governmental demand and supply-side efforts as ultimately delivering energy services at lower cost than the technologies in use today, global warming can actually be reduced while yielding a net economic benefit.

Pessimists, on the other hand, do not believe that government efforts to promote energy efficiency will be very successful. First, they fear that technology-forcing standards (like the CAFE) will generate self-defeating problems such as new source bias, that poorly thought out design standards will retard rather than promote technological change, or that money will simply be wasted by bureaucrats promoting cost-ineffective measures. Second, government must bear the real marketing costs necessary to speed up the slow diffusion of energy-efficient technologies, reducing the net savings. Third, they argue that easy efficiency measures will soon be exhausted, meaning that even a successful, short-term government effort to promote efficiency cannot be sustained. Finally, pessimists tend to feel that renewable energy options do not have the dramatic economic promise that optimists claim.

In spite of their disagreements, however, both optimists and pessimists agree on the general direction that government policy should take to reduce the costs of slowing global warming. First, there should be an increased commitment of government R&D funds to non-carbon-based and renewable energy sources. The earlier that cost-competitive technology alternatives become available, the lower will be the cost of reducing greenhouse gases. As we noted in chapter 9, early cost savings become especially important over time, because they free up capital for investment, which raises future productivity.[53]

Beyond R&D funding, there is disagreement over whether government should make efforts to promote clean energy sources. However, most economists feel that if it does so, to the extent possible such efforts should rely on an incentive-based approach. Thus, government should not try to sort out whether photovoltaic-powered electric vehicles or biomass-based ethanol fuels will be a cheaper, greenhouse-friendly transportation option and then develop and implement a promotional strategy; the better approach is simply to impose a non-regressive carbon tax on all energy sources and then let the issue be decided in the market. However, as I have stated repeatedly, taxes (or tradeable permit systems) are not always politically feasible or easy to im-

---

[52]The quote is from Hogan (1990). The next few paragraphs are distilled from Manne and Richels (1990a), Williams (1990), and Manne and Richels (1990b), as well as Joskow (1992).

[53]Hogan (1990) also argues that expensive energy may retard the rate of technological progress in the nonenergy sector, because such progress in the past has been energy-intensive.

plement; thus, a role will remain for direct promotion of clean technologies in attacking the global warming problem.

20.7 Summary

This chapter ends with a story suggesting two things. First, a more-or-less optimistic outcome to the global warming problem is potentially achievable. Second, major pitfalls need to be avoided along the way.

During the mid-1970s, in the face of the OPEC oil price hikes, the U.S. Congress became concerned about energy security. It took three principal measures: (1) funding substantial R&D in renewable technologies, (2) instituting a 15% tax credit for energy investments, and, (3) requiring public utilities to purchase any power produced by qualifying independent facilities at the utility's "avoided" or marginal cost of production.

The state of California took the most aggressive stance toward developing alternative energy sources, instituting its own 25% energy investment tax credit and a property tax exemption for solar facilities, and requiring utilities to provide ten-year, avoided-cost contracts to independent power producers. These contracts were based on the high energy prices of the early 1980s. At the time, they appeared to shield ratepayers from further fuel increases; in retrospect, they protected alternative energy producers from the dramatic decline in oil prices.

This attractive environment fueled a rush of investors, many looking only for lucrative tax shelters. In fact, at the height of California's efforts to promote alternative energy, investors were guaranteed a return on their investment *through the tax benefits alone*. The federal credit required only that the project be in service (even limited service) for five years, while the California tax credits could not be recovered by the government if the project failed to generate any power after its first year.

Into this environment, a variety of technology and design options were introduced, most of dubious value and most failed. Many of the better ideas, however, were based on work that had been begun under the federal R&D programs. Eventually, two success stories emerged: wind and solar thermal electricity. Figure 20.6 illustrates the dramatic progress made in reducing costs for these two technologies over the last fifteen years. Solar thermal is now close to a competitive $.05 per kWh; wind power has achieved this goal.

A closer look at the solar thermal case is instructive.[54] The private company LUZ International designed and built virtually all of California's plants in six years. In the early 1990s, LUZ was producing 95% of the world's solar electricity—355 MW, or enough to service about 140,000 households.

LUZ's impressive cost performance was driven by two factors. First, each plant took only a year to build and place into service, providing immediate feedback to scientists and engineers. (Wind power benefited from a similar ability to move rapidly through design changes.) Second, economic pressure was placed on LUZ. For its later plants, the ten-year, fixed-price contract was no longer available, while tax credits began to dry up in the mid-to-late 1980s. Thus, LUZ did not have the option of selling obsolete technology to the utilities.

---

[54]This section is based on Lotker (1991) and "A Bright Light Goes Out," *Nature,* December 5, 1990, p. 345.

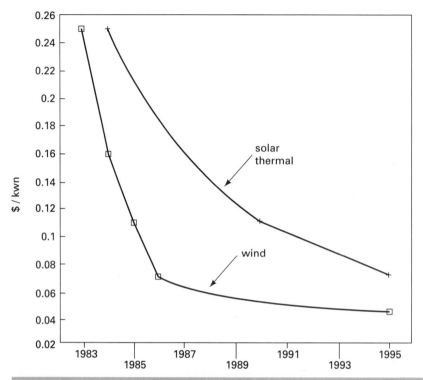

FIGURE 20.6 Costs of Wind and Solar Thermal

Source: Data for this figure are mid-range estimates in Robert H. Williams (1990), "Low-Cost Strategies for Coping with CO_2 Emission Limits," *The Energy Journal,* 11, no. 2, 51–74. Wind figures for 1995 are estimated. The solar thermal estimated for 1995 is from SEG X, which has now been canceled, and the 1995 estimate includes a portion of natural gas-fired power. See "A Bright Light Goes Out," *Nature,* December 5, 1990, p. 345.

In fact, uncertainty in state and federal policy precipitated LUZ' bankruptcy in 1991. The governor canceled the company's property tax exemption (based on a mistaken estimate of the cost to the state). At the same time, uncertain that federal credits would be renewed in 1992, LUZ built its last plant in only seven and one-half months, going $30 million over budget. While its current plants will continue to operate, the company was unable to raise cash for further expansion; citing uncertainty, investors dropped out.

In spite of the substantial direct subsidies LUZ received, a case can be made that the company still was disadvantaged vis à vis even greater subsidies received by conventional power sources. For example, natural gas purchases are exempted from sales taxes under California law; utilities do not take the risk of swings in fossil fuel prices into consideration when choosing new generating capacity; as discussed in chapter 17, they have only recently begun to incorporate environmental costs (adders) into capacity choices; and LUZ was constrained by law to build inefficiently small plants.[55]

---

[55]Lotker (1991).

There is little doubt that, without aggressive governmental action in the early 1980s, wind and solar thermal electricity today would not be commercial options for producing power. As evidenced, both industries are highly concentrated in California. As noted, virtually all of the world's solar thermal power is produced in the state, while California is also the leader in wind technology, currently producing about 80% of the world's wind power. The state today has enough wind capacity to meet the needs of the city of San Francisco; California's largest utility has announced that it will rely solely on wind power and energy efficiency to meet increased demand into the twenty-first century.

The optimistic moral of this story is that government policy can be effective in promoting clean technology. The pessimistic moral is that it can spend much more money than necessary to do so. The research and development and tax credit policies of the mid-to-late 1970s were untargeted and poorly designed. Spurred on by fears of $40-a-barrel oil, as well as unrealistic promises from the supporters of renewable energy, the programs set out to secure new sources of energy soon at any price. As a result, a lot of money went for uneconomic demonstration projects and into the hands of tax farmers rather than wind farmers.

In addition, governmental efforts in the 1970s were motivated primarily by energy security, not environmental concerns. Yet, as a result of these programs, in the 1990s we now have two competitive, clean technologies on the shelf to address pollution control. To put a last optimistic spin on the story: If a shotgun approach to technology promotion like that applied in the 1970s nevertheless yielded competitive, clean options within a decade, a more focused approach can probably achieve similar results at lower cost.

There is some evidence that government policy makers learned the lessons of the 1970s. The magazine *Nature* reports that today "conversations among the National Renewable Energy Laboratory researchers all tend toward the same course: five minutes of science and an hour of policy. No more going for the environmental soft spot; now they argue that renewables make good business sense."[56] By keeping government attention focused on clean technologies, we have the best chance of combating global warming at a low cost and maybe even at a profit.

The last five chapters have examined the question "How can we do better?" in protecting the quality of our environment, where doing better has been defined as achieving a given level of pollution reduction at lower cost and with greater certainty. We have explored two ideas: incentive-based regulation and clean technology promotion. We have argued first that IB regulation, where technically and politically feasible, provides more cost-effective pollution control and better incentives for technological change than does the dominant command-and-control system.

However, we have also seen that the regulatory process itself—whether CAC or IB—is costly and conflict-ridden. As a result, recent economic attention has been focused on policies designed to promote technologies that reduce pollution in the first place. The path dependence theory suggests that government can and should use selective subsidies tied to cost reductions as a cost-effective complement to regulation; by tying subsidies to performance, a means is provided to avoid government failure in promoting clean technology.

The next section of the book turns to global problems. An optimistic view of the

[56]"The Future Is Now (Again)," *Nature,* December 5, 1991.

world sees rapid economic development in poor countries based on clean technologies, leading to a stabilization in the world population as living standards rise and birth rates fall. But even under this scenario, the global population will double in the next half century to around 11 billion people before it stabilizes. Can the global ecosystem survive this impact? Clearly, the rapid development of clean technology is a prerequisite to a sustainable future. My own view is that without cheap, readily available solar energy, it will be difficult for poor countries to achieve rapid enough economic growth to stabilize population growth without poisoning the global environment in the process. In my mind, the most important task for environmental economists is to help design and implement policies to speed up the diffusion of clean technologies.

APPLICATION 20.0

Promoting Electricity Conservation[57]

Suppose that you are in charge of the demand side management program at Megabucks Power and your state public utility commission has just decided that you can now count energy-efficiency measures as equivalent to investments in new generating capacity. This means you can recover efficiency investment costs plus a normal profit through higher electric rates for your customers.

You have the following information at your fingertips: Megabucks currently produces 1 billion kWh and anticipates needing another 100 million next year to service new residences. You are currently charging $.05 per kWh; new generating capacity (a coal plant) would come in at $.06 per kWh. Buying the coal plant would mean Megabucks could sell 1.1 billion kWh for an average price of $.0509 per kWh [$.0509 per kWh = (1 b kWh * $.05 per kWh + .1 b kWh * $.06 per kWh) / 1.1 b kWh)].

Fortunately, there is a CT at hand. It is possible to *reduce demand* by 100 million kWh through a program that weatherizes one quarter of the (identical) houses in your service area. Best of all, weatherization can be obtained at a cost of only $.03 per kWh or an overall investment of $3 million [$3 m = .1 b kWh * .03 per kWh].

Your challenge: Which of your customers pays for the $3 million program? Your assistant, Mr. Offthecuff, has a plan. "Let's select one quarter of the houses at random and provide the weatherization service for free. We can recover the costs by raising electricity rates for everybody. Overall, our customers will be better off since collectively they will save $3 million" [($.06-$.03) per kWh * .1 b kWh].

Good idea?

Key Ideas in Each Section

This chapter looks at technology options and government energy policy in the areas of electric generation and transport. The energy path that the United States follows over the next few decades will depend on the interaction of technology, economics, and government policy.

20.1 U.S. energy use per capita fluctuates based on the price of oil, government-mandated efficiency measures, and economic growth. **OPEC** oil shocks have had an im-

---

[57]This application is adopted from Katz (1989).

portant effect on energy use over the last twenty years. Americans today use about 6% less energy per capita than they did in 1974, but still about twice as much as several European countries and Japan.

20.2 Technology options for electricity (and heat) break down into six main categories. (1) **Demand-side management (DSM)** (energy efficiency) has substantial cost-effective savings potential. (2) New **clean coal technologies** may soon reduce conventional pollutants from coal plants but not greenhouse gas emissions. (3) **Nuclear power** faces unresolved **high- and low-level waste** storage issues, as well as widespread political opposition. (4) **Natural gas** is the most greenhouse-friendly fossil fuel but has a somewhat limited supply. (5) **Hydroelectric** supply can be expanded but at a cost to flooded ecosystems. (6) **Solar power** can be divided into **passive** and **active** categories, with the latter including **photovoltaics** and **solar thermal.** (7) **Wind** is a very attractive candidate, especially in the Midwest. Wind and solar will require improved means of **electricity storage.**

20.3 Based on environmental advantage and cost-effectiveness, CT candidates for electric power generation include efficiency, wind power, and solar power. Two steps to promote these CTs are (1) level the playing field by reducing subsidies for "dirty" technologies and/or internalizing externalities through IB regulation, and (2) invest in the new technologies directly. Here, however, **equity issues, strategic behavior, free riding, rebound effects,** and the right mix between R&D and market development all need to be considered.

20.4 Technology options for transport break down into three categories. (1) On net, fuel efficiency appears to be relatively cheap. Economic benefits include increased **energy security** and lower oil prices through the **monopsony** effect. Costs include reduced performance and possibly safety. (2) Fuel switching options include **methanol, natural gas, ethanol,** and **electric vehicles (EVs).** Of these, EVs and ethanol from waste biomass are two potential CTs. (3) Mode switching from autos to mass transit yields as a significant benefit an increase in residential density, reducing the growth in vehicle miles per capita. **High-speed rail** is a CT alternative to short-haul air travel.

20.5 Fuel efficiency appears to be a CT under our definition. Tools to promote efficiency include the **CAFE** standards, **gas taxes,** and **feebates,** each of which has advantages and disadvantages. In the area of fuel switching, R&D in ethanol from waste biomass, and technology-forcing regulation for EVs may be justified. The ongoing subsidy for ethanol produced from corn illustrates the danger of poorly targeted and open-ended subsidies. Finally, in the area of mode switching, when subsidies to auto transport are considered, transit systems may be considered CTs. To encourage mode switching, tools such as an **auto-emissions tax, congestion (peak-load) pricing** and **dedicated traffic lanes** can be used.

20.6 Economists are divided in their evaluation of the costs of slowing global warming. **Optimists** and **pessimists** differ both on the existence of clean energy technology and the extent to which government can effectively promote it. At a minimum, however, an increased government commitment to R&D in non-carbon fuels, a reduction in subsidies for fossil fuels, and more effective IB regulation are agreed on.

20.7 The development of solar thermal and wind power in California supports an optimistic view regarding a government energy policy but also illustrates the potential for government to waste available funds.

References

Adler, Sy (1991). "The Transformation of The Pacific Electric Railway." *Urban Affairs Quarterly,* 27, no. 1, 36–50.

Bohi, Douglas R., Dallas Burtraw, Alan J. Krupnick and Charles G. Stalon (1990). "Emissions Trading in the Electric Utility Industry." *Discussion Paper QE90-15.* Washington, DC: Resources for the Future.

Cantor, Robin and James Hewlett (1988). "The Economics of Nuclear Power." *Resources and Energy,* vol. 10, 315–335.

Carter, Luther (1987). *Nuclear Imperatives and Public Trust: Dealing with Nuclear Waste.* Washington, DC: Resources for the Future.

Collinge, Robert A. and Anne Stevens (1990). "Targeting Methanol or Other Alternative Fuels: How Intrusive Should Public Policy Be?" *Contemporary Policy Issues,* vol. 8, 54–61.

Davis, William B. (1991). "Economic Incentives to Improve Vehicle Fuel Use and Emissions." NRDC/Sierra Club Testimony Before the California Energy Resources and Development Commission. San Francisco, CA: NRDC.

Dubin, Jeffrey A. and Geoffrey S. Rothwell (1990). "Subsidy to Nuclear Power Through Price-Anderson Liability Limit." *Contemporary Policy Issues,* vol. 8, 73–78.

Durham, Catherine A., Bonnie G. Colby and Molly Longstreth (1988). "The Impact of State Tax Credits and Energy Prices on Adoption of Solar Energy Systems." *Land Economics,* 64, no. 4, 347–355.

Fickett, Arnold P., Clark W. Gellings and Amory B. Lovins (1990). "Efficient Use of Electricity." In *Readings From Scientific American.* New York: W. H. Freeman.

Flavin, Christopher (1987). *Reassessing Nuclear Power: The Fallout from Chernobyl.* Washington, DC: Worldwatch.

Friskin, Francis (1991). "The Contributions of Metropolitan Government to the Success of Toronto's Public Transit System." *Urban Affairs Quarterly,* 27, no. 2, 227–248.

Fulkerson, William, Roddie R. Judkins, and Manoi K. Sanghvi (1990). "Energy from Fossil Fuels." In *Readings From Scientific American.* New York: W. H. Freeman.

Geller, Howard, Daniel Lashoff, Alden Meyer and Mary Beth Zimmerman (eds.) (1992). *America's Energy Choices.* Cambridge, MA: Union of Concerned Scientists.

Goldstein, David B. (1991). "Energy and Capital Cost Savings from New Rail Transit Systems: An Illustration of Least-Cost Methods for the Transportation Sector." NRDC/Sierra Club Testimony Before the California Energy Resources and Development Commission. San Francisco, CA: NRDC.

Greene, David L. (1990). "CAFE or Price?" *The Energy Journal,* 11, no. 3, 37–57.

Greene, David L. and K. G. Duleep (1992). "Costs and Benefits of Automotive Fuel Economy Improvement: A Partial Analysis." *ORNL-6704.* Oak Ridge, TN: Oak Ridge National Laboratory.

Hafele, Wolf (1990). "Energy from Nuclear Power." In *Readings From Scientific American.* New York: W. H. Freeman.

Hall, Darwin C. (1992). "Oil and National Security." *Energy Policy,* 20, no. 11, 1089–1096.

Hall, Darwin C. (1990). "Preliminary Estimates of Cumulative Private and External Costs of Energy." *Contemporary Policy Issues,* vol. 8, 283–308.

Hobbs, Benjamin F. (1991). "The 'Most-Value' Test: Economic Evaluation of Electricity Demand-Side Management Considering Customer Value." *The Energy Journal,* 12, no. 2, 67–91.

Hogan, William W. (1990). "Comments on Manne and Richels: 'CO$_2$ Emission Limits.'" *The Energy Journal,* 11, no. 2, 51–74.

Holtzclaw, John W. (1991). "Explaining Urban Density and Transit Impacts on Auto Use." NRDC/Sierra Club Testimony Before the California Energy Resources and Development Commission. San Francisco, CA: NRDC.

Joskow, P. L. (1992). "Comment on Carbon Taxes and Economic Welfare." *Brookings Papers on Economic Activity, Microeconomics 1992.* Washington, DC: Brookings.

Katz, Myron B. (1989). "Utility Conservation Incentives: Everyone Wins." *The Electricity Journal,* October, 26–35.

Koplow, Douglas (1993). *Federal Energy Subsidies: Energy, Environmental and Fiscal Impacts.* Washington, DC: Alliance to Save Energy.

Lareau, Thomas (1990). "The Economics of Alternative Fuel Use: Substituting Methanol for Gasoline." *Contemporary Policy Issues,* vol. 8, 138–155.

Lave, Lester, Chris Hendrickson and Francis Clay McMichael (1995). "Environmental Implications of Electric Cars." *Science,* vol. 268, 993–995.

Lenssen, Nicholas (1991). *Nuclear Waste: The Problem That Won't Go Away.* Washington, DC: Worldwatch.

Lotker, M. (1991). "Barriers to Commercialization of Large-Scale Solar Electricity: Lessons Learned From the LUZ Experience." Sandia National Laboratory. Washington, DC: NTIS.

Lovins, Amory (1995). "Hypercars: The Next Industrial Revolution." In *Transportation and Energy: Strategies for a Sustainable Transportation System,* eds. Daniel Sperling and Susan Shaheen. Washington, DC: American Council for an Energy Efficient Economy.

Lowe, Marcia (1991). "Rethinking Urban Transport." In *State of the World, 1992.* Washington, DC: Worldwatch.

Lucke, Robert and Eric Toder (1987). "Assessing the U.S. Federal Tax Burden on Oil and Gas Extraction." *The Energy Journal,* 8, no. 4, 51–65.

MacKenzie, James J. (1994). *The Keys to the Car: Electric and Hydrogen Vehicles for the 21st Century.* Washington, DC: World Resources Institute.

MacKenzie, James J. and Michael P. Walsh (1992). *Driving Forces.* Washington, DC: World Resources Institute.

Mackenzie, James, J., Roger C. Dower and Donald D. T. Chen (1992). *The Going Rate: What It Really Costs to Drive.* Washington, DC: World Resources Institute.

Manne, Alan S. and Richard G. Richels (1990a). "The Costs of Reducing U.S. CO_2 Emissions: Further Sensitivity Analysis." *The Energy Journal,* 11, no. 4, 69–78.

Manne, Alan S. and Richard G. Richels (1990b). "CO_2 Emission Limits: An Economic Cost Analysis for the U.S.A." *The Energy Journal,* 11, no. 2, 51–74.

New York State Energy Office (1991). *Draft New York State Energy Plan, 1991 Biennial Update.* Albany, NY: NYSEO.

Office of Technology Assessment (1991a). *Energy Technology Choices: Shaping Our Future.* Washington, DC: U. S. GPO.

Office of Technology Assessment (1991b). *Improving Automobile Fuel Economy.* Washington, DC: U. S. GPO.

Office of Technology Assessment (1990). *Replacing Gasoline: Alternative Fuels for Light Duty Vehicles.* Washington, DC: U. S. GPO.

Ottinger, Richard L., et al. (1990). *Environmental Costs of Electricity.* New York: Oceana Publications.

Pearce, David (1991). "The Role of Carbon Taxes in Adjusting to Global Warming." *The Economic Journal,* 101, no. 407, 938–948.

Walton, A. L. and Darwin C. Hall (1990). "Solar Power." *Contemporary Policy Issues,* vol. 8, 283–308.

Walls, Margaret A. and Alan J. Krupnick (1990). "Cost-Effectiveness of Methanol Vehicles." *Resources,* 100.

Walls, Margaret A., Alan J. Krupnick and Michael A. Toman (1989). "Ethanol Fuels and Non-Market Benefits: Is a Subsidy Justified?" *Discussion Paper ENR89-07.* Washington, DC: Resources for the Future.

Weinberg, Carl J. and Robert H. Williams (1990). "Energy from the Sun." In *Readings From Scientific American.* New York: W. H. Freeman.

Williams, Robert H. (1990). "Low-Cost Strategies for Coping with CO_2 Emission Limits." *The Energy Journal,* 11, no. 2, 51–74.

World Bank (1992). *World Development Report, 1992.* New York: Oxford University Press.

Zweibel, Ken (1990). *Harnessing Solar Power: The Photovoltaics Challenge.* New York: Plenum Press.

PART

Can We Resolve Global Issues?

To this point, this book has focused primarily on environmental quality within a single wealthy country, the United States. We have explored the normative debate over the "right" level of pollution; considered political-economic realities that can constrain the effectiveness of government action to achieve these goals; and in the last five chapters, analyzed two broad approaches to "doing better"—incentive-based regulation and clean technology promotion. In this final part of the book, we will extend the lessons learned to resolving issues of global environmental concern: ozone depletion, global warming, loss of species diversity, and management of the global commons— the ocean and Antarctica.

As one steps outside the national border of a developed country, two things are immediately apparent. First, we are an awesomely wealthy people. A personal example brought this home to me. When I was working in Africa, my driver was admiring my work boots, and wanted to know what they cost. I admitted that the salary he earned in three months, and on which he supported his entire family, would barely be enough to buy them.

The second fact: As significant as our environmental problems are, they pale in comparison to those faced by people in poor countries. Hardship and suffering from water and air pollution, soil erosion and degradation, and deforestation and flooding are serious, dramatic, and widespread in the less developed world.

This part of the book will explore the complex links between widespread poverty in poor countries (working in part through high population growth rates), high levels of consumption in rich countries, and environmental degradation at both the global level and in the less developed world. We will also consider a variety of policies that governments in both rich and poor countries can take to reverse this environmental decline. Finally, we end with a look at the economics of global environmental agreements.

The stakes are high. By the year 2100 our grandchildren may be living on a planet supporting a stable population of 10 billion people, in an environmentally sustainable fashion. This is almost *double* the earth's current population. On the other hand, our grandchildren may be sharing the globe with a population of 16 billion people (and rising), in a world whose environmental life support systems will surely be stressed beyond recovery. The ultimate outcome depends in large measure on the actions of those of us who have sometimes contemplated buying boots at $100 a pair.

21

Poverty, Population, and the Environment

21.0 Introduction

In John Steinbeck's famous book *The Grapes of Wrath,* the main character Tom Joad returns to the family farm in Oklahoma during the dustbowl of the early 1930s to find his family evicted by the local land company, and their house abandoned. He asks his now-crazy neighbor, Muley, "What's the idear of kickin' folks off?" Muley replies:

> You know what kinda years we been havin'. Dust coming up and spoilin' ever'thing so a man didn't get enough crop to plug up an ant's ass. An' the folks that owns the lan' says, 'We can't afford to keep no tenants.' An' they says, 'The share a tenant gets is just the margin a profit we can't afford to lose.' An' they says, 'If we put all our land in one piece we can jus' hardly maker her pay.' So they tractored all the tenants off the lan'.[1]

Joad's family hits the road for California, the promised land, only to arrive mid-winter with thousands of others, finding "no kinda work for three months," misery, and starvation. In the final scene of the book, one of the women, whose baby has just been born dead from malnourishment, breast-feeds a starving fifty-year-old man.

Joad's story illustrates the process of economic development in a nutshell. In the United States, the 1930s, 1940s, and 1950s saw a transition from small-scale, labor-intensive farming to highly mechanized, chemical-intensive, large-scale agriculture. In the process, particularly during the depression, tens of thousands of farmers were pushed off the land through evictions, as large landowners consolidated small plots of land into larger, technically more efficient units. From 1950 to 1990, the number of farm residents in the United States dropped from 23 million to 4.5 million. Many of these farmers were African Americans from the South, who subsequently migrated to industrial cities in the North and Midwest.

---

[1]John Steinbeck, *The Grapes of Wrath* (New York: Viking Press, 1939), p. 64.

This **agrarian transition** away from an economy based on traditional small farming to one based on large-scale, market oriented agriculture has to date been a universal feature of market-driven economic development. The **traditional economic development** challenge is to productively absorb the millions of workers—holding now-useless farming skills, often illiterate or semiliterate—who are "freed up" from agriculture. In the traditional model, increases in agricultural productivity keep food prices low, benefiting urban consumers. At the same time, surplus labor from the agricultural sector fuels growth in other areas, leading to a rise in general living standards and "successful development."

The worldwide depression of the 1930s, the backdrop for *The Grapes of Wrath,* made this a difficult task. In the United States, we have been rather fortunate. For a period of about thirty years after the depression ended, much of the displaced, unskilled agricultural labor was absorbed by the booming manufacturing economy of the 1950s and 1960s. However, even in the United States, the process is not yet complete. As our economy began to "deindustrialize" in the late 1970s and 1980s (see chapter 9), high-paying, unskilled jobs began to dry up. Since then, absorbing the low-skilled sons and daughters of low-skilled agricultural migrants, many of them from minority groups, has again emerged as a development challenge.

The tragic experience of Joad's family is unfortunately a common one in many developing countries. On the one hand, traditional agriculture has become less and less viable, in part because of government policies like subsidized credit favoring large-scale agriculture. On the other hand, many (but not all) poor countries have been stuck in a virtual depression for the last ten to fifteen years. Over the last few decades years or so, large-scale, capital-intensive agriculture has displaced tens of millions of Third World farmers. These workers then either migrated onto less suitable, ecologically sensitive land, became landless agricultural laborers (often able to find "no kinda work" for many months), or else moved to urban shanty towns in search of jobs in the stagnant industrial or state sectors.

The central point of this chapter is that "solving" the economic development problem—providing productive work and income for displaced farmers and their children—is in fact part and parcel of addressing local and global environmental concerns. **Sustainability,** defined in chapter 6 as *preventing the deterioration* of average living standards for future generations, cannot be achieved unless poverty is directly addressed, because poverty and environmental degradation go hand in hand. Yet, the environmental consequences of economic growth can no longer be ignored; overall living standards do not rise automatically with economic growth as conventionally defined.

The specter of rapid population growth hanging over this entire picture is intimately connected with desperately high rates of poverty. As we will discuss below, poor people have very rational economic reasons for preferring large families. A basic lesson is thus that providing cheap birth control—throwing condoms at the problem—is only one part of a successful strategy for reducing fertility in developing countries. In addition, providing health, education, and employment opportunities for the poor majority, especially for young women, and then coupling this with comprehensive family planning services, all are needed to create an effective package for reducing population growth rates.

Beyond poverty and population, the environmental damage people do depends not only on our absolute numbers but also on the natural capital depleted and waste products generated by each person. The average person born in the United States, Europe, or Japan has a dramatically larger impact on the global environment than does a child from a poor country. Yesterday—spent driving my daughter to school, writing this book at my computer (with occasional trips to the refrigerator), taking the family out for a burger at dinnertime, and watching TV in my nice warm house—I arguably contributed more to global warming, ozone depletion, *and* tropical deforestation than a typical Brazilian would in a month or two. As an upper-middle-class American, I consume more than *100 times the resources* used by the average individual from a poor country.

This of course is just another way of restating the IPAT equation from chapter 7. Total environmental damage can be decomposed into three parts: the number of people, consumption per capita, and the damage done by each unit of consumption. The "population" problem is indeed concentrated in poor countries; 90% of world population growth in the next century will occur in the developing world. However, through legal and illegal immigration, poor country population pressure spills over into affluent countries. For example, largely as a result of legal immigration, the U.S. population is expected to increase by 50% (to 393 million) by the year 2050.[2]

By contrast, the "consumption" problem is currently centered in the rich countries. This too will begin to change as a growing number of poor country residents aspire to the consumption levels found in rich countries. The point here is not to make you or I feel guilty about our affluent lifestyle. Rather, we need to recognize that one needs to focus as much attention on reducing the environmental impact of high consumption in rich countries as reducing population growth in poor countries.

This chapter will provide an overview of these complex and interrelated topics: poverty, rapid population growth in the South, overconsumption in the North, environmental degradation, and sustainable economic development.

21.1 Poverty and the Environment

In rich countries, it is commonly assumed that environmental quality can be improved only by sacrificing material consumption. Indeed, this is the whole premise behind benefit-cost analysis laid out in the first part of the book. In poor countries, by contrast, a broad-based growth in income will, in many respects, tend to improve the quality of the environment. Four of the close connections between poverty and the environment follow.

1. For poor people, many environmental problems are problems of poverty. The biggest environmental health threat facing most people in poor countries is **unsafe drinking water,** compounded by **inadequate sewage** facilities. In 1990, around 1 billion people were without access to safe water, and over 1.7 billion were without adequate sanitation. Billions of illnesses each year and millions of deaths are attributed to water pollution.[3]

[2]March 1996 U.S. Census Estimates, Middle Series, at http://www.census.gov/population/projections/nation/npaltsrs.txt.
[3]World Bank (1992).

Exposure to **indoor air pollution** (smoke) from cooking and heating sources ranks close to urban air pollution as a concern. Some 400 million people worldwide are exposed to unsafe levels of indoor smoke, as against 700 million for outdoor air pollutants, but exposure to indoor pollution is typically more intense. Smoke inhalation contributes to about 4 million deaths per year among infants and children.[4] Figure 21.1 illustrates how these basic environmental conditions improve with increases in income.

FIGURE 21.1   Safe Water and Sanitation by Income

Population without safe water

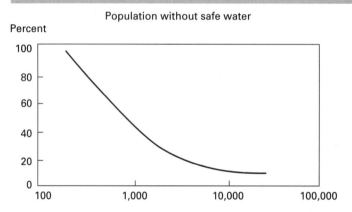

Urban population without adequate sanitation

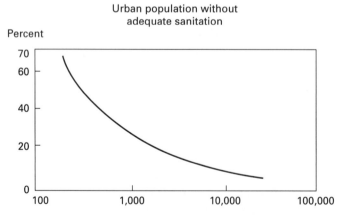

Source: From *World Develpment Report 1992* by The World Bank. Copyright © 1992 by The International Bank for Reconstruction and Development/The World Bank. Reprinted by permisssion of Oxford University Press, Inc.

---

[4]World Bank (1992).

2. Poor people cannot afford to conserve resources. Out of economic necessity, poor people often put an unsustainable burden on the natural capital in their immediate environment. Urban residents scour the immediate countryside for fuel—firewood or animal dung—leading to deforestation or the elimination of fertilizer sources. Landless farmers are pushed into overfarming small plots, farming on steep mountain slopes that soon wash out, or farming in clear-cut rain forests incapable of sustaining agriculture.

While poor people in search of subsistence often stress their immediate environment beyond easy repair, the much higher consumption levels of rich country residents have a substantially larger global impact. For example, commercial ranching for beef exports to European markets has had a bigger impact on Brazilian deforestation than small farmers.[5] Similarly, the dust bowl that helped drive Joad's family out of Oklahoma resulted from improper farming practices driven by a rising demand for wheat. We will address the impact of rich country consumption on environmental degradation below. But subsistence needs also play an important role.

3. Richer people "demand" more pollution control. As per capita income rises in a country, people begin to express a more effective demand for pollution control. Figure 21.2 illustrates cross country data gathered from market-oriented countries for four types of pollutants—ambient concentrations of particulate matter and sulfur dioxide, and per capita production of municipal waste and carbon dioxide. The two regulated air pollutants first rise as per capita income grows but then begin to fall. By contrast, unregulated or lightly regulated pollutants such as carbon dioxide and municipal waste grow along with per capita income.

How can we explain the **inverted U-shape** for the air pollutants?[6] Partly it has to do with **education**. As income rises, so do levels of awareness regarding environmental threats. Partly, it has to do with expanding democracy. As income rises, political participation tends to increase, and as a result, people are provided the opportunity to express a **political demand for pollution control.** (When data from the former Communist regimes are included, the inverted U-shape disappears.) Partly, it has to do with a **shift in industrial composition**—wealthier countries rely more on services and other relatively "clean" industries, while less developed countries have more basic manufacturing and mining. Finally, the relationship can be explained by **relative risk considerations:** When life spans are short due to inadequate nutrition or access to basic health care, concerns about respiratory, neurological, and reproductive diseases, or cancer from pollution, are dampened.

Figure 21.2 also reveals, however, that lightly regulated or unregulated pollutants increase in tandem with income and production levels. (We should recall, in addition, that at least some of the "reduced" sulfur dioxide and particulate emissions documented in Figure 21.2 have in fact reemerged as hazardous solid waste in the form of ash and sulfur sludges.) Hazardous waste production is also probably highly correlated with per capita

---

[5]Browder (1988: 251).

[6]Technically, air pollution (as a by-product of consumption) appears to be a normal good initially, and then becomes an inferior good. For discussions of the inverted U-shape for air pollutants, see World Bank (1992), Grossman and Krueger (1991), and Selden and Song (1992). Hettige, Lucas, and Wheeler (1992) find a decline in the growth rate of toxic intensity in manufacturing due to a shift in sectoral composition.

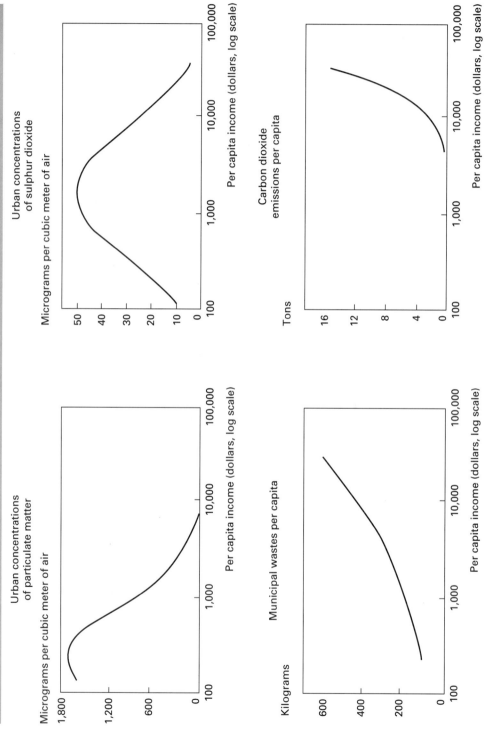

FIGURE 21.2 Regulated and Unregulated Pollutants by Income (Per Capita)

Source: From *World Development Report 1992* by The World Bank. Copyright © 1992 by The International Bank for Reconstruction and Development/The World Bank. Reprinted by permission of Oxford University Press, Inc.

income. As regulations on these pollutants become more stringent, will their per capita generation also begin to decline in wealthier countries? The graphs in Figure 21.2 provide an optimistic, but by no means conclusive assessment.

4. Population growth slows with increased income. The final link between poverty and the environment lies in income growth as a means of population control. As we shall see in the next section, as societies grow wealthier, almost universally families have fewer children.

These four interconnections between poverty and the environment reveal that, in poor countries, one need not "trade off" rising material living standards for improved environmental quality. In fact, the *only* effective way to improve environmental conditions is to alleviate the tremendous poverty faced by many of the people in these nations.

21.2 The Population Picture in Perspective

When my grandparents were born at the turn of the twentieth century, there were about 1.6 billion people alive on the planet. When my parents were born, around 1930, that number had risen to 2 billion. On my own birthday in 1960, I joined some 3 billion inhabitants. When my first daughter turned two in 1990, global population had climbed to 5.3 billion. If she has a child, her daughter or son will be born in a world with around 7.5 billion other people. And if my grandchild lives to be 80, she will likely die, at the end of the twenty-first century, on a planet supporting somewhere between 10 billion and 20 billion people.

Figure 21.3 provides a graphical representation of world population growth spanning these five generations, 200 years. Under the United Nations' 1996 "median" scenario, in which effective population control is achieved over the next few decades, global population will stabilize at around 10 billion people. This is a bit less than twice the number alive today.

Note that "median" doesn't mean this prediction will come true without serious changes—in particular, it requires fairly rapid, widespread adoption of birth control. By contrast, a world in which fertility rates fall only slowly leads to a 2050 population of 11.1 billion and still rising.[7] On the other hand, one could imagine a highly optimistic scenario. If we achieve and begin moving well below global zero population growth by 2020, this gets us down to 7.7 billion in 2050. The point here is that relatively small changes in fertility over the next two decades will have major impacts on global population by mid-century.

The "pessimistic" growth line is there for illustrative purposes—if fertility rates fail to decline at all, then global population will continue to rise, at the extreme, to 20 billion by the year 2100.[8] The actual number is highly uncertain; at some point, growth would be forcibly checked by large-scale famine, disease, war, or ecological disaster.

---

[7]"World Population Prospects: The 1996 Revision," October 1996, United Nations Population Division (New York: Department for Economic and Social Information and Policy Analysis).

[8]A 1% growth rate after the year 2000 would generate a year 2100 population of 16 billion; at 1.5%, "projected" population rises to 26 billion. The World Bank (1992: Figure 1.1) provides the pessimistic projection discussed in the text.

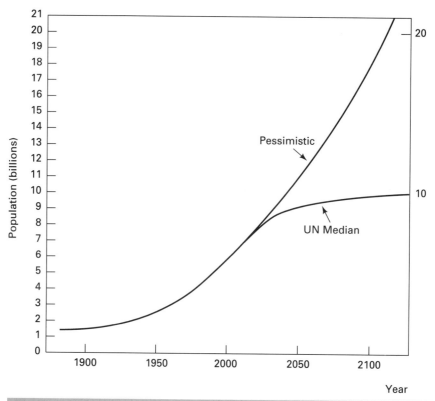

FIGURE 21.3 World Population, 1900–2100

(In an interesting recent book, *How Many People Can the Earth Support?* the author culled results from some sixty studies—dating back to 1679!—and found answers that tended to range from 4 billion to 16 billion.[9])

Given the magnitude of the environmental problems we face today, it is almost inconceivable to imagine the impact that 10 billion of us will have on the planetary ecosystem, let alone 20 billion. Population pressure must clearly be counted as a major global environmental threat in the medium and long term. At the more local level, population growth is increasingly overwhelming the ability of poor country governments to provide educational, health, and sanitary services. As poverty deepens in these countries, environmental stresses multiply for the reasons discussed in the previous section.

In chapter 7 we discussed the **Malthusian** perspective on population growth—named after the famous eighteenth-century economist Thomas Malthus. Reviewing briefly, Malthus predicted that a population growing at a geometric rate would soon outstrip the (slower) growth of food supply, leading to a catastrophic "natural check" on population—war, famine, or disease.

---

[9]Cohen (1995).

Yet Malthus' gloomy prediction has yet to come true on a global scale; population growth continues even in the face of substantial poverty worldwide. To date, we have avoided a Malthusian fate because of impressive technological developments in the field of agriculture—the so-called "Green Revolution" also discussed in chapter 7.

Moreover, Malthus' basic assumption, that population growth grows geometrically, also does not always hold. Not including immigration, wealthy countries have very low population growth rates, often *below* zero. The availability of effective birth control, not foreseen by Malthus, has meant that families are able to control their "natural" reproductive tendencies if they so desire. In general, the motivation to control family size appears to be greater for wealthier families.

The complex link between rising incomes and lower population growth is discussed below. But its presence has lead some observers to argue that poor countries are merely passing through a high-population growth phase. This phase resulted from a decline in death rates due in turn to the introduction of modern medicine in the 1940s and 1950s. As average incomes rise in these countries, it is argued, birth rates will fall and a "natural" **demographic transition** to low population growth will occur.

Indeed, as illustrated in Table 21.1, population growth rates worldwide were low, less than 1% from 1900 to 1950. As modern health-care practices spread in the 1950s, however, growth rates in the developing world exploded to well over 2%. After cresting in the late 1960s, population growth rates have fallen in many places including China and India, the middle-income countries, and the developed countries. The population problem has "taken care of itself" to a remarkable extent in countries like Korea, which experienced rapid and widely shared economic growth. Population growth rates in that country fell from 2.4% in 1960–1970 to 0.9% in 1990.[10]

The mid-1990s have seen generally good news on the population front. The population projections for 2050 presented in Figure 21.3 are *about a billion people lower* than those I presented in the first edition of the book only four years ago. Why? The decade between 1985 and 1995 saw large, unexpected fertility declines in South Central Asia

TABLE 21.1 Population Growth Rates, by Country Income			
	1900–1950	*1960–1970*	*1980–1990*
World	.8%	2.0%	1.7%
China	—	1.6	1.4
India	—	2.3	2.1
Other Low Income	—	2.4	2.6
Middle Income	—	2.7	2.0
Oil Exporters	—	4.0	3.3
Other High Income	—	1.0	0.6
United States	—	1.2	0.9

Source: From *World Development Report 1992* by The World Bank. Copyright © 1992 by The International Bank for Reconstruction and Development/The World Bank. Reprinted by permission of Oxford University Press, Inc.

---

[10]Wattenberg (1990) expresses the anti-Malthusian view.

and Africa. From 1994 to 1996, the UN lowered its global estimate of the number of children per woman from 3.10 to 2.96.

Again, these small changes add up to a big drop in projected numbers over a half century. Nafis Sadik, director of the UN Population Fund, credits the fertility decline to the fact that many countries began lifting family planning restrictions in the early 1980s.[11]

Yet the worldwide population growth rate still remains double that of the pre-1950 period and is over 2% in most lower- and lower-middle-income countries. Population growth actually accelerated in most of the oil-exporting countries, and no overall progress was made in the low-income group, dominated by the very poor, subSaharan African countries. Over the next decade, tragically, population growth in some African countries may be slowed by the spread of the AIDS virus. Yet AIDS will have little impact on world population growth.[12]

Moreover, birth rate declines in some developing countries have begun to stall out. For example, the average number of children in Costa Rica dropped from 7 in 1960, to 3.7 in 1978, but had fallen to only 3.1 by 1990.[13] The key question is What factors lay behind the general movement toward lower population growth rates illustrated in Table 21.1, and will they persist?

In view of the fact that rising incomes lead to lower population growth rates, modern adherents of Malthus' view—that population growth would ultimately lead to misery—have changed his theory somewhat. **Neomalthusians** agree that, *in the past*, economic growth has caused fertility rates to stabilize. However, they argue that a **vicious cycle** is developing today in poor countries: poverty generating high rates of population growth generating more poverty, which then leads to higher levels of population growth, and so on. Neomalthusians do not believe that, for most developing countries, economic growth alone is likely to break this cycle.[14] They argue that without implementing aggressive measures to control population growth, the demographic transition to low population growth rates experienced by rich countries is unlikely to occur in most poor countries.

Supporting this claim, in recent years classic Malthusian conditions have again begun to prevail at the global level. Between 1984 and 1990, grain output per acre improved little, and over the decade, population growth began to move ahead of growth in food production. During the 1980s, world food output per person fell 6% and is projected to fall an additional 21% over the 1990s.[15]

In spite of dramatic productivity gains from the Green Revolution, it has not been able to reduce poverty and malnutrition substantially in many poor countries. Thus, as the technological gains from the new agricultural methods introduced over the last forty years begin to wind down, there is concern that the neomalthusian cycle of poverty → population growth → poverty, and so on will overwhelm the effects of

---

[11]Charles Hanley "UN Summit—Population," AP Wire story, June 1997.

[12]Researchers disagree as to the impact that AIDS will have on population growth on the African continent. A minority of demographers have suggested the possibility of an actual decline in population over the next two decades. See "African Apocalypse," *Time*, July 6, 1992.

[13]World Bank (1984: 71); World Bank (1992).

[14]See, for example, Daly (1990).

[15]Brown and Young (1990).

economic growth in poor countries. In this case, the demographic transition will fail to materialize naturally. And unless effective population control measures are taken, global population would continue to increase well above the 10 billion level until some "natural" check—famine, war, disease, or ecological disaster—emerges.

21.3 An Economic Approach to Family Size

At several points in this chapter, I have asserted that higher incomes tend to be associated with lower population growth rates. As a general rule this is true, both across countries and within countries. In Colombia, Malaysia, and Brazil, for example, the poorest 20% of households support, on average, 30% of the nation's children. By contrast, the wealthiest 20% of households have only 9% of the children.[16] Yet the relationship is not a hard and fast one. For example, as is illustrated by Table 21.1, the high-income oil-exporting countries tend to have high fertility rates, while low-income countries such as Sri Lanka and China have reduced their population growth rates to low levels. In the United States, poor families (including welfare families) are *not* larger than average.

Many factors determine family size—religious and cultural norms obviously play a prominent role. Yet the strength of the **poverty-fertility relationship** suggests that *economic* factors are quite important as well. Evidently, people choose to vary their family size depending upon their income level. So, this suggests the following

---

PUZZLE

Suppose you are a farm worker, recently married, living in Pakistan. In a good year, you might make $200. Infant mortality rates are high—your children will have a one in ten chance of dying during their first year. The likelihood of your children attending more than a couple of years of school is also very small. Nationwide, only 38% of boys and 27% of girls attend primary school, and you are among the least likely to have access to such services. Systems of public welfare, "social security" retirement pensions, and public health care are very limited.

1. What are the economic benefits and costs to you, the parent, of having children?
2. On strictly economic terms, would you prefer to have two babies or five?

SOLUTION

Economic benefits. In poor countries like Pakistan, families are the primary social safety net. If you should become too sick or old to work, your children will be your basic source of support. Thus an important motive for having children is for **economic insurance.** A second reason is that children's labor, controlled by the parent, can help provide a direct **income supplement** for the family.

---

[16]Birdsall and Griffin (1988). These results hold when household poverty is measured on a per capita basis. Families with more children tend to be "richer" in absolute terms.

Children as young as six or seven can be (and are) employed in agriculture and manufacturing, sometimes to the (meager) economic benefit of their parents.

Economic costs. Raising children is a costly endeavor, both in terms of money and time. In economic terms, parents' child-rearing efforts, and the monetary resources they devote to this endeavor, can be thought of as an investment in the future productivity of their children.

Now let us turn to the issue of desired family size. The fact that children provide economic insurance and an income supplement does not *necessarily* mean that a big family is advantageous. Given limited resources, a family could potentially obtain comparable economic benefits following one of two approaches: a **high-investment strategy** with one or two children, or a **low-investment strategy** with many children.

The high-investment strategy would involve focusing all available resources on one or two children—insuring they survived infancy, were provided with a healthy diet, and went on to attend school. Such a child might well land a good job and increase family income substantially. In contrast, the low-investment strategy would be to have many children, recognizing that one or more would likely die young, but that the remainder would survive to contribute a small amount to the family income and insurance network. In short, the low-investment strategy is to substitute quantity for quality.[17]

While in principle, both strategies are open to all, for our farm laborer with his limited resources and restricted access to public services, the high-investment strategy is very difficult to pursue. Moreover, it is tremendously risky. Suppose, that after five years of intensive investment, a single child dies. Thus, the answer to the puzzle above is probably five children rather than two. Yet, as income rises, the high-investment strategy begins to be more attractive. Resources for the long-term (fifteen- to eighteen-year) investment are more readily available, and access to better health care means that the chances of premature death decline.

The analysis of the poverty-fertility link in this section suggests an effective route to population control: Changing parents' economic family plan from a low- to high- investment strategy, where the focus is on the "quality" rather than the "quantity" of children.

21.4 Controlling Population Growth

The benefit-cost model of family size is a very crude one, omitting as it does very important issues of culture, kinship, religion, love, and affection. Yet it does a good job explaining the strong relationship between poverty and fertility observed in many places around the world. In particular, because there are *good economic reasons* for poor people to have large families, simple provision of low-cost birth control is unlikely to solve the population problem (though it would certainly help). Can we use this benefit-cost model to suggest other effective policies for controlling population growth?

---

[17]This basic model was originally proposed by Becker and Lewis (1973). For a more current perspective, see Dasgupta (1995).

1. Balanced Growth and Redistribution   The poverty-fertility relationship seems to provide a straightforward way to control population: Eliminate poverty! Unfortunately, if this were easy to do, nations would have done so already. It does remains true, however, that balanced and rapid economic development that raises the material welfare of the poor majority is one of the most effective population control measures available. Korea's precipitous drop in population growth, noted above, can be attributed primarily to the country's dramatic economic success in the 1960s and 1970s. The gains from economic growth, based on labor intensive manufacturing, were widely shared.[18]

In addition to balanced growth, another way to reduce poverty and thus population growth rates is through **redistribution of wealth** from the rich to the poor. Redistribution often takes the form of publicly provided social services: education, health care, public pension plans. Another possibility is **land reform**—the breaking up of huge, underutilized estates into smaller units, made accessible to landless farmers. Land reform has long been urged in Latin America and other parts of the developing world. This form of redistribution can help to stabilize rural-to-urban migration, increase food production, decrease poverty, reduce population growth rates, and reduce environmental pressure on marginal agricultural lands.[19]

Redistribution can occur between poor and rich classes within countries, or between poor and rich countries. For example, land reform is sometimes financed (involuntarily) by the wealthy landowning class, when their land is taken by the government at below market prices; land reform can also be financed by the developing nation's taxpayers in general, when the landowners are fully compensated by the government; or it can be financed by international development organizations, with money from rich countries.

Forster (1992) has suggested an innovative way for the international community to promote land reform. She advocates **debt-for-farmland swaps,** in which poor countries are forgiven some of their debt to rich countries in exchange for land reform financing. Landless farmers who are pressuring environmentally sensitive areas, such as rain forests or steep terrains, could be resettled with these funds onto productive arable land.

Debt-for-farmland swaps (and their kin, debt-for-nature swaps discussed in detail in the next chapter) in some sense involve a redistribution of wealth from rich country residents (bank shareholders and taxpayers) to poor countries. Yet they can also be viewed as an investment in a sustainable future. Forster (1992) estimates that debt-for-farmland-swaps could preserve tropical rain forests for an investment of $11 per hectare, as opposed to reforestation costs of $750 to $1,100 per hectare.

At the broad, macro level, rapid and balanced economic development, combined with redistributionist policies are clearly the best "contraceptive." Yet both growth and redistribution have been hard to achieve in many parts of the world. Fortunately, it is possible for even poor countries to substantially reduce population growth rates through more targeted policies in the areas of health, education, and family planning.

---

[18]Repetto (1985). Women also entered the workforce at a rapid rate, which as discussed below, is an important factor in reducing population growth rates.
[19]Moene (1992) argues in a general equilibrium context that these beneficial effects are most likely to occur in land-poor countries when land is redistributed to landless farmers, rather than small farmers.

2. Reduced infant and childhood mortality   Improved public health is an important factor in reducing long-run population growth rates. Our benefit-cost approach to family size suggested that improved health care would help slow population growth for one principal reason: The risk associated with investing in a child's health and education would be reduced, encouraging families to substitute quality for quantity.[20]

In the short run, however, reducing childhood and infant mortality accelerates population growth, as parents take some time to adjust their desired number of babies to the new conditions. As noted in Table 21.1 above, during the 1950s and 1960s, population growth rates in poor countries exploded, often doubling, as common diseases were brought under control by modern medicine, but fertility rates remained high.[21] Since then, fertility and thus population growth rates have fallen around the world, though they still remain a severe problem in most poor countries. Part of the demographic transition, described in Section 21.2 above, is reflected in this adjustment on the part of parents to lower childhood mortality rates.

Childhood and infant mortality can be attacked at relatively low cost by providing public health and education services. For example, one of the most common causes of infant death in poor countries is dehydration from diarrhea. This disease can be treated using a simple prescription: clean water with a little sugar.

3. Education   Our economic model of family size tells us that population growth will slow when parents follow a strategy of "high investment" in their children. A key element making such a strategy possible is **access to education.** This is true for three reasons. First, the availability of education directly lowers the cost of pursuing a high-investment strategy to all parents, educated and uneducated alike. Second, as parents become educated themselves, a strategy of substituting quality for quantity also becomes easier, since the parents can provide guidance to the children.

Finally, as parents become educated, their wages tend to rise. This increases the **opportunity cost of parents' time,** making a low-investment strategy less attractive. This is true because a low-investment, "quantity" strategy requires a bigger commitment of time devoted to child rearing than does a high investment, "quality" strategy. Another way to look at this is that, as the parents' wages rise, family income and economic insurance are better served by parents working, than by raising more children.

For this reason, education is particularly important for women, since they do most of the child rearing. One of the best ways to control fertility is to have women participating in the *modern sector* of the economy. (All poor women work. However, employment in agricultural or household labor does not appear to reduce fertility.)[22] As the opportunity cost of the woman's time rises, a quantity strategy becomes less and less attractive for the family as a unit.

---

[20]In addition, in high mortality areas, only when mortality rates drop do parents have to concern themselves at all with birth control. Falling infant mortality rates thus initiate behavioral changes, which make fertility control more likely (Birdsall and Griffin [1988]).

[21]The adjustment process is compounded because, as Birdsall and Griffin (1988) report, parents don't replace dead children on a less than one-to-one basis and typically don't fully "insure" against infant mortality by having larger families.

[22]Birdsall and Griffin (1988).

Education for women appears to have a strong impact on fertility control for other reasons as well. To this point, we have treated the "family" as a homogeneous unit, yet men and women play different roles in the family and may have different ideas about the desirability of limiting family size. In the developing world, as in rich countries, the responsibility for taking birth control measures—whether abstinence, prolonged breast-feeding, or a technological approach—generally falls on the woman. Thus, the direct consumers of birth control devices and fertility control information are generally women, providing another argument for improved female education.

More importantly, however, most of the world's societies are male-dominated, **patriarchal cultures.** In such societies, women often must obtain approval from their husbands in order to control their fertility. This distinction is important, because holding all things equal, it is probably true that women prefer to have fewer children than men do. This is likely for a number of reasons: Women do the vast majority of the hard work involved in child rearing; child rearing interferes with women's other economic activities; and childbirth represents a significant health risk for many women. Thus, policies that strengthen women's status and bargaining position within the family itself, for example, better education or access to paid employment, are likely to have important effects on fertility decisions, independent of their impact on *overall* family income and economic insurance.

4. Family planning   Having argued above that poor people may have good reasons for having large families, it is also true that a big obstacle to pursuing a high-investment strategy is lack of access to family planning services. There remains a large unsatisfied demand for birth control worldwide. Birdsall and Griffin (1988) report that outside of subSaharan Africa, close to 50% of women in poor countries desire no more children, and around two thirds of those who want a larger family would prefer to postpone bearing their next child. At the same time, one source estimates that in three quarters of the world's poor countries, birth control is not affordable for the average individual.[23]

In general, better-educated, wealthier, urban women are better able to actually achieve fertility control. But, effective outreach programs have been able to reduce and, in some cases, almost eliminate urban/rural gaps. Programs that rely on well-trained workers, provide follow-up and support to clients, provide a variety of contraceptive methods, and imbed family planning in a more comprehensive system of public health services have proven quite effective in lowering fertility rates. In one well-studied case in Bangladesh, such a program increased contraceptive use from 10% to 31% in two years, reducing the number of births by about 25%.[24]

A comprehensive program of public health, education (especially targeted at women), and family planning can be an effective way to reduce population growth, even

---

[23]"Cost Said to Rule Out Birth Control for Many," *New York Times*, July 2, 1991. The study was done by the Population Crisis Committee and defines a supply of affordable birth control as requiring less than 1% of annual income.

[24]This paragraph is drawn from Birdsall and Griffin (1988).

in the absence of rapid, balanced growth, and/or explicitly redistributionist policies. Poor countries that have been able to successfully pursue some combination of these policies include Costa Rica, Cuba, Mexico, Colombia, Sri Lanka, Indonesia, China, Zimbabwe, and the southern Indian state of Kerala. Family planning programs, along with economic growth, have been credited with dramatic fertility declines in Taiwan and Thailand.[25]

Current funding for population control in poor countries is around $4.7 billion, with developed countries contributing only about 20% of the total. The World Bank (1992: 174) estimates that given an expenditure of an additional $7 billion per year, world population might stabilize at 10 billion instead of 12.5 billion people in the next century. For comparison, this is about a third of what Americans spend in barbershops, beauty shops, baths, and health clubs each year. Given this, *investment in family planning is one of the most cost-effective measures available for addressing global environmental problems ranging from global warming to loss of biodiversity.*

5. Coercive Policies.   The policies described above all function by encouraging parents to *voluntarily* control family size. Some nations, notably China and India, have used coercive birth control methods. China, a country a little larger than the United States but with less good-quality agricultural land, is home to just over 1 billion people, over four times as many as live in the United States. Even if the Chinese achieve zero population growth today, because of the country's age distribution, the number of people in the country is likely to increase to 1.9 billion before stabilizing.

Prior to 1980, China's Communist government had achieved impressive reductions in fertility primarily by pursuing the noncoercive strategies discussed above: raising the status of the poor through growth and redistribution, and providing education, health care, family planning services, and retirement benefits. The number of children per family fell from over 5.0 in 1970, to 2.7 in 1979.

In 1980, in order to head off a surge in population as the Chinese baby boom reached childbearing age, the government instituted its one-child policy. Urban dwellers were legally limited to a single child, while rural families were allowed to have two or more children. The policy was enforced with a mixture of subsidies, fines, peer pressure, and, on occasion, physical coercion. Families who had only one child were provided monthly stipends, given access to better schools, and taxed at a lower rate. Economically coercive fines, which might amount to over a year's salary, were imposed for a child over the legal limit. Pregnant women were harassed by neighborhood committees, and, forced abortions, while not widespread, have occurred.

By 1990, the average number of children per family had fallen to 2.5. In 1992, after a two-year campaign to boost sterilizations, the number had reportedly dropped to 1.9—zero population growth. The *New York Times* reports that the average Chinese view the policy as unpleasant but needed, something like income taxes. Public acceptance of the policy is higher in urban than rural areas.

One ugly by-product of the one-child policy has been a rise in sex selection of male infants through abortions of female fetuses and an increase in female infanticide. Chinese census figures from the late 1980s indicate about a half-million anticipated female births are failing to show up on the records each year. However, most of these "missing" girls are probably given up for adoption or raised in secret. In China,

---

[25]World Bank (1984).

sons are especially important from the point of view of economic insurance, since daughters traditionally "marry out" of the family.

China's one-child policy—relying on voluntary measures, severe economic and social pressure, and a degree of physical coercion—has worked, though sometimes at a tragic human cost. Noncompliance, although evident, is not widespread. Because China is such a huge country, the overall impact of China's family planning and birth control program has been tremendous. If the birth rates evident in 1970 had persisted, over the period 1970 to 1990 an additional 240 million Chinese—equivalent to the population of the United States—would have been born.[26]

The physically coercive aspects of the Chinese program, while never dominant, have been "accepted" for two mutually enforcing reasons: The Chinese government exercises effective authoritarian political control over the population, *and* the goal of the policy appears to be generally supported. Many Chinese people appear to have accepted a sustainability argument that sacrifice on the part of current generations is necessary to preserve a decent quality of life for the future.

By contrast, in the 1970s the democratically elected Indian government initiated an aggressive birth control policy that included financial incentives for sterilization. Charges of economic coercion and evidence of forced sterilization brought the program to a halt and have since generated considerable public suspicion of all government birth control programs.[27]

It is unlikely that, outside of China, coercive population control methods are likely to be applied. In many parts of the world, they are morally unacceptable. In addition, except under unusual circumstances of an effective, authoritarian regime, and widespread if grudging popular support, such policies are unlikely to be effective. Indeed they are likely to be counterproductive. Luckily, they are also not necessary to stabilize the global population at a sustainable level. Noncoercive, relatively cheap, and in many cases cost-effective measures exist to nudge parents into voluntarily pursuing a high-investment family strategy.

The good news is thus that we need not wait around to see if the near future holds a "natural" demographic transition to a sustainable world population or a vicious neomalthusian cycle of population growth and misery. Neither do we need to follow a coercive path. Instead, policies that raise the material welfare of poor people by promoting balanced growth and redistribution, as well as targeted policies in the areas of health care, education, and family planning, should be sufficient to reach the goal of stabilizing the planetary population at a sustainable level.

21.5 Consumption and the Global Environment

Population control advocates (like me) are sometimes accused by people in poor countries of racism or even genocide. Why, they ask, do you recommend aggressive, if noncoercive, steps to limit the numbers of (mostly) black or brown people in poor

---

[26]The information on the one-child policy presented here is drawn from the *New York Times*: "China, With Ever More Mouths to Feed, Pushes Anew for Small Families," June 16, 1991; "A Mystery from China's Census: Where Have Young Girls Gone?" June 17, 1991; "China's Crackdown on Births: A Stunning and Harsh Success," April 25, 1993; and "Births Punished by Fine, Beating or Ruined Home," April 25, 1993.
[27]Jacobson (1987).

countries, when, in fact, the vast majority of global ecological damage can be traced directly or indirectly to the affluent lifestyles of the (mostly) white people in rich countries?

There are two elements to the **consumption-pollution link.** The first is straightforward. Because inhabitants of rich countries are responsible for over two thirds of global economic activity, at least two thirds of global pollution can be laid at our doorstep. The western European countries, the United States, and Japan comprise about 15% of the world's population but consume 71% of the world's output.[28] As a result, rich country consumption has to date been responsible for most of the global atmospheric pollution—global warming, ozone depletion, acid rain, and radioactive contamination. Rich countries have had by far the biggest impact on polluting and overfishing the oceans. And rich country inhabitants have generated mountains of toxic wastes that are now, on occasion, finding their way to poor countries for disposal.

In addition to generating global pollution problems, there is a second element to the consumption-pollution link. High levels of consumption demand in rich countries have been responsible for an unsustainable drawdown in environmental quality and the stock of natural capital in many poor countries. We will see an example of this when we trace the so-called "hamburger connection" to rain-forest depletion later in this chapter. The expansion of beef ranching in Costa Rica has led to a destruction of the nation's rain-forest resource without sufficiently by compensating investment in created capital.

Many poor countries rely on the export of primary resources or agricultural commodities to earn money for imported fuel, food, consumer goods, and weapons. In principle, this trade is environmentally sustainable. However, sustainability requires that any drawdown in the stock of natural capital—whether oil or mineral reserves, rain-forest resources, topsoil, or air and water quality—be compensated for by investment in created capital. As we discussed in chapters 6 and 7, if a nation's natural capital is depleted faster than new capital is created, then unsustainable development occurs.

The overwhelming demand for resources in rich countries—ranging from gasoline, to steel, to bananas, to beef—has in many cases depleted the natural capital stock in poor countries, *without* commensurate investment in created capital. Why has this occurred? Historically, colonial governments tended to drain resource-generated wealth from their colonies, investing little in human capital or infrastructure. In the postcolonial period, falling relative prices for primary resources, low taxes on politically powerful resource-based industries, and high levels of spending on military and imported consumption goods by ruling elites have constrained investment in created capital. Finally, as we will see in the next section, the burden of debt repayment has led to a flow of created wealth *from* poor to rich countries over the last fifteen years.

The point here is not to assign blame to rich countries or ruling elites for the poverty in the former colonies. Rather, the point is simply to recognize that high lev-

---

[28]World Bank (1992: Table A.2).

els of rich country demand can have as much to do with environmental damage in poor countries as do high population growth rates. Thus growing, transporting, and cooking a year's worth of my favorite breakfast—a banana (Ecuador), a cup of coffee (Guatemala), and a chocolate donut (cocoa, Ghana; sugar, Honduras) uses up about $400 of market resources. This process contributes much more to environmental degradation in those countries—pesticide contamination of water, loss of topsoil, deforestation, and global warming—than does providing breakfast for a person whose *entire yearly income* is $400 or less.

This is also not to say that trade in agricultural commodities or any other goods are, on balance, bad for the environment. We will take up the issue of trade policy in the next chapter. Rather, to insure sustainability, the gains from trade must be invested in created capital sufficient to offset the drawdown in natural capital. *If they are not,* then rich country consumption leads to unsustainable development in poor countries as surely as does rapid population growth.

This section has discussed the two ways in which high levels of consumption in rich countries and environmental problems, both global and those in poor countries, are linked. At the global level, an obvious and direct correspondence exists between consumption and pollution. However, high levels of demand in rich countries have indirectly promoted a drawdown of the stock of natural capital and environmental quality in poor countries. If natural capital depleted through resource or pollution-intensive exports is not being replaced by investment in created capital, high-consumption levels in rich countries can fuel unsustainable resource depletion in poor countries. Many argue that this kind of unsustainable development has in fact been occurring. Given these links, are the critics of population control right? Are neo-malthusians, perhaps motivated by unconscious racism, focusing on the wrong problem?

I argue instead that *both* overpopulation and overconsumption represent serious threats to the global environment and sustainable development in poor countries. There is mounting evidence that rapid population growth is dramatically compounding the problem of economic development, thereby putting tremendous pressure on local environments. Moreover, as the poor both grow in number and aspire to living standards found in the developed world, their impact on global environmental problems will become more and more significant. By the year 2025, for example, poor countries are expected to surpass the rich countries as the main contributor to global warming.

Yet we are indeed being shortsighted, at best, if we insist solely on blaming the reproductive behavior of poor people in poor countries both for their own environmental problems and for the global ones to which they contribute. High levels of consumption in affluent countries are primarily responsible for the global environmental crisis and have indirectly promoted an unsustainable drawdown of natural capital in many poor countries.

Earlier in the book (chapter 11) we discussed a variety of tools for addressing the overconsumption problem in wealthier countries. So far in this chapter, we have examined theoretical links between poverty, population growth, northern consumption patterns, and the prospect for sustainable development. We now turn to a concrete example.

21.6 Sustainable Development in Costa Rica?

Costa Rica (location in Figure 21.4) is a country of about 2.8 million people. It is considered to be a "lower-middle-income" country, with per capita income of $1,900 per year. We focus on Costa Rica here, because in many respects it is a developmental "success story." The statistics in Table 21.2 summarize Costa Rica's recent economic history, as well as comparable data for some neighboring countries.

Let us begin with the crude, often inaccurate, yet commonly employed measure of development: Gross domestic product (GDP) per person. GDP was defined in chapter 6 as the sum total of all market income generated in an economy in a given year. GDP does not include nonmarket production (child rearing and housework, for example) or negative environmental externalities, nor does it account for a drawdown in the stock of natural capital.

Nevertheless, a comparison of GDP growth with population growth from 1980 to 1990 paints an initially optimistic portrait: Aggregate GDP growth averaging 3.0% per year outstripped population growth of 2.4% per year. This meant that by the end of the decade, economic output and material wealth *per person* was higher than at the beginning. As we shall see below, this does not necessarily mean that the average Costa Rican was "better off"—GDP *does not* include environmental costs and the wealth gains may have been unevenly distributed—but the larger slice of pie per person at least made it *possible* for average material living standards to rise.

By contrast, if we look at two other Central American countries, Mexico and Honduras, population growth outstripped GDP growth, meaning that the economies of these countries were producing less wealth per person at the end of the decade than at the beginning. This virtually insured that the average person in these countries was worse off in 1990 than in 1980.

FIGURE 21.4 Central America

TABLE 21.2 Development in Central America, 1980–1990							
	1980–1990 Growth Rates				*1965–1989 Growth Rates*		
	Per Capita Income (1990)	*GDP*	*Population*	*Food per Capita*	*Debt per Capita*	*Forest*	*Pasture*	*Fertilizer*
Costa Rica	$ 1,900	3.0%	2.4%	–0.90%	$1,347	2.8%	3.5%	4.5%
Mexico	2,490	1.0	2.0	0.02	1,123	1.2	0.0	7.1
Honduras	590	2.3	3.4	–1.70	682	1.9	0.9	2.6
All Low	320	3.9	2.6	0.05		0.4	0.0	9.2
All High	19,590	2.3	0.6	0.01		0.1	–0.1	1.5

Source: From *World Development Report 1992* by The World Bank. Copyright © 1992 by The International Bank for Reconstruction and Development/The World Bank. Reprint by permission of Oxford University Press, Inc.

Costa Rica's biggest development triumph is not reflected in Table 21.2. While the country still had a fairly high population growth rate of 2.4% in the 1980s, this figure has been falling dramatically. From 1965 to 1980, the population grew at a rate of 2.7%; the growth rate is projected to fall to 1.9% during the 1990s.[29]

Many observers credit Costa Rica's development successes partially to its democratic political culture. Due to the absence of native Indians to serve as slaves, Costa Rica—like the states of the northern United States—originally developed a system of agriculture based on small farmers who owned their own land. Although the rise of banana and coffee plantations in the late 1800s, and more recently cattle exports, has greatly increased land concentration, Costa Rica's small-farmer history shaped a relatively egalitarian culture.[30]

By contrast, much of Latin America developed along the lines of the southern United States, with a plantation-style agriculture. Small farmers under this system were originally enslaved Indians, later tenants or sharecroppers, with little political or economic power. This social structure generated massive concentrations of land and economic power in the hands of a relatively small elite, deep racial divides, and in the twentieth century, a dominant military presence in government required to maintain these unequal economic and political relationships.

Costa Rica's egalitarian historical legacy has left it with several advantages for sustainable development: a relatively effective governmental bureaucracy, few military expenses (the army was actually banned in 1949), a commitment to education, especially of women, and an advanced welfare system that focuses on basic health-care delivery to poor citizens. These latter two aspects of Costa Rican policy have been very important in reducing population growth rates.

Yet even in Costa Rica, it is uncertain whether recent economic progress can be considered sustainable.[31] First, the figures in Table 21.2 on fertilizer growth—4.5%

---

[29]World Bank (1992).

[30]This explanation of Costa Rican exceptionalism is widely accepted. See, for example, Bieszaz, et al. (1982).

[31]For a contrary view, see Pearce and Atkinson (1993), who find that national savings has exceeded the depreciation of human-made and natural capital in recent years in Costa Rica.

per year from 1965 to 1989—reveal that the agrarian transition discussed above is well underway in Costa Rica. Capital- and chemical-intensive farming has been displacing traditional small-scale agriculture, leading to a growth in landlessness and urban migrants. From 1970 to 1983, the percentage of the Costa Rican labor force in agriculture declined from 42.2% to 33%.[32] In spite of the spread of capital-intensive agriculture, however, food production per capita has actually been falling, at around 1% per year. How can we explain this?

Part of the explanation lies in the **hamburger connection.**[33] Increasing beef consumption in the developed world, along with major subsidy programs for ranching financed by international lending agencies and governments, has fueled the growth of the export beef industry in Latin America.[34] As Table 21.2 reveals, pasture land in Costa Rica grew at an astounding 3.5% per year over the 1980s.[35] Much of this came at the expense of rain-forest (down 2.8% per year over the decade) or marginal hillside lands, but ranching also has expanded significantly into prime agricultural land. Leonard (1987) estimates that cattle ranching has extended to include about half of Central America's good agricultural land.[36] Ranching requires very little labor: Carriere (1991: 192) reports that pasture requires only 6 days of labor per hectare annually, compared, for example, to 37 days for beans or 137 days for coffee.

This kind of economic growth is potentially unsustainable for a variety of reasons. First, ranching in the rain forest leads to rapid destruction of natural capital. Deforested areas in Costa Rica can often maintain pasture for only six years or so before the resource is degraded.[37] Recall that depleting the stock of natural capital is not necessarily unsustainable. However, sustainability does require that any drawdown of natural capital be compensated for by an increase in created capital, an issue we will consider below.

Ranching in prime agricultural lands also exacerbates problems of unemployment and hunger. Low employment levels in ranching mean that few workers displaced from prime land will be reemployed in the agricultural sector, and the displaced who formerly grew some or all of their own food are now likely to face hunger as either urban migrants or farmers pushed on to ecologically sensitive land, further depleting the nation's natural capital. In addition, greater poverty leads to higher population growth rates, exacerbating sustainability problems.

Finally, little of the beef is destined for local markets, so most Costa Ricans do not benefit from lower beef prices. In fact, due to crowding out from the beef industry, we have seen that domestic food production per capita has actually *dropped.* In addition,

---

[32]Leonard (1987).

[33]Pearce and Myers (1990) use this term.

[34]Leonard (1987: 88) reports that in the early 1970s half of all agricultural credit in Costa Rica was going to support the livestock industry, and that aid agencies, at least until recently, strongly advocated cattle production. This is in spite of the fact that on a per acre basis, livestock generate low-export earnings. Leonard also suggests that ranching has succeeded on prime farmland in part because of the absence of infrastructure necessary to develop higher value-added crops. Pearce and Myers (1990) discuss the importance of subsidies for livestock development in Brazil.

[35]By contrast, land devoted to agriculture grew at only .4% per year.

[36]Carriere (1991) provides data for Costa Rica.

[37]Carriere (1991).

to the extent that expensive beef does replace inexpensive beans as a primary protein source in the culturally preferred local diet, the poor are likely to suffer from greater protein deficiencies.

Could the country benefit at all from the growth of this industry? Yes. Some beef processing and shipping centers will provide urban employment. More importantly, profits earned from the export beef industry might be reinvested in Costa Rica—developing jobs, education, and infrastructure. In other words, Costa Rica *could* use the profits from the ranching industry to finance its agrarian transition, effectively replacing its depleted natural capital with created capital.

Unfortunately, investment levels have been low in all of Latin America, including Costa Rica, since the late 1970s. A variety of reasons explain this, but significant among these has been the tremendous burden of debt that Latin American countries owe to American, Japanese, and European banks.

During the 1970s, First World banks loaned tremendous sums of money to government agencies and private companies in poor countries around the world. Latin America's external debt rose from $7.2 billion in 1960 to $315.3 billion in 1982. It is not fully clear what motivated this irresponsible lending binge; however, little of the money was productively invested. Much of it financed imports of consumer goods from First World countries or else disappeared into private bank accounts. As a result, by 1982, most countries were struggling just to make interest payments on the debt.[38]

During the 1980s, a series of rescheduling and compromises were worked out, but over the decade capital continued to flow out of the poor countries. In 1990, for example, Latin American countries paid out over $18 billion in interest payments and $15 billion in principal to First World banks.[39]

Costa Rica has one of the highest per capita external debts in the world. On average, each individual (via the government) owes First World banks over $1,300, more than two thirds of the average yearly income in the country. In 1990, Costa Rica paid out about 10% of the total value of its exports as payment on this debt.[40] This ate up most of the profits from its cattle ranching and other export industries, meaning that little was left over to help finance the agrarian transition. Thus, natural capital stocks were being depleted by the ranchers without compensation in the form of created capital.

To summarize: At the beginning of this section I noted that the rising GDP per capita observed in Costa Rica during the 1980s need not have translated into increased material welfare for the average individual in the short term, nor to sustainable development in the longer run. A closer look at the economic growth pattern based on cattle ranching revealed why.[41] First, the expansion of the export beef sector involved a direct drawdown on a segment of the nation's natural capital—the rain forest. Second, by creating more unemployed, land-hungry farmers, the growth in ranching both put an additional stress on forest resources and exacerbated population

[38]O'Brien (1991) provides the figures on the debt growth.
[39]World Bank (1992: Table 22).
[40]World Bank (1992).
[41]For a more formal discussion of the conditions in which trade leads to unsustainable development, see Pezzey (1993). In one case, he finds that trade, relative to autarky, reduces sustainability in an "impatient" country.

growth pressures. Finally, due to the debt burden, the depletion of natural capital was not compensated for by an increase in created capital. Instead, a substantial portion of the export profits flowed abroad to First World banks.

The growth of the export beef industry in Costa Rica in the 1980s was, by most measures, unsustainable development. Yet the situation in Costa Rica is brighter than most developing countries. In Costa Rica, one can at least identify a primary obstacle to sustainable development as the debt owed to banks in wealthy countries. Absent that burden, the country has the underlying political resources necessary to manage its agrarian transition through investment in people and capital. Given its tradition of effective government, one could also envision the Costa Rican state trimming back subsidy programs that have helped fuel unsustainable ranching practices. (International aid agencies are already under pressure to do so.) Finally, Costa Rica has a well-developed welfare state capable of delivering the health-care and education services needed to slow population growth rates.

For many other less developed countries, debt has also had a devastating impact on capital creation. As such, it has served as a major drag on sustainable development. For example, due in part to the debt burden, investment in physical capital in Mexico and Honduras was actually negative during the 1980s.[42] Yet, the sustainability challenge in most developing countries is *primarily a political one.* Highly unequal concentrations of wealth and political power in poor countries mean that government actions—for example, to promote cattle ranching—often are not taken with the welfare of the majority in mind. Yet, as we have seen, the well-being of the poor majority is a prerequisite for sustainability.

21.7 Envisioning a Sustainable Future

When one surveys the often overwhelming and interrelated problems of environmental degradation, poverty, population growth, overconsumption, and political powerlessness in poor countries, hopes for a future brighter than the present seem dim. Yet, what promise does exist comes from an increasing ecological recognition that the earth is genuinely a single spaceship. In just the last decade, citizens in rich countries have started to become aware that the life-support systems of our own affluent lifestyles, and those of our children, are critically affected by the economic security of poor children in Sao Paolo, Brazil, in the Ghanaian countryside, and indeed throughout the world. Global environmental threats such as greenhouse warming, ozone depletion, and biodiversity loss due to deforestation, as well as increasing legal and illegal immigration by the poor, remind us that we ignore our less fortunate sisters and brothers at our own peril.

This recognition is indeed quite recent and has just begun to take hold. The term "sustainable development" itself gained widespread currency only in 1987 with the publication of a book by the United Nations called, suitably, *Our Common Future.* Also known as the **Bruntland Commission Report,** after the commission's chair Gro

---

[42]From 1980 to 1990, Mexico's rate of gross domestic investment was −3.5%, for Honduras, −0.7 %; World Bank (1992). For empirical confirmation of the debt overhang effect on investment, see Borensztein (1991), and Cohen (1993). For a general discussion of the debt problem, see the Symposia in the *Journal of Economic Perspectives,* Winter, 1990.

Bruntland, the report sought to serve warning—a brighter future can be imagined, but it will not come without hard and conscious work upon our part.

The report called for urgent national and international action on four key **sustainability steps** described below.[43] Underlying all the policy discussion is one common thread: rich countries will have to bear much of the investment cost of achieving a sustainable future.

1. Population and Human Resources   Rapid population growth clearly undercuts sustainable development efforts. The Bruntland Commission reports that between 1985 and the year 2000, cities in Third World countries will grow by about 60%, nearly three quarters of a billion people. Thus, just to maintain current, and in many cases desperately inadequate infrastructure, shelter, and educational facilities, poor countries must increase investment in these areas by over one half in the short term. Fortunately, we are learning how to effectively control population growth. But the process itself—focusing on reducing infant deaths, providing education services, and effective family planning—is not cheap.

2. Food Security   Joad's story in *The Grapes of Wrath* illustrates the agrarian transition underlying the traditional model of economic development: low-productivity, labor-intensive small farmers, driven off the land by high-productivity capital-intensive agriculture. And, to the extent that industrial jobs are available in the urban centers to absorb displaced farmworkers, the process "works," in spite of tremendous hardships suffered by families like Joad's.

Unfortunately, such industrial jobs are not emerging in many poor countries. Instead, the cities are teeming with unemployed and underemployed workers. As a result, there is little rationale for governments to actively promote capital-intensive agriculture in poor countries to displace even more farmworkers; instead, policy should focus on improving the productivity of small farmers. In addition, much of the "modern" farm sector has focused on the production of export crops, rather than food production for domestic consumption. Poor countries need to boost domestic food production to improve food security and basic nutrition.

One of the best ways to both encourage small farmers and increase food output is to reduce subsidies that keep urban food prices artificially low. (Higher food prices are necessary to keep farmers in business.) Yet, this can only be achieved politically if money is available to cushion the blow to poor urban residents of food price hikes. Such a policy again will require resources that poor countries do not have.

3. Improved Technology   The Bruntland Commission's third focus was on the need for cleaner technology. Under the UN's median assumptions, world population is liable to grow to *at least* 10 billion people before stabilizing in the mid-twenty-first century. Thus, our children will grow into middle age on a planet supporting *at least* double the current population. Now imagine doubling the world's stock of

---

[43]World Commission on Environment and Development (1987: Overview). I take some liberties with the commission's format. The authors place the urban challenge on par with population growth. I subsume the former under the latter. They also subdivide technology needs into energy and clean manufacturing.

For a discussion of the feasibility of the Bruntland Commission strategy for sustainable development in an input-output framework, see advanced topic chapter T3.

conventional automobiles, coal-fired power plants, hazardous and nuclear waste, or land devoted to housing and agriculture. Under this kind of scenario, sustainability is simply impossible. Welfare for most people would necessarily decline.

Thus, the development of clean energy and manufacturing technologies (as discussed in chapters 19 and 20) is a fundamental prerequisite for a sustainable future. This is true because population growth cannot be stabilized without improving the material welfare of poor people in poor countries. Cheap energy and cheap basic manufactured goods are essential to achieve a sustainable global population. Yet, unless this material production can be achieved with substantially less environmental impact than it generates today, ecological degradation will undermine sustainability directly.

In essence, poor countries will have to "leapfrog" the dirty, resource-intensive development pattern successfully pursued by the rich countries, to both raise incomes and stabilize population growth. They can only do so, however, if new, clean technologies are developed and made available by those in rich countries with the resources to do so.

4. Resource Conservation   Because of open access to common property and high market discount rates, natural resources are often depleted at an unsustainable rate. Thus, there is a need for action to preserve much of the stock of natural capital remaining in poor countries, for the benefits of future generations. However, given massive poverty in these countries, even when national preserves are set aside, few resources are available for preventing their immediate, if technically illegal, exploitation. Poor countries will be able to do little to conserve natural resources on their own.

In summary, the Bruntland Commission Report yields two lessons. First, through the vision it provides of a sustainable planetary future, it suggests a framework for analyzing national and international environmental policy. In the next few chapters, we will look at a variety of tools available for coping with the worldwide environmental crisis. We now have four questions we will want to ask of such policies: What are the impacts on population growth? On improving food security? On promoting the development and diffusion of clean technology? On resource conservation? The answers, of course, will be complex, and often contradictory, but these sustainability steps are the four fronts on which simultaneous progress must be made.

The second lesson of *Our Common Future* is that it truly is our common future. Whether the planet will ultimately accommodate 10 billion people in a sustainable fashion, or 15 billion or 20 billion in a downward spiral of environmental degradation, conflict, and impoverishment, is a decision entirely in our hands. And by our hands, I mean the people who are reading this book. We are the beneficiaries of four hundred years of "dirty" development; we are also the richest people ever to walk the face of the earth. As such, we are the ones with the ability to design policies to channel global resources into resolving these four problems, and we are the ones who will determine whether our favored historical position is ultimately sustainable or not.

Where are the resources to come from? One attractive source is military spending. In 1995, the world was spending close to $900 billion a year on arms, in many cases with poor countries buying from rich ones. Table 21.3 illustrates that for twenty-three days of global military expenditure, substantial progress could be made addressing problems of population growth and resource conservation.

TABLE 21.3   Military Expenditures and Development

Policy	Cost (Billions $1995)	Days of Military Expenditure
Action Plan of Tropical Forests	$1.9	.8
Action Plan for Desertification	6.5	2.8
Worldwide Clean Water Project	43.0	18.4
Contraceptives to All Who Desire Them Worldwide	1.5	.6
TOTAL	36.8	22.5

Source: Program cost data from the World Commission on Environment and Development (1987), *Our Common Future* (New York: University Press); military spending information from Arias Oscar, Jordana Friedman, and Caleb Rossiter, "Less Spending, More Security," Year 2000 Campaign to Redirect World Military Spending to Human Development, http://www.connix.con/~clouette/cpa/arias.html.

The political challenge involved in diverting resources from military to environmental spending is formidable. Even more difficult will be policies that curtail consumption in rich countries (for example, through debt relief) to invest in sustainable development in poor countries. And yet, I personally am more optimistic that the challenge can be met today than I was twenty years ago, when as a student I first confronted the relentless mathematics of population growth, and its intimate relationship with the desperate poverty found worldwide.

In the 1970s and 1980s, a belief often prevailed that the rich could grow richer while the poor grew poorer; that we in the wealthy countries could in some sense wall-off the poverty and population problems of the Third World.[44] Today, worldwide environmental threats—global warming, ozone depletion, and loss of biological diversity—have made this a less and less tenable position. For the first time in history, rich countries now have a direct and increasingly important economic stake in helping poor countries to stabilize their population growth rates. Because this can be done most effectively by improving the lives of the poorest on the planet, the prospects for a sustainable future, while perhaps not bright, are nevertheless real.

21.8 Summary

This chapter has outlined the fundamental connections between poverty, population growth, overconsumption, and sustainable development. The first step was to characterize the general challenge of economic development as productively absorbing labor freed up in the agrarian transition from small-scale, labor-intensive farming to large-scale, capital-intensive agriculture. It is important to note that, while the agrarian transition has to date been a universal feature of development, the speed at which it occurs is greatly affected by government policies, such as subsidized credit for large farmers, or subsidies that depress food prices and thus discourage food production by small farmers.

---

[44]See for example, Lucas (1976).

Due to an increasing awareness of the importance both of natural capital as an input into economic growth, and of negative environmental externalities as an outcome of economic growth, interest has shifted away from traditional development models to those focusing on sustainable development. Because sustainability is defined in terms of the welfare of the average individual over time, and the average individual in less developed countries is quite poor, sustainable development must concentrate attention on the status of the poor.

Sustainable development will tend to increase environmental quality for four reasons. First, exposure to two of the most pressing environmental problems in poor countries—polluted water and indoor air pollution (smoke)—are a direct result of poverty. Second, poor people cannot afford to conserve resources, and so they often put unsustainable pressure on their local environment. Third, as incomes rise, for a variety of reasons, certain regulated pollutant concentrations decline. Finally, income growth is one of the most effective population control measures available.

There is a debate over the extent of the population problem. On one side are those who foresee a "natural" demographic transition to a stable global population as economic progress proceeds in poor countries. By contrast, neomalthusians have argued that a vicious cycle is developing, in which poverty leads to high population growth rates that engender more poverty. Such a cycle, they argue, has already begun to overwhelm the beneficial effects of economic growth in many places. As a result, they are worried that the demographic transition is stalling out, and that global population will rise far above the 10 billion figure before being checked by physical or social limits.

The debate between neomalthusians and proponents of a natural demographic transition is about whether the global population will rise in the next 100 years to 10 billion to 11 billion, or 14 billion to 20 billion. From a policy point of view, however, there is little disagreement. Both sides agree that effective, noncoercive population control methods can speed up the demographic transition, and should be implemented.

Controlling population growth is not as simple as dispensing low-cost birth control devices, though this certainly helps. Poor people often have good economic reasons for having large families. Parents around the world depend on children for economic insurance and income supplements. Because of limited opportunities, and risk, poor families tend to pursue a low-investment, "quantity" strategy when choosing family size. Encouraging families to adopt a high-investment, "quality" strategy is the crux of an effective population control program.

Balanced economic growth and/or general economic redistribution are the most effective ways to alleviate poverty, and thus make a high-investment strategy feasible for many families. However, such outcomes, desirable for many reasons, have often been difficult to achieve. Yet, even poor countries have had success in achieving lower birth rates by pursuing a mixture of three policies: (1) reducing infant and childhood mortality, (2) improving access to education, especially for women, and (3) providing comprehensive family planning services. (Of course, these policies are also a form of redistribution of income and can help promote balanced growth). Finally, coercive measures, both economic and physical, have been employed by China and India to control population growth. Aside from important moral issues, outside of China such programs may be counterproductive.

The pressure that people place on their environment depends not only on absolute numbers but also on the number of goods they consume and the damage that each good does. While in poor countries, overpopulation is the primary threat to both local and global environmental quality, in rich countries, consumption behavior is the problem. The consumption-pollution link arises from both the disproportionate share of global consumption engaged in by rich countries and the *potential* for an unsustainable drawdown of natural capital and environmental resources fueled by rich country consumption.

Costa Rica illustrates both the potential for and the obstacles to achieving sustainable development. While the country made substantial progress in reducing population growth rates in the 1980s, the increasing importance of its export beef industry threatens to counteract these sustainability gains. First, the industry has drawn down Costa Rica's rain forest stock directly. At the same time, profits from this industry have been siphoned off to repay the tremendous debt accumulated in the 1970s and have not been fully reinvested in created capital within the country. Moreover, cattle ranching has displaced many small farmers, who have increased pressure both on rain-forest lands and urban environments. Increased poverty among the landless farmers, as well as reduced production of food per capita, may also lead to higher birth rates, reducing progress made in reducing population growth.

Is a sustainable future possible? The Bruntland Commission provided an outline of the steps necessary to get us from here to there. They include controlling population growth, creating food security, improving technology, and conserving natural capital. All these options will be expensive and ultimately must be funded primarily by rich countries. The increasing recognition that rich country welfare depends on sustainable progress in poor countries makes this program at least potentially feasible from a political perspective. One possible pool of resources to finance the sustainable development program can be found in current world expenditures on military hardware and personnel.

APPLICATION 21.0

High Income Counties and Hazardous Waste

Some recent evidence (Bohara et al. [1996]) shows that hazardous waste sites in the United States display an inverted U-shape relationship with county income. That is, as income in a county rises, the number of hazardous waste sites at first increases and then decreases, with a turning point of between $17,000 and $21,000 per capita. (The authors also find evidence of "environmental racism" [chapter 5]. Controlling for income, a higher white population saw a significant drop in the number of hazardous waste sites.)

Do you take the evidence on income to mean that richer counties ultimately generate less hazardous waste? Why or why not?

APPLICATION 21.1

Childhood Mortality and Population Growth

Reducing the rate of infant and childhood mortality in poor countries clearly leads to a short-run increase in population growth. Use the economic model of family size developed in this chapter to explain why population growth experts nevertheless advocate improved public health measures as an important component of a population control strategy.

Key Ideas in Each Section

21.0 In large measure, successful **traditional economic development** means productively absorbing the labor freed up in the **agrarian transition.** Because poverty and environmental degradation go hand in hand, economic development is required for **sustainability;** however, sustainable development must also recognize the environmental costs of economic growth.

21.1 There are four connections between poverty and environmental quality. (1) Poor people suffer from **unsafe drinking water, inadequate sewage,** and **indoor air pollution.** (2) Poor people degrade local resources because they cannot afford not to. (3) Some regulated pollutants display an **inverted U-shape** as a function of income, due to **education, relative risk considerations, political demand for pollution control,** and a **shift in industrial composition.** (4) Wealthier people tend to have lower rates of **population growth.**

21.2 Median and "highly pessimistic" **population growth scenarios** are laid out in this section. Under the former, world population will stabilize at twice its current level; under the latter, it will quadruple over the next century to 20 billion. Growth predictions change rapidly with small changes in fertility rates.

To date the **Malthusian** population trap, resulting from an arithmetic growth in food supply and a geometric growth in population, has been avoided. This is due in part to the Green Revolution and in part to the **demographic transition** to low birth rates in rich countries. However, a **neomalthusian vicious cycle,** in which population growth leads to poverty that sustains high population growth, is supported by recent trends in global food production per capita.

21.3 The **poverty-fertility relationship** is explained by an economic model in which all parents seek **economic insurance** and an **income supplement** from children. Due to lack of resources and risk, poor parents choose a **low-investment (quantity) strategy,** rather than a **high-investment (quality) strategy.**

21.4 Based on the model, population growth can be controlled in the following ways: (1) balanced economic growth and/or **redistribution of income** (perhaps via **land reform,** or a **debt-for-farmland swap**); (2) reduced **infant and childhood mortality;** (3) **Access to education** (educated parents have a **higher opportunity cost of time;** education can also enhance women's status and decision-making ability in a **patriarchal culture**); and (4) comprehensive **family planning.** These measures designed to change parental behavior by increasing opportunity have proven successful. In addition to such measures, China has employed more **coercive** forms of population control in its **one-child policy.**

21.5 There are two elements to the **consumption-pollution link.** (1) Because rich countries consume most of the world's resources, we are responsible for most of the world's global pollution problems. (2) Rich country demand can lead to an unsustainable drawdown in natural capital in poor countries.

21.6 The **hamburger connection** between Costa Rican producers and rich country consumers is used to illustrate how export agriculture in a debt-burdened context might lead to unsustainable development. Although the country's gross domestic product (GDP) grew faster than its population in the 1980s, economic expansion based on cattle ranching has degraded rain-forest resources and increased the number of landless farmers. To the extent that compensating investment in created capital has not occurred, growth in the beef industry has lowered net national welfare.

21.7 The **Bruntland Commission Report** for the United Nations identified four **sustainability steps** necessary to achieve sustainable development. (1) Slow **population growth;** (2) boost **food security** by improving the productivity of small farmers; (3) develop and diffuse **clean technology;** and (4) engage in effective **resource conservation.** Each of these steps will cost money, much of which will have to come from rich countries. One source of funding would be to divert funds from global military spending.

References

Ahmad, Yusuf J., Salah El Serafy and Ernst Lutz (1989). *Environmental Accounting for Sustainable Development.* Washington, DC: World Bank.

Becker, Gary S. and Lewis H.G (1973). "Interaction Between Quality and Quantity of Children." *Journal of Political Economy,* 81, 279–288.

Bieszaz, Richard, Karen Bieszaz, and Mavis Bieszaz (1982). *The Costa Ricans.* Englewood Cliffs, NJ: Prentice Hall.

Birdsall, Nancy M. and Charles C. Griffin (1988). "Fertility and Poverty in Developing Countries." *Journal of Policy Modeling,* 10, no. 1, 29–55.

Bohara, Alok, Kishore Gawande, Robert Berrens and Pingo Wang (1996). "Environmental Kuznets Curves for U.S. Hazardous Waste Sites." *Working Paper.* Albuquerque: University of New Mexico.

Borensztein, Eduardo (1991). "Will Debt Reduction Increase Investment?" *Finance and Development,* 28, no. 1, 25–27.

Browder, John O. (1988). "Public Policy and Deforestation in the Brazilian Amazon." In *Public Policies and the Misuse of Forest Resources,* eds. Robert Repetto and Malcolm Gillis. Cambridge: Cambridge University Press.

Brown, Lester R. and John E. Young (1990).

"Feeding the World in the Nineties." In *State of the World 1990.* Lester R. Brown, ed. New York: Norton.

Carriere, Jean (1991). "The Crisis in Costa Rica: An Ecological Perspective." In *Environment and Development in Latin America,* eds. David Goodman and Michael Redclift. New York: Manchester University Press.

Cohen, Daniel (1993). "Low Investment and Large LDC Debt in the 1980's." *American Economic Review,* 83, no. 3, 437–449.

Cohen, Joel (1995). *How Many People Can the Earth Support?* London: W. W. Norton.

Daly, Herman (1990). "How Big is the Population Factor?" *EPA Journal,* July/August, 31.

Dasgupta, Partha (1995). "Population, Poverty and the Local Environment," *Scientific American,* 272, no. 2, 40–46.

Forster, Nancy R. (1992). "Protecting Fragile Lands: New Reasons to Tackle Old Problems." *World Development,* 20, no. 4, 371–382.

Grossman, Gene M. and Alan B. Krueger (1991). "Environmental Impacts of a North American Free Trade Agreement," *Working Paper 3914.* Cambridge: National Bureau of Economic Research.

Hettige, H.. Lucas, R. E. B. Lucas, and D.

Wheeler (1992). "The Toxic Intensity of Industrial Production: Global Patterns, Trends and Trade Policies." *American Economic Review,* 82, no. 2, 478–481.

Howarth, Richard B. and Richard B. Noorgard (1990). "Intergenerational Resource Rights, Efficiency and Social Optimality." *Land Economics,* 66, no. 1, 1–11.

Jacobson, Jodi L. (1987). *Planning the Global Family.* Washington, DC: Worldwatch.

Leonard, H. Jeffrey (1987). *Natural Resources and Economic Development in Central America.* Oxford: Transaction Books.

Lucas, George (ed.) (1976). *Lifeboat Ethics* New York: Harper and Row.

Moene, Karl Ove (1992). "Poverty and Land Ownership." *American Economic Review,* 82, no. 1, 52–64.

Musambachime, Mwelma (1990). "The Impact of Rapid Population Growth on Economic Decline: The Case of Zambia." *Review of African Political Economy,* 448, no. 2, 81–91.

O'Brien, Phillip J. (1991). "Debt and Sustainable Development in Latin America." In *Environment and Development in Latin America,* eds. David Goodman and Michael Redclift. New York: Manchester University Press.

Pearce, David and Giles D. Atkinson (1993). "Capital Theory and the Measurement of Sustainable Development: An Indicator of 'Weak' Sustainability." *Ecological Economics,* 8, no. 2, 103–108.

Pearce, David and Norman Myers (1990). "Economic Values and the Environment of Amazonia." In *The Future of Amazonia: Destruction or Sustainable Development?* eds. David Goodman and Anthony Hall. New York: St. Martins Press.

Pezzey, John (1993). "Sustainability Policies in Models of Trade with Exhaustible Resources." Paper presented at the American Economic Association Meetings, Anaheim.

Repetto, Robert (1989). "Nature's Resources as Productive Assets." *Challenge,* 32, no. 5, 16–27.

Repetto, Robert (1985). "Population, Resource Pressures, and Poverty. In *The Global Possible: Resources, Development and the New Century.* Robert Repetto, ed. New Haven: Yale University Press.

Selden, Thomas M. and Daqing Song (1992). "Environmental Quality and Development: Is There a Kuznets Curve for Air Pollution?" Paper presented at the 1993 American Economic Association Meetings.

Solow, Robert (1992). *An Almost Practical Step Toward Sustainability.* Washington, DC: Resources for the Future.

Wattenberg, Ben J. (1990). "How Big is the Population Factor?" *EPA Journal,* July/August, 30.

World Bank (1992). *World Development Report 1992: Development and the Environment.* New York: Oxford University Press.

World Commission on Environment and Development (1987). *Our Common Future.* New York: Oxford University Press.

CHAPTER 22

Environmental Policy in Poor Countries

22.0 Introduction

At the end of chapter 21, we identified four interrelated **sustainability steps** that need to be pursued in poor countries if the ultimate vision of a sustainable future for human beings is to be realized. These four policy goals are (1) stabilizing population growth, (2) achieving food security, (3) promoting the development and adoption of clean technology, and (4) conserving natural capital. This chapter moves on to consider a variety of other steps that poor and rich countries can take to promote the four policy goals.

As in our discussion of environmental policy in the United States, we need to be fully aware of the constraints that government policy makers in poor countries face. Because the potential for government failure in poor countries is large, due in part to much stronger business influence over policy, the first half of this chapter analyzes measures designed to harness the profit motive in pursuit of sustainable development. First, poor country governments should eliminate environmentally destructive subsidy policies. Second, by strengthening property rights, governments can reinforce profit-based motives for conservation.

While government can do a lot by selectively disengaging itself from market transactions, and improving private incentives for conservation, government ultimately must be counted on to take an effective, proactive role in promoting sustainable development. This chapter thus goes on to examine the role that regulatory and clean technology strategies must play.

Finally, we end with a trio of related topics: resource conservation, debt relief, and international trade. The basic message is that achieving the four sustainability steps is not cheap; without substantial aid from wealthy countries, it is doubtful whether sustainable development in poor countries can be achieved.

22.1 The Political Economy of Sustainable Development

Before jumping into specifics, we need to pause to consider the constraints under which government policy operates. Part II of this book focused considerable attention on the obstacles to effective government action in the United States, raised both by imperfect information and the opportunity for political influence.

The United States is a wealthy country, with a fairly efficient marketplace and government. By contrast, the average person in a less developed country is a very poor person, and this poverty undermines the efficiency of both markets and governments. Per capita annual income in low-income countries in 1992 was $320, or about 87 cents per person per day. In the world's poorest countries, this falls to 22 cents per day, on average. But even these abysmal figures disguise the true extent of poverty, since there is considerable wealth inequality *within* countries.

In general, most countries have a small **political-economic elite** who control a disproportionate share of national income and wield disproportionate influence over political events. Even in a developed country like the United States, the top 20% of the population owns over 70% of the nation's wealth and takes in 44.3% of the annual income.[1] The income distribution in poor countries is typically much more uneven. For example, in 1980, the top 20% of the population in four central American countries— El Salvador, Guatemala, Nicaragua, and Honduras—received between 54% and 66% of the national income.[2]

This kind of tremendous economic and political disparity often has a historical basis in the period of colonial rule. For example, throughout Latin America, the current, dramatic concentration of landownership in the hands of a small percentage of the population can be traced to the *hacienda* system established by the Spanish colonists. Or consider another example. Britain granted Zambia independence in 1964 after exploiting that nation's rich copper deposits for 40 of its 70 years of colonial rule. At independence, only 100 Africans out of a population of 3.5 million had received a college education, and fewer than 1,000 were high school graduates.[3]

At the risk of very gross oversimplification, the typical class structure in a developing country can be represented by the pyramid in Figure 22.1.[4] At the top are a small group of wealthy landholders, industrialists, and military officers, often educated in western universities. Businessmen in this group include both local capitalists and local managers of multinational corporations. Below them come the urban middle class: teachers, professionals, state employees, factory workers, miners, and soldiers. The vast majority of the population are the poor: urban shanty-town dwellers subsisting on part-time work, rural small farmers, and landless laborers.

Sustainable development—increasing NNW for the average individual—by definition requires focusing on the lower class, since they are the average individuals. Moreover, it is this group, who out of brute necessity, often run down the local stock of natural

---

[1] *Statistical Abstract of the United States,* 1992. Washington, DC: U.S. Dept. of Commerce.
[2] Leonard (1987: 51).
[3] Musambachime (1990).
[4] For a succinct review article on "Third World Politics," see Weaver et al. (1990).

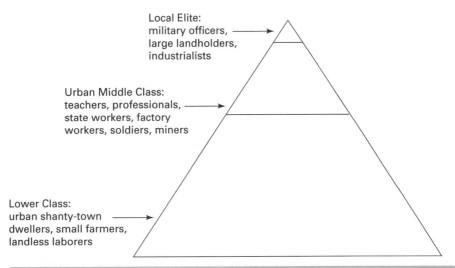

Local Elite:
military officers,
large landholders,
industrialists

Urban Middle Class:
teachers, professionals,
state workers, factory
workers, soldiers, miners

Lower Class:
urban shanty-town
dwellers, small farmers,
landless laborers

FIGURE 22.1 Class Structure in Poor Countries (Generalized)

capital in a nonsustainable fashion. As we begin to evaluate development/environmental policy in poor countries, the question we thus need to ask is, Does the policy improve or exacerbate the position of the poor?

Unfortunately, because the lower class generally has little political power in developing countries, this question is seldom central to policy design. Elite-dominated governments, often maintaining their power through military force, rarely provide democratic avenues for those adversely impacted by government policy to register their protests. Yet, for environmental progress, the ability to protest is vital.

As was argued in chapter 12, the primary environmental lesson from the Communist experience is that a lack of democracy will stifle the recognition of environmental problems. Absent substantial pressure from those affected, government will have neither the power nor the inclination to force economic decision makers—whether state bureaucrats, managers of private corporations, or ordinary citizens—to recognize and internalize the external environmental costs generated by their actions. Perhaps for this reason, increasing landlessness among small farmers, leading to severe pressure on marginal rural lands and massive urban migration, has not, until recently, been viewed as the major environmental problem that it indeed has become.

In addition to nonrecognition of important problems, when government leaders are not democratically accountable, opportunities for corruption multiply. This is especially true when even top government officials in poor countries fail to achieve a standard of living common to the middle class in western countries. Not surprisingly, given their very low pay and level of training, corruption among low-level bureaucrats in poor countries is not uncommon. Thus, as a general rule, government bureaucracies in poor countries are not particularly efficient. (The few developing countries for which this is not true tend to be economically quite successful.)[5] As a result, even

---

[5]Though not necessarily in a sustainable fashion. Examples include Taiwan, Korea, China, Singapore, Botswana, and Costa Rica.

when development/environmental problems are in fact recognized, and policies set up to attack them, progress may be quite slow.

Partly in response to government failures in poor countries, so-called nongovernmental organizations (NGOs) have emerged to deal with issues of rural development, small-farmers rights, urban service provision, and natural resource protection. NGOs include international development and human rights groups, the international arms of environmental and conservation groups, local environmental groups, peasant and rural workers unions, and urban activist groups.

To summarize: For a variety of reasons including colonial history, small political-economic elites, undemocratic governmental structures, and poorly trained and paid bureaucrats, factors leading to government failure are compounded in poor countries. Given this potential, policies that depend on sophisticated analytical capabilities, or aggressive monitoring and enforcement are not likely to succeed in many parts of the developing world.

Unlike in wealthy countries, the "environmental movement" is very small in poor countries. Thus progress toward sustainable development must spring from either environmental concern on the part of ruling elites or a nonenvironmental interest on their part in population control, food security, technological innovation, or resource conservation. No strong groundswell drives the political process in a sustainable direction.

The lack of popular environmental counterpressure also means that business interests have a much freer hand in affecting environmental policy in poor countries. Both **domestic** and **multinational businesses** operate in the developing world. Domestic firms are owned and operated by residents of the poor country; multinational firms operate in many countries around the globe and are typically headquartered in a developed country.

Multinational companies have a particularly strong presence in resource-based industries in less developed countries. Between 80% and 90% of world trade in tea, coffee, cocoa, cotton, forest products, tobacco, jute, copper, iron ore, and bauxite is under the control of three to six such companies. However, multinationals have also invested heavily in manufacturing in poor countries, especially in chemicals.[6]

The influence of business, whether domestic or multinational, on environmental policy goals can be positive. For example, businesses can create jobs leading to balanced growth and a subsequent reduction in population growth rates. Or they can import or develop new clean technology. However, the influence can also be negative. Businesspeople may bribe officials to obtain subsidized access to timber or other resources, and understate profits to avoid taxation.[7] Or businesses might promote subsidized credit programs, allowing them to import capital-intensive agricultural technologies that displace farmworkers, on net, leading to an increase in unemployment and poverty. Or business might use its resources to discourage the passage and/or enforcement of environmental or resource protection legislation.

---

[6]World Commission on Environment and Development (1987: 85).

[7]In Papua, New Guinea, for example, Thompson (1992) reports that prior to 1986, no logging company had ever declared a profit or paid income tax. Estimates of losses from transfer pricing in the country ranged from $42 million to $55 million per year.

The point here is to neither condemn nor praise business as an agent of environmental change in poor countries.[8] Rather, the point is simply to remember that business managers, whether multinational or domestic, are not interested in sustainable development. They are interested in profit. To the extent that profit opportunities promote sustainable development, business will do so as well. However, businesses will just as eagerly pursue profit-driven options that are ultimately unsustainable.

Likewise, the point is not to condemn governments in poor countries as hopelessly corrupt or inefficient. There are many examples of government success as well as failure in the developing world. Ultimately, we *must* rely on poor country governments to undertake effective action if we seek to achieve a sustainable future. There is simply no other choice.

22.2 Ending Environmentally Damaging Subsidies

Both rich and poor countries around the world maintain a broad array of **subsidies** for particular industries with the purported intent of promoting economic development. Some of the forms these subsidies take include special tax breaks, privileged access to imported parts and materials, protection from international competition, low-cost access to natural resources, the provision of subsidized or interest-free loans, and investment in infrastructure.

Unfortunately, many of these subsidy policies have had the effect of undermining the four steps to sustainability discussed above. This section will look closely at the forest industry, where government policy has often worked to promote a rapid and unsustainable exhaustion of the resource. To begin with, governments often sell public timber to logging companies at prices that are "too low." By this I mean that governments **fail to capture all the resource rent** associated with the timber. As discussed in chapter 6, for timber harvesting to be sustainable, *all* of the resource rent must be retained in the host country and invested in created capital.

Repetto (1988a: 20) reports that in the recent past, the governments of Ghana, Indonesia, and the Philippines have received less than 38% of the total rents from timber production in the form of sales revenue and taxes.[9] By failing to capture all the rents, governments make logging artificially profitable, and this speeds up the depletion of the resource. In addition, once timber sales have been consummated and roads built, it has proven very difficult for governments to enforce environmental contract terms in remote areas, or to monitor illegal cutting and smuggling of timber.[10]

Many governments also engage in **infrastructure development** to support forestry—building roads and ports, and surveying and grading timber. In the extreme, taxpayers actually pay firms to harvest timber. This has occurred in the United States, where the Forest Service sells timber at prices that do not cover its administrative and

---

[8]There is substantial debate over the role that multinational corporations in particular play in promoting or hindering sustainable development. In my own research (Goodstein [1989]), I found that absentee ownership of coal resources hindered development in Appalachia, vis à vis the rest of the southern United States I argue that the most important impact of absentee ownership was the restriction in the growth of a local business class interested in promoting manufacturing development.

[9]The figures for Indonesia and the Philippines are from 1979 to 1982, and for Ghana, 1971 to 1974.

[10]Thompson (1992) details how difficult this process can be for the case of Papua, New Guinea.

road-building expenses. In 1995, this direct subsidy from the Forest Service was close to $230 million.[11]

Poor countries have also **subsidized "downstream" industries,** which process raw timber into lumber and other finished wood and paper products. Subsidies include substantial tax breaks and subsidized credit, as well as placing bans on the export of unfinished logs. Many of these policies have not been successful, however, due to high tariffs in rich countries designed to protect *their* wood processing industries. Moreover, due to a lack of domestic competition, wood processing industries in poor countries tend to be very inefficient and require continuous subsidies. In addition, their existence puts further pressure on the government to artificially lower timber prices to maintain employment.[12]

Governments have also sponsored **colonization projects** to resettle landless farmers in rain-forest areas. Such conversion efforts have been judged a sustainable success in peninsular Malaysia, where about 12% of the country's forest has been converted to permanent tree crops like rubber and palm oil since 1950.[13] However, efforts in Brazil and Indonesia have failed, with the land being abandoned after deforestation. In part, this failure has resulted from poor soil quality. In addition, the policies have been hampered by inadequate, though still substantial, government efforts to develop distribution and marketing channels for small farmers in remote areas. Subsidies for these programs, from the government and the World Bank, ranged as high as $10,000 per household in Indonesia, a country with a GNP per capita of $560.[14]

Finally, as was discussed in the Costa Rican case in chapter 21, governments, with the assistance of international groups like the World Bank, have been quite active in promoting the spread of **cattle ranching** in forested areas. This process has advanced furthest in the Brazilian Amazon, where cattle ranching has caused over 70% of total deforestation.[15] Under the theory that ranching would serve as a spur to the general economic development of the Amazon, and concerned about securing its national borders through settlement, the Brazilian government pumped over $730 million into the beef industry between 1966 and 1983. However, Browder (1988) shows that in 1985, few of the government-supported Amazon ranches could have survived without continuing subsidies.

To summarize: With the ostensible goal of supporting resource-based economic development (and influenced by factors as diverse as national defense and personal gain), policy makers in poor countries have established an array of subsidies for logging companies, forest product industries, small farmers, and large ranchers. With a few exceptions, such policies have failed to generate stand-alone industries and have continually drained capital from other sectors. With limited economic progress, population growth has not declined. Because of the policy emphasis on ranching instead of basic foodstuffs, and the failure of small farm programs to take root, food security has not improved. And little clean technology has been developed or introduced.

---

[11]See *Wall Street Journal,* February 19, 1997, and Repetto (1988b).

[12]Deacon (1992) points out, however, that export bans on raw logs may still on balance reduce the rate of deforestation.

[13]Gillis (1988).

[14]Repetto (1988a).

[15]Browder (1988).

At the same time, subsidy policies have led to unsustainable declines in natural capital—the forest resource. In addition, they have generated environmental damage ranging from siltation and flooding, to forest fires, to a tremendous loss of biodiversity. Finally, native inhabitants of the forests have lost access to their means of subsistence, and their cultural survival is threatened.

This section has explored in detail some of the subsidy policies that promote rapid deforestation around the world, for little if any net economic benefit to poor countries. Subsidies for other products that aggravate environmental damage include energy, pesticides and fertilizer, and irrigation water. In Egypt, India, Brazil, China, and Mexico, for example, electric power is sold at less than 60% of production cost, with the government making up the difference through tax revenues.[16] The increased demand for power sparked by lower prices has brought with it associated environmental damage from hydroelectric, coal, and nuclear power plants.

Environmentally damaging subsidies are not unique to poor countries, as our discussion of the U.S. Forest Service above, and of energy and agricultural subsidies in chapters 19 and 20, make clear. And just as subsidy elimination is difficult in rich countries, so it will be in poor countries. Subsidies can seldom be eliminated without some form of **compensation** for the losers.

In addition, compensation is often required on the grounds of basic **fairness** when subsidies benefit the poor. For example, a major obstacle to food security arises when governments hold prices for basic foods, for example, bread or cooking oil, below their market-clearing price. Low prices drive farmers into bankruptcy. Recognizing this effect, and interested in boosting agricultural output, the former USSR decontrolled bread prices in December 1991. Figure 22.2 illustrates what happened. Prices

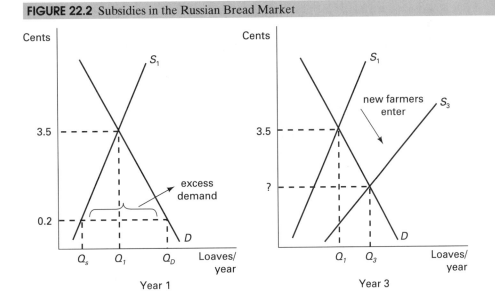

FIGURE 22.2 Subsidies in the Russian Bread Market

[16]World Bank (1992: 68–69).

were initially controlled at around .2 cents per pound, leading to a restriction in the available supply, the development of shortages and long lines, and black markets. (Average monthly income in Russia is about $20.)

By June 1992, prices had jumped to 3.5 cents per pound, more than a sixteenfold increase. In the long run (two years or so), more farmers would be expected to enter the wheat market, shifting the supply curve out and driving bread prices down to some intermediate level. Yet, the sudden decontrol has meant at least several years of suffering for Russians, particularly those unable to work.

To cushion the blow of increased prices, the government has provided income supplements. One family interviewed by the *New York Times* was receiving child-support payments for food, clothing and day care from the government totaling $4.40 per month. But political pressures in early 1993 still led to at least symbolic action to restore price controls on basic goods.[17]

Russia is a relatively wealthy country, yet removing food subsidies there has led to considerable hardship. In poor countries, eliminating food price controls without increasing the income of the poor can lead to starvation. During the early 1980s, at least a dozen food riots shook poor countries as governments, under the prodding of the International Monetary Fund, lifted price controls without taking adequate measures to boost poor people's income.[18]

On political and sometimes, equity grounds, removing environmentally damaging subsidies requires resources to compensate people who lose out. Nevertheless, eliminating such subsidies present a cheap way to improve environmental quality in poor countries. Removing subsidies requires no ongoing governmental expense, and sustainability can be enhanced through the productive use of the resources freed up. For example, if tax breaks for pesticide use were eliminated, the increased government revenues could be used to fund agricultural extension workers, helping farmers to reduce the amount of pesticide they employed.

22.3 Establishing and Enforcing Property Rights

Way back in chapter 3 we identified one of the primary causes of pollution and resource degradation to be open access to common property. Recall that the **open access problem** arose when individuals considered only the private benefit and costs from exploiting a shared resource—air, land, or water—without taking into account the external social costs imposed on others. Recall also that traditional societies managed common property problems through informal social controls and moral sanctions.

However, as traditional control mechanisms have broken down, and both population and consumption pressures have risen, the free access problem has emerged as the underlying source of environmental degradation worldwide. When the **property rights** or titles to resources such as land or fisheries are not clearly defined, the people who exploit the resource have little incentive to engage in profit-based conservation or invest in long-lived environmental protection measures such as erosion control. To improve this situation, government has three options:

---

[17]"In Choppy Russian Economy, A Family Jury Rigs a Budget," *New York Times,* January 20, 1992; and "Russia Says Curbs on Profit Are Not a Change in Policy," *New York Times,* January 7, 1993.
[18]Tibesar and White (1990).

1. Communal Ownership   Where an existing community is managing the property sustainably, government policy can protect and enforce the existing communal property right. Often this will mean restricting access to outsiders and may require imposing limitations on the use of sophisticated technology. For example, in one case, cooperative fishing agreements in southern Brazil broke down when nylon fishing nets were adopted by some members of the group, giving them an "unfair" advantage. In addition, under Brazilian law, the group could not exclude outsiders, who also used such nets.[19] The primary advantage of communal ownership patterns, when they can be preserved, is that they tend to be quite sustainable.

2. State Ownership   Government can declare the land a national forest, reserve, or park, or regulate an ocean fishery. However, a simple declaration is inadequate. Government must also devote the necessary resources to protecting the boundaries of the reserve in order to prevent unauthorized uses. This kind of enforcement task can be extremely difficult for most poor countries. Even in a country with a relatively efficient bureaucracy such as Costa Rica, by 1985 one source estimated that landless farmers had already cleared one quarter of the total forest reserves that the government had set aside for protection.[20] (See chapter 23 for an analysis of efforts to improve this situation.)

A recent effort by Chile to manage its ocean fisheries involves an overall quota system, controls on boats and fishing gear, and a licensing scheme. In this case, assistance to strengthen enforcement and monitoring capabilities will be provided by Nordic countries and the World Bank.[21]

3. Private Ownership   The final option is to assign property rights to private individuals. However, this process also is more difficult than it seems on the surface. First, it is not free, since government resources must be put to work delineating and enforcing private property rights. More importantly, privatization can easily contribute to increased poverty.

Privatizing commonly held property will often hurt those who previously had access under traditional law. For example, privatization of rural land in Kenya led to married sons and wives losing their traditional land rights, since they were not represented in the process. And in many instances, privatization schemes provide an advantage to wealthy and/or educated individuals to increase their wealth at the expense of the poor.[22] This type of privatization is counterproductive from a sustainability point of view, since it tends to increase poverty and downgrade women's social status, thus increasing population growth rates while reducing food security. Privatization efforts designed to boost profit-based conservation must therefore be conducted carefully so as to increase rather than decrease both the social status of women and general employment opportunities.

---

[19]World Bank (1992: 70).

[20]The estimate is from Fundacion Neotropica, an environmental organization in Costa Rica, cited in Carriere (1991).

[21]World Bank (1992: 84).

[22]Barrows and Roth (1990).

Privatizing forested land can also have ambiguous environmental impacts. For example, as a way to clearly establish ownership uses, many poor countries require that settlers clear the land in order to take title (as was the practice on the U.S. frontier). This process of course encourages deforestation. Yet without actual occupation and use of the land, settlers and government officials would have a hard time validating whose claim to a piece of land is legitimate. Even where clearance is not required, establishing legal title to land in many poor countries can take years. As a result, farmers tend to clear the land anyway in order to establish *de facto* control.

Yet, because they risk losing their land, farmers who have not attained legal title tend to underinvest in **profit-based conservation** measures (see chapter 6) like erosion control, as well as investments that increase farm output.[23] To encourage such measures, governments can speed up the titling process; for example, by employing more surveyors and land clerks and by providing better law enforcement to prevent illegal evictions. This will increase the security of farmers' private property rights and should encourage them to invest more in their land.

The advantage of private ownership, once secure title has been transferred, is that it promotes profit-based conservation. (However, as was discussed in chapter 6, profit-based conservation may not be sufficient to insure sustainability.) Some of this advantage of private ownership can be captured through long-term leases of state-owned property to private companies. Repetto (1988a) argues that one factor promoting tropical deforestation is the relatively short life of most timber contracts. Since the companies are not guaranteed access to a second cut in twenty or thirty years' time, they have no incentive to practice sustainable forest management.[24] He thus recommends that lease periods be substantially lengthened.

Clarifying and strengthening property rights is a way to directly reduce environmental damage by "internalizing externalities." When property rights are clearly defined, then the owner—a community, the government, or an individual—bears a larger part of the social costs of environmental resource degradation or depletion. Individual and community ownership schemes have an advantage in this respect over government ownership, since people at the local level are directly affected by resource degradation. As a result, they have a greater incentive than do government managers to maintain the productivity of that piece of the environment they "own."

Ownership at the individual or community level will thus tend to promote profit-based conservation, while conservation under state ownership depends on the strength of environmental concern within the governing elite. As we have argued above, such concern may be quite weak, and even where strong, the enforcement capabilities of poor country governments can make resource conservation and environmental protection difficult.

Yet privatization alone is no panacea. In a study of East African farmers, Barrows and Roth (1990) concluded that due to a lack of credit, marketing infrastructure, technical assistance, and in some cases *increased* uncertainty under the new legal structure, the displacement of traditional communal land holdings by private farms has

---

[23]Southgate formalizes this argument (1990).

[24]Deacon (1992), however, points out that this may not be a sufficient condition to insure sustained yield management. Timber companies may fear higher taxes or expropriation in the future. He argues that macro conditions of overall investment security matter more than do formal property-right arrangements.

had little impact on agricultural investment. They conclude that privatization is most useful when it serves as a safeguard against the taking of small-farmer land by politically powerful individuals.

The first two sections of this chapter have focused on ways in which poor country governments can improve environmental quality either by selectively reducing environmentally damaging subsidies, or by strengthening communal and private property rights in order to promote profit-based conservation. We now move on to a consideration of more proactive government policy: regulation and clean technology promotion.

22.4 Regulatory Approaches

Environmental regulation is a new phenomenon in the developed world, with most of the major laws having been passed within the last twenty-five years. Regulation is even more recent in poor countries: Mexico, for example, passed its comprehensive federal environmental law only in 1988.

Chapters 16 and 17 have already provided an in-depth look at the theory of regulation. It was argued there that in general, an **incentive-based** system (pollution taxes or marketable permits) is both more cost-effective in the short run, and better at encouraging technological advancement in the long run, than a so-called **command-and-control** approach to pollution control. Recall that a stereotypical command-and-control system features (1) uniform emission standards for all sources and (2) the installation of government-mandated pollution control technologies. The inflexibility in the approach means that cost-saving opportunities that can be captured by incentive-based systems are not exploited, and that incentives for improved technology are limited. This lesson holds for poor countries as well, with a couple of *caveats*.

First, as we learned in chapter 15, monitoring and enforcement is the weakest link in the regulatory process in rich countries. This observation holds even stronger in poor countries. Mexico, for example, has been trying to beef up its enforcement efforts, partly been in response to the negotiation of the North American Free Trade Agreement, discussed later in this chapter. Yet, in spite of some highly publicized efforts, including plant shutdowns, enforcement remains quite weak by U.S. standards. One spot survey of six U.S. companies operating along the border found that none of them held required environmental permits.[25] Thus, the primary focus of regulatory policy in the developing world must be **enforceability.**

Pollution taxes can improve enforcement, because government benefits materially from enforcing the law. This is especially true if the enforcement agency is allowed to keep some portion of the fines. Command-and-control systems also have some enforceability advantages, when regulators can force firms to install low marginal cost ("automatic") pollution control technologies. However, recall that even such automatic technologies, like catalytic converters or power plant scrubbers, break down and require maintenance.

In poor countries with efficient court systems, one way to improve enforcement would be to encourage the use of citizen suits against polluters, discussed in chapter

---

[25]U.S. General Accounting Office (1992).

17. Another recommendation has been to allow foreign nongovernmental organizations to sue U.S.-based multinational corporations in U.S. courts for violations of poor country environmental laws.[26]

The second rule that poor country governments must heed in selecting regulatory instruments is to seek **administrative simplicity.** For example, during the mid-1980s severe particulate pollution from state-owned and multinational chemical plants, steel mills, and other industrial and power facilities in Cubatao, Brazil, led to the evacuation of many residents to a nearby soccer stadium. While in principle, a marketable permit or particulate tax system might have been introduced to control the pollution, instead the authorities directed the firms to install scrubbers and switch to low-sulfur oil—classic command-and-control tactics.[27] It is doubtful that local authorities had either the technological capabilities or the staff to develop, monitor, and enforce a sophisticated incentive-based system. This is particularly true since extensive field testing of tradeable permit or pollution tax systems in rich countries has not yet occurred.

In practice, avoiding administrative complexity and insuring enforceability means that pure incentive-based systems (pollution taxes or marketable permit systems) may not be feasible. However, the use of **indirect pollution taxes** will often be a good approach. In contrast to direct pollution taxes, which tax the emission of pollutants directly, indirect pollution taxes impose fees on inputs to, or outputs from, a polluting process. Examples include energy or fuel taxes (discussed in chapter 20), or taxes on timber production.

The example of taxes on timber sold to mills (called **royalties**) is an interesting one, since it illustrates some of the problems raised by indirect taxation of pollution. The idea is that by taxing rain-forest timber production, logging will become less profitable, leading to a reduction in this activity. This in turn may be desirable because logging contributes to environmental damage ranging from siltation and flooding, to loss of biodiversity, to an aggravation of global warming. The situation is illustrated in Figure 22.3.

In a classic supply-and-demand analysis, increased royalties raise costs to firms, causing some to drop out of the market. This shifts the supply curve up to S', and the timber brought to market drops to T'. This appears to be the desired result of the policy. However, an offsetting effect may in fact lead to a much smaller reduction in the actual area logged. As royalties are raised, fewer tree species become profitable to harvest. Yet to get at the remaining profitable species, firms may still need to clear-cut the same acreage. Firms then remove the profitable species, leaving much of the timber that would formerly have been brought to market behind, a process called *high grading.* Thus, although increased royalties will have a big effect on the timber brought to market, they may have a smaller impact on the acreage logged.

To solve this problem, one might suggest a more direct pollution tax—a royalty based on the acreage logged. Such a tax would get at the problem in an up-front

---

[26]Naysnerski and Tietenberg (1992) make the first suggestion. Harvard Law Review (1990) argues a more ambitious variant of the second.

[27]World Bank (1992: 131).

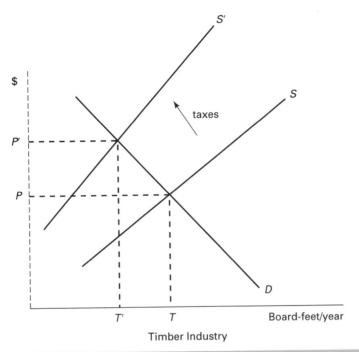

FIGURE 22.3 Increased Royalties and Logging Activity

way. But monitoring logging activity is much harder than slapping a tax on logs as they come to the mill, so the indirect tax wins out on enforceability grounds. Another alternative would be to vary royalties by species, with higher taxes on high-value trees, as is done in the Malaysian state of Sarawak. This reduces high grading and thus can have a bigger impact on acreage reduction.[28] In summary, the lesson from the timber royalty case is that indirect pollution taxes *are not* direct pollution taxes, and their ultimate effect on pollution or resource degradation cannot be taken for granted. The impact of indirect taxes on the environmental problem at hand must be carefully considered.

This is not to say, however, that indirect pollution taxes are a bad idea. Well-designed indirect taxes can have a substantial impact on environmental problems. In addition to such measures, cost-saving flexibility can be built into command-and-control regulatory structures wherever possible. To see how the use of an indirect tax combined with flexibility in a command-and-control regulatory approach can reduce the costs of pollution control, we turn to the case of air pollution control in Mexico City.

---

[28]Though it need not. In fact, which system reduces overall logged acreage more will depend on which system reduces logging profitability more. Repetto (1988a) provides the information on the royalty structure in Sarawak.

FIGURE 22.4 Air Pollution Control in Mexico City, Marginal Costs from Vehicles

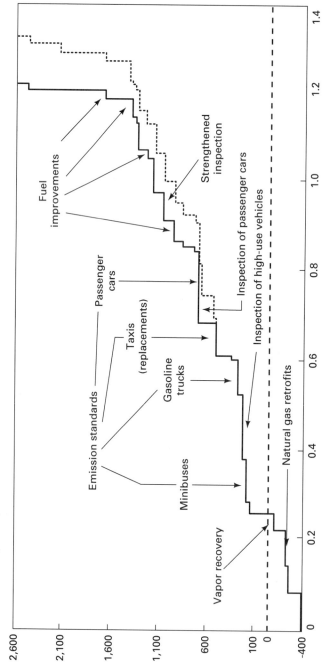

Incremental cost of reducing emissions
(thousands of dollars per ton)

Reduction in toxicity-weighted emissions
(millions of tons)

- - - - Incremental cost with tax

——— Incremental cost without tax

Source: From *World Development Report 1992* by The World Bank. Copyright ® 1992 by The International Bank for Reconstruction and Development/The World Bank. Reprinted by permission of Oxford University Press, Inc.

Mexico City is home to both 20 million people and over half of Mexico's non-oil manufacturing output. Air pollution in the city is among the worst in the world. A 1982 study suggested that simply breathing the air had a health effect comparable to smoking forty cigarettes per day.[29] During the winter of 1991 the pollution problem was at an all-time high: Athletes were warned not to train outside, birds dropped dead out of the trees, and vendors began selling oxygen on the street. The government has begun to take steps to control the problem, including the shutdown of some major private and public-owned industrial facilities, and incentive-based measures such as increased parking fees in the central city.[30]

In a 1991 study, Eskeland constructed a marginal cost of reduction curve for air pollution from motor vehicles in the city, reproduced in Figure 22.4. The curve starts out at the left with measures that actually save money: retrofitting some high-use public vehicles to natural gas and recovering refueling vapors. However, the options for further improvement—first emission standards, then strengthened inspection, and then improvements in fuel—become increasingly costly. Eskeland estimates that using these command-and-control measures alone, pollution could be reduced by 1.2 million tons per year, at a cost of about $1,800 per ton for the last unit removed.

However, as indicated by the dotted line, if the measures were coupled with a relatively low **gasoline tax** (of around $.05 per liter), the same pollution reduction could be achieved at lower cost. As you can see in the graph, Eskeland estimates marginal savings of around $300 per ton of air pollution for the last ton reduced. The reason: The gas tax would reduce overall driving, and forestall the need for more expensive command-and-control measures to achieve a given reduction in pollution. In fact, the government has since raised gasoline taxes by a substantially higher margin than the study recommended.

However, because a gasoline tax is not a direct emissions tax, it is not fully cost-effective. For example, both dirty and clean cars are taxed at the same rate. The equal marginal cost of reduction principle necessary for cost-effectiveness (chapter 16), is thus not satisfied. As a result, Eskeland (1991) recommends that cleaner cars receive a rebate of some of their gas tax when they are inspected, thus encouraging their purchase. In another move toward cost-effectiveness, the Mexican government has required taxi drivers to buy new, cleaner vehicles every three years. This measure generates a large environmental bang for the buck because taxis are driven ten times as far per year as are private cars.

The government has also pursued one symbolic but highly cost-ineffective regulatory policy: the Day Without a Car program. Under this program, travel by car, depending on the license plate number, is banned on a specified workday. This brief description provides a good opportunity to present a

---

[29]The study was done by the U.S. Embassy and is cited in Lepkowski (1987).
[30]"Smog City," and "Pay to Breathe," *The Economist,* May 18, 1991, and February 16, 1991.

PUZZLE

Will the Day Without a Car program necessarily cause families to reduce overall driving?

SOLUTION

By now, you have probably figured out that the answer to these puzzles always seems to be no. First, car travel is unlikely to fall by one fifth, because people will simply drive more on other days of the week to accomplish their shopping and recreational tasks. This substitution effect will cause the overall decline in driving to be small. Moreover, some families, for whom compliance with the regulation is very costly, will likely buy a second car. Access to a second vehicle would actually *increase* driving for such a family.[31] Of course, the program may yield other benefits, in particular, raising public awareness.

This section has argued that for reasons of enforceability and ease of administration, poor countries will most often rely on command-and-control regulatory methods, combined with indirect pollution taxes. Often, the two measures can complement one another. In addition, careful analysis will often reveal fairly simple ways to increase the cost-effectiveness of both indirect pollution taxes and command-and-control regulatory systems. Examples from Mexico City include gas tax rebates for clean cars at inspection time, and tight regulation of highly polluting sources like taxi cabs.

22.5 Sustainable Technology: Development and Transfer

In addition to regulation, promoting the adoption of more sustainable technology is the other proactive tool that poor countries governments have to improve environmental quality. Chapters 18 through 20 provide a general discussion of **clean technology.** There we defined a clean technology as one capable of delivering comparable services at comparable long-run private costs to existing technology, *and* doing so in an environmentally superior fashion. In poor countries, we need to tack on an additional condition. In the interests of controlling population growth by reducing poverty, technologies that the government promotes should also (1) increase employment and/or (2) improve the economic position of the poor, especially women. So-called **sustainable technologies** are clean technologies that also help reduce poverty.[32]

This section addresses three questions about promoting sustainable technology. First, how can sustainable technologies be identified? Second, how are they developed? Third, what steps can be taken to promote their diffusion?

---

[31]Eskeland (1991) makes these points.

[32]Sustainable technologies differ from appropriate or intermediate technologies in that they need not be small-scale or locally produced. Sustainable technologies can *include* traditional, intermediate, conventional, or emerging technologies, or any blend.

Technologies can be judged sustainable only after field testing and may only be sustainable under certain conditions. For example, Ton and Jong (1991) take a detailed look at the introduction of irrigation pumps and a new type of rice into a drought-stricken region of northern Mali. The new technology increased yields dramatically *and* increased employment. Overall food security thus rose. The increased yields also made it possible for the communities to afford the imported capital necessary for production, at least in principle. (Outside support from the United Nations had not yet been withdrawn.) However, the greater centralization of production fostered by the pumps concentrated economic power in the hands of males of a wealthier ethnic group, thus increasing both gender and income inequality.

Is this technology sustainable? At this point it is hard to tell. Over time, one would need to answer the following two questions. First, in the absence of outside aid, can the villagers afford to operate and maintain their more capital-intensive production method? In other words, is the technology really profitable and thus self-sustaining? Second, do the income and food security benefits of higher yields outweigh the increase in inequality? In other words, are women and the ethnic minority group on balance better off after the introduction of the new technology? If the answer to both of these questions is yes, then we would judge the technology sustainable.

Bhalla and James (1991) report that three very modern technologies—photovoltaic electricity (discussed in chapter 20), electronic load controllers for small-scale hydropower, and laser-guided leveling of irrigated fields—have proven to be clean technologies when applied under the right circumstances in poor countries. That is, they are both cost-effective and clear environmental winners. (Level fields conserve irrigation water.) In addition, photovoltaics and load controllers appear to have had no direct negative impact on employment, thus qualifying as sustainable technologies. Laser-guided leveling on the other hand reduces the number of workers needed in the irrigation process. However, *if* the water freed up from improved irrigation is used to grow more crops, overall employment will expand.

This example reflects a more general point: Calculating the overall employment impact of a new technology is a difficult, though not impossible, task. Even if a technology leads to direct job loss, the increased efficiency *may* free up resources that can be invested elsewhere in the poor country economy, creating more jobs.[33] Nevertheless, *assuming* this kind of effect is not good policy. Governments should stay away from promoting cost-effective technologies that substantially reduce employment.

Sustainable technologies need not be sophisticated. Examples include erosion control methods such as building rock or clay dikes or planting trees, and efficient cooking stoves, which reduce charcoal use by several hundred percent. These technologies can dramatically improve environmental quality while boosting the material well-being of people in poor countries.[34] The short-term cost-effectiveness of these technologies is essential. Poor people cannot afford to adopt new techniques unless their advantages are clear-cut and substantial.

[33]Moreover, there are indirect effects on employment as well. For example, a shift to photovoltaics might reduce the number of workers not only in the coal-powered electricity industry but also in upstream production in firms that manufacture power plants or in coal mines. Similarly, it would boost employment in the semiconductor industry. Economists use a technique called input-output analysis to examine the direct and indirect employment effects of new technologies. See advanced topic chapter T3, and chapter 9.

[34]Wardman and Salas (1991) and Tibesar and White (1990).

How are sustainable technologies developed? In chapter 21, it was stressed that rich countries must bear much of the cost of research and development of technically sophisticated clean technologies—photovoltaic cells being a good example. However, external aid is often needed to establish and promote simple sustainable technologies as well. A **nongovernmental organization (NGO)** called Plan International financed a project in the African country of Burkina Faso, which serves as a good example. The NGO found that reintroducing traditional erosion control techniques, using mostly locally crafted implements, boosted yields of peanuts and grains by over 100% over the period 1985 to 1987. After this period, outside agronomical assistance was gradually withdrawn, and the project became self-sustaining. The Burkina Faso government, while supportive of the project, simply had no money to invest in it.[35]

While potentially beneficial technologies will often have to be developed with assistance from the rich countries, the actual users of the technology must be closely involved in the design process. This is true first because poor country residents, particularly farmers, often have the greatest knowledge of potential solutions to a given problem. Second, if the technologies do not suit the needs of the users, they will never be adopted, no matter how "sustainable" they are in theory.

Poor country governments, sometimes in combination with international development agencies and NGOs, can employ a wide range of tools to promote sustainable technologies, ranging from design standards for technology, to technical assistance programs, to consumer and producer subsidies, to research and development grants. The advantages and disadvantages of these options, summarized in Table 22.1, were discussed in detail in chapter 16 and will not be further reviewed here.

While government efforts to promote technologies are important, the private sector and **multinational corporations** in particular will typically play the dominant role in diffusing new techniques of production and consumption. Sometimes these technologies are sustainable, sometimes not. One beneficial influence of direct foreign

TABLE 22.1 Policies for Sustainable Technology

Policy	*Small-scale Sustainable Technologies*
Design Standards	Energy and Water Efficiency
Technical Assistance	Waste Reduction in Manufacturing, Alternative and Agroforestry, Passive Solar, Wind Power, Energy and Water Efficiency
Small Grants/Loans/Tax Credits	Energy and Water Efficiency, Active Solar, Passive Solar, Agriculture and Agroforestry, Wind Power, Energy and Water Efficiency
Policy	*Large-scale Sustainable Technologies*
R&D	Agriculture and Agroforestry
Infrastructure Investment	Mass transit, Agriculture and Agroforestry, Active Solar, Wind Power, Telecommunications

---

[35]Wardman and Salas (1991). Yield increases were measured vis à vis the surrounding countryside. Yields were also improved by importing a superior variety of sorghum. In addition, the project included agroforestry and husbandry components.

investment by multinational corporations in manufacturing is that they may bring with them cleaner production technologies. For example, Wheeler and Martin (1993) found that multinational investment has promoted the diffusion of relatively clean technology in the paper and pulp industries.

On average, multinationals, with higher profits, higher visibility, and easier access to technology, probably have somewhat better environmental and safety records than do domestic firms in poor countries. Nevertheless, and not surprisingly, multinational operations in the developing world are generally much dirtier and dangerous than are their similar facilities in rich countries.[36]

The most well-known example of this so-called double standard was illustrated in the wake of a 1984 chemical explosion in Bhopal, India, at a plant owned by a subsidiary of Union Carbide. More than 2,000 people were killed and up to 200,000 injured, many severely, by a toxic gas cloud. While the Bhopal plant was technologically similar to a sister plant in West Virginia, safety systems in Bhopal were very poorly maintained.[37] In another particularly egregious example of a corporate double standard, the drug company Ciba-Geigy subjected six Egyptian boys to a pesticide spray to test exposure levels.[38]

Multinationals do not automatically transfer clean technology. In a study of pesticide use in Mexico, Goodman (1987) argues that multinationals *could* help solve the problem by promoting safer techniques developed in the United States, *and* that such efforts are in the long-run interests of such firms if they seek to avoid expensive regulation in Mexico. However, the companies do not see it his way. Instead, multinational pesticide firms to date have preferred a low profile and have done little to modernize Mexican pesticide practices.

Multinationals have also promoted highly unsustainable technologies in poor countries. For many years, for example, Nestlé Corporation heavily advertised bottle feeding of babies in poor countries, as a "modern" alternative to breast-feeding. This was a disastrous and often deadly practice for poor infants, whose families are without access to clean water or funds to purchase adequate amounts of formula. Nestlé reduced its aggressive advertising only after a prolonged boycott effort by consumers in rich countries.[39]

More generally, manufacturing and agricultural production methods imported from rich countries by multinationals tend to be fairly capital-intensive. A chemical plant in Mexico is very much like a chemical plant in Ohio. If taxes on these firms are low and/or their profits are not reinvested locally, the use of this capital-intensive technology may lead to little net increase in employment or reduction in poverty, while at the same time aggravating environmental problems.

How can poor countries nudge the technologies introduced by the private sector in the direction of sustainability? First, improved environmental regulation and enforcement would help insure that technology choices are "clean" relative to current practice. In addition, shareholders and consumers in rich countries can exert pressure on multinationals to adopt more sustainable policies and technologies.

[36]These points are developed respectively by Pearson (1987) and Castleman (1987).
[37]Lepkowski (1987).
[38]"How a Drug Company Deals With Disputes Over Its Medicines," *Wall Street Journal,* June 1, 1984.
[39]"Nestlé: Battling the Boycotts," *New York Times,* July 28, 1991.

Regulating technologies for their employment impact on sustainability, however, is quite difficult. (Again, imperfect information rears its ugly head.) As a result, widespread command-and-control regulation of the actual production techniques employed by multinational or domestic firms in order to boost employment is likely to be ineffective and may even be counterproductive. For example, Bhopal's chemical plant did not have a computerized safety monitor standard in developed countries, in part because Indian law required firms to choose labor-intensive over capital-intensive production techniques where possible.[40] Poor countries should instead focus on extracting reasonable tax, technology licensing, or reinvestment concessions from multinational firms, to promote sustainable development efforts elsewhere in the economy.

This section has defined a sustainable technology as a clean technology, which also helps reduce poverty. The rapid diffusion of such technologies in poor countries is crucial if they hope to outrun a neomalthusian cycle in which increased poverty leads to high rates of population growth, generating more poverty, and so on. Such technologies must also alleviate poverty in a clean way, because environmental degradation in many poor countries is already quite severe. With global population doubling in the next fifty years, dramatically exacerbating environmental decline, poor countries must "leapfrog" the path of dirty development followed by their rich neighbors. Sustainable technology may deliver the means to do so.

However, developing, identifying, and diffusing sustainable technologies are expensive tasks, which will not be accomplished without a major and ongoing commitment of resources from rich countries. At the same time, the recipient countries must be a full partner in the process. On my desk I have a beautiful picture of a modern windmill on a hilltop in eastern Zimbabwe, built there by a Danish aid group to electrify a remote village. Unfortunately, the windmill had been inoperative for over a year when I took the picture in 1982. The village was unable to raise the money to buy spare parts, which had to be imported from Denmark. The lesson: A successful sustainable technology depends much more on the social needs, capabilities, and organizations of the people it is intended to serve than it does on the provision of hardware.

22.6 Resource Conservation and Debt Relief

Several times over the last few chapters I have remarked that it has proved difficult for poor countries to successfully conserve natural resources—forests, wetlands, range lands, and fisheries—by simply setting aside reserves and parks. Problems are faced both in establishing such protected areas and in managing the regions once they have been created.

Over the last few years, we have seen fierce battles in the United States over wilderness set-asides to protect the habitat of the spotted owl in the Pacific Northwest, to reduce logging in the Tongass National Forest in Alaska, and to prohibit oil development in the Arctic National Wildlife Refuge. Similar **development-environment strug-**

---

[40]And, in part, because it was more expensive. See Lepkowski (1987). Stewart (1990) provides a somewhat more favorable interpretation of the overall Indian experience in technology regulation.

gles are played out in poor countries, but the stakes there are more dramatic. Both desperately poor people and wealthy development companies desire access to the resource, and together they can form a potent anticonservation political force.

Even when a protected area has been established, the government faces the often overwhelming **enforcement** task of preventing game poaching, illegal logging, and the invasion of landless farmers. Thus, there has been an increasing recognition among environmentalists that protecting natural resources in poor countries requires directly addressing the economic needs of the poor people who depend on, and threaten, those resources. This section will explore two related policy options for strengthening the link between resource protection and economic opportunity—sustained yield resource development and debt-for-nature swaps.

Sustained yield resource development means using available renewable natural capital in an ecologically sustainable way. Under a sustained yield rule, harvests cannot exceed the regenerative capacity of the land or fishery (see Chapter 7). To illustrate this concept, let us consider the economics of deforestation in the Amazon rainforest in Brazil.

As illustrated in Figure 22.5, three primary forms of activity exist in the Amazon, which sometimes follow in sequence. First, the jungle is clear-cut, by either logging companies, small farmers, or commercial ranchers. The latter two groups tend to simply burn the fallen timber. Small farmers, sometimes following roads built by loggers, grow crops for a few years. However, these early migrants often move on, either abandoning their land or selling out to cattle farmers. This technology is known as shifting cultivation or slash-and-burn agriculture.

FIGURE 22.5 The Deforestation Process

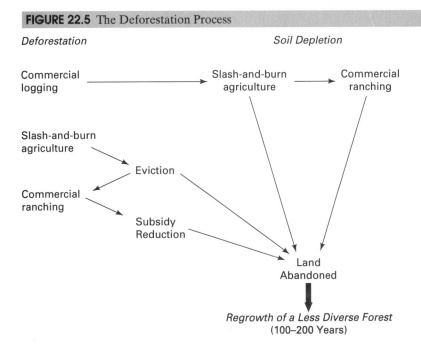

There is ongoing debate as to the motivation for land abandonment by both small farmers and cattle ranchers: Some argue that the poor-quality tropical soils make rain-forest farming unsustainable; others maintain that poor and politically powerless pioneers are unable to hold on to the property that they farm as a second wave of wealthier migrants move in. Finally, reductions in subsidies have led to some abandonment by ranchers.[41]

When populations and farm plots are small, slash-and-burn agriculture can generate a sustained yield, since the jungle is given time to recover. However, as population pressure has increased, and ranchers have moved in to follow the farmers, the system has in some cases become ecologically untenable.

How could sustained yield resource development proceed in the Amazon? As we will see, the rain forest *does* have substantial economic value that might be exploited in an ecologically sustainable fashion. Doing so will require applying a successful mix of the policies described above: eliminating unsustainable subsidies, clarifying property rights, and promoting sustainable technologies via measures like technical assistance programs, infrastructure development, and subsidized credit programs. The problem is compounded, however, by the fact that much of the benefit of sustained yield development accrues to people outside of the rain forest, particularly to those in rich countries. Getting us to pay "our share" for the public good of rain-forest protection becomes an added policy challenge.

What sustained yield values does the rain forest hold? First, experience has shown that there are profitable, **sustained yield farming and ranching methods** suitable for tropical forest soils, which do not require shifting cultivation.[42] Governments can encourage farmers to adopt these sustainable technologies both by promoting them directly through technical assistance programs and targeted credit subsidies, and by eliminating subsidies for unsustainable practices. Deforestation will be slowed if farmers and ranchers can eliminate their voracious need for more and more land and become more prosperous (leading to smaller families).

More generally, the *standing* forest is increasingly viewed as a resource with substantial economic value. From a commercial perspective, Pearce and Myers (1990) reports that the **harvesting of wild products,** such as meat and fish, and primates (for medical research), could generate an annual income of $200 per hectare, more than is earned either by one-time clear-cutting or by unsustainable cattle ranching.[43] Developing this potential would require both nurturing a marketing and transportation infrastructure, and clarifying property rights within the rain forest. Some kind of communal or private ownership would be necessary to avoid the overharvesting of profitable wild resources such as nuts, meat, or vegetable oils on commonly held property.

The rain forest holds two other important commercial products: **medicine** and a **gene pool for agriculture.** Tropical forest species form the basis for pharmaceutical products whose annual sales were valued at $12 billion in the early 1980s.[44] The forest

---

[41]See Schneider (1993) and Carriere (1991).

[42]Barrow and Roth (1990).

[43]Pearce (1990) reports that commercial logging returns about $150/hectare, while Browder (1988) finds ranching income to average $112.50/hectare.

[44]Pearce and Myers (1990) citing Norman Myers (1984), *The Primary Source: Tropical Forests and Our Future* (New York: Norton).

undoubtedly contains many more valuable species, thousands of which may be lost each year. However, the medical value of the rain forest lies not only in its biodiversity; the native Amazon people also have a medical knowledge base that is also being threatened by deforestation. Finally, the huge gene pool represented by the forest is economically important for breeding disease-resistant and high-yield agricultural crops.

In addition to these commercial benefits, the forest yields a variety of utilitarian environmental services. One of these is as a **carbon sink;** a substantial portion of the world's carbon dioxide is tied up in the rain-forest biomass. When the forests are burned, the CO_2 is released into the atmosphere, contributing to global warming. In addition, the rain forest serves as a **rainfall regulator,** by recycling much of its own moisture. As deforestation proceeds, the Amazon basin may well likely dry out, affecting rainfall patterns throughout Brazil.

Finally, many people have expressed considerable moral interest in protecting the rain forest, its natural species, and its human cultures. From an economic point of view, this concern represents an **existence value** for the rain forest. (see Chapter 8). Especially in rich countries, people have expressed a willingness to pay for rain forest preservation independent of the material economic services that the tropical forest might provide.

The benefits from medical, agricultural, environmental, and existence value services provided by the rain forest accrue primarily to those living outside of the Amazon, and indeed, Brazil. Thus rain-forest protection is a classic **public good,** as described in chapter 3. Many of us have been solicited by environmental groups to contribute money to efforts to "save the rain forest." While each of us has a material stake in such a project, we also have an incentive to **free ride** on the efforts of others to provide the public good. As a result, economic theory predicts that rain-forest protection groups will raise less than the amount of money we as a society are really willing to pay for such efforts.

This in turn means that private-sector efforts to promote sustained yield development in the Amazon will be inefficiently low, on a simple benefit-cost basis. Traditionally, economists have argued that government needs to step in and use its power to tax in order to provide an efficient quantity of public goods—whether a national park, clean air, or national defense. In an international context, this implies that in order to protect the narrow economic interests of their citizens, rich country governments will have to raise aid money for rain-forest protection. Of course, such aid might also be justified on the grounds of economic sustainability and fairness to future generations.

In summary, in poor and densely populated countries, the only feasible way to conserve natural resources is often to link conservation with enhanced economic opportunity. Governments can do this by using the variety of tools discussed in this chapter. Around the world, dozens of such efforts have been launched in recent years, including a successful effort to both cultivate tourism and reduce its environmental impact in the Nepalese Himalayas, and a less successful attempt to protect the wintering grounds of the monarch butterfly in Mexico.[45] However, such efforts are currently

---

[45]Brandon and Wells (1992).

underfunded. Because rich countries are often major beneficiaries of resource preservation, an efficient level of conservation will only be achieved if a mechanism is established by which rich country residents pay for the benefits they receive.

One example of such an approach lies in debt relief. As was discussed in chapter 21, during the 1970s and early 1980s, the developing countries accumulated a huge quantity of debt, owed to private banks in rich countries. Merely paying the interest on this debt remains a tremendous burden on poor countries today. For example, we saw that Cost Rica pays out about 10% of its export earning each year in debt service. The debt burden poses a major obstacle to sustainable development, since it reduces investment in the created capital which poor countries desperately need.

One way to relieve the debt burden and simultaneously invest in resource conservation is through a **debt-for-nature swap.** Under a debt-for-nature swap, a rich country group (government, nongovernmental organization, or bank) will pay off a portion of the loan, typically at a deep discount. Banks are willing to sell this debt at a paper loss, since they suspect they will not be repaid in full anyway. In exchange, poor country governments must agree to invest a certain amount of money into a resource conservation program at home. These programs tend to focus on beefing up enforcement and supporting sustained yield resource development at existing preserves. The actual ownership of the natural resource does not change hands.[46]

The developing country benefits in several ways. First, the debt is reduced.[47] Second, it can undertake needed conservation measures at home. Finally, the conservation program can be financed using local money, not scarce foreign currency (dollars, yen, or deutschemark). It is thus "cheaper" from the poor country's perspective. Figure 22.6 provides the details of a 1992 swap between the Brazilian government and the U.S.-based NGO, the Nature Conservancy.

Debt-for-nature swaps are one way in which residents of rich countries can express their demand for resource preservation in poor countries. However, their use has been fairly limited. Consummated deals through 1992 had reduced total debt in the Third World by around $400 million, well under one percent of total Third World debt of $1.3 trillion. About one quarter of these swaps have been financed by private parties, primarily conservation NGOs. The rest of the efforts have been paid for by rich country governments, mostly the United States.[48]

The limited use of the option reflects in part resistance on the part of poor country governments, who are concerned that environmentalists from rich countries will "lock up" their resource base. Probably more significant is the fact that NGOs in rich countries have been able to raise only limited funds for such purposes. Due to the free-rider problem, discussed above, such an outcome is predicted for private groups who seek to provide public goods. At the same time, government efforts have been limited for lack of political support.

---

[46]Deacon and Murphy (1992).

[47]Sachs (1990) and Bulow and Rogoff (1990) both point out that the actual debt burden may not fall by the full value of the swap. Since the swap strengthens the position of the creditor nation (and suggests the likelihood of further swaps), the value of the debt on secondary markets may rise. Issuing bonds to pay for the swaps in local currency is also inflationary.

[48]Deacon and Murphy (1992).

(1) The Nature Conservancy buys $2.2 million in Brazilian debt owed to a private bank. The banks agrees to a price of $850,000 for the debt, $.38 to the dollar.

(2) The Nature Conservancy donates the debt to FUNATURA, a Brazilian conservation NGO. FUNUTURA, in turn, uses it to buy $2.2 million in long-term Brazilian government bonds, paying 6 percent interest, or $132,000 per year.

(3) These funds accrue to a partnership between the Nature Conservancy, FUNUTARA, and IBAMA (the Brazilian EPA). Their goal is to manage the Grande Serpao Veredas National Park, in the interior highland of the country. Endangered mammals who have taken refuge in the park include the jaguar, the pampas deer, the manned wolf, the giant anteater, and the harpie eagle.

(4) The management strategy includes purchasing "buffer zone" lands around the park, hiring park rangers, and promoting sustained yield resource development. Early priorities include such basic measures as the purchase of a motor boat and a four-wheel drive vehicle, and the construction of a park headquarters.

FIGURE 22.6 A Debt-for-Nature Swap in Brazil

Source: Fundaçao Pró-Natureza and The Nature Conservancy (1991), *Grande Sertao Veredas National Park Debt Conversion Proposal*, Revised Draft Washington, DC: Nature Conservancy.

Bigman (1990) recommends a major expansion of the debt-for-nature concept, in which debtor nations would pay most of their debt in local currency into an international environment fund. This fund would finance sustainable development and family planning measures. Under his scheme, rich country governments would compensate banks for unpaid debt at 50% of its current market value, through a tax on gasoline.[49] If debt-for-nature schemes are in fact effective in conserving resources in poor countries, and the record is too recent to fully judge, a significant expansion could well be justified on benefit-cost grounds.

22.7 Trade and the Environment

The issue of trade and the environment made U.S. headlines during the debate over the **North American Free Trade Agreement (NAFTA).** NAFTA, a 1993 agreement between Canada, Mexico, and the United States, is designed to reduce tariff and subsidy trade barriers and eliminate restrictions on foreign investment and capital mobility. Passage of NAFTA in the United States was hotly contested, in part because of fears it would exacerbate environmental decline in all three countries.

There are essentially three environmental arguments against freer trade and one environmental argument in favor. The argument for the free trade act is that, by stimulating investment and economic growth in Mexico, poverty will be reduced.[50] As we learned in chapter 21, **poverty reduction** in poor countries can have important environmental benefits, as water and air quality improve, pressures on nonrenewable

---

[49]Bulow and Rogoff (1990) present a similar, if less ambitious proposal, to reduce public debt. They also argue that the potential for government relief of private debt makes both banks and poor countries reluctant to settle the matter. Sachs (1990), by contrast, makes the case for relief of both private and public debt, through a negotiated reduction in interest rates.

[50]Grossman and Krueger (1991). For a generally supportive view of the impact of trade on the environment, see Dean (1992) and Bhagwati (1993).

resources decline, more resources are available for investment in health care, education, and family planning, and parents are provided with the option of pursuing a quality rather than a quantity strategy for family size. In the case of NAFTA in particular, Pastor (1992) argues that the agreement process has already strengthened both democratic and environmental political movements within Mexico.

Environmental critics of the treaty have lodged three principal objections.[51] First, they argue that it will not reduce poverty. Free trade will likely force the Mexican government to significantly reduce **subsidies for corn farmers.** Hundreds of thousands of small farmers would then lose their livelihoods, as cheap northern grain entered the market. (Canada and the United States. have built up tremendously productive farm sectors through their own subsidy policies.) Levy and van Wijnbergen (1992) and Robinson et al. (1992) predict job losses of around 700,000 to 800,000 in the corn sector.

Koechlin and Larudee (1992), comparing job loss in the corn sector with job creation in manufacturing, predict a *net increase* in Mexican unemployment of between 120,000 and 1.6 million. While urban dwellers in Mexico would benefit from lower corn prices, they would also suffer from substantially increased migration to the cities and downward pressure on wages. As a result, it is quite possible that they too will be worse off.[52] With greater poverty will come higher birth rates, and more pressure on local resources.

Levy and van Wijnbergen (1992) argue that this problem could be dealt with by increasing public investment in rural roads and irrigation projects for small farmers. By increasing productivity and land values, small farmers would be able to survive with lower corn prices. The authors find that such a program would actually cost less than the current corn subsidy program, which benefits wealthy commercial farmers as well as poor subsistence farmers. However, *if* such a program is not undertaken in conjunction with NAFTA, environmental gains from poverty reduction are unlikely to materialize.

The second charge against the treaty is that Mexico, with its **weak environmental enforcement** apparatus, will face dramatic and escalating pollution problems as a result of increased investment in manufacturing and vegetable production. There is evidence, for example, that pesticide pollution will increase in Mexico (but decrease in Florida) following a trade agreement.[53] This judgment is thus made: Environmental improvements that accompany reductions in poverty will not compensate for the direct increase in pollution. On balance, it is argued, freer trade will lead to *deteriorating* environmental conditions in poor countries.

Again, the response from supporters of trade is: Strengthen enforcement activities; don't restrict trade. NAFTA does contain a "side agreement" on environmental issues, which in principle gives U.S. parties the ability to prod businesses that "persistently" violate Mexican environmental laws to comply. However, the process is so complex and restrictive, it is unlikely to see much use.[54]

---

[51]For an overview of environmental objections to free trade, see Daly (1993).

[52]Levy and Van Wijnbergen (1992: 16); Koechlin and Larudee (1992).

[53]Abler and Pick (1993).

[54]See "Run for the Border," *In These Times,* September 6, 1993; and "Some Questions and Answers on NAFTA," *Wall Street Journal,* November 17, 1993.

The final environmental charge against a free trade agreement is that environmental regulations in rich countries will be weakened as (1) **business mobility increases,** and (2) foreign governments and companies issue **trade-based challenges to environmental laws.** This process is known as a **downward leveling** of regulatory standards. In chapter 9 we learned that differences in the stringency of environmental regulation in fact appear to have little influence on business location decisions. Much more important are wage differences and access to markets. Given this, U.S. lawmakers appear to have little to lose by maintaining strong environmental standards. Indeed, Mexico could begin stringently enforcing its laws without sacrificing investment from the United States.

Unfortunately, it is not always reality but perception that matters in regulatory decisions. Much of the public and many policy makers appear to believe that strong environmental standards discourage investment. Evidence from the few industries where environmental regulation *has* discouraged investment can be used as a stick by industry to weaken standards.

Free trade agreements can also lead to downward leveling since they give foreign governments and corporations the ability to challenge certain regulations as trade barriers. Table 22.2 provides a list of several recent challenges. One of the most widely cited has been a case in which the U.S. government imposed a ban on the import of Latin American tuna. The embargo was enacted because these countries were not using fishing techniques required by U.S. law to reduce the incidental killing of dolphins and other marine animals. Mexico challenged the embargo under the terms of the General Agreement on Tariffs and Trade (GATT). A GATT court ruled in Mexico's favor, arguing that member nations were not allowed to dictate production methods beyond their borders. The United States was forced to rescind the ban or face international trade sanctions.

TABLE 22.2   Trade Challenges to Environmental Regulation

Measure	Trade Agreement	Challenger	Decision
U.S. Ban on Latin American Tuna Imports	GATT	Mexican Govt.	Ban Declared Illegal
Danish Requirement That Drinks Be Sold in Reusable Deposit Containers	Treaty of Rome	U.K. Govt., European Beer Manufacturers	Deposit Requirement Upheld, Reuse Weakened
U.S. Ban on Asbestos	U.S.-Canada FTA	Quebec Govt.	Ban Overturned on Other Grounds; Trade Issue Referred to GATT.
Canadian Requirement that Fish Must be Sampled Prior to Export, to Promote Conservation	U.S.-Canada FTA	—	Requirement Declared Illegal
Canadian Review of Natural Gas Export License	U.S.-Canada FTA	U.S. Energy Companies	Review Dropped
U.S. Standards for Reformulated Gasoline	WTO	Venezuelan Government	Standards Revised

Sources: Based on data from Shrybman (1992); and "U.S. Defeated in Its Appeal of Trade Case," *New York Times,* May 30, 1996, p. D1.

As Table 22.2 illustrates, by prohibiting import and export bans, restrictions, and tariffs, free trade agreements can tie regulators' hands. In effect, environmental decisions made by democratically elected bodies (congresses and parliaments) can be overruled by a very closed international legal process, whose primary treaty charge is to promote free trade for the sake of efficiency gains. Moreover, as we will discuss further in the next chapter, international trade agreements like the GATT, as written, may weaken international environmental agreements such as the one designed to protect the ozone layer. GATT may have to be amended if such environmental treaties are to use trade sanctions as enforcement tools.[55]

This section has provided a look at the debate over the environmental impact of free trade agreements. Clearly, trade can be a vital component of any strategy to promote sustainable development. When trade works to reduce poverty, it provides environmental benefits in the form of greater investment in air and water quality, reduced pressure on the local environment, and lowered population growth rates.

However, the economic growth that accompanies free trade agreements need not reduce poverty. In the Mexican case, the "losers" from NAFTA are likely to be the large class of small corn farmers. As a result, the treaty may well lead to a net increase in Mexican unemployment, more rural to urban migration, and a reduction in urban wages.

More generally, we saw in chapter 21 that trade in natural resource–based industries can foster unsustainable development. This occurs when the *full* resource rent is not reinvested in created capital in the developing country. In a world in which poor country governments are both debt-burdened and have difficulty collecting and productively investing tax revenues from resource-based industries, such an outcome is not unlikely.[56]

Critics have also charged that, in spite of the environmental benefits which accompany growth, the direct increase in pollution will lead to a decline in environmental quality in poor countries. Finally, they charge that environmental regulations in rich countries will be weakened as business mobility increases and legal challenges are lodged by international competitors.

Is free trade good or bad for the environment? Freer trade is generally championed by economists because it tends to increase efficiency, and as we know from chapter 4, more efficient production means a bigger overall economic pie. The environmental challenge is to channel the efficiency gains from trade into investment in a sustainable future. From this perspective, freer trade should be viewed as a means to an end—stabilizing population growth, enhancing food security, transferring sustainable technology, and conserving resources—not as an end in itself. Yet at this point, trade agreements have only just begun to acknowledge environmental and sustainability concerns.[57]

---

[55]French (1993). For an analysis of the potential impact of NAFTA on U.S. standards, see Center for International Environmental Law (1993).

[56]Pezzey (1993) develops a formal model of the impact of trade on sustainability.

[57]French (1993).

22.8 Summary

Environmental policy in poor countries cannot be narrowly viewed as "controlling pollution." The complex and conflicting problems of poverty, population growth, and environmental and resource degradation require a broader focus: promoting sustainable development. This task in turn can be broken down into four subareas: controlling population growth, insuring food security, promoting clean and sustainable technology, and conserving natural resources.

This chapter has considered several general steps that governments can take in these directions. These include reducing environmentally damaging subsidies; working to clarify and enforce communal or private property rights; regulating pollution in as cost-effective a manner as possible; promoting the development and transfer of sustainable technology; conserving natural capital by encouraging sustained yield resource development; and insuring that the gains from trade are funneled into measures promoting sustainable development.

One recurring theme in this chapter has been the question of who will pay for these programs. Until recently, many poor countries have questioned the wisdom of environmental or natural resource protection, reasoning that they could not afford to engage in such measures. There is an increasing recognition, however, that improving environmental quality is often a good economic investment. The financial reality remains unchanged, however. Poor countries still cannot afford to make many of these investments.

As an example, the people of Burkina Faso would benefit greatly if the erosion control measures discussed in Section 22.5 above were widely disseminated, boosting agricultural productivity and incomes, and slowing down population growth rates and rural to urban migration. Yet the country is desperately poor. As a result, such programs are proceeding at a snail's pace, funded through private donations by people in affluent countries.

Ultimately, sustainable development in poor countries is unlikely to occur without a substantial commitment of resources by those of us in rich countries. This commitment can take a variety of forms: research and development in clean and sustainable technologies ranging from solar and wind power to biotechnology to improved refrigerators and stoves; funding of family planning efforts; debt relief in the form of debt-for-nature or debt-for-farmland swaps; international aid for rural development projects; financial and technical assistance in the implementation of environmental regulatory programs; the removal of trade barriers to poor country products; and adjustment aid to help poor countries reduce their own environmentally damaging subsidies.

In some instances, this kind of resource commitment is justified on the basis of narrow self-interest. Global pollution problems such as the greenhouse effect and ozone depletion *will not* be adequately addressed without such efforts. Natural resources that we in rich countries value—medical products, agricultural gene pools, wild animal species, wilderness—*will be* rapidly exhausted if we do not pay our share for their protection.

Beyond narrow self-interest, however, resources must be committed by those of us in rich countries if we want to insure a high quality of life for our children and grandchildren. Environmental quality is already perceived to be severely threatened.

In the absence of a massive effort to promote sustainable development on a global basis, it appears likely that population growth rates will not soon stabilize, and clean technologies will develop and diffuse only slowly. In that case, my granddaughter and yours may well inhabit a world with 20 billion people, where population pressures and pollution levels are on average at least four times as intense as we experience today.

The environmental impact of continuing population and consumption growth may be simply to intensify the problems of local air and water pollution, disposal of solid and hazardous waste, exposure to toxic chemicals, and the disappearance of green spaces and wild creatures. On the other hand, such trends may lead to new and unimagined changes in the global environment. Within the last decade, two such threats have emerged: global warming and ozone depletion. The final chapter of the book turns to the increasingly critical issue of global environmental regulation.

APPLICATION 22.0

Subsidy Removal: Environmental and Social Impact[58]

Some have argued that removing government controls that keep food prices down is a necessary step to insure food security. In addition, some maintain, the subsequent increase in price will also reduce soil erosion by giving farmers stronger incentives (and access to capital) to invest in long-term erosion control measures.

1. It seems counterintuitive to argue that increasing the price that consumers face for food will, in many cases, actually improve access to food. How can you explain this line of reasoning?
2. In the short run, who would suffer most from lifting price controls on food? How can this problem be addressed?
3. Can you think of a reason why rising food prices might actually increase soil erosion?

APPLICATION 22.1

Environmental Regulation and Nontariff Barriers

In 1989, the United States imposed a ban on the export of unprocessed logs from public lands in the Pacific Northwest, with the purported intent of slowing down deforestation of the spotted owl ecosystem. Japan has objected to the ban, arguing that it is a "thinly disguised nontariff barrier" to trade. "The ban does not meet the environmental objective, since it does not apply to processed wood products. [Rather] it will raise the price of unprocessed wood to Japan (the U.S. is the largest timber supplier to Japan) and encourage ailing U.S. wood processing industries."[59]

From the U.S. perspective, of course, aiding our wood-processing industries might seem like a good idea, particularly if the burden of higher prices is borne by a princi-

---

[58]This problem draws in part on an unpublished paper by S. Barret (1990) called "Macroeconomic Policy Reforms and the Third World Soil Conservation," summarized in Dean (1992).

[59]This summary of the Japanese objection is found in Dean (1992).

pal competitor. The danger, of course, is that this kind of action might prompt retaliation by the Japanese in the form of trade restrictions on U.S. products.

To sort out whether environmentally motivated regulations or product standards are genuine, or are instead thinly disguised trade barriers, Dean (1990: 16) makes the following suggestion: Standards or regulations must not only meet the environmental objective but also do so in a least-cost way.

1. Do you think the Japanese objection, as stated, is correct?
2. Do you think the ban is an environmental measure or a trade barrier?
3. Dean argues that if a regulation or product standard does not meet the environmental objective in a least-cost way, then we may be justified in assuming it to be a trade barrier. Do you agree?

Key Ideas in Each Section

22.0 This chapter considers sustainability policy in poor countries. The basic message is that none of these policies is cheap; in many cases, success will require investment aid from wealthy countries.

22.1 We begin with a brief consideration of the possibility of government failure due to imperfect information and political influence, both compounded by a lack of resources and small **political-economic elites.** Both **multinational** and **domestic business** can have substantial political influence in poor countries.

22.2 Removing **environmentally damaging subsidies** in industries such as timber, energy, and agriculture is the first policy considered. For example, tropical deforestation is promoted by (1) **failure to capture resource rents** ("low" timber prices); (2) **infrastructure development;** (3) **subsidized "downstream" industries;** (4) **colonization projects;** and (5) **subsidized cattle ranching.** When subsidies are removed, **compensation** is often required both on political and **fairness** grounds.

22.3 Reducing **open access to common property** is a second policy. This can be achieved by strengthening **property rights,** whether **communal, state,** or **private.** When ownership rights are strengthened, owners are more likely to engage in **profit-based conservation.** Private and communal owners in poor countries often have greater incentives, and more resources, than do state managers for good management. Yet privatization can penalize the poor and is itself a difficult task for poor country governments to manage well.

22.4 The general points made in chapters 16 and 17 about **incentive-based** versus **command-and-control** regulation hold true in poor countries. However, special attention must be paid to **enforceability** and **administrative simplicity. Indirect pollution taxes,** such as **timber royalties** or **gasoline taxes,** are thus appealing, but because they don't tax pollution directly, their environmental effect must be carefully considered. Flexible or targeted CAC measures are also good regulatory strategies.

22.5 A **sustainable technology** is a **clean technology** that also improves the economic position of the poor majority. Government can promote the development and diffusion of sustainable technology using tools such as **subsidies** and **infrastructure investment.** Major sources of technology transfer are **nongovernmental organizations** (NGOs) and **multinational corporations.** Poor countries can encourage the transfer of clean technology by instituting environmental regulation and by obtaining adequate tax concessions from multinationals for reinvestment elsewhere in the economy.

22.6 Two obstacles to resource conservation in poor countries are the intensity of the **development-environment conflict** and the difficulty of **enforcement.** One way to address these problems is through **sustained yield resource development.** Examples from the rain forest include s**ustained yield farming and ranching; harvesting of wild products;** prospecting for **pharmaceuticals** and **agricultural genes;** and tourism. However, the forest also delivers nonmarketable (**public**) goods, such as a **carbon sink, rainfall regulator,** and **existence value.** The **free-rider problem** means that, without some collective mechanism for rich countries to pay for preservation, inefficiently low levels of preservation will occur. One such mechanism is a **debt-for-nature swap.**

22.7 If the **North American Free Trade Agreement** (**NAFTA**) in fact leads to **poverty reduction** in Mexico as its supporters maintain, it may improve environmental quality. However, if **corn subsidies are** eliminated as a result of the treaty, poverty may in fact deepen. In addition, through **weak environmental enforcement** and a **downward leveling** of regulatory standards (in turn arising from **increased business mobility** and **trade-based regulatory challenges**), NAFTA may undermine environmental quality in all three countries.

References

Abler, David G. and Daniel Pick (1993). "NAFTA, Agriculture and the Environment in Mexico." *American Journal of Agricultural Economics,* vol. 75.

Barrows, Richard and Michael Roth (1990). "Land Tenure and Investment in African Agriculture: Theory and Evidence." *The Journal of Modern African Studies,* 28, no. 2, 265–298.

Bhagwati, Jagdish (1993.) "The Case for Free Trade." *Scientific American,* November, 41–49.

Bhalla, Ajit S. and Dilmus D. James (1991). "Integrating New Technologies with Traditional Economic Activities in Developing Countries: An Evaluative Look at 'Technology Blending.'" *The Journal of Developing Areas,* vol. 25, 477–496.

Bigman, David (1990). "A Plan to End LDC Debt and Save the Environment Too." *Challenge,* 33, no. 4, 33–37.

Brandon, Katrina Eadie and Michael Wells (1992). "Planning for People and Parks: Design Dilemmas." *World Development,* 20, no. 4, 557–570.

Browder, John O. (1988). "Public Policy and Deforestation in the Brazilian Amazon." In *Public Policies and the Misuse of Forest Resources,* eds. Robert Repetto and Malcolm Gillis. Cambridge: Cambridge University Press.

Bulow, Jeremy and Kenneth Rogoff (1990). "Cleaning Up Third World Debt Without Getting Taken to the Cleaners." *Journal of Economic Perspectives,* 4, no. 1, 31–42.

Carriere, Jean (1991). "The Crisis in Costa Rica: An Ecological Perspective." In *Environment and Development in Latin America,* eds. David Goodman and Michael Redclift. New York: Manchester University Press.

Castleman, Barry (1987). "Workplace Health

Standards and Multinational Corporations in Developing Countries." In *Multinational Corporations, Environment and the Third World,* ed. Charles S. Pearson. Chapel Hill, NC: Duke University Press.

Center for International Environmental Law (1993). "Integrating Labor and Environmental Concerns into the North American Free Trade Agreement." Washington, DC: CIEL.

Daly, Herman (1993). "The Perils of Free Trade." *Scientific American,* November, 50–57.

Deacon, Robert T. (1992). "Controlling Tropical Deforestation: An Analysis of Alternative Policies." *Working Paper in Economics 4-92.* Santa Barbara: UC, Santa Barbara.

Deacon, Robert T. and Paul Murphy (1992). "The Structure of an Environmental Transaction: The Debt-for-Nature Swap." Paper presented at the American Economic Association Meetings, Anaheim, CA, January 1993.

Dean, Judith (1992). "Trade and the Environment: A Survey of the Literature." *Policy Research Working Paper WPS966.* Washington, DC: World Bank.

Eskeland, Gunnar S. (1991). "Demand Management in Environmental Protection: Fuel Taxes and Air Pollution in Mexico City." Paper presented at the American Economic Association Meetings, January 1992.

French, Hillary (1993). "Reconciling Trade and the Environment." In *State of the World, 1993,* ed. Lester Brown. New York: W. W. Norton.

Fundacao Pro-Natureza and The Nature Conservancy (1991). *Grande Sertao Veredas National Park Debt Conversion Proposal, Revised Draft.* Washington, DC: Nature Conservancy.

Gillis, Malcolm (1988). "Malaysia: Public Polices and the Tropical Forest." In *Public Policies and the Misuse of Forest Resources,* eds. Robert Repetto and Malcolm Gillis. Cambridge: Cambridge University Press.

Goodman, Louis W. (1987). "Foreign Toxins: Multinational Corporations and Pesticides in Mexican Agriculture." In *Multinational*

Corporations, Environment and the Third World, ed. Charles S. Pearson. Chapel Hill, NC: Duke University Press.

Goodstein, Eban (1989). "Land Ownership, Development and Poverty in Southern Appalachia." *The Journal of Developing Areas,* 23, no. 4, 519–534.

Grossman, Gene M. and Alan B. Krueger (1991). "Environmental Impacts of a North American Free Trade Agreement." *Economics Discussion Paper 158.* Princeton, NJ: Woodrow Wilson School.

Harvard Law Review (1990). "Developments—International Environmental Law: Extraterritorial Environmental Regulation." *Harvard Law Review,* 104, no. 7, 1609–1638.

Koechlin, Timothy and Mehrene Larudee (1992). "The High Cost of NAFTA." *Challenge,* 19–26.

Leonard, H. Jeffrey (1987). *Natural Resources and Economic Development in Central America.* Oxford: Transaction Books.

Lepkowski, Wil (1987). "The Disaster at Bhopal—Chemical Safety in the Third World." In *Multinational Corporations, Environment and the Third World,* ed. Charles S. Pearson. Chapel Hill, NC: Duke University Press.

Levy, Santiago and Sweder van Wijnberen (1992). "Transition Problems in Economic Reform: Agriculture in the U.S. Mexico Free-trade Agreement." In *Economy-Wide Modeling of the Economic Implications of a FTA with Mexico and a NAFTA with Canada and Mexico.* Washington, DC: U.S. International Trade Commission.

Musambachime, Mwelma (1990). "The Impact of Rapid Population Growth on Economic Decline: The Case of Zambia." *Review of African Political Economy,* 448, no. 2, 81–91.

Naysnerski, Wendy and Tom Tietenberg (1992). "Private Enforcement of Federal Environmental Law." *Land Economics,* 68, no. 1, 28–48.

Pastor, Robert A. (1992). "NAFTA as the Center of an Integration Process: The Nontrade Issues." In *North American Free Trade: Assessing the Impact,* eds. Nora Lustig, Barry Bosworth and Robert Z. Lawrence. Washington DC: Brookings.

Pearce, David and Norman Myers (1990). "Economic Values and the Environment of Amazonia." In *The Future of Amazonia: Destruction or Sustainable Development?* eds. David Goodman and Anthony Hall. New York: St. Martins Press.

Pearson, Charles S. (1987). "Introduction." In *Multinational Corporations, Environment and the Third World,* ed. Charles S. Pearson. Chapel Hill, NC: Duke University Press.

Pezzey, John (1993). "Sustainability Policies in Models of Trade with Exhaustible Resources."Paper presented at the American Economic Association Meetings, Anaheim, CA.

Repetto, Robert (1988a). "Overview." In *Public Policies and the Misuse of Forest Resources,* eds. Robert Repetto and Malcolm Gillis. Cambridge: Cambridge University Press.

Repetto, Robert (1988b). "Subsidized Timber Sales from National Forest Lands in the United States." In *Public Policies and the Misuse of Forest Resources,* eds. Robert Repetto and Malcolm Gillis. Cambridge: Cambridge University Press.

Robinson, Sherman, Mary E. Burfisher, Raul Hinojosa-Ojeda and Karen E. Thierfelder (1992). "Agricultural Policies and Migration in a U.S.-Mexico Free Trade Area: A Computable General Equilibrium Analysis." In *Economy-Wide Modeling of the Economic Implications of a FTA with Mexico and a NAFTA with Canada and Mexico.* Washington, DC: U.S. International Trade Commission.

Sachs, Jeffrey (1990). "A Strategy for Efficient Debt Reduction." *The Journal of Economic Perspectives,* 4, no. 1, 19–29.

Schneider, Robert (1993). "Land Abandonment, Property Rights, and Agricultural Sustainability in the Amazon." *LATEN Dissemination Note #3.* Washington, DC: World Bank Latin America Technical Department.

Shrybman, Steven (1992). "Trading Away the Environment." *World Policy Journal,* Winter, 93–110.

Southgate, Douglas (1990). "The Causes of Land Degradation Along 'Spontaneously' Expanding Agricultural Frontiers in the Third World." *Land Economics,* 66, no. 1, 93–101.

Stewart, Frances (1990). "Technology Transfer for Development." In *Science and Technology: Lessons for Development Policy,* eds. Robert E. Evanson and Gustav Ranis. Boulder, CO: Westview Press.

Thompson, Herbert (1992). "The Forestry-Timber-Logging Industry in Papua New Guinea." *Capitalism, Nature, Socialism,* 3, no. 3, 49–70.

Tibesar, Arthur and Rodney White (1990). "Pricing Policy and Household Energy Use in Dakar, Senegal." *The Journal of Developing Areas,* 24, no. 1, 33–48.

Ton, Kees and Kees de Jong (1991). "Irrigation Technology and Social Change: An Analysis of Social Variables of Technology." *Journal of Developing Areas,* vol. 25, 197–206.

U.S. General Accounting Office (1992). *U.S. Mexico Trade: Assessment of Mexico's Environmental Controls for New Companies.* Washington, DC: U.S. GAO.

Wardman, Anna and Luci G. Salas (1991). "The Implementation of Anti-Erosion Techniques in the Sahel: A Case Study From Kaya, Burkina Faso." *The Journal of Developing Areas,* 26, no. 1, 65–80.

Weaver, Frederick S., Frank W. Holmquist, and Michael D. Ford (1990). "Third World Politics: Three Textbook Versions." *The Journal of Developing Areas*, 25, no. 1, 107–116.

Wheeler, David and John Martin (1993). "Prices, Policies and the International Diffusion of Clean Technology: The Case of Wood Pulp Production." Paper presented at the American Economic Association Meetings, Anaheim, CA.

World Bank (1992). *World Development Report 1992: Development and the Environment.* New York: Oxford University Press.

World Commission on Environment and Development (1987). *Our Common Future.* New York: Oxford University Press .

CHAPTER 23

The Economics of Global Agreements

23.0 Introduction

This book began with a discussion of a looming environmental problem with worldwide repercussions: global warming. Due to the buildup of carbon dioxide and other industrial gases in the atmosphere, most scientists agree that the planet will grow measurably warmer over the next fifty years. How much warmer remains in question, but the distinct possibility exists that global warming may cause catastrophic changes in rainfall patterns and lead to a significant increase in sea level. If so, it will emerge as the single biggest environmental challenge that humans will face in the twenty-first century.

Since our early introduction to the greenhouse effect, we have explored four difficult, but general, environmental economic questions. The answers to these questions can help us address the global warming problem. First, how much pollution—in this case, global warming—is too much? We considered three broad answers to this normative question: efficiency, safety, and ecological sustainability. Efficiency advocates would have us carefully balance the very real costs of slowing global warming against the obvious benefits. Both safety and ecological proponents find benefit-cost analysis too narrow a basis for choice, and advocate a freeze if not a rollback of carbon dioxide emissions, in spite of the high cost.

The second issue: What are some of the obstacles to effective government action in achieving our goals? Suppose we set a target to stabilize carbon dioxide emissions at 1990 levels. Are we in fact likely to get there? Government policy makers are hampered by imperfect information. In addition, the possibility of political influence over environmental policy emerges when regulators must make discretionary choices. Our twenty-five-year experience with environmental regulation indicates that ambitious pollution reduction goals have proven difficult to achieve. Enforcement in particular has proven a weak link in the regulatory chain.

Our third question was Can we do better? The book suggested two possible answers: (1) smarter regulation and (2) a shift in government focus to the promotion of clean technology. Incentive-based regulation carries the promise of reducing pollution in a more cost-effective and technologically dynamic fashion than the current reliance on command-and-control methods. In the greenhouse case, this means carbon taxes or marketable permit systems can help us achieve our goals at lower cost than mandating particular types of carbon dioxide emission technology.

In addition to better regulation, the government can initiate a proactive policy promoting the rapid development and diffusion of clean technology. To qualify as clean, a technology must be found cost-competitive, either immediately or after only a short period of subsidy. If the government follows this selection rule, the policy of promoting clean technology will also be cost-effective. Clean technologies with substantial power to reduce carbon dioxide emissions include energy efficiency, solar electric, and wind power.

The fourth and final question: Is an effort to combat global warming consistent with the need for sustainable development in poor countries? On the one hand, boosting the incomes of the poor majority of the planet in order to increase food security and ultimately reduce population growth rates will work against this goal in the short term. Yet, the consumption of the poorest half of the planet's inhabitants is not currently the main greenhouse problem. Moreover, reduced population growth is a vital step in any program to control global warming. At the same time, promotion and diffusion of sustainable technology, and greater efforts to conserve forest resources will directly reduce carbon dioxide emissions.

This chapter of the book considers one last and formidable obstacle toward progress on global environmental issues such as slowing the greenhouse effect: the need for coordinated international action. International action, in turn, will result only from *effective* international agreements. Such agreements are, unfortunately, hard to achieve, and once reached, can prove difficult to enforce.

We begin by analyzing the incentives that a nation has first to join an international pollution control agreement, and second to comply with the terms of that agreement once it is signed. We then turn to a discussion of the tools available for enforcing such treaties. The chapter then moves on to analyze two international agreements, on ozone depletion and biodiversity. We end by coming full circle, with a consideration of the prospects for an effective treaty to halt global warming.

23.1 Agreements as Public Goods

Effective international agreements are hard to develop. The basic problem is that agreement on burden-sharing is difficult to achieve. In principle, each country might contribute its **true willingness to pay** for a treaty.[1] This willingness to pay in turn would depend on both the benefits received and the ability to pay, which might vary widely between nations. For example, low-lying Bangladesh and Egypt have a tremendous stake in slowing global warming and preventing a sea-level rise. Yet both countries are poor and would have a difficult time financing strong measures to reduce CO_2 emissions. On the other hand, a landlocked, wealthy country like Switzerland has a high ability to pay but may have fewer immediate interests at stake.

A poor country's willingness to pay to join an agreement will typically be much smaller than a rich country's, simply because it has a much lower national income. Yet poor country participation will often be vital. For example, if China were to industrial-

---

[1]For a further discussion of willingness to pay, see chapter 8.

ize further, using its vast coal reserves, global warming would accelerate considerably. Given China's low willingness to pay for a reduction in global warming (as a result of its low income), a **compensation fund** would have to be established for China to sign a greenhouse treaty. Those with a high willingness to pay (typically rich countries) would have to pay for China to adopt less polluting and expensive energy sources. Otherwise, it would not be in China's interests to sign the treaty.

If each nation did contribute its true willingness to pay, then the agreement process would generate an efficient level of global pollution control. However, a country's underlying willingness to pay for an agreement is not well-defined in the first place and is certainly not transparent to negotiators from other nations. Therefore, each nation's bargainers will have an incentive to *understate* their true interest in a treaty in the hopes that others will shoulder more of the burden. In the extreme, a country might not sign a global warming or other environmental treaty at all *but still benefit* from the efforts of other nations.

This is just another form of the **free-rider problem** we have encountered several times in the book, beginning in chapter 3. From an economic point of view, an international pollution control agreement is a **public good,** which has to be provided voluntarily by the private nations of the world. Reducing global warming is a public good, because there is no way to exclude free riders from enjoying the benefits provided by the treaty.

The public good nature of environmental treaties has two implications. First, treaties will tend to be **too weak** from a benefit-cost point of view, since signatory nations are reluctant to reveal and commit their true willingness to pay in the bargaining process. Second, once signed, nations will have a strong **incentive to cheat** on the agreement. Unilateral cheating is another way to free ride on the pollution control efforts of others. Of course, if everyone cheats, the agreement will collapse.

While the theory of public goods predicts that international environmental treaties will be both weak and susceptible to enforcement problems, agreements nevertheless do get signed and efforts are made to insure compliance. Table 23.1 lists some of the most significant environmental treaties now in effect.[2]

23.2 Monitoring and Enforcement

In chapter 3, we noted two ways to overcome the free rider problem: government provision of the public good and social pressure. Within a single country, government typically supplies the public good of environmental protection, using its ability to tax, fine, and jail to prevent free riding (pollution) by private individuals and corporations. In the United States, for example, environmental laws are passed by Congress, and the regulatory details are then worked out and enforced by the Environmental Protection Agency and the Justice Department.

At the international level, the treaty is the equivalent of an environmental law. However, *no* international government exists that can flesh out the treaties and then coerce nations into undertaking the broadly agreed-upon steps, nor is there likely to be one soon. The United Nations has no authority over its member nations in the environmental arena.[3]

[2]For a good general discussion of these issues, see Sand (1990).
[3]For a further discussion, see French (1992).

TABLE 23.1 Global Environmental Agreements		
Formal Name (Common Name)	*Year Signed*	*Prominent Nonmembers, 1992*
The Antarctic Treaty System	1959	Self-Limited Membership
Nuclear Test Ban Treaty	1963	France, China
The Convention on International Trade in Endangered Species of Wild Flora and Fauna (CITES Treaty)	1973	Burma, Cambodia, Laos, Vietnam
New Management Procedure of International Whaling Commission (Whaling Moratoria)	1974	
Law of the Sea	1982	United States, United Kingdom, West Germany (not currently in force)
Montreal Protocol on Substances that Deplete the Ozone Layer (Montreal Protocol)	1987	
The Base Convention on Transboundary Movement of Hazardous Wastes and Their Disposal (Basel Convention)	1989	African Nations
Rio Convention on Global Warming	1992	
Rio Convention on Biodiversity	1992	United States

Nevertheless, each treaty does set up its own **inter-governmental organization (IGO),** which is charged with overseeing the agreement. Countries seldom agree to give IGOs the authority to actually enforce treaty agreements; this would be giving away to much sovereignty. However, IGOs can be still be given substantive powers. One of these is to set **non-binding standards** that states are "expected" but not required to meet. The second is to **monitor** compliance with agreements.

For example, in a 1991 revision of the Antarctic treaty, an environmental committee has been appointed to which each nation must submit information on its management procedures. Environmental Impact Statements (see Chapter 7) are also now required for new activities, including tourism, sponsored by a member nation. Social pressure can then be brought to bear on states that either fail to achieve the standards or are out of compliance with the broader terms of the treaty. The environmental group Greenpeace has effectively "shamed" countries with particularly poor environmental records on the continent.[4]

Such **social pressure** is the second way in which free riding has traditionally been controlled. However, a well-orchestrated public relations campaign encouraging the United States to join with the "community of nations" was insufficient to get it to sign a biodiversity treaty in 1992 in Rio de Janeiro. Such moral pressures are even less

[4]See "Mining Banned," and "Antarctic: Exploration or Exploitation?" *The New Scientist,* October 12, 1991, and June 22, 1991.

likely to be effective in insuring compliance once treaties have been signed. Nevertheless, bad publicity and community pressure, as in the Antarctic case mentioned above, remain among the important tools of international negotiation.

Given the lack of an international pollution control agency, and the limited effectiveness of social pressure, the burden of enforcement will fall on measures written into the treaty itself. Treaty members must agree in advance on the sanctions to be levied against noncomplying members or nonmembers. In the absence of such sanctions, compliance is liable to be very poor. For example, the CITES treaty regulating trade in endangered species relies primarily on national enforcement efforts. According to the World Wildlife Federation, an environmental group which voluntarily monitors CITES, about one third of the member nations have never filed the required biennial progress report. Most nations who do report have done so in a very tardy manner. The basic problem is a lack of committed resources. Even in a rich country like the United States, a lack of trained customs officials means that up to 60,000 parrots have entered the country illegally in a single year.[5]

There are two basic enforcement tools: restricting access to a compensation fund and imposing trade sanctions. The simplest mechanism is to establish a **compensation fund** to act as a carrot for both joining a treaty and complying with its terms. Such compensation funds, however, can only induce compliance by poor countries.

Trade sanctions are the most powerful tool available. As we shall see below, their mere existence played an important part in the success of the agreement to control depletion of the ozone layer. Sanctions tend to be restricted to goods related to the treaty. This is useful, since it minimizes the possibility that the imposition of sanctions for enforcement purposes will degenerate into a trade war. For example, under the CITES treaty, a ban on trade in wildlife products from Thailand was imposed in 1991 to encourage that country to crack down on illegal exports. At least nineteen international environmental agreements authorize some form of trade sanction.[6]

23.3 The Ozone Layer and Biodiversity

This section will examine two environmental treaties: the 1987 Montreal Protocol to control the depletion of the ozone layer, and the 1992 Rio Earth Summit agreement on biodiversity. We will focus on the factors that promoted agreement and the enforcement mechanisms built in. In the ozone case, we also have a compliance record to examine.

OZONE DEPLETION

The earth's upper atmosphere is surrounded by a thin shield of a naturally occurring chemical known as ozone. Ozone at ground level is better known as smog and is quite harmful. By contrast, the **ozone layer** surrounding the earth serves a beneficial role by screening out the sun's harmful ultraviolet rays. Exposure to ultraviolet rays causes skin cancer and eye disease, reduces the productivity of agriculture, and can kill small terrestrial and marine organisms at the base of the food chain. Over the last twenty

---

[5]Heppes and McFadden (1987).
[6]French (1992).

years, it has become apparent that the ozone layer is threatened by the buildup of human-made chemicals in the upper atmosphere.

These chemicals, known as chlorofluorocarbons (CFCs), were invented in the 1940s.[7] They have since served as aerosol propellants, coolants in refrigerators and air conditioners, foam-blowing agents, and gaseous cleansers for medical and computer equipment. They are also very long-lived, stock pollutants. CFCs released into the atmosphere from discarded refrigerators today will continue to break down the ozone layer for up to a hundred years.

The potential for significant ozone depletion by CFCs was first established in 1974. In spite of the serious health and ecological effects of ozone depletion, uncertainty about the scientific link between depletion and CFCs slowed international regulatory action. Although the United States unilaterally banned CFCs as aerosol propellants in 1977, few other countries followed suit. In 1982, a benefit-cost analysis published in the prestigious *American Economic Review,* while acknowledging substantial uncertainty, argued *against* regulating CFC use on efficiency grounds.[8] This position was also advanced by CFC manufacturers.

Nevertheless international concern over the problem was mounting, fueled by a 1985 British study documenting a huge, seasonal **ozone hole** over Antarctica. Less severe, but measurable depletion was occurring throughout the middle latitudes. In 1987, building on six years of United Nations efforts, twenty-four countries signed the **Montreal Protocol** to Protect Against Atmospheric Ozone Reduction. Just *after* the protocol was signed, a conclusive scientific link between ozone depletion and CFCs was at last established.

The treaty called for a ten-year, 50% reduction in CFC production by each country from a 1986 baseline. The treaty made some concessions to poor countries, who would otherwise be locked into their current levels of low consumption, and who were hardly responsible for the global problem in the first place. Developing countries were given a ten-year grace period before cutbacks would have to be made. In addition, rich countries were urged, but not required, to set up an assistance fund to ease the transition.[9]

These incentives were insufficient to attract India and China, both of whom viewed the benefits of cheap refrigeration from CFCs as too high to forego. As a result, a 1990 revision of the Protocol required rich countries to establish a fund of $260 million to finance the adjustment to CFC replacements in poor countries, with $60 million contributed by the primary CFC producer, the United States. This fund provided a sufficient inducement to join for most of the remaining nonmember countries, including India and China.

As a way to discourage free riding by nonmembers, the treaty mandated trade restrictions on CFCs. Parties to the treaty were required to ban imports and exports of CFCs, many products containing CFC, products produced with CFCs, and technologies for producing CFCs, to nonmember countries. These trade sanctions limited the gains from nonmembership and thus reduced free riding. However, these restrictions

---

[7]Halons, used in fire extinguishers, are also human-made ozone-depleting gases. Much of the discussion below applies to halons as well as CFCs.
[8]Bailey (1982).
[9]Somerset (1989).

could conceivably be challenged under the General Agreement on Tariffs and Trade (GATT) as an obstacle to free trade.[10]

The half-dozen companies that produce the great bulk of CFCs worldwide ultimately supported the 1987 Montreal Protocol, although they viewed the goal of a 50% reduction as greater than necessary. But by 1988, faced with mounting evidence of ozone depletion, the major producer DuPont announced its intentions to phase out CFCs altogether by the year 2000. In 1990, the Protocol nations also revised the treaty to call for a complete ban by the year 2000. In 1992, after a finding that an accelerated phaseout might save an additional million lives through reduced skin cancer, the treaty nations agreed to eliminate CFC production by 1996. The compensation fund was also boosted to $500 million.[11]

Compliance with the early terms of the treaty by the rich countries was quite good; the accelerated phaseout adopted in 1992 was possible because several nations were already ahead of schedule. As discussed in chapter 17, the United States adopted an incentive-based regulatory approach—tradeable permits combined with indirect pollution taxes—to meet its treaty obligations. Because of the ten-year grace period provided to developing countries, it is difficult to evaluate global compliance. We do know that CFC smuggling (in the form of freon) is a growing problem. However, poor countries do not appear to have taken the opportunity to artificially *boost* CFC consumption in order to increase their final allotted quota, as they might have done.[12]

Munasinghe and King (1992) suggest that CFC reduction efforts could be more effective in poor countries if some changes were made to the compensation fund. Currently, it gives no incentive for early cutbacks, nor does it reward countries who cut back in a cost-effective or environmentally sound manner.[13] Thus, the fund might consider favoring investments in CFC recycling over investments in the production of CFC substitutes, some of which are also ozone-depleting, a point discussed further below.

The first two sections of this chapter suggested, on theoretical grounds, that the prospects for obtaining enforceable international agreements on the environment were not good. In many ways, the Montreal Protocol contradicts such a gloomy picture. In spite of scientific uncertainty, initial international agreement was obtained. The threat of trade sanctions helped overcome the free-rider problem. A sufficient compensation fund was eventually established to bring poor countries on board. The pollution control target was dramatically tightened as scientific knowledge advanced, and compliance has been remarkably good.

Several factors help explain the success of the Protocol. The dramatic discovery of the ozone hole over the Antarctic provided an initial boost to the treaty process, as did predictions of a comparable Arctic hole in 1992. Once the agreement had been signed, however, two additional factors worked in its favor. First, because there were only six main corporations involved in the production of CFCs, monitoring the

---

[10]French (1993). A nonsignatory to the Protocol could challenge the Protocol under GATT.

[11]The treaty contains at least one loophole: Production can be continued to service existing equipment and for "essential uses." See "Ozone Protection Treaty Strengthened," *Science News,* December 12, 1992; and "The Resistible Rise of Skin Cancer," *New Scientist,* May 16, 1992.

[12]Munasinghe and King (1992).

[13]Munasinghe and King (1992) argue that early cutbacks are justified on efficiency grounds; that is, the marginal benefits far outweigh the costs.

progress of the CFC phaseout has been relatively easy. Second, clean technological substitutes for CFCs have developed quickly as a result of the imminent ban. Early predictions of prohibitively high compliance costs proved faulty.

What are these substitutes? In 1990, DuPont estimated that by the year 2000, about 29% of the CFC market would be served by conservation and recycling, and 32% by a switch to organic compounds and water (for cleaning and foam blowing). The environmental impact of these techniques is much more benign than the CFCs they replace. The remaining 39% of the market, primarily in refrigeration, would require the development of new synthetic chemicals.[14] The industry has since developed hydrofluorocarbon (HFC) and hydrochlorofluorocarbon (HCFC) substitutes. HFCs are "ozone friendly" but not as efficient a coolant. Unfortunately, HCFCs also deplete the ozone layer, though at a rate well below CFCs. HCFC production was frozen at 1991 levels under the 1992 update of the Montreal Protocol and is slated to be phased out in 2030.[15]

To sum up: The Montreal Protocol has proven to be a stunningly successful environmental treaty. Beginning with initial meetings in 1980, through the 50% cuts agreed to in 1987, and the accelerated phaseout decided on in 1992, it took "only" sixteen years to effectively ban the production of CFCs. The dark side is that this was not fast enough. Because CFCs are so long-lived (and because of HCFCs and other ozone depleters), the ozone problem will get worse before it gets better. Under a year 2000 CFC ban, scientists estimated that the concentration of ozone-depleting chemicals would triple over 1989 levels by the year 2010; the Antarctic ozone hole was continuing to grow as of 1997.[16] Given the dramatic elevation in skin cancers and blindness likely to emerge even given the 1996 phaseout, CFCs have already earned their place in the history books as one of the most destructive pollutants released into the environment. Through their contribution to refrigeration, however, they have also been one of the most beneficial chemicals ever developed.

BIODIVERSITY

Protecting **biodiversity** means protecting endangered species—not only cuddly mammals but also the entire ecosystems in which they live. As we discussed in the last chapter on deforestation, preserving the stock of genetic material found in natural ecosystems is important not only for its **existence value** but also for two utilitarian reasons: **pharmaceuticals and agricultural breeding.** As an example, a strain of Mexican maize, discovered in 1977, had a natural immunity to two serious viral diseases. Hybrid corn seeds based on the genetic material in the maize are now available from U.S.-based seed companies.

The fact that Mexico will receive no compensation for this profitable innovation helps explain why the valuable resource of biodiversity is threatened.[17] Historically, ge-

---

[14]Manzer (1990).

[15]HCFCs deplete the ozone at 2% to 10% the rate of CFCs. This information and the HFC quote are from "Atmosphere of Uncertainty: Businesses Dependent on CFC's Cooperate, Innovate and Wait," *Scientific American,* April 1990. HFCs have also been found to cause benign cancers in rats at very high doses. The EPA has judged them "safe." See "EPA Sees No Problem with CFC Substitutes," *Chemical and Engineering News,* September 28, 1992. On phaseout of HCFCs, see "Ozone Protection Treaty Strengthened," *Science News,* December 12, 1992.

[16]"Substitute CFCs Will Stoke Global Warming," *New Scientist,* May 13, 1989.

[17]Sedjo (1992).

netic material has been viewed as an **open access** common property resource. Seed and drug companies based in rich countries would send prospectors to tropical countries that are host to the vast majority of the world's species. (A single tree in an Amazon rain forest contained forty-three species of ants, more than in the entire British Isles!) They would return with samples to be analyzed for prospective commercial uses. If a plant or animal then generated a profitable return, the country from which it originated would receive no benefit. Host country residents, not being able to realize any of the commercial value of biodiversity, have thus been little interested in conservation.

This situation has begun to change a bit, thanks in large part to improvements in technologies that have made large-scale screening and cataloging of species economically attractive. Costa Rica has recently struck several deals with a U.S.-based drug company, Merck, as well as several U.S. foundations and universities to develop a "forest prospecting industry." The long-run goal is to train a Costa Rican workforce capable of regulating biological prospectors. Costa Rica will then grant access to its forests conditional on receiving a share of profits from any agricultural or pharmaceutical innovations.[18] Building a strong institutional base for this industry is important, so that Costa Rica can prevent illegal prospecting, as well as forestall efforts by corporations to synthesize a new drug based on a botanical finding, and then fail to report it.

Essentially what Costa Rica is doing is shifting a free access common property resource into a state-owned resource, by beefing up its technical **enforcement capabilities.** This in turn greatly strengthens the incentive for profit-based conservation (see chapter 22). Costa Rica is well-placed to do this on its own, because, as we noted in chapter 21, it has a relatively efficient bureaucracy, has a highly literate population, already has an extensive national park network, and has strong links with U.S.-based conservation groups.

Global efforts to protect biodiversity have taken the form of a treaty signed at the Earth Summit in Rio De Janeiro in 1992. The initiative has three central features. First, nations are required to inventory and monitor their biological assets. Second, conservation efforts centered around sustained yield resource development (see chapter 22) are to be pursued, conditional on financial support from wealthy countries. Finally, the treaty specified that a product developed from the genetic resources of a country remained the intellectual property of the host nation, unless a company had agreed to a profit-sharing mechanism in advance.[19] In other words, under the treaty a country like Mexico would have a legal right to block the sale of hybrid corn seeds developed from Mexican maize, unless it was guaranteed a share of the profits. How such a provision will be enforced remains an open question.

At the Rio Summit, developing nations tried to get the rich countries to agree to commit 0.7% of their annual GDP to sustainable development projects, up from 0.4%. (from $55 billion to $98 billion annually). However, no such firm commitment was forthcoming. An additional $5 billion in annual aid over the next five years was pledged at the summit, with 80% coming from Japan, 16% from the European Community, and 4% from the United States. Some of this aid will help finance the conservation programs under the biodiversity treaty.

---

[18]"Prospectors for Tropical Medicines," *New Scientist,* October 19, 1991.
[19]Hathaway (1992).

The Rio agreement was weakened by developing countries that objected to initial attempts to list particular species and habitats as endangered (the approach taken in the 1973 CITES treaty on wildlife trade). Ultimately, the agreement was signed by 158 nations, with one significant holdout: the United States. The United States had several objections, but primary was the provision that assigned property rights to genetic resources to host countries.

Under the agreement, these rights must be purchased by foreign and domestic firms. As we noted in chapter 22, whenever common property resources are privatized, those who previously had free access will lose out. In this case, multinational seed and pharmaceutical companies, many of them U.S.-based, were the losers. A U.S. biotech industry spokesperson put it this way: "It seems to us highway robbery that a Third World country should have the right to a protected invention simply because it supplied a bug, or a plant or animal in the first place. It's been weighted in favor of developing nations." While Japan and Britain shared some of the U.S. reservations, these two nations ultimately signed on under pressure from domestic environmental groups. In 1993, newly elected President Clinton reversed the U.S. stand taken at the conference and announced we would sign the treaty.[20]

The Rio agreement is important from a symbolic point of view, in that the rich countries formally acknowledged the need for a transfer of resources in order to protect biodiversity. Few are optimistic, however, that the treaty as currently framed will do more than slow down the massive acceleration in species extinction we are currently witnessing.

First, the treaty itself contains no requirement that rich countries contribute to the conservation fund. While significant monies were committed at Rio, no ongoing financial mechanism was established. Second, while the Rio treaty formally assigns to each country the property rights to its genetic resources, no enforcement mechanism is set up. What if biotech companies ignore or circumvent the international law? Without the kind of technical enforcement capability that Costa Rica is building up, the property rights provision of the treaty is liable to be fairly hollow.

The prospects for strengthening the Rio biodiversity treaty are not good for two related reasons. First, it is very hard to assess compliance with and progress toward an agreement whose goal is to "protect biodiversity." As the treaty acknowledges, the problem of species extinction is a diverse and deeply rooted one, ultimately driven by rapid population growth and desperate poverty in poor countries. In short, effectively preserving biodiversity means *achieving sustainable development* throughout the less developed world. As discussed in chapter 22, this will require a substantial increase in the transfer of technology and other resources from wealthy countries to poor ones.

The second obstacle to an effective international agreement is closely related. The loss of biodiversity is unlikely to galvanize the massive aid efforts from the developed world essential to such an effort. The daily extinctions of dozens of species of plants,

---

[20]The United States was also concerned about efforts to regulate international trade in genetically engineered products on safety grounds, and the control over the conservation fund set up by the treaty. See "U.S. to Oppose Treaty on Protection of Resources," *New York Times,* May 30, 1992. The quote is from "Biodiversity Convention a 'Lousy Deal' Says US," *New Scientist,* July 4, 1992. Clinton's decision is reported in "Not Just Hot Air," *Time,* May 3, 1993.

insects, and animals in the tropical rain forest may deprive my children of important medicines and agricultural products. However, this threat is a negative and distant one: The loss of biodiversity may reduce well-being, but it does not threaten many human lives. By contrast, action to ban CFCs in the ozone case was forthcoming because of the potential for direct and positive harm: massive increases in skin cancer and blindness.

To sum up: the framework laid at Rio for protecting biodiversity was certainly helpful, but success on the scale of the Montreal Protocol is unlikely to be duplicated. Instead, follow-up meetings are likely to focus, unproductively, on rich country funding levels. As a result, nongovernmental conservation organizations, multinational drug and agricultural companies, and host country governments will now have to take the lead in protecting biodiversity for its own sake. As the next section discusses, however, protecting tropical forests might be an important side-benefit of a global warming agreement.

23.4 The Prognosis for Slowing Global Warming

The prospects for progress on an effective international agreement to control global warming fall midway between the examples of the Montreal Protocol and Rio biodiversity treaty. Like ozone depletion, and unlike the loss of biodiversity, global warming represents a distinct, positive threat to a wide range of nations. Also like ozone depletion, the greenhouse threat arises from several well-defined atmospheric pollutants—primarily carbon dioxide (CO_2) and methane. Thus a treaty can be structured around the concrete goal of controlling these pollutants, instead of an ill-defined target of "preserving ecosystems." The prospect of **positive harm** to our children and the existence of a **well-defined problem,** both improve the prospects for an effective agreement.

However, a global warming treaty shares many of the problems faced in the biodiversity case. Foremost among these is the vastly **decentralized** nature of the problem. Unlike the case of CFCs, there are millions of producers of carbon dioxide and methane. Virtually no sector of a modern economy operates without producing CO_2, and methane pollution arises from sources as diverse as natural gas pipelines, rice paddies, and cattle ranches. Enforcement thus looms as a major obstacle to an effective treaty.

In addition, as in the loss of biodiversity, both **deforestation** and rapid **population growth** in poor countries are important sources of the greenhouse effect. This means that "solving" global warming is also tied up with the momentous task of achieving sustainable development in the less developed world. To illustrate this point, Table 23.2 presents three CO_2 control strategies, analyzed by Chapman and Drennen (1991).

Policy (1) illustrates the likely outcome under a strategy focused purely on rich countries. Under this scenario, the developed countries maintain the drop in per capita fossil fuel use displayed from 1980 to 1986 of 0.5% per year. Developing countries meanwhile continue to increase per capita fuel use at 1.7% per year and continue with population growth rates of 2%. Here, CO_2 levels double over the next sixty-five years.

TABLE 23.2   Global Warming and Sustainable Development

Policy	Estimated Date of Carbon Doubling[a]
(1) Continuation of trends in per capita fossil fuel use: declines in rich countries, increases in poor countries	2059
(2) Reduce population growth and increase income growth in developing countries; increase energy taxes globally	2309
(3) Number (2) plus 10 million acres forested annually	Never

[a]From an 1860 preindustrial baseline.
Source: Duane Chapman and Thomas Drennen (1991), "Equity and Effectiveness of Possible CO_2 Treaty Proposals," *Contemporary Policy Issues,* vol. 8, 16–28. Used with permission.

By contrast, policy (2), which achieves "sustainable development" in poor countries—a long-run increase in income and a reduction in population growth rates to 0.8%—coupled with increased global fuel taxes, forestalls a doubling of CO_2 levels for 250 years. Adding in a forestry program of policy (3) to trap carbon dioxide further improves the picture. It is apparent that, unlike the Montreal Protocol, an effective treaty to slow down global warming cannot focus solely on regulatory control of industries (and consumers) in the rich countries. Instead, it must also tackle a broad range of interrelated and difficult development issues: poverty, population growth, and deforestation. Fortunately, the ultimate task still remains the narrow and quantifiable one of reducing carbon and methane emissions.

With this background, the bare bones of a successful treaty must do three things: (1) mandate **numerical emission reduction targets** for carbon dioxide and methane; (2) provide a mechanism by which rich countries effectively **transfer technology and resources** to poor countries to finance sustainable development; and (3) provide strong **enforcement** mechanisms. The best tool for accomplishing these three goals simultaneously would be an international **marketable permits system.**

How would this work? An initial treaty would first put an annual cap on targeted global emissions of a greenhouse pollutant, say CO_2. A share of the annual total would then be allocated to each nation. Some have suggested that carbon permits be allocated based on a nation's population; others have suggested an initial fifty-fifty split between rich and poor countries. At any rate, for the system to work, poor countries would have to emerge from the process with an excess supply of permits, while rich countries would have an excess demand.

The next step in the process would be for rich nations to trade expertise and technology to poor nations in exchange for permits. Trade would be authorized only for measures that lead to demonstrable reductions in greenhouse gas emissions. To lessen the opportunity for corruption, trade in cash would be discouraged. Poor country A thus might trade 1 million pounds of CO_2 for a shipment of photovoltaic solar cells, a boatload of condoms, 100 forestry professors, and an environmental economist.[21]

---

[21]Economists have traditionally argued that in a world of perfect information, payment in cash is preferable to payment-in-kind of the type discussed here. This is because it is assumed the recipient better knows how to spend his money than the donor. In this case, however, the global agreement specifies expenditures for a certain purpose, and payment in kind is easier to monitor than payment in cash. For a general argument along these lines, see Blackorby and Donaldson (1988).

Each country would then be responsible for reducing CO_2 emissions to the level specified by the tradeable permits held. This could be done through an "internal" marketable permit system, carbon taxes, command-and-control regulation, or programs to promote investment in clean technology. An intergovernmental organization (IGO) established by the initial treaty would have to have broad compliance monitoring powers. Holley (1991) suggests **chain monitoring** in which the countries are ranked by CO_2 emissions, and each nation is monitored by the next biggest emitter.[22] Presumably, such monitors would have an economic incentive to insure their (larger) competitors were not cheating on an agreement.

Finally, a permit system could be enforced by restricting trade in permits to countries who were either exceeding their permitted emissions or violating other terms of the agreement. Poor country sales would be restricted, as would rich country purchases. One beauty of the permit system is that it gives countries something that can then be taken away if they refuse to comply. Finally, the treaty would have to authorize more **comprehensive trade sanctions** against a nation that repeatedly or willfully failed to meet its permitted emission requirements. Figure 23.1 illustrates one version of the total process.

The prospects for this kind of comprehensive agreement are not good. First, such a treaty would mean a measurable reduction in general consumption levels in rich countries. As discussed in chapter 20, such a shift in resources need not imply either increases in unemployment, or indeed, decreases in happiness. Nevertheless, a massive foreign aid program is politically unpopular in rich countries. Second, an effective treaty would both require nations to allow foreign or intergovernmental monitoring of compliance, and authorize the imposition of full-scale trade embargoes for willful noncompliance. To date, countries have seldom agreed to give up this much sovereignty.

Finally, uncertainty as to the magnitude of the problem provides an excuse for inaction. However, as in the ozone case, greenhouse gases are very long-lived. Thus, by the time the magnitude of global warming is confirmed, it may well be too late to take any effective action.

At the Rio de Janeiro Earth Summit in 1992, the U.S. government pleaded uncertainty and successfully weakened the **global warming convention** that was ultimately signed. The European nations were originally pressing for a schedule of timetables and cutbacks aimed at substantially *reducing* global CO_2 emissions. President Bush, by threatening to boycott the Rio Summit altogether, was able instead to achieve a much weaker agreement. Ultimately, the nations made only a nonbinding commitment to "try" and stabilize carbon emissions at 1990 levels by the year 2000.[23]

Five years later, in Kyoto, Japan, the United States, along with other developed nations, did sign on to a new treaty with binding numerical targets—around a 5% cutback from 1990 levels, to be achieved between 2008 and 2012. International carbon trading is also a feature of the treaty, but the details have yet to be worked out. United States' compliance with the treaty, however, is not guaranteed. The U.S. Senate has said it will refuse to ratify the Kyoto Treaty unless developing nations

---

[22]The biggest emitter, the United States, would in turn monitor several medium-sized countries. For a good discussion of greenhouse compliance, see di Primo et al. (1992).

[23]"How Bush Achieved Global Warming Pact with Modest Goals," *Wall Street Journal,* May 27, 1992.

Treaty Sets
Annual Global Carbon Emission Total

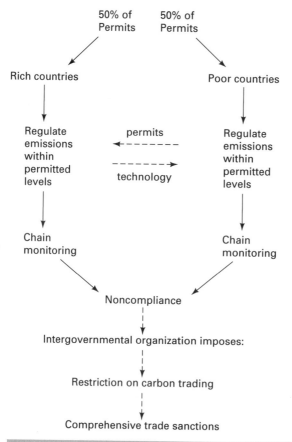

FIGURE 23.1 Model Greenhouse Treaty

also agree to make CO_2 reductions, and President Clinton announced he would not bring the treaty to the Senate for ratification until at least 1999.

Whether urgent international action on global warming is in fact justified is the subject of an important economic (and ethical) debate, explored in chapters 1 and 20. But the general consensus is that the *initial* steps to control CO_2 emissions (improved energy efficiency, fuel switching away from coal, and the control of natural gas leaks) will not be particularly costly. Indeed, as noted in chapter 1, most of the economists working on global warming issues have publicly called for action based on efficiency arguments.[24] Given this, the U.S. lack of leadership in the 1990s has been unfortunate from a global benefit-cost perspective.

[24]"Now, With Treaty On Climate Signed, Countries Promise Stricter Measures," *New York Times,* June 13, 1992. President Clinton announced in 1993 that we would meet the Rio target by 2000. See "Not Just Hot Air," *Time,* May 3, 1993.

As the Montreal Protocol case illustrates, a treaty process is a long, drawn-out affair. The original 1992 European position on global warming, though much stronger than the final Rio statement, was a far cry from the effective agreement outlined in Figure 23.1. It dealt only with step one, establishing numerical reduction targets, but did not address in a serious way the other two requirements: resources for sustainable development and enforcement. Our nation's actions at Rio, and later at Kyoto, undercut the substantial insurance value that would have been provided by an agreement which at least addressed the first of the three necessary steps. The treaty process must be well-advanced in the event that the additional, bolder steps are to be seriously contemplated.

Nevertheless, as the biggest greenhouse gas emitter, the U.S. position is illustrative of the general problem of forging agreements outlined in the introduction to this chapter. Relative to its much more energy-efficient Japanese and European competitors, the U.S. economy has more to lose from a global warming treaty. Thus, the opposition to the process has been strongest from our country.

I stated above that one of the factors favoring a global warming treaty is that the greenhouse effect is liable to inflict positive and significant harm on the citizens of many nations. As an example of a clear and present danger yielding an impressive international response, we can look to the appearance of the ozone hole in 1985 that spurred nations into signing the Montreal Protocol. If the greenhouse effect does in fact lead to a substantial increase in global temperature, we would indeed be lucky if some bad weather materializes sooner rather than later. If instead, we warm only slowly, an effective global warming treaty is likely to come too late.

23.5 Summary

This chapter identifies a basic obstacle to effective international action on global environmental problems: the public good nature of an agreement. Free riding means that agreements are likely to be too weak from an efficiency perspective and to be susceptible to noncompliance. International bodies set up to administer agreements may monitor compliance but have few enforcement powers. One informal tool is community pressure. Formal enforcement mechanisms must be written into a treaty and include restricted access to a compensation fund and targeted trade sanctions.

The Montreal Protocol to protect the ozone layer represents the most successful environmental treaty to date. In a period of sixteen years, nations moved from skepticism about the need to regulate CFCs at all, to banning the bulk of production. The treaty's success can be traced to three factors: (1) the rapidly mounting evidence of a significant health threat; (2) the centralized nature of CFC production, which minimized enforcement problems; and (3) the speedy development of low cost CFC substitutes.

By contrast, the Rio biodiversity agreement has value primarily as a symbol of concern. The treaty formally recognizes two key points: (1) Rich nations must finance sustained yield resource development projects in poor countries if biodiversity is to be preserved, and (2) an important obstacle to profit-based conservation has been free access by multinational firms to genetic resources. However, the treaty is very weak on enforcement mechanisms, and rich nations have little political incentive to pay the necessary price to beef up the treaty.

The prospects for a global warming treaty are enhanced by the positive threat posed and the focus on a handful of pollutants. However, as in the biodiversity case, solving the problem would in fact require achieving sustainable development in poor countries—increasing incomes in a clean fashion while reducing population growth. An effective treaty would mandate emission reductions, provide a means to transfer technology and resources to poor countries, and have a built-in enforcement mechanism. An international tradeable permits system has these three features. In addition, enforcement would have to be guaranteed by the threat of comprehensive trade sanctions.

Scientists are unlikely to soon develop evidence as dramatic as the ozone hole to propel an effective global warming treaty forward. As a result, a serious political interest in combating global warming may emerge only if and when a series of droughts strike rich countries. Because carbon dioxide is such a long-lived pollutant, at that point, nations will have to move very quickly to implement an effective treaty.

This book has ended, as it began, with a discussion of global warming. Today, I have compounded this problem by actions as simple as driving to work and turning on my computer. Yet global warming is just one of the pressing environmental problems we will face in the coming years. From the siting of waste facilities at the community level, to regulatory policy at the national level, to sustainable development around the globe, environmental challenges abound. While these problems are formidable, for our children's sake, we have no option but to face them squarely. This book has provided some tools for doing so.

At the risk of repeating myself (again!), let me summarize the three-step approach that we have developed:

Step 1. Set your environmental goal.
Efficiency, safety, or ecological sustainability?
Step 2. Recognize the constraints on effective government action.
Imperfect information, political influence, and inadequate enforcement.
Step 3. Look for ways to do better.
Incentive-based regulation and clean technology promotion.

Now, get to work.

APPLICATION 23.0

After the Warming

In the BBC science-fiction drama, *After the Warming,* an historian looks back from the year 2050 at our efforts to deal with the problem of global warming. It turns out that we do adopt a fairly effective tradeable permit system for greenhouse gases, beginning in the late 1990s. (Unfortunately, due to positive feedback in the form of disrupted ocean currents, year 2050 residents find themselves having to redouble their efforts to keep the planet from overheating.)

Nations that violated the treaty, the historian informs us, lost their carbon-trading rights until they came back into compliance.

1. Would this enforcement mechanism work for developing countries? Developed countries? Why or why not?

2. The show describes the growth of a powerful and rather efficient "Planetary Management Authority" (sort of like "The Federation" on *Star Trek*), which uses advanced technology to monitor compliance and make enforcement decisions. Is it likely that compliance could be effectively monitored by a centralized world agency?

Key Ideas in Each Section

23.0 This chapter discusses the economics of global pollution control agreements.

23.1 Each country has a true **willingness-to-pay** for a pollution control agreement that is a function of both its income and the environmental benefits it is likely to receive. However, because agreements are **public goods**, the **free-rider problem** means they will be both **too weak** from an efficiency (and safety) point of view and provide **incentives for cheating.**

23.2 Monitoring compliance is typically the responsibility of an **intergovernmental organization (IGO)** set up by each treaty. IGOs can also issue **nonbinding standards** and **monitor** compliance. The three main enforcement tools are **social pressure,** restricted access to **compensation funds,** and targeted **trade sanctions.**

23.3 This section describes two agreements. First, the **Montreal Protocol** initiated a global phaseout of **chlorofluorocarbons (CFCs)** to protect the earth's **ozone layer.** The treaty succeeded due to (1) the clear and present danger from the **ozone hole,** (2) a narrowly defined problem, and (3) ease of enforcement due to limited number of producers. Second, the Rio Convention on Biodiversity seeks to protect **biodiversity** (important for **existence value** and as a gene pool) by encouraging member nations to inventory reserves, take conservation measures, and provide host countries with a share in **pharmaceutical and agricultural breeding** profits. The treaty has little more than symbolic value due to (1) a clear but distant danger of negative harm, (2) a broadly defined problem, and (3) inability to take action without funding from rich countries.

23.4 How likely is an effective **global warming treaty?** Pros include the likelihood of **positive harm** and the existence of **well-defined** pollutants. Cons arise from highly **decentralized** producers and the fact that a greenhouse treaty would have to confront sustainability issues ranging from **deforestation** to **population growth.** An effective treaty would have three components: (1) **numerical emission targets;** (2) **technology and resource transfers;** and (3) **good enforcement.** A **marketable permit system,** combined with **chain monitoring** and **comprehensive trade sanctions,** is one model that fits these requirements. The Rio Convention on Global Warming falls well short of such a treaty; an updated and somewhat strengthened version is expected to be in place in the late 1990s.

References

Bailey, Martin (1982). "Risks, Costs and Benefits of Fluorocarbon Regulation." *American Economic Review,* 72, no. 2, 247–250.

Blackorby, Charles and David Donaldson (1988). "Cash Versus Kind, Self Selection and Efficient Transfers." *American Economic Review,* 78, no. 4, 691–700.

Chapman, Duane and Thomas Drennen (1991). "Equity and Effectiveness of Possible CO_2 Treaty Proposals." *Contemporary Policy Issues,* vol. 8, 16–28.

di Primo, Juan C., Gotthard Stein and Herman F. Wagner (1992). "Verifying Compliance with an International Convention on Greenhouse Gasses." *Environment,* 34, no. 2, 4–6.

French, Hillary (1993). "Reconciling Trade and the Environment." In *State of the World, 1993.* ed. Lester Brown. New York: W. W. Norton.

French, Hillary (1992). "Strengthening Global Environmental Governance." In *State of the World, 1992.* ed. Lester Browne New York: W. W. Norton.

Hathaway, Oona (1992). "Whither Biodiversity? The Global Debate Over Biological Variety Continues." *Harvard International Review,* 15, no. 2, 58–60.

Heppes, John B. and Eric J. McFadden (1987). "The Convention on Trade in Endangered Species: The Prospects for Preserving Our Biological Heritage." *Boston University International Law Journal,* 5, no. 2, 229–246.

Holley, Susan E. (1991). "Global Warming: Construction and Enforcement of a Global Accord." *Stanford Environmental Law Journal,* vol. 10, 44.

Manzer, L. E. (1990). "The CFC-Ozone Issue: Progress on the Development of Alternatives to CFCs." *Science,* 7, no. 6, 31–35.

Munasinghe, Mohan and Kenneth King (1992). "Accelerating Ozone Layer Protection in Developing Countries." *World Development,* 20, no. 4, 609–618.

Sand, Peter (1990). *Lessons Learned in Global Environmental Governance.* Washington, DC: World Resources Institute.

Sedjo, Roger A. (1992). "Property Rights, Genetic Resources and Biotechnological Change." *Journal of Law and Economics,* 35, no. 1, 199–213.

Somerset, Margaret (1989). "An Attempt to Stop the Sky from Falling: The Montreal Protocol to Protect Against Atmospheric Ozone Reduction." *Syracuse Journal of International Law and Commerce,* 15, no. 39, 391–429.

PART

V

Advanced Topics

This last part of the book contains four short chapters which expand on ideas developed earlier in the text. The first two chapters deal with the implications of "nonstandard" benefit and cost functions. Topic T1 addresses the issue of efficient pollution regulation when the functions are non-convex; this chapter expands on material in chapter 4. T2 extends the analysis in chapter 16 to consider some advantages of pollution taxes over marketable permits (and vice versa) when there is uncertainty regarding costs and benefits.

Topic T3 takes up the challenge of identifying clean technologies in the life-cycle context discussed in chapter 18. A simple model is developed to illustrate, in principle, how economists keep track of all the direct and indirect pollution generated by a particular technology.

Finally, topic T4 illustrates in greater detail the concept of incentive-compatible regulation discussed briefly in chapter 12. It shows how, in principle, the right mix of incentives can be built into a regulatory design to insure that truthful information about compliance costs is forthcoming from regulated parties.

The Importance
of Being Convex

T1.0 Introduction

This chapter starts out with a puzzle. Consider the four diagrams in Table T1.1, representing the marginal benefits of pollution reduction.

PUZZLE

Tell a story about the remaining damages that are being caused by the pollutants A, B, C, and D as cleanup progresses.

SOLUTION

Pollutant A is our standard case, representing declining marginal benefits of cleanup. Here, the initial cleanup efforts yield large benefits, but as the environment becomes cleaner, additional benefits of cleanup fall. We might call this the **buffering model** of pollution damage: At high levels of pollution the buffering capacity of the environment is exceeded and damages are large. By contrast, as pollution levels fall, the environment naturally begins to neutralize harmful effects. Throughout the book, we have always assumed a buffering model of environmental damage, but in this chapter, we will consider some alternatives.

Pollutant B represents a **linear model** of pollution damage. Each unit of cleanup yields the same level of benefit. In other words, the marginal damages of pollution are constant. Linear pollution damage is also often assumed for exposure to carcinogenic material. I also employed the linear model in a paper I wrote on oil spill damages (Goodstein [1992]). I had found that oil tanker accidents increased significantly on Saturdays. In the paper, I analyzed the environmental impact of diverting tanker traffic away from Saturdays via a harbor tax. I assumed a linear relationship between reduction in traffic on Saturdays and reduction in elevated spill levels—for every 10% reduction in traffic, a 10% reduction in the damage from elevated Saturday spill rates. The diagram I used thus looked very much like that for pollutant B.

Pollutant C represents a very interesting case. At first, cleanup yields no marginal benefits. But beyond point P^*, benefits are suddenly quite high, and then begin to decline in the standard fashion. This is a **saturation model** of pollution damage. At cleanup levels below P^* (the saturation level), the environment is essentially "dead." For example, a lake may be unable to support fish. Cleanup to levels above the saturation level, however, will yield great initial benefits as the first fish species return. Subsequent cleanup will also generate benefits but at a decreasing rate. Other examples of a saturation model include the impact on visibility of particulates in the air, and congestion externalities.

Pollutant D is a weird one. Here the marginal benefit curve initially begins below the horizontal axis! Cleanup starts out being harmful, actually increasing pollution damage. Beyond P', however, the standard buffering relationship kicks in. How can pollution reduction increase pollution damage? Repetto (1987) provides an example. As we learned in chapter 14, nitrogen oxide (NOx) combines with volatile organic compounds and sunlight to form ground-level ozone or smog. It turns out that for chemical reasons, at high NOx concentrations, ozone formation is actually inhibited. In fact, ozone concentrations in the direct vicinity of an NOx source are typically lower than in areas farther away where the NOx is dilute. For this reason, initial cleanup of NOx (holding all other factors constant) will actually lead to increased smog.

Pollutants C and D have what are known as **non-convex** cleanup functions. The purpose of this chapter is to explain what is meant by non-convexity and illustrate its significance for policy purposes. The bottom line is that, when non-convexities are present in either cost or benefit functions, there will no longer be a single intersection of the marginal benefit and marginal cost curves. Thus, marginal analysis will not continue to provide a reliable guide to the efficient level of pollution control. This may become a problem, since small changes that appear desirable on a benefit-cost basis can now lead one *away* from the most efficient outcome.

T1.1 Non-Convex Damages and Costs

First of all, where does this word "non-convex" come from and what does it mean? Non-convexity (and convexity) refer to the *shape* of the benefit and cost of cleanup functions. To see this, however, we need to look at the *total,* not the marginal, functions. Figure T1.2 reproduces a figure from chapter 4, where we discussed the relationship between the total and marginal benefits and costs of cleanup for the case of cigarette smoke in the office.

Both sets of curves illustrate the same information. The total costs of pollution reduction rise at an increasing rate; another way of saying this is that the additional cost

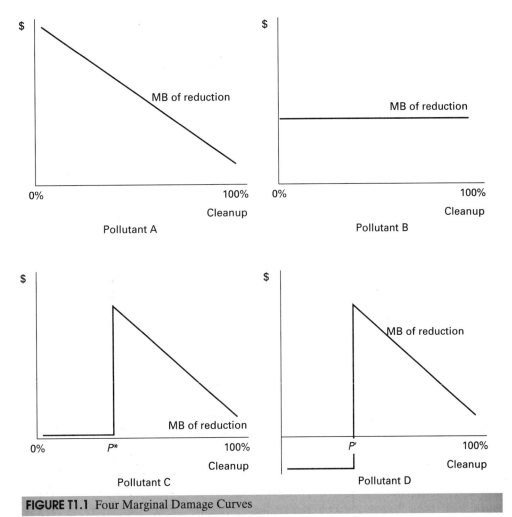

FIGURE T1.1 Four Marginal Damage Curves

of each cigarette given up rises. Similarly, the total benefits of cleanup rise at a decreasing rate; thus, the marginal benefits of pollution reduction are falling.

How can we move from one set of curves to another? The marginal cost curve represents the change in total costs. Thus, as Figure T1.2 illustrates, the marginal cost of the first cigarette reduced, $4, is just the change in the total cost curve between 0 and 1 cigarette reduced. Similarly, the marginal benefit of the fourth cigarette reduced, $6, is the change in the total benefits curve between 3 and 4 cigarettes reduced. The marginal curves graph the total change in y for a 1-unit change in x. But this is just the "rise" over the "run" of the total curve. Thus, the marginal curves graph the slopes of the total curves. In calculus terms, the marginal curves graph the first derivative of the totals.

Moreover, the area *under* the marginal cost curve equals the total cost. For example, the marginal cost of the first cigarette reduced, $4, plus the marginal cost of the second, $6, just equals the total costs of two cigarettes reduced, $10. But $4 is just the

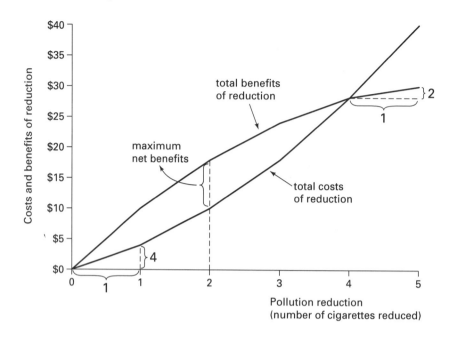

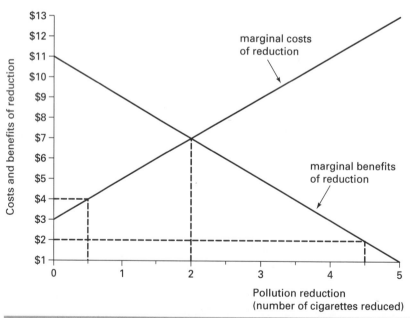

FIGURE T1.2 Marginals and Totals Compared: Costs and Benefits of Pollution Reduction

area under the marginal curve between 0 and 1, while $6 is the area under the curve between 1 and 2.

Finally, note that *the efficient pollution level does not occur where total costs equal total benefits* (between 4 and 5 cigarettes reduced). At this point, since total benefits and costs are equal, the net monetary benefits to "society" are zero. Instead, the efficient level occurs where the total benefit curve lies farthest above the total cost curve. Here, the net monetary benefits to Brittany and Tyler combined are maximized. At the point where total benefits and cost are equal, we know we have reduced pollution "too much" under an efficiency standard. At this point the *marginal* costs of reduction exceed the *marginal* benefits, given the conventional shapes of the benefit and cost curves.

The "conventional" shapes of the total benefit and cost of reduction curves are those portrayed in Figure T1.2. They have a smooth, lens-like shape. This is a **convex** shape: The benefit curve is convex downward, and the cost curve is convex upward. Convexity requires the costs of cleanup to rise at an increasing rate and the benefits to rise at a decreasing rate (a buffering model) over the whole range of cleanup.[1] If we have convexity of the cost and benefit curves, this allows us to pinpoint the efficient level of pollution using marginal analysis. That is, if we find the MB of reduction exceeds the MC, then we know more reduction is in order and vice versa.

By contrast, let us now look at the total benefit curve associated with the saturation model. Figure T1.3 illustrates this case. The first three tons of pollution reduction have no impact on, let us say, water quality in a lake. However, the fourth ton provides a big increase in benefits as the first fish species returns. As before, the marginal cost curve still graphs the slope of the total cost curve except at the point 3 tons, where the total curve takes a sharp turn and the slope is undefined.

Here, the total benefits of the cleanup curve are non-convex. The curve *does not* have the smooth, lens-like shape found in Figure T1.2. The benefits of reduction *do not* increase at a decreasing rate over the whole range of cleanup. As a challenging exercise, see if you can graph the total benefits of cleanup associated with NOx reduction. There is enough information in Figure T1.1, pollutant D, to do so.

T1.2 Efficient Cleanup and Non-Convexity

Now that we know what non-convexity is, why is it important? When either the benefit or the cost of the cleanup function is non-convex, it complicates the identification of the efficient pollution level. To see this, consider our saturation model of pollution damage, but this time let us add in a marginal cost of reduction curve. Figure T1.4 illustrates three different cases.

For cases 1 and 2, the non-convexity doesn't change our approach: We can still use **marginal analysis** to identify the efficient pollution level. In case 1, the MC and MB curves intersect only once, at point *X*. The non-convexity is, thus, out of the relevant range of analysis. In case 2 there is also only a single intersection, at a zero level of cleanup. (Economists call case 2 a *corner-solution*.) In both of these cases, controlling pollution at the level where MB equals MC will lead to efficient pollution control.

---

[1]This is a sufficient but not necessary condition. In addition, the smooth lens shape is required for strict convexity. The linear model, where total benefits and costs change at a constant rate, is also convex but not strictly so. For a more technical discussion, see Chiang (1984).

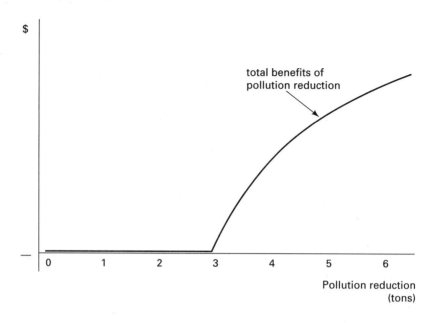

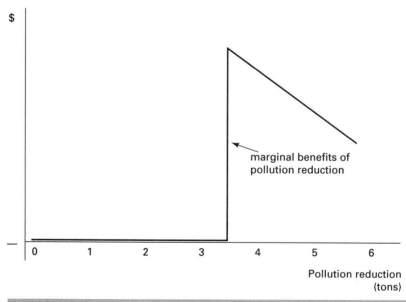

FIGURE T1.3 The Saturation Model

Case 3, by contrast, illustrates the problem. Here, the MB and MC curves inter-sect three times, at points *A*, *B*, and *C*. As it turns out, one of these is the efficient pol-lution level. But which one? Marginal analysis can be used to tell us something about these points.

First, A and C are **locally efficient.** In other words, small moves away from either point will lead to a drop in net monetary benefits to society. If one moves to the right

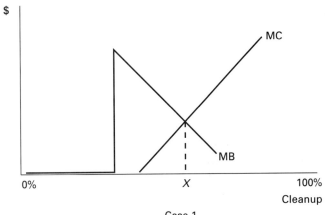

Case 1

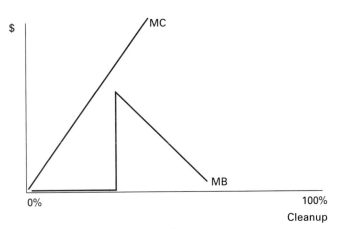

Case 2

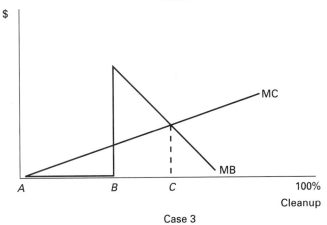

Case 3

FIGURE T1.4 Non-convexity and Efficiency

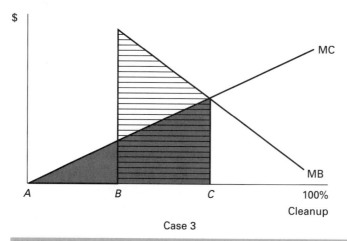

Case 3

FIGURE T1.5 Comparing Total Costs and Benefits

of *A*, the additional costs of pollution control exceed the (zero) additional benefits. Thus, in the neighborhood of *A*, *A* is the most efficient point. Similarly, movements to the left of *C* lead to a sacrifice of marginal benefits that exceed the costs of reduction, while a shift to cleanup levels greater than *C* generate marginal costs that are greater than benefits. *C* is, thus, also locally efficient.

By contrast, moving away from *B* in *either* direction improves efficiency. To the left, marginal costs exceed marginal benefits, so further reduction is in order. To the right, marginal benefits exceed marginal costs, implying a need for greater cleanup.

Thus, marginal analysis tells us that *A* and *C* both maximize net benefits *locally* but that *B* is clearly inefficient. How do we choose between points *A* and *C*? We are forced at this point to abandon marginal analysis and look at the total costs and benefits of pollution reduction. At point *A*, the total costs and benefits are both just zero since no cleanup occurs. *C* will, thus, be preferred to *A* if total benefits minus total costs are positive.

As noted above, total benefits and costs can be calculated from the area under the marginal benefit and cost curves. Figure T1.5 illustrates that *C* will be more efficient than *A* if the area under the marginal benefit curve (the hatched area) is greater than the area under the marginal cost curve (the gray area). On the other hand, if the gray area exceeds the hatched area, then net benefits at pollution level *C* are actually less than zero, and point *A* is more efficient.

In intuitive terms, what is this diagram saying about saturation pollutants? From the perspective of efficiency, one should either cleanup to above the level of the saturation level or not at all. It also cautions us against blindly accepting the following argument: "The lake is dead anyway, so why bother with pollution control?" While reducing pollution control (moving to point *A*) will be more efficient locally, it *may* be better on a benefit-cost basis to invest in aggressive cleanup, to point *C*.

T1.3 Summary

This chapter has introduced the concept of non-convex cleanup functions and illustrated that non-convexity complicates the identification of an efficient pollution level. Under some conditions, marginal analysis will not be sufficient to identify an efficient outcome. Why is this important? It may make effective regulation more difficult, because small, benefit-cost-based improvements may, in fact, not be leading in the most efficient direction.

In the real world, how important are non-convex damage and cost functions? Economists differ on how widespread they are, but non-convexities are undoubtedly important for particular pollutants.[2] For example, the relationship between ground-level ozone and both of its precursors, NOx and volatile organic compounds, is non-convex. This means, as Repetto (1987) notes, that a strategy of tightly controlling either one or the other, but not both, might actually be efficient, depending upon control costs.

APPLICATION T1.0

Follow Through

1. Follow through on the suggestion in the text: Graph the total benefits of cleanup associated with NOx reduction. There is enough information in Figure T1.1, pollutant D, to do so.

2. Based on the discussion of the way in which ozone is formed, how can you explain the shape of the two portions of the total cost curve?

Key Ideas in Each Section

T1.0 Marginal pollution damages will vary depending upon the underlying effect of pollutants. Three possibilities are (1) the **buffering model,** (2) the **linear model** and (3) the **saturation model.**

T1.1 A **convex** damage or cost function will have a smooth, lens-like shape for the *total* function. Benefits from cleanup under a saturation model are non-convex.

T1.2 When cleanup benefits are non-convex, **marginal analysis** can identify only **locally efficient** options. To identify the globally efficient option, total costs and benefits of cleanup must be compared.

References

Burrows, Paul (1986). "Nonconvexity Induced by External Costs on Production: Theoretical Curio or Policy Dilemma?" *Journal of Environmental Economics and Management,* vol. 13, 101–128.

Chiang, Alpha C. (1984). *Fundamental Methods of Mathematical Economics.* New York: McGraw-Hill.

Goodstein, Eban (1992). "Saturday Effects in Tanker Oil Spills." *Journal of Environmental Economics and Management,* vol. 23, 276–288.

Repetto, Robert (1987). "The Policy Implications of Non-convex Environmental Damages: A Smog Control Case Study." *Journal of Environmental Economics and Management,* vol. 14, 13–29.

---

[2]Burrows (1986) provides a review of the main theoretical arguments for non-convexities in both cost and damage functions. He argues that the general problem of non-convexity is overstated. He also notes that even when non-convexities are present, iterative strategies based on marginal analysis will often lead to efficiency gains over alternate approaches.

T O P I C

2

Imperfect Regulation in an Uncertain World

T2.0 Introduction

Chapter 17 provided an extended discussion of the two types of incentive-based regulation: marketable permits and pollution taxes. We found that, although tradeable permit systems and taxes are quite similar in many respects, there are also important differences, summarized in Table T2.1.

To review briefly, when permit systems are initiated through permit giveaways, they are much less costly than pollution taxes for the affected firms. Permits also generate a much more certain level of pollution control than taxes, and they do not need to be adjusted for inflation or population increases and economic growth. However, permit systems have the drawbacks associated with market power, thin markets, the determination of permit life, and relocation incentives. In addition, taxes generate strong incentives for monitoring and enforcement and, if used to replace income taxes, can increase labor market efficiency.

The discussion in chapter 16, comparing permits and taxes, was based on the assumption of **perfect information:** That is, regulators were assumed to know *everything* about both the benefits and cost of pollution control. However, we know from our discussion of the real-world practice of regulation in chapter 12 that this assumption is far from the truth. In this advanced topic chapter, we introduce uncertainty into the analysis. This will highlight another important difference between permits and taxes, based on the **costs of regulatory mistakes.**

T2.1 Minimizing the Costs of Being Wrong

We noted above that permits have the advantage of providing a more certain level of pollution control than do emission taxes. This is because taxes have to be adjusted if regulators find pollutant levels resulting from a given tax are lower or higher than expected. Let us explore this issue a bit more fully, with the aid of Figure T2.1.

Figure T2.1 illustrates the marginal costs and marginal benefits of pollution re-

TABLE T2.1 Taxes and Marketable Permits Compared	
Advantages of Permits	*Advantages of Taxes*
If permits are given away, lower cost to firms.	Issues of thin markets, market power, permit life, and relocation incentives are avoided.
More certain pollutant level.	If revenues are used to cut income taxes, labor market efficiency will be improved.
No need for adjustment to account for economic growth or inflation.	If revenues are partially retained by enforcement agencies, enforcement incentives are strengthened.

duction for two particular cases. The first panel, with a steep marginal benefit curve, illustrates a pollutant with a **safety threshold.** Cleanup need not be pursued above C', even on safety grounds, since the additional benefits are low. But for cleanup levels below C', damages from additional pollution begin to mount steeply. An example of a pollutant with a safety threshold is the ozone-depleting chlorofluorocarbon (CFC) discussed in chapter 23. Because the ozone layer has already been saturated with long-lived CFCs released in the past, any *additional* CFC production generates high marginal damages in the form of skin cancers and eye disease.

The second panel of Figure T2.1, by contrast, illustrates a situation where *costs* are quite sensitive to the level of the cleanup. Pollution reduction to a level of C'' can be pursued relatively cheaply, but beyond C'', costs begin to mount rapidly. Global warming probably fits this picture: Carbon dioxide emissions can be reduced fairly

FIGURE T2.1 IB Regulation, Two Special Cases

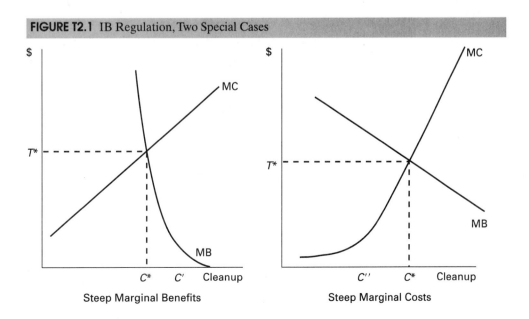

Steep Marginal Benefits   Steep Marginal Costs

cheaply by pursuing energy efficiency and switching to natural gas, but once these opportunities are exhausted, more expensive options will have to be exercised.

If regulators knew with certainty the location of the curves in Figure T2.1, then they could achieve efficient pollution reduction to C^* using *either* form of incentive-based regulation. They might issue just enough marketable permits to achieve the desired cleanup or, alternatively, charge a pollution tax of T^*. However, in the real world, regulators seldom, if ever, have such perfect information. The point of this chapter is to determine, following Weitzman (1974), what approach regulators should use when they are uncertain about the location of the curves *and* are pursuing efficiency as their goal. We will see that when the **marginal benefit curve is steep,** regulators should use a marketable permit system. By contrast, when the **marginal cost curve is steep,** a pollution tax system is preferred.

When the marginal benefit curve is steep, regulators will want to keep tight control over the actual quantity of pollutant released into the environment to insure that the threshold is not far exceeded. Under these circumstances, a marketable permit system is preferred to a pollution tax because of the costs of being wrong. We can see this graphically in Figure T2.2.

In Figure T2.2, the efficient level of cleanup is C^*. However, suppose that regulators miss the mark and issue 20% more permits than they should, so that firms clean up only to $\hat{C}$. Then the monetary loss to society is represented by the gray area—the difference between the foregone benefits and increased costs of cleaning up to C^*. By contrast, suppose regulators opted for a pollution tax. Efficiency requires a tax of T^*, but if the regulators are too low by 20%, we get a tax of T'. Facing this tax, firms clean up only to C',

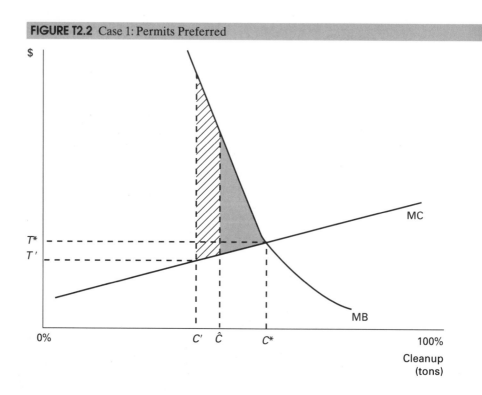

FIGURE T2.2 Case 1: Permits Preferred

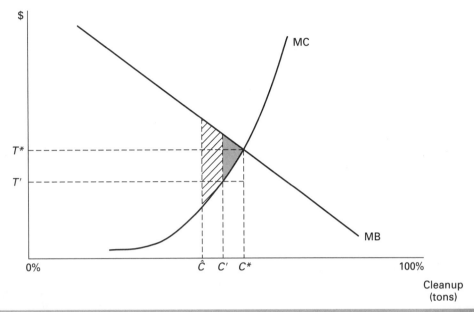

FIGURE T2.3 Case 2: Taxes Preferred

and society loses net benefits equal to the gray area *plus* the hatched area as a result. The basic idea here is that a permit approach, because it allows for greater control over actual cleanup levels, keeps pollution relatively close to the safety threshold.

By contrast, when the social costs of being wrong arise more from increased compliance costs and less from the benefits of reduction, a tax policy will be preferred. We can see this in Figure T2.3.

If regulators undershoot the efficient tax by 20% and set it at T', firms will decrease cleanup only a little, to C'. Because the marginal cost of reduction curve is so steep, firm behavior will not be very responsive to the lower tax. As a result, monetary losses to society will be restricted to the gray area—the difference between lower control costs and higher foregone benefits from cleanup to only C'. By contrast, if regulators mandate a cleanup level that is 20% too low, then firms are forced to make bigger changes in their behavior, reducing pollution to $\hat{C}$. In this case, overall monetary losses to society become the gray area *plus* the hatched area. The intuition here is that, with a steep marginal cost curve, firms will not change their pollution behavior much with decreased (or increased) pollution taxes. As a result, losses to society from either under- or over-regulation using taxes will not be too big.

What if both the marginal benefit and marginal cost curves are steep? Then a clear-cut advantage for either method, based on the costs of being wrong, disappears.

T2.2 Summary

This chapter has considered an important distinction between marketable permits and pollution taxes when regulators are uncertain about the precise location of the marginal benefit and cost of pollution reduction curves (virtually always!). In such a case, regulators will not be able to specify correctly either the number of permits or the efficient tax. If efficiency is the regulatory goal, then regulators should be concerned about minimizing the costs of any mistakes.

When the marginal benefit curve for cleanup is steep, regulators should opt for a tradeable permit system to keep the actual quantity of pollution close to the threshold. When the marginal cost of reduction curve is steep, a tax system is preferred since a firm's pollution behavior will not be particularly responsive to a tax set too high or too low. If these rules are followed, the efficiency costs arising from imperfect regulation in an uncertain world will be minimized.

APPLICATION T2.0

Still More on Efficient Gunk Control

Suppose that gunk has marginal benefits of reduction equal to $20 - 2x$, and marginal costs of reduction equal to $5 + x/2$, where x is the tons of gunk reduced.

1. Graph the MB and MC curves to find the efficient level of gunk reduction.
2. As a result of imperfect information, regulators are considering two inefficient policies: a tax 10% below the efficient tax level; and a marketable permit system, with the number of permits to be issued 10% below the efficient reduction level. Use your graph to show the monetary loss to society as a whole of the different policies. Which is more efficient?
3. Suppose regulators did not know exactly where the MB curve lay but did know that gunk was a threshold pollutant. Should they use a permit system or tax if they are interested in efficient regulation? Why?

Key Terms and Ideas

T2.0 In a world of **perfect information,** both marketable permit systems and taxes are capable of achieving efficient regulation. With uncertainty, however, differences between the two IB systems emerge based on the potential **cost of regulatory mistakes.**

T2.1 If the **marginal benefit curve is steep** due to a **safety threshold** effect, a permit system is preferred for efficient regulation. By contrast, if the **marginal cost curve is steep,** meaning firm pollution behavior is relatively unresponsive to small changes in tax levels, a tax is preferred.

Reference

Weitzman, M. L. (1974). "Prices Versus Quantities." *Review of Economic Studies,* vol. 41, 447–491.

TOPIC 3

Input-Output Models and Life-Cycle Analysis

T3.0 Introduction

In our definition of clean technology (CT) in chapter 18, we said that, among other things, a CT had to be "environmentally superior" to conventional technology. We suggested that a measure of environmental superiority might be based on a so-called **life-cycle** approach, which identified the major environmental impacts of a product from cradle to grave. One problem with doing life-cycle analysis is deciding at what stage a product is actually born. Consider a rubber tire. We might go all the way back to the production of petroleum necessary to create synthetic rubber. But why stop there? Why not include as well the manufacture of the drilling equipment necessary to produce the petroleum? Or the manufacture of the machine tools needed to produce the equipment to manufacture the drilling rigs?

This point came up again in our chapter 19 discussion of waste reduction in manufacturing and agriculture and recycling. Any time total resource use in the economy falls, both direct and indirect benefits are obtained. The **direct environmental benefits** of, for example, improved wastewater recycling in a jewelry factory are reduced emissions of heavy metals. However, **indirect environmental benefits** arise when metals recovered from the recycling process are reused. These indirect benefits include the pollution prevented by (1) lower levels of mining, smelting, and transporting the metals; (2) lower levels of production and transport of mining equipment; (3) lower levels of production of machinery necessary to make mining equipment; and so on as we move farther "upstream" in the production process.

This advanced topic chapter illustrates a method economists have developed to capture all of the complex environmental interactions in an economic system. Using what is called **input-output (I-O) analysis,** it is possible to describe completely all of the direct and indirect pollution created by a particular technology. I-O analysis allows us, at least in theory, to do a thorough life-cycle analysis of a product or production technique.[1]

In practice, however, I-O analysis is very data-intensive, requiring information about many technical relationships between inputs, outputs, and pollutants in an economy. For this reason, and in spite of its theoretical appeal, I-O is not now widely used for life-cycle analyses of any detail, for example, comparing paper with plastic bags. Instead, most detailed life-cycle analyses done today are of a partial nature, in which analysts try to identify the "major" indirect environmental effects of a production technique or product. Because of cost and data limitations, life-cycle analysts have to *assume* that most of the indirect effects of different technologies are comparable.

This chapter will develop a simple I-O model to make two general points about life-cycle impacts: (1) Technologies that reduce overall input use (**input-reducing technologies**) are always clean technologies; (2) technologies that substitute one "clean" input for another "dirty" one (**input-substituting technologies**) may or may not be clean technologies. In such a case, a detailed I-O study would have to be done to establish with certainty whether a proposed CT was really clean.

Unfortunately, case (2) is the one that almost always holds in the real world. For example, suppose I use a more efficient, compact, fluorescent lightbulb and save a lot of energy. It might be *possible* (but, in fact, isn't likely) that switching to the product would generate a big increase in the emission of a deadly hazardous waste in a distant, upstream production process. Given this possibility of large and distant indirect environmental effects of a new technology and the difficulty in identifying *all* these effects via a detailed I-O study, can any technology really be called a clean one with certainty?

While recognizing that there are few real-world examples of pure input-reducing technologies, clean technology proponents argue that processes that are *more* input-reducing are more likely to be clean technologies.[2] Defining what is meant by "more input-reducing" is itself not easy and can be done only on a case-by-case basis. For example, as we discussed in chapter 19, recycling products that would otherwise be made from virgin timber or minerals is likely to substantially reduce net indirect pollution (including any unsustainable drawdown of natural capital) in the extraction and transport phases of production.

Of course, without an I-O study of sufficient detail, no one can say for certain that this is true. But in the real world, as we have seen quite often, policy decisions must always be made with less than perfect information. Under these circumstances, rules of thumb can be helpful. The ordering of the **three R's** discussed in chapter 19—(1) **reduce**, (2) **reuse**, (3) **recycle**—provides a guide that emphasizes input-reducing technologies over input-substituting technologies.

To summarize: Most technological change involves substituting one input for another. Under these circumstances, establishing whether the new technology is truly cleaner requires an I-O analysis to trace all the direct and indirect environmental ef-

---

[1]Input-output analysis can also be used to calculate the direct and indirect *employment* effects of different technologies. One such I-O study looking at waste management options for New York City was discussed in chapter 9.

[2]Clean technology proponents are not alone in relying on approximations to input-reducing technological change. Economists who study productivity changes in industry often assume that pure input-reducing (Hicks-Neutral) technological change occurs.

fects of the new technology. In practice, this can seldom be done. However, this does not mean we need to abandon the search for clean technology. Instead, technologies with apparent environmental benefits should be subject to partial life-cycle analyses. These can identify any major indirect impacts that might disqualify a potential clean technology candidate.

The first section of this chapter develops a simple I-O model and shows that input-reducing technological change is always clean. The next section illustrates how the indirect effects of an input-substituting technology may offset positive direct environmental benefits. The chapter ends with a discussion of how I-O models are used in practice to address macro-level questions about the direct and indirect pollution effects of different technological choices.

T3.1 Input-Reducing Technology

Input-output analysis earns its name because it traces all of the complex relationships between the inputs and outputs of an economic system. I-O models allow us to account for the fact that many outputs are also inputs into other outputs! The first step in doing an input-output analysis is to develop an **I-O table** for the economy being studied. Table T3.1 shows an I-O table for a very simple economy with only two "products," corn and enriched soil, and one pollutant, dirty water.[3]

Corn is grown in high-quality soil, and as a result of erosion and nutrient uptake, the farming process uses up some of the soil. Enriched soil is also "produced" by feeding corn to animals who then generate manure for fertilizer. Table T3.1 illustrates these input-output relationships in the following way. If we read down the first column, we find that in the production of 1 ton of corn, .4 tons of corn (as seed) and .2 tons of soil are used up. In addition, as a result of erosion in the corn-farming process, 200 gallons of stream water are polluted with sediment.

Reading down the second column, we find that to produce each ton of manure-enriched soil, we require .1 tons of corn as animal feed and no enriched soil. Through the runoff of nitrates in the fertilizer, 100 gallons of stream water are polluted for each ton of soil "produced."

The trick behind input-output analysis is to recognize a simple accounting fact: The total output of the economy (corn and enriched soil) must equal the intermediate

TABLE T3.1 I-O Table for a Corn-Soil Economy

		OUTPUTS	
		Corn	Enriched Soil
I N P U T S	Corn (tons)	.4	.1
	Enriched Soil (tons)	.2	0
	Dirty Water (1,000 gallons)	.2	.1

---

[3]This model was inspired by a slightly more complex one in Duchin (1990), who also lays out the general theoretical framework for expanding a conventional I-O model to include pollutants.

consumption of these products by producers plus their final consumption by consumers. In other words, the supply of each product has to equal demand. Now, of course, consumers don't eat soil. But consumers do decide how much to invest in preserving natural capital. As we shall see below, consumers may decide either to build up or run down the stock of soil in the economy. So, we now have two relationships that must hold true:

total corn produced = corn used to produce corn + corn used to produce soil
+ corn eaten by people

total soil "produced" = soil used to produce corn + soil used to produce soil
+ net increase (or decrease) in the stock of soil

Let us now employ some simple algebra to see how input-output analysis works. If we let x^c and x^s equal the total output of corn and soil each year and y^c and y^s equal the final consumer "demand" for these products on an annual basis, then our two verbal equations above become:

$$\text{Supply} = \text{Demand}$$
$$\text{Corn: } x^c = .4x^c + .1x^s + y^c$$
$$\text{Soil: } x^s = .2x^c + 0 + y^s$$

Here are two equations and four unknowns. To solve the system, we need to specify a level of final demand. Suppose consumers would like to eat 10 tons of corn and desire to keep the stock of natural capital (enriched soil) constant. If they do this, the economy will be a sustainable one, assuming zero population growth. Given this final demand for corn and soil, $y^c = 10$ and $y^s = 0$.

If we substitute these values and do a little algebra, we obtain a solution: $x^c = 17.3$ and $x^s = 3.5$. In other words, the economic goal is to satisfy a final demand for corn of 10 tons and yet maintain the stock of enriched soil constant. To do this, total corn production must be 17.3 tons and total production of enriched soil to replace that used up must be 3.5 tons. Total water pollution in the economy is, thus, $17.3 * 200 + 3.5 * 100 = 3,810$ gallons.

So far, we have illustrated that the final demand for corn and soil preservation will determine how much of these products are also demanded in the intermediate production stages. Let us now use this little model to evaluate whether a proposed new technology is indeed a clean one. Suppose that farmers figure out a way to reduce soil erosion so that, under the new method, only .1 tons of soil are required to produce a ton of corn. With less erosion, water pollution drops to 100 gallons per ton of corn produced. What are the environmental benefits of this proposed CT?

We might look just at the direct benefits: The original economy is producing 17.3 tons of corn at 200 gallons of pollution per ton. Reducing pollution to 100 gallons per ton should cause a direct fall in total pollution from 3,810 to 2,080 gallons. But recall that some of this corn was, in fact, going to feed animals to produce manure to replenish the soil, which itself caused pollution. Because erosion has been reduced by the new approach (an input-reducing technology), the economy can now devote fewer resources to replenishing the soil. This will mean that both the manure and corn sectors can "shrink," yielding even greater indirect environmental benefits. Yet, the economy will still produce the same final consumption levels as before.

To see this, we can rewrite our two I-O equations using the new farming technology (replacing the coefficient on x^c in the second equation with .1):

$$\text{Supply} = \text{Demand}$$
$$\text{Corn:} \ x^c = .4x^c + .1x^s + y^c$$
$$\text{Soil:} \ x^s = .1x^c + 0 + y^s$$

Consumers are still interested in eating 10 tons of corn and maintaining the natural stock of soil quality constant. So, substituting in $y^c = 10$ and $y^s = 0$ as before and solving, we now get: $x^c = 16.9$ and $x^s = 1.7$. With the more efficient farming method, total corn production falls to 16.9 tons, while enriched soil production falls to 1.7 tons. As a result, total water pollution actually falls to $16.9 * 100 + 1.7 * 100 = 1,860$ gallons. Thus, including the indirect benefits of lowered corn and manure output leads to a pollution reduction of 220 gallons beyond the direct effect.

This example illustrates a general point: Whenever a technology simply reduces input use, it will also reduce pollution in the connected sectors of the economy. Thus, an **input-reducing technology will always be a clean technology.** Moreover, the combined indirect and direct environmental benefits will be larger than the simple direct effect.[4]

T3.2 Input-Substituting Technology

Unfortunately, very few technological innovations involve simple reductions in input use. More often, one type of resource is substituted for another. Under these circumstances, direct and indirect environmental effects may offset one another. Let us return to our original I-O model to illustrate this point. Suppose that farmers have been using cow manure to enrich their soil. However, it is discovered that pig manure, in terms of direct effects, is more environmentally sound. For each ton of soil enriched, only 50 rather than 100 gallons of stream water are polluted. The catch: Pigs eat twice as much corn as cows. Is pig manure a clean (!!) technology?

Our input-output table now looks like this:

TABLE T3.2   I-O Table for an Input-Substituting Technology

		OUTPUTS	
		Corn	Enriched Soil
I N P U T S	Corn (tons)	.4	.2
	Enriched Soil (tons)	.2	0
	Dirty Water (1,000 gallons)	.2	.05

With the pig technology, .2 tons of corn are required for every ton of soil enriched, but soil enrichment generates only 50 gallons of pollution per ton. If we write

---

[4]Proofs of these propositions for a general linear model can be found in Axtell (1991). If one moves to a system that allows input substitution in other sectors, this claim holds only as a local approximation.

down our I-O equations that specify total output must equal intermediate consumption plus final consumption, we now get:

$$Supply = Demand$$
$$Corn: x^c = .4x^c + .2x^s + y^c$$
$$Soil: x^s = .2x^c + 0 + y^s$$

Consumers are still interested in eating 10 tons of corn and maintaining the stock of soil quality constant. So, substituting in $y^c = 10$ and $y^s = 0$ as before and solving, we now get: $x^c = 17.9$ and $x^s = 3.6$. Relative to the original case we evaluated above, both corn and manure production have to rise to accommodate the pigs' larger appetites and still replace all of the natural capital (soil) that is exhausted.

What happens to water pollution? Table T3.3 provides a comparison:

TABLE T3.3   Is Pig Manure a Clean Technology?

Pollution (gallons)	Cow Manure	Pig Manure
Nitrate from Manure	$3.5 * 100 = 350$	$3.6 * 50 = 180$
Sediment from Farming	$17.3 * 200 = 3,460$	$17.9 * 200 = 3,580$
Total	$3,810$	$3,760$

Manure production has to rise (from 3.5 to 3.6 tons) to satisfy the increased demand for corn. However, nitrate pollution from the manure still falls thanks to the inherent cleanliness of pigs. By contrast, sediment pollution from corn farming rises substantially. However, on a *total* gallons polluted basis, pig manure has to rate as a clean technology since pollution falls from 3,810 to 3,760. Yet, its advantage is much smaller than one might have thought based on a 50% reduction in pollution per ton. Here the indirect pollution from increased production of the substitute resource (corn) offsets the direct gains.

Yet, can we really characterize the pig technology as "clean"? Note that nitrate pollution falls when the pig technology is adopted, but sediment pollution increases. If we add them together, the net result is a decrease in pollution. But what if sediment pollution has more serious ecological or health effects than nitrate pollution? While life-cycle analysis in an I-O framework can (on paper) identify both the direct and indirect pollution generated by a technology, it provides no guidance as to how to weigh their disparate impacts.

One way to do this is to estimate marginal dollar damages associated with each pollutant, then add up the damages and see which technology is "cleaner." Chapter 8 of this book discussed techniques for estimating damage values, and chapter 17 described how such an approach is being used in the electric utility industry to influence the choice of generating technology. However, uncertainty in these benefit estimates places one more obstacle in the way of doing reliable life-cycle analyses.

The last two sections have discussed a very simple I-O model illustrating two general points: (1) Input-reducing technologies are always CTs; and (2) technologies that involve substituting one "clean" input for another "dirty" one may or may not be CTs. While, in principle, the true answer can be determined only via I-O analysis, such analyses are seldom carried out for specific technologies because the data are too poor. Instead, CT proponents argue from a theoretical perspective that technologies that are "more" input-reducing are more likely to be clean. A less complete form of life-cycle analysis than I-O can then be used to identify major indirect effects that might disqualify a potential CT candidate.

T3.3 I-O in the Real World

The little model explored above has only illustrative value. However, economists have developed much more elaborate I-O models that contain economies with dozens of economic sectors and several major pollutants. Linear (matrix) algebra techniques are used to solve these models and calculate the direct and indirect pollution content of different sets of technologies in a fashion conceptually similar to the approach taken above.

While an economy with dozens of sectors is more realistic than one with only two, still, applied I-O analyses are not useful for answering detailed questions such as Are cloth diapers "cleaner" than disposable ones? Instead, real-world applications of I-O focus on broader questions. Two of these are discussed below.

Bingham et al. (1987) examined the general balance between direct and indirect air pollution attributable to the final demand of consumers. Table T3.4 illustrates their results.

For air pollutants, the authors found that overall the direct contribution from consumption is a little over 50% of the total, ranging to a low of 10% for particulates. The direct contribution of consumption to other negative externalities—water pollution, habitat destruction, scenic impacts—would certainly be lower than 50%, since consumers produce substantial direct air pollution via the automobile, home heating, and electricity. As a result, indirect pollution probably accounts for well over 50% of the total pollution generated in final consumption.

Bingham et al. (1987) also found that total pollution in 1972 rose roughly on a one-to-one basis with increased consumption. Thus, the wealthiest 10% of American

TABLE T3.4   Air Pollutant Discharges Due to Consumption, 1972

	Distribution of Pollutant Generation Due to Consumption (10^6 mg/yr)		
	Direct	*Indirect*	*Percent of Total Indirect*
Particulates	0.7	6.3	90
Sulfur oxides	1.0	14.7	93
Nitrogen oxides	4.7	9.7	67
Hydrocarbons	10.4	8.4	44
Carbon monoxide	52.7	26.5	33
Total pollutants	69.5	65.6	48

Source: Taylor H. Bingham, Donald W. Anderson, and Phillip C. Cooley (1987), "Distribution of the Generation of Air Pollution," *Journal of Environment Economics and Management.* vol. 14, 30–40. Used with permission.

families generated four to six times as much air pollution as did the poorest 10%. At the same time, as we discussed in chapter 5, poorer families are more likely to suffer from air pollution exposure.

A more recent I-O study was conducted by Duchin and Lange (1992) for the United Nations. The authors were asked to explore the environmental outcomes associated with the vision of "sustainable development" outlined in the Bruntland Commission Report discussed in chapter 21. Briefly, the Bruntland Commission called for accelerated transfer of clean technology from rich to poor countries. This would allow these nations to grow in a relatively clean way. Along with increased incomes would then come a decline in population growth rates. If the process worked according to plan, then within thirty to forty years, poverty and population growth in poor countries would be dramatically reduced, unsustainable pressures on natural capital would be scaled back, and all this would come at a fairly low pollution cost.

Duchin and Lange used a forty-four-sector model of the world economy divided into seventeen regions. They included three air pollutants: carbon dioxide (global warming), sulfur oxides (acid rain and sulfate air pollution), and nitrogen oxides (global warming, acid rain, and smog). They then made a series of relatively optimistic, but still feasible, assumptions about both economic growth in poor countries and the rate of technology transfer from rich to poor countries.

The authors project GDP to grow 150% worldwide from 1990 to 2020. On the technology side, over the same period, the authors assume improvements in the efficiency of input use on the order of 20% to 50% in sectors such as transportation, electricity, and construction. Most of this technological change is input-reducing and thus clean, but input-substitution does occur in some sectors. For example, chemical use in the paper industry is assumed to increase with increased recycling.

In the *absence* of rapid and widespread technological improvements (their baseline scenario), Duchin and Lange (1992) estimate that air pollutant emissions in all three categories will increase by more than 250% worldwide between 1990 and 2020. Yet, even under the optimistic scenario, emissions are also projected to rise, with carbon dioxide emissions up 73%, sulfur oxide emissions up 26%, and nitrogen oxide emissions up 74%. Nevertheless, taking into account all direct and indirect environmental effects, accelerated transfer of (mostly) input-reducing technology can clearly have a major impact on air pollution levels around the world.

One may debate whether the environmental cost of economic growth under the optimistic scenario is still unsustainably high. Duchin and Lange believe that it is. They conclude that input-reducing efficiency improvements in known technologies are unlikely to allow for sustainable development as defined by the Bruntland Commission. They thus argue that, rather than relying solely on efficiency improvements in existing technologies, completely new clean technologies will have to be created to accommodate growth in a sustainable fashion. Two such technologies they discuss are mass transit and solar (photovoltaic) electricity.

T3.4 Summary

This chapter illustrates how, in theory, one can trace all of the direct and indirect environmental effects of a new technology using input-output analysis. In practice, I-O analysis is too data-intensive to be helpful in micro-level decisions. However, at a theoretical level, I-O models suggest that, in general, technologies that are more input-reducing are more likely to be clean. Defining what is meant by "more input-reducing" has to be done on a case-by-case basis. I-O models are also helpful in gaining insight into macro-level questions. The two examples mentioned here involved estimates of the general magnitude of indirect air pollution effects and the degree to which the rapid diffusion of more efficient technologies can promote sustainable development.

APPLICATION T3.0

Doing Input-Output

Consider the following I-O table, slightly modified from the one in the text:

OUTPUTS

		Corn	Enriched Soil
I N P U T S	Corn (tons)	.5	.1
	Enriched Soil (tons)	.3	0
	Dirty Water (1,000 gallons)	.3	.2

1. What does the number ".1" in the table mean? What does the number ".3" (the one on the top) mean?

2. Suppose that, as in the text, consumers wish to consume 10 tons of corn and maintain the current stock of enriched soil. What do the two I-O equations look like?

3. Solve the two equations to get the total output of corn and soil needed to satisfy both intermediate and final consumer demand.

4. Now suppose that to accommodate population growth and still maintain a sustainable agricultural base, consumers decide to increase the stock of enriched soil by 1 ton. (They still want to consume 10 tons of corn.) What happens to total corn and soil output?

5. What happens to water pollution in question 4 relative to question 3? Is the decision to boost the stock of enriched soil, in fact, sustainable? If it is not, can you think of a sustainable way to accommodate population growth?

Key Ideas in Each Section

T3.0 In principle, all of the **direct** and **indirect environmental benefits** of a new technology can be computed using **input-output (I-O) analysis.** In reality, I-O is too data-intensive to do small-scale **life-cycle** analyses. However, I-O does show that **input-reducing technologies** are cleaner than **input-substituting technologies,** justifying the waste reduction hierarchy of the **three R's: reduce, reuse, recycle.**

T3.1 This section uses a simple **I-O table** to illustrate that **input-reducing technologies are always clean** and that the indirect environmental benefits are quite important.

T3.2 This section illustrates that apparently clean input-substituting technologies may not be when indirect benefits are taken into account.

T3.3 Two economy-wide I-O studies are discussed. The first one demonstrates that direct air pollution from consumption accounts for, on average, around 50% of the total. The second study evaluates the Bruntland Commission strategy of transferring clean technology to poor countries. The authors conclude that even substantial input-reducing technological change for conventional technologies will be insufficient to insure a sustainable future. They, thus, call for greater investment in new clean technologies.

References

Axtell, Robert (1991). "Cascading Market Inefficiency Through Indirect Effects in the Joint Production of Goods and Externalities." Paper presented at the Eastern Economic Association Meetings, Pittsburgh, PA, March.

Bingham, Taylor H., Donald W. Anderson and Phillip C. Cooley (1987). "Distribution of the Generation of Air Pollution." *Journal of Environmental Economics and Management,* vol. 14, 30–40.

Duchin, Faye (1990). "The Conversion of Biological Materials and Wastes to Useful Products." *Structural Change and Economic Dynamics,* 1, no. 2, 243–261.

Duchin, Faye and Glenn-Marie Lange (1992). *Strategies for Environmentally Sound Economic Development.* New York: Institute for Economic Analysis.

Incentive-Compatible Regulation

T4.0 Introduction

In chapter 12, we identified imperfect information as one of the primary obstacles to effective government regulation of the environment. We noted that, due to budget limitations, the Environmental Protection Agency gathers or generates less than full information about most problems before acting. In particular, the agency can sponsor only limited research of its own; as a result, it must often turn to industry for data about the expected compliance costs of regulation. Yet, asking for information about costs from the very industry one is regulating has elements of asking the fox to guard the henhouse. The incentives for cheating are rather high.

In chapter 12, we discussed two potential solutions to this problem. One was to build up the institutional capability of the EPA to increase its ability to detect inaccurate reports of compliance costs. The second was to design regulatory policy to minimize any gains from lying. So-called **incentive-compatible regulation** insures that the *incentives* faced by the regulated parties are *compatible* with the goal of the regulator. This advanced topic chapter illustrates how incentive-compatible regulation can work.

T4.1 Incentives to Lie

To motivate the problem, consider the EPA's recent efforts to regulate sulfur dioxide (SO_2) emissions from power plants. Suppose the agency seeks to regulate SO_2 at the efficient level, where the marginal benefits of reduction just equal marginal costs. *If* the EPA knew what the costs and benefits were, it might then achieve the efficient pollution level in one of two ways. First, it could issue or auction off marketable permits up to the SO_2 target. Or, it could set an emission tax to achieve the same goal. However, as we shall show below, if firms are expecting a marketable permit system, they have an incentive to overstate compliance costs. By the same token, if they expect a tax, an incentive exists to understate compliance costs.

Figure T4.1 illustrates a marginal cost–marginal benefit diagram for analyzing pollution control. This diagram differs from the ones used previously in the book because the horizontal axis is flipped around. Instead of measuring pollution reduction (cleanup) as we have done before, it now measures pollution emitted. As a result, the MC of reduction curve now slopes downward, reflecting the fact that, at high pollution levels, per unit cleanup is cheaper. Similarly, the MB of reduction curve now slopes upward: At high pollution levels, the per unit benefits of cleanup are also high.

The true marginal benefits and costs of SO_2 reduction are reflected by the curves labeled MB and MC. If EPA had access to this information, efficiency would require a pollution level of P^*. This, in turn, could be achieved either by auctioning off P^* marketable permits (at a market-clearing price of T^*) or by setting a pollution tax at T^*.

However, suppose the EPA must rely on power companies for information about how much it will cost firms to switch over to less polluting production methods. If faced with a marketable permit system, industry has a clear incentive to lie and *overstate* the cost (MC'). If the industry does so and the EPA uses the industry estimates, the agency will increase the number of permits it sells to P'. This will drive down the price of permits to T' and allow an inefficiently high level of pollution, reducing the firm's cleanup costs.

By contrast, suppose that agency is planning to use a pollution tax to control SO_2 emissions and firms know this. Then, as illustrated in Figure T4.2, companies have the incentive to *understate* their costs, for example, claiming MC''. The EPA will consider the efficient pollution level to be P'' and set what it *thinks* is the appropriate tax at T''. By doing this, the emission tax will be reduced (from T^*). However, with a low tax of T'', *actual* pollution will rise to P'''. Again, pollution levels will be inefficiently high and a firm's cleanup costs will be reduced.

Now, after the fact, regulators will be able to tell they have been lied to. How? In the marketable permits case, permit prices will be only T', reflecting real control costs, when the agency expects them to rise to T''. In the tax case, the pollution level will be P''' again, reflecting real control costs, when the agency expects it to be P''. Thus, one

FIGURE T4.1 Imperfect Information and Permits

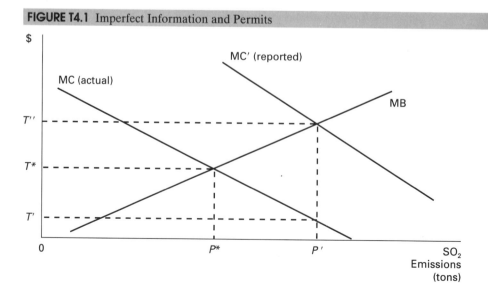

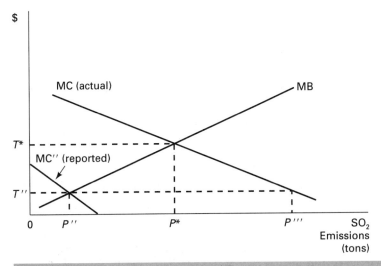

FIGURE T4.2 Imperfect Information and Taxes

approach to solving the problem of imperfect information would be to adjust either the number of permits or the tax level based on the observed outcomes. For example, if the observed pollution level is higher than the regulator predicted, the regulator can raise the pollution tax.

Through such a process, called iteration, the regulator might be able to arrive at the efficient tax level or number of permits. However, in practice, it is not easy to adjust either the number of permits or the tax level once they have been established. As was detailed in chapter 12, setting regulatory policy is a cumbersome and politically charged process not amenable to trial and error. Are we then stuck with a recognition that firms will tend to overstate costs if facing a marketable permit system and understate them if facing pollution taxes? Fortunately, no.

T4.2 Incentives to Tell the Truth

An incentive-compatible approach developed by Kwerel (1977) can be used to encourage truthful behavior.[1] This approach mixes a marketable permit system with a tax system to precisely balance the different incentives firms have to lie about compliance costs. It works in the following way. Regulators tell firms that they will combine an auction of marketable permits with a subsidy payment for any pollution reduced over and above the number of permits the firm holds (an **excess emission reduction subsidy**). To see this clearly, we need to use a little mathematical notation. So, let:

p = industry pollution level
L = number of permits made available
z = price of permits
e = subsidy level for emission reductions

[1]Greunspecht and Lave (1989) provide a more general review of the literature on environmental regulation under imperfect information.

The industry's total pollution control costs are thus:

cleanup costs + permit costs − excess emission reduction subsidy
(area under $z * L$ $e * (L - p)$
MC curve)

The trick here is that regulators set the subsidy level, *e*, at the intersection of the MB curve and the *reported* MC curve. Thus, by the costs that they report, firms directly affect not only the number of permits that are issued but also the subsidy they will receive for any excess emission reductions.

With this setup, we can see how the incentive-compatible mechanism works to encourage truth telling. First, let us consider what happens if firms overstate their costs. At first glance, this seems like a good strategy. Figure T4.3 illustrates the situation. By overstating their costs, the firms know that regulators will provide a large number of permits (*L*) and set a high emission reduction subsidy at *e*−. Both of these seem favorable. The catch is that, unlike the case of a straight marketable permit system, the large supply of permits will not cause their price to fall. Instead, the high emission subsidy will cause the permit price that firms have to pay to be driven *up*. As long as *e* is greater than the price of permits, *z*, each firm would do better buying another permit, holding emissions constant, and collecting the subsidy for the extra "reduction." But this high demand for permits will cause permit prices to get bid up to *e*−.

As a result, in equilibrium, the permit price *z* must just equal *e*−. Because the price of an additional permit just equals the emission subsidy, firms will not come out ahead financially from the subsidy policy and, thus, do not benefit from a high *e*−. However, as long as the true MC of reduction is less than the subsidy, firms would lose money if they did not reduce pollution and receive the subsidy. As a result, they *will* cut back pollution to *P* even though they hold *L* permits.

The final equilibrium will, thus, look like this: *L* permits auctioned off at a price

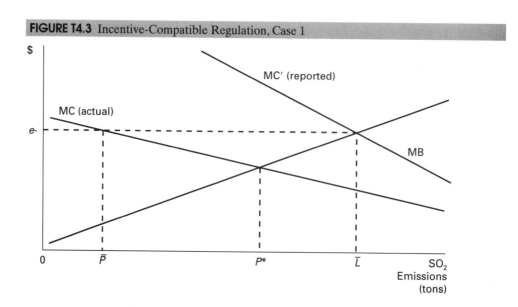

FIGURE T4.3 Incentive-Compatible Regulation, Case 1

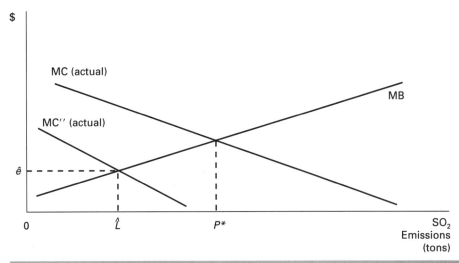

FIGURE T4.4 Incentive-Compatible Regulation, Case 2

just equal to the emission subsidy $e-$, with firms polluting at a level of P. But P is a lower level of pollution and one more costly to achieve than P^*. Overstating compliance costs will, thus, lead firms to bear higher pollution reduction costs than they would if they told the truth.

Is there an incentive to understate costs? Figure T4.4 illustrates this possibility. If firms underreport costs, then $\hat{L}$ permits will be available, and firms will receive a subsidy for emission reductions below $\hat{L}$ of $\hat{e}$. However, since the true marginal costs of reduction exceed the subsidy for excess emission reductions, firms will pollute up to the limit of $\hat{L}$ and not take any subsidies. But, again, this is a stricter and more costly standard than they would have faced if they had told the truth. Understating costs is clearly not a good strategy for firms.

We have just demonstrated that both overstating and understating compliance costs ultimately lead to higher costs for firms than telling the truth. Thus, under this hybrid regulatory mechanism, firms have no incentive to lie. In a nutshell, the advantages to inflating costs that accrue under a straight marketable permit system are here negated by the emission reduction subsidy which forces up permit prices.

T4.3 Summary

This chapter has provided an introduction to incentive-compatible regulation. We first established that firms have an incentive to overstate compliance costs when faced with marketable permit regulation and to understate costs when faced with pollution taxes. A mechanism was then suggested that precisely balanced these offsetting tendencies by combining a tax-based subsidy policy with a marketable permit system. This hybrid regulatory structure is incentive-compatible, because firms are provided an incentive to tell the truth, which is compatible with the regulatory goal of efficient regulation.

APPLICATION T4.0

CAC and Incentives for Truth Telling

In 1987, the EPA estimated that the costs of controlling hazardous air pollutant emissions from coke ovens in the steel industry would be about $4 billion; by 1991 that estimate had fallen to between $250 million and $400 million. In the late 1970s, projections for benzene emission control were on the order of $350,000 per plant; in actuality, chemical companies found they were able to use substitutes that "virtually eliminated control costs."[2]

We showed in this chapter that industry has an incentive to overstate costs if faced with marketable permit regulation. Does the same incentive hold for command-and-control regulation, which was used in the two cases above?

1. Assume (a) that the EPA's intitial cost estimates above were based on industry sources and (b) that the EPA sought to regulate these pollutants at the efficient level.[3] Use a diagram to provide a possible explanation for why the cost estimates were so high. (Show that under command-and-control regulation, where a uniform emission standard is set, that industry has an incentive to overstate true costs.)

Key Ideas in Each Section

T4.0 This chapter illustrates a way in which regulators can design a system to **elicit truthful information** about control costs from regulated firms. Such a system of regulation is called **incentive-compatible.**

T4.1 Under a permit system, firms have an incentive to overstate control costs; under a tax system the reverse is true.

T4.2 A hybrid regulatory approach, which combines a marketable permit system with an **excess emission reduction subsidy,** precisely balances the offsetting incentives firms have to lie about control costs.

References

Gruenspecht, A. and Lester Lave (1989). "The Economics of Health, Safety and Environmental Regulation." In *Handbook of Industrial Organization, Volume II,* eds. R. Schmalansee and R. Willig. New York: North Holland.

Kwerel, Evan (1977). "To Tell the Truth: Imperfect Information and Optimal Pollution Control." *Review of Economic Studies,* 44, no. 3, 595–601.

Mason, Keith (1991). "The Economic Impact." *The EPA Journal,* January–February.

---

[2]Mason (1991).

[3]In fact, these air pollutants are typically regulated under a safety standard. However, control costs still enter agency decisions as to the stringency of regulation.

Author Index

A

Abler, David G., 486*n*, 492
Ackerman, Frank, 173, 375, 386
Adler, Sy, 411, 424
A.D. Little, Inc., 340*n*, 357
Ahmad, Yusuf J., 83*n*, 103, 459
Alberine, Anna, 265*n*, 270
Anderson, Donald W., 78, 386, 538
Andrews, Richard N. L., 191*n*, 195
Arora, Seema, 251–52, 256, 386
Arrow, Kenneth, 29*n*, 31, 126
Arthur, Brian W., 335*n*, 357
Aschauer, David A., 173
Atkinson, Giles D., 86*n*, 103, 449*n*, 460
Atkinson, Scott, 306, 312, 317, 332
Austin, David, 78, 332
Axtell, Robert, 533*n*, 538

B

Bagwell, Laurie Simon, 199*n*, 212
Bailey, Martin N., 153*n*, 173, 500*n*, 512
Baliga, Sanjay, 367*n*
Barbera, Anthony J., 153*n*, 154, 173
Barnes, Patricia, 329*n*, 333
Barret, S., 490*n*
Barrows, Richard, 469*n*, 492, 470–71,
        482*n*
Baumol, William, 171, 173
Bear, Dinah, 126
Becker, Gary S., 440*n*, 459
Behrens, William, 126
Bell, Frederick, 138–39, 140*n*, 146
Benbrook, Charles M., 369*n*, 386
Berardi, Stephen J., 95, 256, 271, 386
Berman, Daniel, 351, 357
Berman, Eli, 163, 173
Bernheim, Douglas, 199*n*, 212
Berrens, Robert, 459
Bezdek, Roger H., 156*n*, 159, 173, 175,
        319*n*, 333
Bhagwati, Jagdish, 485*n*, 492
Bhalla, Ajit S., 492
Bieszaz, Karen, 449*n*, 459

Bieszaz, Mavis, 459
Bieszaz, Richard, 459
Bigman, David, 485, 492
Bingham, Taylor H., 69*n*, 78, 359–60,
        386, 535–36, 538
Birdsall, Nancy M., 439*n*, 442*n*, 443,
        459
Bishop, Richard C., 113, 126, 139, 146
Blackorby, Charles, 506*n*, 512
Blair, R., 126
Blecker, Robert A., 212
Blinder, Alan, 64*n*, 68, 78, 171, 173, 209,
        212
Bohara, Alok, 457, 459
Bohi, Douglas R., 321*n*, 322, 323, 332,
        403, 424
Bohm, Peter, 304, 312
Bold, Frederick, 353*n*, 357
Bolin, Bert, 126
Borenstein, Eduardo, 459
Bowles, Samuel, 153*n*, 173
Boyd, Hayden, 54*n*, 61
Boyle, Kevin J., 130, 146
Brady, Gordon L., 264*n*, 271, 304, 312
Brajer, Victor, 69*n*, 78
Brandon, Katrina, 483*n*, 492
Brazee, Richard, 147
Breslow, Marc, 159*n*, 173
Bridges, James S., 363*n*, 386
Brimelow, Peter, 42*n*
Bromley, Daniel W., 35*n*, 43, 50*n*, 61,
        136*n*, 147, 263*n*, 271
Brooks, Nancy, 70*n*, 78
Brookshire, David S., 131–32, 147
Browder, John S., 433*n*, 459, 466, 492
Brown, Gardner W., Jr., 307*n*, 312
Brown, Lester R., 108*n*, 126, 438*n*, 459
Brown, Michael H., 246*n*, 256
Bryner, Gary C., 217*n*, 218*n*, 230*n*, 236
Buente, David T., 286*n*
Bui, Linda T. M., 163, 173
Bullard, Robert D., 70, 74*n*, 78
Bulow, Jeremy, 484*n*, 485*n*, 492
Burfisher, Mary E., 494
Burrows, Paul, 523

Burtraw, Dallas, 66, 78, 149, 173, 313,
        319*n*, 321, 322, 323, 327*n*, 332,
        337*n*, 424
Byrd, Denise C., 324, 333

C

Campen, James, 191, 195
Cantor, Robin, 395*n*, 424
Canzoneri, Diana, 387
Carlin, Alan, 151, 173, 251*n*, 256, 259*n*,
        261*n*, 262*n*
Carnevale, Richard A., 368*n*, 386
Carriere, Jean, 450*n*, 459, 482*n*, 492
Carson, Richard T., 41*n*, 44, 132*n*, 137*n*,
        138, 147
Carter, Luther, 396*n*, 424
Cason, Timothy N., 251–52, 256, 386
Castleman, Barry, 479*n*, 492–93
Chakrabarti, Alok K., 153*n*, 173
Chapman, Duane, 162*n*, 173, 512
Chestnut, Lauraine G., 147
Chiang, Alpha C., 523
Ciriacy-Wantrup, S. V., 113, 126
Clarke, Marjorie, 376*n*, 386
Claussen, Eileen, 332
Cline, William R., 4*n*, 9*n*, 18
Clough, Kerrigan, 74*n*, 78
Coase, Ronald, 53, 61
Cobb, Clifford, 82*n*, 83*n*, 97*n*, 103,
        205–6, 209*n*, 212
Cobb, John J., 97, 98, 103
Cohen, Daniel, 436*n*, 459
Cohen, Joel, 459
Cohen, Mark A., 278, 291
Colborn, Theo, 251, 256
Colby, Bonnie G., 424
Collinge, Robert A., 415*n*, 424
Collins, Mark, 113*n*, 126
Common, Mick, 109*n*, 126
Commoner, Barry, 262*n*, 267, 271
Cooley, Phillip C., 386, 538
Cooper, Susan, 388
Copeland, Brian R., 74*n*, 78
Costanza, Robert, 103, 126, 143, 147

545

Subject Index